orth Carolina CRIMES

A Guidebook on the Elements of Crime

Fifth Edition

2001

Edited and Revised by

Robert L. Farb

Institute of Government

The University of North Carolina at Chapel Hill

orth Carolina

CRIMES

A Guidebook on the Elements of Crime

INSTITUTE of GOVERNMENT

Established in 1931, the Institute of Government provides training, advisory, and research services to public officials and others interested in the operation of state and local government in North Carolina. A part of The University of North Carolina at Chapel Hill, the Institute also administers the university's Master of Public Administration Program.

Each year approximately 14,000 city, county, and state officials attend one or more of the 230 classes, seminars, and conferences offered by the Institute. Faculty members annually publish up to fifty books, bulletins, and other reference works related to state and local government. Each day that the General Assembly is in session, the Institute's *Daily Bulletin*, available in print and electronically, reports on the day's activities for members of the legislature and others who need to follow the course of legislation. An extensive Web site (http://ncinfo.iog.unc.edu/) provides access to publications and faculty research, course listings, program and service information, and links to other useful sites related to government.

Support for the Institute's operations comes from various sources, including state appropriations, local government membership dues, private contributions, publication sales, and service contracts. For more information about the Institute, visit the Web site or call (919) 966-5381.

The University of North Carolina at Chapel Hill
CB# 3330 Knapp Building
Chapel Hill, NC, 27599-3330

First edition 1977. Fifth Edition 2001
This publication is printed on permanent, acid-free paper in compliance with the North Carolina General Statutes.
Printed in the United States of America

07 06 05 04 03 7 6 5 4 3

ISBN 1-56011-384-7
Printed on recycled paper

Summary of Contents

(Note: The detailed Table of Contents follows; each chapter also includes a Chapter Contents.)

Table of Contents

Preface

This is the fifth edition of a book first published in 1977. The organization of this book remains essentially the same as the fourth edition, which was published in 1995. The text has been updated to include discussion of new offenses and case law.

North Carolina Crimes embodies the work and involvement of many Institute of Government faculty and staff over twenty years. For this edition, I thank Institute of Government faculty member Jessica Smith, who read drafts of the text and offered useful comments. I also thank the many Institute of Government staff members and others who contributed to the editing, production, and distribution of this book.

I welcome comments about this book's scope, organization, or content. Comments may be sent to me at **farb@iogmail.iog.unc.edu** or by regular mail at the Institute of Government, CB# 3330, Knapp Building, The University of North Carolina at Chapel Hill, Chapel Hill, NC 27599-3330.

Robert L. Farb

Chapel Hill
February 2001

Introduction

Purpose of This Book

North Carolina Crimes is a guidebook for North Carolina substantive criminal law, designed primarily for use by law enforcement officers. Its main purpose is to help the law enforcement officer decide which offense should be charged, if any, and what evidence should be gathered to prepare a case for trial. The book is also written to be helpful to magistrates, attorneys, and judges, although citations to legal authority are limited (regional reporters are not cited, for example), and little material is presented on technical matters, such as indictment problems. In short, *North Carolina Crimes* is not a comprehensive treatise but a practical guide to substantive criminal law in North Carolina.

Readers of the book should not rely on it as a source for the form of words to be used in charging an offense. Another Institute of Government publication, *Arrest Warrant and Indictment Forms* (formerly *Arrest Warrant Forms)*, serves that purpose.

This fifth edition incorporates statutory changes made through the 2000 session of the General Assembly and case law through volume 352 of the *North Carolina Reports* and volume 139 of the *North Carolina Court of Appeals Reports*. It supersedes all earlier editions and supplements.

Coverage of the Book

The book attempts to cover all of the criminal offenses that may be encountered more than rarely by law enforcement officers in North Carolina, except for offenses in such special subjects as motor vehicle law (which is covered in a limited manner), alcoholic beverage control law, and fish and game law. [For an in-depth discussion of motor vehicle law, see Ben F. Loeb, Jr., and James C. Drennan, *Motor Vehicle Law and the Law of Impaired Driving in North Carolina* (Chapel Hill: Institute of Government, The University of North Carolina at Chapel Hill, 2000)] Even outside those special areas, many offenses are omitted because there seemed to be little practical use for information about them. Many such offenses are referred to here, however, if they are related to more common offenses, as the section below indicates.

Because the criminal law is constantly changing, readers may wish to check *Administration of Justice Bulletins*, published by the Institute of Government (formerly under the title *Administration of Justice Memorandum*) for changes in the statutes. After each legislative session the Institute of Government publishes an *AOJ Bulletin* summarizing new legislation affecting criminal law and procedure. These publications are useful in updating *North Carolina Crimes* until a supplement is published. They may be ordered from the Institute of Government's publications office at (919) 966-4119 or (919) 966-4120; the texts of these publications also are available from the Institute of Government's criminal law Web site at http://www.iog.unc.edu/programs/crimlaw/aoj.htm.

A useful reference about punishments is John Rubin and Ben F. Loeb, Jr., *Punishment for North Carolina Crimes and Motor Vehicle Offenses* (Chapel Hill: Institute of Government, The University of North Carolina at Chapel Hill, 1999).

How to Use This Book

Readers may find a particular offense by consulting (1) the detailed table of contents at the beginning of the book, which lists all discussed offenses; (2) the directory of statutes, which lists all discussed statutory offenses in statutory order at the back of the book; or (3) the descriptive-word index, also at the back of the book.

The book has introductory chapters on states of mind, defenses, participants in crime, and punishment under structured sentencing and then has separate chapters on various major categories of offenses. The material on each offense within a category is divided into five sections: (1) the statute, if any, dealing with the offense; (2) the elements of the offense; (3) the punishment for the offense; (4) notes on legal points about and case law concerning the offense that are not evident in the listing of elements; and (5) the names of related offenses not in the chapter. Here are a few comments on those sections.

1. Statute. If a statute deals with the offense at all, even if it only sets out the punishment, it is reproduced. Readers should be careful to check the General Statutes for amended versions of the reproduced statutes. If the offense is recognized only in cases decided by the state's courts and is not mentioned anywhere in the North Carolina General Statutes—that is, if it is a common-law crime—this section shows the notation, "This is a common-law offense."

2. Elements of the offense. Usually an offense is broken down into elements of offenses according to the pattern established by a North Carolina Supreme Court case or by the North Carolina Pattern Jury Instructions. In some cases, the breakdown of elements appearing here is original. Remember that there is not necessarily a single "right" way to list elements. One person might regard one element of the crime of misdemeanor larceny as being "takes personal property belonging to another," while another person might break that phrase down into three elements: "(1) takes (2) personal property (3) belonging to another."

3. Punishment. The punishment set out is the crime's offense classification under structured sentencing. (See Chapter 5, "Punishment under Structured Sentencing," for a detailed discussion of the particular meaning of an offense classification.) If a statute does not specify the punishment for a particular misdemeanor (thus leaving its punishment to be determined by G.S. 14-3, a statute that sets out general provisions on punishment), then G.S. 14-3(b) provides that the offense may be treated as a Class H felony if it was "infamous, done in secrecy and malice, or with deceit and intent to defraud" [see Chapter 4 for a discussion of G.S. 14-3(b)]. Generally, the note on punishment will indicate if this statutory provision is applicable.

4. Notes. The notes include points about the offense that are not obvious from the elements. Many of the notes will be keyed to the elements—for example, there may be a note about Element (1) of an offense. Many elements do not have a note; this merely means that nothing needs to be said about them that is not obvious. This section contains significant discussion of the law of each crime as defined by decisions of the North Carolina Supreme Court, the North Carolina Court of Appeals, and sometimes other courts. Frequently, particular offenses are compared in this section.

5. Related offenses not in this chapter. This section is essential to get the most from the book. The related offenses listed include those crimes that are not dealt with in the same chapter of this book as the offense being discussed. Thus a reader looking under "Common-Law Robbery" will not find armed robbery listed as a related offense, because armed robbery is dealt with in the same chapter and can be found by checking the table of contents that begins the chapter. On the other hand, felonious larceny is listed as a related offense because it appears in another chapter. Such a listing, when it appears, shows in parentheses the chapter that discusses the related offense; the table of contents for that chapter will list the related offense. The section on related offenses also shows related crimes that did not seem sufficiently important or frequent to be included in the book. When such an offense is listed, it appears without enclosing quotation marks or a book chapter reference but with its General Statutes citation number. For example, under the related offenses to "Child Abuse (Misdemeanor)" appears: Exposing child to fire (G.S. 14-318). Such a listing, with the statutory citation and without enclosing quotation marks, shows that the offense is *not* included in this book. In Chapter 24, "Drug Offenses," there are very few related offenses, so the heading is not used where it does not apply. Note that the chapter includes a section entitled "Other Controlled Substance Offenses."

In summary, a reader of this book who finds that the description of an offense does not fit the situation at hand should check all of the other crimes that appear in the same chapter and also the related offenses list appearing at the end of that crime's discussion.

Citations to Legal Authority

As mentioned above, this book does not attempt to give complete legal authority for every point made, but it does cite some legal authorities to be used as starting points for those who might want to look further. Sometimes citations are to cases that merely illustrate the point being discussed. The later history of a case, such as an affirmance by a higher court, is not included. Cases should be checked before being cited as authority.

Here are some examples of the shorthand citations used, with explanations of their meaning.

G.S. 14-120.	This means Chapter 14, Section 120, of the General Statutes of North Carolina.
501 U.S. 560.	This means the case beginning at page 560 of volume 501 of the *United States Reports*, the official set of books which reports the decisions of the United States Supreme Court.
338 N.C. 168.	This means the case beginning at page 168 of volume 338 of the *North Carolina Reports*, which reports the decisions of the North Carolina Supreme Court.
116 N.C. App. 1.	This means the case beginning at page 1 of volume 116 of the *North Carolina Court of Appeals Reports*, which reports decisions of the North Carolina Court of Appeals.
39 N.C. L. Rev. 121, 149.	This indicates a passage to be found on page 149 of an article that begins on page 121 in volume 39 of the *North Carolina Law Review*.
***LaFave*, vol. 2, p. 4**	This means the material beginning on page 4 of volume 2 of *Substantive Criminal Law* (1986), by W. LaFave and A. Scott, Jr. This book is available from the West Group (formerly West Publishing).

Perkins, p. 355. This means the material beginning on page 355 of *Criminal Law* (3d edition, 1982) by R. Perkins and R. Boyce, a basic criminal law treatise. This book is available from the West Group (formerly West Publishing).

N.C.P.I.—Crim. 206.30. This means item number 206.30 in *North Carolina Pattern Jury Instructions for Criminal Cases.*

Black's Law Dictionary This means *Black's Law Dictionary,* seventh edition. [St. Paul, Minn.: West Group (1999)].

Miscellaneous Points of Interpretation

Age. A person is "under the age of 12 years" who has not yet reached his or her twelfth birthday. A person "at least 18 years old" or "18 years or older" has reached his or her eighteenth birthday. A person "over 12 and under 16 years of age" has reached his or her twelfth birthday but has not reached his or her sixteenth birthday.

A person attains a given age on the anniversary date of his or her birthday, regardless of the particular time of day the person was born, (120 N.C. App. 874). Thus a person becomes thirteen years old just after midnight on the date of his or her birthday.

He/she. The use of sex-specific pronouns is generally avoided throughout this publication. Unless otherwise specified, a crime may be committed by either a male or a female.

"Person" includes corporation. The word "person" in a criminal statute (and the word "person" used to describe elements of offenses in this book) includes a corporation. See G.S. 12-3(6). Thus a corporation may be convicted of a crime just like a natural person. However, a corporation is charged and served with criminal process in a different manner than a natural person. See G.S. 15A-773.

North Carolina
CRIMES
A Guidebook on the Elements of Crime

1
States of Mind

Chapter Contents

1
States of Mind

Generally

As a general rule, a criminal offense consists of both an act (or omission) and a criminal state of mind. This necessary state of mind is sometimes called a "guilty mind" or "*mens rea*" (as discussed below, for a few kinds of crimes no guilty mind is required; those are cases of "strict liability" for crime). The necessary state of mind for a criminal offense varies from offense to offense. Often the law on states of mind is not entirely clear, but the notes below briefly describe various states of mind that are referred to in the definitions of North Carolina crimes (some other states of mind less generally used are discussed under the offenses to which they apply). Many of these notes will be referred to later in this book when the necessary state of mind for a particular criminal offense is discussed.

Definitions

"Intentionally." A person acts (or fails to act) intentionally when it is his or her purpose to so act (or fail to act) (103 N.C. 323), and the person intentionally causes a result (for example, serious bodily injury)—either when that result was the purpose of the act or omission or when he or she is aware that result is nearly certain to flow from the act or omission (*Perkins*, p. 834). As a practical matter, intent ordinarily must be proved circumstantially by showing facts from which the intent may be inferred (211 N.C. 93). It can be inferred that a person intends the natural and probable consequences of his or her act (261 N.C. 558); for example, when a person shoots at another, it can be inferred that the person intends to cause serious bodily injury, since that is the natural consequence of a shooting. The doctrine of "transferred intent" permits the conviction of a defendant for a homicide or assault who shot with the intent to harm the intended victim but in fact harmed an unintended victim (331 N.C. 239; 293 N.C. 462) and also permits the conviction of a defendant for discharging a firearm into occupied property when shooting at a person but in fact shooting into an occupied property (125 N.C. App. 505).

"Knowingly." A person acts (or fails to act) knowingly when the person is aware or conscious of what he or she is doing (278 N.C. 623). Similarly, a person has knowledge about the circumstances surrounding his or her act (for example, that a claim for insurance was false) or about the results of an act (for example, that serious bodily injury would occur) when he or she is aware of or conscious of those circumstances or of those results (218 N.C. 258). A person does not act "knowingly" if he or she merely *should* have known; the person must actually know (212 N.C. 361). North Carolina does not accept the doctrine, accepted in some jurisdictions, that knowledge includes "willful blindness" of a highly probable fact, that is, deliberate avoidance of knowledge (324 N.C. 190).

"Willfully." Generally North Carolina courts have said that an act or omission is done willfully when done intentionally and without an honest belief that there is an excuse or justification for it (215 N.C. 303; 306 N.C. 138). It is not necessary for the person to know that he or she is breaking the law in order for the act to be willful (210 N.C. 742; 86 N.C. App. 25).

In 1995 the North Carolina Court of Appeals ruled that "willfully" also requires that the act or omission be done "purposely and designedly in violation of law" (118 N.C. App. 130). This definition conflicts with the general rule discussed in the previous paragraph, and it is uncertain which of these rules will prevail.

An act is not willful if it is done negligently or accidentally (*Perkins*, p. 875), and a failure to perform a duty is not willful if the defendant does not have the means to perform it (as when a defendant does not make alimony payments because of lack of money) (229 N.C. 248).

Consider this example of justification excusing what would otherwise be willful behavior: the court of appeals ruled that punishing a dog in a way that would otherwise be cruelty to an animal was not willful cruelty because the act was justified as necessary to train the dog (22 N.C. App. 144).

"Maliciously." North Carolina courts have recognized three meanings of "malice." The meaning of the term depends on whether malice is an element of murder or of another offense. A killing is done maliciously when (1) it is done with ill will, hatred, spite, or resentment toward the victim (sometimes called express or particular malice) (297 N.C. 168; 307 N.C. 184); (2) the act that causes death is inherently dangerous to human life and is done so recklessly or wantonly that it reflects disregard of life and social duty (311 N.C. 391; 98 N.C. App. 600; 105 N.C. App. 377); or (3) it is done intentionally and without justification or excuse (in a murder case, this third type of malice may be inferred from the intentional infliction of a wound with a deadly weapon) (307 N.C. 184; 322 N.C. 152; 111 N.C. App. 110). However, when the term is used in connection with offenses other than murder, such as crimes of damage to property, North Carolina courts say it means only the first type of malice, express malice (275 N.C. 342).

"With malice aforethought." "With malice aforethought" means the same thing as "with malice" and nothing more. It does not require premeditation (13 N.C. 425).

"Wantonly." An act is done wantonly when it is done with conscious and intentional disregard of and indifference to the rights and safety of others and without care for the consequences (284 N.C. 67; 306 N.C. 138), even though the offender had not formed an intention to harm anyone (98 N.C. 641).

"Negligently." The meaning of the word "negligently" varies depending on whether the term is used in the criminal law or in the law that determines civil liability (203 N.C. 69). Criminal negligence (sometimes called culpable negligence) implies a greater deviation from reasonable conduct than does civil negligence; it means recklessness or carelessness that shows a thoughtless disregard of consequences or a heedless indifference to the safety and rights of others (232 N.C. 717; 336 N.C. 762; 112 N.C. App. 770).

"Strict liability." The North Carolina Supreme Court has said that "performance of an act which is expressly forbidden by statute may constitute an offense in itself without regard to the question of intent" (201 N.C. 32). Most offenses for which such "strict liability" is imposed are regulatory offenses—for example, motor vehicle offenses. A person may, for example, be convicted of speeding even though the person had not intended to speed or did not know that he or she was speeding—and even if the speedometer erroneously informed the person that he or she was not speeding.

2
Bars and Defenses

Chapter Contents

2
Bars and Defenses

Bars to prosecution

Generally

A defendant charged with an offense may sometimes prevent successful prosecution by demonstrating facts, unrelated to his or her guilt or innocence of the crime charged, that cut off—or "bar"—prosecution. Among these bars are double jeopardy, ex post facto, lack of jurisdiction, expiration of the statute of limitations, and state-granted immunity. Each of these bars is discussed briefly below.

Double Jeopardy

The Fifth Amendment to the United States Constitution provides that no person shall be "twice put in jeopardy" for the "same offense," which means that if a defendant charged with an offense can show that he or she already has been put "in jeopardy" for that "same offense," the state may not again prosecute that defendant. This raises two questions: How far down the prosecution road may the state go in trying a defendant before it is regarded as putting him or her in jeopardy? And how closely related to the present charge must the previous offense be in order to be regarded as the "same offense"? As a general matter, a defendant has not been put in jeopardy until the jury is sworn (437 U.S. 28) or, in nonjury cases, until the trial begins—which means the swearing in of the first witness or presentation of the first evidence (420 U.S. 377; 327 N.C. 244). Even so, a defendant may be retried after jeopardy attaches if the first trial had to be called off in midstream (a "mistrial") because of "manifest necessity," if the jury could not reach a unanimous verdict (a "hung jury"), or the defendant caused the retrial by appealing a conviction and obtaining a new trial. In North Carolina, one offense generally is treated as being the same as another only when all of the elements needed to be proved for conviction of the one offense are among those that must be proved for conviction of the other offense (301 N.C. 153). This means, for example, that a defendant who has been tried for armed robbery could later be tried for an assault with a deadly weapon with intent to kill that he or she committed during that robbery, since it would not have been necessary, in trying to prove armed robbery, to show that the defendant had an intent to kill.

Ex Post Facto

The ex post facto provisions of the United States and North Carolina constitutions prohibit: (1) the enactment of a statute that makes criminal an act that was not a crime when it was committed; (2) changing the elements of an offense after it was committed and to the defendant's disadvantage; (3) increasing the punishment for a crime after the act constituting the crime was committed (298 N.C. 604); and (4) altering the rules of evidence to allow less or different testimony than the law required when the crime was committed (529 U.S. 513). However, some changes in the rules of evidence or criminal procedure do not violate ex post facto provisions (305 N.C. 92; 110 U.S. 574).

Lack of Jurisdiction

To say that the state lacks jurisdiction to try a person for an offense means that the offense is not part of the state's concern. The state has no jurisdiction to try a person for an act made criminal by North Carolina law unless it was committed entirely or partially within the state. If some part of a crime is committed in North Carolina, though other parts of the crime are committed outside the state, North Carolina has jurisdiction to try the person for the offense (305 N.C. 196; 104 N.C. App. 298; 81 N.C. App. 499).

The following statutes deal with the problem of deciding where or whether an act occurred in North Carolina:

§15-130. Assault in one county, death in another.

In all cases of felonious homicide when the assault has been made in one county within the State, and the person assaulted dies in any other county thereof, the offender shall be indicted and punished for the crime in the county wherein the assault was made.

§15-131. Assault in this State, death in another.

In all cases of felonious homicide, when the assault has been made within this State, and the person assaulted dies without the limits thereof, the offender shall be indicted and punished for the crime in the county wherein the assault was made, in the same manner, to all intents and purposes, as if the person assaulted had died within the limits of this State.

§15A-134. Offense occurring in part outside North Carolina.

If a charged offense occurred in part in North Carolina and in part outside North Carolina, a person charged with that offense may be tried in this State if he has not been placed in jeopardy for the identical offense in another state.

Expiration of Statute of Limitations

A statute of limitations provides that if a criminal charge is not brought against a defendant within a certain time, it may not be prosecuted at all. North Carolina has no statute of limitations on prosecution for a felony (275 N.C. 264). G.S. 15-1 provides a two-year statute of limitations for misdemeanors (except for malicious misdemeanors). The two-year period begins to run when the final act that is part of the offense is completed (258 N.C. 533). In order to beat the two-year misdemeanor deadline, the state must issue a valid criminal process (244 N.C. 68; 118 N.C. App. 130). Issuance of a constitutionally void criminal process does not satisfy the statute (272 N.C. 491). The defense is waived if the defendant fails to plead it or to request jury instructions (133 N.C. 709), pleads guilty (193 N.C. 747), or fails to introduce evidence that the time limit has expired (222 N.C. 28).

State-Granted Immunity

North Carolina statutes (G.S. 15A-1051 through -1054) make it possible for the court or prosecutor to give a person immunity from prosecution for a certain offense in exchange for that person's agreement to plead guilty to another offense or to provide testimony against another defendant. When this kind of immunity has been granted, the person may not be prosecuted for that offense, regardless of the evidence against him or her.

Defenses that justify

Generally

Sometimes a person may not be guilty of a crime he or she has been charged with, even if the person did the act charged and knew what he or she was doing, if there was a reason for committing the act that the law recognizes as a valid justification. Examples of defenses based on such justification are discussed briefly below.

Self-Defense as a Defense to Murder

A person may kill an attacker if he or she reasonably believes that the killing is necessary in order to keep the attacker from killing him or her or doing him or her great bodily harm (208 N.C. 127). If the defendant reasonably believed at the time that the killing was the only way to save himself or herself from death or great bodily harm, the defendant can claim self-defense, even if it might later be shown that he or she was not actually in such danger (223 N.C. 770; 338 N.C. 168). However, a person generally may not successfully assert self-defense if he or she provoked the attack (229 N.C. 718) unless, after entering the fight, he or she withdrew and let the other person know of the withdrawal (225 N.C. 117; 338 N.C. 363; 4 N.C. App. 469). Old cases ruled that in some circumstances a person must retreat as far as possible before resorting to self-defense (223 N.C. 770). However, the modern view is that a person who did not provoke the attack may kill or use a lesser degree of deadly force without retreating if the person reasonably believes the attack threatens death or great bodily injury (338 N.C. 168; 117 N.C. App. 141). Also, a person who did not provoke the attack need not retreat if on his or her own premises (288 N.C. 34; 24 N.C. App. 673). A law enforcement officer lawfully performing a duty, such as making an arrest, need not retreat either [177 N.C. 559; G.S. 15A-401(d)(2)].

The law describes two kinds of self-defense as a defense to murder. The law of "perfect" self-defense excuses a killing altogether if, at the time of the killing, (1) it appeared to the defendant, and the defendant believed, it was necessary to kill to save himself or herself from death or great bodily harm; (2) this was a reasonable belief; (3) the defendant was not the aggressor; (4) and the defendant did not use excessive force (303 N.C. 526; 341 N.C. 585). If elements (1) and (2) are present but either (3) or (4) are absent, the defendant is said to have an "imperfect" right of self-defense. With "imperfect" self-defense a killing is not completely excused, and the defendant is guilty of at least voluntary manslaughter (303 N.C. 526; 331 N.C. 695).

See John Rubin, *The Law of Self-Defense in North Carolina* (Chapel Hill: Institute of Government, The University of North Carolina at Chapel Hill, 1996).

Self-Defense as a Defense to Assault

A person may use force against another when the amount of force the person uses appears to him or her to be reasonably necessary in order to protect himself or herself from the other person's assault, even when the other person's assault is not deadly (230 N.C. 54). A person may not, however, use more force than appears reasonably necessary or continue to use it after the need has disappeared (253 N.C. 37). Also, if a person voluntarily entered or remained in a fight in which the person used force to defend himself or herself, the person may not successfully assert this defense (228 N.C. 228). Closely related to this point is the North Carolina rule that a private citizen may not be convicted of resisting arrest if the arrest itself was not legal (240 N.C. 476; see "Resisting, Delaying, or Obstructing an Officer," Chapter 18). However, a person may not use deadly force or a deadly weapon to resist an illegal arrest by a law enforcement officer who is using reasonable force, when the person knows or should know that the officer is a law enforcement officer attempting to make an arrest [G.S. 15A-401(f)].

See John Rubin, *The Law of Self-Defense in North Carolina,* cited above.

Defense of Others

A person may generally intervene and use force against another when it appears reasonably necessary in order to protect a third person from death or great bodily harm (134 N.C. 698; 265 N.C. 312), and possibly lesser harm. But a person may do this only if he or she reasonably believes that the third person himself or herself would have been justified in using the force—for example, if the person being protected had picked the fight, then the one who intervened could not claim this defense if he or she knew the person being protected could not have used force lawfully in self-defense (239 N.C. 89; 270 N.C. 622; 337 N.C. 615). A person may intervene on behalf of his or her spouse or a family member (and possibly other persons) even if the attack does not present a threat of death or great bodily harm (75 N.C. 174; 222 N.C. 178).

Defense of Property

This defense may be divided into two categories: defense of property generally and defense of habitation or home. A person may generally use force to protect the person's own property or property of another person he or she is acting for, but the person may never use more force than the amount that is reasonably necessary to prevent interference with the property (258 N.C. 44). A person may never use deadly force unless there is danger to life (258 N.C. 44), except as described in the next paragraph.

Under North Carolina's case law, a person defending his or her home or habitation may use deadly force against another person attempting to enter the home or habitation if the defender reasonably believes there is a danger of death or great bodily harm to any occupant, or reasonably believes the assailant intends to commit a felony (222 N.C. 428; 267 N.C. 409; 299 N.C. 103). The common-law rule of thumb has been that at least part of the intruder's body must be inside the habitation before deadly force may be used, though there is authority that the property holder may open the door to shoot the assailant outside when reasonably necessary (267 N.C. 409). Although deadly force is allowed to prevent entry, once entry is accomplished, the rules about defense of the person, except for retreat, apply (297 N.C. 151; 78 N.C. App. 100). However, if an assailant enters a person's habitation, leaves, or is repelled, and attempts to re-enter, the rule stated above about use of deadly force to prevent entry applies to the second attempt to enter (105 N.C. App. 518).

The previous paragraph discusses common-law rules about defense of habitation. For offenses committed on or after October 1, 1994, the following statute describes when deadly force may be used against an intruder into a home. The statute essentially codifies existing common-law rules about defense of habitation (except for the additional authority to terminate an intruder's unlawful entry):

§14-51.1. Use of deadly physical force against an intruder.

(a) A lawful occupant within a home or other place of residence is justified in using any degree of force that the occupant reasonably believes is necessary, including deadly force, against an intruder to prevent a forcible entry into the home or residence or to terminate the intruder's unlawful entry (i) if the occupant reasonably apprehends that the intruder may kill or inflict serious bodily harm to the occupant or others in the home or residence, or (ii) if the occupant reasonably believes that the intruder intends to commit a felony in the home or residence.

(b) A lawful occupant within a home or other place of residence does not have a duty to retreat from an intruder in the circumstances described in this section.

(c) This section is not intended to repeal, expand, or limit any other defense that may exist under the common law.

Public Authority

An act done in the lawful exercise of public authority cannot be a crime even if the same act done without that authority would have been a crime (*Perkins*, p. 1093). That is one reason, for example, a law enforcement officer is not guilty of assault for handcuffing an unruly arrestee nor guilty of possession of a controlled substance for buying drugs as part of an investigation (106 N.C. 728). But the person loses this defense by going beyond his or her authority (172 N.C. 895). G.S. 15A-401(d) and (e) describe the limits of authority in using force to arrest. (See also the discussion of resisting an unlawful arrest, under "Self-Defense as a Defense to Assault," above.) A specific statute (G.S. 20-145) exempts from speed limits ambulances, fire trucks in emergencies, law enforcement officers who are pursuing violators, and a few others.

Domestic Authority

In some instances people without public authority also claim authority, by virtue of their private position, to do acts that would otherwise be crimes. The parent and the teacher who stands in the parents' place are the primary examples of people with this domestic authority. A parent may use force to discipline his or her child if permanent injury is not inflicted and the parent does not act maliciously (95 N.C. 588). The same rule generally applies to a teacher or anyone else standing in the parent's place (113 N.C. 635), although the force must be applied within the "sphere of the person's authority" (136 N.C. 610). However, G.S. 115C-390 allows local school boards to restrict teachers' authority to use force to discipline students and maintain order. Domestic authority also seems to permit the use of nondeadly force by those in charge of places of assembly (theaters and common carriers, for example) to expel (but not punish) people who should not be there or are acting improperly (*Perkins*, p. 1105).

Prevention of Crime

Although this provision is infrequently applied in North Carolina, common law seems to permit a citizen to use force to prevent a felony or a breach of the peace (*Perkins*, p. 1108), including the use of deadly force to prevent a felony dangerous to life (8 N.C. 457; 13 N.C. 58). In addition, a citizen is authorized to detain, and then turn over to law enforcement officers, anyone the citizen has probable cause to believe has committed in his or her presence a felony, a breach of the peace, a crime involving physical injury to another, or theft or destruction of property (G.S. 15A-404; 68 N.C. App. 209). The detention must be reasonable, and the suspect must be surrendered to a law enforcement officer as early as possible.

Defenses showing lack of blameworthiness

Generally

Sometimes a defendant charged with an offense may show his or her innocence, even though the defendant did the illegal act and the act is not justified, by establishing that the circumstances were such that he or she should not be blamed for the act—the person might either have lacked a guilty mind or have been forced into the act. These are excuse defenses—that is, defenses showing that a person was not responsible for what he or she did. Examples of such defenses are described briefly below.

A defendant may offer defenses other than those described below to show that lack of responsibility for what he or she did. For example, a defendant may claim that a shooting was accidental, and as a result he or she did not have the required state of mind to be convicted of any resulting homicide charge (330 N.C. 249).

Insanity

A person may be found not guilty of a crime by establishing that (1) when committing the offense, he or she had a mental disease, a mental defect, or low intelligence and (2) as a result was incapable of knowing the nature and quality of the act or knowing that the act was wrong (293 N.C. 413; 306 N.C. 90; 328 N.C. 477).

A person is presumed to be sane, and the defendant has the burden of proving to the satisfaction of the jury insanity at the time of the act (314 N.C. 374). Accordingly, even uncontradicted evidence of a defendant's insanity does not entitle him or her to a directed verdict of not guilty by reason of insanity (300 N.C. 223; 328 N.C. 477). The presumption of sanity does not relieve the state of its burden of proving all of the essential elements of each charged crime (328 N.C. 477).

Immaturity

In North Carolina, generally a person under 16 who commits a crime is not subject to trial in adult courts [G.S. 7B-1501(7), -1601]; instead, the person is under the jurisdiction of the juvenile court. But if a juvenile was 13 years of age or older when he or she committed a Class A felony (first-degree murder is the only Class A felony), the juvenile *must* be tried as an adult. A juvenile 13 years of age or older at the time any other felony offense is committed *may*, in the judge's discretion, be tried as an adult would be for that felony (G.S. 7B-2200). In addition, a child under 6 may not even be brought before the juvenile court as a delinquent [G.S. 7B-1501(7)]. Immaturity as a defense to sexual offenses is discussed in Chapter 8.

Unconsciousness or Automatism

A person charged with a crime may establish his or her innocence by showing that he or she was physically unable to control the actions that constitute the criminal act, either because of unconsciousness or because of a sickness or an outside force (287 N.C. 266; 309 N.C. 239).

Unconsciousness is not a defense if it results from insanity, a mental defect, voluntary intoxication, or voluntary use of drugs (336 N.C. 684; 350 N.C. 701). It is a defense if it results from epilepsy, a blow to the head, fever, sleepwalking, involuntary intoxication, or involuntary use of drugs (296 N.C. 693). The defendant has the burden of proving the defense to the satisfaction of the jury (287 N.C. 266).

Duress or Necessity

Courts use these terms interchangeably, and the test of availability as a defense is the same: A person may escape criminal liability for an act if he or she committed the act because of a reasonable fear that he, she, or another would suffer immediate death or serious bodily injury if he or she did not act (289 N.C. 644). The rationale underlying this defense is based on the public policy that "law ought to promote the achievement of higher values at the expense of lesser values, and [that] sometimes the greater good for society will be accomplished by violating the literal language of a criminal law" (103 N.C. App. 264). So, for example, this defense would excuse from prosecution a passerby who broke into a car because he or she saw that an occupant of the car was in physical distress and needed immediate medical assistance.

This defense is not available to any charge of intentional homicide (305 N.C. 532; 307 N.C. 274) and probably is not available to any charge of homicide except a felony murder when the defendant did not actually do the killing (289 N.C. 644; 64 N.C. App. 536).

One traditional form of the duress defense is coercion of a wife by her husband—under common law a wife who committed a criminal act in the presence of her husband and at his command was presumed to have committed the act under duress from him (244 N.C. 701). However, this doctrine is clearly obsolete (33 N.C. App. 511; 133 N.C. App. 543).

According to our courts, this defense is not intended to excuse criminal activity by those who disagree with decisions and polices of the lawmaking branches of government. Thus this defense could not be claimed by anti-abortion protesters who trespassed onto an abortion clinic's property in an effort to save fetuses from abortion (103 N.C. App. 264).

This defense may not be successfully asserted when the offense continues to be committed after the duress has ended. For example, a defendant charged with impaired driving could not assert the defense that he or she was attempting to escape from a group of people chasing the defendant on foot when the incident occurred thirty minutes before the defendant was stopped and charged; the assailants were left behind long before the defendant's observation by a law enforcement officer (94 N.C. App. 386).

There is a special five-factor test to prove this defense to a charge of escape from a prison or jail (see 60 N.C. App. 191).

Entrapment

If a person was entrapped into committing an offense by a law enforcement officer or some other person acting on behalf of a public agency, the person is not guilty of that crime. To establish entrapment, it must be shown that (1) the idea for committing the crime did not originate with the defendant and (2) someone acting for a governmental agency persuaded or tricked the defendant into doing the offense when he or she otherwise would not have done it (307 N.C. 1; 77 N.C. App. 61). It is commonly said that a person has not been entrapped if he or she already had a "predisposition" to commit the crime and that "merely providing an opportunity" to commit the crime does not amount to entrapment (307 N.C. 1). Generally, predisposition to commit a crime may be demonstrated by a person's ready compliance, acquiescence in, or willingness to cooperate in a criminal plan when law enforcement officers simply provide the person an opportunity to commit such a crime (97 N.C. App. 589). The defendant has the burden of proving entrapment "to the satisfaction of the jury" (307 N.C. 1). A defendant may not raise entrapment as a defense if he or she denies committing the underlying acts of the alleged crime (302 N.C. 623; 95 N.C. App. 56). However, a defendant may raise the defense if he or she denies having the intent to commit the offense (306 N.C. 566; 95 N.C. App. 56).

Ignorance or Mistake

Although generally it is true that "ignorance of the law is no excuse" (45 N.C. App. 438), in some cases a person's ignorance of facts can be a defense. If a person made a reasonable mistake of fact—for example, thinking that the car the person drove away was his or her own (when it actually only looked the same)—the person is not guilty when what the person did would not have been a crime if the fact had been as the person believed. Such a mistake may negate an element of a charged criminal offense. In some cases, however, the person's knowledge does not matter (such as whether a defendant knows the victim's age in a statutory rape case), and a mistake of fact is not a defense.

Voluntary Intoxication

The fact that the defendant was voluntarily intoxicated on alcohol or drugs when he or she committed an offense is not a complete defense. But sometimes a person may be voluntarily intoxicated to such a degree that his or her condition prevents formation of the "specific intent" that is a necessary element of a particular offense (304 N.C. 511; 333 N.C. 687; 335 N.C. 477). If so, the defendant cannot be found guilty of the specific-intent offense, but he or she may be found guilty of a lesser-included offense. The leading example of specific intent is the intent to kill formed after premeditation and deliberation required for a homicide to constitute first-degree murder. A person who was so intoxicated that he or she could not premeditate and deliberate could not be convicted of first-degree murder based on the theory of specific intent formed after premeditation and deliberation. A voluntarily intoxicated defendant who commits a homicide and is charged based on the theory of specific intent formed after premeditation and deliberation could be convicted of second-degree murder instead because the malice required for that offense is not a "specific intent."

Voluntary intoxication may be a valid defense to any offense requiring "specific intent" as an essential element. Examples include *attempted* rape (note: "specific intent" is an essential element of any attempt) (307 N.C. 198); felonious breaking and entering (27 N.C. App. 137); and burglary (313 N.C. 554). Voluntary intoxication is not a defense to offenses that do not have as an element "specific intent." For example, the voluntary intoxication defense is unavailable to a first-degree murder charge based on the theory of commission by lying in wait. Specific intent formed after premeditation and deliberation is not an element of proving first-degree murder committed by lying in wait (326 N.C. 368; 330 N.C. 446). The North Carolina Supreme Court has suggested, but not conclusively ruled, that voluntary intoxication may not be a defense to first-degree murder based on the theories of poisoning, imprisonment, starvation, or torture (320 N.C. 179; 330 N.C. 446). This defense is unavailable for second-degree murder (334 N.C. 356), discharging a firearm into occupied property (339 N.C. 114), or rape (307 N.C. 198). Voluntary intoxication does not apply to acting in concert theory (or other theories of participation in crime; see Chapter 3), because the defense applies only to an element of a crime, and these theories describe the nature of a person's participation in a given offense but are not crimes themselves (334 N.C. 356).

A more detailed discussion of this defense is provided by John Rubin, "The Voluntary Intoxication Defense," *Administration of Justice Memorandum* No. 93/01 (Institute of Government, May 1993).

Diminished Capacity

A defendant whose mental condition is diminished at the time of an alleged offense but does not satisfy the criteria for the insanity defense, may still have a partial defense to some crimes. The diminished capacity defense allows a defendant to introduce evidence of mental or emotional conditions that shows the defendant could not form the required state of mind to commit the charged crime. The North Carolina Supreme Court has allowed diminished capacity as a defense to the element in first-degree murder that provides that the defendant formed the specific intent to kill after premeditation and deliberation (322 N.C. 243; 331 N.C. 462). Like voluntary intoxication, diminished capacity may be available as a defense to other offenses requiring specific intent as an element.

For a comprehensive discussion of the diminished capacity defense, see John Rubin, "The Diminished Capacity Defense," *Administration of Justice Memorandum* No. 92/01 (Institute of Government, Sept. 1992).

3
Participants in Crimes

Chapter Contents

3
Participants in Crimes

Crimes often are committed by only one person. However, sometimes two or more people participate in committing a crime. In such a case, the participants might play similar or different roles in carrying out the offense. This chapter explains basic common-law doctrines that categorize the various types of roles a person can play in committing a crime. These doctrines do not establish separate offenses. They merely describe the nature of a person's participation in a given offense (301 N.C. 407).

Principals—Committing the Entire Crime

Statute

This is a common-law concept.

Elements

A person is a principal to a crime based on this concept when
(1) with the required state of mind
(2) he or she commits all of the acts necessary to constitute a crime.

Punishment

A person who is a principal to a crime is guilty of that crime and is punishable as provided for that crime.

Notes

Generally. The term "principal" is used to describe a person who participates directly in committing a crime. The most important way of being a principal, of course, is by committing all of a crime, either alone or with other people. One can also be a principal by committing part of a crime that others complete or by helping someone else commit a crime (292 N.C. 711). These other ways of being a principal are discussed on the following pages. The law divides principals into two types: principals in the first degree and principals in the second degree. A principal in the first degree is one who commits an entire crime, who acts indirectly to cause a crime, or who acts in concert with others to commit a crime. A principal in the second degree is one who aids and abets in the commission of a crime (301 N.C. 407). Principal concepts apply to felony offenses, but not to misdemeanors. "Aiding and Abetting Misdemeanor," discussed later in this chapter, covers situations involving persons participating indirectly in misdemeanors.

Element (1). Often a person is guilty of a crime only if he or she has a certain state of mind (for example, *intending* to do what the person did, or *recklessly* doing what the person did), although in some cases a person may be found guilty without regard to state of mind. In any event, a person may be a principal to a crime only by committing it with the state of mind required by law for that particular offense. See Chapter 1, "States of Mind".

Element (2). When, in addition to having the required state of mind, a person also does all of the acts that constitute elements of the crime, the person is a principal; that is, the person has committed the crime.

Related offenses not in this chapter

None.

Principals—Acting Indirectly

Statute

This is a common-law concept.

Elements

A person is a principal to a crime based on this concept when
- (1) with the required state of mind, *and*
- (2) without being present
- (3) he or she causes the occurrence that constitutes the crime
- (4) (a) by using a tool or device that brings about the occurrence in the person's absence, *or*
  - (b) by using a person who is not himself or herself guilty but brings about the occurrence in the principal's absence, *or*
  - (c) by using a combination of (a) and (b), above, *or*
  - (d) by being an accessory before the fact.

Punishment

A person who is a principal to a crime is guilty of that crime and is punishable as provided for that crime.

Notes

Generally. As explained above, the type of principal participation does not establish a separate crime; it is only a statement of circumstances in which a person may be found guilty of a given crime (301 N.C. 407).

Element (2). Anyone who is present and commits the crime is also guilty.

Element (4)(a). If the defendant sets in motion the force that results in the crime, such as by laying a trap or leaving poison, the defendant can be guilty even though not present when the crime is completed (114 N.C. 910; *Perkins*, p. 737).

Element (4)(b). If the defendant employs another to commit the act and the other person cannot be found guilty because of insanity, immaturity, or absence of knowledge of what he or she was doing, then the defendant is guilty as a principal (276 N.C. 641; *Perkins*, p. 737). If the other person is not innocent, the defendant is an accessory before the fact (if the defendant is not present when the act is committed) or an aider and abettor (if the defendant is present when the act is committed).

Element (4)(d). See "Accessory before the Fact to Felony."

Related offenses not in this chapter

"Solicitation of Another to Commit a Felony" (Chapter 4)
"Conspiracy" (Chapter 4)
"Attempt" (Chapter 4)

Principals—Acting in Concert

Statute

This is a common-law concept.

Elements

A person is a principal to a crime based on this concept when
(1) with the required state of mind
(2) he or she
  (a) participates in at least one of the acts necessary to the commission of the crime, *or*
  (b) is present when the offense is committed and the person's participation indicates a shared or common purpose with someone whose actions satisfy all elements of the offense, *and*
(3) one or more of the co-participants engages in the acts not engaged in by the defendant that constitute the remainder of the crime.

Punishment

A person who is a principal to a crime is guilty of that crime and is punishable as provided for that crime.

Notes

Generally. Being a principal by acting in concert is not a separate crime; it is only a statement of one of the circumstances in which a person can be found guilty of a given crime (301 N.C. 407). It is not necessary that the defendant do any particular act constituting at least part of a crime to be convicted of that crime under the acting-in-concert principle, as long as the defendant is acting together with another who does the acts necessary to constitute the crime pursuant to a common plan or purpose to commit the crime (297 N.C. 349; 333 N.C. 501; 338 N.C. 315). A judge may instruct the jury on both theories of acting in concert and aiding and abetting when facts in a case support both theories (313 N.C. 80). See also the notes under "Principals—Committing the Entire Crime."

Element (1). If two people join in a purpose to commit a crime, and the crime has as an element a specific intent to do something (for example, the specific intent to kill as an element of first-degree murder committed by premeditation and deliberation), proof of the each person's specific intent is not required; all that needs to be established is that one of the principals had that specific intent (345 N.C. 184).

Elements (2) and (3). A defendant can be a principal by acting in concert with another person if he or she commits an act that satisfies one or more elements of a crime. For example, if a defendant threatened a victim with violence, and an accomplice took personal property from the victim, the defendant would still be a principal in the first-degree robbery.

However, even if the defendant's conduct does not constitute even one element of a crime, the doctrine of acting in concert can apply if the defendant is present when the offense is committed and the defendant's conduct indicates a shared or common purpose with a co-participant whose actions constitute the elements of the offense (297 N.C. 349; 299 N.C. 652; 338 N.C. 315). The "presence" element of this offense may be satisfied by actual or constructive presence. Being in close proximity to the place where a crime was committed may show that a defendant was constructively present (301 N.C. 394; 330 N.C. 167).

If two people join in a purpose to commit a crime, each of them—if actually or constructively present during the commission of the crime—is guilty not only as a principal if the other commits that particular crime, but each also is guilty of any other crime committed by the other in pursuing the common purpose or as a natural or probable consequence thereof (345 N.C. 184).

Charging Issues. In charging a substantive offense (such as murder), it is unnecessary to allege the theory of acting in concert (345 N.C. 43).

Related offenses not in this chapter

"Conspiracy" (Chapter 4)
"Subornation of Perjury" (Chapter 18)
Inciting to Riot (various offenses) (Chapter 17)

Aiding and Abetting Felony

Statute

This is a common-law concept. Many statutes specifying particular offenses include aiding and abetting as a form of the offense.

Elements

A person is guilty of a felony based on this concept when

(1) a felony is committed by another person (the principal in the first degree), *and*

(2) he or she

  (a) knowingly advises, instigates, encourages, or helps the other principal commit the felony, *or*

  (b) shares the criminal purpose of the other principal and, to the knowledge of the other principal, aids or is in a position to aid the other principal when the felony is committed, *or*

  (c) is present with the opportunity and duty to prevent the act and fails to do so.

Punishment

A person who aids or abets a felony is guilty of that felony and is punishable as provided for that felony.

Notes

Generally. A judge may instruct the jury on both the theory of acting in concert and the theory of aiding and abetting when facts in a case support both theories (313 N.C. 80).

Element (1). A principal in the first degree and an aider and abettor do not have to be tried in the same manner, nor must the outcome of each prosecution be the same. The principal in the first degree need not be convicted before a person may be found guilty of aiding and abetting that principal (141 N.C. 722). The defendant may be convicted even if a principal in the first degree is acquitted in another trial of the same crime (113 N.C. 716; 283 N.C. 261; but see 122 N.C. App. 497, which distinguished these cases and ruled that a conviction for aiding and abetting a named principal must be set aside when that principal later was found not guilty). To convict the aider and abettor it need only be established that the crime was committed by someone (283 N.C. 261). Also, it is permissible at the same trial for one principal to be convicted and another acquitted or convicted of a lesser or greater charge (335 N.C. 647). [This last statement marks a change in the doctrine of North Carolina's courts; until the decision in 335 N.C. 647, the state supreme court had said that if the other principal is acquitted at the same trial in which the aider and abettor defendant is being tried, the defendant may not be convicted (214 N.C. 123), nor may the defendant be convicted of a greater degree of crime than the degree for which the other principal is convicted (250 N.C. 85).] The principal and aider and abettor need not be found guilty of the same offense. For example, when a principal pled guilty to voluntary manslaughter, the defendant as an aider and abettor was properly convicted at a later trial of second-degree murder (24 N.C. App. 717).

Element (2)(a). The mere presence of the defendant does not make him or her an aider or abettor (255 N.C. 412; 304 N.C. 447; 310 N.C. 126), even if the defendant has a secret intent to assist if it becomes necessary. The defendant must actually have aided or encouraged the principal in the first degree (238 N.C. 94).

Element (2)(b). Even if the defendant is not immediately present, he or she can satisfy this element by standing by in a position in which he or she can help and the principal in the first degree knows that (299 N.C. 284; 306 N.C. 288; 109 N.C. App. 136).

Element (2)(c). Criminal liability as an aider and abettor applies to a person who fails to prevent a crime when he or she has the opportunity and duty to do so. For example, it has included when (1) a mother failed to stop another person from assaulting her child (306 N.C. 466) and (2) a mother failed to prevent illegal sexual intercourse between an adult and her child in her presence (109 N.C. App. 136).

Withdrawal before completion of offense. If a person who would otherwise be guilty as an aider and abettor withdraws before the offense is completed, the person may avoid guilt as a principal, but only if withdrawal is communicated to the other participant at the time, so as to remove any encouragement (268 N.C. 303).

Charging Issues. In charging a substantive offense, it is unnecessary to allege the theory of aiding and abetting (37 N.C. App. 528).

Related offenses not in this chapter

"Solicitation of Another to Commit a Felony " (Chapter 4)
"Conspiracy" (Chapter 4)
"Accessory after the Fact to Felony" (Chapter 4)

Aiding and Abetting Misdemeanor

Statute

This is a common-law concept.

Elements

A person is guilty of a misdemeanor based on this concept when
- (1) a misdemeanor is committed by another person, *and*
- (2) he or she
  - (a) knowingly advises, induces, encourages, or aids the other person to commit the misdemeanor, *or*
  - (b) has the opportunity and duty to prevent the act and fails to do so.

Punishment

A person who aids or abets a misdemeanor is guilty of that misdemeanor and is punishable as provided for that misdemeanor.

Notes

Element (1). See the note on Element (1) under "Aiding and Abetting Felony."

Element (2). Anyone who helps commit a misdemeanor is guilty as a principal in the second degree. Aiding and abetting a misdemeanor includes what would be accessory before the fact to a misdemeanor (184 N.C. 723) (e.g., counseling or procuring the commission of a crime). Whether the person is present when the misdemeanor is committed is immaterial. See the notes on Element (2) under "Aiding and Abetting Felony" and "Accessory after the Fact to Felony."

Element (2)(b). See the notes on Element (2)(c) under "Aiding and Abetting Felony."

Related offenses not in this chapter

"Accessory after the Fact to Felony" (Chapter 4)
"Solicitation of Another to Commit a Felony" (Chapter 4)
"Conspiracy" (Chapter 4)

Accessory before the Fact to Felony

Statute

§14-5.2. Accessory before fact punishable as principal felon.

All distinctions between accessories before the fact and principals to the commission of a felony are abolished. Every person who heretofore would have been guilty as an accessory before the fact to any felony shall be guilty and punishable as a principal to that felony. However, if a person who heretofore would have been guilty and punishable as an accessory before the fact is convicted of a capital felony, and the jury finds that his conviction was based solely on the uncorroborated testimony of one or more principals, coconspirators, or accessories to the crime, he shall be guilty of a Class B2 felony.

Elements

A person is a principal to a crime based on this concept when

(1) before a felony is committed by another person, he or she counsels, procures, commands, or knowingly aids the other person to commit the felony
(2) the felony is committed by the other person, *and*
(3) he or she is not present when the other person commits the felony.

Punishment

Under G.S. 14-5.2, an accessory before the fact to a felony is guilty as a principal to the felony and is punishable as provided for that felony. The only exception to this rule is a defendant who is guilty as an accessory before the fact to a capital felony (first-degree murder is the only such felony) who a jury finds was convicted solely on the uncorroborated testimony of another principal, co-conspirator, or accessory; such a defendant is guilty of a Class B2 felony (see 340 N.C. 119).

Notes

Generally. G.S. 14-5.2 provides that an accessory before the fact to a felony is guilty as a principal to the felony (307 N.C. 213).

Element (1). The prosecution must prove that the defendant's conduct caused or directly contributed to the principal's commission of the felony (319 N.C. 620). A defendant is an accessory before the fact only if assistance occurs *before* the crime. If assistance occurs during the crime, the defendant is an aider and abettor (see "Aiding and Abetting Felony"). This offense is aimed at the person who is not actually or constructively present when the principal crime is committed.

Element (2). A person may not be convicted of an offense based on accessory before the fact if *all* the principals are acquitted (91 N.C. App. 198). [Compare with the discussion of inconsistent verdicts under Element (1) of "Aiding and Abetting Felony."] Such acquittal means the accessory before the fact is also acquitted, since there is no proof of commission of the crime by the principal (61 N.C. 400; 109 N.C. App. 373). Even if the accessory-before-the-fact defendant has pled guilty and the principal is acquitted, this rule applies and the plea must be set aside (109 N.C. App. 373). An accessory before the fact may be convicted of a more serious offense than other principals convicted for the same criminal act. For example, a defendant was properly convicted of first-degree murder based on accessory before the fact although all the principals had pled guilty to second-degree murder (338 N.C. 244; 340 N.C. 119).

When an accessory before the fact becomes an aider and abettor. If the defendant counseled, procured, commanded, or knowingly helped the principal commit the felony and then was present when the felony was committed or stood by with intent to render assistance, he or she would be guilty under the aiding and abetting principle (255 N.C. 42; 16 N.C. App. 527; see "Aiding and Abetting Felony").

Guilt for crimes other than that counseled, procured, or planned. If the principal who is counseled or assisted by the defendant to commit a crime commits a different crime from the one counseled by the defendant, or additional crimes, the defendant still is guilty as an accessory before the fact if the other principal's criminal act is a natural and probable consequence of the crime counseled by the defendant (87 N.C. 514). [Note, there is some authority for the rule that an accessory before the fact must answer for *all* crimes flowing from the accomplished event (113 N.C. App. 774).] For example, when a defendant provided information so that others could commit breaking and entering and larceny, and while committing those crimes the principals also committed arson and murder, the accessory before the fact was properly convicted of all crimes committed by the principals (113 N.C. App. 774; see also 345 N.C. 184).

Relationship to conspiracy. To prove conspiracy, the prosecution must show, as an element, that there was an agreement to commit an offense. However, accessory before the fact to felony does not require, as an element, evidence of any such agreement. Therefore, a defendant may be convicted of both conspiracy and the principal offense under the accessory-before-the-fact principle if the defendant's conduct satisfies the elements of both offenses (294 N.C. 1; 313 N.C. 132).

Relationship to solicitation. Solicitation to commit murder is a lesser-included offense of murder that is committed as an accessory before the fact (345 N.C. 43). Thus a conviction of solicitation to commit murder is not permitted when a murder conviction is obtained under the theory of accessory before the fact.

Related offenses not in this chapter

"Solicitation of Another to Commit a Felony" (Chapter 4)
"Conspiracy" (Chapter 4)
"Accessory after the Fact to Felony" (Chapter 4)
Inciting to Riot (various offenses) (Chapter 17)
"Subornation of Perjury" (Chapter 18)

4
General Crimes

Chapter Contents

4
General Crimes

Attempt

Statute

This is a common-law offense. Some statutes specifying particular offenses include attempt as a form of the offense, so before making a charge the law enforcement officer should check the appropriate offense that has been attempted.

Elements

A person guilty of attempt to commit a certain crime

(1) specifically intends to do something that is a crime, *and*

(2) at the time the person has that intent, he or she performs a substantial overt act calculated and designed to bring about the crime, *and*

(3) the act comes so close to bringing the crime about that in the ordinary course of things the person would have completed the crime had he or she not been stopped or thwarted.

Punishment

An attempt to commit a felony or misdemeanor is punishable under the next lower classification as the offense attempted, unless a different classification is specifically stated in a statute (G.S. 14-2.5). For example, an attempt to commit a Class G felony would be punishable as a Class H felony. An attempt to commit a Class 1 misdemeanor would be a Class 2 misdemeanor. Unless a different classification is stated, an attempt to commit a Class A or B1 felony is a Class B2 felony, an attempt to commit a Class B2 felony is a Class C felony, an attempt to commit a Class I felony is a Class 1 misdemeanor, and an attempt to commit a Class 3 misdemeanor is also a Class 3 misdemeanor. For a few offenses, the defining statute provides that an attempt is to be punished as if the offense had been actually committed. When that is the case, this issue will be discussed under the offense. For example, G.S. 14-87 provides that armed robbery is a Class D felony and that attempted armed robbery also is a Class D felony (see "Armed Robbery" in Chapter 12).

Before structured sentencing some *attempted* misdemeanors, if "infamous, done in secrecy and malice, or [committed] with deceit and intent to defraud," could be punished as felonies pursuant to G.S. 14-3(b). Under structured sentencing this is no longer the case. Attempts committed on or after October 1, 1994, have specific punishments pursuant to G.S. 14-2.5, and therefore G.S. 14-3(b) does not apply.

Notes

Element (1). A defendant may attempt to commit either a felony or a misdemeanor (*Perkins*, p. 611; see, for example, 220 N.C. 411). The intent may be inferred from evidence of previous commissions of the crime attempted (224 N.C. 527). The precise nature of the intended crime need not be proved; for example, it would not be necessary to prove what particular object a person charged with attempted larceny intended to take (82 N.C. 556). A charge of attempt cannot be based on an "attempt to attempt" or on an attempt to commit some other crime that is itself a form of attempt (158 N.C. 627), such as assault (199 N.C. 778) or embracery (that is, an attempt to influence a judge or jury by corrupt means) (95 N.C. 685).

Element (2). Intent alone cannot constitute an attempt; there must be a direct act toward commission of an offense (224 N.C. 347).

Element (3). To be sufficient to establish an attempt, the act must amount to the "commencement of the consummation" of the attempted crime; the act must be more than mere preparation (183 N.C. 687; 334 N.C. 54).

Attempted first-degree murder—elements. A person commits the crime of attempted first-degree murder if the person (1) specifically intends to kill another person unlawfully; (2) commits an overt act calculated to carry out that intent, beyond mere preparation; (3) acts with malice, premeditation, and deliberation; and (4) falls short of committing the murder (131 N.C. App. 199).

Attempted second-degree murder is not a crime. The crime of attempted second-degree murder does not exist because a specific intent to kill is not an element of second-degree murder, and an attempt requires an intent to commit the substantive offense (351 N.C. 448).

Impossibility. As a general rule, the fact that the defendant would have been unable to commit the crime even if he or she had gone through with it does not prevent a conviction for attempt, as long as the defendant specifically intended to commit the crime and did all the acts necessary to commit the crime under the circumstances as he or she reasonably saw them (183 N.C. 687; 307 N.C. 1). A defendant may be convicted of attempting to possess cocaine when (1) the defendant intends to possess cocaine; (2) the defendant acts in a manner to accomplish that intent by driving to an area known for drug sales, approaching people the defendant believes to be cocaine dealers, and exchanging money for what the defendant thinks is cocaine (but was in fact pieces of Brazil nut represented by undercover officers to be rock cocaine); and (3) the defendant's efforts fall short of completing the offense of possession of cocaine (122 N.C. App. 294).

Related offenses not in this chapter

"Simple Assault" (Chapter 7)
"Assault Inflicting Serious Injury" (Chapter 7)
"Discharging Barreled Weapon or Firearm into Occupied Property" (attempt) (Chapter 7)
"Indecent Liberties with a Child" (attempt) (Chapter 8)
"Armed Robbery" (attempt) (Chapter 12)
"Being Found in a Building with Intent to Commit Any Felony or Larceny" (Chapter 13)
"Safecracking" (attempt) (Chapter 13)
"Obtaining Property by False Pretenses" (attempt) (Chapter 14)
"Subornation of Perjury" (Chapter 18)
"Attempt and Conspiracy to Violate Controlled Substances Act" (Chapter 24)
See discussion of attempt under specific offenses throughout the book.

Solicitation of Another to Commit a Felony

Statute

This a common-law offense.

Elements

A person guilty of this offense
(1) entices, advises, counsels, incites, induces, orders, or commands another to commit a felony
(2) with the specific intent that the other person commit the crime.

Punishment

Solicitation to commit a felony is punishable as a felony two classes lower than the felony solicited, unless a different classification is specifically stated in a statute [G.S. 14-2.6(a)]. For example, solicitation to commit a Class G felony would be a Class I felony. Unless a different classification is provided, solicitation to commit a Class A or B1 felony is a Class C felony, solicitation to commit a Class B2 felony is a Class D felony, solicitation to commit a Class H felony is a Class 1 misdemeanor, and solicitation to commit a Class I felony is a Class 2 misdemeanor [G.S. 14-2.6(a)]. Solicitation to commit any misdemeanor is punishable as a Class 3 misdemeanor, unless a different classification is specifically stated in a statute [G.S. 14-2.6(b)].

Before structured sentencing a solicitation that would otherwise be a misdemeanor, if "infamous, done in secrecy and malice, or [committed] with deceit and intent to defraud," could be punished as a Class H felony pursuant to G.S. 14-3(b). Under structured sentencing this is no longer the case. Solicitation now has specific punishments pursuant to G.S. 14-2.6, and therefore G.S. 14-3(b) does not apply to a solicitation occurring on or after October 1, 1994.

Notes

Element (1). Solicitation has occurred even if the person solicited is a law enforcement officer who has no intention to consider carrying out the crime (25 N.C. App. 567).

Element (2). The offense of solicitation is committed even if the crime solicited is not carried out; the solicitation itself is the offense (210 N.C. 283).

Charging one or more instances of solicitation. A single solicitation may continue over a period of time and involve several contacts when the person solicited gives no definite refusal to the solicitor's request. But a definite refusal coupled with a lapse of some time may end the transaction so that a new request upon another occasion may constitute a new offense (292 N.C. 711). In such a case, a defendant may be charged with more than one solicitation.

Relationship to attempt, accessory before the fact, and conspiracy. Solicitation also could be an attempt in some circumstances (*Perkins*, p. 649). Solicitation and attempt to commit the same offense are separately punishable (100 N.C. App. 286). A solicitation could make the defendant an accessory before the fact and, therefore, a principal to the crime, if the offense solicited is carried out. Solicitation is not a lesser-included offense of conspiracy (100 N.C. App. 240). Solicitation to commit murder is a lesser-included offense of murder that is committed as an accessory before the fact (345 N.C. 43). Thus a conviction of solicitation to commit murder is not permitted when a murder conviction is obtained under the theory of accessory before the fact.

Solicitation to commit a misdemeanor. North Carolina case law has recognized the offenses of solicitation to commit misdemeanor assault (117 N.C. App. 654) and solicitation to commit common law obstruction of justice (100 N.C. App. 286). It is unclear whether solicitation to commit other kinds of misdemeanors would be recognized (*LaFave*, vol. 2, pp. 4–5).

Related offenses not in this chapter

Inciting to Riot (various offenses) (Chapter 17)
"Subornation of Perjury" (Chapter 18)
Offering Bribes (various offenses) (Chapter 18)
"Procuring for Prostitution" (Chapter 20)

Conspiracy

Statute

This is a common-law offense.

Elements

A person guilty of this offense
(1) enters into an agreement with at least one other person
(2) to commit an unlawful act
(3) with intent at the time by the defendant and at least one of the others that the agreement be carried out.

Punishment

Conspiracy to commit a felony is punishable as a felony one class lower than the felony the defendant conspired to commit, unless a different classification is stated. Conspiracy to commit a Class A or B1 felony is a Class B2 felony, conspiracy to commit a Class B2 felony is a Class C felony, and conspiracy to commit a Class I felony is a Class 1 misdemeanor, unless a different classification is provided by another statute [G.S. 14-2.4(a)].

Conspiracy to commit a misdemeanor is punishable as a misdemeanor one class lower than the misdemeanor the defendant conspired to commit, unless a different classification is stated [G.S. 14-2.4(b)]. Conspiracy to commit a Class 3 misdemeanor is a Class 3 misdemeanor, unless a different classification is stated.

Some statutes provide that a conspiracy to commit a particular crime is a form of that crime and carries the same punishment. For example, the drug trafficking offenses discussed in Chapter 24 provide that a conspiracy to commit such an offense is punished the same as the completed drug trafficking offense.

Notes

Element (1). There must be an agreement; if one of two people, such as an undercover officer, is only pretending to enter an agreement but has no intent to carry it out, there is no conspiracy (275 N.C. 651) (in such a case, the offense of solicitation may have occurred). An agreement may take the form of written or spoken words, a mutual understanding (102 N.C. App. 174), or a nonverbal act [for example, handing a knife to a co-conspirator in an assault would be a nonverbal act sufficient to show agreement (67 N.C. App. 223)].

Element (2). The agreement must be to do something unlawful (106 N.C. App. 342). Some old cases suggest that it could be something that is unlawful but not criminal (such as noncriminal fraud) (*Perkins*, p. 695), but conspiracy charges probably should be brought only against those who agree to commit criminal acts.

Element (3). Even if one of several parties to the agreement has no intent to carry out the crime, it is a conspiracy if at least two parties do have that intent (275 N.C. 651). If the state is able only to identify and charge one conspirator, trial and conviction of that single conspirator is not precluded; trial may proceed if the state can prove the existence of other conspirators (24 N.C. App. 591).

Whether or not there is one conspiracy or several conspiracies depends on the nature of the agreement or agreements. A defendant who enters into a single agreement to commit multiple offenses may be convicted of only one count of conspiracy (of course, the defendant may still be convicted of any offenses actually committed pursuant to the conspiracy) (106 N.C. App. 342). Separate agreements to commit separate offenses may be prosecuted as separate conspiracy offenses even if the crimes were committed together (334 N.C. 467; 335 N.C. 1). The number of separate agreements, not the number of offenses the conspirators agree to commit, determines the number of conspiracy charges (313 N.C. 572; 335 N.C. 1; 84 N.C. App. 150; 112 N.C. App. 838; 122 N.C. App. 666). Factors such as time intervals between discussions, participants, objectives, and number of meetings also help determine the number of conspiracies (106 N.C. App. 342).

Lack of need for overt act. Generally a conspiracy is complete once the agreement is made. Therefore, it is irrelevant to this charge whether the substantive crime is ever committed (329 N.C. 654). Unlike many other states, North Carolina does not require an overt act in furtherance of the conspiracy before the crime of conspiracy can occur (272 N.C. 528).

Acts committed within and outside the state. A person may be charged with this offense if any co-conspirator commits within the state an overt act in furtherance of the unlawful agreement, even if the conspiracy was entered into outside the state (261 N.C. 181; 104 N.C. App. 298).

Acquittal of co-conspirators. Generally, if all of the other alleged co-conspirators are acquitted, then the sole remaining defendant may not be convicted (264 N.C. 571; 204 N.C. 503). However, a defendant's conspiracy conviction remains valid even though all alleged co-conspirators are found not guilty at a later trial (119 N.C. 375, distinguishing 204 N.C. 503).

Relationship to solicitation. A defendant can be guilty of solicitation even if the other party is unwilling to agree, but that is not true with conspiracy.

Guilt as principal. A conspirator must be actually or constructively present when the crime is committed in order to be guilty as an aider and abettor or as an actor in concert (301 N.C. 407). Evidence of the conspiracy may be used to establish that a conspirator who was present during the crime aided and abetted or acted in concert, or to show that an absent conspirator was an accessory before the fact (301 N.C. 407). The agreement to commit an offense required to prove conspiracy is not an element of accessory before the fact to a felony. Consequently a defendant may be convicted of both conspiracy and the principal offense as an accessory before the fact if the defendant's conduct satisfies the elements of both offenses (294 N.C. 1; 313 N.C. 132). See Chapter 3, "Participants in Crimes."

Conspiracy to commit crime when one of co-conspirators could not be convicted of crime if acting alone. A person may be convicted of a conspiracy with another to commit a crime even though that person could not be convicted of the crime if acting alone. For example, a person may be convicted of conspiracy with another to commit the crime of larceny by employee even though the person could not be convicted of that crime if acting alone because he or she is not an employee (126 N.C. App. 524).

Lesser-included offenses. Conspiracy to possess heroin is a lesser-included offense of conspiracy to possess heroin with intent to sell and deliver (60 N.C. App. 1).

Related offenses not in this chapter

"Attempt and Conspiracy to Violate Controlled Substances Act" (Chapter 24)
Drug "Trafficking" offenses (Chapter 24)
Conspiracy to break or enter jail with intent to injure prisoner (G.S. 14-221)

Continuing Criminal Enterprise—Non-Drug Offenses

Statute

§14-7.20. Continuing criminal enterprise.

(a) Any person who engages in a continuing criminal enterprise shall be punished as a Class H felon and in addition shall be subject to the forfeiture prescribed in subsection (b) of this section.

(b) Any person who is convicted under subsection (a) of this section of engaging in a continuing criminal enterprise shall forfeit to the State of North Carolina:

(1) The profits obtained by the person in the enterprise, and
(2) Any of the person's interest in, claim against, or property or contractual rights of any kind affording a source of influence over, such enterprise.

(c) For purposes of this section, a person is engaged in a continuing criminal enterprise if:

(1) The person violates any provision of this Chapter, the punishment of which is a felony; and
(2) The violation is a part of a continuing series of violations of this Chapter:
    a. Which are undertaken by the person in concert with five or more other persons with respect to whom the person occupies a position of organizer, a supervisory position, or any other position of management; and
    b. From which the person obtains substantial income or resources.

Elements

A person guilty of this offense

(1) commits any felony in General Statutes Chapter 14 (Criminal Law)
(2) that is part of a continuing series of violations of General Statutes Chapter 14
(3) that are undertaken in concert with five or more other persons
(4) over whom the person occupies a position of organizer, supervisor, or other position of management *and*
(5) the person obtains substantial income or resources from the continuing violations.

Punishment

Class H felony. Additionally, property set out in G.S. 14-7.20(b) must be forfeited.

Notes

Generally. This offense is very similar to "Continuing Criminal Enterprise—Drug Offenses" (Chapter 24). For cases interpreting a similar federal statute, see 526 U.S. 813; 517 U.S. 292; 135 F.3d 291; 471 U.S. 773; 885 F.2d 195; 791 F.2d 1120; 751 F.2d 250; 506 F.2d 1323; and 621 F. Supp. 383.

Element (1). This offense is limited to felonies defined by General Statutes Chapter 14. Therefore, drug offenses (in G.S. Ch. 90), motor vehicle offenses (in G.S. Ch. 20), and offenses defined in other chapters of the General Statutes would not be covered by this offense.

Related offenses not in this chapter

"Continuing Criminal Enterprise—Drug Offenses" (Chapter 24)

Accessory after the Fact to Felony

Statute

§14-7. Accessories after the fact; trial and punishment.

If any person shall become an accessory after the fact to any felony, whether the same be a felony at common law or by virtue of any statute made, or to be made, such person shall be guilty of a crime, and may be indicted and convicted together with the principal felon, or after the conviction of the principal felon, or may be indicted and convicted for such crime whether the principal felon shall or shall not have been previously convicted, or shall or shall not be amenable to justice. Unless a different classification is expressly stated, that person shall be punished for an offense that is two classes lower than the felony the principal felon committed, except that an accessory after the fact to a Class A or Class B1 felony is a Class C felony, an accessory after the fact to a Class B2 felony is a Class D felony, an accessory after the fact to a Class H felony is a Class 1 misdemeanor, and an accessory after the fact to a Class I felony is a Class 2 misdemeanor. The offense of such person may be inquired of, tried, determined and punished by any court which shall have jurisdiction of the principal felon, in the same manner as if the act, by reason whereof such person shall have become an accessory, had been committed at the same place as the principal felony, although such act may have been committed without the limits of the State; and in case the principal felony shall have been committed within the body of any county, and the act by reason whereof any person shall have become accessory shall have been committed within the body of any other county, the offense of such person guilty of a felony as aforesaid may be inquired of, tried, determined, and punished in either of said counties: Provided, that no person who shall be once duly tried for such felony shall be again indicted or tried for the same offense.

Elements

A person is guilty of this offense
(1) when a felony was in fact committed by another person (the principal), *and*
(2) after the felony was committed, the person knowingly gave the principal personal assistance in escaping or attempting to escape detection, arrest, or punishment
(3) knowing that the principal committed the crime.

Punishment

This offense is punishable two classes lower than the felony committed by the principal felon, except that accessory after the fact to a Class A or B1 felony is a Class C felony, accessory after the fact to a Class B2 felony is a Class D felony, accessory after the fact to a Class H felony is a Class 1 misdemeanor, and accessory after the fact to a Class I felony is a Class 2 misdemeanor.

Notes

Element (1). See the note on Element (1) under "Aiding and Abetting Felony" (Chapter 3). There can be no conviction of this offense if the named principal is acquitted (91 N.C. App. 198).

Element (2). The offense can occur only *after* the principal offense has been completed (260 N.C. 749). Merely not arresting a felon or not turning in the offender would not satisfy this element, but giving the felon money or telling lies to conceal his or her whereabouts would (*Perkins*, p. 749).

Element (3). To be guilty of this offense the defendant must have known that the person aided has committed a felony (221 N.C. 153; 307 N.C. 62).

Participant not accessory after the fact; trial for both aiding and abetting felony and accessory after the fact to that felony. Co-participants in a crime who help themselves or one another to escape from a crime cannot be found guilty of being accessories after the fact. A participant in a crime (for example, a person who is a principal as an aider and abettor) cannot also be convicted as an accessory after the fact to that crime (260 N.C. 749; 298 N.C. 673; 104 N.C. App. 350). Even though such a person could not be convicted as an aider and abettor and an accessory after the fact based on a single crime, the person can be charged and tried for both (104 N.C. App. 350). If convicted of both, judgment for one must be set aside.

Lesser-included offenses. Accessory after the fact to a felony is not a lesser-included offense of the principal felony (254 N.C. 450).

Related offenses not in this chapter

"Aiding and Abetting Felony" (Chapter 3)
"Misdemeanor Possession of Stolen Goods" (Chapter 11)
"Felonious Possession of Stolen Goods" (Chapter 11)
"Receiving Stolen Goods—Misdemeanor" (Chapter 11)
"Receiving Stolen Goods—Felony" (Chapter 11)
"Altering or Removing Serial Number" (Chapter 11)
"Buying, Selling, or Possessing Property with Altered Serial Number" (Chapter 11)
Misprision of felony (common law) (*Perkins*, p. 572)
Harboring or aiding certain persons (G.S. 14-259)

Compounding a Felony

Statute

This is a common-law offense.

Elements

A person is guilty of this offense

(1) when another person (the principal) has committed a felony, *and*
(2) the person knows that the principal has committed a crime, *and*
(3) (a) agrees not to prosecute, *or*
    (b) agrees not to inform, *or*
    (c) agrees to dismiss the prosecution
(4) in exchange for something of value.

Punishment

Class 1 misdemeanor.

Notes

Element (1). It must be proved that the person whom the defendant agreed not to proceed against actually committed a felony (142 N.C. 665). This offense seems to occur only when the offense compounded is a felony, but there is some indication that it could apply as well to a misdemeanor (*Perkins*, p. 578).

Element (2). This element probably is satisfied even when the defendant does not specifically know of the felony, if the defendant has inferred it, and the fact that he or she agreed not to proceed against the felony should be sufficient evidence of knowledge (*Perkins*, p. 580).

Element (3). An agreement is the heart of this offense. The offense has not been committed if a person merely refrains from proceeding against the felony in hopes of receiving a reward, but without an agreement (*Perkins*, p. 581). It appears that the agreement need not be with the one who committed the felony.

Element (4). Mere failure to proceed against a person does not constitute compounding; compounding must be done in exchange for something of value. That "consideration" could be for the benefit of either the defendant or someone else. And the "consideration" can include return of the victim's own property. That is, compounding could include an agreement by the victim not to press charges or not to testify if the offender will pay restitution.

Application to public officials. A public official can be guilty of compounding just as a private citizen can (121 N.C. 606).

Related offenses not in this chapter

Offering Bribes (various offenses) (Chapter 18)
Misprision of felony (common law) (*Perkins*, p. 572)
Willfully failing to discharge duties (G.S. 14-230)

Committing an Infamous or Related Misdemeanor

Statute

§14-3. Punishment of misdemeanors, infamous offenses, offenses committed in secrecy and malice, or with deceit and intent to defraud, or with ethnic animosity.

Section (a) of this statute is not reproduced here.

(b) If a misdemeanor offense as to which no specific punishment is prescribed be infamous, done in secrecy and malice, or with deceit and intent to defraud, the offender shall, except where the offense is a conspiracy to commit a misdemeanor, be guilty of a Class H felony.

Section (c) of this statute is not reproduced here.

Elements

A person guilty of a misdemeanor may have the punishment for a conviction increased when

(1) the committed misdemeanor is
(2) one as to which no specific punishment is prescribed, *and*
(3) is infamous, or done in secrecy and malice, or done with deceit and intent to defraud.

Punishment

Class H felony.

Notes

Generally. This is a punishment enhancement rather than a criminal offense. To enhance punishment of a misdemeanor as infamous, done in secrecy and malice, or done with deceit and intent to defraud, the applicable factors must be alleged in the criminal pleading (116 N.C. App. 89).

Elements (1) and (2). The group of misdemeanors to which this provision may apply was reduced by implementation of structured sentencing. Structured sentencing provides specific statutory punishments for most offenses, including attempts and solicitation (see discussion of those offenses earlier in this chapter). For example, attempted common-law robbery (Ch. 12) was formerly punished under this statute because it was an infamous misdemeanor, but now that offense is specifically punished as a Class H felony pursuant to G.S. 14-2.5. After structured sentencing, this provision applies only to a misdemeanor offense "as to which no specific punishment is prescribed." This provision would apply only to misdemeanors like common-law obstruction of justice and common-law forgery, which have no punishment prescribed by a specific statute. The statute specifically excludes from its coverage conspiracy to commit a misdemeanor.

See G.S. 14-3(a) to determine how to classify misdemeanors that were not assigned a classification under structured sentencing. See G.S. 14-2.4, -2.5, and -2.6 for classifications of conspiracies, attempts, and solicitations (all of these offenses are discussed earlier in this chapter).

Element (3). One of these factors must be alleged in the criminal pleading in order to enhance punishment (116 N.C. App. 89). The factor alleged must be a necessary element of the underlying offense, rather than a particular circumstance of the individual case (307 N.C. 1; 317 N.C. 557). An offense is "infamous" if it is an act of depravity, involves moral turpitude, and reveals a heart devoid of social duty and a mind fatally bent on mischief (317 N.C. 557).

Related offenses not in this chapter

"Common-Law Robbery" (attempt) (Chapter 12)
"Common-Law Forgery" (Chapter 14)
"Common-Law Uttering of Forged Paper" (Chapter 14)
"Common-Law Obstruction of Justice" (Chapter 18)

Committing a Misdemeanor Because of Prejudice

Statute

§14-3. Punishment of misdemeanors, infamous offenses, offenses committed in secrecy and malice, or with deceit and intent to defraud, or with ethnic animosity.

Sections (a) and (b) of this statute are not reproduced here.

(c) If any Class 2 or Class 3 misdemeanor is committed because of the victim's race, color, religion, nationality, or country of origin, the offender shall be guilty of a Class 1 misdemeanor. If any Class A1 or Class 1 misdemeanor offense is committed because of the victim's race, color, religion, nationality, or country of origin, the offender shall be guilty of a Class I felony.

Elements

A person guilty of a misdemeanor may have the punishment for a conviction increased when he or she

(1) commits all elements of an underlying misdemeanor offense
(2) because of the victim's race or color or religion or nationality or country of origin.

Punishment

If the underlying offense is a Class 2 or Class 3 misdemeanor, the offense is punishable as a Class 1 misdemeanor. If the underlying offense is a Class A1 or Class 1 misdemeanor, the offense is punishable as a Class I felony.

Notes

Generally. This is a punishment enhancement rather than a criminal offense. To enhance punishment of a misdemeanor that was motivated by prejudice, that motivation must be alleged and proven.

Element (1). Any Class A1, 1, 2, or 3 misdemeanor may be enhanced under this statute. Generally, however, assaults, property offenses, and trespass offenses are likely to be the underlying misdemeanors. A felony offense is not eligible for this kind of enhancement. Compare with "Ethnic Intimidation," discussed in Chapter 7, which must involve a misdemeanor assault or misdemeanor damaging or defacing of property.

Element (2). To qualify for this punishment enhancement, an offense must be committed because of the *victim's* race, color, religion, nationality, or country of origin. "Ethnic Intimidation," in Chapter 7, applies to assaultive and property damage offenses committed because of the personal characteristics of the victim *or* another person.

Related offenses not in this chapter

"Ethnic Intimidation" (Chapter 7)

See the offenses in Chapter 7, "Assaults and Threats."

See the offenses in Chapter 11, "Larceny, Possession of Stolen Goods, Embezzlement, and Related Offenses."

See the offenses in Chapter 16, "Trespass, Property Damage, and Littering."

5
Punishment under Structured Sentencing

Chapter Contents

5
Punishment under Structured Sentencing

Generally

This chapter briefly describes the application of structured sentencing to both felonies and misdemeanors so that interested readers can learn what a particular felony or misdemeanor classification means in terms of actual punishments for individual defendants. Readers interested in a more complete discussion should consult Stevens H. Clarke, *Law of Sentencing, Probation, and Parole in North Carolina* (Chapel Hill: Institute of Government, The University of North Carolina at Chapel Hill, 1997); John Rubin and Ben F. Loeb, Jr., *Punishments for North Carolina Crimes and Motor Vehicle Offenses* (Chapel Hill: Institute of Government, The University of North Carolina at Chapel Hill, 1999), from which much of this chapter is drawn; and North Carolina Sentencing and Policy Advisory Commission, *Structured Sentencing Training and Reference Manual* (Revised January 2000). Note that supplements also are available for the Institute of Government publications. All of these publications are available from the Institute of Government's Publications Sales Office: telephone (919) 966-4119; fax (919) 962-2707; e-mail khunt@iogmail.iog.unc.edu; or visit the Institute's Web site at http://ncinfo.iog.unc.edu.

Structured sentencing became effective for offenses committed on or after October 1, 1994. The only misdemeanors currently not subject to structured sentencing are impaired driving under G.S. 20-138.1; commercial impaired driving under G.S. 20-138.2; a second or subsequent conviction of a zero tolerance offense under G.S. 20-138.2A (commercial drivers) or G.S. 20-138.2B (school bus and child care vehicle drivers); and failing to comply with health control measures under G.S. 130A-25. Also exempt from structured sentencing are felony convictions in which defendants are sentenced as violent habitual felons under G.S. 14-7.12.

Felonies

The centerpiece of structured sentencing for felonies is the statutory table of punishments, commonly referred to as the sentencing grid, in G.S. 15A-1340.17(c). It is included as Table 1 at the end of this chapter. Two other tables necessary to determine the appropriate sentence for a felony are also included: Table 2, dealing with maximum sentences, and Table 3, dealing with prior record level.

A sentencing court essentially must take seven steps to determine the appropriate sentence for felonies under structured sentencing. These steps (with the appropriate source to consult) are as follows:

- Determine the offense class for each felony conviction (listed under each offense in this book as "Punishment")
- Determine the prior record level for the defendant (Table 3)
- Consider aggravating and mitigating factors [see G.S. 15A-1340.16(d), (e)]
- Select a minimum sentence from the applicable minimum sentence range (Table 1)
- Determine the maximum sentence (Table 2)
- Determine the sentence disposition (active, intermediate, or community) (Table 1)
- Consider the appropriateness of restitution (see discussion later in this chapter and Table 5)

Each of these steps is summarized below. The main exceptions also are noted below, under the heading "Special Provisions."

The sentencing court will inform the defendant of (1) the active jail or prison term imposed; (2) the active term's minimum and maximum length; and (3) whether that term will be activated or suspended. If the active term is suspended, the defendant will be informed of the type of alternative disposition (intermediate or community) he or she will receive. This procedure will be followed for each offense conviction, unless a particular conviction is consolidated or set to run concurrently with other convictions.

Offense Class

The first step in determining the appropriate sentence for a felony is to identify the class of the felony. There are ten classes of felonies under structured sentencing (A, B1, B2, C, D, E, F, G, H, and I). For each felony listed in this book, the class of the offense is indicated under the "Punishment" section of the discussion. For example, a violation of G.S. 14-32(c) ("Assault with Deadly Weapon with Intent to Kill"; see Chapter 7) is a Class E felony. A violation of G.S. 20-138.5 ("Habitual Impaired Driving"; see Chapter 25) is a Class G felony.

Prior Record Level

The second step is to determine the defendant's prior record level. A defendant is assigned to one of six prior record levels (I through VI) based on the number of points he or she receives under structured sentencing. For example, a defendant with five to eight points is in prior record level III. The six prior record levels, and the point ranges for each level, are indicated in the prior-record-level worksheet issued by the Administrative Office of the Courts (AOC-CR-600, Dec. 1997), which appears as Table 3 at the end of this chapter. The felony portion of this form is derived from G.S. 15A-1340.14, while the misdemeanor portion comes from G.S. 15A-1340.21. The form will be used by the prosecutor and the judge to make a record of an individual defendant's criminal history. Readers of this book should check for updated versions of this form from the AOC before using the example in this book in court.

A defendant is assigned points in one of three ways. First, if a defendant has any prior convictions, points are assigned to each conviction based on the offense class of the conviction. For example, a prior conviction for a Class H felony is assigned two points. The point values for each offense class are indicated in Table 3. In calculating points for prior convictions, the following structured sentencing rules must be kept in mind.

Prior misdemeanors. In determining a defendant's prior record level for the purpose of felony sentencing, prior convictions of Class 2 and 3 misdemeanors do not count; nor do prior misdemeanor offenses of any class under Chapter 20 of the General Statutes, except misdemeanor death by vehicle under G.S. 20-141.4(a2); impaired driving under G.S. 20-138.1; and commercial impaired driving under G.S. 20-138.2. See G.S. 15A-1340.14(b).

Current classification of prior conviction. Under the structured sentencing rules for felonies, the classification of the prior offense is the classification assigned to that offense at the time the *current* offense was committed. For example, if the defendant has a prior conviction for second-degree burglary, the points assigned to the conviction would depend on the current classification of the offense (now Class G), not the classification in effect at the time the conviction occurred. See G.S. 15A-1340.14(c).

Multiple prior convictions. If the defendant was convicted of more than one offense in a single superior court during one calendar week, only the conviction with the highest point total is counted. If the defendant was convicted of more than one offense during a single session (i.e., day) of district court, only the most serious conviction is counted. See G.S. 15A-1340.14(d).

Convictions from other jurisdictions. Unless the prosecution or defendant proves otherwise, a conviction from another jurisdiction is classified as a Class I felony if that jurisdiction classifies the offense as a felony. Similarly, unless the prosecution proves otherwise, a conviction from another jurisdiction is classified as a Class 3 misdemeanor if the other jurisdiction classifies the offense as a misdemeanor. See G.S. 15A-1340.14(e).

Second, one point is added if all the elements of the present offense are included in the prior offense. In essence, the current offense must be the same as or a lesser-included offense of the prior offense committed by the defendant. This additional point may be counted whether or not the prior offense was used in determining the prior record level. See G.S. 15A-1340.14(b)(6).

Third, and last, one point is added if the defendant was on probation, parole, or post-release supervision; was serving an active sentence; or was an escapee when he or she was arrested for the current offense. See G.S. 15A-1340.14(b)(7).

Aggravating and Mitigating Factors

Table 1, the sentencing grid, contains three ranges of imprisonment for felonies: presumptive, aggravated, and mitigated. To determine the range in which to sentence a defendant, the court must consider any evidence of aggravating and mitigating factors. The statutory *aggravating* factors are set forth in G.S. 15A-1340.16(d). The statutory *mitigating* factors are set forth in G.S. 15A-1340.16(e).

If the court finds that aggravating factors are present and outweigh any mitigating factors, it may depart from the presumptive range of imprisonment contained in Table 1 and impose a term of imprisonment from the aggravated range. Likewise, if the court finds that mitigating factors outweigh aggravating factors, it may impose a term of imprisonment from the mitigated range. If the court selects a term from the aggravated or mitigated range, the court must make written findings of the aggravating and mitigating factors. The court must make such findings regardless of whether it imposes an active or suspended term of imprisonment. See G.S. 15A-1340.16(b), (c).

Minimum Sentence

Once the class of felony, prior record level, and aggravating and mitigating factors are determined, the court must select a minimum term of imprisonment from Table 1. To determine the minimum term, the court must locate the class of felony at issue along the left-hand side of the grid and the prior record level along the top of the grid. The cell in which the felony class and prior record level intersect shows the possible sentences that the court may impose. The court then must determine whether to impose a term of imprisonment from the presumptive, aggravated, or mitigated ranges (expressed in months) shown in the particular cell. Lastly, the court must select a minimum term of imprisonment from within the applicable range.

Maximum Sentence

The judgment of the court also must contain a maximum term of imprisonment. The maximum term is set by statute based on the minimum term imposed by the court. For Class B1 through E felonies, the maximum term of imprisonment is 120 percent of the minimum term rounded to the next highest month, plus 9 months. For Class F through I felonies, the maximum term of imprisonment is 120 percent of the minimum term rounded to the next highest month. See G.S. 15A-1340.17(d), (e), (e1).

A minimum/maximum table containing these calculations is shown as Table 2. The numbers in the table to the left of the dash represent the minimum term of imprisonment imposed by the court, expressed in months. The numbers to the right of the dash represent the corresponding maximum term required by statute. The table is in two parts—the first part lists maximum sentences for Class B1 through E felonies, and the second lists the maximums for Class F through I felonies.

Sentence Disposition

The next step is to determine the sentence disposition, which is prescribed in Table 1. Each cell in the grid contains a sentence disposition, signified by the letter "A," "I," or "C," or a combination of these letters. "A" represents active punishment (jail or prison); "I" represents intermediate punishment (a form of probation—more strict supervision than unsupervised probation but less restrictive than jail or prison); and "C" represents community punishment (the least restrictive form of probation). The court must impose the sentence disposition indicated in the applicable cell. Some cells in the grid prescribe two possible dispositions, separated by a slash (for example, "I/A"). In those cases, the court can impose either disposition.

Active punishment. This is an unsuspended term of imprisonment (G.S. 15A-1340.11). If the court imposes an active punishment, the minimum and maximum term of imprisonment previously determined by the court must be activated. The maximum term may be reduced by earned time credit (awarded by the Department of Correction or local jail), but the term of imprisonment may not be reduced (except for credit for time served awaiting trial) below the minimum term imposed by the court. See G.S. 15A-1340.13(d).[1]

Ordinarily, if the only disposition prescribed in a particular cell is "A,"

1. A defendant convicted of a Class B1 through E felony is automatically released from prison 9 months before the end of his or her maximum term of imprisonment and is placed on post-release supervision. The defendant may be released sooner if he or she receives any earned-time credit but may not be released before serving the

the court must impose active imprisonment. Upon a finding of extraordinary mitigation, however, the court may impose an intermediate punishment even when only an active punishment is prescribed. Extraordinary mitigation is authorized only when the offense is a Class B2, C, or D felony; the offense is not a drug-trafficking offense under G.S. 90-95(h) or a drug-trafficking conspiracy offense under G.S. 90-95(i); *and* the defendant is in prior record level I or II. See G.S. 15A-1340.13(g), (h).

In cases involving drug-trafficking offenses, the court is not required to impose an active punishment (regardless of the class of offense or the defendant's prior record level) if the court finds that the defendant provided "substantial assistance" within the meaning of G.S. 90-95(h)(5). Drug trafficking is discussed further below under the heading "Special Provisions."

When sentencing a defendant for multiple offenses, the court may consolidate sentences, run them concurrently, or run them consecutively. Unless otherwise specified by the court, sentences run concurrently. If the court consolidates offenses for sentencing, the most serious offense is controlling—the sentence disposition and the minimum and maximum terms of imprisonment must conform to the structured sentencing rules for that offense. If the court imposes consecutive sentences, the minimum term of imprisonment is the sum of the minimum terms imposed for the offenses, and the maximum term is the sum of the maximum terms for the offenses. See G.S. 15A-1340.15, -1354.[2]

A defendant sentenced for a felony to active punishment is normally committed to the custody of the Department of Correction. However, upon request of the sheriff or board of county commissioners, the court may, in its discretion, sentence the person to a local confinement facility in that county. See G.S. 15A-1352(c).

Intermediate punishment. This is supervised probation involving at least one of the following: (1) special probation; (2) assignment to a residential program; (3) house arrest with electronic monitoring; (4) intensive probation; or (5) assignment to a day-reporting center [G.S. 15A-1340.11(6)].

If the court imposes an intermediate punishment, the court must suspend the minimum and maximum term of imprisonment and impose a period of supervised probation with at least one of the conditions described in G.S. 15A-1340.11(6). For intermediate punishments for felonies, the court is authorized to impose a period of probation ranging from 18 to 36 months; the court may depart from this range upon finding that a longer or shorter period is necessary. See G.S. 15A-1343.2(d)(4).

As a condition of intermediate punishment, the court is authorized to impose special probation, also known as a split sentence. Under special probation, the court suspends the term of imprisonment, places the defendant on probation, and requires the defendant to submit to a period of

---

minimum term of imprisonment imposed by the court (absent credit for time served). See G.S. 15A-1368.2. The period of post-release supervision is 9 months for most people convicted of a Class B1 through E felony. But a defendant is subject to a far longer period of supervised release—5 years—if he or she has been convicted of a Class B1 through E felony and is required to register as a sex offender under G.S. Chapter 14, Article 27A. If the defendant violates a condition of post-release supervision during that period, he or she can be returned to prison "up to the time remaining on his [or her] maximum imposed term." G.S. 15A-1368.3(c)(1).

2. If the court imposes consecutive terms of imprisonment for more than one Class B1 through E felony, the maximum term for each second and subsequent Class B1 through E felony is reduced by 9 months.

imprisonment as a condition of probation. The period of imprisonment pursuant to special probation may not exceed 6 months or one-fourth of the maximum term of imprisonment imposed, whichever is less. See G.S. 15A-1351(a).

Community punishment. A community punishment is defined as any sentence that does not include an active or intermediate punishment. See G.S. 15A-1340.11(2). The court must suspend any term of imprisonment; it may not impose an active term of imprisonment or special probation requiring a period of imprisonment.

A community punishment may include unsupervised probation or supervised probation with any authorized condition other than one defined as an intermediate punishment. For community punishments for felonies, the court is authorized to impose a period of probation ranging from 12 to 30 months; the court may depart from this range upon finding that a longer or shorter period is necessary. See G.S. 15A-1343.2(d)(3). A community punishment also may consist of a fine only, without probation. See G.S. 15A-1340.17(b).

Fines. The court may impose a fine as part of any disposition, whether active, intermediate, or community. Unless otherwise provided by statute, the amount of the fine is in the court's discretion. See G.S. 15A-1340.17(b).

Restitution

The last step is to consider the appropriateness of restitution. Article 81C of G.S. Chapter 15A (G.S. 15A-1340.34 through –1340.38) governs restitution in all criminal cases. The restitution requirements differ, however, depending on whether or not the offense is subject to the Crime Victims' Rights Act (G.S. 15A-830 through -841). The felonies subject to the Crime Victims' Rights Act are (i) any Class A through F felony; (ii) a Class F through I felony if it is in violation of certain statutes (see Table 5 at the end of this chapter); or (iii) an attempt to commit one of the above felonies if the attempt is punishable as a felony.

The discussion below outlines the main differences concerning restitution between offenses subject to the Crime Victims' Rights Act and other criminal offenses. Note that a statute governing a particular offense may contain more specific restitution requirements.

For offenses subject to the Crime Victims' Rights Act, the court *must* order restitution to the victim or victim's estate [G.S. 15A-1340.34(b)]. If probation is imposed, restitution ordered to the victim must be made a condition of probation. Even if the defendant is sentenced to active imprisonment, it appears that the court must order restitution to the victim or victim's estate. If a restitution order to a victim is for more than $250, it is enforceable as a civil judgment and, in some circumstances, may be subject to immediate execution (G.S. 15A-1340.38).

In cases not subject to the Crime Victims' Rights Act, the court must consider whether restitution is appropriate, but the court is not required to order it [G.S. 15A-1340.34(a), (c)]. Thus the court may make restitution a condition of probation. It appears that the court also may impose restitution as part of a sentence of active imprisonment. In cases not subject to the Crime Victims' Rights Act, however, a restitution order is not enforceable as a civil judgment. The victim or victim's estate may bring a civil suit for damages resulting from the crime [G.S. 15A-1340.37(a)], but in such a suit the amount of restitution imposed is not admissible in evidence and the defendant has the right to contest the amount of damages claimed (G.S. 1-15.1).

In both kinds of cases, if the defendant is sentenced to active imprisonment, the court also must consider whether to recommend to the Department of Correction that restitution be made from any work-release earnings. G.S. 15A-1340.36(c). For Class B1 through E felonies, restitution is a mandatory condition of post-release supervision [G.S. 15A-1340.34(b)].

The losses and injuries for which restitution may be ordered are described in G.S. 15A-1340.35. In determining the amount of restitution, the court must have adequate proof of the injuries or losses claimed and must take into account the defendant's ability to pay (G.S. 15A-1340.36). The court also may (but is not required to) order restitution to people other than the victim or to organizations (G.S. 15A-1340.37).

Special Provisions

A number of provisions depart from the basic structured sentencing scheme for felonies, described above. These departures are noted in the punishment charts where applicable. The principal exceptions are as follows:

Class A felonies. Class A felonies are punishable by death or life without parole, regardless of the defendant's prior record level. The only Class A felony is first-degree murder under G.S. 14-17. For a discussion of capital sentencing issues, see Robert L. Farb, *North Carolina Capital Case Law Handbook* (Chapel Hill: Institute of Government, The University of North Carolina at Chapel Hill, 1996).

Habitual felon. A defendant who is convicted for the fourth time of a felony within the meaning of G.S. 14-7.1 (which describes how a person becomes an habitual felon) is sentenced as though he or she was convicted of a Class C felony (unless the offense for which he or she was convicted is a Class A, B1, or B2 felony). For example, a defendant found to be an habitual felon after being convicted of felonious breaking or entering under G.S. 14-54 is sentenced as though he or she was convicted of a Class C felony, not a Class H felony, which is the classification of that offense. (A defendant's status as an habitual felon is determined by a jury at a hearing held after a conviction, unless the defendant admits to being an habitual felon.) Prior convictions used to establish habitual felon status cannot be used in determining the prior record level in sentencing for the Class C felony.

Violent habitual felon. A defendant convicted for the third time of a violent felony within the meaning of G.S. 14-7.7 must be sentenced to life without parole, regardless of the defendant's prior record level. Provisions for review of a sentence of imprisonment for life without parole upon conviction of a Class A felony also apply here.

Firearm enhancement. Subject to certain exceptions, a defendant who used, displayed, or threatened to use or display a firearm during the commission of a Class A through E felony must be sentenced to an additional 60 months imprisonment. See G.S. 14-2.2(a).

Drug trafficking. Drug trafficking is punished according to a separate table of punishments, containing minimum and maximum terms of imprisonment that depart from the sentencing grid. Minimum fines also are prescribed for drug-trafficking offenses. See G.S. 90-95(h) and trafficking offenses in Chapter 24.

Misdemeanors

The focus of structured sentencing for misdemeanors is the statutory table of punishments in G.S. 15A-1340.23 (See Table 4 at the end of this chapter). All misdemeanors, except those mentioned at the beginning of this chapter, are subject to structured sentencing. See G.S. 15A-1340.10.

A sentencing court essentially must take five steps to determine the appropriate sentence for a misdemeanor. These steps (with the appropriate source to consult) are as follows:

- Determine the offense class for each misdemeanor conviction (listed under each offense in this book as "Punishment")
- Determine the prior conviction level for the defendant (Table 4)
- Select a sentence length from the appropriate sentence range (Table 4)
- Determine the sentence disposition (active, intermediate, or community) (Table 4)
- Consider the appropriateness of restitution (see discussion later in this chapter and Table 5)

The sentencing court will inform the defendant of (1) the active jail or prison term imposed and (2) whether that term will be activated or suspended. If the active term is suspended, the defendant will be informed of the type of alternative disposition (intermediate or community) he or she will receive. This procedure will be followed for each offense conviction, unless a particular conviction is consolidated or set to run concurrently with other convictions.

Offense Class

The first step in determining the appropriate sentence for a misdemeanor is to identify the class of the misdemeanor. There are four classes of misdemeanors under structured sentencing (A1, 1, 2, and 3). For each misdemeanor listed in this book, the class of the offense is indicated under the "Punishment" section of the discussion. For example, "Assault by Pointing Gun" (G.S. 14-34; see Chapter 7) is a Class A1 misdemeanor. "Passing a Stopped School Bus" (G.S. 20-217; see Chapter 25) is a Class 2 misdemeanor.

Some misdemeanor offenses have no classification and no punishment listed in the General Statutes. Under G.S. 14-3(a), those offenses are generally considered Class 1 misdemeanors. Such misdemeanors that are "infamous, done in secrecy and malice, or committed with deceit and intent to defraud" may be punished as Class H felonies pursuant to G.S. 14-3(b). Some misdemeanor offenses have a punishment but no classification listed. Under G.S. 14-3(a), those offenses are classified as follows: as a Class 1 misdemeanor if punishable by more than 6 months imprisonment; as a Class 2 misdemeanor if punishable by more than 30 days but not more than 6 months imprisonment; and as a Class 3 misdemeanor if punishable by imprisonment of 30 days or less or by a fine only.

Prior Conviction Level

The second step is to determine the defendant's prior conviction level. A defendant is assigned to one of three prior conviction levels (I through III) based on the total number of prior felony and misdemeanor convictions. The three prior conviction levels, and the number of convictions applicable to each level, are indicated in Table 4.

Each conviction, whether a felony or misdemeanor (including driving while impaired and other misdemeanors under Chapter 20 of the North Carolina General Statutes), counts as one conviction. If the defendant was convicted of more than one offense in a single week of superior court, only one of the convictions counts. If the defendant was convicted of more than one offense during a single session (i.e., day) of district court, only one of the convictions counts. Infractions do not count. See G.S. 15A-1340.21.

A prior offense may be counted as a conviction only if the offense is classified as a felony or misdemeanor at the time the defendant committed the current offense. Thus if an offense had been changed from a misdemeanor to an infraction (for example, speeding 50 m.p.h. in a 35 m.p.h. zone) when a defendant committed a new misdemeanor, a prior conviction for that offense would not count in misdemeanor sentencing [G.S. 15A-1340.21(b)].

Sentence Length

Once the class of misdemeanor and prior conviction level are determined, the court must determine the length of any term of imprisonment. (If the court selects a community punishment as the sentence disposition, discussed under the next heading, it may impose a judgment consisting of a fine only; in those circumstances, it would be unnecessary for the court to specify any term of imprisonment.) To determine the length of any term of imprisonment, the court must locate the class of misdemeanor at issue along the left-hand side of Table 4 and the prior conviction level along the top of Table 4. The cell in which the misdemeanor class and prior conviction level intersect shows the possible terms of imprisonment (expressed in days) that the court may impose. The court must select a single term of imprisonment from the range shown in the applicable cell; there is no minimum and maximum term of imprisonment, as in felony sentencing.

Sentence Disposition

The next step is to determine the sentence disposition, which is prescribed in Table 4. Each cell in Table 4 contains a sentence disposition, signified by the letter "A," "I," or "C," or a combination of these letters. "A" represents active punishment (jail or prison); "I" represents intermediate punishment (a form of probation—more strict supervision than unsupervised probation but less restrictive than jail or prison); and "C" represents community punishment (the least restrictive form of probation). The court must impose the sentence disposition indicated in the applicable cell. Some cells prescribe more than one possible disposition, separated by a slash (for example, "C/I/A"). In those cases, the court can impose any single one of the indicated dispositions.

Active punishment. If the court imposes an active punishment, the term of imprisonment previously determined by the court must be activated. A defendant's term of imprisonment may be reduced by earned-time credit up to 4 days per month of incarceration (awarded by the Department of Correction or local jail). See G.S. 15A-1340.20(d).

When sentencing a defendant for multiple offenses, the court may consolidate sentences or run them concurrently. Subject to certain limitations, the court may also impose consecutive sentences. Unless otherwise specified by the court, sentences run concurrently. If the court consolidates offenses for sentencing, the most serious offense is controlling—the sentence disposition and the term of imprisonment must conform to the structured sentencing rules for that offense. If the court imposes consecutive sentences, the length of imprisonment cannot exceed twice the longest term of imprisonment authorized for the most serious misdemeanor conviction. Consecutive sentences cannot be imposed, however, if all of the convictions are for Class 3 misdemeanors. See G.S. 15A-1340.22, -1354(a).

A defendant sentenced for a misdemeanor to active punishment of 90 days or less must be committed to a local jail facility. The court may choose local confinement or commitment to the custody of the Department of Correction if the defendant is sentenced to more than 90 days of active punishment. See G.S. 15A-1352(a).

An active sentence may be imposed for any misdemeanor, even if an active sentence would not otherwise be authorized, if the sentence does not exceed the total amount of time that the defendant has spent in pretrial confinement awaiting trial for that misdemeanor. In effect, a sentence of "credit for time served" may be imposed for any misdemeanor [G.S. 15A-1340.20(c1)].

Intermediate punishment. This is supervised probation involving at least one of the following: (1) special probation; (2) assignment to a residential program; (3) electronic monitoring; (4) intensive probation; or (5) assignment to a day-reporting center [G.S. 15A-1340.11(6)].

If the court imposes an intermediate punishment, the court must suspend the term of imprisonment and impose a period of supervised probation with at least one of the conditions described in G.S. 15A-1340.11(6). For intermediate punishments for misdemeanors, the court is authorized to impose a period of probation ranging from 12 to 24 months; the court may depart from this range upon finding that a longer or shorter period is necessary. See G.S. 15A-1343.2(d)(2).

As a condition of intermediate punishment, the court is authorized to impose special probation, also known as a split sentence. Under special probation, the court suspends the term of imprisonment, places the defendant on probation, and requires the defendant to submit to a period of imprisonment as a condition of probation. The period of imprisonment pursuant to special probation may not exceed 6 months or one-fourth of the maximum term of imprisonment imposed, whichever is less. See G.S. 15A-1351(a).

Community punishment. A community punishment is defined as any sentence that does not include an active or intermediate punishment. See G.S. 15A-1340.11(2). The court must suspend any term of imprisonment; it may not impose an active term of imprisonment or special probation requiring a period of imprisonment.

A community punishment may include unsupervised probation or supervised probation with any authorized condition other than one defined as an intermediate punishment. For community punishments for misdemeanors, the court is authorized to impose a period of probation ranging from 6 to 18 months; the court may depart from this range upon finding that a longer or shorter period is necessary. See G.S. 15A-1343.2(d)(1). A community punishment also may consist of a fine only, without probation. See G.S. 15A-1340.23(b).

Fines. The court may impose a fine as part of any disposition, whether active, intermediate, or community. Unless otherwise provided by statute, the maximum fine for each class of misdemeanor is as indicated in Table 4.

Restitution

The last step is to determine the appropriateness of restitution. The restitution requirements in G.S. 15A-1340.34 through -1340.38 (discussed earlier in this chapter in connection with felonies) apply equally to misdemeanors. Thus the sentencing court must determine whether a misdemeanor is subject to the Crime Victims' Rights Act (G.S. 15A-830 through -841), which for certain offenses mandates restitution to the victim and allows enforcement of the restitution order as a civil judgment. For misdemeanors not subject to the Crime Victims' Rights Act, the court must consider the appropriateness of restitution, but the court is not required to order it.

The main difference with restitution in misdemeanor versus felony cases is that far fewer misdemeanors are subject to the Crime Victims' Rights Act. Only the following misdemeanors are covered: (i) assault with a deadly weapon; (ii) assault inflicting serious injury; (iii) assault by pointing a gun; (iv) domestic criminal trespass; and (v) stalking.

Further, the Crime Victims' Rights Act applies to the above misdemeanors only if the defendant and victim were in one of six different "personal relationships" (for example, as current or former spouses) described in G.S. 50B-1(b). Table 5 at the end of this chapter lists the offenses subject to the Crime Victims' Rights Act.

Table 1
Felony Sentence Dispositions and Minimum Prison/Jail Term Ranges
(shown in months)

A = active punishment I = intermediate punishment C = community punishment

Prior Record Level

Felony Class	I 0 Pts	II 1–4 Pts	III 5–8 Pts	IV 9–14 Pts	V 15–18 Pts	VI 19+ Pts	
Class A	Death or life without parole						
Class B1	**A**	**A**	**A**	**A**	**A**	**A**	**Disposition**
	240–300	288–360	336–420	384–480	Life without parole	Life without parole	*Aggravated Range*
	192–240	**230–288**	**269–336**	**307–384**	**346–433**	**384–480**	**Presumptive Rar**
	144–192	173–230	202–269	230–307	260–346	288–384	*Mitigated Range*
Class B2	**A**	**A**	**A**	**A**	**A**	**A**	
	157–196	189–237	220–276	251–313	282–353	313–392	
	125–157	**151–189**	**176–220**	**201–251**	**225–282**	**251–313**	
	94–125	114–151	132–176	151–201	169–225	188–251	
Class C	**A**	**A**	**A**	**A**	**A**	**A**	
	73–92	100–125	116–145	133–167	151–188	168–210	
	58–73	**80–100**	**93–116**	**107–133**	**121–151**	**135–168**	
	44–58	60–80	70–93	80–107	90–121	101–135	
Class D	**A**	**A**	**A**	**A**	**A**	**A**	
	64–80	77–95	103–129	117–146	133–167	146–183	
	51–64	**61–77**	**82–103**	**94–117**	**107–133**	**117–146**	
	38–51	46–61	61–82	71–94	80–107	88–117	
Class E	**I/A**	**I/A**	**A**	**A**	**A**	**A**	
	25–31	29–36	34–42	46–58	53–66	59–74	
	20–25	**23–29**	**27–34**	**37–46**	**42–53**	**47–59**	
	15–20	17–23	20–27	28–37	32–42	35–47	
Class F	**I/A**	**I/A**	**I/A**	**A**	**A**	**A**	
	16–20	19–24	21–26	25–31	34–42	39–49	
	13–16	**15–19**	**17–21**	**20–25**	**27–34**	**31–39**	
	10–13	11–15	13–17	15–20	20–27	23–31	
Class G	**I/A**	**I/A**	**I/A**	**I/A**	**A**	**A**	
	13–16	15–19	16–20	20–25	21–26	29–36	
	10–13	**12–15**	**13–16**	**16–20**	**17–21**	**23–29**	
	8–10	9–12	10–13	12–16	13–17	17–23	
Class H	**C/I/A**	**I/A**	**I/A**	**I/A**	**I/A**	**A**	
	6–8	8–10	10–12	11–14	15–19	20–25	
	5–6	**6–8**	**8–10**	**9–11**	**12–15**	**16–20**	
	4–5	4–6	6–8	7–9	9–12	12–16	
Class I	**C**	**C/I**	**I**	**I/A**	**I/A**	**I/A**	
	6–8	6–8	6–8	8–10	9–11	10–12	
	4–6	**4–6**	**5–6**	**6–8**	**7–9**	**8–10**	
	3–4	3–4	4–5	4–6	5–7	6–8	

Source: G.S. 15A-1340.17(c). Class B2, C, and D ranges are for offenses committed on or after December 1, 1995. For shorter ranges applying before that date, see the repealed version of this statute.

Table 2
Felony Minimum and Maximum Prison/Jail Terms
(shown in months)

Felony Classes B1, B2, C, D, and E

15–27	56–77	97–126	138–175	179–224	220–273	261–323	302–372
16–29	57–78	98–127	139–176	180–225	221–275	262–324	303–373
17–30	58–79	99–128	140–177	181–227	222–276	263–325	304–374
18–31	59–80	100–129	141–179	182–228	223–277	264–326	305–375
19–32	60–81	101–131	142–180	183–229	224–278	265–327	306–377
20–33	61–83	102–132	143–181	184–230	225–279	266–329	307–378
21–35	62–84	103–133	144–182	185–231	226–281	267–330	308–379
22–36	63–85	104–134	145–183	186–233	227–282	268–331	309–380
23–37	64–86	105–135	146–185	187–234	228–283	269–332	310–381
24–38	65–87	106–137	147–186	188–235	229–284	270–333	311–383
25–39	66–89	107–138	148–187	189–236	230–285	271–335	312–384
26–41	67–90	108–139	149–188	190–237	231–287	272–336	313–385
27–42	68–91	109–140	150–189	191–239	232–288	273–337	314–386
28–43	69–92	110–141	151–191	192–240	233–289	274–338	315–387
29–44	70–93	111–143	152–192	193–241	234–290	275–339	316–389
30–45	71–95	112–144	153–193	194–242	235–291	276–341	317–390
31–47	72–96	113–145	154–194	195–243	236–293	277–342	318–391
32–48	73–97	114–146	155–195	196–245	237–294	278–343	319–392
33–49	74–98	115–147	156–197	197–246	238–295	279–344	320–393
34–50	75–99	116–149	157–198	198–247	239–296	280–345	321–395
35–51	76–101	117–150	158–199	199–248	240–297	281–347	322–396
36–53	77–102	118–151	159–200	200–249	241–299	282–348	323–397
37–54	78–103	119–152	160–201	201–251	242–300	283–349	324–398
38–55	79–104	120–153	161–203	202–252	243–301	284–350	325–399
39–56	80–105	121–155	162–204	203–253	244–302	285–351	326–401
40–57	81–107	122–156	163–205	204–254	245–303	286–353	327–402
41–59	82–108	123–157	164–206	205–255	246–305	287–354	328–403
42–60	83–109	124–158	165–207	206–257	247–306	288–355	329–404
43–61	84–110	125–159	166–209	207–258	248–307	289–356	330–405
44–62	85–111	126–161	167–210	208–259	249–308	290–357	331–407
45–63	86–113	127–162	168–211	209–260	250–309	291–359	332–408
46–65	87–114	128–163	169–212	210–261	251–311	292–360	333–409
47–66	88–115	129–164	170–213	211–263	252–312	293–361	334–410
48–67	89–116	130–165	171–215	212–264	253–313	294–362	335–411
49–68	90–117	131–167	172–216	213–265	254–314	295–363	336–413
50–69	91–119	132–168	173–217	214–266	255–315	296–365	337–414
51–71	92–120	133–169	174–218	215–267	256–317	297–366	338–415
52–72	93–121	134–170	175–219	216–269	257–318	298–367	339–416
53–73	94–122	135–171	176–221	217–270	258–319	299–368	340 or more*
54–74	95–123	136–173	177–222	218–271	259–320	300–369	
55–75	96–125	137–174	178–223	219–272	260–321	301–371	

*Where minimum term is 340 months or more, maximum is 120% of minimum rounded to next highest month, plus 9 months.

Table 2 (continued)
Felony Minimum and Maximum Prison/Jail Terms
(shown in months)

Felony Classes F, G, H, and I							
3–4	9–11	15–18	21–26	27–33	33–40	39–47	45–54
4–5	10–12	16–20	22–27	28–34	34–41	40–48	46–56
5–6	11–14	17–21	23–28	29–35	35–42	41–50	47–57
6–8	12–15	18–22	24–29	30–36	36–44	42–51	48–58
7–9	13–16	19–23	25–30	31–38	37–45	43–52	49–59
8–10	14–17	20–24	26–32	32–39	38–46	44–53	

Source: G.S. 15A-1340.17(e), (e1).

Table 3

STATE OF NORTH CAROLINA

_______________ County

File No.

In The General Court Of Justice
☐ District ☐ Superior Court Division

STATE VERSUS

Name And Address Of Defendant

Social Security No | *SID No.*

Race | *Sex* | *DOB*

WORKSHEET
PRIOR RECORD LEVEL FOR FELONY SENTENCING AND PRIOR CONVICTION LEVEL FOR MISDEMEANOR SENTENCING
(STRUCTURED SENTENCING)

G.S. 15A-1340.14, 15A-1340.21

NOTE: *This Worksheet is provided to assist the attorney for the state in calculating and presenting the defendant's prior record level or prior conviction level. Record the defendant's prior record on the reverse side of this form or attach a copy of the defendant's prior record pursuant to G.S. 15A-1340.14(f). If sentencing for a felony, count the number of prior convictions in each offense class and enter those totals in the chart in section I below. For multiple prior convictions at one session of court, see G.S. 15A-1340.14(d). The only Class 1 misdemeanor offenses under Chapter 20 that are assigned points for determining prior record level for felony sentencing are misdemeanor death by vehicle [G.S. 20-141.4(a2)] and, for sentencing for felony offenses committed on or after December 1, 1997, impaired driving [G.S. 20-138.1] and commercial impaired driving [G.S. 20-138.2]. First Degree Rape and First Degree Sexual offense convictions prior to October 1, 1994, are Class B1 convictions.*

I. SCORING PRIOR RECORD/FELONY SENTENCING

NUMBER	TYPE	FACTORS	POINTS
	Prior Felony Class A Conviction	X10	
	Prior Felony Class B1 Conviction	X 9	
	Prior Felony Class B2 or C or D Conviction	X 6	
	Prior Felony Class E or F or G Conviction	X 4	
	Prior Felony Class H or I Conviction	X 2	
	Prior Class A1 or 1 Misdemeanor Conviction *(see note above)*	X 1	
		SUBTOTAL ▶	
If all the elements of the present offense are included in any prior offense whether or not the prior offenses were used in determining prior record level.		+ 1	
If the offense was committed: (a) while on supervised or unsupervised probation, parole, or post-release supervision; or (b) while serving a sentence of imprisonment; or (c) while on escape		+ 1	
		TOTAL ▶	

II. CLASSIFYING PRIOR RECORD/CONVICTION LEVEL

MISDEMEANOR

NOTE: *If sentencing for a misdemeanor, total the number of prior conviction(s) listed on the reverse and select the corresponding prior conviction level.*

No. Of Prior Convictions	Level
0	I
1-4	II
5 +	III

PRIOR CONVICTION LEVEL ▶ ☐

☐ The Court has determined the number of prior convictions to be __________ and the level to be as shown above.

FELONY

NOTE: *If sentencing for a felony, locate the prior record level which corresponds to total points determined in section I above.*

Points	Level
0	I
1 - 4	II
5 - 8	III
9 - 14	IV
15 - 18	V
19 +	VI

PRIOR RECORD LEVEL ▶ ☐

☐ The Court finds the prior convictions, prior record points and the prior record level of the defendant to be as shown herein.

Date | *Name Of Presiding Judge (Type Or Print)* | *Signature Of Presiding Judge*

AOC-CR-600, Rev. 12/97

(Over)

Table 3 (continued)

III. PRIOR CONVICTION

NOTE: *Federal law precludes making computer printout of DCI-CCH (rap sheet) part of permanent public court record.*

Offense	File No.	Date of Conviction	County *(name state, if not N.C.)*	Class

AOC-CR-600, Side Two, Rev. 12/97

Table 4
Misdemeanor Sentence Dispositions and Prison/Jail Term Ranges
A = active punishment   I = intermediate punishment   C = community punishment

Misdemeanor Class (Fine)	Level I: No Prior Convictions	Level II: 1 to 4 Prior Convictions	Level III: 5 or More Prior Convictions
Class A1 (fine discretionary)	C/I/A 1–60 days	C/I/A 1–75 days	C/I/A 1–150 days
Class 1 (fine discretionary)	C 1–45 days	C/I/A 1–45 days	C/I/A 1–120 days
Class 2 (maximum fine $1,000)	C 1–30 days	C/I 1–45 days	C/I/A 1–60 days
Class 3 (maximum fine $200)	C 1–10 days	C/I 1–15 days	C/I/A 1–20 days

Source: G.S. 15A-1340.23(c).

Table 5
Felonies (Class F through I) and Misdemeanors Subject to Restitution Requirements under Crime Victims' Rights Act

Statute	Description of Offense	Punishment
14-16.6(b)	Assault with deadly weapon on executive or legislative officer	Class F felony
14-16.6(c)	Assault inflicting serious bodily injury on executive or legislative officer	Class F felony
14-18	Involuntary manslaughter	Class F felony
14-32.1(e)	Aggravated assault on handicapped person	Class F felony
14-32.2(b)(3)	Patient abuse: conduct resulting in serious bodily injury	Class F felony
14-32.3(a)	Abuse by caretaker of disabled/elder adult in domestic setting:	
	resulting in serious injury	Class F felony
	resulting in injury	Class H felony
14-32.3(b)	Neglect by caretaker of disabled/elder adult in domestic setting:	
	resulting in serious injury	Class G felony
	resulting in injury	Class I felony
14-32.3(c)	Exploitation by caretaker of disabled/elder adult in domestic setting: resulting in loss of more than $1,000	Class H felony
14-32.4	Assault inflicting serious bodily injury	Class F felony
14-33(a)	Simple assault, simple assault and battery, or simple affray	Class 2 misdemeanor*
14-33(c)(1)	Assault:	
	inflicting serious injury	Class A1 misdemeanor*
	with deadly weapon	Class A1 misdemeanor*
14-33(c)(2)	Assault on female	Class A1 misdemeanor*
14-33.2	Habitual misdemeanor assault	Class H felony
14-34	Assault by pointing gun	Class A1 misdemeanor*
14-34.2	Assault with deadly weapon on government official or on company or campus police officer	Class F felony
14-34.6(b)	Assault on firefighter or emergency personnel:	
	inflicting serious bodily injury	Class I felony
	with deadly weapon other than firearm	Class I felony
14-34.6(c)	Assault with firearm on firefighter or emergency personnel	Class F felony
14-41	Abduction of minor	Class F felony
14-43.2	Involuntary servitude	Class F felony
14-43.3	Felonious restraint	Class F felony
14-51, -52	Second-degree burglary	Class G felony
14-58	Second-degree arson	Class G felony
14-87.1	Common-law robbery	Class G felony
14-134.3(a)	Domestic criminal trespass	Class 1 misdemeanor*
14-190.17	Second-degree sexual exploitation of minor	Class F felony
14-190.17A	Third-degree sexual exploitation of minor	Class I felony
14-190.19	Participating in prostitution of minor	Class F felony
14-202.1	Taking, or attempting to take, indecent liberties with child	Class F felony
14-277.3	Stalking:	
	First offense	Class 1 misdemeanor*
	While court order in effect prohibiting similar behavior	Class A1 misdemeanor*
	Second or subsequent conviction within 5 years	Class I felony
14-288.9	Assault on emergency personnel: with dangerous weapon or substance	Class F felony
20-138.5	Habitual impaired driving	Class F felony
20-141.4(a1)	Felony death by vehicle	Class G felony

NOTE: The restitution provisions governing sentencing for crimes subject to the Crime Victims' Rights Act apply to offenses committed on or after Dec. 1, 1998. This table does not show the punishments in effect for offenses committed before that date.

All Class A through E felonies (not listed in this table) are subject to the Crime Victims' Rights Act. An attempt to commit a Class A through E felony or one of the Class F through I felonies listed here is also subject to the Crime Victims' Rights Act if the attempt is punishable as a felony. Unless a different classification is otherwise stated, an attempt to commit a felony is punishable one class lower than the felony attempted. *See* G.S. 14-2.5. An attempt to commit a Class I felony is normally a Class 1 misdemeanor, so it is normally not subject to the Crime Victims' Rights Act.

*A misdemeanor is subject to the Crime Victims' Rights Act only if the defendant and victim have a personal relationship as defined in G.S. 50B-1(b).

SOURCE: G.S. 15A-830(a)(7), -834.

6
Homicide

Chapter Contents

6
Homicide

First-Degree Murder

Statute

§14-17. Murder in the first and second degree defined; punishment.

A murder which shall be perpetrated by means of poison, lying in wait, imprisonment, starving, torture, or by any other kind of willful, deliberate, and premeditated killing, or which shall be committed in the perpetration or attempted perpetration of any arson, rape or a sex offense, robbery, kidnapping, burglary, or other felony committed or attempted with the use of a deadly weapon shall be deemed to be murder in the first degree, a Class A felony, and any person who commits such murder shall be punished with death or imprisonment in the State's prison for life without parole as the court shall determine pursuant to G.S. 15A-2000, except that any such person who was under 17 years of age at the time of the murder shall be punished with imprisonment in the State's prison for life without parole. Provided, however, any person under the age of 17 who commits murder in the first degree while serving a prison sentence imposed for a prior murder or while on escape from a prison sentence imposed for a prior murder shall be punished with death or imprisonment in the State's prison for life without parole as the court shall determine pursuant to G.S. 15A-2000. All other kinds of murder, including that which shall be proximately caused by the unlawful distribution of opium or any synthetic or natural salt, compound, derivative, or preparation of opium, or cocaine or other substance described in G.S. 90-90(a)4., when the ingestion of such substance causes the death of the user, shall be deemed murder in the second degree, and any person who commits such murder shall be punished as a Class B2 felon.

Elements

A person guilty of this offense
- (1) kills
- (2) another living human being
- (3) (a) (i) with malice *and*
  - (ii) with a specific intent to kill formed after premeditation and deliberation; *or*
  - (b) by poisoning, lying in wait, imprisonment, starvation, or torture; *or*
  - (c) while committing or attempting arson, rape, sex offense, robbery, burglary, kidnapping, or any felony in which a deadly weapon is used.

Punishment

Class A felony punishable by death or imprisonment for life without possibility of parole. Before the jury may impose the death penalty, it must find beyond a reasonable doubt that one or more of the "aggravating circumstances" listed in G.S. 15A-2000 (the murder was heinous, atrocious, or cruel, or was committed during a robbery, for example) exist and that the aggravating circumstances outweigh any "mitigating circumstances," such as the defendant's age or lack of significant prior criminal history. This determination of the sentence takes place in a separate hearing after the defendant is found guilty. For a discussion of capital sentencing issues, see Robert L. Farb, *North Carolina Capital Case Law Handbook* (Chapel Hill: Institute of Government, The University of North Carolina at Chapel Hill, 1996).

If a defendant under age seventeen is convicted of first-degree murder, the mandatory sentence is life imprisonment without parole. However, if the defendant under age seventeen committed the offense while serving a prison sentence for a prior murder or while on escape from a prison sentence for a prior murder, he or she may be punished by the death penalty.

Notes

Elements (1) and (2). To kill oneself is suicide, which is not a crime in North Carolina (G.S. 14-17.1). To shoot someone who is already dead is not murder; the victim must be living in order for the act to be murder. To destroy a fetus that has not yet been separated from its mother is not murder but abortion (G.S. 14-44), which is lawful under certain circumstances. Killing a viable unborn fetus is not murder; murder would be committed only when injuries were inflicted before birth and if the fetus is born alive and then dies of the injuries (324 N.C. 87). A defendant who intended to kill one person but mistakenly killed another is still guilty of murder (215 N.C. 598).

Element (3)(a)(i). The law of homicide recognizes three forms of malice: (1) the express emotions of hatred, ill will, and spite (297 N.C. 168); (2) commission of an inherently dangerous act (or omission to act when there is a legal duty to do so) in such a reckless and wanton manner "as to manifest a mind utterly without regard for human life and social duty and deliberately bent on mischief" (351 N.C. 386; 311 N.C. 391; 190 N.C. 674; 98 N.C. App. 600; 105 N.C. App. 377); and (3) a condition of the mind which prompts a person to take the life of another intentionally, or to intentionally inflict serious bodily injury which proximately results in death, without just cause, excuse, or justification (307 N.C. 184). See the definition of "Maliciously" in Chapter 1.

The second form of malice, that based in an inherently dangerous act, was found when the defendant—even though two other people became violently ill after using the drugs in the defendant's presence—supplied drugs to the victim, who later died (98 N.C. App. 600).

The third form of malice can be inferred from the intentional infliction of a wound with a deadly weapon (288 N.C. 632; 297 N.C. 247; 307 N.C. 184; 309 N.C. 674). This is the case even if the alleged homicide involved a mercy killing (321 N.C. 186). Malice may also be inferred from the use of hands alone to inflict a fatal injury when an adult assaults an infant (320 N.C. 51). See the discussion of what constitutes a deadly weapon under the offense "Assault with a Deadly Weapon" in Chapter 7.

Element (3)(a)(ii). "Specific intent to kill" means that the defendant intended his or her actions to result in the victim's death; it is not enough that the defendant merely committed an intentional act that resulted in the victim's death (333 N.C. 52).

"Premeditation" means thinking about something beforehand, for some length of time, however short; "deliberation" refers to an intention to kill formed while defendant was in a "cool state of blood" (183 N.C. 795; 296 N.C. 623; 326 N.C. 253). "Cool state of blood" does not mean absence of passion and emotion; a person may be capable of forming murderous intent, premeditating and deliberating, yet be prompted and to a large extent controlled by passion at the time of the offense (328 N.C. 231). Rather, it means that a killing was committed with a fixed design to kill, regardless of whether the defendant was angry or gripped with passion at the time of the act (296 N.C. 623; 326 N.C. 253). It also means that the defendant's anger or emotion was not so strong as to overcome the defendant's reason (330 N.C. 425). Premeditation and deliberation need not last for any perceptible length of time (175 N.C. 777; 275 N.C. 615). Premeditation and deliberation are generally established from the circumstances and manner of the killing (282 N.C. 58).

Circumstantial evidence, rather than direct evidence, generally proves premeditation and deliberation (338 N.C. 363). Circumstances showing premeditation and deliberation include: lack of provocation (303 N.C. 293); the defendant's conduct before and after killing (326 N.C. 40; 328 N.C. 598; 332 N.C. 520); statements of ill will toward the victim on the part of the defendant (313 N.C. 132); the defendant's previous assault of the victim (327 N.C. 178); previous difficulties between the defendant and the victim (326 N.C. 253); threats before and during the killing; the brutal nature of the killing (such as in strangulation, 328 N.C. 505; 332 N.C. 565); blows dealt after the victim is helpless; and the nature and number of the victim's wounds (328 N.C. 231; 331 N.C. 559; 338 N.C. 168) (for general lists and discussions of these circumstances, see 309 N.C. 78; 328 N.C. 175; 333 N.C. 407).

When a specific intent to kill is an element of first-degree murder, a defendant may be so drunk as to be unable to form this intent, even though the drunkenness was voluntary (274 N.C. 62; 298 N.C. 1; 330 N.C. 446; 337 N.C. 1). It is also possible that a defendant's mental disorder, although not sufficient to establish the legal defense of insanity, may limit the defendant's ability to deliberate, premeditate, and form a specific intent to kill (322 N.C. 243; 336 N.C. 617). See Chapter 2, "Bars and Defenses."

Element (3)(b). Evidence of first-degree murder committed by any of these means consists of evidence that the defendant killed a person by poison, lying in wait, imprisonment, starving, or torture, and that the defendant's act was the proximate cause of death. Neither specific intent to kill, nor premeditation and deliberation are elements of this category of murder, and they therefore need not be proven (317 N.C. 193; 320 N.C. 179; 328 N.C. 368). Nor must malice be proven as an element of this kind of murder (328 N.C. 1; 329 N.C. 466; 351 N.C, 251). The commission of an act of torture implies the requisite malice, and no separate showing is necessary (329 N.C. 466 at 481). Thus murder by the other acts described in this element also do not require an explicit showing of malice.

Lying in wait requires ambush and surprise of the victim (327 N.C. 210, 217). It may mean stationing oneself in advance or lying in ambush to attack a victim, but a defendant can be lying in wait even though not concealed (298 N.C. 135). A victim may even be aware of the attacker's presence; there would be adequate surprise in such a circumstance if the victim does not expect to be attacked (326 N.C. 368, 375). Lying in wait does not require that an attacker wait at the site of the killing for some period of time; "a moment's deliberate pause" before killing a victim unaware of the impending assault, and consequently without an opportunity for self-defense, satisfies the definition of murder by lying in wait (326 N.C at 376).

Torture is the act or process of inflicting great, severe, or extreme pain, usually by more than a single act (328 N.C. 1; 348 N.C. 474).

Element (3)(c). Murder perpetrated under this element is referred to as felony murder. Evidence of this type of first-degree murder consists of evidence of commission or attempt of one of the listed felony offenses and an act that was the proximate cause of the victim's death. Only an interrelationship between the underlying felony and the murder are required; the underlying felony need not "cause" the death, and the homicide need not be committed to escape or to complete the underlying felony (337 N.C. 615). If the killing was done in the course of attempting one of the felonies specified in the statute, no proof of premeditation or deliberation is necessary (225 N.C. 486), and whether the killing was intentional is immaterial (231 N.C. 301). Additionally, if the underlying offense is one of those listed in the statute, the state is not required to prove malice under the felony murder theory, because malice is implied from the underlying felony or the use of a deadly weapon (292 N.C. 455; 315 N.C. 444; 329 N.C. 466). The fact that the killing was accidental is no defense if it was committed in the course of one of the named felonies (264 N.C. 508). Discharging a firearm into occupied property constitutes a felony in which a deadly weapon is used, thereby supporting a felony murder conviction if death results (316 N.C. 78). A felony was committed with the use of a deadly weapon when the defendant carried a gun while committing felonious larceny, even though it was not used to commit the larceny (315 N.C. 191). The offense of felony child abuse constitutes a felony in which a deadly weapon was used if the defendant uses his or her hands to kill a child, thereby supporting a conviction of first-degree murder based on the felony murder theory (346 N.C. 471).

A felony committed after the victim dies may be adequate to prove felony murder. The "continuous transaction" doctrine applies to felony murder. This means that when a series of incidents form one continuous transaction, several criminal offenses for which the defendant is responsible may arise from that transaction (315 N.C. 191). Applying this doctrine, a person may commit felony murder when the felony (a sexual assault or arson, for example) occurs before, during, or soon after the victim's death, as long as the felony and murder are incidents that form one continuous transaction (303 N.C. 321; 329 N.C. 423, 435; 332 N.C. 116). A time interval of three-and-one-half hours between the commission of a murder and the commission of arson of the murder victim's dwelling is sufficient evidence of the "continuous transaction" doctrine (342 N.C. 249).

The prosecution need not elect for submission to a jury between theories of felony murder and murder with specific intent formed after premeditation and deliberation if its proof satisfies the elements of both types of murder (314 N.C. 649).

Each party to a conspiracy to commit one of the named felonies who is actually or constructively present during the commission of such a felony is guilty of first-degree murder if one of them kills while committing the felony (301 N.C. 407). One who aids and abets another in the commission of felony murder is also guilty as a principal (328 N.C. 598).

The prosecution may attempt to prove first-degree murder by felony murder based on the commission of more than one felony. For example, a jury may convict a defendant of first-degree murder based on predicate felonies of both armed robbery and felonious breaking and entering. However, if an appellate court finds insufficient evidence to support one of the felonies on which the felony murder was based, and it is impossible to determine if the jury convicted the person based on the erroneously submitted felony, a new trial may be ordered (326 N.C. 434).

For felony murder to apply, the defendant, co-conspirators, aiders, or others acting in concert with the defendant must have committed the homicide. A defendant may not be held responsible on this theory for a homicide committed by an adversary (a law enforcement officer, for example) or victim (330 N.C. 536).

Proximate cause. To constitute this offense (and, indeed, to constitute any form of homicide), the defendant's act must be the "proximate cause" of the death. Proximate causation can be shown without proving that a defendant's act was the sole or immediate cause of death. Rather, the act need only be a *contributing* cause of death if the direct cause is "a natural result of the criminal act" (290 N.C. 292; 301 N.C. 374). Thus if the defendant inflicts a dangerous wound that is a contributing cause of death, he or she is liable for murder. Proximate cause would exist even if a victim died from negligent medical treatment after an assault, unless the negligent treatment was the sole cause of death (290 N.C. 292; 115 N.C. App. 25). Proximate cause also would exist when the defendant's criminal act was a contributing cause of the victim's death, even if a victim chose surgery against medical advice and died (118 N.C. App. 200), refused on religious grounds to accept blood transfusions and died (135 N.C. App. 499), or there was a voluntary decision by family members to remove the victim from life support systems (110 N.C. App. 319). A defendant who wounds someone and leaves the victim outdoors in a helpless condition in cold weather may be guilty of homicide if the victim dies from exposure to the cold (234 N.C. 716). Also, it is not a defense that a victim's pre-existing physical condition (i.e., alcoholism) made the victim peculiarly vulnerable to an assault; the defendant's assault is considered to be the proximate cause of death, even if the assault would not have been fatal without the pre-existing condition (255 N.C. 412; 298 N.C. 673; 115 N.C. App. 25). If a defendant intentionally wounds a victim, foreseeability of death is not a component of proximate cause (115 N.C. App. 25; 278 N.C. 210, overruled on other grounds, 331 N.C. 583). The common-law rule that a person could not be convicted of murder if the victim died more than a year and a day after the criminal act has been abolished (328 N.C. 613).

Lesser-included offenses. Involuntary manslaughter is a lesser-included offense of first- and second-degree murder and voluntary manslaughter (314 N.C. 649; 327 N.C. 74). Second-degree murder is a lesser-included offense of premeditated and deliberate first-degree murder (327 N.C. 259). The lesser-included offense of second-degree murder must be submitted to the jury in a prosecution for first-degree murder based solely on a theory of premeditation and deliberation if evidence reasonably would support a verdict on the lesser charge (307 N.C. 274; 326 N.C. 298; 328 N.C. 515; 337 N.C. 224). Misdemeanor and felony assaults and attempted first-degree murder are not lesser-included offenses of murder involving assault when the "short-form" murder indictment is used (334 N.C. 54; 131 N.C. App. 199).

Attempted first-degree murder. An attempt to commit this offense is a Class B2 offense (G.S. 14-2.5). When the defendant assaulted the victim in his car, and later drove to the home of the victim's cousin and—with accomplices—shot at the victim eight times, there was sufficient evidence of attempted first-degree murder (131 N.C. App. 199).

Constitutionality. The murder by torture provision is not unconstitutionally vague (329 N.C. 466).

Related offenses not in this chapter

Destroying unborn child (G.S. 14-44, -45.1)
Producing miscarriage (G.S. 14-45, -45.1)
Concealing dead body of newborn child (G.S. 14-46)

Second-Degree Murder

Statute

See G.S. 14-17, reproduced under "First-Degree Murder."

Elements

A person guilty of this offense
(1) kills
(2) another living human being
(3) with malice.

Punishment

Class B2 felony.

Notes

Generally. All the elements of second-degree murder were discussed in connection with "First-degree Murder." To charge this offense, it is *not* necessary to show a specific intent to kill; thus voluntary intoxication is no defense to this charge (283 N.C. 444; 334 N.C. 356). See the note on voluntary intoxication under "Defenses Showing Lack of Blameworthiness" in Chapter 2.

Element (3). Because malice can be inferred from the intentional use of a deadly weapon to inflict harm, the offense of second-degree murder can be established by showing a voluntary unlawful killing committed with a deadly weapon (275 N.C. 108). The deadly weapon whose use gives rise to the inference of malice may be a weapon that is deadly by its very nature, such as a gun (183 N.C. 795), or because of the way it is used, such as hands and feet used against an infant or a disabled or feeble person (309 N.C. 512; 13 N.C. App. 499; 35 N.C. App. 48). In exceptional cases, reckless use of an automobile may establish malice for second-degree murder (190 N.C. 674; 311 N.C. 391; 199 N.C. App. 689; 131 N.C. App. 48; 105 N.C. App. 377; 109 N.C. App. 64; 351 N.C. 386). Also, cruel and reckless acts that indicate a total disregard for human life, such as extreme and brutal child abuse, are sufficient to supply the malice necessary for second-degree murder (295 N.C. 559). There was sufficient evidence of second-degree murder when a defendant supplied illegal drugs to a victim with knowledge that the drugs were inherently dangerous (the defendant witnessed two other people become violently ill after using the drugs in the defendant's presence) (98 N.C. App. 600).

Death resulting from distribution of illegal drugs. If a defendant unlawfully distributes opium, cocaine, or a derivative of either substance, and ingestion of that substance causes the user's death, the defendant is guilty of second-degree murder (see G.S. 14-17 above).

Lesser-included offenses. Involuntary manslaughter is a lesser-included offense of first- and second-degree murder and voluntary manslaughter (314 N.C. 649; 327 N.C. 74). See the discussion of this note under "First-Degree Murder." Felony death by vehicle is not a lesser-included offense of second-degree murder based on a vehicular homicide (131 N.C. App. 48).

Possible charges in homicide involving impaired driving offense. When a defendant willfully violates the DWI law and such violation is a proximate cause of death, at least three different charges are possible, depending upon the state of mind of the defendant. Possible charges are second-degree murder, involuntary manslaughter, and felony death by vehicle. As noted in Element (3) just above, second-degree murder is a possible charge only if evidence shows recklessness amounting to malice. To convict such a defendant of involuntary manslaughter (described below in this chapter), there must be evidence that the defendant willfully, intentionally, or recklessly violated a motor vehicle law designed to protect the safety of others—that is, the defendant was culpably negligent (37 N.C. App. 445). Driving while impaired is per se culpable negligence in North Carolina (314 N.C. 633). The final possible charge is felony death by vehicle (also described below in this chapter), when the defendant's culpable act is impaired driving.

Proximate cause. See the discussion of this note under "First Degree Murder."

Attempted second-degree murder is not a crime. The crime of attempted second-degree murder does not exist because a specific intent to kill is not an element of second-degree murder, and an attempt requires an intent to commit the substantive offense (351 N.C. 448).

Related offenses not in this chapter

See the offenses listed under "First Degree Murder."

Voluntary Manslaughter

Statute

§14-18. Punishment for manslaughter.

Voluntary manslaughter shall be punishable as a Class D felony, and involuntary manslaughter shall be punishable as a Class F felony.

Elements

A person guilty of this offense
(1) kills
(2) another living human being
(3) without malice.

Punishment

Class D felony.

Notes

Elements (1) and (2). See the discussion of these elements under "First-Degree Murder."

Element (3) generally. Voluntary manslaughter is distinguished from second-degree murder by the absence of malice in voluntary manslaughter. The law recognizes two types of unlawful killings that result from intentional conduct but might not involve malice: (a) a killing committed in the sudden heat of passion caused by adequate provocation that would arouse an ordinary person beyond his or her power of control (270 N.C. 622) and (b) a killing committed during the exercise of an "imperfect" right of self-defense (295 N.C. 559; 303 N.C. 526). (See the definition of "Maliciously" in Chapter 1). These circumstances do not completely justify or excuse a killing. Rather, they displace the element of malice, reducing the offense from second-degree murder to voluntary manslaughter. Classic examples of voluntary manslaughter are a killing committed by a defendant who discovers his or her spouse in an act of adultery and a killing caused by the use of excessive force in self-defense.

"Sudden heat of passion" means emotions such as "rage, anger, hatred, furious resentment, or terror, rendering the mind incapable of cool reflection" (338 N.C. 494). A killing is done in the sudden heat of passion only if it is done before the defendant has had time to cool down. For example, a killing committed in anger aroused during a sudden, mutual fight will reduce a homicide to voluntary manslaughter (152 N.C. 822; 280 N.C. 51). But if a person arms himself or herself in expectation of being assaulted and then kills during the assault, the person has not killed in the sudden heat of passion (51 N.C. 381). A killing committed when the defendant finds his or her spouse in an act of adultery is manslaughter if done at the time the act is discovered in progress or immediately thereafter, but not when there has been time for the defendant's passion to cool (48 N.C. 74; 286 N.C. 304; 64 N.C. App. 656).

An assault against a defendant or a close relative of the defendant is recognized as adequate provocation (299 N.C. 103). Finding one's spouse in an act of adultery is adequate provocation (286 N.C. 304), but mere discovery of the fact of adultery is not (30 N.C. 330). Mere words or insulting gestures—such as throwing a cigarette butt at a defendant—that are not accompanied by threatening conduct are not adequate provocation to reduce murder to manslaughter (226 N.C. 62; 287 N.C. 147; 65 N.C. App. 107). Trespass on one's land is not by itself adequate provocation for killing, and the killing of a mere trespasser is murder rather than manslaughter (53 N.C. 463).

The distress that prompts a person to commit a mercy killing to end an ill relative's extreme physical suffering does not constitute adequate provocation; thus it does not negate malice, and a mercy killing is properly categorized as first-degree murder rather than voluntary manslaughter (321 N.C. 186).

Voluntary manslaughter is committed in the exercise of imperfect self-defense when a person uses excessive force in self-defense or is an aggressor, without murderous intent, in bringing on a fight or difficulty (280 N.C. 51; 295 N.C. 559; 303 N.C. 526). See the discussion of self-defense in Chapter 2, "Bars and Defenses."

Proximate cause. See the discussion of this note under "First-Degree Murder."

Relation to other offenses. See the discussion in the "Lesser-included offenses" note under "First-Degree Murder."

Related offenses not in this chapter

See the related offenses listed under "First-Degree Murder."

Involuntary Manslaughter

Statute

See G.S. 14-18, reproduced under "Voluntary Manslaughter."

Elements

A person guilty of this offense

(1) kills

(2) another living human being

(3) unlawfully

(a) by an unlawful act that does not amount to a predicate felony for felony murder or is not inherently dangerous to life, *or*
(b) by engaging in any other conduct in such a reckless and careless manner as to show a thoughtless disregard for consequences or a heedless indifference to the rights and safety of others, *or*
(c) by culpable omission to perform a legal duty.

Punishment

Class F felony.

Notes

Elements (1) and (2). See the discussion of these elements under "First-Degree Murder."

Element (3) generally. The kinds of conduct described in Elements (3) (a), (b), and (c) are not actually elements of this offense. The requirement of this element is that the killing be unlawful; (a), (b), and (c) are three alternative grounds on which the prosecution may allege and prove unlawfulness (314 N.C. 649). Involuntary manslaughter is an unlawful killing without malice, premeditation and deliberation, or an intention to kill or inflict serious bodily injury (336 N.C. 762).

Element (3)(a). This ground pertains to two kinds of cases: (1) cases not covered by the felony-murder rule because the killing occurs in the course of an unlawful act that is not a felony covered by that rule (that is, another type of felony or a misdemeanor) [see the note on Element (3)(c) under "First-Degree Murder"] and (2) cases in which malice is not present because the killing results from the commission of an unlawful act that is not naturally dangerous to life (see the definition of "Maliciously" in Chapter 1).

A common example of the first kind of case is a killing caused by an intentional or reckless violation of a statute or ordinance designed for the protection of human life or limb (295 N.C. 559; 336 N.C. 762). Examples include a killing resulting from a violation of a motor vehicle law (that is, a DWI offense) (242 N.C. 540; 257 N.C. 270; 260 N.C. 663); a killing committed when a gun discharges accidentally while a defendant is pointing it at the victim (279 N.C. 716); a killing caused by misdemeanor child abuse (295 N.C. 559; 309 N.C. 132); and a killing by dogs allowed to run free in criminally negligent violation of a local ordinance (336 N.C. 762). Some courts refer to the intentional, willful, or wanton violation of a statute or ordinance designed to protect human life or limb as culpable, gross, or criminal negligence (336 N.C. 762). This is a kind of negligence greater than mere carelessness.

An example of the second kind of unlawful killing constituting voluntary manslaughter would be a killing caused by a light blow to an unexpectedly vulnerable victim (*Perkins*, p. 110).

Element (3)(b). A defendant is guilty of involuntary manslaughter even though the act that caused death is lawful, if the act was carried out in a reckless and careless manner with respect to the rights and safety of others. Such reckless and careless acts may also be described as culpable negligence (112 N.C. App. 770). Mishaps with firearms are common examples of this type of involuntary manslaughter (241 N.C. 356; 260 N.C. 186; 279 N.C. 676; 291 N.C. 700). However, if a defendant fires a gun *intentionally* under circumstances naturally dangerous to life, the crime is murder rather than manslaughter (286 N.C. 304). An accidental killing committed during a lawful activity not resulting from a defendant's intentional or negligent conduct is not a crime at all (254 N.C. 101).

Element (3)(c). To be liable for involuntary manslaughter for *failing* to act to prevent harm to a victim, a defendant must have a legal duty to protect the victim. Thus a parent who negligently fails to feed a child is guilty of involuntary manslaughter if the child dies of starvation, because the law imposes a duty on parents to care for their children (if the parent *intentionally* fails to feed the child, the crime is first-degree murder) (18 N.C. App. 433).

Proximate cause. See the discussion of this note under "First-Degree Murder." The defendant's act must proximately cause the victim's death. A proximate cause is a cause without which the victim's death would not have occurred; it need not have been the only cause, nor the last or nearest cause of death (336 N.C. 762, 771). "Forseeability" is an essential part of proximate cause in an involuntary manslaughter case (forseeability apparently is not an essential part of proximate cause in an intentional homicide; see the note on "Proximate cause" under "First-Degree Murder"). The defendant need not have foreseen the exact injury that occurred but, in the exercise of reasonable care, might have foreseen some injury resulting from his or her act or omission, or that generally injurious consequences might have been expected. Thus the state is not required to prove that a defendant foresaw that the victim would die from an assault; the state must prove only that the defendant foresaw that some serious injury might result. There was sufficient evidence of "forseeability" when the defendant was aware of the fifty-seven-year-old victim's heart condition and would have reasonably foreseen that two stab wounds would be injurious to her—the victim died from the stress on her heart caused by the defendant's assault (343 N.C. 399). The intervening negligence of a third person (particularly applicable in vehicular homicide cases) may insulate a defendant from criminal liability when that third person's negligence is the sole proximate cause of the victim's death (260 N.C. 663; 77 N.C. App. 36; 65 N.C. App. 122).

Possible charges in homicide involving impaired driving offense. See the discussion of this note under "Second-Degree Murder." When a defendant commits the offense of impaired driving that proximately causes a victim's death and involuntary manslaughter is charged, the state need not prove that the defendant's impairment caused the defendant to violate some other rule of the road that caused the victim's death (314 N.C. 633). Impaired driving constitutes the necessary intentional or reckless violation of a statute designed to protect human life.

Relation to other offenses. In a case in which a defendant's impaired driving renders a resulting killing unlawful, misdemeanor death by vehicle is a lesser-included offense of involuntary manslaughter, but felony death by vehicle is not (90 N.C. App. 614; 71 N.C. App. 581; 33 N.C. App. 93; 31 N.C. App. 93). Felony death by vehicle and involuntary manslaughter in this circumstance share the same essential elements (90 N.C. App. 614).

Related offenses not in this chapter

See the offenses listed under "First-Degree Murder."

Death by Vehicle—Felony

Statute

§20-141.4. Felony and misdemeanor death by vehicle.

(a) Repealed by Session Laws, 1983, c. 435, s. 27.

(a1) Felony Death by Vehicle.—A person commits the offense of felony death by vehicle if he unintentionally causes the death of another person while engaged in the offense of impaired driving under G.S. 20-138.1 or G.S. 20-138.2 and commission of that offense is the proximate cause of the death.

(a2) Misdemeanor Death by Vehicle.—A person commits the offense of misdemeanor death by vehicle if he unintentionally causes the death of another person while engaged in the violation of any State law or local ordinance applying to the operation or use of a vehicle or to the regulation of traffic, other than impaired driving under G.S. 20-138.1, and commission of that violation is the proximate cause of the death.

(b) Punishments.—Felony death by vehicle is a Class G felony. Misdemeanor death by vehicle is a Class 1 misdemeanor.

(c) No Double Prosecutions.—No person who has been placed in jeopardy upon a charge of death by vehicle may be prosecuted for the offense of manslaughter arising out of the same death; and no person who has been placed in jeopardy upon a charge of manslaughter may be prosecuted for death by vehicle arising out of the same death.

Elements

A person guilty of this offense
- (1) kills
- (2) another living human being
- (3) unintentionally
- (4) (a) while engaged in the offense of impaired driving under G.S. 20-138.1, *or*
  - (b) while engaged in the offense of impaired driving in a commercial vehicle under G.S. 20-138.2, *and*
- (5) commission of the impaired driving offense is the proximate cause of death.

Punishment

Class G felony.

Notes

Generally. This offense was established as part of the Safe Roads Act of 1983. See the notes on "Impaired Driving" in Chapter 25. The statute covers killings committed when the defendant drives a vehicle while impaired. To convict on this charge, it is not necessary to prove reckless or careless driving, as is required to establish involuntary manslaughter.

Element (5). As in manslaughter and murder, a defendant is guilty of death by vehicle only if the defendant's culpable act—in this case, impaired driving—is the proximate cause of death.

Possible charges in homicide involving impaired driving offense. See the discussions of this note under "Second-Degree Murder" and "Involuntary Manslaughter."

Relation to other offenses. This is not a lesser-included offense of involuntary manslaughter (90 N.C. App. 614) or second-degree murder (131 N.C. App. 48). Misdemeanor death by vehicle is not a lesser-included offense of felony death by vehicle. See the discussion of this note under "Involuntary Manslaughter."

Proximate cause. See the discussion of this note under "Involuntary Manslaughter."

Related offenses not in this chapter

"Impaired Driving" (Chapter 25)

Death by Vehicle—Misdemeanor

Statute

See subsection (a2) of G.S. 20-141.4, reproduced under "Death by Vehicle—Felony."

Elements

A person guilty of this offense

(1) kills
(2) another living human being
(3) unintentionally
(4) while committing a violation of any state law or local ordinance applying to the operation and use of a vehicle or to the regulation of traffic, other than impaired driving under G.S. 20-138.1, *and*
(5) commission of that offense is the proximate cause of death.

Punishment

Class 1 misdemeanor.

Notes

Generally. This statute covers killings committed while the defendant operates a vehicle in violation of either state law or local ordinance. To convict for this crime, it is not necessary to prove reckless or careless driving, as is required to establish involuntary manslaughter (71 N.C. App. 581).

Element (5). See the note on Element (5) under "Death by Vehicle—Felony."

Proving violation of local ordinances. See the provisions of G.S. 160A-79 and G.S. 153A-50 on pleading and proving a city or county ordinance.

Relation to other offenses. This is a lesser-included offense of involuntary manslaughter, but not of felony death by vehicle. See the discussion of this note under "Involuntary Manslaughter."

Proximate cause. See the discussion of this note under "Involuntary Manslaughter."

Related offenses not in this chapter

See the offenses listed in Chapter 25, "Motor Vehicle Offenses."

7
Assaults and Threats

Chapter Contents

7 Assaults and Threats

Simple Assault

Statute

§ 14-33. Misdemeanor assaults, batteries, and affrays, simple and aggravated; punishments.

(a) Any person who commits a simple assault or a simple assault and battery or participates in a simple affray is guilty of a Class 2 misdemeanor.

(b) Unless his conduct is covered under some other provision of law providing greater punishment, any person who commits any assault, assault and battery, or affray is guilty of a Class 1 misdemeanor if, in the course of the assault, assault and battery, or affray, he:

(1) through (3) Repealed by Session Laws 1995, c. 507, s. 19.5(b);
(4) through (7) Repealed by Session Laws 1991, c. 525, s. 1;
(8) Repealed by Session Laws 1995, c. 507, s. 19.5(b);
(9) Commits an assault and battery against a sports official when the sports official is discharging or attempting to discharge official duties at a sports event, or immediately after the sports event at which the sports official discharged official duties. A "sports official" is a person at a sports event who enforces the rules of the event, such as an umpire or referee, or a person who supervises the participants, such as a coach. A "sports event" includes any interscholastic or intramural athletic activity in a primary, middle, junior high, or high school, college, or university, any organized athletic activity sponsored by a community, business, or nonprofit organization, any athletic activity that is a professional or semiprofessional event, and any other organized athletic activity in the State.

(c) Unless the conduct is covered under some other provision of law providing greater punishment, any person who commits any assault, assault and battery, or affray is guilty of a Class A1 misdemeanor if, in the course of the assault, assault and battery, or affray, he or she:

(1) Inflicts serious injury upon another person or uses a deadly weapon;
(2) Assaults a female, he being a male person at least 18 years of age;
(3) Assaults a child under the age of 12 years;
(4) Assaults an officer or employee of the State or any political subdivision of the State, when the officer or employee is discharging or attempting to discharge his official duties;
(5) Repealed by Session Laws 1999-105, s. 1, effective December 1, 1999; or
(6) Assaults a school employee or school volunteer when the employee or volunteer is discharging or attempting to discharge his or her duties as an

employee or volunteer, or assaults a school employee or school volunteer as a result of the discharge or attempt to discharge that individual's duties as a school employee or school volunteer. For purposes of this subdivision, the following definitions shall apply:

a. "Duties" means:
   1. All activities on school property;
   2. All activities, wherever occurring, during a school authorized event or the accompanying of students to or from that event; and
   3. All activities relating to the operation of school transportation.

b. "Employee" or "volunteer" means:
   1. An employee of a local board of education; or a charter school authorized under G.S. 115C-238.29D, or a nonpublic school which has filed intent to operate under Part 1 or Part 2 of Article 39 of Chapter 115C of the General Statutes;
   2. An independent contractor or an employee of an independent contractor of a local board of education, charter school authorized under G.S. 115C-238.29D, or a nonpublic school which has filed intent to operate under Part 1 or Part 2 of Article 39 of Chapter 115C of the General Statutes, if the independent contractor carries out duties customarily performed by employees of the school; and
   3. An adult who volunteers his or her services or presence at any school activity and is under the supervision of an individual listed in sub-sub-subdivision 1. or 2. of this sub-subdivision.

Elements

A person guilty of this offense
(1) commits an assault on another.

Punishment

Class 2 misdemeanor.

Notes

Forms of assault. Assault is not defined by statute; instead, it is defined by common (or case) law (270 N.C. 655). Assault may take many different forms. Its basic definition in North Carolina is an overt act or attempt, or the unequivocal appearance of attempt, with force and violence, to immediately physically injure another person, with the show of force or menace of violence being sufficient to put a reasonable person in fear of immediate physical injury (270 N.C. 655; 89 N.C. App. 372; 115 N.C. App. 687; N.C.P.I.—Crim. 208.40). The key component is a show of force sufficient to place another in reasonable fear of immediate physical harm. An assault may be the actual unlawful physical touching of another person (battery), or it may be an attempt to unlawfully touch another. Historically, there was a requirement that a defendant actually intend to harm the victim in order for an assault to occur (82 N.C. 549; 162 N.C. 632; *Perkins*, pp. 161–67). Today, however, a defendant's intent to harm is not always necessary for an assault to occur. As the above definition indicates, in some cases there is an assault because the show of force is sufficient to place the victim in reasonable fear of physical harm, regardless of the defendant's intent to harm.

North Carolina also recognizes two other means of committing an assault.

1. *Assault by show of violence*. This form of assault occurs when (a) the defendant shows an apparent ability to inflict injury (even if there is no actual ability); (b) the act is such that a reasonable person would fear harm from it; and (c) the act causes the victim to do something the victim would not have done or not do something he or she would have done, such as leaving a place or taking a different route (231 N.C. 313; 245 N.C. 185; 270 N.C. 655; 28 N.C. App. 490). The key difference between assault by show of violence and

regular assault is that this form of assault causes the victim to do something they would not have otherwise done.

2. *Assault by criminal negligence*. This form of assault occurs, with no intent on the part of the defendant to assault the victim, when (a) an act resulting in injury to another arises from conduct that shows a reckless disregard of the consequences and (b) bodily injury was a foreseeable consequence of the act (202 N.C. 755; 120 N.C. App. 182). This form of assault may occur when driving a car in a criminally negligent manner (184 N.C. 753; 202 N.C. 755; 242 N.C. 59).

Battery. A battery is the actual striking of another (or other unlawful application of force to another, such as poisoning). The statutes, however, use assault and battery interchangeably, often using the term "assaults" for acts that must involve a striking (such as assault inflicting serious injury). When a battery is committed, the state is not required to show that the victim was placed in fear (266 N.C. 103; 18 N.C. App. 208; 27 N.C. App. 576). The term "assault" is used in this book to include battery.

Aiding and abetting by failure to defend. A parent can be convicted of aiding and abetting an assault on his or her child if the parent was present when the child was assaulted and did not take reasonable steps to prevent the assault. This rule arises because of the special relationship between parent and child (306 N.C. 466).

Fine and imprisonment proper. Versions of G.S. 14-33 applicable before enactment of structured sentencing made it improper to impose both an active jail term and a fine for simple assault. G.S. 14-33 no longer contains such a limitation.

Relation to second-degree rape. Simple assault is not a lesser-included offense of attempted second-degree rape (97 N.C. App. 597).

Assault and battery against a sports official. Section (b)(9) of this statute provides for an aggravated assault offense when a person commits an assault and battery against a sports official during, or immediately after, an athletic event where the official was discharging or attempting to discharge official duties. Sports officials include officials enforcing rules, such as referees, umpires, and coaches. Virtually all athletic contests are covered: community to interscholastic, intramural, intercollegiate, and professional events fall within the scope of this statute. Assault and battery against a sports official is punishable as a Class 1 misdemeanor, while simple assault is a Class 2 misdemeanor.

Multiple assault convictions when assaulting same victim. To find a defendant guilty of two separate assaults of the same victim, there must be a distinct interruption in the original assault followed by a second assault. Evidence in a prosecution of two counts of assault with a deadly weapon inflicting serious injury was insufficient to show a distinct interruption in the original assault followed by a second assault; thus dismissal of one count was required (138 N.C. App. 185).

Related offenses not in this chapter

"Simple Affray" (Chapter 17)
"Disorderly Conduct" (Chapter 17)
Hazing of student (G.S. 14-35)

Assault Inflicting Serious Injury

Statute

See subsection (c)(1) of G.S. 14-33, reproduced under "Simple Assault."

Elements

A person guilty of this offense
(1) commits an assault on another, *and*
(2) inflicts serious injury.

Punishment

Class A1 misdemeanor.

Notes

Element (1). See the notes on "Forms of assault" and "Battery" under "Simple Assault."

Element (2). Serious injury may be (a) physical injury that causes great pain and suffering or (b) serious mental injury (326 N.C. 777). Whether an injury is serious is a question of fact (261 N.C. 558; 326 N.C. 777). However, when evidence is not conflicting on this issue, a court may give a jury a peremptory instruction on whether a particular injury is serious (60 N.C. App. 92).

The following have been found by a jury to be serious injuries: shards of glass in the arm and shoulder of a victim of a drive-by shooting into the victim's vehicle, coupled with an officer's observation that the victim was shaken (337 N.C. 182); gunshot wound in the wrist (7 N.C. App. 564); swelling on back of skull (5 N.C. App. 635); cut nose and knocked-out teeth (1 N.C. App. 539) badly-bruised shoulder, inability to move arm properly for three days, pain and suffering (338 N.C. 502). Mental injury amounting to serious injury was properly found when a victim was sexually assaulted, for several days, with devices used to degrade and dehumanize, and after the assault the victim required hospital admission and treatment for severe depression, suicidal tendencies, anorexia, insomnia, and feelings of hopelessness and helplessness (326 N.C. 777).

Proving serious injury for this offense requires less evidence than proving serious bodily injury for "Assault Inflicting Serious Bodily Injury," an offense discussed later in this chapter.

Related offenses not in this chapter

"Aggravated Misdemeanor Affray" (Chapter 17)
Inciting to Riot (various offenses) (Chapter 17)
"Disorderly Conduct" (Chapter 17)
"Resisting, Delaying, or Obstructing an Officer" (Chapter 18)
Hazing of students (G.S. 14-35)

Assault with a Deadly Weapon

Statute

See subsection (c)(1) of G.S. 14-33, reproduced under "Simple Assault."

Elements

A person guilty of this offense
(1) commits an assault on another
(2) with a deadly weapon.

Punishment

Class A1 misdemeanor.

Notes

Element (1). See notes on "Forms of assault" and "Battery" under "Simple Assault."

Element (2). A deadly weapon is any instrument that under the circumstances of its use is likely to cause death or serious bodily injury (1 N.C. App. 539). Whether a weapon is deadly may depend on its nature and size, how it is used [for example, did it leave cut marks (228 N.C. 228)?], and the strength of the defendant compared to the victim (102 N.C. App. 419). If the deadly character of the weapon depends on such factors, the jury decides whether the weapon is deadly (120 N.C. 603). Some weapons, such as guns, are deadly by their very nature (316 N.C. 111) and the judge should instruct the jury that they are deadly weapons.

Examples of deadly weapons include a pistol (183 N.C. 795); a pistol used to strike rather than shoot at a victim (87 N.C. App. 626); a knife (51 N.C. App. 387); a belt with metal buckle used for hours on a child (244 N.C. 701); hands or feet used against an infant or a feeble person (309 N.C. 512; 13 N.C. App. 499; 102 N.C. App. 419) or used in a particularly vicious manner against a weaker person (61 N.C. App. 610; 104 N.C. App. 766); an automobile (261 N.C. 558); a firebomb (315 N.C. 1); and a fire used to burn a house and harm a person inside (315 N.C. 749). If the weapon is not deadly by its very nature, the criminal pleading needs only (a) to allege that it is a deadly weapon without describing it further (for example, by saying "a stick, a deadly weapon") or (b) to describe it so as to necessarily demonstrate its deadly character (293 N.C. 633).

Difference from assault by pointing gun. See the note on this point under "Assault by Pointing Gun." "Assault with a Deadly Weapon" may also, of course, be committed with weapons other than guns.

Relation to other offenses. This offense is not a lesser-included offense of discharging a firearm into a motor vehicle (330 N.C. 249). For assaults with deadly weapons against (certain) employees and security officers, see "Assault with Firearm or Other Deadly Weapon on Governmental Officers or Employees, or Company or Campus Police Officers" and "Simple Assault and Aggravated Assaults on Firefirghters or Specified Medical Personnel," discussed later in this chapter.

Related offenses not in this chapter

"Armed Robbery" (Chapter 12)
"Aggravated Misdemeanor Affray" (Chapter 17)
Incitement to Riot (various offenses) (Chapter 17)
"Disorderly Conduct" (Chapter 17)

"Transporting, Possessing Weapon during Emergency" (Chapter 17)
"Possession of Firearm by Felon" (Chapter 19)
"Possession of Weapon on School Grounds" (Chapter 19)
"Carrying Concealed Weapon" (Chapter 19)
"Manufacture, Possession, etc., of Machine Gun, Sawed-Off Shotgun, or Weapon of Mass Destruction" (Chapter 19)
Criminal use of laser device (G.S. 14-34.8)
"Carrying Gun into Assembly or Establishment Where Alcoholic Beverages Are Sold and Consumed" (Chapter 19)
Use of dangerous weapon by prisoner in assault (G.S. 14-258.2)

Assault on a Female

Statute

See subsection (c)(2) of G.S. 14-33, reproduced under "Simple Assault."

Elements

A person guilty of this offense
(1) is a male at least 18 years old, *and*
(2) commits an assault
(3) on a female.

Punishment

Class A1 misdemeanor.

Notes

Constitutionality. This offense has been held constitutional (not in violation of the Equal Protection Clause of the Fourteenth Amendment to the U.S. Constitution) even though a male defendant is subject to a greater penalty than a female who commits the same act (39 N.C. App. 395).

Element (1). The jury may estimate a defendant's age solely by observing his appearance in court, without relying on any additional evidence of age (298 N.C. 263). Even so, the state should present evidence of the defendant's age. Circumstantial evidence may be adequate for a jury's decision (324 N.C. 539).

Element (2). See the notes on "Forms of assault" and "Battery" under "Simple Assault."

Relation to other offenses. This offense is not a lesser-included offense of either first-degree statutory rape (306 N.C. 629), or of attempted second-degree rape (318 N.C. 669; 322 N.C. 733).

Related offenses not in this chapter

"Aggravated Misdemeanor Affray" (Chapter 17)
See the offenses in Chapter 8, "Sexual Assaults."

Assault on Child under 12

Statute

See subsection (c)(3) of G.S. 14-33, reproduced under "Simple Assault."

Elements

A person guilty of this offense
(1) commits an assault
(2) on a child under the age of 12 years.

Punishment

Class A1 misdemeanor.

Notes

Element (1). See the notes on "Forms of assault" and "Battery" under "Simple Assault." As a general rule, the person who is in charge of a child (a parent or school teacher, for example) is not criminally liable for inflicting moderate punishment to correct the child. Moderate punishment is punishment that does not cause lasting injury (68 N.C. 322). G.S. 115C-390 allows teachers to use reasonable force, including corporal punishment, to restrain or correct pupils. Force is unreasonable if it is motivated by anger or malice or if it causes permanent injury (113 N.C. 635).

Element (2). If the child actually is under the age of 12, it is immaterial whether the defendant believed that the child was 12 or over. See the note on Element (2) under "First-Degree Statutory Rape" (Chapter 8).

Generally. If the victim is 12 or older but under 16 and the defendant is the child's parent or guardian, child abuse might be charged.

Relation to other offenses. This offense is not a lesser-included offense of first-degree rape of a child of age 12 or less (306 N.C. 629).

Related offenses not in this chapter

"Indecent Liberties with a Child" (Chapter 8)
"Aggravated Misdemeanor Affray" (Chapter 17)

Assault on Governmental Officer or Employee

Statute

See subsection (c)(4) of G.S. 14-33, reproduced under "Simple Assault."

Elements

A person guilty of this offense
(1) commits an assault
(2) on an officer or employee of the State or any political subdivision of the State
(3) who is discharging or attempting to discharge his or her official duties.

Punishment

Class A1 misdemeanor.

Notes

Element (1). See notes on "Forms of assault" and "Battery" under "Simple Assault."

Element (2). When the General Assembly created this offense in 1991, it repealed offenses addressing assaults on specific officials, including law enforcement officers, custodial officers of the Department of Correction, judges, school administrators and teachers, and county social services employees. Assault on any of these officials is now encompassed by this offense, along with assault on all other local or state government employees or officers (but see the discussion of "Assault on or Threat to Court Officer" later in this chapter). It would seem that the defendant must know that the person who he or she assaults is a state officer or employee. In interpreting a similarly written statute concerning assault on law enforcement officers, the North Carolina Supreme Court ruled that the state must prove that the defendant knew that the person he or she assaulted was a law enforcement officer (315 N.C. 1). It is not clear that the defendant must know that the officer or employee is discharging, or attempting to discharge, a duty of his or her office. See Element (3) below.

Coverage for company police and campus police under this offense is not always clear. Historically, there were questions about whether company police and campus police could be considered "law enforcement officers" for purposes of the offense of assault on a law enforcement officer (a prior version of this statute). Under the new version of the statute, if an officer is employed in his or her security work by an agency of state or local government, then he or she clearly would be covered by this statute. For example, a campus police officer at The University of North Carolina at Chapel Hill would be covered because he or she is a state employee. This offense probably would be available when the victim is a campus police officer at a private university or a security officer for a business *only* if the officer is an off-duty government officer.

When off-duty members of a city police force were assaulted while working as security guards for a restaurant, charges of assault on a law enforcement officer were proper under the following circumstances: the officers were working in full police uniform and were carrying sidearms, the officers' employment with the restaurant had been made through the city police department, the officers were required to follow police department rules and guidelines, and they were attempting to place the defendant under arrest (an official duty of office while working for the city) when they were assaulted (108 N.C. App. 349; see also 332 N.C. 461). In similar circumstances, there might also be a violation of this statute.

Element (3). The statute specifies that the assault may occur either while an officer or employee is discharging a duty of his or her office, or while attempting to discharge such a duty. Assaults *because* of a duty discharged by the officer or employee are not covered by this offense. For example, assaulting a judge in the grocery store at a shopping mall because of what happened in court a week ago would not be covered by this statute (but see the discussion of "Assault on or Threat to Court Officer" later in this chapter).

The duty being discharged must be a *lawful* duty; if, for example, the officer or employee was making an illegal arrest, then this element would not be satisfied. See the note on Element (2) under "Resisting, Delaying, or Obstructing an Officer" (Chapter 18). A criminal pleading for this offense need allege only that the officer or employee was discharging a duty of his or her office, not what the specific duty was; in this respect the offense differs from the offense of resisting, delaying, or obstructing an officer (7 N.C. App. 132).

Charging both assault on a governmental officer or employee and resisting arrest. The general rule is that a person may not be convicted of both this offense and resisting, delaying, or obstructing an officer if the same assaultive conduct is the basis of both offenses (282 N.C. 157; 298 N.C. 191; 33 N.C. App. 698; 33 N.C. App. 722), because double jeopardy prohibits a person from being punished twice for the same criminal conduct, absent a contrary legislative intent (see the discussion of double jeopardy as a bar to prosecution in Chapter 2, "Bars and Defenses"). The best practice may be to charge both offenses based on the same conduct and permit the prosecutor to (1) choose the best offense for prosecution; (2) determine whether, given the facts, separate charges based on different conduct are possible; or (3) attempt to prosecute for both offenses based on the following argument. It may be argued that the legislature has clearly expressed "its intent to prescribe and punish exactly the same conduct under two separate statutes," so the general rule should no longer stand (315 N.C. 444 , 450–63; see generally 459 U.S. 359). Consequently, a trial court in a single trial may impose punishment for conviction of each statute separately even though the same conduct is the basis for each charge (315 N.C. at 450–63; 322 N.C. 666, 678). It is clear that a defendant may be convicted of resisting, delaying, or obstructing a public officer and assault on a governmental officer on the basis of *different* conduct arising out of the same incident (298 N.C. 191). For example, a defendant's hitting an officer and later resisting that officer's attempt to handcuff him or her may be two episodes of conduct arising out of the same incident that lead to two separate convictions.

Relation to other offenses. See "Assault on or Threat to Court Officer," discussed later in this chapter.

Related offenses not in this chapter

"Aggravated Misdemeanor Affray" (Chapter 17)
"Resisting, Delaying, or Obstructing an Officer" (Chapter 18)
Use of dangerous weapon by prisoner in assault (G.S. 14-258.2)
Injuring or killing law-enforcement agency animal (G.S. 14-163.1)

Assault on School Personnel

Statute

See subsection (c)(6) of G.S. 14-33, reproduced above in "Simple Assault."

Elements

A person guilty of this offense
(1) commits an assault
(2) on a school employee or school volunteer
(3) (a) who is discharging or attempting to discharge his or her duties,
or
(b) as a result of the employee's or volunteer's discharge or attempt to discharge his or her duties.

Punishment

Class A1 misdemeanor.

Notes

Element (1). See the notes on "Forms of assault" and "Battery" under "Simple Assault."

Element (2). See the definition of "employee" and "volunteer" in G.S. 14-33(c)(6)a. and b., reproduced under "Simple Assault."

Element (3). Assault committed because of a duty discharged by the employee or volunteer is covered by this offense.

Relation to other offenses. This offense, to the extent it includes governmental employees such as teachers, overlaps with the offense of "Assault on Governmental Officer or Employee," discussed earlier in this chapter. However, that offense, unlike this offense, does not cover an assault on a teacher committed as a result of the discharge of his or her duties (for example, a parent assaulting a teacher at a shopping mall because the teacher had disciplined his child at school).

Related offenses not in this chapter

None.

Assault with Firearm or Other Deadly Weapon on Governmental Officers or Employees, or Company or Campus Police Officers

Statute

§14-34.2. Assault with a firearm or other deadly weapon upon governmental officers or employees, company police officers, or campus police officers.

Unless a person's conduct is covered under some other provision of law providing greater punishment, any person who commits an assault with a firearm or any other deadly weapon upon an officer or employee of the State or of any political subdivision of the State, a company police officer certified pursuant to the provisions of Chapter 74E of the General Statutes, or a campus police officer certified pursuant to the provisions of Chapter 17C or Chapter 116 of the General Statutes, in the performance of his duties shall be guilty of a Class F felony.

Elements

A person guilty of this offense

(1) commits an assault
(2) with
  (a) a firearm, *or*
  (b) any other deadly weapon
(3) (a) on an officer or employee of the State or any political subdivision of the State, *or*
  (b) a certified company police officer, *or*

(c) a certified campus police officer
(4) who is performing a duty of the official's office.

Punishment

Class F felony.

Notes

Element (1). See the notes on "Forms of assault" and "Battery" under "Simple Assault."

Element (2)(a). A firearm is a weapon that propels shot, shells, or bullets by the action of an explosion within it (*Black's Law Dictionary*, p. 648.), and thus includes a shotgun, rifle, or pistol. It would not seem to include an air rifle, an air pistol, or a pistol that shoots blanks. This offense can occur even if the firearm is not fired.

Element (2)(b). For a definition of deadly weapon, see the note on Element (2) under "Assault with a Deadly Weapon."

Elements (3)(a), (b), and (c). See the notes for Element (2) under "Assault on Governmental Officer or Employee." Company and campus police officers are explicitly covered by this offense, while their inclusion as possible victims of "Assault on Governmental Officer or Employee" is not always clear. In interpreting a previous version of this statute, North Carolina's courts ruled that the defendant must know that the victim is one of the designated kinds of officers or employees (315 N.C. 1; 38 N.C. App. 509). This statute is likely to be interpreted similarly. Previous versions of this statute had made it a crime to commit these kinds of assaults against firefighters, emergency medical services personnel, ambulance attendants, and paramedics, among others. To the extent that such officials are public employees, company police, or campus police, assaults on them will come under this statute. They also may be covered under "Simple Assault and Aggravated Assault on Firefighters or Specified Medical Personnel."

Element (4). This offense is committed only if the officer or employee assaulted is engaged in a lawful duty. However, to be covered by this statute, the duty performed need not be a duty required by law; it need only be a duty permitted by law. For example, a law enforcement officer investigating a minor traffic accident that the officer has no statutory duty to investigate is still discharging a duty of his or her office (88 N.C. App. 139).

A criminal pleading for this offense need only allege that the victim was discharging a duty of his or her office, not what the specific duty was (37 N.C. App. 133; 40 N.C. App. 318); in this respect the offense differs from "Resisting, Delaying, or Obstructing an Officer" (Chapter 18). When the victim is a law enforcement officer, the duty need not be making an arrest; the officer could be patrolling, checking licenses, or engaged in any other official task. See the note on Element (4) under "Resisting, Delaying, or Obstructing an Officer" (Chapter 18). When an officer fired his pistol at the defendant in attempting to make an arrest, the officer was performing a duty of his office for purposes of this statute, and it was a violation of this statute for the defendant to return fire with a firearm (291 N.C. 480). However, if an officer uses excessive force in making an arrest, the person the officer is attempting to arrest can use reasonable force in self-defense (34 N.C. App. 572).

Multiple victims and offenses based on one shot. The North Carolina Supreme Court has indicated that a defendant may be convicted of two counts of assault for firing one shot at two officers (341 N.C. 173, describing ruling in 291 N.C. 480).

Multiple convictions based on same act of shooting one officer. The North Carolina Court of Appeals, declining to follow prior case law (50 N.C. App. 736; 121 N.C. App. 355) because it conflicted with North Carolina Supreme Court rulings, ruled that a defendant may be convicted and sentenced for both (1) assault with a deadly weapon with intent to kill and (2) assault with a deadly weapon on a law enforcement officer, based on the same act of shooting one officer. The court ruled that each offense had an element that was not contained in the other offense, and thus double jeopardy principles did not bar both convictions.

Relationship with other offenses. Several of the assault offenses discussed in this chapter overlap and must be carefully compared to determine whether a defendant's acts satisfy all the elements of each offense. Some apply only when a firearm is used, while others include deadly weapons as well. Another issue is which assault victims are covered.

Related offenses not in this chapter

See the offenses listed in Chapter 19, "Weapons Offenses."
Interference with firefighters (G.S. 58-82-1)

Assault with Firearm on Law Enforcement Officer, Probation or Parole Officer, or Detention Facility Employee

Statute

§ 14-34.5. Assault with a firearm on a law enforcement, probation, or parole officer or on a person employed at a State or local detention facility.

(a) Any person who commits an assault with a firearm upon a law enforcement officer, probation officer, or parole officer while the officer is in the performance of his or her duties is guilty of a Class E felony.

(b) Anyone who commits an assault with a firearm upon a person who is employed at a detention facility operated under the jurisdiction of the State or a local government while the employee is in the performance of the employee's duties is guilty of a Class E felony.

Elements

A person guilty of this offense
(1) commits an assault
(2) with a firearm
(3) on a law enforcement officer, probation officer, parole officer, or state or local government detention facility employee
(4) who is performing his or her duties.

Punishment

Class E felony.

Notes

Element (1). See the notes on "Forms of assault" and "Battery" under "Simple Assault".

Element (3). The term "law enforcement officer" probably is not limited to officers who are public employees. This offense would likely be applicable to assaults with firearms on company police officers ["company police officers" is a statutory term that includes most campus police officers at public and private colleges and universities, railroad police officers, and any other privately employed law enforcement officer; G.S. 74E-6(b)].

Although G.S. 14-34.5 does not define "law enforcement officer," another statute and certain court decisions suggest that company police officers are covered by the term under some circumstances. G.S. 74E-6(c) authorizes company police officers to make arrests and to charge infractions on specified types of property, so they appear to fit the definition of law enforcement officer in G.S. 14-288.1(5), which includes any "person authorized under the laws of North Carolina to make arrests and . . . acting within his territorial jurisdiction." Also, the North Carolina Court of Appeals has characterized company police officers as "public, although limited police officer[s]" in contrasting them with private detectives (17 N.C. App. 701). They probably would be considered law enforcement officers when enforcing state law but not when acting solely to protect private interests of their employers (205 N.C. 51). They would be considered law enforcement officers when they both enforce state law and protect their employer's private interests at the same time. See the note on Element (2) under "Assault on Governmental Officer or Employee."

Element (4). See the note on Element (4) of "Assault with Firearm or Other Deadly Weapon on Governmental Officers or Employees, or Company or Campus Police Officers."

Related offenses not in this chapter

None.

Simple Assault and Aggravated Assault on Firefighters or Specified Medical Personnel

Statute

§ 14-34.6. Assault or affray on a firefighter, an emergency medical technician, medical responder, emergency department nurse, or emergency department physician.

(a) A person is guilty of a Class A1 misdemeanor if the person commits an assault or an affray on any of the following persons who are discharging or attempting to discharge their official duties:

(1) An emergency medical technician.
(2) A medical responder.
(3) An emergency department nurse.
(4) An emergency department physician.
(5) A firefighter.

(b) Unless a person's conduct is covered under some other provision of law providing greater punishment, a person is guilty of a Class I felony if the person violates subsection (a) of this section and (i) inflicts serious bodily injury or (ii) uses a deadly weapon other than a firearm.

(c) Unless a person's conduct is covered under some other provision of law providing greater punishment, a person is guilty of a Class F felony if the person violates subsection (a) of this section and uses a firearm.

I. Simple Assault or Affray on Firefighter or Specified Medical Personnel

Statute

See G.S. 14-34.6(a), reproduced under "Simple Assault and Aggravated Assault on Firefighters or Specified Medical Personnel."

Elements

A person guilty of this offense
- (1) commits an assault or affray
- (2) on a firefighter, emergency medical technician, medical responder, emergency department nurse, or emergency department physician
- (3) who is discharging or attempting to discharge an official duty.

Punishment

Class A1 misdemeanor.

Notes

Element (1). See the notes on "Forms of assault" and "Battery" under "Simple Assault" and the discussion of "Simple Affray" in Chapter 17.

Element (2). An "emergency medical technician" is defined in G.S. 131E-155(5) as a person who has completed an educational program in emergency medical care approved by the Department of Health and Human Resources and has been certified as an emergency medical technician by the department. A "medical responder" is defined in G.S. 131E-155(5a) as a person who has completed an educational program in emergency medical care and first aid approved by the Department of Health and Human Resources and has been certified as a medical responder by the department.

II. Assault Inflicting Serious Bodily Injury or Using a Deadly Weapon Other than a Firearm on Firefighter or Specified Medical Personnel

Statute

See G.S. 14-34.6(a) and (b), reproduced under "Simple Assault and Aggravated Assault on Firefighters or Specified Medical Personnel."

Elements

A person guilty of this offense
- (1) commits an assault or affray, *and*
- (2) inflicts serious bodily injury or uses a deadly weapon
- (3) on a firefighter, emergency medical technician, medical responder, emergency department nurse, or emergency department physician
- (4) who is discharging or attempting to discharge an official duty.

Punishment

Class I felony.

Notes

Element (2). Although "serious bodily injury" is not defined, a court would likely use the definition of that term in G.S. 14-32.4: "bodily injury that creates a substantial risk of death, or that causes serious permanent disfigurement, coma, a permanent or protracted condition that causes extreme pain, or permanent or protracted loss or impairment of the function of any bodily member or organ, or that results in prolonged hospitalization." Note that this definition requires greater proof of injury than the term "serious injury," which appears in many other assault statutes. See the discussion of deadly weapon under Element (2) of "Assault with a Deadly Weapon".

III.
Assault or Affray with Firearm on Firefighter or Specified Medical Personnel

Statute

See G.S. 14-34.6(a) and (c), reproduced under "Simple Assault and Aggravated Assault on Firefighters or Specified Medical Personnel."

Elements

A person guilty of this offense

(1) commits an assault or affray, *and*
(2) uses a firearm
(3) on a firefighter, emergency medical technician, medical responder, emergency department nurse, or emergency department physician
(4) who is discharging or attempting to discharge an official duty.

Punishment

Class F felony.

Related offenses not in this chapter

None.

Assault on or Threat to Court Officer

Note: The offenses described in the statutes below, as applied to court officers, became effective for acts committed on or after December 1, 1999.

Statute

§14-16.6. Assault on executive, legislative, or court officer.

(a) Any person who assaults any legislative officer, executive officer, or court officer, or any person who makes a violent attack upon the residence, office, temporary accommodation or means of transport of any one of those officers in a manner likely to endanger the officer, shall be guilty of a felony and shall be punished as a Class I felon.

(b) Any person who commits an offense under subsection (a) and uses a deadly weapon in the commission of that offense shall be punished as a Class F felon.

(c) Any person who commits an offense under subsection (a) and inflicts serious bodily injury to any legislative officer, executive officer, or court officer, shall be punished as a Class F felon.

§14-16.7. Threats against executive, legislative, or court officers.

(a) Any person who knowingly and willfully makes any threat to inflict serious bodily injury upon or to kill any legislative officer, executive officer, or court officer, shall be guilty of a felony and shall be punished as a Class I felon.

(b) Any person who knowingly and willfully deposits for conveyance in the mail any letter, writing, or other document containing a threat to inflict serious bodily injury upon or to kill any legislative officer, executive officer, or court officer, shall be guilty of a felony and shall be punished as a Class I felon.

§14-16.8. No requirement of receipt of the threat.

In prosecutions under G.S. 14-16.7 of this Article it shall not be necessary to prove that any legislative officer, executive officer, or court officer actually received the threatening communication or actually believed the threat.

§14-16.9. Officers-elect to be covered.

Any person who has been elected to any office covered by this Article but has not yet taken the oath of office shall be considered to hold the office for the purpose of this Article and G.S. 114-15.

§14-16.10. Definitions.

The following definitions apply in this Article:

(1) Court officer. — Magistrate, clerk of superior court, acting clerk, assistant or deputy clerk, judge, or justice of the General Court of Justice; district attorney, assistant district attorney, or any other attorney designated by the district attorney to act for the State or on behalf of the district attorney; public defender or assistant defender; court reporter; court counselor as defined in G.S. 7B-1501(5).
(2) Executive officer. — A person named in G.S. 147-3(c).
(3) Legislative officer. — A person named in G.S. 147-2(1), (2), or (3).

I. Assault on Court Officer

Statute

See G.S. 14-16.6(a), reproduced under "Assault on or Threat to Court Officer."

Elements

A person guilty of this offense
(1) assaults
(2) a court officer.

Punishment

Class I felony.

Notes

Element (1). See the notes on "Forms of assault" and "Battery" under "Simple Assault."

Element (2). A court officer is defined in G.S. 14-16.10(1) as a magistrate, clerk of superior court, acting clerk, assistant or deputy clerk, judge, or justice of the General Court of Justice; district attorney, assistant district attorney, or any other attorney designated by the district attorney to act for the state or on behalf of the district attorney; public defender or assistant defender; court reporter; or court counselor as defined in G.S. 7B-1501(5). Unlike other assaults on public officials discussed in this chapter, there is no requirement that a court officer be performing a duty of office when assaulted.

Statute applicable to executive officers and legislators. This statute also applies to executive officers and legislators, as defined in G.S. 14-16.10.

Additional conduct included within statute. This statute also prohibits a violent attack upon the residence, office, temporary accommodation, or means of transport of any covered officer in a manner likely to endanger the officer.

II. Assault on Court Officer Using Deadly Weapon or Inflicting Serious Injury

Statute

See G.S. 14-16.6(b) and (c), reproduced under "Assault on or Threat to Court Officer."

Elements

A person guilty of this offense
(1) assaults
(2) a court officer
(3) using a deadly weapon or inflicts serious injury.

Punishment

Class F felony.

Notes

Element (1). See the notes on "Forms of assault" and "Battery" under "Simple Assault."

Element (2). See the note on Element (2) of "Assault on Court Officer."

Element (3). For a definition of deadly weapon, see the note on Element (2) of "Assault with a Deadly Weapon." For a definition of serious injury, see the note on Element (2) under "Assault Inflicting Serious Injury."

Statute applicable to executive officers and legislators. This statute also applies to executive officers and legislators, as defined in G.S. 14-16.10.

Additional conduct included within offense. This statute also prohibits using a deadly weapon or inflicting serious injury during a violent attack upon the residence, office, temporary accommodation, or means of transport of any covered official.

III. Threat to Kill or Inflict Serious Injury on Court Officer

Statute

See G.S. 14-16.7(a), reproduced under "Assault on or Threat to Court Officer."

Elements

A person guilty of this offense
(1) knowingly, *and*
(2) willfully
(3) makes a threat
(4) to inflict serious bodily injury *or* to kill
(5) a court officer.

Punishment

Class I felony.

Notes

Element (1). See the definition of "knowingly" in Chapter 1, "States of Mind."

Element (2). See the definition of "willfully" in Chapter 1, "States of Mind."

Element (5). See the note on Element (2) of "Assault on Court Officer."

Statutes applicable to executive officers and legislators. This statute also applies to executive officers and legislators, as defined in G.S. 14-16.10.

Additional conduct prohibited. G.S. 14-16.7(b) also prohibits making a similar threat by mail.

No requirement of receiving or believing threat. G.S. 14-16.8 provides that it is unnecessary to prove that the victim received the threatening communication or actually believed the threat.

Related offenses not in this chapter

None.

Assault by Pointing Gun

Statute

§14-34. Assaulting by pointing gun.

If any person shall point any gun or pistol at any person, either in fun or otherwise, whether such gun or pistol be loaded or not loaded, he shall be guilty of Class A1 misdemeanor.

Elements

A person guilty of this offense
(1) intentionally
(2) points a gun at another.

Punishment

Class A1 misdemeanor.

Notes

Element (1). Even though the defendant might actually have pointed a gun at someone, the offense has not occurred unless the defendant intended to do so (243 N.C. 306). If the defendant intends to point the gun at one person and mistakenly points it at someone else (transferred intent), he or she has committed this offense (43 N.C. App. 564). See the definition of "intentionally" in Chapter 1. If a person points a gun at another with legal justification, then the pointing is not an offense under this statute (244 N.C. 353; 103 N.C. App. 720). For example, if a law enforcement officer points a gun at another in the good faith discharge of the officer's official duties, then this offense has not been committed. The absence of legal justification is not an element of the offense; instead an offender must raise the issue as a defense (96 N.C. App. 366).

Element (2). The statute provides that this offense occurs regardless of the defendant's purpose in pointing the gun ("in fun or otherwise") and regardless of whether the gun was loaded. If the gun is pointed with the intent to harm or put in fear, the charge of assault with a deadly weapon should be considered.

Difference from assault with deadly weapon. An assault by pointing a gun could also be an assault with a deadly weapon *if* the pointing amounts to a form of assault, e.g., if the defendant intends to injure the victim or put the victim in fear (see the note on "Forms of assault" under "Simple Assault"). But this charge is proper even if the pointing does not amount to an assault.

Manslaughter. A person could be guilty of involuntary manslaughter under the misdemeanor-manslaughter rule [see the note on Element (3) under "Involuntary Manslaughter" (Chapter 6)] if the person was violating the statute and the gun discharged accidentally (227 N.C. 594).

Related offenses not in this chapter

See the offenses in Chapter 19, "Weapons Offenses."
"Transporting, Possessing Weapon during Emergency" (Chapter 17)
Criminal use of laser device (G.S. 14-34.8)

Habitual Misdemeanor Assault

Statute

§14-33.2. Habitual misdemeanor assault.

A person commits the offense of habitual misdemeanor assault if that person violates any of the provisions of G.S. 14-33(c) or G.S. 14-34 and has been convicted of five or more prior misdemeanor convictions, two of which were assaults. A person convicted of violating this section is guilty of a Class H felony.

Elements

A person guilty of this offense
(1) commits an assault listed in G.S. 14-33(c) or G.S. 14-34, *and*
(2) has been convicted of five or more misdemeanor convictions, *and*
(3) two of those prior misdemeanor convictions were assaults.

Punishment

Class H felony.

Notes

Element (1). This offense may be charged only if the predicate assault is one of the misdemeanors listed in G.S. 14-33(c) or G.S. 14-34. Thus commission of any of the following assaults would satisfy this element: (1) assault inflicting serious injury; (2) assault with a deadly weapon; (3) assault on a female; (4) assault on a child under 12; (5) assault on a government official; (6) assault on aschool personnel; or (7) assault by pointing a gun. Felony assaults and some other misdemeanor assaults—such as simple assault or assault on a sports official—do not satisfy this element.

Elements (2) and (3). The precise combination of offenses in the defendant's prior record must be present: five prior *misdemeanor* convictions, two of which were assaults. For example, this element would not be satisfied if a defendant had five prior convictions, and two were assaults—but one of the assaults was a felony assault. This element also would not be satisfied if a defendant had five prior misdemeanor convictions, but only one of them was an assault conviction. Any prior misdemeanor assault conviction may satisfy Element (3), including a simple assault conviction, even though a simple assault offense would not satisfy Element (1).

References in a criminal pleading to prior convictions should include the date and court of conviction. The following is an example of the portion of a charge alleging Elements (2) and (3): "The defendant has been previously convicted of the misdemeanor assault of assault on a female on October 12, 1992, in Wake County District Court. The defendant has been previously convicted of the misdemeanor assault of assault on a female on December 12, 1993, in Wake County District Court. The defendant has been previously convicted of the misdemeanor of speeding 80 mph in a 55 mph zone on March 1, 1989, in Durham County District Court. The defendant has been previously convicted of the misdemeanor of domestic criminal trespass on October 12, 1992, in Wake County District Court. The defendant has been previously convicted of the misdemeanor of concealment of merchandise on May 12, 1995, in Wake County District Court."

In alleging and proving prior convictions in superior court, a prosecutor must comply with G.S. 15A-928. G.S. 15A-928(b), which requires that an indictment or information for this kind of offense must allege prior convictions in either (1) a separate count of the indictment or information charging the substantive offenses, or (2) in a separate indictment or information.

Under G.S. 15A-928(c), a defendant on trial for this offense in superior court must be arraigned in the jury's absence before the close of presentation of the state's case. If the defendant admits the prior convictions, Elements (2) and (3) are established, and proof of the convictions and jury instructions about them are not allowed. If the defendant denies the prior conviction or a particular conviction, then the state has the burden of proving the conviction(s) before the jury.

Comparison with habitual felon statute; ex post facto issue. The offense of habitual misdemeanor assault constitutes a separate substantive felony offense, unlike the habitual felon statute (G.S. 14-7.1), which is a punishment enhancement statute. A habitual misdemeanor assault conviction may be used as a felony conviction to establish habitual felon status. The use of a prior conviction that occurred before the date of the enactment of G.S. 14-33.2 to prove the offense of habitual misdemeanor assault is not an ex post facto violation (139 N.C. App. 209).

Related offenses not in this chapter

None.

Assault with Deadly Weapon with Intent to Kill

Statute

§14-32. Felonious assault with deadly weapon with intent to kill or inflicting serious injury; punishments.

(a) Any person who assaults another person with a deadly weapon with intent to kill and inflicts serious injury shall be punished as a Class C felon.

(b) Any person who assaults another person with a deadly weapon and inflicts serious injury shall be punished as a Class E felon.

(c) Any person who assaults another person with a deadly weapon with intent to kill shall be punished as a Class E felon.

Elements

A person guilty of this offense
(1) commits an assault on another
(2) with a deadly weapon
(3) with intent to kill.

Punishment

Class E felony.

Notes

Element (1). See the notes on "Forms of assault" and "Battery" under "Simple Assault."

Element (2). See the note on Element (2) under "Assault with a Deadly Weapon."

Element (3). Intent to kill may be inferred from the nature of the assault (261 N.C. 558; 307 N.C. 42) or from prior conduct of the defendant, such as the defendant's previous threats and assaults against the victim (59 N.C. App. 477).

Multiple convictions based on same act of shooting one officer. The North Carolina Court of Appeals, declining to follow prior case law (50 N.C. App. 736; 121 N.C. App. 355) because it conflicted with North Carolina Supreme Court rulings, ruled that a defendant may be convicted and sentenced for both (1) assault with a deadly weapon with intent to kill and (2) assault with a deadly weapon on a law enforcement officer, based on the same act of shooting one officer. The court ruled that each offense had an element that was not contained in the other offense, and thus double jeopardy principles did not bar both convictions.

Multiple charges and punishments. A defendant may be charged with this offense and attempted first-degree murder, but it is unclear whether the defendant may be convicted and punished for both offenses.

Related offenses not in this chapter

Inciting to Riot (various offenses) (Chapter 17)
"Aggravated Misdemeanor Affray" (Chapter 17)
See the offenses listed in Chapter 19, "Weapons Offenses."

Assault with Deadly Weapon Inflicting Serious Injury

Statute

See subsection (b) of G.S. 14-32, reproduced under "Assault with a Deadly Weapon with Intent to Kill."

Elements

A person guilty of this offense
(1) commits an assault on another
(2) with a deadly weapon, *and*
(3) inflicts serious injury.

Punishment

Class E felony.

Notes

Element (1). See the notes on "Forms of assault" and "Battery" under "Simple Assault."

Element (2). See the note on Element (2) under "Assault with a Deadly Weapon."

Element (3). See the note on Element (2) under "Assault Inflicting Serious Injury."

Related offenses not in this chapter

See the offenses listed under "Assault with Deadly Weapon with Intent to Kill."

Assault with Deadly Weapon with Intent to Kill Inflicting Serious Injury

Statute

See subsection (a) of G.S. 14-32, reproduced under "Assault with Deadly Weapon with Intent to Kill."

Elements

A person guilty of this offense
(1) commits an assault on another
(2) with a deadly weapon
(3) with intent to kill, *and*
(4) inflicts serious injury.

Punishment

Class C felony.

Notes

Element (1). See the notes on "Forms of assault" and "Battery" under "Simple Assault."

Element (2). See the note on Element (2) under "Assault with a Deadly Weapon." The use of a deadly weapon may sometimes be inferred from the nature of the victim's injuries (67 N.C. App. 703).

Element (3). Intent to kill may be inferred from the circumstances of the assault, including the use of a deadly weapon, the manner in which the assault was carried out, and the degree of injury (227 N.C. 34; 261 N.C. 558; 281 N.C. 447).

Element (4). See the note on Element (2) under "Assault Inflicting Serious Injury."

Multiple charges and punishments. A defendant may be charged with this offense and attempted first-degree murder, but it is unclear whether the defendant may be convicted and punished for both offenses. A defendant may be convicted and punished for this offense and secret assault, even though both offenses are based on the same assault (126 N.C. App. 78).

Related offenses not in this chapter

See the offenses listed under "Assault with Deadly Weapon with Intent to Kill."

Assault Inflicting Serious Bodily Injury

Statute

§14-32.4. Assault inflicting serious bodily injury.

Unless the conduct is covered under some other provision of law providing greater punishment, any person who assaults another person and inflicts serious bodily injury is guilty of a Class F felony. "Serious bodily injury" is defined as bodily injury that creates a substantial risk of death, or that causes serious permanent disfigurement, coma, a permanent or protracted condition that causes extreme pain, or permanent or protracted loss or impairment of the function of any bodily member or organ, or that results in prolonged hospitalization.

Elements

A person guilty of this offense
(1) commits an assault on another, *and*
(2) inflicts serious bodily injury.

Punishment

Class F felony.

Notes

Element (1). See the notes on "Forms of assault" and "Battery" under "Simple Assault"

Element (2). Note that the definition of "serious bodily injury" in the statute set out above requires proof of a more severe injury than has been required by appellate cases for "serious injury" in offenses, such as "Assault Inflicting Serious Injury."

Relation to other offenses. Note that the punishment (Class F felony) for this offense is less severe than the punishment (Class E felony) for "Assault with Deadly Weapon Inflicting Serious Injury." Although the offense of assault with a deadly weapon inflicting serious injury has an element—the use of a deadly weapon—that is not an element of this offense, the *serious injury* element in assault with a deadly weapon inflicting serious injury requires less proof than the *serious bodily injury* element in this offense. Both offenses could be charged in factually appropriate cases, although it is unclear whether a defendant may be convicted of and punished for both offenses.

Related offenses not in this chapter

None.

Assault Inflicting Serious Bodily Injury on Law Enforcement Officer, Probation or Parole Officer, or Detention Facility Employee

Statute

§14-34.7. Assault on a law enforcement, probation, or parole officer or on a person employed at a State or local detention facility.

(a) Unless covered under some other provision of law providing greater punishment, a person is guilty of a Class F felony if the person assaults a law enforcement officer, probation officer, or parole officer while the officer is discharging or attempting to discharge his or her official duties and inflicts serious bodily injury on the officer.

(b) Anyone who assaults a person who is employed at a detention facility operated under the jurisdiction of the State or a local government while the employee is in the performance of the employee's duties and inflicts serious bodily injury on the employee is guilty of a Class F felony, unless the person's conduct is covered under some other provision of law providing greater punishment.

Elements

A person guilty of this offense
(1) commits an assault
(2) on a law enforcement officer, probation officer, parole officer, or state or local government detention facility employee
(3) who is discharging or attempting to discharge his or her official duties, *and*
(4) inflicts serious bodily injury on the officer.

Punishment

Class F felony.

Notes

Element (1). See the notes on "Forms of assault" and "Battery" under "Simple Assault."

Element (2). See the note on Element (3) under "Assault with Firearm on Law Enforcement Officer, Probation or Parole Officer, or Detention Facility Employee."

Element (3). See the note on Element (4) under "Assault with Firearm or Other Deadly Weapon on Governmental Officers or Employees, or Company or Campus Police Officers."

Element (4). Although the term "serious bodily injury" is not defined, a court would likely use the definition of that term in G.S. 14-32.4: "bodily injury that creates a substantial risk of death, or that causes serious permanent disfigurement, coma, a permanent or protracted condition that causes extreme pain, or permanent or protracted loss or impairment of the function of any bodily member or organ, or that results in prolonged hospitalization."

Related offenses not in this chapter

None.

Secret Assault

Statute

§14-31. Maliciously assaulting in a secret manner.

If any person shall in a secret manner maliciously commit an assault and battery with any deadly weapon upon another by waylaying or otherwise, with intent to kill such other person, notwithstanding the person so assaulted may have been conscious of the presence of his adversary, he shall be punished as a Class E felon.

Elements

A person guilty of this offense

(1) commits an assault and battery on another
(2) with a deadly weapon
(3) in a secret manner
(4) with intent to kill, *and*
(5) with malice.

Punishment

Class E felony.

Notes

Element (1). The statute specifies that a battery must occur for this offense to be committed. The state must prove that the assault and battery was committed against a particular individual (330 N.C. 298). See the notes on "Forms of assault" and "Battery" under "Simple Assault."

Element (2). See the notes on Element (2) under "Assault with a Deadly Weapon."

Element (3). An assault occurs in a secret manner when the victim did not know of an impending attack or that the defendant had the intention of attacking the victim, even though the victim might have known of the defendant's presence (287 N.C. 207; 1 N.C. App. 296; 101 N.C. App. 317). Examples include a sudden shooting through a window (203 N.C. 442), a sudden attack on the driver from a concealed position in a car's back seat (190 N.C. 177), and a shooting from ambush (189 N.C. 695).

Element (4). Intent to kill may be inferred from the nature of the assault (261 N.C. 558). See the notes on Element (3) under "Assault with Deadly Weapon with Intent to Kill" and "Assault with Deadly Weapon with Intent to Kill Inflicting Serious Injury."

Element (5). An act is done with malice when it is done with hatred, ill will, or spite or when it is done with that "condition of mind that prompts a person to take the life of another intentionally without just cause, excuse, or justification" (183 N.C. 795). See the definitions of "maliciously" and "with malice aforethought" in Chapter 1.

Multiple charges and punishments. A defendant may be convicted and punished for this offense and assault with deadly weapon with intent to kill inflicting serious injury, even though both offenses are based on the same assault (126 N.C. App. 78).

Related offenses not in this chapter

See the offenses in Chapter 19, "Weapons Offenses."
Use of dangerous weapon by prisoner in assault (G.S. 14-258.2)

Simple Assault on Handicapped Person

Statute

§14-32.1. Assaults on handicapped persons; punishments.

(a) For purposes of this section, a "handicapped person" is a person who has:

(1) A physical or mental disability, such as decreased use of arms or legs, blindness, deafness, mental retardation or mental illness; or
(2) Infirmity

which would substantially impair that person's ability to defend himself.

(b) through (d) Repealed by Session Laws 1993, c. 767, s. 31.

(e) Unless his conduct is covered under some other provision of law providing greater punishment, any person who commits any aggravated assault or assault and battery on a handicapped person is guilty of a Class F felony. A person commits an aggravated assault or assault and battery upon a handicapped person if, in the course of the assault or assault and battery, that person:

(1) Uses a deadly weapon or other means of force likely to inflict serious injury or serious damage to a handicapped person; or
(2) Inflicts serious injury or serious damage to a handicapped person; or
(3) Intends to kill a handicapped person.

(f) Any person who commits a simple assault or battery upon a handicapped person is guilty of a Class 1 misdemeanor.

Elements

A person guilty of this offense

(1) commits an assault
(2) on a handicapped person.

Punishment

Class 1 misdemeanor.

Notes

Element (1). See the notes on "Forms of assault" and "Battery" under "Simple Assault."

Element (2). The statute provides that a person is handicapped who has a mental or physical disease or an infirmity that substantially impairs the person's ability to defend himself or herself.

Related offenses not in this chapter

None.

Aggravated Assault on Handicapped Person

Statute

See subsection (e) of G.S. 14-32.1, reproduced under "Simple Assault on Handicapped Person."

Elements

A person guilty of this offense

(1) commits an assault
(2) on a handicapped person, *and*
(3) (a) uses a deadly weapon or other means of force likely to cause serious injury to a handicapped person, *or*
  (b) inflicts serious injury on a handicapped person, *or*
  (c) intends to kill a handicapped person.

Punishment

Class F felony.

Notes

Element (1). See the notes on "Forms of assault" and "Battery" under "Simple Assault."

Element (2). See the note on Element (2) under "Simple Assault on Handicapped Person."

Element (3)(a). See the note on Element (2) under "Assault with a Deadly Weapon."

Element (3)(b). See the note on Element (2) under "Assault Inflicting Serious Injury."

Element (3)(c). See the notes on Element (3) under "Assault with Deadly Weapon with Intent to Kill" and "Assault with Deadly Weapon with Intent to Kill Inflicting Serious Injury."

Related offenses not in this chapter

None.

Discharging Barreled Weapon or Firearm into Occupied Property

Statute

§14-34.1. Discharging certain barreled weapons or a firearm into occupied property.

Any person who willfully or wantonly discharges or attempts to discharge:

(1) Any barreled weapon capable of discharging shot, bullets, pellets, or other missiles at a muzzle velocity of at least 600 feet per second; or

(2) A firearm

into any building, structure, vehicle, aircraft, watercraft, or other conveyance, device, equipment, erection, or enclosure while it is occupied is guilty of Class E felony.

Elements

A person guilty of this offense

(1) willfully or wantonly discharges or attempts to discharge a firearm or a barreled weapon

(2) into property

(3) that is occupied when the weapon is discharged.

Punishment

Class E felony.

Notes

Element (1). This offense would not occur if the defendant accidentally, rather than intentionally, shot into the property. A firearm is a weapon that propels shot, shell, or bullets by the action of an explosive within it (*Black's Law Dictionary,* p. 648), and thus includes a shotgun, rifle, or pistol. A barreled weapon includes only weapons capable of discharging shot, bullets, pellets, or other missiles at a muzzle velocity of at least 600 feet per second. Thus any air rifle or air pistol with the required muzzle velocity would be covered. Note that this offense can occur even when no assault has occurred.

Element (2). The statute specifies the property as "any building, structure, vehicle, aircraft, watercraft, or other conveyance, device, equipment, erection, or enclosure." It is hard to imagine any structure or vehicle not covered by this statute. A firearm is discharged "into" occupied property even if the firearm is located inside the property, as long as the defendant is not inside the property. For example, a person commits this offense when standing outside a car and holding and firing a pistol through the car window even though the pistol is inside the car when fired (321 N.C. 464; 321 N.C. 663).

Element (3). The property is occupied if someone actually is present there (see 270 N.C. 588, a burglary case). But even if it is occupied, the person is guilty of this offense only if he or she knows, or has reasonable grounds to believe, that it is occupied (284 N.C. 67). Although it need not be alleged in the criminal pleading, it must be proved at trial that the defendant either knew that the property was occupied or had reasonable grounds to believe that it was (34 N.C. App. 271). Evidence was sufficient that a defendant had reasonable grounds to believe that cars were occupied when the defendant fired a semiautomatic weapon in a club's parking lot where he knew there were parked vehicles and also knew that people had left the club and were present in the parking lot (342 N.C. 589).

Attempt. The statute attaches the same punishment to an attempt to commit this offense.

Felony murder. If death proximately results to a victim of this offense, the offender is guilty of felony murder (304 N.C. 609).

Multiple convictions and punishments allowed. Three distinct shots fired from a pistol into an occupied car supported three convictions and punishments for this offense (341 N.C. 173; see also 350 N.C. 483). A defendant may be convicted and punished for both discharging a barreled weapon or firearm into occupied property and assault with a deadly weapon (88 N.C. App. 428).

Related offenses not in this chapter

"Malicious Damage to Occupied Property by Use of Explosive or Incendiary" (Chapter 16)
"Possession of Firearm by Felon" (Chapter 19)
"Manufacture, Possession, etc., of Machine Gun, Sawed-Off Shotgun, or Weapon of Mass Destruction" (Chapter 19)

Assault on Emergency Personnel

Statute

§14-288.9. Assault on emergency personnel; punishments.

(a) An assault upon emergency personnel is an assault upon any person coming within the definition of "emergency personnel" which is committed in an area:

(1) In which a declared state of emergency exists; or
(2) Within the immediate vicinity of which a riot is occurring or is imminent.

(b) The term "emergency personnel" includes law-enforcement officers, firemen, ambulance attendants, utility workers, doctors, nurses, and other persons lawfully engaged in providing essential services during the emergency.

(c) Any person who commits an assault upon emergency personnel is guilty of a Class 1 misdemeanor. Any person who commits an assault upon emergency personnel with or through the use of any dangerous weapon or substance shall be punished as a Class F felon.

Elements

A person guilty of this offense

(1) commits an assault
(2) on a law enforcement officer, firefighter, doctor, utility worker, or other person providing essential services
(3) in an area in which a state of emergency has been declared or within the immediate vicinity of a riot.

Punishment

Class 1 misdemeanor.

Notes

Element (1). See the notes on "Forms of assault" and "Battery" under "Simple Assault."

Element (2). "Emergency personnel" has generally meant paramedics and officials who respond to accidents, fires, and other life-threatening events in everyday life. That, however, is not the group of people covered by this statute. To be covered by this statute, the person who is assaulted must be providing service during a declared state of public emergency. And the statute covers assaults on any person providing essential services during the emergency; thus it may include persons like utility workers or Red Cross workers. It is not clear whether the defendant must know that the victim is a designated kind of emergency worker to commit this offense.

For possible offenses involving emergency personnel acting outside of a state of emergency, see "Simple Assault and Aggravated Assault on Firefighters or Specified Medical Personnel."

Element (3). A state of emergency may be declared by certain city and county officials and by the governor under the authority of the Riot and Civil Disorder Act (G.S. Ch. 14, Art. 36A) when an emergency exists because of civil disorder or natural disaster. See the notes under "Misdemeanor Riot" (Chapter 17) for the definition of a riot.

Related offenses not in this chapter

"Resisting, Delaying, or Obstructing an Officer" (Chapter 18)
"Disorderly Conduct" (Chapter 17)
Inciting to Riot (various offenses) (Chapter 17)
"Aggravated Misdemeanor Affray" (Chapter 17)
Interference with firefighters (G.S. 58-82-1)

Assault on Emergency Personnel with Dangerous Weapon

Statute

See G.S. 14-288.9, reproduced under "Assault on Emergency Personnel."

Elements

A person guilty of this offense
- (1) commits an assault
- (2) on a law enforcement officer, firefighter, doctor, utility worker, or other person who is providing essential services
- (3) in an area where a state of emergency has been declared or within the immediate vicinity of a riot, *and*
- (4) uses a dangerous weapon or substance to commit the assault.

Punishment

Class F felony.

Notes

Elements (1) through (3). See the notes on these elements under "Assault on Emergency Personnel."

Element (4). G.S. 14-288.1(2) defines "dangerous weapon or substance" to include "any deadly weapon, ammunition, explosive, incendiary device, radioactive material . . . or any instrument or substance designed for a use that carries a threat of serious bodily injury or destruction of property; or any instrument or substance . . . capable of being used to inflict serious bodily injury, when the circumstances indicate [that it] will be so used; or any part or ingredient in any instrument or substance . . . when the circumstances indicate a probability that such part or ingredient will be so used."

Related offenses not in this chapter

See the offenses listed under "Assault on Emergency Personnel."

Child Abuse (Misdemeanor)

Statute

§14-318.2. Child abuse a Class 1 misdemeanor.

(a) Any parent of a child less than 16 years of age, or any other person providing care to or supervision of such child, who inflicts physical injury, or who allows physical injury to be inflicted, or who creates or allows to be created a substantial risk of physical injury, upon or to such child by other than accidental means is guilty of the Class 1 misdemeanor of child abuse.

(b) The Class 1 misdemeanor of child abuse is an offense additional to other civil and criminal provisions and is not intended to repeal or preclude any other sanctions or remedies.

Elements

A person guilty of this offense
- (1) (a) is a parent of a child less than 16 years of age, *or*
  - (b) is a person providing care or supervision of a child less than 16 years of age, *and*
- (2) (a) inflicts physical injury on, *or*
  - (b) allows physical injury to be inflicted on, *or*
  - (c) creates or allows to be created a substantial risk of physical injury to
- (3) that child
- (4) other than by accident.

Punishment

Class 1 misdemeanor.

Notes

Element (1). The statute applies only to people who stand in special relationships that create some duty toward the child.

Element (2). Any "physical injury" is covered by this section—an injury need not be a serious injury [see the note on Element (2) under "Assault Inflicting Serious Injury"]. Any contact that caused physical pain would probably be a physical injury. Element (2)(c), above, does not require that an injury actually occur; it is satisfied if the defendant leaves the child in circumstances in which abuse is likely to occur.

Element (4). The statute is not intended to apply to injuring children accidentally. "Battered child syndrome" is a circumstance of continuous injury to a child that permits the inference that the injury did not occur by accident, but that someone caring for the child was responsible for it (295 N.C. 559, 570; 309 N.C. 132, 137–38).

Predicate for manslaughter. A violation of this statute that results in death to the child can support a conviction for involuntary manslaughter or second-degree murder (295 N.C. 559).

Justification. The general rule is that a person who is in charge of a child (a parent or schoolteacher, for example) cannot be criminally liable for inflicting moderate punishment to correct the child. Moderate punishment is punishment that does not inflict lasting injury (68 N.C. 322). G.S. 115C-390 allows teachers to use reasonable force, including corporal punishment, to restrain or correct pupils. Force is unreasonable if it is motivated by anger or malice or if it causes permanent injury (113 N.C. 635).

Child-abuse reporting. G.S. 7B-301 requires any person or institution suspecting that a child has been abused to report the incident to the local director of the local social services department, but it does not impose a criminal penalty for failure to report. However, a common-law rule provides that if a statute either prohibits an act or commands the performance of an act, and the statute does not impose a sanction for violations, then a violation of the act is a general misdemeanor (75 N.C. 15; 94 N.C. 918; 228 N.C. 371). Under structured sentencing, such a violation would be a Class 1 misdemeanor.

Related offenses not in this chapter

"Indecent Liberties with a Child" (Chapter 8)
See the offenses in Chapter 8, "Sexual Assaults."
Permitting child to use firearm (G.S. 14-316)
Exposing child to fire (G.S. 14-318)
Illegally receiving or giving compensation for placing child for adoption (G.S. 48-37)

Child Abuse Inflicting Serious Injury (Felony)

Statute

§14-318.4. Child abuse a felony.

(a) A parent or any other person providing care to or supervision of a child less than 16 years of age who intentionally inflicts any serious physical injury upon or to the child or who intentionally commits an assault upon the child which results in any serious physical injury to the child is guilty of a Class E felony, except as otherwise provided in subsection (a3) of this section.

(a1) Any parent of a child less than 16 years of age, or any other person providing care to or supervision of the child, who commits, permits, or encourages any act of prostitution with or by the juvenile is guilty of child abuse and shall be punished as a Class E felon.

(a2) Any parent or legal guardian of a child less than 16 years of age who commits or allows the commission of any sexual act upon a juvenile is guilty of a Class E felony.

(a3) A parent or any other person providing care to or supervision of a child less than 16 years of age who intentionally inflicts any serious bodily injury to the child or who intentionally commits an assault upon the child which results in any serious bodily injury to the child, or which results in permanent or protracted loss or impairment of any mental or emotional function of the child, is guilty of a Class C felony. "Serious bodily injury" is defined as bodily injury that creates a substantial risk of death, or that causes serious permanent disfigurement, coma, a permanent or protracted condition that causes extreme pain, or permanent or protracted loss or impairment of the function of any bodily member or organ, or that results in prolonged hospitalization.

(b) The felony of child abuse is an offense additional to other civil and criminal provisions and is not intended to repeal or preclude any other sanctions or remedies.

Elements

A person guilty of this offense

(1) (a) is a parent of a child less than 16 years of age, *or*
(b) is a person providing care or supervision to a child less than 16 years of age, *and*

(2) (a) intentionally inflicts on or to the child, *or*
(b) intentionally commits an assault on the child which results in

(3) serious physical injury.

Punishment

Class E felony.

Notes

Elements (2)(a) and (2)(b). The state must prove only that the defendant intentionally inflicted injury that proved to be serious; the state need not prove that the defendant intended to inflict serious injury (316 N.C. 168, a case decided under a former version of the statute but equally applicable to this version). See the note on Element (4) under "Child Abuse (Misdemeanor)" for a discussion of "battered child syndrome." When an adult has exclusive custody of a child for a period of time and that child suffers injuries that are neither self-inflicted nor accidental, evidence is sufficient to support an inference that the adult inflicted the injuries (316 N.C. 168; 320 N.C. 51; 72 N.C. App. 167).

Element (3). See the note on Element (2) of "Assault Inflicting Serious Injury" for a discussion of what constitutes serious injury.

Child-abuse reporting. G.S. 7B-301 requires any person or institution suspecting that a child has been abused to report the incident to the director of the county social services department, but it does not impose a criminal penalty for failure to do so. However, a common-law rule provides that if a statute either prohibits an act or commands the performance of an act, and the statute does not impose a sanction for a violation, then a violation of the act is a general misdemeanor (228 N.C. 371; 94 N.C. 918; 75 N.C. 15). Under structured sentencing, this would be a Class 1 misdemeanor.

Felony murder. The commission of felony child abuse with hands used as a deadly weapon to kill a child was sufficient evidence to support a conviction of first-degree felony murder (346 N.C. 471).

Related offenses not in this chapter

See the offenses listed under "Child Abuse (Misdemeanor)."

Child Abuse Inflicting Serious Bodily Injury or Mental or Emotional Injury (Felony)

Statute

See subsection (a3), reproduced under "Child Abuse Inflicting Serious Injury (Felony)."

Elements

A person guilty of this offense

(1) (a) is a parent of a child less than 16 years of age, *or*
    (b) is a person providing care or supervision to a child less than 16 years of age, *and*
(2) (a) intentionally inflicts on or to the child, *or*
    (b) intentionally commits an assault on the child which results in
(3) (a) serious bodily injury, *or*
    (b) permanent or protracted loss or impairment of any mental or emotional function.

Punishment

Class C felony.

Notes

Elements (2)(a) and (2)(b). See the note on Elements (2)(a) and (2)(b) of "Child Abuse Inflicting Serious Injury (Felony)."

Element (3)(a). "Serious bodily injury" is defined as bodily injury that creates a substantial risk of death, or that causes serious permanent disfigurement, coma, a permanent or protracted condition that causes extreme pain, or permanent or protracted loss or impairment of the function of any bodily member or organ, or that results in prolonged hospitalization. This definition is the same as contained in G.S. 14-32.4 (assault inflicting serious bodily injury).

Related offenses not in this chapter

See the offenses listed under "Child Abuse (Misdemeanor)."

Child Abuse—Prostitution (Felony)

Statute

See subsection (a1), reproduced under "Child Abuse Inflicting Serious Injury (Felony)."

Elements

A person guilty of this offense

(1) (a) is a parent of a child less than 16 years of age, *or*
    (b) is a person providing care or supervision to a child less than 16 years of age, *and*
(2) commits or permits or encourages

(3) an act of prostitution with *or* by the child.

Punishment

Class E felony.

Notes

Element (1). See the note on Element (1) under "Child Abuse (Misdemeanor)."

Element (3). See the definition of prostitution in the note for Element (1) under "Prostitution and Assignation" (Chapter 20).

Related offenses not in this chapter

See the offenses in Chapter 20, "Prostitution and Loitering for Prostitution."
"Indecent Liberties with a Child" (Chapter 8)
"Sexual Activity by a Substitute Parent" (Chapter 8)
"Sexual Activity by a Custodian" (Chapter 8)
Illegally receiving or giving compensation for placing child for adoption (G.S. 48-37)

Child Abuse—Sexual Act (Felony)

Statute

See subsection (a2), reproduced under "Child Abuse Inflicting Serious Injury (Felony)."

Elements

A person guilty of this offense
(1) is a parent or legal guardian of a child less than 16 years of age, *and*
(2) (a) commits a sexual act upon the juvenile, *or*
(b) allows another to commit a sexual act upon the juvenile.

Punishment

Class E felony.

Notes

Element (1). Only an actual parent or legal guardian may commit this offense. Thus a schoolteacher or a baby-sitter could not be charged with this offense. It is not clear whether this offense applies to a stepparent who has not adopted the child.

Element (2) generally. This offense applies only to acts committed against a juvenile under age 16. A parent or guardian can commit this offense without actually committing a sexual act. If the parent or guardian allows another to commit the act, the parent or guardian may be charged.

Element (2)(a). "Sexual act" probably includes cunnilingus, analingus, fellatio, anal intercourse, and vaginal intercourse. G.S. 14-27.1(4) excludes vaginal intercourse from the definition of sexual act, but that statute does not appear to apply to this offense.

Related offenses not in this chapter

See the offenses in Chapter 8, "Sexual Assaults."
"Taking Indecent Liberties with a Child" (Chapter 8)
"Sexual Activity by a Substitute Parent" (Chapter 8)
"Sexual Activity by a Custodian" (Chapter 8)
"Crime against Nature" (Chapter 9)
Illegally receiving or giving compensation for placing child for adoption (G.S. 48-37)

Contributing to a Juvenile's Being Delinquent, Undisciplined, Abused, or Neglected

Statute

§14-316.1. Contributing to delinquency and neglect by parents and others.

Any person who is at least 16 years old who knowingly or willfully causes, encourages, or aids any juvenile within the jurisdiction of the court to be in a place or condition, or to commit an act whereby the juvenile could be adjudicated delinquent, undisciplined, abused, or neglected as defined by G.S. 7B-101 and G.S. 7B-1501 shall be guilty of a Class 1 misdemeanor.

It is not necessary for the district court exercising juvenile jurisdiction to make an adjudication that any juvenile is delinquent, undisciplined, abused, or neglected in order to prosecute a parent or any person, including an employee of the Department of Juvenile Justice and Delinquency Prevention under this section. An adjudication that a juvenile is delinquent, undisciplined, abused, or neglected shall not preclude a subsequent prosecution of a parent or any other person including an employee of the Department of Juvenile Justice and Delinquency Prevention, who contributes to the delinquent, undisciplined, abused, or neglected condition of any juvenile.

Elements

A person guilty of this offense

(1) is at least 16 years old *and*
(2) knowingly or willfully
(3) causes or encourages or aids
(4) a juvenile within the jurisdiction of the court
(5) (a) to be in a place or condition, *or*
    (b) to commit an act
(6) whereby the juvenile could be adjudicated
    (a) delinquent as defined in G.S. 7B-1501(7), *or*
    (b) undisciplined as defined in G.S. 7B-1501(27), *or*
    (c) abused as defined in G.S. 7B-101(1), *or*
    (d) neglected as defined in G.S. 7B-101(5).

Punishment

Class 1 misdemeanor.

Notes

Element (4). "Juvenile" is defined generally in G.S. 7B-101(14) in the article concerning abused and neglected juveniles and in 7B-1501(17) in the article concerning delinquent and undisciplined juveniles. A delinquent juvenile is generally within the court's jurisdiction when the juvenile is at least 6 years old and less than 16 years old [G.S. 7B-1501(7); 7B-1601]. An undisciplined juvenile is generally within the court's jurisdiction when the juvenile is at least 6 years old and less than 18 years old [G.S. 7B-1501(27); 7B-1600]. An abused or neglected juvenile is generally within the court's jurisdiction when the juvenile is less than 18 years old [G.S. 7B-101(1), (14), and (15); 7B-200].

Element (6). The statute expressly provides that it is unnecessary to prove that the child actually was adjudicated delinquent, undisciplined, abused, or neglected. Such adjudication only must be possible.

Element (6)(a). A delinquent juvenile is a juvenile at least 6 years old and less than 16 years old who commits a crime or infraction under state law or under a local government ordinance, including a violation of the motor vehicle laws [G.S. 7B-1501(7)].

Element (6)(b). An undisciplined juvenile is (a) a juvenile at least 6 years old and less than 16 years old who is unlawfully absent from school; or is regularly disobedient to and beyond the disciplinary control of the juvenile's parent, guardian, or custodian; or is regularly found in places where it is unlawful for a juvenile to be; or has run away from home for a period of more than 24 hours or (b) a juvenile 16 or 17 years old who is regularly disobedient to and beyond the disciplinary control of the juvenile's parent, guardian, or custodian; or is regularly found in places where it is unlawful for a juvenile to be; or has run away from home for a period of more than 24 hours [G.S. 7B-1501(27)].

Element (6)(c). The definition of an abused juvenile under G.S. 7B-101(1) of the North Carolina Juvenile Code is *not* identical to the definition of child abuse under the criminal child-abuse statutes, G.S. 14-318.2 and 14-318.4, although there are substantial similarities [see "Child Abuse (Misdemeanor)," "Child Abuse Inflicting Serious Injury (Felony)," "Child Abuse Inflicting Serious Bodily Injury or Mental or Emotional Injury (Felony)," "Child Abuse—Prostitution (Felony)," and "Child Abuse—Sexual Act (Felony)" in this chapter]. In determining whether to charge this particular offense, the definition of abuse under the Juvenile Code should be consulted. G.S. 7B-101(1) defines an abused juvenile, in part, as a juvenile younger than age 18 whose parent or other person responsible for the juvenile's care inflicts or allows to be inflicted on the juvenile serious, nonaccidental physical injury; creates or allows to be created a substantial risk of such injury; uses or allows to be used cruel or grossly inappropriate devices to modify behavior; commits, permits, or encourages the commission of a variety of listed sexual assaults, prostitution, and obscenity offenses by, with, or upon the juvenile; or creates or allows to be created serious emotional damage to the juvenile.

Element (6)(d). A neglected juvenile is a juvenile under age 18 "who does not receive proper care, supervision, or discipline from the juvenile's parent, guardian, custodian, or caretaker; or who has been abandoned; or who is not provided necessary medical care; or who is not provided necessary remedial care; or who lives in an environment injurious to the juvenile's welfare; or who has been placed for care or adoption in violation of law" [G.S. 7B-101(15)].

Constitutionality. This statute is not unconstitutionally vague (276 N.C. 499).

Relation to other offenses. Contributing to the delinquency of a minor is not a lesser-included offense of second-degree rape (100 N.C. App. 641). Convictions for both contributing to the delinquency of a minor and second-degree rape occurring during the same transaction are not barred by double jeopardy (100 N.C. App. 641). Negligence by a parent resulting in the death of a child may constitute involuntary manslaughter (See Chapter 6) (18 N.C. App. 433).

Related offenses not in this chapter

See the offenses in Chapter 8, "Sexual Assaults."
"First-Degree Statutory Rape" (Chapter 8)
"First-Degree Statutory Sexual Offense" (Chapter 8)
"Statutory Rape of Person Who Is 13, 14, or 15 Years Old" (Chapter 8)
"Statutory Sexual Offense against Person Who Is 13, 14, or 15 Years Old" (Chapter 8)
"Indecent Liberties with a Child" (Chapter 8)
"Incest between Near Relatives" (Chapter 9)
"Incest between Uncle and Niece or Nephew and Aunt" (Chapter 9)
"Sexual Activity by a Substitute Parent" (Chapter 8)
"Sexual Activity by a Custodian" (Chapter 8)
"Involuntary Manslaughter" (Chapter 6)
Selling cigarettes to minors (G.S. 14-313)
Selling or giving weapons to minors (G.S. 14-315)
Permitting young children to use dangerous firearms (G.S. 14-316)
Permitting minors to enter barrooms or billiard rooms (G.S. 14-317)
Exposing children to fire (G.S. 14-318)
Discarding or abandoning iceboxes (G.S. 14-318.1)
Illegally receiving or giving compensation for placing child for adoption (G.S. 48-37)

Patient Abuse and Neglect

Statute

§14-32.2. Patient abuse and neglect; punishments.

(a) It shall be unlawful for any person to physically abuse a patient of a health care facility or a resident of a residential care facility, when the abuse results in death or bodily injury.

(b) Unless the conduct is prohibited by some other provision of law providing for greater punishment,

(1) A violation of subsection (a) above is a Class C felony where intentional conduct proximately causes the death of the patient or resident;
(2) A violation of subsection (a) above is a Class E felony where culpably negligent conduct proximately causes the death of the patient or resident;
(3) A violation of subsection (a) above is a Class F felony where such conduct is willful or culpably negligent and proximately causes serious bodily injury to the patient or resident.
(4) A violation of subsection (a) is a Class A1 misdemeanor where such conduct evinces a pattern of conduct and the conduct is willful or culpably negligent and proximately causes bodily injury to a patient or resident.

(c) "Health Care Facility" shall include hospitals, skilled nursing facilities, intermediate care facilities, intermediate care facilities for the mentally retarded, psychiatric facilities, rehabilitation facilities, kidney disease treatment centers, home health agencies, ambulatory surgical facilities, and any other health care related facility whether publicly or privately owned.

(c1) "Residential Care Facility" shall include adult care homes and any other residential care related facility whether publicly or privately owned.

(d) "Person" shall include any natural person, association, corporation, partnership, or other individual or entity.

(e) "Culpably negligent" shall mean conduct of a willful, gross and flagrant character, evincing reckless disregard of human life.

(e1) "Abuse" means the willful or culpably negligent infliction of physical injury or the willful or culpably negligent violation of any law designed for the health or welfare of a patient or resident.

(f) Any defense which may arise under G.S. 90-321(h) or G.S. 90-322(d) pursuant to compliance with Article 23 of Chapter 90 shall be fully applicable to any prosecution initiated under this section.

(g) Criminal process for a violation of this section may be issued only upon the request of a District Attorney.

(h) The provisions of this section shall not supersede any other applicable statutory or common law offenses.

Elements

A person guilty of this offense
- (1) physically abuses
- (2) (a) a patient of a health care facility, *or*
  - (b) a resident of a residential care facility, *and*
- (3) the abuse results in
- (4) death or bodily injury, *and*
- (5) (a) intentional conduct proximately causes the death of the patient or resident, *or*
  - (b) culpably negligent conduct proximately causes the death of the patient or resident, *or*
  - (c) the conduct is willful or culpably negligent and proximately causes serious bodily injury to the patient or resident
  - (d) the conduct evinces a pattern of conduct, and the conduct is willful or culpably negligent and proximately causes bodily injury to the patient or resident.

Punishment

If elements (1) through (4) and (5)(a) exist, it is a Class C felony. If elements (1) through (4) and (5)(b) exist, it is a Class E felony. If elements (1) through (4) and (5)(c) exist, it is a Class F felony. If elements (1) through (4) and (5)(d) exist, it is a Class A1 misdemeanor.

Notes

Element (1). "Abuse" is defined in G.S. 14-32.2(e1), reproduced above.

Elements (2)(a) and (2)(b). "Health care facility" and "residential care facility" are defined in G.S. 14-32.2(c) and (c1), respectively, reproduced above.

Elements (5)(b), (c), and (d). "Culpably negligent" is defined in G.S. 14-32.2(e), reproduced above.

Criminal process may be issued only on request of district attorney. G.S. 14-32.2(g) provides that criminal process (arrest warrant, criminal summons, or citation) charging a violation of this statute may only be issued on the request of a district attorney.

Related offenses not in this chapter

None.

Domestic Abuse, Neglect, or Exploitation of Disabled or Elder Adults

Statute

§14-32.3. Domestic abuse, neglect, and exploitation of disabled or elder adults.

(a) Abuse. — A person is guilty of abuse if that person is a caretaker of a disabled or elder adult who is residing in a domestic setting and, with malice aforethought, knowingly and willfully: (i) assaults, (ii) fails to provide medical or hygienic care, or (iii) confines or restrains the disabled or elder adult in a place or under a condition that is cruel or unsafe, and as a result of the act or failure to act the disabled or elder adult suffers mental or physical injury.

If the disabled or elder adult suffers serious injury from the abuse, the caretaker is guilty of a Class F felony. If the disabled or elder adult suffers injury from the abuse, the caretaker is guilty of a Class H felony.

A person is not guilty of an offense under this subsection if the act or failure to act is in accordance with G.S. 90-321 or G.S. 90-322.

(b) Neglect. — A person is guilty of neglect if that person is a caretaker of a disabled or elder adult who is residing in a domestic setting and, wantonly, recklessly, or with gross carelessness: (i) fails to provide medical or hygienic care, or (ii) confines or restrains the disabled or elder adult in a place or under a condition that is unsafe, and as a result of the act or failure to act the disabled or elder adult suffers mental or physical injury.

If the disabled or elder adult suffers serious injury from the neglect, the caretaker is guilty of a Class G felony. If the disabled or elder adult suffers injury from the neglect, the caretaker is guilty of a Class I felony.

A person is not guilty of an offense under this subsection if the act or failure to act is in accordance with G.S. 90-321 or G.S. 90-322.

(c) Exploitation. — A person is guilty of exploitation if that person is a caretaker of a disabled or elder adult who is residing in a domestic setting, and knowingly, willfully and with the intent to permanently deprive the owner of property or money: (i) makes a false representation, (ii) abuses a position of trust or fiduciary duty, or (iii) coerces, commands, or threatens, and, as a result of the act, the disabled or elder adult gives or loses possession and control of property or money.

If the loss of property or money is of a value of more than one thousand dollars ($1,000) the caretaker is guilty of a Class H felony. If the loss of property or money is of a value of one thousand dollars ($1,000) or less, the caretaker is guilty of a Class 1 misdemeanor.

(d) Definitions. — The following definitions apply in this section:

(1) Caretaker. — A person who has the responsibility for the care of a disabled or elder adult as a result of family relationship or who has assumed the responsibility for the care of a disabled or elder adult voluntarily or by contract.

(2) Disabled adult. — A person 18 years of age or older or a lawfully emancipated minor who is present in the State of North Carolina and who is physically or mentally incapacitated as defined in G.S. 108A-101(d).

(3) Domestic setting. — Residence in any residential setting except for a health care facility or residential care facility as these terms are defined in G.S. 14-32.2.

(4) Elder adult. — A person 60 years of age or older who is not able to provide for the social, medical, psychiatric, psychological, financial, or legal services necessary to safeguard the person's rights and resources and to maintain the person's physical and mental well-being.

I. Abuse of Disabled or Neglected Adult

Statute

See G.S. 14-32.3(a), reproduced above.

Elements

A person guilty of this offense
- (1) is a caretaker of a
- (2) disabled adult or elder adult (hereinafter, victim)
- (3) who is residing in a domestic setting, *and*
- (4) with malice, knowingly and willfully
- (5) (a) assaults, *or*
  - (b) fails to provide medical care or hygienic care, *or*
  - (c) confines or restrains the victim in a place or under a condition that is cruel or unsafe, *and*
- (6) as a result of the act or failure to act the victim suffers
  - (a) serious mental or physical injury from the abuse, *or*
  - (b) mental or physical injury from the abuse.

Punishment

If elements (1) through (5) and (6)(a) exist, it is a Class F felony. If elements (1) through (5) and (6)(b) exist, it is a Class H felony.

Notes

Element (1). "Caretaker" is defined in G.S. 14-32.3(d)(1), reproduced above.

Element (2). "Disabled adult" and "elder adult" are defined in G.S. 14-32.3(d)(2) and (d)(4), respectively, reproduced above.

Element (3). "Domestic setting" is defined in G.S. 14-32.3(d)(3), reproduced above.

Element (4). The statutory words "malice aforethought" do not require proof of premeditation and deliberation, because those words mean the same as malice under the common law. See the definitions of "maliciously" and "with malice aforethought" in Chapter 1.

Element (6)(a). For a definition of serious injury, see the note on Element (2) under "Assault Inflicting Serious Injury."

II. Neglect of Disabled or Neglected Adult

Statute

See G.S. 14-32.3(b), reproduced above.

Elements

A person guilty of this offense
- (1) is a caretaker of a
- (2) disabled adult or elder adult (hereinafter, victim)
- (3) who is residing in a domestic setting, *and*
- (4) wantonly or recklessly or with gross carelessness
- (5) (a) fails to provide medical care or hygienic care, *or*
  - (b) confines or restrains the victim in a place or under a condition that is unsafe, *and*
- (6) as a result of the act or failure to act the victim suffers

(a) serious mental or physical injury from the neglect, *or*
(b) mental or physical injury from the neglect.

Punishment

If Elements (1) through (5) and (6)(a) exist, it is a Class G felony. If Elements (1) through (5) and (6)(b) exist, it is a Class I felony.

Notes

Element (1). "Caretaker" is defined in G.S. 14-32.3(d)(1), reproduced above.

Element (2). "Disabled adult" and "elder adult" are defined in G.S. 14-32.3(d)(2) and (d)(4), respectively, reproduced above.

Element (3). "Domestic setting" is defined in G.S. 14-32.3(d)(3), reproduced above.

Element (4). See Chapter 1 for a definition of "wantonly."

Element (6)(a). For a definition of serious injury, see the note on Element (2) under "Assault Inflicting Serious Injury."

III. Exploitation of Disabled or Neglected Adult

Statute

See G.S. 14-32.3(c), reproduced above.

Elements

A person guilty of this offense
(1) is a caretaker of a
(2) disabled adult or elder adult (hereinafter, victim)
(3) who is residing in a domestic setting, *and*
(4) knowingly, willfully, and with intent to permanently deprive the owner of property or money
(5) (a) makes a false representation, *or*
(b) abuses a position of trust or fiduciary duty, *or*
(c) coerces or commands or threatens, *and*
(6) as a result of the act, the victim gives or loses possession and control of property or money.

Punishment

Class H felony if the value of the loss of property or money is more than $1,000. Class 1 misdemeanor if the value of the loss of property or money is $1,000 or less.

Notes

Element (1). "Caretaker" is defined in G.S. 14-32.3(d)(1), reproduced above.

Element (2). "Disabled adult" and "elder adult" are defined in G.S. 14-32.3(d)(2) and (d)(4), respectively, reproduced above.

Element (3). "Domestic setting" is defined in G.S. 14-32.3(d)(3), reproduced above.

Related offenses not in this chapter

None.

Ethnic Intimidation

Statute

§14-401.14. Ethnic intimidation; teaching any technique to be used for ethnic intimidation.

(a) If a person shall, because of race, color, religion, nationality, or country of origin, assault another person, or damage or deface property of another, or threaten to do any such act, he shall be guilty of a Class 1 misdemeanor.

(b) A person who assembles with one or more persons to teach any technique or means to be used to commit any act in violation of subsection (a) of this section is guilty of a Class 1 misdemeanor.

Elements

A person guilty of this offense
- (1) because of race, color, religion, nationality or country of origin
- (2) (a) assaults another person, *or*
  - (b) damages property of another, *or*
  - (c) defaces property of another, *or*
  - (d) threatens to do (a), (b), or (c).

Punishment

Class 1 misdemeanor.

Notes

Element (1). The statutory language supports charging this offense when the underlying assault or property damaging offense is done because of (1) the victim's race, color, religion, or country of origin or (2) the race, color, religion, or country of origin of a person other than the victim of the underlying offense. For example, the second alternative is supported by evidence that an offender assaults a white victim because the victim's spouse is African-American.

"Teaching" ethnic intimidation made an offense. Subsection (b) of this statute provides that it is a Class 1 misdemeanor for a person to "assemble" with one or more persons to "teach any technique or means to be used to commit any act" of ethnic intimidation.

Sentencing enhancement for ethnic animosity. G.S. 14-3(c) provides: "If any Class 2 or Class 3 misdemeanor is committed because of the victim's race, color, religion, nationality, or country of origin, the offender shall be guilty of a Class 1 misdemeanor. If any Class A1 or Class 1 misdemeanor is committed because of the victim's race, color, religion, nationality, or country of origin, the offender shall be guilty of a Class I felony." This statute is discussed as "Committing a Misdemeanor Because of Prejudice" in Chapter 4. Note: this sentencing enhancement is limited to situations in which a crime is committed because of the victim's personal characteristics, unlike ethnic intimidation, which can be committed because of the race, color, religion, nationality, or country of origin of *a person other than the victim* of the crime (e.g., if an offender committed simple assault against one person because of the race of that person's spouse, this sentencing enhancement would not apply).

Relation to other offenses. If the underlying assault or property offense is a Class 2 or 3 misdemeanor, this may be an appropriate charge. If the underlying offense is a Class 1 misdemeanor, it may be better to simply charge that offense, because the punishment is the same as ethnic intimidation and there will be fewer elements to prove. Class A1 misdemeanor offenses have more severe punishments than does ethnic intimidation.

Constitutional issues. This statute raises issues of First Amendment rights of free speech and assembly that have not yet been tested in North Carolina's courts. However, the United States Supreme Court has found a similar statute in Wisconsin to be constitutional (508 U.S. 476).

Related offenses not in this chapter

"Committing a Misdemeanor Because of Prejudice" (Chapter 4)
See the offenses in Chapter 11, "Larceny, Possession of Stolen Goods, Embezzlement, and Related Offenses."

Going Armed to the Terror of the People

Statute

This is a common-law offense (272 N.C. 535; 32 N.C. App. 495).

Elements

A person guilty of this offense
(1) arms himself or herself with unusual and dangerous weapons
(2) for the purpose of terrifying others, *and*
(3) goes about on public highways
(4) in a manner to cause terror to others.

Punishment

Class 1 misdemeanor.

Notes

Generally. This common-law offense has been charged only rarely in North Carolina, so the extent of its application remains untested.

Element (1). Any gun is an "unusual and dangerous weapon" for the purpose of this offense (272 N.C. 535).

Element (2). When this charge is made, the criminal pleading must allege that the defendant's purpose is to terrorize (32 N.C. App. 495).

Element (3). It appears that the offense would not occur if the defendant remained on private premises.

Element (4). For this offense to be committed, it is not necessary that the defendant actually assault anyone, and it may not be necessary that anyone actually be terrified, as long as the defendant acts "in such a manner as will naturally cause a terror to the people" (272 N.C. 535).

Related offenses not in this chapter

"Aggravated Misdemeanor Affray" (Chapter 17)
"Unlawful Assembly" (Chapter 17)
"Disorderly Conduct" (Chapter 17)
"Misdemeanor Riot" (Chapter 17)
See the offenses in Chapter 19, "Weapons Offenses."
See the offenses in G.S. Ch. 14, Art. 4A, concerning prohibited secret societies. Specific statutes in this article make offenses of wearing masks, hoods, etc.,

on public property and burning crosses on the property of another.

Malicious Injury by Use of Explosive or Incendiary

Statute

§14-49. Malicious use of explosive or incendiary; punishment.

(a) Any person who willfully and maliciously injures another by the use of any explosive or incendiary device or material is guilty of a Class D felony.

(b) Any person who willfully and maliciously damages any real or personal property of any kind or nature belonging to another by the use of any explosive or incendiary device or material is guilty of a Class G felony.

Elements

A person guilty of this offense
- (1) willfully and maliciously
- (2) injures another
- (3) by use of an explosive or incendiary device or material.

Punishment

Class D felony.

Notes

Element (1). See the definition of "willfully" and "maliciously" in Chapter 1.

Element (2). Unlike assault inflicting serious injury, this offense apparently can be charged even when the injury is not serious.

Element (3). G.S. 14-50.1 defines "explosive or incendiary device or material" as "nitroglycerine, dynamite, gunpowder, other high explosive, incendiary bomb or grenade, other destructive incendiary device, or any other destructive incendiary or explosive device, compound, or formulation; any instrument or substance capable of being used for destructive explosive or incendiary purposes against persons or property, when the circumstances indicate some probability that such instrument or substance will be so used; or any explosive or incendiary part or ingredient in any instrument or substance included above, when the circumstances indicate some probability that such part or ingredient will be so used."

Related offenses not in this chapter

"Burglary with Explosives" (Chapter 13)
"Malicious Damage to Occupied Property by Use of Explosive or Incendiary" (Chapter 16)
"Malicious Damage by Use of Explosive or Incendiary" (Chapter 16)
"Making False Bomb Report" (Chapter 16)
"Transporting, Possessing Weapon during Emergency" (Chapter 17)
"Manufacture, Possession, etc., of Machine Gun, Sawed-Off Shotgun or Weapon of Mass Destruction" (Chapter 19)

Malicious Throwing of Corrosive Acid or Alkali

Statute

§14-30.1. Malicious throwing of corrosive acid or alkali.

If any person shall, of malice aforethought, knowingly and willfully throw or cause to be thrown upon another person any corrosive acid or alkali with intent to murder, maim or disfigure and inflicts serious injury not resulting in death, he shall be punished as a Class E felon.

Elements

A person guilty of this offense
(1) throws corrosive acid or alkali on another, *and*
(2) in so doing inflicts serious injury on the other person
(3) with malice aforethought
(4) with intent to murder, maim, or disfigure the other person.

Punishment

Class E felony.

Notes

Element (1). This offense would not apply if the substance thrown were something other than acid or alkali.

Element (2). See the note on Element (2) under "Assault Inflicting Serious Injury," earlier in this chapter.

Other elements. See the notes under "Castration or Maiming of Privy Member."

Consent. See the note on "Consent" under "Castration or Maiming of Privy Member."

Related offenses not in this chapter

None.

Maiming of Tongue or Eye

Statute

§14-30. Malicious maiming.

If any person shall, of malice aforethought, unlawfully cut out or disable the tongue or put out an eye of any other person, with intent to murder, maim or disfigure, the person so offending, his counselors, abettors and aiders, knowing of and privy to the offense, shall be punished as a Class C felon.

Elements

A person guilty of this offense
(1) (a) cuts out or disables the tongue of another, *or*
(b) puts out an eye of another person
(2) with malice
(3) with the intent to murder, maim, or disfigure the person,
(4) resulting in permanent injury to the tongue or eye.

Punishment

Class C felony.

Notes

Element (1)(b). It is not clear whether the disabling of an eye would be regarded as putting out an eye.

Element (2). The statutory phrase suggesting this element is "with malice aforethought," but those words mean only "with malice" and do not imply any need for deliberation or premeditation (13 N.C. 425). See the definitions of "maliciously" and "with malice aforethought" in Chapter 1.

Other elements. See the notes under "Castration or Maiming of Privy Member."

Consent. See the note on "Consent" under "Castration or Maiming of Privy Member."

Related offenses not in this chapter

Mayhem (common-law offense, described in the note on "Common-law mayhem" under "Castration or Maiming of Privy Member")

Maiming of Nose, Lip, Ear, or Limb

Statute

§14-29. Castration or other maiming without malice aforethought.

If any person shall, on purpose and unlawfully, but without malice aforethought, cut, or slit the nose, bite or cut off the nose, or a lip or an ear, or disable any limb or member of any other person, or castrate any other person, or cut off, maim or disfigure any of the privy members of any other person, with intent to kill, maim, disfigure, disable or render impotent such person, the person so offending shall be punished as a Class E felon.

Elements

A person guilty of this offense
- (1) (a) cuts or slits the nose of another person, *or*
  - (b) bites or cuts off the nose, lips, or ear of another person, *or*
  - (c) disables a limb or member of another person
- (2) on purpose
- (3) with the intent to kill, maim, disfigure, disable, or render impotent the other person.

Punishment

Class E felony.

Notes

Element (1)(b). For this offense to be committed, it is not necessary that the entire ear be bitten or cut off; severing a part of it satisfies this element (23 N.C. 121). However, biting an ear that merely requires stitches is insufficient (130 N.C. App. 466).

Element (1)(c). "Disable" suggests that the injury must be such as to make the limb or member work less well. The nose, lip, eye, or tongue is not included as a limb or member under this statute (188 N.C. 781).

Element (2). The North Carolina Supreme Court has said that "[t]he words 'on purpose' have the same significance as the word 'maliciously'" (255 N.C. 42). See the note on Element (2) under "Castration or Maiming of Privy Member."

Element (3). To commit this offense, the defendant must intend to maim; maiming by negligence does not satisfy the requirement (38 N.C. App. 357).

Application to castration or maiming of privy member. The words of the statute also make this offense apply to castration or maiming of a privy member, but it appears that any case charged under this statute also could be charged under the more serious offense of "Castration or Maiming of Privy Member." This offense is a lesser-included offense of "Castration or Maiming of Privy Member" (3 N.C. App. 323).

Other elements. See the notes under "Castration or Maiming of Privy Member."

Consent. See the notes on "Consent" under "Castration or Maiming of Privy Member."

Related offenses not in this chapter

Mayhem (common-law offense, described in the note on "Common-law mayhem" under "Castration or Maiming of Privy Member," below)

Castration or Maiming of Privy Member

Statute

§14-28. Malicious castration.

If any person, of malice aforethought, shall unlawfully castrate any other person, or cut off, maim or disfigure any of the privy members of any person, with intent to murder, maim, disfigure, disable or render impotent such person, the person so offending shall be punished as a Class C felon.

Elements

A person guilty of this offense

(1) (a) castrates another person, *or*
 (b) cuts off a privy member of another person, *or*
 (c) maims a privy member of another person, *or*
 (d) disfigures a privy member of another person
(2) with malice
(3) with intent to murder, maim, disfigure, disable, or render impotent the other person
(4) resulting in permanent injury to the privy member.

Punishment

Class C felony.

Notes

Element (1)(a). *Webster's Third New International Dictionary* defines "castration" as removing a person's testes or ovaries.

Element (1)(b), (c), and (d). "Privy member" is no longer defined in most dictionaries. However, it probably means male private parts. There was sufficient evidence of this offense when it was committed during a continuous transaction with the murder of the victim, even though his testicles had been cut off after his death (350 N.C. 411).

Element (1)(d). Disfigurement occurs when the natural personal appearance is impaired (23 N.C. 121).

Element (2). The statutory words suggesting this element are "with malice aforethought," but those words mean only "with malice" and do not imply any need for deliberation or premeditation (13 N.C. 425). See the definitions of "maliciously" and "with malice aforethought" in Chapter 1.

Element (3). The intent to maim or disfigure may be inferred from an act that maims or disfigures (3 N.C. App. 323).

Element (4). To make this charge, permanent injury must have been inflicted (226 N.C. 403).

Consent. It is not a defense that the maimed person consented to the act (255 N.C. 42).

Common-law mayhem. Common-law mayhem is slightly different from castration or maiming of privy member and maiming of nose, lip, ear, or limb and maiming of tongue or eye, although those offenses cover almost all circumstances in which common-law mayhem might be charged. Its elements are "(1) depriving, (2) anyone, (3) maliciously, (4) of a corporal member useful for fighting" (255 N.C. 42).

Related offenses not in this chapter

Mayhem (common-law offense, described in the note on "Common-law mayhem," above)

Communicating Threats

Statute

§14-277.1. Communicating threats.

(a) A person is guilty of a Class 1 misdemeanor if without lawful authority:
- (1) He willfully threatens to physically injure the person or that person's child, sibling, spouse, or dependent or willfully threatens to damage the property of another;
- (2) The threat is communicated to the other person, orally, in writing, or by any other means;
- (3) The threat is made in a manner and under circumstances which would cause a reasonable person to believe that the threat is likely to be carried out; and
- (4) The person threatened believes that the threat will be carried out.

(b) A violation of this section is a Class 1 misdemeanor.

Elements

A person guilty of this offense
- (1) without lawful authority
  - (a) willfully threatens to injure another person or that person's child, sibling, spouse, or dependent
  - (b) willfully threatens to damage another's property, *and*
- (2) communicates that threat to the threatened person
- (3) in a manner to make a reasonable person believe that it is likely to be carried out, *and*
- (4) the threat is believed by the threatened person.

Punishment

Class 1 misdemeanor.

Notes

Element (1). A 1999 legislative amendment added a provision that a threat directed at a person may include not only a threat to injure that person, but also a threat to injure that person's child, sibling, spouse, or dependent.

Element (2). The threat must be communicated to the person; if it is said only to a third person and never communicated to the person threatened, this offense ordinarily has not occurred. However, this offense probably would occur if the defendant communicated the threat to a third person and intended that the third person convey the threat to the intended victim, and the third person actually conveyed the threat to the victim.

Element (3). If the threat is clearly a joke or an exaggeration or if it is impossible to carry out, the offense does not occur. A conditional threat is covered by this statute if the defendant has no right to impose the condition. For example, when a defendant threatened to hit the victim if the victim came "any closer" to the defendant, this statute applied because the defendant had no right to impose that condition (37 N.C. App. 714).

Element (4). The person threatened must actually believe that the defendant would carry out the threat.

Charging this offense and assault by pointing gun. The defendant can be charged with and convicted of both communicating threats and assault by pointing gun, even if both offenses arose from the same incident, without being subjected to double jeopardy (40 N.C. App. 730).

Related offenses not in this chapter

"Extortion" (Chapter 12)
"Picketing Courthouse" (Chapter 18)
Sending threatening letters (G.S. 14-394)

Harassing Phone Calls

Statute

§14-196. Using profane, indecent or threatening language to any person over telephone; annoying or harassing by repeated telephoning or making false statements over telephone.

(a) It shall be unlawful for any person:
- (1) To use in telephonic communications any words or language of a profane, vulgar, lewd, lascivious or indecent character, nature or connotation;

(2) To use in telephonic communications any words or language threatening to inflict bodily harm to any person or to that person's child, sibling, spouse, or dependent or physical injury to the property of any person, or for the purpose of extorting money or other things of value from any person;
(3) To telephone another repeatedly, whether or not conversation ensues, for the purpose of abusing, annoying, threatening, terrifying, harassing or embarrassing any person at the called number;
(4) To make a telephone call and fail to hang up or disengage the connection with the intent to disrupt the service of another;
(5) To telephone another and to knowingly make any false statement concerning death, injury, illness, disfigurement, indecent conduct or criminal conduct of the person telephoned or of any member of his family or household with the intent to abuse, annoy, threaten, terrify, harass, or embarrass;
(6) To knowingly permit any telephone under his control to be used for any purpose prohibited by this section.

(b) Any of the above offenses may be deemed to have been committed at either the place at which the telephone call or calls were made or at the place where the telephone call or calls were received. For purposes of this section, the term "telephonic communications" shall include communications made or received by way of a telephone answering machine or recorder, telefacsimile machine, or computer modem.

(c) Anyone violating the provisions of this section shall be guilty of a Class 2 misdemeanor.

Elements

I. *Using Threatening Language on Phone* [G.S. 14-196(a)(2), reproduced above]

A person guilty of this offense

A person guilty of this offense
(1) in a telephone call
(2) (a) threatens to inflict bodily harm to a person or that person's child, sibling, spouse, or dependent, *or*
(b) threatens injury to another's property, *or*
(c) extorts something of value from another.

II. *Repeating Phone Calls for Harassment* [G.S. 14-196(a)(3), reproduced above]

A person guilty of this offense
(1) telephones another repeatedly
(2) for the purpose of annoying, threatening, terrifying, harassing, or embarrassing a person at the called number.

III. *Failing to Hang Up for Purpose of Disrupting Phone Service* [G.S. 14-196(a)(4), reproduced above]

A person guilty of this offense
(1) makes a telephone call, *and*
(2) fails to hang up or disengage the connection
(3) with the intent to disrupt the service of another.

IV. *Making False Statements by Phone to Harass* [G.S. 14-196(a)(5), reproduced above]

A person guilty of this offense
(1) telephones another, *and*
(2) knowingly makes any false statement

(3) concerning death, injury, illness, disfigurement, indecent conduct, or criminal conduct
(4) of the person telephoned or any member of the person's family or household
(5) with the intent to abuse, annoy, threaten, terrify, harass, or embarrass.

V. *Permitting Use of Phone for Harassment* [G.S. 14-196(a)(6), reproduced above]

A person guilty of this offense
(1) knowingly permits any telephone under his or her control
(2) to be used for a purpose prohibited in I–IV, above.

Punishment

Class 2 misdemeanor.

Notes

Constitutionality of G.S. 14-196(a)(1) and (a)(3). Subsection (a)(1) of the statute, which forbids using "indecent" language on the telephone, has been held invalid because it may include speech that is protected by the First Amendment to the U.S. Constitution (446 F. Supp. 608, *affirmed*, 596 F.2d 1205). On the other hand, the constitutionality of subsection (a)(3) has been upheld (59 N.C. App. 38).

Victim. The victim of these offenses may be an organization, such as a sheriff's department, as well as a person (59 N.C. App. 38).

Location of offense. Subsection (b) of the statute provides that the offenses defined are committed either where the call was made or where it was received.

Recorded conversation as evidence. A telephone conversation between the defendant and the victim recorded with the victim's consent is admissible in evidence against the defendant charged with these offenses; making such a recording does not violate federal or state law (270 N.C. 357; 355 U.S. 107).

Entrapment. In one case, someone had been making indecent telephone calls to women who placed a certain kind of newspaper advertisement. The police placed the same kind of an advertisement and listed a telephone number in the police department, which they used to trace the defendant's telephone when he called and used indecent language. The court held that the defendant could not claim entrapment in this situation and that evidence so obtained could be used to convict him (270 N.C. 357).

Calls made or received by or through telefacsimile machine and computer modem; relationship with G.S. 14-196.3 (cyberstalking). G.S. 14-196(b) provides that the statute applies to communications made or received by a telephone answering machine or recorder, telefacsimile machine, or computer modem. Thus some communications may be a violation of both this statute and cyberstalking, G.S. 14-196.3, discussed below.

Related offenses not in this chapter

"Extortion" (Chapter 12)
"Picketing Courthouse" (Chapter 18)
"False Report to Law Enforcement Agencies or Officers" (Chapter 18)
False ambulance request (G.S. 14-286.1, -111.1, -111.2)
Threatening letters (G.S. 14-394)
False report of emergency (G.S. 14-401.8)

False fire alarm (G.S. 14-286)
False bomb report (G.S. 14-69.1)

Cyberstalking

Statute

§14-196.3. Cyberstalking.

(a) The following definitions apply in this section:

(1) Electronic communication.—Any transfer of signs, signals, writing, images, sounds, data, or intelligence of any nature, transmitted in whole or in part by a wire, radio, computer, electromagnetic, photoelectric, or photo-optical system.

(2) Electronic mail.—The transmission of information or communication by the use of the Internet, a computer, a facsimile machine, a pager, a cellular telephone, a video recorder, or other electronic means sent to a person identified by a unique address or address number and received by that person.

(b) It is unlawful for a person to:

(1) Use in electronic mail or electronic communication any words or language threatening to inflict bodily harm to any person or to that person's child, sibling, spouse, or dependent, or physical injury to the property of any person, or for the purpose of extorting money or other things of value from any person.

(2) Electronically mail or electronically communicate to another repeatedly, whether or not conversation ensues, for the purpose of abusing, annoying, threatening, terrifying, harassing, or embarrassing any person.

(3) Electronically mail or electronically communicate to another and to knowingly make any false statement concerning death, injury, illness, disfigurement, indecent conduct, or criminal conduct of the person electronically mailed or of any member of the person's family or household with the intent to abuse, annoy, threaten, terrify, harass, or embarrass.

(4) Knowingly permit an electronic communication device under the person's control to be used for any purpose prohibited by this section.

(c) Any offense under this section committed by the use of electronic mail or electronic communication may be deemed to have been committed where the electronic mail or electronic communication was originally sent, originally received in this State, or first viewed by any person in this State.

(d) Any person violating the provisions of this section shall be guilty of a Class 2 misdemeanor.

(e) This section does not apply to any peaceable, nonviolent, or nonthreatening activity intended to express political views or to provide lawful information to others. This section shall not be construed to impair any constitutionally protected activity, including speech, protest, or assembly.

I. Using Electronic Mail or Electronic Communication to Threaten to Inflict Bodily Harm or Property Damage or to Extort Money

Statute

See G.S. 14-196.3(b)(1), reproduced above.

Elements

A person guilty of this offense

(1) uses in electronic mail or electronic communication
(2) words or language
(3) (i) threatening to inflict bodily harm to any person or that person's child, sibling, spouse, or dependent, *or*
 (ii) threatening to inflict physical injury to the property of any person, *or*
 (iii) for the purpose of extorting money or other things of value from any person.

Punishment

Class 2 misdemeanor.

Notes

Effective date. This offense became effective for acts committed on or after December 1, 2000.

Element (1). See the definitions of "Electronic communication" and "Electronic mail" in G.S. 14-196.3(a), reproduced above.

Elements (3)(i) and (3)(ii). A person who makes these threats also may be guilty of communicating threats under G.S. 14-277.1 (discussed earlier in this chapter), which is a Class 1 misdemeanor.

Element (3)(iii). A person who extorts money or other things of value also may be guilty of extortion under G.S. 14-118.4 (discussed in Chapter 12), which is a Class F felony.

Relationship with G.S. 14-196 (harassing phone calls). Because G.S. 14-196 (harassing phone calls), discussed earlier in this chapter, applies to communications received through a telefacsimile machine or computer modem, some communications may be a violation of both G.S. 14-196 and cyberstalking.

Aider and abettor. G.S. 14-196.3(b)(4) provides that a person who knowingly permits an electronic communication device to be used for any purpose prohibited by this statute is also guilty of this offense.

Venue. G.S. 14-196.3(c) provides that an offense is considered to have been committed where the electronic mail or electronic communication was originally sent, originally received in North Carolina, or first viewed by a person in North Carolina.

Related offenses not in this chapter

"Communicating Threats" (Chapter 7)
"Extortion" (Chapter 12)

II. Repeatedly Using Electronic Mail or Electronic Communication for Harassment

Statute

See G.S. 14-196.3(b)(2), reproduced above.

Elements

A person guilty of this offense
(1) electronically mails or electronically communicates to another repeatedly
(2) for the purpose of abusing, annoying, threatening, terrifying, harassing, or embarrassing any person.

Punishment

Class 2 misdemeanor.

Notes

Effective date. This offense became effective for acts committed on or after December 1, 2000.

Element (1). See the definitions of "Electronic communication" and "Electronic mail" in G.S. 14-196.3(a), reproduced above.

Element (2). A person who makes a threat also may be guilty of communicating threats under G.S. 14-277.1 (discussed earlier in this chapter), which is a Class 1 misdemeanor.

Relationship with G.S. 14-196 (harassing phone calls). See the note on this subject under "I. Using Electronic Mail or Electronic Communication to Threaten to Inflict Bodily Harm or Property Damage or to Extort Money."

Aider and abettor. See the note on this subject under "I. Using Electronic Mail or Electronic Communication to Threaten to Inflict Bodily Harm or Property Damage or to Extort Money."

Venue. See the note on this subject under "I. Using Electronic Mail or Electronic Communication to Threaten to Inflict Bodily Harm or Property Damage or to Extort Money."

Related offenses not in this chapter

"Communicating Threats" (discussed earlier in this chapter)

III. Using Electronic Mail or Electronic Communication to Send False Statement

Statute

See G.S. 14-196.3(b)(3), reproduced above.

Elements

A person guilty of this offense
(1) electronically mails or electronically communicates to another, *and*
(2) knowingly makes a false statement
(3) concerning death, injury, illness, disfigurement, indecent conduct, or criminal conduct of the person electronically mailed or any member of the person's family or household

(4) with the intent to abuse, annoy, threaten, terrify, harass, or embarrass.

Punishment

Class 2 misdemeanor.

Notes

Effective date. This offense became effective for acts committed on or after December 1, 2000.

Element (1). See the definitions of "Electronic communication" and "Electronic mail" in G.S. 14-196.3(a), reproduced above.

Relationship with G.S. 14-196 (harassing phone calls). See the note on this subject under "I. Using Electronic Mail or Electronic Communication to Threaten to Inflict Bodily Harm or Property Damage or to Extort Money."

Aider and abettor. See the note on this subject under "I. Using Electronic Mail or Electronic Communication to Threaten to Inflict Bodily Harm or Property Damage or to Extort Money."

Venue. See the note on this subject under "I. Using Electronic Mail or Electronic Communication to Threaten to Inflict Bodily Harm or Property Damage or to Extort Money."

Related offenses not in this chapter

"Communicating Threats" (discussed earlier in this chapter).

Stalking

Statute

§14-277.3. Stalking

(a) Offense.—A person commits the offense of stalking if the person willfully on more than one occasion follows or is in the presence of another person without legal purpose and with the intent to cause death or bodily injury or with the intent to cause emotional distress by placing that person in reasonable fear of death or bodily injury.

(b) Classification.—A violation of this section is a Class 1 misdemeanor. A person who commits the offense of stalking when there is a court order in effect prohibiting similar behavior is guilty of a Class A1 misdemeanor. A second or subsequent conviction for stalking occurring within five years of a prior conviction of the same defendant is punishable as a Class I felony.

Elements

A person guilty of this offense
(1) willfully and on more than one occasion
(2) (a) follows, *or*
 (b) is in the presence
(3) of another person
(4) without legal purpose
(5) (a) with the intent to cause death or bodily injury, *or*
 (b) with the intent to cause emotional distress by placing that person in reasonable fear of death or bodily injury.

Punishment

A first offense is a Class 1 misdemeanor. An offender who commits the offense when a court order prohibiting similar behavior is in effect is guilty of a Class 1 misdemeanor. A second or subsequent conviction for stalking occurring within five years of a prior conviction of the same defendant is punishable as a Class I felony.

Notes

Element (1). See the definition of "willfully" in Chapter 1.

Element (5)(b). The term "reasonable fear" is defined under an objective standard as that which frightens an ordinary, prudent person under the same or similar circumstances (137 N.C. App. 710).

Related offenses not in this chapter

See the offenses listed in Chapter 16, "Trespass, Property Damage, and Littering."

Violation of Domestic Violence Protective Order

Statute

§50B-4.1. Violation of valid protective order a misdemeanor.

(a) A person who knowingly violates a valid protective order entered pursuant to this Chapter or by the courts of another state or the courts of an Indian tribe shall be guilty of a Class A1 misdemeanor.

(b) A law enforcement officer shall arrest and take a person into custody without a warrant or other process if the officer has probable cause to believe that the person knowingly has violated a valid protective order excluding the person from the residence or household occupied by a victim of domestic violence or directing the person to refrain from doing any or all of the acts specified in G.S. 50B-3(a)(9).

(c) When a law enforcement officer makes an arrest under this section without a warrant, and the party arrested contests that the out-of-state order or the order issued by an Indian court remains in full force and effect, the party arrested shall be promptly provided with a copy of the information applicable to the party which appears on the National Crime Information Center registry by the sheriff of the county in which the arrest occurs.

Elements

A person guilty of this offense
- (1) knowingly
- (2) violates
- (3) a valid protective order entered pursuant to
  - (a) Chapter 50B of the General Statutes, *or*
  - (b) a court of another state, *or*
  - (c) a court of an Indian tribe.

Punishment

Class A1 misdemeanor.

Notes

Element (1). See the definition of "knowingly" in Chapter 1.

Element (3)(a). Chapter 50B of the General Statutes allows a person (hereinafter, plaintiff) who has a "personal relationship" with another person (hereinafter, defendant) to bring a civil action against the defendant for acts of domestic violence committed against the plaintiff or a minor child who resides with or is in the plaintiff's custody. "Personal relationship" includes: (1) current or former spouses; (2) people of the opposite sex who live together or have lived together; (3) parent and child (however, an aggrieved party may not obtain an order of protection against a child under 16); (4) a person acting *in loco parentis* to a minor child and the minor child (however, an aggrieved party may not obtain an order of protection against a child under 16); (5) grandparent and grandchild (however, an aggrieved party may not obtain an order of protection against a grandchild under 16); (6) current or former household members; (7) people who have a child in common; and (8) people of the opposite sex who are or have been in a dating relationship [see G.S. 50B-1(b) for the complete definition]. Acts of "domestic violence" include, among others, attempting to cause bodily injury, intentionally causing bodily injury, or placing the plaintiff or member of the plaintiff's family or household in fear of imminent serious bodily injury [see G.S. 50B-1(a) for the complete definition]. The plaintiff may obtain a domestic violence protective order from a district court judge or, under certain circumstances, a designated magistrate. The order may prohibit the defendant from doing a wide variety of things, including not assaulting, threatening, abusing, or harassing the plaintiff or the plaintiff's children (residing with or in the plaintiff's custody) and staying away from the plaintiff's residence and place of work. In addition, the order may give the plaintiff exclusive possession of a residence or vehicle. For a complete list of relief that may be granted, see G.S. 50B-3(a).

Offense when making false statement regarding protective order. G.S. 50-B-4.2 provides that a person who knowingly makes a false statement to a law enforcement agency or officer that a protective order remains in effect is guilty of a Class 2 misdemeanor.

Related offenses not in this chapter

None.

Throwing Objects at Sporting Events

Statute

§14-281.1. Throwing, dropping, etc., objects at sporting events.

It shall be unlawful for any person to throw, drop, pour, release, discharge, expose or place in an area where an athletic contest or sporting event is taking place any substance or object that shall be likely to cause injury to persons participating in or attending such contests or events or to cause damage to animals, vehicles, equipment, devices, or other things used in connection with such contests or events. Any person violating the provisions of this section shall be guilty of a Class 3 misdemeanor.

Elements

A person guilty of this offense
(1) throws or drops or pours or releases or discharges or exposes or places
(2) any substance or object
(3) in an area where an athletic contest or sporting event is taking place
(4) in a manner likely to
  (a) injure participants in the contest or event, *or*
  (b) injure spectators at the contest or event, *or*
  (c) damage animals, vehicles, equipment, devices, or other things used in connection with the contest or event.

Punishment

Class 3 misdemeanor.

Notes

Element (3). The area in which the contest or event is taking place includes the stands. It is not certain whether the offense applies in the stadium parking lot or on roads leading to the athletic event.

Element (4). For this offense to be committed, the substance or object need not actually injure someone or damage equipment; it need only be *likely* to cause injury or damage.

Related offenses not in this chapter

"Injury to Real Property" (Chapter 16)
"Defacing Public Building" (Chapter 16)
"Injury to Personal Property" (Chapter 16)
"Disorderly Conduct" (Chapter 17)
Injuring houses, churches, fences, and walls (G.S. 14-144)

8
Sexual Assaults

Chapter Contents

8
Sexual Assaults

First-Degree Forcible Rape

Statute

§14-27.2. First-degree rape.

(a) A person is guilty of rape in the first degree if the person engages in vaginal intercourse:

(1) With a victim who is a child under the age of 13 years and the defendant is at least 12 years old and is at least four years older than the victim; or

(2) With another person by force and against the will of the other person, and:

a. Employs or displays a dangerous or deadly weapon or an article which the other person reasonably believes to be a dangerous or deadly weapon; or

b. Inflicts serious personal injury upon the victim or another person; or

c. The person commits the offense aided and abetted by one or more other persons.

(b) Any person who commits an offense defined in this section is guilty of a Class B1 felony.

Elements

A person guilty of this offense

(1) has vaginal intercourse

(2) with a person

(3) by force, *and*

(4) against that person's will, *and*

(5) the defendant

(a) used or displayed a dangerous or deadly weapon (or what reasonably appeared to be a dangerous or deadly weapon), *or*

(b) inflicted serious personal injury on the victim, *or*

(c) inflicted serious personal injury on another person, *or*

(d) was aided and abetted by one or more other persons.

Punishment

Class B1 felony. G.S. 15A-1340.16B provides that a defendant convicted of a Class B1 felony must be sentenced to life imprisonment without parole, despite the sentencing dispositions set out in G.S. 15A-1340.17, if: (1) the offense was committed against a victim who was 13 years of age or younger at the time of the offense; (2) the defendant has one or more prior convictions of a Class B1 felony; and (3) the court finds that there are no mitigating factors under G.S. 15A-1340.16(e). The state may be constitutionally required to allege and to prove before a jury the factors set out in (1) and (2) above, even though G.S. 15A-1340.16B appears to allow the state to prove them at a sentencing hearing (120 S. Ct. 2348).

Notes

Generally. Since the elements (other than the sexual act) are the same as first-degree sexual offense, the cases cited here may be rape or sexual offense cases.

Statute gender-neutral. The previous statute applied only when the victim was a female and the defendant was a male, though case law held that a female could be guilty as an aider and abettor in the rape of another female (121 N.C. 579; 269 N.C. 453). Under this statute, however, the defendant may be either a male or female. Thus a female would be guilty if she forced a male at gunpoint to have sexual intercourse with her. This offense, however, involves only vaginal intercourse. Thus a male could not be prosecuted under this offense for illegally having sex with another male, and a female could not be prosecuted under this offense for illegally having sex with another female. Such activity may be prosecuted under other offenses, however.

Element (1). "Vaginal intercourse" means the same as the older terms "carnal knowledge" and "sexual intercourse." It means the penetration of the female sexual organ by the male sexual organ (249 N.C. 134). The slightest penetration is sufficient to violate the statute (277 N.C. 197); neither proof of erection (314 N.C. 337) nor proof of emission of semen are required (G.S. 14-27.10; 232 N.C. 374; 317 N.C. 417). Penetration of the vulva or labia is sufficient penetration of a female's sexual organ; penetration of the vagina is not required (317 N.C. 417). The victim's testimony that the defendant had sexual intercourse with her is sufficient to establish penetration (301 N.C. 512).

Element (2). Effective for offenses committed on or after July 5, 1993, a person may be prosecuted for rape or sexual offense against his or her spouse (G.S. 14-27.8; 1993 Session Laws, Ch. 274). This legislation repealed the "spousal defense" to rape and sexual offense in North Carolina. This defense, before repeal, most recently had provided that a person could be prosecuted for rape or sexual offense against a spouse only if the couple was living apart when the offense was committed.

Element (3). Proof of actual force is not required—constructive force by threat, fear, or duress is sufficient. *Threatened* use of force can be holding a gun or knife on the victim to procure submission (269 N.C. 453) or threatening serious bodily harm that reasonably induces fear (293 N.C. 1; 56 N.C. App. 163). The force does not include the conduct that constitutes the sexual act itself (72 N.C. App. 300, but see 332 N.C. 262, where court reserved ruling on this issue). A child's general fear of a parent's authority over the child can constitute constructive force (319 N.C. 34; 104 N.C. App. 226). Sexual acts with a person who the defendant knows is mentally defective may constitute force (thus forming an exception to the statement above that cites 72 N.C. App. 300 (131 N.C. App. 156).

Element (4). Evidence of physical resistance is not necessary to prove lack of consent (293 N.C. 559). If penetration occurs with the victim's consent, no rape has occurred though the victim later withdraws consent during the same act of intercourse (297 N.C. 293).

Element (5)(a). Threatened use of the weapon is sufficient (318 N.C. 114). Use of the weapon need not continue throughout the crime (289 N.C. 55). The defendant may be convicted under this statute even if he or she only displays the weapon and never threatens to use it (304 N.C. 293; 306 N.C. 718; 310 N.C. 428).

A deadly weapon is any instrument which by its nature or under the circumstances of its use is likely to cause death or serious bodily injury (1 N.C. App. 539). Some weapons are deadly by their very nature (gun; long, sharp knife), and the judge instructs the jury that they are deadly. Other weapons are considered deadly depending on how they are used and the jury decides whether they are deadly (120 N.C. 603); these include a pocket knife (304 N.C. 293), pen (304 N.C. 680), pencil, safety razor (309 N.C. 594), or vise grips (310 N.C. 157). See the discussion of Element (2) under "Assault with a Deadly Weapon" in Chapter 7.

The term "dangerous weapon" is not defined; it may be practically the same as a "deadly weapon" (303 N.C. 293), or it may be something less harmful than a deadly weapon.

This element would be satisfied if the weapon reasonably appeared to the victim to be dangerous or deadly even though it in fact was not—for example, a toy pistol (306 N.C. 288). It was sufficient to prove that an object was a deadly weapon when a rape victim testified that the defendant held a long, cold metallic object against her head that she thought was a knife, though in fact the object could have been a screwdriver (301 N.C. 18).

Element (5)(b). "Serious personal injury" may be proven by showing mental injury or bodily injury (307 N.C. 198; 336 N.C. 58; 97 N.C. App. 559; 101 N.C. App. 12) or death (347 N.C. 412). Mental injury must extend for some appreciable time beyond the crime itself, and it must be an injury beyond that normally experienced in every forcible rape (or sexual offense, if applicable) (336 N.C. 58). Hysteria and crying for only a relatively short time after the crime are not sufficient to establish mental injury (307 N.C. 198). When a victim continued to have appetite loss, severe headaches, nightmares, and difficulty sleeping months after being raped, she experienced serious mental injury satisfying this element (101 N.C. App. 12). An elderly victim suffered mental injury when she was sexually assaulted in her home, was too frightened to return to her home, and moved to her niece's home and was still there nine months later at the time of trial (342 N.C. 409, adopting concurring opinion in 117 N.C. App. 192).

Bodily injury is defined as "such physical injury as causes great pain and suffering" (258 N.C. 89). Whether the injury is serious is a question of fact (261 N.C. 558). The statute does not require that the injury be inflicted to procure the victim's submission; rather, this element is satisfied if the injury is inflicted at any time during the incident (332 N.C. 544). The injury can even be inflicted after the sexual act if it is so related to the sexual act that the infliction of injury and the sexual act form a continuous transaction (314 N.C. 232).

Element (5)(c). See the discussion immediately above on the meaning of serious personal injury. Although the statute does not say so, the other person injured should have some direct connection with the victim of the rape and usually should be present or close by. The statute does not specifically require that the infliction of injury be designed to further the rape, though that may have been the intent of this provision.

Element (5)(d). See "Aiding and Abetting Felony," in Chapter 3, for a discussion of what acts constitute aiding and abetting. Note that the aider and abettor need not actually have sexual intercourse with the victim during the rape; he or she may simply assist another or stand by to assist if needed (306 N.C. 288; 109 N.C. App. 136). The aider and abettor also would be guilty of first-degree forcible rape (310 N.C. 608; 109 N.C. 136). Mere presence does not constitute aiding and abetting (304 N.C. 447; 310 N.C. 126); the aider and abettor must say or do something to show assent to the criminal purpose and contribution to its execution (109 N.C. App. 136). A mother was properly convicted of rape as an aider and abettor when her child engaged in vaginal intercourse with another person in the mother's presence and the mother did not take any reasonable steps to prevent the vaginal intercourse (109 N.C. App. 136). See the note concerning " Aiding and abetting by failure to defend" under "Simple Assault" in Chapter 7.

Attempt. An attempt to commit this crime is a Class B2 felony (G.S. 14-2.5). See "Attempt," in Chapter 4, for a discussion of what constitutes attempt. If the defendant did not achieve penetration, the crime would be attempted first-degree rape.

Victim's virginity. Virginity is not an element of any of the rape offenses.

Defendant under 14. Old case law had held that a male under 14 was presumed incapable of sexual intercourse and could not be convicted of offenses involving sexual intercourse (60 N.C. 293), though this presumption was rebuttable (275 N.C. 411). Any such presumption has now been removed by statute (G.S. 14-27.9).

Lesser-included offenses. Simple assault is *not* a lesser-included offense of attempted second-degree rape (97 N.C. App. 597), but see G.S. 15-144.1 and 117 N.C. App. 78. Assault on a female is *not* a lesser-included offense of rape or attempted first- or second-degree forcible rape (318 N.C. 669; 322 N.C. 733), but see G.S. 15-144.1 and 117 N.C. App. 78. Indecent liberties is *not* a lesser-included offense of forcible or statutory rape, sexual offense, crime against nature, or incest (303 N.C. 507; 319 N.C. 34). Crime against nature is *not* a lesser-included offense of forcible or statutory rape or sexual offense (309 N.C. 224).

Multiple prosecutions. Double jeopardy does not preclude simultaneous convictions for rape (forcible or statutory), sexual offense, indecent liberties with a child, crime against nature, and incest arising out of the same transaction (319 N.C. 34; 319 N.C. 656; 322 N.C. 415).

Punishment for separate acts. Each separate act of sexual intercourse that constitutes rape is a separate, punishable offense (319 N.C. 656; 133 N.C. App. 543; 31 N.C. App. 556; 87 N.C. App. 199, affirmed, 322 N.C. 108). A defendant was properly convicted and punished for two separate counts of first-degree rape when he was guilty as the principal by committing forcible sexual intercourse (aided and abetted by another) and as an aider and abettor to another who also committed forcible sexual intercourse (310 N.C. 608).

Evidence of recent possession of property stolen during rape. If a larceny and a rape occur about the same time as part of a criminal enterprise committed by the same person, the doctrine of recent possession raises a permissible inference that the jury may consider in determining whether a defendant who possesses recently stolen property also may have committed the rape (301 N.C. 18).

Evidence rule shielding victim's past sexual behavior. North Carolina Evidence Rule 412 (G.S. 8C-1, Rule 412) applies to all rape and sexual offense cases (and their lesser-included offenses). The rule prohibits inquiry into the victim's past sexual behavior unless the behavior (1) was between the victim and the defendant; (2) is evidence of specific sexual behavior that would prove that the defendant did not commit the act (for example, the victim's boyfriend had sexual intercourse with her about the time of the alleged rape, which explains the presence of semen in the victim's vagina); (3) is evidence of a distinctive pattern of sexual behavior that so closely resembles the defendant's version of the encounter with the victim that it tends to prove that the victim consented to the act(s) charged; or (4) is evidence of sexual behavior offered as the basis of expert psychological or psychiatric opinion that the victim fantasized or invented the act(s). Even if past sexual behavior fits one of the four categories, it may not be proved by reputation or opinion evidence. The rule also provides for an *in camera* (not open to the public) hearing to determine the admissibility of this type of evidence before it may be offered in open court. For more information about Evidence Rule 412, see Robert L. Farb and Anne S. Kim, "North Carolina's Evidence Shield Rule in Rape and Sex Offense Cases," *Administration of Justice Memorandum* No. 94/02 (Institute of Government, March 1994).

Indictment and time of offense involving children. Generally an indictment must include a designated date or time period within which the alleged offense occurred [G.S. 15A-924(a)(4)]. However, in a case involving a sexual assault (any offense in this chapter) on a child, the need for specificity of dates for offenses is less important because children cannot be expected to be exact regarding times and dates (311 N.C. 739; 328 N.C. 72; 106 N.C. App. 106, reversed on other grounds, 334 N.C. 92; 114 N.C. App. 610). A child's uncertainty as to time or date on which a charged offense was committed affects the weight or believability of the evidence at trial, rather than the admissibility of the evidence. Therefore it is not improper to use an approximate date or time frame in an indictment; for example, the defendant committed an offense against a child "on or about" a particular date or between one date and another. Unless a defendant demonstrates deprivation of his or her defense because of lack of specificity (for example, presenting an alibi defense for a certain date), specificity in indictments is not required (328 N.C. 72).

Related offenses not in this chapter

"Crime against Nature" (Chapter 9)
"Fornication and Adultery" (Chapter 9)
"Assault on a Female" (Chapter 7)
Kidnapping (various offenses) (Chapter 10)
"Incest between Near Relatives" (Chapter 9)
"Incest between Uncle and Niece or Aunt and Nephew" (Chapter 9)
Failure of sexual offender to register with sheriff (G.S. 14-208.11)
Contaminating food or drink with intent to commit rape [G.S. 14-401.16(c)]

Second-Degree Forcible Rape

Statute

§14-27.3. Second-degree rape.

(a) A person is guilty of rape in the second degree if the person engages in vaginal intercourse with another person:

(1) By force and against the will of the other person; or
(2) Who is mentally defective, mentally incapacitated, or physically helpless, and the person performing the act knows or should reasonably know the other person is mentally defective, mentally incapacitated, or physically helpless.

(b) Any person who commits the offense defined in this section is guilty of a Class C felony.

Elements

A person guilty of this offense
(1) has vaginal intercourse
(2) with a person
(3) and the intercourse is
  (a) by force and against the person's will, *or*
  (b) with someone who is
    (i) mentally defective, *or*
    (ii) mentally incapacitated, *or*
    (iii) physically helpless,
    which is (or should be) known by the defendant.

Punishment

Class C felony.

Notes

Statute gender-neutral. See the note on this subject under "First-Degree Forcible Rape."

Elements (1) and (2). See the notes on these elements under "First-Degree Forcible Rape."

Element (2). See the note on this element under "First-Degree Forcible Rape."

Element (3)(a). See the notes on Elements (3) and (4) under "First-Degree Forcible Rape."

Element (3)(b). "Mentally defective" means that the victim is mentally retarded or has a mental disorder, either of which condition leaves the victim incapable of appraising the conduct or resisting or communicating an unwillingness to submit (G.S. 14-27.1). "Mentally incapacitated" means that some act has been committed on the victim that leaves the victim incapable of appraising the nature of the conduct or resisting the act (G.S. 14-27.1). "Physically helpless" means that the victim is unconscious or physically unable to resist the act or to communicate an unwillingness to submit (G.S. 14-27.1). A sleeping victim is "physically helpless" (320 N.C. 387). A victim so intoxicated as to be unable to resist may also be "physically helpless" (73 N.C. App. 487). The statute does not require that the defendant be the one who made the victim mentally incapacitated or physically helpless.

Attempt. An attempt to commit this offense is a Class D felony (G.S. 14-2.5). See "Attempt," in Chapter 4, for a discussion of what constitutes attempt. If the defendant did not achieve penetration, the crime would be attempted second-degree rape.

Defendant under 14. See the note on this topic under "First-Degree Forcible Rape."

Victim's virginity. See the note on this topic under "First-Degree Forcible Rape."

Lesser-included offenses. Attempted second-degree rape is a lesser-included offense of second-degree rape. See also the note on this topic under "First-Degree Forcible Rape."

Multiple prosecutions. See the note on this topic under "First-Degree Forcible Rape."

Related offenses not in this chapter

See the offenses listed under "First-Degree Forcible Rape."

First-Degree Statutory Rape

Statute

See subsection (a)(1) of G.S. 14-27.2, reproduced under "First-Degree Forcible Rape."

Elements

A person guilty of this offense
- (1) has vaginal intercourse
- (2) with a child under the age of 13 years
- (3) who is at least four years younger than the defendant, *and*
- (4) the defendant is at least 12 years old.

Punishment

Class B1 felony. See the additional discussion in "Punishment" under "First-Degree Forcible Rape."

Notes

Statute gender-neutral. See the note on this subject under "First-Degree Forcible Rape." For example, an adult woman who has consensual vaginal intercourse with a 12-year-old boy is guilty of this offense (109 N.C. App. 136).

Element (1). See the note on this element under "First-Degree Forcible Rape."

Element (2). A child is under the age of 13 years until the day of his or her thirteenth birthday. The defendant is not excused by being misled or mistaken about the victim's age (224 N.C. 760). If the victim is 13 or older, the defendant might still be guilty of "Indecent Liberties with a Child."

Element (3). The age difference must be measured from the defendant's birthday to the victim's birthday. Thus if the defendant was born on February 1, 1978, the victim was born on January 10, 1982, and the date of the offense was October 1, 1994, the offense does not constitute first-degree statutory rape, since there is not a difference of four full years in age. If the victim had been born a month later, this element would be satisfied.

Element (4). Although it is better for the state to offer testimony as to the defendant's age, a jury may find this element satisfied by determining a defendant's age based on its own observations of him or her, even when the defendant does not testify (298 N.C. 783; 111 N.C. App. 845).

Victim's consent and use of force. Consent is not a defense (269 N.C. 57). To establish this crime, it is not necessary to prove that the intercourse was by force or against the victim's will (226 N.C. 266).

Attempt. An attempt to commit this crime is a Class B2 felony (G.S. 14-2.5). See "Attempt," in Chapter 4, for a discussion of what constitutes attempt. If the defendant did not achieve penetration, the crime would be attempted first-degree rape.

Defendant under 14. See the note on this subject under "First-Degree Forcible Rape."

Victim's virginity. See the note on this subject under "First-Degree Forcible Rape."

Lesser-included offenses. "Indecent Liberties with a Child" (discussed later in this chapter), "Assault on Child under 12" (Chapter 7), "Assault on a Female" (Chapter 7), and Incest (various offenses) (Chapter 9) are *not* lesser-included offenses of first-degree statutory rape (306 N.C. 629; 319 N.C. 34), but see G.S. 15-144.1. In some cases a defendant could be guilty of first-degree statutory rape and one or more of these other offenses. See also the note on this subject under "First-Degree Forcible Rape."

Multiple prosecutions. See the note on this topic under "First-Degree Forcible Rape."

Related offenses not in this chapter

See the offenses listed under "First-Degree Forcible Rape"
Child abuse (various offenses) (Chapter 7)
"Assault on Child under 12" (Chapter 7)

Statutory Rape of Person Who Is 13, 14, or 15 Years Old

Statute

§14-27.7A. Statutory rape or sexual offense of person who is 13, 14, or 15 years old.

(a) A defendant is guilty of a Class B1 felony if the defendant engages in vaginal intercourse or a sexual act with another person who is 13, 14, or 15 years old and the defendant is at least six years older than the person, except when the defendant is lawfully married to the person.

(b) A defendant is guilty of a Class C felony if the defendant engages in vaginal intercourse or a sexual act with another person who is 13, 14, or 15 years old and the defendant is more than four but less than six years older than the person, except when the defendant is lawfully married to the person.

I. Statutory Rape of Person Who Is 13, 14, or 15 Years Old by a Defendant Who Is at Least Six Years Older than the Victim

Elements

A person guilty of this offense
(1) has vaginal intercourse
(2) with a child who is 13, 14, or 15 years old, *and*
(3) the defendant is at least six years older than the child.

Punishment

Class B1 felony. See the additional discussion in "Punishment" under "First-Degree Forcible Rape."

II. Statutory Rape of Person Who Is 13, 14, or 15 Years Old by a Defendant Who Is More than Four but Less than Six Years Older than the Victim

Elements

A person guilty of this offense
(1) has vaginal intercourse
(2) with a child who is 13, 14, or 15 years old, *and*
(3) the defendant is more than four but less than six years older than the child.

Punishment

Class C felony.

Notes

Generally. These offenses were created by the General Assembly in 1995, effective for offenses committed on or after December 1, 1995. They effectively extend the reach of our statutory rape laws to older victims.

Statute gender-neutral. See the note on this topic under "First-Degree Forcible Rape."

Element (1). See the note on this element under "First-Degree Forcible Rape."

Element (2). A child is under a particular age until the day of that birthday. For example, a child is under the age of 15 until the day of his or her fifteenth birthday. As with first-degree statutory rape, a defendant is not excused by being misled or mistaken about the victim's age (224 N.C. 760, which would likely apply to this offense). If the victim is not one of the ages covered here or under "First-Degree Statutory Rape," the defendant might still be guilty of "Indecent Liberties with a Child," "Taking Indecent Liberties with a Student by School Personnel," or "Sexual Activity Between School Personnel and Student," discussed later in this chapter.

Element (3). This element differentiates the two offenses listed inder I. and II., above. For I., the defendant must be at least six years older than the alleged victim. For II., the defendant must be more than four but less than six years older than the alleged victim. The age difference must be measured from the defendant's birthday to the victim's birthday. Thus if the defendant was born on February 10, 1981, the victim was born on January 10, 1986, and the date of the offense was October 1, 2000, the defendant committed the second offense above: "II. Statutory Rape of Person Who Is 13, 14, or 15 Years Old by a Defendant Who Is More than Four but Less than Six Years Older than the Victim." The victim was 14 years old on the date of the offense, and the defendant was four years and eleven months older than the victim.

See the note on Element (4) under "First-Degree Statutory Rape," concerning proof of a defendant's age.

Marriage exception. The statute specifically provides that these offenses do not apply if the defendant and alleged victim are lawfully married. Note, however, that other offenses may apply to conduct between married parties.

Victim's consent and use of force. As with first-degree statutory rape, consent is not a defense (351 N.C. 611). To establish this crime, it is not necessary to prove that the intercourse was by force or against the victim's will.

Victim's virginity. See the note on this topic under "First-Degree Forcible Rape."

Attempt. See "Attempt," in Chapter 4, for a discussion of what constitutes attempt and how it would be punished. If the defendant did not achieve penetration, the crime would be attempted rape under G.S. 14-27.7A.

Lesser-included offenses. See the note on this topic under "First-Degree Statutory Rape."

Multiple prosecutions. See the note on this topic under "First-Degree Forcible Rape."

Related offenses not in this chapter

See the offenses listed under "First-Degree Forcible Rape."
Child abuse (various offenses) (Chapter 7)

First-Degree Forcible Sexual Offense

Statute

§14-27.4. First-degree sexual offense.

(a) A person is guilty of a sexual offense in the first degree if the person engages in a sexual act:

(1) With a victim who is a child under the age of 13 years and the defendant is at least 12 years old and is at least four years older than the victim; or

(2) With another person by force and against the will of the other person, and:

a. Employs or displays a dangerous or deadly weapon or an article which the other person reasonably believes to be a dangerous or deadly weapon; or

b. Inflicts serious personal injury upon the victim or another person; or

c. The person commits the offense aided and abetted by one or more other persons.

(b) Any person who commits an offense defined in this section is guilty of a Class B1 felony.

Elements

A person guilty of this offense

(1) engages in a sexual act other than vaginal intercourse
(2) with a person
(3) by force, *and*
(4) against that person's will, *and*
(5) the defendant
  (a) used or displayed a dangerous or deadly weapon (or what reasonably appeared to be a dangerous or deadly weapon), *or*
  (b) inflicted serious personal injury on the victim, *or*
  (c) inflicted serious personal injury on another person, *or*
  (d) was aided and abetted by one or more other persons.

Punishment

Class B1 felony. See the additional discussion in "Punishment" under "First-Degree Forcible Rape."

Notes

Generally. Since the elements (other than the sexual act) are the same as for first-degree rape, the cases cited here may be rape or sexual offense cases.

Statute gender-neutral. The wording of this statute means that the defendant may be male or female and the victim may be male or female, depending on the kind of sexual act on which the charge is based.

Element (1). "Sexual act" is defined to include cunnilingus, analingus, fellatio, and anal intercourse but not vaginal intercourse, which is the act required if rape is to be charged [G.S. 14-27.1(4)]. Cunnilingus means the stimulation by tongue or lips of any part of the woman's genitalia; penetration is not required under this statute, although penetration is required as a separate element of the offense of crime against nature (303 N.C. 666). Analingus means stimulation of a person's anal opening by tongue or lips (101 N.C. App. 593). As with cunnilingus, penetration by the tongue or lips into the anus is not required under the sexual offense statute (316 N.C. 714). Fellatio is any touching of the male sexual organ by the lips, tongue, or mouth of another person (93 N.C. App. 1).

"Sexual act" also includes insertion of "any object" into another's genital or anal opening. "Object" means an inanimate object as well as a hand or finger or other part of the body (302 N.C. 342; 326 N.C. 581). Only the slightest penetration of the opening by the object is necessary to satisfy this element. A separate statute provides that anal intercourse occurs upon penetration, however slight, and that there need not be any proof of emission of semen (G.S. 14-27.10). G.S. 14-27.10 requires that evidence of anal intercourse constituting this offense show penetration (316 N.C. 714).

Elements (2), (3), (4), and (5)(a), (b), and (c). See the discussion of these elements under "First-Degree Forcible Rape."

Element (5)(d). See Aiding and Abetting (various offenses), in Chapter 3, for a discussion of what acts constitute aiding and abetting. Note that the aider and abettor need not actually commit the sexual act during the sexual offense; he or she may simply assist another (304 N.C. 534) or stand by to assist if needed (306 N.C. 288). The aider and abettor also would be guilty of first-degree forcible sexual offense. Mere presence does not constitute aiding and abetting (304 N.C. 447; 310 N.C. 126).

Attempt. An attempt to commit this crime is a Class B2 felony. See "Attempt," Chapter 4, for a discussion of what constitutes attempt. If penetration is a required element of a particular sexual offense and the defendant did not achieve penetration, the charge should be attempted sexual offense.

Victim's virginity. Virginity is not an issue for any of the sexual offenses.

Defendant under 14. Old case law held that a male under 14 was presumed incapable of sexual acts and could not be convicted of offenses involving sexual intercourse (60 N.C. 293), though the presumption was rebuttable (275 N.C. 411). Any such presumption has now been removed by statute (G.S. 14-27.9).

Comparison with crime against nature. Cunnilingus, fellatio, analingus, and anal intercourse—all of which constitute sexual acts for this offense—are also forms of "Crime against Nature" (Chapter 9). The crime against nature statute does not require that the act be committed without consent. If cunnilingus, fellatio, analingus, or anal intercourse was committed by force, the defendant could be charged either with forcible sexual offense (first- or second-degree, depending on whether a deadly weapon was used, etc.) or with crime against nature, or both. If the act was done with consent, possible charges would be crime against nature and, if the victim and defendant fall into applicable age groups, one of the statutory sexual offenses described in this chapter. All of the sexual offense crimes carry a greater punishment than crime against nature, which is a Class I felony.

Lesser-included offenses. Crime against nature and indecent liberties are *not* lesser-included offenses of first- or second-degree sexual offense (303 N.C. 507; 309 N.C. 224). See also the note on this topic under "First-Degree Forcible Rape."

Multiple prosecutions. See the note on this topic under "First-Degree Forcible Rape."

Punishment for separate acts. In cases of first- and second-degree sexual offense, each unlawful sexual act committed by a defendant against a single victim during a single incident constitutes a separate crime for which the defendant may be separately charged and convicted. For example, if a defendant engaged in cunnilingus and anal intercourse with the female victim, two separate counts of sexual offense may be charged (319 N.C. 656; 87 N.C. App. 199). But see 132 N.C. App. 453 (when both cunnilingus and inserting object into minor's genital area occurred during single transaction, only one conviction allowed).

Evidence rule shielding victim's past sexual behavior. See the note on this topic under "First-Degree Forcible Rape."

Related offenses not in this chapter

"Crime against Nature" (Chapter 9)
"Fornication and Adultery" (Chapter 9)
"Assault on a Female" (Chapter 7)
Kidnapping (various offenses) (Chapter 10)
Contaminating food or drink with intent to commit sexual offense [G.S. 13-410.16(c)]

Second-Degree Forcible Sexual Offense

Statute

§14-27.5. Second-degree sexual offense.

(a) A person is guilty of a sexual offense in the second degree if the person engages in a sexual act with another person:

(1) By force and against the will of the other person; or
(2) Who is mentally defective, mentally incapacitated, or physically helpless, and the person performing the act knows or should reasonably know that the other person is mentally defective, mentally incapacitated, or physically helpless.

(b) Any person who commits the offense defined in this section is guilty of a Class C felony.

Elements

A person guilty of this offense

(1) engages in a sexual act other than vaginal intercourse
(2) with a person, *and*
(3) the act is
  (a) by force and against the person's will, *or*
  (b) with someone who is
    (i) mentally defective, *or*
    (ii) mentally incapacitated, *or*
    (iii) physically helpless,
    which is (or should be) known by the defendant.

Punishment

Class C felony.

Notes

Statute gender-neutral. See the note on this subject under "First-Degree Forcible Sexual Offense."

Element (1). See the note on this element under "First-Degree Forcible Sexual Offense."

Element (2). See the note on this element under "First-Degree Forcible Rape."

Element (3)(a). See the discussion of Elements (3) and (4) under "First-Degree Forcible Rape."

Element (3)(b). See the note on this element under "Second-Degree Forcible Rape."

Attempt. An attempt to commit this crime is a Class D felony (G.S. 14-2.5). See "Attempt," in Chapter 4, for a discussion of what constitutes attempt. If penetration is a requirement of a particular sexual offense and the defendant did not achieve penetration, the crime would be attempted second-degree sexual offense.

Victim's virginity. See the note on this subject under "First-Degree Forcible Sexual Offense."

Defendant under 14. See the note on this subject under "First-Degree Forcible Sexual Offense."

Comparison with crime against nature. See the note on this subject under "First-Degree Forcible Sexual Offense."

Lesser-included offenses. See the note on this subject under "First-Degree Forcible Sexual Offense."

Multiple prosecutions. See the note on this subject under "First-Degree Forcible Rape."

Punishment for separate acts. See the note on this subject under "First-Degree Forcible Sexual Offense."

Related offenses not in this chapter

See the offenses listed under "First-Degree Forcible Sexual Offense."

First-Degree Statutory Sexual Offense

Statute

See subsection (a)(1) of G.S. 14-27.4, reproduced under "First-Degree Forcible Sexual Offense."

Elements

A person guilty of this offense

(1) engages in a sexual act other than vaginal intercourse
(2) with a child under the age of 13 years
(3) who is at least four years younger than the defendant, *and*
(4) the defendant is at least 12 years old.

Punishment

Class B1 felony. See the additional discussion in "Punishment" under "First-Degree Forcible Rape."

Notes

Statute gender-neutral. See the note on this subject under "First-Degree Forcible Sexual Offense."

Element (1). See the note on this element under "First-Degree Forcible Sexual Offense."

Element (2). A child is under the age of 13 years until the day of his or her thirteenth birthday. The defendant is not excused by being misled or mistaken as to the victim's age (224 N.C. 760). If the victim is 13 or older, the defendant might still be guilty of "Statutory Sexual Offense against Person Who Is 13, 14, or 15 Years Old" or "Indecent Liberties with a Child" (both are discussed below) or "Crime against Nature" (Chapter 9).

Element (3). The age difference must be measured from the defendant's birthday to the victim's birthday. Thus if the defendant was born on February 10, 1984, the victim was born on January 10, 1988, and the date of the offense was October 1, 2000, this crime was not committed, since there is not a full four years difference in age. If the victim had been born a month later, this element would be satisfied. There is no lesser statutory sexual offense that applies when the age difference is less than four years, though "Crime against Nature" might apply, as discussed in the note "Comparison with crime against nature" under "First-Degree Forcible Sexual Offense."

Element (4). See the note on this element under "First-Degree Statutory Rape."

Victim's consent. Consent is not a defense to a statutory sex offense charge (269 N.C. 57); it is not necessary in such cases to show that the act was by force and against the victim's will (226 N.C. 266).

Attempt. An attempt to commit this crime is a Class B2 felony (G.S. 14-2.5). See "Attempt," in Chapter 4, for a discussion of what constitutes attempt. If penetration is a requirement of a particular sexual offense, and if the defendant did not achieve penetration, the crime would be attempted sexual offense.

Victim's virginity. See the note on this subject under "First-Degree Forcible Sexual Offense."

Defendant under 14. See the note on this subject under "First-Degree Forcible Sexual Offense."

Comparison with crime against nature. See the note on this subject under "First-Degree Forcible Sexual Offense."

Lesser-included offenses. See the note on this subject under "First-Degree Forcible Sexual Offense."

Multiple prosecutions. See the note on this topic under "First-Degree Forcible Rape."

Related offenses not in this chapter

See the offenses listed under "First-Degree Forcible Sexual Offense."
Child Abuse (various offenses) (Chapter 7)
"Assault on Child under 12" (Chapter 7)

Statutory Sexual Offense against Person Who Is 13, 14, or 15 Years Old

Statute

See G.S. 14-27.7A, reproduced under "Statutory Rape of Person Who Is 13, 14, or 15 Years Old."

I. Statutory Sexual Offense against Person Who Is 13, 14, or 15 Years Old by a Defendant Who Is at Least Six Years Older than the Victim

Elements

A person guilty of this offense
- (1) engages in a sexual act other than vaginal intercourse
- (2) with a child who is 13, 14, or 15 years old, *and*
- (3) the defendant is at least six years older than the child.

Punishment

Class B1 felony. See the additional discussion in "Punishment" under "First-Degree Forcible Rape."

II. Statutory Sexual Offense against Person Who Is 13, 14, or 15 Years Old by a Defendant Who Is More than Four but Less than Six Years Older than the Victim

Elements

A person guilty of this offense
- (1) engages in a sexual act other than vaginal intercourse
- (2) with a child who is 13, 14, or 15 years old, and
- (3) the defendant is more than four but less than six years older than the child.

Punishment

Class C felony.

Notes

Generally. These offenses were created by the General Assembly in 1995, effective for offenses committed on or after December 1, 1995. They effectively extend the reach of our statutory sexual offense laws to older victims.

Statute gender-neutral. See the note on this topic under "First-Degree Forcible Sexual Offense."

Element (1). See the note on this element under "First-Degree Forcible Sexual Offense."

Element (2). A child is under a particular age until the day of that birthday. For example, a child is under the age of 15 until the day of his or her fifteenth birthday. As with first-degree statutory sexual offense, a defendant is not excused by being misled or mistaken about the victim's age (224 N.C. 760, which would likely apply to this offense). If the victim is not one of the ages covered here or under "First-Degree Statutory Sexual Offense," the defendant might still be guilty of "Indecent Liberties with a Child," "Taking Indecent Liberties with Student by School Personnel," or "Sexual Activity between School Personnel and Student," discussed later in this chapter, or "Crime against Nature" (Chapter 9).

Element (3). This element differentiates the two offenses listed above at I. and II. For I., the defendant must be at least six years older than the alleged victim. For II., the defendant must be more than four but less than six years older than the alleged victim. The age difference must be measured from the defendant's birthday to the victim's birthday. Thus if the defendant was born on February 10, 1981, the victim was born on January 10, 1986, and the date of the offense was October 1, 2000, the defendant committed the second offense above, "II. Statutory Sexual Offense against Person Who Is 13, 14, or 15 Years Old by a Defendant Who Is More than Four but Less than Six Years Older than the Victim." The victim was 14 years old on the date of the offense, and the defendant was four years and eleven months older than the victim.

See the note on Element (4) under "First-Degree Statutory Rape," concerning proof of a defendant's age.

Marriage exception. The statute specifically provides that these offenses do not apply if the defendant and alleged victim are lawfully married. Note, however, that other offenses may apply to conduct between married parties.

Victim's consent. See the note on this topic under "First-Degree Statutory Sexual Offense."

Victim's virginity. See the note on this topic under "First-Degree Forcible Sexual Offense."

Comparison with crime against nature. See the note on this topic under "First-Degree Forcible Sexual Offense."

Attempt. See "Attempt," in Chapter 4, for a discussion of what constitutes attempt and how it should be punished. If penetration is a requirement of a particular sexual offense, and if the defendant did not achieve penetration, the crime would be attempted sexual offense.

Lesser-included offenses. See the note on this topic under "First-Degree Forcible Sexual Offense."

Multiple prosecutions. See the note on this topic under "First-Degree Forcible Rape."

Related offenses not in this chapter

See the offenses listed under "First-Degree Forcible Sexual Offense."
Child Abuse (various offenses) (Chapter 7)

Sexual Activity by a Substitute Parent

Statute

§14-27.7 Intercourse and sexual offenses with certain victims; consent no defense.

(a) If a defendant who has assumed the position of a parent in the home of a minor victim engages in vaginal intercourse or a sexual act with a victim who is a minor residing in the home, or if a person having custody of a victim of any age or a person who is an agent or employee of any person, or institution, whether such institution is private, charitable, or governmental, having custody of a victim of any age engages in vaginal intercourse or a sexual act with such victim, the defendant is guilty of a Class E felony. Consent is not a defense to a charge under this section.

(b) If a defendant, who is a teacher, school administrator, student teacher, or coach, at any age, or who is other school personnel, and who is at least four years older than the victim engages in vaginal intercourse or a sexual act with a victim who is a student, at any time during or after the time the defendant and victim were present together in the same school, but before the victim ceases to be a student, the defendant is guilty of a Class G felony, except when the defendant is lawfully married to the student. The term "same school" means a school at which the student is enrolled and the school personnel is employed or volunteers. A defendant who is school personnel, other than a teacher, school administrator, student teacher, or coach, and is less than four years older than the victim and engages in vaginal intercourse or a sexual act with a victim who is a student, is guilty of a Class A1 misdemeanor. This subsection shall apply unless the conduct is covered under some other provision of law providing for greater punishment. Consent is not a defense to a charge under this section. For purposes of this subsection, the terms "school", "school personnel", and "student" shall have the same meaning as in G.S. 14-202.4(d).

Elements

A person guilty of this offense

(1) assumes the position of a parent in the home of a person less than 18 years old, *and*
(2) has vaginal intercourse or engages in a sexual act
(3) with a person less than 18 years old residing in the home.

Punishment

Class E felony.

Notes

Statute gender-neutral. The wording of the statute means that both the defendant and the victim may be male or female, depending on the kind of sexual activity on which the charge is based.

Element (1). Apparently an actual parent would not be liable under this statute, since a parent would not be someone who "has assumed the position of a parent." The actual parent might be guilty of incest (Chapter 9). The kinds of persons probably covered by this phrase would be stepparents, live-in boyfriends and girlfriends, guardians, etc. The statute does not require that the sexual activity take place in the home.

Element (2). See the note on Element (1), discussing "vaginal intercourse," under "First-Degree Forcible Rape." See the note on Element (1), defining "sexual act," under "First-Degree Forcible Sexual Offense."

Element (3). Presumably the same rule applies here as in statutory rape—that the defendant is not excused by being misled or mistaken as to the victim's age (224 N.C. 760).

Consent. The statute specifies that consent is not a defense to this charge.

Defendant under 14. See the note on this subject under "First-Degree Forcible Sexual Offense."

Comparison with crime against nature. Cunnilingus, fellatio, analingus, and anal intercourse—all of which are sexual acts for purposes of this offense—are also forms of "Crime against Nature" (Chapter 9). Whether the victim consents is not an element of this offense or of crime against nature. Thus for these specified sexual acts the prosecutor could proceed under either this statute (Class E felony) or crime against nature (Class I felony), or both. Unlike a charge of crime against nature, however, a charge of cunnilingus or analingus would not require proof of penetration to prove sexual activity by a substitute parent. See the note on this subject under "First-Degree Forcible Sexual Offense."

Related offenses not in this chapter

"Crime against Nature" (Chapter 9)
"Incest between Near Relatives" (Chapter 9)
"Incest between Uncle and Niece or Aunt and Nephew" (Chapter 9)
"Fornication and Adultery" (Chapter 9)
"Assault on a Female" (Chapter 7)
Child Abuse (various offenses) (Chapter 7)
"Assault on Child under 12" (Chapter 7)
Failure of sexual offender to register with sheriff (G.S. 14-208.11)

Sexual Activity by a Custodian

Statute

See G.S. 14-27.7(a), reproduced under "Sexual Activity by a Substitute Parent."

Elements

A person guilty of this offense
(1) has custody of the victim or is an agent or employee of a person or institution having custody of the victim, *and*
(2) has vaginal intercourse or engages in a sexual act
(3) with the person who is in custody.

Punishment

Class E felony.

Notes

Statute gender-neutral. See the note on this subject under "Sexual Activity by a Substitute Parent," immediately above.

Element (1). The defendant might be a police officer, a jailer, a prison guard, an employee of a hospital or nursing home, or someone else in a similar position. The agency that employs the defendant might be either public or private, charitable or not, as long as it has custody of the victim. If the defendant is an employee of such an institution, it is not necessary that he or she have anything in particular to do with maintaining custody of the victim. The statute would seem to also apply to people employed by foster homes and similar places. Whether a patient is voluntarily or involuntarily committed to a hospital, he or she is still in the hospital's custody; a nurse was properly convicted of this offense when he had sexual intercourse with a patient who was voluntarily in a hospital (319 N.C. 258). An employee of a youth home that provided food, shelter, and adult supervision to abused and neglected juveniles was properly convicted of this offense (138 N.C. App. 109).

Element (2). See the note on Element (1), discussing "vaginal intercourse," under "First-Degree Forcible Rape." See the note on Element (1), defining "sexual act," under "First-Degree Forcible Sexual Offense."

Element (3). The victim's age is irrelevant; also, the statute does not require that sexual activity take place in the institution where the victim is kept in custody.

Consent. The statute specifies that consent is not a defense to this charge.

Comparison with crime against nature. See the note on this subject under "Sexual Activity by a Substitute Parent."

Defendant under 14. See the note on this subject under "First-Degree Forcible Sexual Offense."

Related offenses not in this chapter

See the offenses listed under "Sexual Activity by a Substitute Parent."

Sexual Activity between School Personnel and Student

Statute

See G.S. 14-27.7(b), reproduced under "Sexual Activity by a Substitute Parent."

I. Sexual Activity with Student by Teacher, School Administrator, Student Teacher, or Coach

Elements

A person guilty of this offense
- (1) is a teacher, school administrator, student teacher, or coach, *and*
- (2) engages in vaginal intercourse or a sexual act
- (3) with a student, *and*
- (4) the student and the teacher, school administrator, or coach are at the same school.

Punishment

Class G felony.

Notes

Element (2). The sexual conduct need not occur at a school, and consent is not a defense. See the note on Element (1), discussing "vaginal intercourse," under "First-Degree Forcible Rape." See the note on Element (1), defining "sexual act," under "First-Degree Forcible Sexual Offense."

Element (3). "Student" is defined as a person enrolled in kindergarten or grades 1 through 12 in any school. This offense is not committed if the student is no longer enrolled in the school or is lawfully married to the alleged perpetrator.

Element (4). "School" is defined as any public school, charter school, or nonpublic school under Parts 1 and 2 (G.S. 115C-547 through -562) of Article 39 of Chapter 115C of the General Statutes. This offense may occur only if the student is at the same school as the alleged perpetrator. For example, this offense would not occur if a student at a high school had vaginal intercourse with a teacher at another high school.

Multiple offenses and punishments. G.S. 14-27.7(b) states that this subsection "shall apply unless the conduct is covered under some other provision of law providing for greater punishment." This provision appears to bar a conviction and punishment for this offense as well as second-degree rape, for example, arising from the same conduct. However, it does not appear to bar a trial for both charges, just a conviction and punishment for both.

II. Sexual Activity with Student by School Personnel Other Than Teacher, School Administrator, or Student Teacher (Felony)

Statute

See G.S. 14-27.7(b), reproduced under "Sexual Activity by a Substitute Parent."

Elements

A person guilty of this offense

(1) is included in the definition of "school personnel" and is not a teacher, school administrator, or student teacher, *and*
(2) engages in vaginal intercourse or a sexual act
(3) with a student, *and*
(4) the person is at least four years older than the student, *and*
(5) the person and student are at the same school.

Punishment

Class G felony.

Notes

Element (1). "School personnel" means any person included in the definition contained in G.S. 115C-332(a)(2) and any person who volunteers at a school or a school-sponsored activity. G.S. 115C-332(a)(2) defines "school personnel" as any (1) employee of a local school board, whether full-time or part-time, or (2) independent contractor or employee of an independent contractor of a local school board, if the independent contractor carries out duties customarily performed by school personnel—whether paid with federal, state, local, or other funds—who has significant access to students. School personnel includes substitute teachers, driver training teachers, bus drivers, clerical staff, and custodians.

Elements (2), (3), and (5). See the notes on Elements (2), (3), and (4), respectively, under "I. Sexual Activity with Student by Teacher, School Administrator, Student Teacher, or Coach."

Element (4). The age difference must be measured from the defendant's birthday to the victim's birthday. See the note on Element (3) on "First-Degree Statutory Rape."

Multiple offenses and punishments. See the note on this subject under "I. Sexual Activity with Student by Teacher, School Administrator, Student Teacher, or Coach."

III. Sexual Activity with Student by School Personnel Other Than Teacher, School Administrator, or Student Teacher (Misdemeanor)

Statute

See G.S. 14-27.7(b), reproduced under "Sexual Activity by a Substitute Parent."

Elements

A person guilty of this offense
(1) is included in the definition of "school personnel" and is not a teacher, school administrator, or student teacher, *and*
(2) engages in vaginal intercourse or a sexual act
(3) with a student, *and*
(4) is less than four years older than the student, *and*
(5) the person and student are at the same school.

Punishment

Class A1 misdemeanor.

Notes

See the notes under "II. Sexual Activity with Student by School Personnel Other Than Teacher, School Administrator, or Student Teacher (Felony)."

Related offenses not in this chapter

See the offenses listed under "Sexual Activity by Substitute Parent."

Indecent Liberties with a Child

Statute

§14-202.1. Taking indecent liberties with children.

(a) A person is guilty of taking indecent liberties with children if, being 16 years of age or more and at least five years older than the child in question, he either:
(1) Willfully takes or attempts to take any immoral, improper, or indecent liberties with any child of either sex under the age of 16 years for the purpose of arousing or gratifying sexual desire; or
(2) Willfully commits or attempts to commit any lewd or lascivious act upon or with the body or any part or member of the body of any child of either sex under the age of 16 years.

(b) Taking indecent liberties with children is punishable as a Class F felony.

Elements

A person guilty of this offense
(1) is at least 16 years old, *and*
(2) (a) (i) for the purpose of arousing or gratifying sexual desire
(ii) willfully takes or attempts to take an indecent liberty with, *or*
(b) willfully commits or attempts to commit a lewd or lascivious act upon the body of

(3) a child under the age of 16 years, *and*
(4) the child is five or more years younger than the defendant.

Punishment

Class F felony.

Notes

Element (1). Although it is better for the state to offer testimony as to the defendant's age, a jury may find this element satisfied by determining a defendant's age based on its own observations of him or her, even when the defendant does not testify (298 N.C. 783; 111 N.C. App. 845).

General discussion of Elements (2)(a) and (2)(b). Appellate cases have not provided precise definitions of what conduct is an "indecent liberty" or a "lewd or lascivious act" and how the two terms differ. Both terms deal with improper sexual conduct with a child (302 N.C. 157). *Black's Law Dictionary* (pp. 772; 886; 919) defines "indecent liberties" as improper behavior toward a child, expecially of a sexual nature; "lascivious" as tending to excite, lust, lewd, indecent, obscene; and "lewd" as obscene, indecent, and tending to moral impurity or wantonness.

It appears that the two terms overlap to a great extent, although "indecent liberty" may cover a wider range of conduct than "lewd or lascivious act." The words "lewd or lascivious" seem to refer to conduct that is inherently perverted. In contrast, "indecent liberty" may include both conduct that is inherently perverted and conduct that is not inherently perverted but is depraved because of the defendant's purpose of arousing or gratifying his sexual desire (326 N.C. 561).

A defendant's acts of inserting his tongue in the mouths of two children while kissing them and inserting his tongue in their eyes and noses after getting in bed with them satisfied both Elements (2)(a) and (2)(b) (322 N.C. 753). When a defendant approached a 13-year-old male victim lying in bed and rubbed the victim's genital area, this offense was committed (97 N.C. App. 433).

An indecent liberty or lewd or lascivious act may occur even if the defendant does not touch a child (319 N.C. 34). For example, indecent liberties include masturbating in a child's presence (52 N.C. App. 376; 133 N.C. App. 420); photographing a nude child in a clearly sexually suggestive position (59 N.C. App. 724); secretly videotaping a female teenager trying on clothes (108 N.C. App. 648); and engaging in sex acts with others in the presence of a child (109 N.C. App. 136). A California court ruled that a child's touching of her own genitalia at the defendant's instigation was a constructive touching by the defendant (199 Cal. Rptr. 586).

Consent by a victim is no defense to this crime, and the state need not prove force by the defendant.

Element (2)(a). Note that an attempt to take an indecent liberty also is specifically prohibited. Unlike Element (2)(b), this element also requires proof that the indecent liberty was taken or attempted for the purpose of arousing or gratifying sexual desire.

Element (2)(b). Note that an attempt to commit a lewd or lascivious act also is specifically prohibited. Sexual intercourse with a child is a "lewd or lascivious act" (39 N.C. App. 75). Evidence that a defendant pulled down a child's pants and said, "Let me play with you" was sufficient to convict him of attempting to commit a lewd and lascivious act (67 N.C. App. 168).

Elements (3) and (4). If, for example, the victim was 15 years old and the defendant was 20 years old, the age difference must be measured from the defendant's birthday to the victim's birthday for this element to be satisfied. See the note on this subject under "First-Degree Statutory Rape."

Constitutionality. This statute is not unconstitutionally vague, its age classification is not a denial of equal protection, and the statute does not unconstitutionally restrict protected sexual activity (302 N.C. 157).

Relationship with crime against nature. This statute and the crime against nature statute are complementary but not mutually exclusive. Thus a defendant may be convicted of violating this statute by committing fellatio with a child, though his conduct also violates the crime against nature statute (302 N.C. 157). This statute also prohibits acts that are not prohibited by the crime against nature statute (244 N.C. 455).

Lesser-included offenses. This offense is *not* a lesser-included offense of first- or second-degree rape or first- or second-degree sexual offense (303 N.C. 507; 306 N.C. 629; 309 N.C. 224). See also the note on this topic under "First-Degree Forcible Rape." Assault on a female is not a lesser-included offense of indecent liberties (127 N.C. App. 437).

Multiple prosecutions. See the note on this topic under "First-Degree Forcible Rape."

Offense involving defendant under 16. Effective for offenses committed on or after October 1, 1995, the General Assembly created the offense of indecent liberties between children (G.S. 14-202.2), punishable as a Class 1 misdemeanor. This offense essentially extends the existing indecent liberties offense to defendants under 16 years of age and shortens the required gap between the ages of the defendant and victim from at least five years (in indecent liberties) to at least three years.

A person guilty of indecent liberties between children is

(1) under 16 years of age, *and*
(2) (a) (i) for the purpose of arousing or gratifying sexual desire
(ii) willfully takes or attempts to take an indecent liberty with, *or*
(b) (i) for the purpose of arousing or gratifying sexual desire
(ii) willfully commits or attempts to commit a lewd or lascivious act upon the body of
(3) a child
(4) who is three or more years younger than the defendant.

The notes above would generally apply to this offense as well. However, unlike the note on Element (2)(b) above, Element (2)(b) of indecent liberties between children requires proof of a purpose of arousing or gratifying sexual desire (see 133 N.C. App. 272, which ruled that the evidence was insufficient).

An unemancipated juvenile less than 16 years of age may not be prosecuted as an adult for this misdemeanor offense. Instead, a juvenile petition alleging delinquency may be issued.

Related offenses not in this chapter

See the offenses listed under "First-Degree Forcible Rape."

Taking Indecent Liberties with a Student by School Personnel

Statute

§14-202.4 Taking indecent liberties with a student.

(a) If a defendant, who is a teacher, school administrator, student teacher, or coach, at any age, or who is other school personnel and is at least four years older than the victim, takes indecent liberties with a victim who is a student, at any time during or after the time the defendant and victim were present together in the same school but before the victim ceases to be a student, the defendant is guilty of a Class I felony, unless the conduct is covered under some other provision of law providing for greater punishment. The term "same school" means a school at which the student is enrolled and the school personnel is employed or volunteers. A person is not guilty of taking indecent liberties with a student if the person is lawfully married to the student.

(b) If a defendant, who is school personnel, other than a teacher, school administrator, student teacher, or coach, and who is less than four years older than the victim, takes indecent liberties with a student as provided in subsection (a) of this section, the defendant is guilty of a Class A1 misdemeanor.

(c) Consent is not a defense to a charge under this section.

(d) For purposes of this section, the following definitions apply:

(1) "Indecent liberties" means:
  a. Willfully taking or attempting to take any immoral, improper, or indecent liberties with a student for the purpose of arousing or gratifying sexual desire; or
  b. Willfully committing or attempting to commit any lewd or lascivious act upon or with the body or any part or member of the body of a student.
  For purposes of this section, the term indecent liberties does not include vaginal intercourse or a sexual act as defined by G.S. 14-27.1.

(2) "School" means any public school, charter school, or nonpublic school under Parts 1 and 2 of Article 39 of Chapter 115C of the General Statutes.

(3) "School personnel" means any person included in the definition contained in G.S. 115C-332(a)(2), and any person who volunteers at a school or a school-sponsored activity.

(4) "Student" means a person enrolled in kindergarten, or in grade one through grade 12 in any school.

I.
Taking Indecent Liberties with Student by Teacher, School Administrator, Student Teacher, or Coach

Statute

See G.S. 14-202.4(a), reproduced under "Taking Indecent Liberties with a Student."

Elements

A person guilty of this offense

(1) is a teacher, school administrator, student teacher, or coach, *and*
(2) takes indecent liberties
(3) with a student, *and*
(4) the student and the teacher, school administrator, or coach are at the same school.

Punishment

Class I felony.

Notes

Element (2). The sexual conduct need not occur at a school, and consent is not a defense. For a discussion of the term "indecent liberties," see the note on "General Discussion of Elements (2)(a) and (2)(b)" and the notes on Elements (2)(a) and (2)(b) under "Indecent Liberties with a Child." However, G.S. 14-202.4(d)(1) provides that the term indecent liberties does not include vaginal intercourse or a sexual act [presumably because this kind of sexual activity is prohibited by G.S. 14-27.7(b); see "Sexual Activity Between School Personnel and Student"].

Element (3). "Student" is defined as a person enrolled in kindergarten or grades 1 through 12 in any school. This offense is not committed if the student is no longer enrolled in the school or is lawfully married to the alleged perpetrator.

Element (4). "School" is defined as any public school, charter school, or nonpublic school under Parts 1 and 2 (G.S. 115C-547 through -562) of Article 39 of Chapter 115C of the General Statutes. This offense may occur only if the student is at the same school as the alleged perpetrator. For example, this offense would not occur if a teacher at a high school took indecent liberties with a student at another high school.

Multiple offenses and punishments. G.S. 14-202.4(a) states that a violation is a Class I felony "unless the conduct is covered under some other provision of law providing for greater punishment." This provision appears to bar a conviction and punishment for this offense and a more serious offense arising from the same conduct. However, it does not appear to bar a trial for both charges, just a conviction and punishment for both.

II. Taking Indecent Liberties with Student by School Personnel Other Than Teacher, School Administrator, or Student Teacher (Felony)

Statute

See G.S. 14-202.4(a), reproduced under "Taking Indecent Liberties with a Student."

Elements

A person guilty of this offense

(1) is included in the definition of "school personnel" and is not a teacher, school administrator, or student teacher, *and*
(2) takes indecent liberties
(3) with a student, *and*
(4) the person is at least four years older than the student, *and*
(5) the person and student are at the same school.

Punishment

Class I felony.

Notes

Element (1). "School personnel" means any person included in the definition contained in G.S. 115C-332(a)(2) and any person who volunteers at a school or a school-sponsored activity. G.S. 115C-332(a)(2) defines "school personnel" as any (1) employee of a local school board, whether full-time or part-time, or (2) independent contractor or employee of an independent contractor of a local school board, if the independent contractor carries out duties customarily performed by school personnel—whether paid with federal, state, local, or other funds—who has significant access to students. School personnel includes substitute teachers, driver training teachers, bus drivers, clerical staff, and custodians.

Elements (2), (3), and (5). See the notes on Elements (2), (3), and (4), respectively, under "I. Taking Indecent Liberties with Student by Teacher, School Administrator, Student Teacher, or Coach."

Element (4). The age difference must be measured from the defendant's birthday to the victim's birthday. See the note on Element (3) on "First-Degree Statutory Rape."

Multiple offenses and punishments. See the note on this subject under "I. Taking Indecent Liberties with Student by Teacher, School Administrator, Student Teacher, or Coach."

III. Taking Indecent Liberties with Student by School Personnel Other Than Teacher, School Administrator, or Student Teacher (Misdemeanor)

Statute

See G.S. 14-202.4(a), reproduced under "Taking Indecent Liberties with a Student."

Elements

A person guilty of this offense

(1) is included in the definition of "school personnel" and is not a teacher, school administrator, or student teacher, *and*
(2) takes indecent liberties
(3) with a student, *and*
(4) is less than four years older than the student, *and*
(5) the person and student are at the same school.

Punishment

Class A1 misdemeanor.

Notes

See the notes under "II. Taking Indecent Liberties with Student by School Personnel Other Than Teacher, School Administrator, or Student Teacher (Felony)."

Related offenses not in this chapter

See the offenses listed under "Sexual Activity by Substitute Parent."

Solicitation of Child by Computer to Commit Unlawful Sex Act

Statute

§14-202.3. Solicitation of child by computer to commit an unlawful sex act.

(a) Offense. — A person is guilty of solicitation of a child by a computer if the person is 16 years of age or older and the person knowingly, with the intent to commit an unlawful sex act, entices, advises, coerces, orders, or commands, by means of a computer, a child who is less than 16 years of age and at least 3 years younger than the defendant, to meet with the defendant or any other person for the purpose of committing an unlawful sex act.

(b) Jurisdiction. — The offense is committed in the State for purposes of determining jurisdiction, if the transmission that constitutes the offense either originates in the State or is received in the State.

(c) Punishment. — A violation of this section is a Class I felony.

Elements

A person guilty of this offense

(1) is 16 years of age or older, *and*
(2) knowingly, with the intent to commit an unlawful sex act,
(3) entices or advises or coerces or orders or commands
(4) by means of a computer
(5) a child less than 16 years of age, *and*
(6) at least three years younger than the person
(7) to meet with the person or any other person
(8) for the purpose of committing an unlawful sex act.

Punishment

Class I felony.

Notes

Element (2). An unlawful sex act includes, among others, such criminal offenses as rape, sexual offense, indecent liberties, and crime against nature.

Element (6). The age difference must be measured from the defendant's birthday to the victim's birthday. See the note on Element (3) under "First-Degree Statutory Rape."

Jurisdiction over offense. G.S. 14-202.3(b) provides that the offense may be charged if the computer transmission that constitutes the offense either originates in North Carolina or is received in North Carolina.

Related offenses not in this chapter

None.

Failure to Register as Sex Offender

Statute

Part 1. Registration Programs, Purpose and Definitions

Generally.

G.S. 14-208.5 is not set forth here.

§14-208.6. Definitions.

The following definitions apply in this Article:

(1a) "County registry" means the information compiled by the sheriff of a county in compliance with this Article.

(1b) "Division" means the Division of Criminal Statistics of the Department of Justice.

(1c) "Mental abnormality" means a congenital or acquired condition of a person that affects the emotional or volitional capacity of the person in a manner that predisposes that person to the commission of criminal sexual acts to a degree that makes the person a menace to the health and safety of others.

(1d) "Offense against a minor" means any of the following offenses if the offense is committed against a minor, and the person committing the offense is not the minor's parent: G.S. 14-39 (kidnapping), G.S. 14- 41 (abduction of children), and G.S. 14-43.3 (felonious restraint). The term also includes the following if the person convicted of the following is not the minor's parent: a solicitation or conspiracy to commit any of these offenses; aiding and abetting any of these offenses.

(2) "Penal institution" means:
  a. A detention facility operated under the jurisdiction of the Division of Prisons of the Department of Correction;
  b. A detention facility operated under the jurisdiction of another state or the federal government; or
  c. A detention facility operated by a local government in this State or another state.

(2a) "Personality disorder" means an enduring pattern of inner experience and behavior that deviates markedly from the expectations of the individual's culture, is pervasive and inflexible, has an onset in adolescence or early adulthood, is stable over time, and leads to distress or impairment.

(3) "Release" means discharged or paroled.

(4) "Reportable conviction" means:
  a. A final conviction for an offense against a minor, a sexually violent offense, or an attempt to commit any of those offenses unless the conviction is for aiding and abetting. A final conviction for aiding and abetting is a reportable conviction only if the court sentencing the individual finds that the registration of that individual under this Article furthers the purposes of this Article as stated in G.S. 14-208.5.
  b. A final conviction in another state of an offense, which if committed in this State, would have been an offense against a minor or a sexually violent offense as defined by this section.
  c. A final conviction in a federal jurisdiction of an offense, which is substantially similar to an offense against a minor or a sexually violent offense as defined by this section.

(5) "Sexually violent offense" means a violation of G.S. 14-27.2 (first degree rape), G.S. 14-27.3 (second degree rape), G.S. 14-27.4 (first degree sexual offense), G.S. 14-27.5 (second degree sexual offense), G.S. 14-27.6 (attempted rape or sexual offense), G.S. 14-27.7 (intercourse and sexual offense with certain victims), G.S. 14-178 (incest between near relatives), G.S. 14-190.6 (employing or permitting minor to assist in

offenses against public morality and decency), G.S. 14-190.16 (first degree sexual exploitation of a minor), G.S. 14- 190.17 (second degree sexual exploitation of a minor), G.S. 14-190.17A (third degree sexual exploitation of a minor), G.S. 14-190.18 (promoting prostitution of a minor), G.S. 14-190.19 (participating in prostitution of a minor), or G.S. 14-202.1 (taking indecent liberties with children). The term also includes the following: a solicitation or conspiracy to commit any of these offenses; aiding and abetting any of these offenses.

(6) "Sexually violent predator" means a person who has been convicted of a sexually violent offense and who suffers from a mental abnormality or personality disorder that makes the person likely to engage in sexually violent offenses directed at strangers or at a person with whom a relationship has been established or promoted for the primary purpose of victimization.

(7) "Sheriff" means the sheriff of a county in this State.

(8) "Statewide registry" means the central registry compiled by the Division in accordance with G.S. 14-208.14.

G.S. 14-208.6A is not set forth here.

§14-208.6B. Registration requirements for juveniles transferred to and convicted in superior court.

A juvenile transferred to superior court pursuant to G.S. 7B-2200 who is convicted of a sexually violent offense or an offense against a minor as defined in G.S. 14-208.6 shall register in accordance with this Article just as an adult convicted of the same offense must register.

Part 2. Sex Offender and Public Protection Registration Program.

§14-208.7. Registration.

(a) A person who is a State resident and who has a reportable conviction shall be required to maintain registration with the sheriff of the county where the person resides. If the person moves to North Carolina from outside this State, the person shall register within 10 days of establishing residence in this State, or whenever the person has been present in the State for 15 days, whichever comes first. If the person is a current resident of North Carolina, the person shall register:

(1) Within 10 days of release from a penal institution or arrival in a county to live outside a penal institution; or

(2) Immediately upon conviction for a reportable offense where an active term of imprisonment was not imposed.

Registration shall be maintained for a period of 10 years following release from a penal institution. If no active term of imprisonment was imposed, registration shall be maintained for a period of 10 years following each conviction for a reportable offense.

(b) The Division shall provide each sheriff with forms for registering persons as required by this Article. The registration form shall require:

(1) The person's full name, each alias, date of birth, sex, race, height, weight, eye color, hair color, drivers license number, and home address;

(2) The type of offense for which the person was convicted, the date of conviction, and the sentence imposed;

(3) A current photograph; and

(4) The person's fingerprints.

The sheriff shall photograph the individual at the time of registration and take fingerprints from the individual at the time of registration both of which will be kept as part of the registration form. The registrant will not be required to pay any fees for the photograph or fingerprints taken at the time of registration.

(c) When a person registers, the sheriff with whom the person registered shall immediately send the registration information to the Division in a manner determined by the Division. The sheriff shall retain the original registration form and other information collected and shall compile the information that is a public record under this Part into a county registry.

§14-208.8. Prerelease notification.

(a) At least 10 days, but not earlier than 30 days, before a person who will be subject to registration under this Article is due to be released from a penal institution, an official of the penal institution shall:

(1) Inform the person of the person's duty to register under this Article and require the person to sign a written statement that the person was so informed or, if the person refuses to sign the statement, certify that the person was so informed;

(2) Obtain the registration information required under G.S. 14-208.7(b)(1) and (2), as well as the address where the person expects to reside upon the person's release; and

(3) Send the Division and the sheriff of the county in which the person expects to reside the information collected in accordance with subdivision (2) of this subsection.

(b) If a person who is subject to registration under this Article does not receive an active term of imprisonment, the court pronouncing sentence shall conduct, at the time of sentencing, the notification procedures specified in subsection (a) of this section.

§14-208.9. Change of address.

If a person required to register changes address, the person shall provide written notice of the new address not later than the tenth day after the change to the sheriff of the county with whom the person had last registered. Upon receipt of the notice, the sheriff shall immediately forward this information to the Division. If the person moves to another county in this State, the Division shall inform the sheriff of the new county of the person's new residence.

§14-208.9A. Verification of registration information.

The information in the county registry shall be verified annually for each registrant as follows:

(1) Every year on the anniversary of a person's initial registration date, the Division shall mail a nonforwardable verification form to the last reported address of the person.

(2) The person shall return the verification form to the sheriff within 10 days after the receipt of the form.

(3) The verification form shall be signed by the person and shall indicate whether the person still resides at the address last reported to the sheriff. If the person has a different address, then the person shall indicate that fact and the new address.

(4) If the person fails to return the verification form to the sheriff within 10 days after receipt of the form, the person is subject to the penalties provided in G.S. 14-208.11. If the verification form is returned to the sheriff as undeliverable, the sheriff shall make a reasonable attempt to verify that the person is residing at the registered address. If the person cannot be found at the registered address and has failed to report a change of address, the person is subject to the penalties provided in G.S. 14-208.11, unless the person reports in person to the sheriff and proves that the person has not changed his or her residential address.

G.S. 14-208.10 is not set forth here.

§14-208.11. Failure to register; falsification of verification notice; failure to return verification form; order for arrest.

(a) A person required by this Article to register who does any of the following is guilty of a Class F felony:
(1) Fails to register.
(2) Fails to notify the last registering sheriff of a change of address.
(3) Fails to return a verification notice as required under G.S. 14-208.9A.
(4) Forges or submits under false pretenses the information or verification notices required under this Article.

(a1) If a person commits a violation of subsection (a) of this section, the probation officer, parole officer, or any other law enforcement officer who is aware of the violation shall immediately arrest the person in accordance with G.S. 15A-401, or seek an order for the person's arrest in accordance with G.S. 15A-305.

(b) Before a person convicted of a violation of this Article is due to be released from a penal institution, an official of the penal institution shall conduct the prerelease notification procedures specified under G.S. 14-208.8(a)(2) and (3). If upon a conviction for a violation of this Article, no active term of imprisonment is imposed, the court pronouncing sentence shall, at the time of sentencing, conduct the notification procedures specified under G.S. 14-208.8(a)(2) and (3).

§14-208.12A. Termination of registration requirement.

(a) The requirement that a person register under this Part automatically terminates 10 years from the date of initial county registration if the person has not been convicted of a subsequent offense requiring registration under this Article.

(b) If there is a subsequent offense, the county registration records shall be retained until the registration requirement for the subsequent offense is terminated.

G.S. 14-208.13, -208.14, and -208.15 are not set forth here.

Elements

A person guilty of this offense
(1) is a sex offender who is required to register, *and*
(2) (a) fails to register, *or*
(b) fails to notify the last registering sheriff of a change of address, *or*
(c) fails to return a verification notice as required under G.S. 14-208.9A, *or*
(d) forges or submits under false pretenses the information or verification notices required.

Punishment

Class F felony.

Notes

Elements (1) and (2)(a). G.S. 14-208.7 sets out the registration requirements for a person who has a "reportable conviction," which is defined in G.S. 14-208.6(4). Both statutes are reproduced above. This registration requirement initially became effective January 1, 1996, and is applicable to people convicted or released from a penal institution on or after that date. For a discussion of 1997 legislative changes to the sex offender registration statutes and their effective dates, see John Rubin, "1997 Legislation Affecting Criminal Law and Procedure," *Administration of Justice Bulletin* No. 97/03 (Institute of Government, November 1999, 17–19).

Element (2)(b). The requirement to notify the appropriate sheriff of a change of address is set out in G.S. 14-208.9, reproduced above.

Elements (2)(c) and (2)(d). G.S. 14-208.9A is reproduced above.

Related registration requirements. There are registration requirements for sexually violent predators (see G.S. 14-208.20 through -208.25) and juveniles adjudicated delinquent of certain sex offenses (see G.S. 14-208.26 through -208.32).

Related offenses not in this chapter

None.

9

Crime against Nature, Incest, Indecent Exposure, and Related Offenses

Chapter Contents

9
Crime against Nature, Incest, Indecent Exposure, and Related Offenses

Crime against Nature

Statute

§14-177. Crime against nature.

If any person shall commit the crime against nature, with mankind or beast, he shall be punished as a Class I felon.

Elements

A person guilty of this offense
(1) commits the crime against nature.

Punishment

Class I felony.

Notes

Element (1). Each of the following acts is an example of "the crime against nature": the taking by a male of the sexual organ of another male into his mouth (3 N.C. App. 459); the inserting, by a male, of his sexual organ into the mouth or anus of another male or a female (166 N.C. 247; 264 N.C. 746; 11 N.C. App. 516); the receiving by a male or female of the sexual organ of a male into his or her mouth or anus (175 N.C. 767); fellatio (oral stimulation of the male sexual organ) by a female (40 N.C. App. 385); cunnilingus (penetration of the female sexual organ by the tongue) (295 N.C. 55); and analingus (penetration of the anus by the tongue). While there are no North Carolina appellate cases on sexual acts with animals, the statute expressly includes "the crime against nature, with . . . beast," which could be committed by a male or female. Note that the penetration of the female sexual organ by the male sexual organ is not included, even though, depending on the facts, this act may violate other criminal offenses relating to rape, incest, etc.

Constitutionality. The crime against nature statute is constitutional (299 N.C. 699). Acts in private between a man and woman married to each other apparently are exempt (40 N.C. App. 385; *Perkins*, p. 468). If the statute were interpreted to encompass sexual acts of married couples in private, it probably would be unconstitutional (381 U.S. 479). It is not unconstitutional discrimination to punish only unmarried people for engaging in the crime against nature by consent in private; also, the definition of crime against nature is not unconstitutionally vague (40 N.C. App. 385).

Age and consent. The age or physical maturity of the person upon or with whom the defendant commits the forbidden act is irrelevant to this statute (175 N.C. 767). Whether the other person consents also is irrelevant. The defendant could defend against a charge of crime against nature if he or she could show that he or she was forced or defrauded into committing one of the forbidden acts.

Penetration required. Penetration of or by a sexual organ is required before this offense has been committed (255 N.C. 583), but emission (male sexual climax) is not required (G.S. 14-23). On the other hand, in making a charge of first- or second-degree sexual offense (Chapter 8) on the basis of the act of cunnilingus, penetration is not required; stimulation by tongue or lips of any part of the woman's genitalia is sufficient (303 N.C. 666).

Attempt. Previous law provided that an attempt to commit the crime against nature was punishable the same as if a defendant had actually committed the offense of crime against nature (213 N.C. 45). However, under structured sentencing, an attempt to commit this offense is punished as a Class 1 misdemeanor (G.S. 14-2.5).

Comparison with "Indecent Liberties with a Child." Crime against nature differs from "Indecent Liberties with a Child" (Chapter 8; G.S. 14-202.1) in the following ways: (1) The age of the person upon or with whom the defendant commits this offense is irrelevant; for an offense to constitute taking indecent liberties, the victim must be a child under 16 and the defendant at least 16 and at least five years older than the victim. (2) Taking indecent liberties includes the "natural" heterosexual sex act (penetration of the female sexual organ by the male sexual organ), while crime against nature does not. (3) Taking indecent liberties includes some sexual acts not included in crime against nature, such as various sexual acts that do not involve penetration of the mouth, anus, or female sexual organ—for example, rubbing private parts and fondling breasts.

Comparison with "Sexual Activity by a Substitute Parent." Crime against nature differs from "Sexual Activity by a Substitute Parent" [Chapter 8; G.S. 14-27.7(a)] in the following ways: Penetration of or by the sexual organ is an essential element of crime against nature, but not of sexual activity by a substitute parent. Additionally, sexual activity by a substitute parent requires that the sexual act be performed by a person who has "assumed the role of parent" to the victim. That is not an element of crime against nature (89 N.C. App. 199).

Multiple prosecutions. Double jeopardy does not preclude simultaneous convictions for rape (forcible or statutory), sexual offense, indecent liberties with a child, crime against nature, and incest arising out of the same transaction (319 N.C. 34; 319 N.C. 656; 322 N.C. 415).

Relation to other offenses. Crime against nature is not a lesser-included offense of "First-Degree Sexual Offense" or "Second-Degree Sexual Offense" (Chapter 8; G.S. 14-27.4; 14-27.5)(309 N.C. 224). Nor is it a lesser-included offense of "Sexual Activity by a Substitute Parent" or "Sexual Activity by a Custodian" [Chapter 8; G.S. 14-27.7(a)] (89 N.C. App. 199). "Indecent Liberties with a Child" is not a lesser-included offense of crime against nature (303 N.C. 507; 319 N.C. 34).

Related offenses not in this chapter

"Attempt" (Chapter 4)
"Assault on a Female" (Chapter 7)
Child Abuse (various offenses) (Chapter 7)
See the offenses listed in Chapter 8, "Sexual Assaults."
See the offenses listed in Chapter 20, "Prostitution and Loitering for Prostitution."
See the offenses listed in Chapter 21, "Obscenity and Related Offenses."

Incest between Near Relatives

Statute

§14-178. Incest between certain near relatives.

The parties shall be guilty of a felony in all cases of carnal intercourse between (i) grandparent and grandchild, (ii) parent and child or stepchild or legally adopted child, or (iii) brother and sister of the half or whole blood. Every such offense is punishable as a Class F felony.

Elements

A person guilty of this offense
(1) has sexual intercourse with his or her
(2) (a) grandparent or grandchild, *or*
(b) parent or child or stepchild or legally adopted child, *or*
(c) brother or sister of the half or whole blood, *and*
(3) the person knows of that relationship.

Punishment

Class F felony.

Notes

Element (1). "Carnal intercourse," the term used in this statute, requires penetration, however slight, of the female sexual organ by the male sexual organ (44 N.C. App. 27).

Element (2)(b). A child for purposes of this offense includes an illegitimate child (235 N.C. 636); uncorroborated testimony of the child alone will support conviction (278 N.C. 63).

Element (3). Case law requires proof that the defendant knew of the relationship (278 N.C. 63; 44 N.C. App. 27).

Defenses. This offense can be committed even if no force is used; but force, fraud, or undue influence may be a defense. For example, a girl of 16 submitted to intercourse with her grandfather after sleeping in the same bed with him since early childhood and had a child nine months later. Her grandfather told her she was doing nothing wrong. The court held that even though she was not raped, the relationship with her grandfather and her age could be sufficient for the jury to exonerate her of incest in her suit for damages against the grandfather (176 N.C. 448).

Multiple prosecutions. See the note on this topic under "Crime against Nature."

Lesser-included offenses. "Indecent Liberties with a Child" (Chapter 8) is not a lesser-included offense of incest (303 N.C. 507; 319 N.C. 34).

Related offenses not in this chapter

See the offenses listed under "Crime against Nature."
Failure of sexual offender to register with sheriff (G.S. 14-208.11)

Incest between Uncle and Niece or Nephew and Aunt

Statute

§14-179. Incest between uncle and niece and nephew and aunt.

In all cases of carnal intercourse between uncle and niece, and nephew and aunt, the parties shall be guilty of a Class 1 misdemeanor, and shall be punished by a fine or imprisonment, in the discretion of the court.

Elements

A person guilty of this offense
(1) has sexual intercourse
(2) when the participants in the intercourse are uncle and niece or nephew and aunt, *and*
(3) the person knows of the relationship.

Punishment

Class 1 misdemeanor.

Notes

Element (1). See the note on Element (1) under "Incest between Near Relatives."

Element (2). Intercourse by a man with the daughter of his half-sister has been held to violate this statute (149 N.C. 513).

Element (3). See the note on Element (3) under "Incest between Near Relatives."

Multiple prosecutions. See the note on this topic under "Crime against Nature."

Lesser-included offenses. See the note on this topic under "Incest between Near Relatives."

Related offenses not in this chapter

See the offenses listed under "Crime against Nature."

Bigamy

Statute

§14-183. Bigamy.

If any person, being married, shall marry any other person during the life of the former husband or wife, every such offender, and every person counseling, aiding or abetting such offender, shall be punished as a Class I felon. Any such offense may be dealt with, tried, determined and punished in the county where the offender shall be apprehended, or be in custody, as if the offense had been actually committed in that county. If any person, being married, shall contract a marriage with any other person outside of this State, which marriage would be punishable as bigamous if contracted within this State, and shall thereafter cohabit with such person in this State, he shall be guilty of a felony and shall be punished as in cases of bigamy. Nothing contained in this section shall extend to any person marrying a second time, whose husband or wife shall have been continually absent from such person for the space of seven years then last past, and shall not have been known by such person to have been living within that time; nor to any person who at the time of such second marriage shall have been lawfully divorced from the bond of the first marriage; nor to any person whose former marriage shall have been declared void by the sentence of any court of competent jurisdiction.

Elements

A person guilty of this offense
- (1) is a married person, *and*
- (2) (a) "marries" another person in this state, *or*
  - (b) "marries" another person outside this state and thereafter cohabits with that person in this state.

Punishment

Class I felony.

Notes

Element (1). The statute does not apply to someone whose spouse has died, or has been absent and not known to be living for seven years, or from whom an annulment or divorce has been granted. The defendant's belief that his or her divorce or annulment is valid is apparently no defense to this charge if the divorce was in fact invalid (e.g., because the person who was granted the divorce was not a resident of the state in which it was obtained) (220 N.C. 445; 224 N.C. 183; 325 U.S. 226).

Element (2). If a person who is already married "marries" again—i.e., goes through a marriage ceremony with someone else—this second "marriage" is legally invalid. North Carolina law cannot forbid the second "marriage" if it takes place in another state, but bigamy is committed if the "married" couple thereafter cohabits (lives together as husband and wife) in North Carolina.

The validity of a marriage must be proved by the state and must be determined by the law of the state in which the ceremony was performed. A common-law marriage is not valid in North Carolina (301 N.C. 479). A ceremony solemnized by a Roman Catholic layman who bought for $10 a mail order certificate giving him ministerial status in the Universal Life Church was not a ceremony of marriage to be recognized in a bigamy prosecution (301 N.C. 479). A ceremony conducted by an assistant pastor, who was not an ordained minister or a magistrate but who was authorized by his church to perform marriages, was a ceremony of marriage to be recognized in a bigamy prosecution (99 N.C. App. 107, affirmed, 328 N.C. 86).

Related offenses not in this chapter

None.

Fornication and Adultery

Statute

§14-184. Fornication and adultery.

If any man and woman, not being married to each other, shall lewdly and lasciviously associate, bed and cohabit together, they shall be guilty of a Class 2 misdemeanor: Provided, that the admissions or confessions of one shall not be received in evidence against the other.

Elements

A person guilty of this offense
(1) lewdly and lasciviously cohabits
(2) with a person to whom he or she is not married.

Punishment

Class 2 misdemeanor.

Notes

Generally. This statute makes it a crime for a man and a woman, whether single or married, to cohabit if they are not married to each other. Each commits the offense. One party may be convicted even though the other is acquitted (109 N.C. 764). Cohabitation requires that the couple live together in the manner of husband and wife and have habitual sexual intercourse. A single act of intercourse is not enough to constitute this offense (225 N.C. 13), but two weeks' cohabitation has been considered sufficient (241 N.C. 277).

Evidence. The statute provides "that the admissions or confessions of one [participant] shall not be received in evidence against the other." The courts have held that this language refers only to statements made out of court by either participant (229 N.C. 386). One participant may testify in court against the other, and statements made out of court by the participant may then be introduced to corroborate that participant's in-court testimony. Rarely is there any direct eyewitness testimony as to actual acts of intercourse, except by the participants themselves; a conviction of the offense can be supported entirely by circumstantial evidence (225 N.C. 13).

Related offenses not in this chapter

Occupying hotel room for immoral purposes (G.S. 14-186)

Indecent Exposure

Statute

§14-190.9. Indecent exposure.

(a) Any person who shall willfully expose the private parts of his or her person in any public place and in the presence of any other person or persons, of the opposite sex, or aids or abets in any such act, or who procures another to perform such act; or any person, who as owner, manager, lessee, director, promoter or agent, or in any other capacity knowingly hires, leases or permits the land, building, or premises of which he is owner, lessee or tenant, or over which he has control, to be used for purposes of any such act, shall be guilty of a Class 2 misdemeanor.

(b) Notwithstanding any other provision of law, a woman may breast feed in any public or private location where she is otherwise authorized to be, irrespective of whether the nipple of the mother's breast is uncovered during or incidental to the breast feeding.

(c) Notwithstanding any other provision of law, a local government may regulate the location and operation of sexually oriented businesses. Such local regulation may restrict or prohibit nude, seminude, or topless dancing to the extent consistent with the constitutional protection afforded free speech.

Elements

I. Indecent Exposure

A person guilty of this offense

(1) willfully exposes, or aids and abets, or procures another to expose, the private parts of his or her body
(2) in a public place, *and*
(3) in the presence of a person of the opposite sex.

II. Use of Premises for Indecent Exposure

A person guilty of this offense

(1) knowingly permits a building or land
(2) that the person owns or has control of
(3) to be used for indecent exposure, as outlined in I., above.

Punishment

Class 2 misdemeanor.

Notes

Private parts. Private parts include both the external organs of sex and of excretion—male and female genitalia and anus—but not buttocks (348 N.C. 556). It is not necessary that a person of the opposite sex actually see the defendant's private parts; it is sufficient if the private parts are exposed in the person's presence. (348 N.C. 556; 136 N.C. App. 268). Thus a defendant was properly convicted of this offense when he pulled down his pants in front of a female, was naked from head to foot, and the victim saw his exposed buttocks (348 N.C. 556). The court of appeals has ruled that female breasts are not private parts (7 N.C. App. 166; but see 348 N.C. 556, discussing 7 N.C. App. 166 but neither adopting nor rejecting that ruling). The statute also provides that exposure of a mother's nipple during breast feeding is not a violation.

Public place. Appellate case law (268 N.C. 711; 136 N.C. App. 268) has stated that a public place is a place that is public as distinguished from private, but not necessarily a place devoted to the uses of the public. It is a place that is visited by many people and to which the public may have access. A public place is also a place that is viewable from any location open to the view of the public at large. Exposing one's genitals to a person of the opposite sex while lying on a creek embankment adjacent to a backyard was sufficient to support a conviction when evidence showed that the creek embankment was used by the public, nothing prevented anyone from walking through a private yard to get there, and there were no "No Trespassing" signs anywhere along the creek (136 N.C. App. 268). Exposing one's genitals to a person of the opposite sex while in a car in a shopping center parking lot or on a street is sufficient to support a conviction (268 N.C. 162; 268 N.C. 711).

Nude shows. Females who exhibited their private parts in a nightclub to males who paid a $5 admission charge and the nightclub operator who aided and abetted the women in doing this committed this offense. The exhibition need not be "obscene" within the meaning of G.S. 14-190.1(b) to violate this section (285 N.C. 305).

Local regulation of sexually oriented businesses. A 1998 legislative amendment added subsection (c) to this statute so that local governments are not preempted by state law (see, for example, 280 N.C. 238) from regulating the local operation of sexually oriented businesses. Such regulation may restrict or prohibit nude, seminude, or topless dancing to the extent consistent with constitutional law protecting free speech.

Related offenses not in this chapter

"Stalking" (Chapter 7)
See the offenses listed in Chapter 8, "Sexual Assaults."
See the offenses listed in Chapter 21, "Obscenity and Related Offenses."

Secretly Peeping into Room Occupied by Female Person

Statute

§14-202. Secretly peeping into room occupied by female person.

Any person who shall peep secretly into any room occupied by a female person shall be guilty of a Class 1 misdemeanor.

Elements

A person guilty of this offense
(1) peeps secretly
(2) into a room
(3) occupied by a female.

Punishment

Class 1 misdemeanor.

Notes

Element (1). "Peep" means to "look cautiously or slyly—as if through a crevice—out from chinks and knotholes." In one case, looking through a window into a room occupied by a woman was held to be "peeping" even though the venetian blind on the window (with its slats closed) was six to ten inches short of the window sill and the defendant looked through this gap with his face pressing against the window screen (262 N.C. 93). "Peeping" must be intentional and for the purpose of invading the privacy of the female occupant of the room (295 N.C. 236). This offense may be committed by a male or female.

Element (2). The statute is *not* limited to peeping into bedrooms or dressing rooms.

Element (3). The female in the room must be identified by name in the criminal process against the defendant (263 N.C. 784).

Constitutionality. The statute is not unconstitutionally vague (295 N.C. 236).

Related offenses not in this chapter

See the offenses listed under "Indecent Exposure" in this chapter.

10
Kidnapping and Related Offenses

Chapter Contents

10
Kidnapping and Related Offenses

First-Degree Kidnapping

Statute

§14-39. Kidnapping.

(a) Any person who shall unlawfully confine, restrain, or remove from one place to another, any other person 16 years of age or over without the consent of such person, or any other person under the age of 16 years without the consent of a parent or legal custodian of such person, shall be guilty of kidnapping if such confinement, restraint or removal is for the purpose of:

(1) Holding such other person for ransom or as a hostage or using such other person as a shield; or
(2) Facilitating the commission of any felony or facilitating flight of any person following the commission of a felony; or
(3) Doing serious bodily harm to or terrorizing the person so confined, restrained or removed or any other person; or
(4) Holding such other person in involuntary servitude in violation of G.S. 14-43.2.

(b) There shall be two degrees of kidnapping as defined by subsection (a). If the person kidnapped either was not released by the defendant in a safe place or had been seriously injured or sexually assaulted, the offense is kidnapping in the first degree and is punishable as a Class C felony. If the person kidnapped was released in a safe place by the defendant and had not been seriously injured or sexually assaulted, the offense is kidnapping in the second degree and is punishable as a Class E felony.

(c) Any firm or corporation convicted of kidnapping shall be punished by a fine of not less than five thousand dollars ($5,000) nor more than one hundred thousand dollars ($100,000), and its charter and right to do business in the State of North Carolina shall be forfeited.

Elements

A person guilty of this offense

(1) confines or restrains or removes from one place to another
(2) a person
(3) without the person's consent (or, if the person is under 16, without consent of the person's parent or guardian)
(4) for the purpose of
    (a) holding the victim as hostage, *or*
    (b) holding the victim for ransom, *or*

(c) using the victim as a shield, *or*
(d) facilitating the commission of a felony, *or*
(e) facilitating flight following the commission of a felony, *or*
(f) doing serious bodily harm to the victim or any other person, *or*
(g) terrorizing the victim or any other person, *or*
(h) holding the victim in involuntary servitude in violation of G.S. 14-43.2, *and*

(5) (a) does not release the victim in a safe place, *or*
(b) seriously injures the victim, *or*
(c) sexually assaults the victim.

Punishment

Class C felony.

Notes

Removal not required. Previous law (282 N.C. 490) required that the victim be moved from one place to another before the offense could constitute kidnapping. This statute provides that restraint or confinement, without movement, also may constitute kidnapping.

Element (1). Confinement means "some form of imprisonment within a given area such as a room, a house, or a vehicle" (294 N.C. 503). Threatened use of a deadly weapon can constitute restraint (294 N.C. 503). Restraint can include a restriction on freedom of movement by confinement, but it also includes restrictions on a person's movement without confinement; i.e., physical seizure or tying up with rope or cord (331 N.C. 199; 337 N.C. 212; 115 N.C. App. 674). The restraint or confinement of the victim need not be for a substantial period of time, and removal need not cover a substantial distance (294 N.C. 503; 297 N.C. 660; 111 N.C. App. 310).

Element (3). Without consent can be accomplished by fraud (336 N.C. 321; 304 N.C. 293; 278 N.C. 42). When a defendant persuaded a 15-year-old female and her sister, who had advertised as babysitters, to accompany him in his car to allegedly babysit his children, but in fact the defendant intended to assault them, a fraudulent "taking" occurred, satisfying this element (257 N.C. 348). The victims' and their parents' consent were fraudulently obtained and thus invalid.

Element (4) generally. For this element to be satisfied, the defendant need not actually carry out any of the acts listed in sub-elements (a) through (h) (i.e., hold the victim for ransom, or commit another felony, or do serious bodily harm to the victim, or terrorize the victim, etc.). Instead, this element is satisfied if the defendant has such a *purpose* in restraining, confining, or removing the victim; even if that purpose is not carried out (295 N.C. 655; 315 N.C. 738; 36 N.C. App. 447; 115 N.C. App. 674). Also, the defendant need not have such an illegal purpose when the restraint, confinement, or removal began—it is sufficient to prove that the defendant intended to carry out one of these purposes at *any time during* the confinement, restraint, or removal (315 N.C. 738). However, there is insufficient evidence of kidnapping when the offense that was the alleged purpose of the unlawful restraint occurred before any unlawful restraint occurred; for example, if a defendant assaults a victim and then unlawfully restrains the victim, the assault may not constitute the purpose of the unlawful restraint (136 N.C. App. 185).

Element (4)(a). Holding as hostage means "the unlawful taking, restraining, or confining of a person with the intent that the person, or victim, be held as security for the performance or forbearance of some act by a third person"

(33 N.C. App. 162; 106 N.C. App. 128). When a defendant confined and restrained a law enforcement officer as security for preventing the defendant's arrest by other officers, this element was satisfied (106 N.C. App. 128).

Elements (4)(d) and (e). Facilitating means "to make easier" (333 N.C. 687). Again, it is only necessary that the kidnapping be for the *purpose* of facilitating a felony or flight following the felony (295 N.C. 399). Such an underlying felony is not a lesser-included offense of the kidnapping, and generally the defendant may be convicted of both offenses (295 N.C. 399) (but see discussion below in "Multiple punishment" note).

If a defendant is charged with kidnapping by facilitating the commission of a felony, the underlying felony need not be committed against the victim of the kidnapping. For example, in a case where an infant was kidnapped, the commission of a sexual assault against the infant's mother satisfied this element (111 N.C. App. 310). A kidnapping *after* another felony has been completed may still facilitate the earlier felony (332 N.C. 116; 333 N.C. 687; 115 N.C. App. 674). For example, when a defendant unlawfully broke into an occupied dwelling with the intent to commit murder (thereby committing burglary), then restrained the victim against a dwelling wall and shot her, restraint of the victim against the wall and subsequent removal of the victim from the home constituted a continuing act of kidnapping to facilitate burglary and murder (333 N.C. 687).

An indictment alleging a kidnapping committed for the purpose of facilitating the commission of a felony or facilitating flight following the commission of a felony need not allege the specific felony that was the purpose of the unlawful restraint, removal, or confinement (314 N.C. 432).

Element (4)(g). Terrorizing means causing another person terror. This is not ordinary concern or ordinary fear but some higher degree of fear, such as intense apprehension or fright (315 N.C. 738; 36 N.C. App. 447; 109 N.C. App. 344).

Element (4)(h). Involuntary servitude is the holding of a person against his or her will: (1) for the performance of labor, whether or not for compensation, or whether or not for the satisfaction of a debt, and (2) by actual or threatened coercion or intimidation (G.S. 14-43.2).

Element (5)(a). The release of a victim in a safe place requires a defendant's conscious, willful action to assure the victim's release in a place of safety (309 N.C. 239; 330 N.C. 273; 128 N.C. App. 244). When a defendant released a hostage after being cornered and outnumbered by law enforcement officers, and the hostage was released into the focal point of the officers' weapons, the hostage was not released in a safe place (333 N.C. 156). A murder victim who was found stabbed to death in his own house, with his hands tied behind his back, was never released in a safe place from this restraint (350 N.C. 315). A victim who escaped from the defendant was not released in a safe place (92 N.C. App. 230). A defendant and his accomplice released the victim in a safe place when they gave her money to make a phone call and took her to a motel parking lot where they released her (127 N.C. App. 565).

Element (5)(b). "Serious injury" is almost certainly equivalent to that required to prove serious injury in an assault offense (see, e.g., 320 N.C. 746 and 322 N.C. 117). See the discussion of Element (2) under "Assault Inflicting Serious Injury" in Chapter 7, "Assaults and Threats."

Element (5)(c). "Sexual assault" need not necessarily be rape (295 N.C. 655), but it probably must be the equivalent of one of the sexual assault offenses in G.S. Ch. 14, Art. 7A (see Chapter 8), or crime against nature (G.S. 14-177) committed in a nonconsensual manner (see Chapter 9).

A defendant may *not* be convicted of both first-degree kidnapping and a sexual assault (that is, rape or sex offense) if the sexual assault is the factor in Element (5) that would elevate the offense from second-degree to first-degree kidnapping. In such a case the first-degree kidnapping must be reduced to a conviction of second-degree kidnapping or judgment must be arrested for the sexual assault conviction (313 N.C. 297; 316 N.C. 13; 317 N.C. 283; 318 N.C. 141). Convictions of both offenses only would be proper if the jury finds another factor in Element (5)—such as the defendant's failure to release the victim in a safe place—that would elevate the kidnapping to first-degree.

Multiple punishment. A defendant may be convicted of several offenses arising out of a series of events that form one continuous transaction, as long as the offenses are separate and distinct from one another. As a result, a defendant may be convicted of kidnapping and other crimes arising out of the same episode. If confinement, restraint, or removal is inherent in another felony (e.g., forcible rape and armed robbery), a defendant may *not*, based the same confinement, restraint, or removal, be convicted of both that felony and kidnapping for the purpose of committing that felony (294 N.C. 503; 304 N.C. 93; 318 N.C. 141; 133 N.C. App. 310; 123 N.C. App. 276).

A defendant may be convicted and punished for kidnapping and the underlying felony if the confinement, restraint, or removal that is the basis of the kidnapping is a separate, complete act, independent of, and not inherent in, the other felony (294 N.C. 503; 337 N.C. 212; 347 N.C. 555; 350 N.C. 315). For example, when victims were robbed in one room and then moved to another room and confined, the defendants were properly convicted of both robbery and kidnapping; the victims were moved to a room which did not contain any property that would be taken in a robbery (104 N.C. App. 558). The confinement was an act independent of and apart from the underlying felony. Similarly, when a defendant pulled a victim from one room to another, tied the victim up with an electrical cord, then shocked the victim by cutting open the cord and plugging it in, the defendant was properly convicted of kidnapping for pulling and binding the victim as well as assault with a deadly weapon with intent to kill inflicting serious injury for seriously burning the victim with electrical shocks (115 N.C. App. 674). Under similar circumstances, simultaneous conviction of kidnapping and crime against nature was proper (294 N.C. 503). Likewise, a defendant may be convicted and sentenced for both armed robbery and kidnapping for the purpose of committing armed robbery (295 N.C. 399).

Indictment must allege elements of offense. An indictment for first-degree kidnapping under this statute must allege the elements of the offense as set out in the statute, including one of the aggravating factors in Element (5) (309 N.C. 239). Simply alleging that the defendant kidnapped the victim is insufficient (36 N.C. App. 569). A judge may not instruct on an act (confine, restrain, or remove) or purpose of kidnapping not alleged in the indictment (317 N.C. 532).

Lesser-included offenses. Second-degree kidnapping, felonious restraint, and false imprisonment are all lesser-included offenses of first-degree kidnapping. However, a trial judge may not submit felonious restraint as a lesser-included offense of first- or second-degree kidnapping unless the kidnapping indictment alleges the elements of felonious restraint—transporting the victim in a motor vehicle or other conveyance (128 N.C. App. 688).

Firm or corporation as defendant. A firm or corporation convicted of this offense is subject to a fine of not less than $5,000 and not more than $10,000 and forfeiture of the right to do business in North Carolina.

Constitutionality. G.S. 14-39 is not unconstitutional (294 N.C. 503; 295 N.C. 399).

Related offenses not in this chapter

Involuntary servitude (G.S. 14-43.2)

Second-Degree Kidnapping

Statute

See G.S. 14-39, reproduced under "First-Degree Kidnapping."

Elements

A person guilty of this offense
- (1) confines or restrains or removes from one place to another
- (2) a person
- (3) without the person's consent (or, if the person is under 16, without consent of the person's parent or guardian)
- (4) for the purpose of
  - (a) holding the victim as hostage, *or*
  - (b) holding the victim for ransom, *or*
  - (c) using the victim as a shield, *or*
  - (d) facilitating the commission of a felony, *or*
  - (e) facilitating flight following the commission of a felony, *or*
  - (f) doing serious bodily harm to the victim or any other person, *or*
  - (g) terrorizing the victim or any other person, *or*
  - (h) holding the victim in involuntary servitude in violation of G.S. 14-43.2.

Punishment

Class E felony.

Notes

Generally. The only distinction between first- and second-degree kidnapping is that Element (5) of first-degree kidnapping is not an element of second-degree kidnapping.

Removal not required. See this same note topic under "First-Degree Kidnapping."

Elements (1) through (4). See the discussion of elements (1) through (4) under "First-Degree Kidnapping."

Multiple punishment. See this same note topic under "First-Degree Kidnapping."

Firm or corporation as defendant. See this same note topic under "First-Degree Kidnapping."

Constitutionality. See this same note topic under "First-Degree Kidnapping."

Related offenses not in this chapter

See the offenses listed under "First-Degree Kidnapping."

Felonious Restraint

Statute

§14-43.3. Felonious restraint.

A person commits the offense of felonious restraint if he unlawfully restrains another person without that person's consent, or the consent of the person's parent or legal custodian if the person is less than 16 years old, and moves the person from the place of the initial restraint by transporting him in a motor vehicle or other conveyance. Violation of this section is a Class F felony. Felonious restraint is considered a lesser included offense of kidnapping.

Elements

A person guilty of this offense
(1) unlawfully restrains a person
(2) without the person's consent (or, if the person is under sixteen, without consent of the person's parent or guardian), *and*
(3) transports the person by motor vehicle or other conveyance from the place of the initial restraint.

Punishment

Class F felony.

Notes

Generally. The law creating this offense does not expressly or by implication abolish the common-law crime of false imprisonment.

Relation to other offenses. G.S. 14-43.3 expressly states that this offense is a lesser-included offense of kidnapping. However, a trial judge may not submit felonious restraint as a lesser-included offense of first- or second-degree kidnapping unless the kidnapping indictment alleges the elements of felonious restraint—transporting the victim in a motor vehicle or other conveyance (128 N.C. App. 688).

Related offenses not in this chapter

See the offenses listed under "First-Degree Kidnapping."

False Imprisonment

Statute

This is a common-law offense.

Elements

A person guilty of this offense
(1) intentionally and unlawfully
(2) restrains or detains a person
(3) without the person's consent.

Punishment

Class 1 misdemeanor.

Notes

Generally. False imprisonment is a lesser-included offense of kidnapping (34 N.C. App. 233; 55 N.C. App. 305). The chief distinction between false imprisonment and kidnapping is that a specific purpose is not an element of false imprisonment [see Element (4) of "First-Degree Kidnapping" and "Second-Degree Kidnapping"]. If the purpose of the restraint or detention was to accomplish one of the purposes enumerated in the kidnapping statute, then the offense is kidnapping. If the restraint or detention occurred without any of the purposes specified by statute, the offense is false imprisonment (331 N.C. 199; 109 N.C. App. 344).

Element (1). The defendant is guilty only if detention or restraint of the victim is unlawful. For example, a merchant is not guilty of false imprisonment if the merchant detains in a reasonable manner and for a reasonable length of time a person whom the merchant has probable cause to suspect is a shoplifter [G.S. 14-72.1(c)].

Element (3). To prove that the restraint was against the victim's will, the prosecution must show that the defendant used actual force, threatened force, or fraud resulting in coerced consent (278 N.C. 42; 73 N.C. App. 546).

Relation to first- and second-degree kidnapping. A judge must instruct a jury on this lesser-included offense of first- and second-degree kidnapping only when there is evidence from which the jury could find that false imprisonment was committed. When the prosecutor presents evidence of every element of a kidnapping charge and there is no evidence negating those elements other than the defendant's denial that he or she committed the offense, the jury need not be instructed on the lesser-included offense of false imprisonment (109 N.C. App. 344).

Related offenses not in this chapter

See the offenses listed under "First-Degree Kidnapping."

Abduction of Children

Statute

§14-41. Abduction of children

(a) Any person who, without legal justification or defense, abducts or induces any minor child who is at least four years younger than the person to leave any person, agency, or institution lawfully entitled to the child's custody, placement, or care shall be guilty of a Class F felony.

(b) The provisions of this section shall not apply to any public officer or employee in the performance of his or her duty.

Elements

A person guilty of this offense

(1) without legal justification or defense

(2) abducts or induces

(3) a minor child who is at least four years younger than the person
(4) to leave
(5) a person, agency, or institution lawfully entitled to the child's custody, placement, or care.

Punishment

Class F felony.

Notes

Element (1). A noncustodial parent may be guilty of this offense when that parent abducts his or her child in violation of the terms of a child custody order and the other elements of this offense are satisfied.

Element (3). Although the term "minor child" is not defined in this statute, it would likely be defined as a person under eighteen years of age. See the definition of this term in G.S. 14-269.7.

Related offenses not in this chapter

Enticing minor out of state for purpose of employment (G.S. 14-40)

11
Larceny, Possession of Stolen Goods, Embezzlement, and Related Offenses

Chapter Contents

11
Larceny, Possession of Stolen Goods, Embezzlement, and Related Offenses

Misdemeanor Larceny

Statute

§14-72. Larceny of property; receiving stolen goods or possessing stolen goods.

(a) Larceny of goods of the value of more than one thousand dollars ($1,000) is a Class H felony. The receiving or possessing of stolen goods of the value of more than one thousand dollars ($1,000) while knowing or having reasonable grounds to believe that the goods are stolen is a Class H felony. Larceny as provided in subsection (b) of this section is a Class H felony. Receiving or possession of stolen goods as provided in subsection (c) of this section is a Class H felony. Except as provided in subsections (b) and (c) of this section, larceny of property, or the receiving or possessing of stolen goods knowing or having reasonable grounds to believe them to be stolen, where the value of the property or goods is not more than one thousand dollars ($1,000), is a Class 1 misdemeanor. In all cases of doubt, the jury shall, in the verdict, fix the value of the property stolen.

(b) The crime of larceny is a felony, without regard to the value of the property in question, if the larceny is:

(1) From the person; or

(2) Committed pursuant to a violation of G.S. 14-51, 14-53, 14-54 or 14-57; or

(3) Of any explosive or incendiary device or substance. As used in this section, the phrase "explosive or incendiary device or substance" shall include any explosive or incendiary grenade or bomb; any dynamite, blasting powder, nitroglycerin, TNT, or other high explosive; or any device, ingredient for such device, or type or quantity of substance primarily useful for large-scale destruction of property by explosive or incendiary action or lethal injury to persons by explosive or incendiary action. This definition shall not include fireworks; or any form, type, or quantity of gasoline, butane gas, natural gas, or any other substance having explosive or incendiary properties but serving a legitimate nondestructive or nonlethal use in the form, type, or quantity stolen.

(4) Of any firearm. As used in this section, the term "firearm" shall include any instrument used in the propulsion of a shot, shell or bullet by the action of gunpowder or any other explosive substance within it. A "firearm," which at the time of theft is not capable of being fired, shall be included within this definition if it can be made to work. This definition shall not include air rifles or air pistols.

(5) Of any record or paper in the custody of the North Carolina State Archives as defined by G.S. 121-2(7) and 121-2(8).

(c) The crime of possessing stolen goods knowing or having reasonable grounds to believe them to be stolen in the circumstances described in subsection (b) is a felony or the crime of receiving stolen goods knowing or having reasonable grounds to believe them to be stolen in the circumstances described in subsection (b) is a felony, without regard to the value of the property in question.

(d) Where the larceny or receiving or possession of stolen goods as described in subsection (a) of this section involves the merchandise of any store, a merchant, a merchant's agent, a merchant's employee, or a peace officer who detains or causes the arrest of any person shall not be held civilly liable for detention, malicious prosecution, false imprisonment, or false arrest of the person detained or arrested, when such detention is upon the premises of the store or in a reasonable proximity thereto, is in a reasonable manner for a reasonable length of time, and, if in detaining or in causing the arrest of such person, the merchant, the merchant's agent, the merchant's employee, or the peace officer had, at the time of the detention or arrest, probable cause to believe that the person committed an offense under subsection (a) of this section. If the person being detained by the merchant, the merchant's agent, or the merchant's employee, is a minor under the age of 18 years, the merchant, the merchant's agent, or the merchant's employee, shall call or notify, or make a reasonable effort to call or notify the parent or guardian of the minor, during the period of detention. A merchant, a merchant's agent, or a merchant's employee, who makes a reasonable effort to call or notify the parent or guardian of the minor shall not be held civilly liable for failing to notify the parent or guardian of the minor.

Elements

A person guilty of the offense
- (1) takes personal property belonging to another
- (2) and carries it away
- (3) without the consent of the possessor, *and*
- (4) with the intent to deprive the possessor of its use permanently
- (5) knowing that the taker was not entitled to it.

Punishment

Class 1 misdemeanor.

Notes

Element (1). "Taking" means obtaining possession of the property (273 N.C. 652). The property must be *personal* property, not real property such as a fence or tombstone (218 N.C. 373), and not a thing of value other than personal property (though other statutes may make stealing those items a crime; see related offenses, below). Any animal may now be the subject of larceny (G.S. 14-84). Contraband (for example, illegal drugs) is property covered by the larceny and robbery statutes (334 N.C. 513).

Obtaining the property is "taking" only if it occurs without the possessor's consent (273 N.C. 652) or by a trick (111 N.C. 665)—for example, by stating that the property is only being borrowed, or through the possessor's mistake (*Perkins*, p. 313). However, it is not necessary to allege the fraudulent manner in which the property was taken or to use the words "by trick" in a criminal pleading alleging larceny, even if the defendant obtained possession of the property by trick or fraud (35 N.C. App. 401). Note that if the defendant obtains or attempts to obtain property by a false representation, "Obtaining Property by False Pretenses" (Chapter 14) can be charged (67 N.C. App. 110; 299 N.C. 229).

To be sufficient, a criminal pleading for larceny must allege the identity of the owner of the property or the identity of the person in lawful possession of the property (such as the possessor, bailee, or other person with a special property interest in the stolen property) and the evidence must support the allegation. Proof of mere ownership of the premises from which property was stolen does not by itself establish ownership or possession of, or interest in, the stolen property (313 N.C. 164).

Element (2). Any assumption of control of the property by the defendant, however brief, satisfies this element (65 N.C. 305; 6 N.C. App. 740). The property need not be removed from the possessor's premises (89 N.C. 475)—for example, it was sufficient when the defendant removed an air conditioner from its window base to a point on the floor some four to six inches nearer the door (296 N.C. 101), and when the defendant removed tires from cars parked at a car dealership and left them propped against the hubs (58 N.C. App. 102).

Element (3). This element may be satisfied by the possessor's testimony that he or she did not consent. Larceny violates the right to possess property, not the right to own it. Thus even the owner of property may be guilty of larceny if the owner steals his or her property that is in another person's lawful possession (*Perkins*, p. 297; see dicta in 89 N.C. 466).

Element (4). A mere temporary taking under circumstances in which the possessor is likely to regain possession does not satisfy this element, but taking for temporary use can satisfy the element if the property is taken and then abandoned under circumstances that both make it unlikely that the possessor will recover the property and show the taker's indifference to the possessor's rights (139 N.C. App. 471). The actual deprivation need not be identical to the intended deprivation. For example, a defendant who rents a car for a day with the intent to sell it can satisfy this element by keeping the car with no intent to return it (N.C.P.I.—Crim. 216.15).

Element (5). A person who honestly believes he or she is entitled to property he or she takes is not guilty of larceny, even if not in fact entitled to it (250 N.C. 272).

Multiple offenses. A defendant may be convicted for only one larceny if several pieces of property are taken during one continuous act or transaction (342 N.C. 607; 331 N.C. 317; 78 N.C. App. 572). For example, when a defendant stole a firearm and other property in a single breaking and entering, the defendant could be convicted of only one larceny (331 N.C. 317; 130 N.C. App. 140). A defendant may properly be convicted of multiple counts of larceny if evidence shows separate incidents in which there were separate takings of property (322 N.C. 770; 335 N.C. 741). See the notes concerning "Multiple victims" under "Common-Law Robbery" and "Armed Robbery" (both in Chapter 12) for larceny that occurs as part of a robbery.

Doctrine of possession of recently stolen property. When the defendant possesses property that has been stolen recently, that possession may be a sufficient basis for concluding that he or she participated in larceny if the stolen property was found in the defendant's custody and was subject to his or her control to the exclusion of all other people not party to the larceny (268 N.C. 480; 301 N.C. 669; 311 N.C. 80; 109 N.C. App. 222). Use of the doctrine requires proof that the stolen property was found in the defendant's custody and had been in the defendant's possession or subject to his or her control and disposition since the theft (313 N.C. 516; 316 N.C. 41).

As a general principle, "[t]he possession, in point of time, should be so close to the theft as to render it unlikely that the possessor could have acquired the property honestly" (274 N.C. 594). Thus the evidence was sufficient to convict two defendants when, within several days of a number of larcenies from nearby houses, articles stolen from these houses were found in a house occupied and exclusively controlled at the time by the defendants (282 N.C. 249). On the other hand, the evidence was held insufficient to convict a defendant who was found, one day after a larceny, operating a car owned by his co-defendant that contained various articles stolen in that larceny; three other men (including the owner of the car) were passengers; all had access to the stolen articles; two were not charged as co-conspirators in the larceny; and the car's owner claimed that the stolen articles belonged to him (301 N.C. 669).

In appropriate circumstances, the doctrine of recent possession can apply even if a substantial period of time has elapsed between the theft and the discovery of the defendant's possession of the stolen goods. For example, the doctrine was held to apply when a defendant was found to possess a unique tool not generally traded in his community 27 days after it was stolen and fingerprint evidence tied the defendant to the theft (6 N.C. App. 66). Additionally, the doctrine was found applicable to a case in which the defendant or his girlfriend possessed a stolen watch for up to 4 weeks after it was stolen (313 N.C. 516). It was also applied in a case in which the defendant possessed commercial restaurant equipment 11 to 12 days after it had been stolen, since such property is not usually traded in lawful retail channels (83 N.C. App. 323). However, the doctrine was held inapplicable when a defendant was found to possess audio tapes 19 days after they were stolen and a rifle 30 days after it was stolen, because such items are frequently traded in normal channels (54 N.C. App. 522).

Larceny of vehicles. Larceny of a vehicle, like larceny of other personal property, may be charged as a felony if the vehicle is worth more than $1,000 or is taken from the person or taken pursuant to burglary or breaking and entering; otherwise larceny of a vehicle, like larceny of anything else, is a misdemeanor. However, since the thief then possesses the stolen vehicle, he or she may also be charged with the separate offense of possessing a stolen vehicle, regardless of the vehicle's value; see "Possession of Stolen Vehicle," below in this chapter.

Proof of motor vehicle ownership. Evidence of tag letters and numbers plus a certified copy of the Division of Motor Vehicles registration or certificate of title is prima facie evidence of the ownership of the motor vehicle (G.S. 8-37).

Larceny of certain animals is felonious. Larceny of horses, mules, swine, or cattle is a Class H felony, regardless of the value of the animal taken [G.S. 14-81(a)]. G.S. 14-81(a1) provides that larceny of a dog is a Class I felony, regardless of the value of the animal taken.

Larceny of lost property. A person who finds lost property and takes it for personal use is guilty of larceny if, at the time of finding it, the person knows who the owner is or has a reasonable means of ascertaining the owner—that is, if there is a clue to the owner's identity (188 N.C. 561; *Perkins*, p. 311). Thus when three women divided and kept for their own use money in a deposit bag with "Bank of North Carolina" written on it, after one of them had found the bag on a sidewalk, the finder of the bag was guilty of larceny, and the defendant, who took a share of the money for her own use knowing how it had been obtained, was guilty of receiving stolen property (46 N.C. App. 259).

Comparison with "Embezzlement" (below in this chapter) and "Obtaining Property by False Pretenses" (Chapter 14). See the note on "Relationship to Larceny and Embezzlement" under "Obtaining Property by False Pretenses" in Chapter 14 for a more detailed discussion of this issue. To commit embezzlement a defendant must deprive an owner of property the defendant has been entrusted with; that is not the case for larceny. Larceny requires an intent to deprive the owner of property permanently, while obtaining property by false pretenses does not. Obtaining property by false pretenses requires that the defendant make a false representation to obtain property; larceny does not. Larceny requires that property be wrongfully taken without the owner's consent, while obtaining property by false pretenses frequently involves the initial consent of the property owner.

Comparison with "Shoplifting—Concealing Merchandise" (below in this chapter). Larceny, unlike shoplifting, requires proof that the person intended to permanently deprive the owner (or other lawful possessor) of possession of the property. Shoplifting, unlike larceny, requires proof that the property was willfully concealed on the store's premises. Although it is legally possible to charge a person with larceny who has been stopped in a store's premises with willfully concealed goods, the difficulty of proving the element of intent to permanently deprive under such circumstances makes concealing merchandise the better charge. On the other hand, a person who has willfully concealed goods on a store's premises and then left the store before being stopped is normally charged with larceny because the element of the intent to permanently deprive is readily provable, and larceny is the more serious offense (misdemeanor larceny is a Class 1 misdemeanor and the first offense of concealing merchandise is a Class 3 misdemeanor). It is unclear whether a person may be convicted and punished for both larceny and concealing merchandise based on the same incident.

Comparison with "Larceny by Employee" (discussed later in this chapter). See the note "Charging this offense and comparison with common-law larceny" in "Larceny by Employee."

Limited civil liability for merchant or law enforcement officer. See the note on this topic under "Shoplifting—Concealing Merchandise," below.

Merchant required to make reasonable effort to notify parent of detained minor. See the note on this topic under "Shoplifting—Concealing Merchandise," below.

Related offenses not in this chapter

See Chapter 12, "Robbery, Extortion, and Related Offenses."
See Chapter 13, "Burglary and Breaking or Entering."
"Obtaining Property by False Pretenses" (Chapter 14)
"Food Stamp Fraud" (Chapter 14)
"Welfare Fraud" (Chapter 14)
"Computer Fraud" (Chapter 14)
Medicaid Fraud (various offenses) (Chapter 14)
"Medicaid Card Fraud" (Chapter 14)
Removal of shopping cart from store (G.S. 14-72.3)
Larceny of secret technical process (G.S. 14-75.1)
Larceny of public records (G.S. 14-76)
Larceny of wills (G.S. 14-77)
Larceny of ungathered crops (G.S. 14-78)
Larceny of ginseng (G.S. 14-79)
Larceny of pine needles or pine straw (G.S. 14-79.1)
Larceny of horses, mules, swine, cattle, or dogs (G.S. 14-81)
Taking horses, mules, or dogs for temporary purposes (G.S. 14-82)
Pursuing livestock with intent to steal (G.S. 14-85)
Making, distributing, possessing, or programming device for theft of telecommunication services (G.S. 14-113.5 and -113.6)
Removing or defacing tombstones and monuments (G.S. 14-148)
Tampering with utility meters (G.S. 14-151.1)
Protection of patient property (G.S. 108A-60)

Felonious Larceny

Statute

See G.S. 14-72, reproduced under "Misdemeanor Larceny."

Elements

A person guilty of this offense
(1) takes personal property belonging to another, *and*
(2) carries it away
(3) without the consent of the possessor, *and*
(4) with the intent to deprive the possessor of its use permanently
(5) knowing that the taker was not entitled to it, *and*
(6) (a) the property was worth over $1,000, *or*
(b) the larceny was from the person, *or*
(c) the larceny was committed pursuant to burglary, or breaking out of a dwelling, or breaking or entering a building, or burglary by explosives, *or*
(d) the larceny was of an explosive or incendiary device, *or*
(e) the larceny was of a firearm, *or*
(f) the larceny was of a record or paper in the custody of the North Carolina State Archives.

Punishment

Class H felony.

Notes

Generally. See the notes under "Misdemeanor Larceny."

Elements (1) through (5). See the notes on elements (1) through (5) under "Misdemeanor Larceny."

Element (6) generally. Sub-elements (a) through (f) are alternate ways of proving felonious larceny. Only one of these factors must be present to raise the larceny to a felony. For example, if the larceny was committed pursuant to a burglary under (c), the value of the property taken [sub-element (a)] is irrelevant. Likewise, larceny of a firearm under (e) is a felony regardless of the firearm's value.

Element (6)(a). If a defendant steals several items in a single incident, their value can be added together to establish whether this $1,000 threshold for charging felonious larceny is reached.

In most cases, the value of stolen goods is determined by their fair market value at the time of the theft, not their replacement cost (263 N.C. 730; 318 N.C. 643). Fair market value is the price that a willing buyer would pay a willing seller for the item in question on the open market (*Black's Law Dictionary*, p. 1549; 96 N.C. App. 209). That might be shown by the price of an item of similar age and condition, or the average purchase price of such an item on the open market. The fair market value must be established by direct evidence, not by mere speculation (318 N.C. 643). However, if the stolen property is not commonly traded and has no ascertainable market value (for example, a pay telephone), a jury may determine the property's value from evidence of its replacement cost (107 N.C. App. 237).

Element (6)(b). Larceny is from the person when the property is physically possessed by the person or if it is within protection of the person when it is stolen (328 N.C. 313; *Perkins*, pp. 342, 346). "From the person" was satisfied when a convenience store employee opened a cash register to make change for the defendant, and the defendant reached into and took money from the register. Even though the money was not in the victim's physical possession, it was within the protection of the employee when it was stolen (328 N.C. 313). "From the person" was not satisfied when a defendant took a bank bag from a kiosk in a shopping mall when the kiosk employee was about 25 feet away from the kiosk, because the bank bag was not in the immediate presence of and under the employee's protection or control when it was taken (345 N.C. 146).

Element (6)(c). The statute specifies larceny "committed pursuant to a violation of G.S. 14-51, 14-53, 14-54, or 14-57." It does not include larceny committed pursuant to breaking and entering a motor vehicle under G.S. 14-56; see "Breaking or Entering Vehicle" (Chapter 13). The breaking or entering or burglary that precedes the larceny need not have been committed by the defendant; when others committed a breaking of a store and afterward the defendant acted in concert with them to steal the store's merchandise, the defendant could be found guilty of larceny after breaking or entering (50 N.C. App. 210).

Element (6)(d). See the definition of "explosive or incendiary devices" in G.S. 14-72(b)(3), reproduced above.

Element (6)(e). Larceny of a firearm is a felony regardless of the value of the firearm (311 N.C. 380). See the definition of "firearm" in G.S. 14-72(b)(4), reproduced above.

Larceny of horses, mules, swine, cattle, or dogs. Larceny of horses, mules, swine, or cattle is a Class H felony, regardless of the value of the animal taken [G.S. 14-81 (a)]. Larceny of a dog is a Class I felony, regardless of the value of the animal taken [G.S. 14-81(a1)].

Doctrine of possession of recently stolen property. See the note with this title under "Misdemeanor Larceny."

Multiple offenses. See the note on this topic under "Misdemeanor Larceny."

Forfeiture of vehicles. All conveyances—including vehicles, boats, or airplanes—used in the commission of a larceny of property worth more than $2,000 may be seized and forfeited pursuant to the provisions of G.S. 14-86.1. For example, a vehicle used to carry stolen merchandise from the scene of a break-in would satisfy this requirement of the forfeiture statute.

Larceny of vehicles. See the note with this title under "Misdemeanor Larceny."

Lesser-included offenses. Misdemeanor larceny is a lesser-included offense of felonious larceny (263 N.C. 517). Unauthorized use of a motor-propelled conveyance is a lesser-included offense of larceny (46 N.C. App. 338). Receiving stolen goods is not a lesser-included offense of larceny (330 N.C. 249).

Relationship to receiving stolen goods and possession of stolen goods. A person may be charged with larceny, receiving, and possession of the same property but may be convicted of only one of those offenses (302 N.C. 370; 305 N.C. 225; 47 N.C. App. 303; 113 N.C. App. 69).

Limited civil liability for merchant or law enforcement officer. See the note on this topic under "Shoplifting—Concealing Merchandise," below.

Merchant required to make reasonable effort to notify parent of detained minor. See the note on this topic under "Shoplifting—Concealing Merchandise," below.

Related offenses not in this chapter

See the offenses listed under "Misdemeanor Larceny."

Larceny of Chose in Action

Statute

§14-75. Larceny of chose in action.

If any person shall feloniously steal, take and carry away, or take by robbery, any bank note, check or other order for the payment of money issued by or drawn on any bank or other society or corporation within this State or within any of the United States, or any treasury warrant, debenture, certificate of stock or other public security, or certificate of stock in any corporation, or any order, bill of exchange, bond, promissory note or other obligation, either for the payment of money or for the delivery of specific articles, being the property of any other person, or of any corporation (notwithstanding any of the said particulars may be termed in law a chose in action), that person is guilty of a Class H felony.

Elements

A person guilty of this offense

(1) takes a document representing a "chose in action" belonging to another, *and*
(2) carries it away
(3) without the consent of the possessor, *and*
(4) with the intent to deprive the possessor of its use permanently
(5) knowing that the taker is not entitled to it.

Punishment

Class H felony.

Notes

Elements in general. Except for the nature of the things stolen, discussed below, the elements of this offense are the same as the elements of the larceny of property. See the notes to "Misdemeanor Larceny" and "Felonious Larceny."

Chose in action. At common law, documents representing debts (known as "choses in action"), such as checks, were not recognized as property with the value of the debt. Therefore, a statute had to be enacted to cover the theft of these items. The statute applies only to "any bank note, check or other order for the payment of money issued by or drawn on any bank or other society or corporation . . . , or any treasury warrant, debenture, certificate of stock or other public security, or certificate of stock in any corporation, or any order, bill of exchange, bond, promissory note or other obligation, either for the payment of money or for the delivery of specific articles. . . ."

See 75 N.C. 257 concerning the common-law rule. A blank check appears not to be a chose in action under this statute. Because a blank check has at least some value, however trivial, the theft of a blank check can be charged as misdemeanor larceny. Although no North Carolina case has addressed this issue, see a New Jersey case, 113 N.J. Super. 1, 272 A.2d 539 (1971).

Related offenses not in this chapter

See the offenses listed under "Misdemeanor Larceny."

Unauthorized Use of Motor-Propelled Conveyance

Statute

§14-72.2. Unauthorized use of a motor-propelled conveyance.

(a) A person is guilty of an offense under this section if, without the express or implied consent of the owner or person in lawful possession, he takes or operates an aircraft, motorboat, motor vehicle, or other motor-propelled conveyance of another.

(b) Unauthorized use of an aircraft is a Class H felony. All other unauthorized use of a motor-propelled conveyance is a Class 1 misdemeanor.

(c) Unauthorized use of a motor-propelled conveyance shall be a lesser-included offense of unauthorized use of an aircraft.

(d) As used in this section, "owner" means any person with a property interest in the motor-propelled conveyance.

Elements

A person guilty of this offense
(1) willfully takes or operates
(2) a motor-propelled conveyance
(3) of another
(4) without the consent of the owner or other person in lawful possession.

Punishment

If the conveyance is an aircraft, the offense is a Class H felony. For any other kind of motor-propelled conveyance, the offense is a Class 1 misdemeanor.

Notes

Element (1). Note that this element is satisfied by proof of taking *or* operating. Thus a person may lawfully take a vehicle but later be unlawfully operating it beyond the scope of the owner's or possessor's consent.

Element (4). The consent of one authorized to act for the owner would also be sufficient to grant lawful possession to the user (for example, a person who borrowed a vehicle).

Absence of intent to deprive owner of use. This offense is used in cases of "joyriding," when a larceny charge is inappropriate because of absence of intent to deprive the owner of the vehicle's permanent use. See the note on Element (4) under "Misdemeanor Larceny."

Distinguished from possession of stolen vehicle. In the crime of possession of stolen vehicle, the defendant possesses the vehicle knowing it to be stolen. In the crime of unauthorized use, the defendant exercises control without the owner's consent, and the vehicle or conveyance need not be stolen. See "Possession of Stolen Vehicle."

Included in larceny. Unauthorized use of a motor-propelled conveyance is a lesser-included offense of larceny of a vehicle (46 N.C. App. 338) (see "Misdemeanor Larceny").

Proof of motor vehicle ownership. See the note on "Proof of motor vehicle ownership" under "Misdemeanor Larceny."

Related offenses not in this chapter

Removing boats (G.S. 14-162)

Misdemeanor Possession of Stolen Goods

Statute

See G.S. 14-72(a), reproduced under "Misdemeanor Larceny."

§14-71.1. Possessing stolen goods.

If any person shall possess any chattel, property, money, valuable security or other thing whatsoever, the stealing or taking whereof amounts to larceny or a felony, either at common law or by virtue of any statute made or hereafter to be made, such person knowing or having reasonable grounds to believe the same to have been feloniously stolen or taken, he shall be guilty of a Class H felony, and may be indicted and convicted, whether the felon stealing and taking such chattels, property, money, valuable security or other thing shall or shall not have been previously convicted, or shall or shall not be amenable to justice; and any such possessor may be dealt with, indicted, tried and punished in any county in which he shall have, or shall have had, any such property in his possession or in any county in which the thief may be tried, in the same manner as such possessor may be dealt with, indicted, tried and punished in the county where he actually possessed such chattel, money, security, or other thing; and such possessor shall be punished as one convicted of larceny.

Elements

A person guilty of this offense

(1) possesses stolen property
(2) knowing, or having reasonable grounds to believe, that it was stolen
(3) with a dishonest purpose.

Punishment

Class 1 misdemeanor.

Notes

Generally. This usually will be a preferable charge to "Receiving Stolen Goods—Misdemeanor," below, because "possession" is likely easier to prove than "receiving." Also, for this offense, it is not necessary to prove that someone other than the defendant stole the property as long as circumstances would have led a reasonable person to believe it was stolen (305 N.C. 225). Much of case law applying to the two "Receiving Stolen Goods" offenses, below in this chapter, probably applies to this offense.

Element (1). As with the receiving stolen goods offense, the defendant is not required to hold the property for his or her own benefit; it is sufficient to possess the property in an attempt to help the thief (69 N.C. 29). If a defendant is found to possess more than one stolen item, the number of separate offenses of possession of stolen property for which the defendant may be convicted equals the number of times the defendant obtained possession of the property. Thus if a defendant obtains ten stolen items during eight different times of receipt following break-ins over a six-week period, the defendant is guilty of eight separate offenses of possession of stolen goods (322 N.C. 770).

A person may constructively possess stolen property. That is, the element of possession is satisfied if the defendant has control of the property even if he or she does not physically possess it (95 N.C. 626; 234 N.C. 42; 14 N.C. App. 120; 74 N.C. App. 587; 130 N.C. App. 456). For example, if stolen property was found at a storage unit rented by the defendant, and evidence showed that only the defendant had a key to that storage unit, constructive possession could be inferred.

Element (2). It is not necessary to prove that someone else stole the property in order to convict a defendant for possession of stolen property. See the note on Element (3) under "Receiving Stolen Goods—Misdemeanor."

Element (3). This element requires more than just the knowledge, or reasonable grounds to believe, that the property in question was stolen [Element (2), above]. This means some kind of illegal purpose. It may be inferred from the circumstances of the case (*Perkins*, p. 404). That may be evidence that the defendant intended to convert the property to his or her own use (N.C.P.I.—Crim. 216.47). Or it may be evidence that the receiver or possessor acted with intent to aid the thief (or receiver or possessor) of the goods (316 N.C. 295). It is not necessary that the receiver or possessor gain personally by his or her actions (316 N.C. 295). Evidence that a person received or possessed property with an innocent intent, such as an intent to return the property without reward to its owner, could disprove this element (*Perkins*, p. 403).

Because "dishonest purpose" does not appear in the statutes describing the possession of or receiving stolen property offenses, the term need not be included in a criminal pleading charging a defendant with such an offense (97 N.C. App. 19).

Possessing stolen lost property. See the note concerning "Larceny of lost property" under "Misdemeanor Larceny."

Relationship to larceny and receiving stolen goods offenses. A person may be charged with larceny, receiving, and possession of the same property, but the person may be convicted of only one of those offenses for a single transaction (302 N.C. 370; 305 N.C. 225; 47 N.C. App. 303). Possession is not a lesser-included offense of receiving (302 N.C. 370).

Limited civil liability for merchant or law enforcement officer. See the note on this topic under "Shoplifting—Concealing Merchandise."

Merchant required to make reasonable effort to notify parent of detained minor. See the note on this topic under "Shoplifting—Concealing Merchandise."

Related offenses not in this chapter

See the offenses listed under "Misdemeanor Larceny."
"Accessory after the Fact to Felony" (Chapter 4)
Possession of financial transaction card forgery devices (G.S. 14-113.14)
Failure to follow pawnbroker requirements (G.S. 91A-11)
Failure to follow record requirements for peddlers, itinerant merchants, and specialty market vendors (G.S. 66-257)

Felonious Possession of Stolen Goods

Statute

See G.S. 14-71.1, reproduced under "Misdemeanor Possession of Stolen Goods," immediately preceding this offense, and G.S. 14-72, reproduced under "Misdemeanor Larceny."

Elements

A person guilty of this offense
(1) possesses stolen property
(2) when the larceny was

   (a) of property worth more than $1,000, *or*
   (b) from the person, *or*
   (c) pursuant to burglary, or breaking out of a dwelling, or breaking or entering a building, or burglary by explosives, *or*
   (d) of an explosive or incendiary device, *or*
   (e) of a firearm, *or*
   (f) of a record or paper in the custody of the North Carolina State Archives
(3) knowing, or having reasonable grounds to believe, that the property was stolen in that manner
(4) with a dishonest purpose.

Punishment

Class H felony.

Notes

Generally. This usually will be a preferable charge to "Receiving Stolen Goods—Felony," below, because "possession" is likely easier to prove than "receiving." Also, for this offense, it is not necessary to prove that someone other than the defendant stole the property as long as circumstances would have led a reasonable person to believe it was stolen (305 N.C. 225). Much of case law applying to the two "Receiving Stolen Goods" offenses, below in this chapter, probably applies to this offense.

Element (1). See the note for this element under "Misdemeanor Possession of Stolen Goods," just above.

Element (2). Sub-elements (a) through (f) are identical to sub-elements (a) through (f) of Element (6) of "Felonious Larceny," earlier in this chapter. For further discussion, see the notes on those elements under that offense. Thus the characteristics that distinguish misdemeanor and felonious larceny also distinguish misdemeanor and felonious possession of stolen goods.

Element (3). See the note for Element (2) under "Misdemeanor Possession of Stolen Goods," just above.

Element (4). This is equivalent to felonious intent (316 N.C. 295; 111 N.C. App. 340). See the note for Element (3) under "Misdemeanor Possession of Stolen Goods," just above.

Possessing stolen vehicle. Possessing a stolen vehicle, like possessing any other stolen personal property, may be charged as a felony if the vehicle is worth more than $1,000 or is taken from the person or taken pursuant to burglary or breaking and entering; otherwise it is charged as a misdemeanor. Regardless of the vehicle's value, the defendant may also be charged with possession of stolen vehicle.

Possessing stolen dogs, horses, mules, swine, or cattle. Possessing stolen dogs, horses, mules, swine, or cattle is a felony regardless of their value because the larceny of these animals is a felony regardless of their value. See G.S. 14-81 and 14-71.1.

Proof of motor vehicle ownership. See the note on this topic under "Misdemeanor Larceny."

Forfeiture of vehicles. All conveyances—including vehicles, boats, or airplanes—used to unlawfully conceal, convey, or transport property as part of a felony violation of G.S. 14-71 (receiving stolen goods), G.S. 14-71.1 (possessing stolen goods), or G.S. 20-106 (possessing, receiving, or transferring stolen vehicles) may be seized and forfeited pursuant to the provisions of G.S. 14-86.1.

Possessing stolen lost property. See the note concerning "Larceny of lost property" under "Misdemeanor Larceny."

Lesser-included offenses. Misdemeanor possession of stolen goods is a lesser-included offense of felonious possession of stolen goods.

Limited civil liability for merchant or law enforcement officer. See the note on this topic under "Shoplifting—Concealing Merchandise," below.

Merchant required to make reasonable effort to notify parent of detained minor. See the note on this topic under "Shoplifting—Concealing Merchandise," below.

Related offenses not in this chapter

See the related offenses listed under "Misdemeanor Possession of Stolen Goods."

Receiving Stolen Goods—Misdemeanor

Statute

See G.S. 14-72(a), reproduced under "Misdemeanor Larceny."

§14-71. Receiving stolen goods.

If any person shall receive any chattel, property, money, valuable security or other thing whatsoever, the stealing or taking whereof amounts to larceny or a felony, either at common law or by virtue of any statute made or hereafter to be made, such person knowing or having reasonable grounds to believe the same to have been feloniously stolen or taken, he shall be guilty of a Class H felony, and may be indicted and convicted, whether the felon stealing and taking such chattels, property, money, valuable security or other thing, shall or shall not have been previously convicted, or shall or shall not be amenable to justice; and any such receiver may be dealt with, indicted, tried and punished in any county in which he shall have, or shall have had, any such property in his possession or in any county in which the thief may be tried, in the same manner as such receiver may be dealt with, indicted, tried and punished in the county where he actually received such chattel, money, security, or other thing; and such receiver shall be punished as one convicted of larceny.

Elements

A person guilty of this offense
(1) receives or conceals property
(2) stolen by another
(3) knowing, or with reasonable grounds to believe, that it was stolen, *and*
(4) with a dishonest purpose.

Punishment

Class 1 misdemeanor.

Notes

Misdemeanor possession of stolen goods is a preferable charge. Misdemeanor possession of stolen goods usually will be a preferable charge to misdemeanor receiving stolen goods because "possession" is likely easier to prove than "receiving." Also, for misdemeanor possession of stolen goods, it is not necessary to prove that someone other than the defendant stole the property as long as circumstances would have led a reasonable person to believe it was stolen (305 N.C. 225).

Element (1). To commit this offense, the receiver need not be taking the property for his or her own benefit; the receiver violates this statute by taking the property to help the thief (69 N.C. 29). Property may be constructively received to satisfy this element; that is, it is sufficient that property be delivered to his or her control, rather than into his or her physical possession (234 N.C. 42; 95 N.C. 626; 14 N.C. App. 120). The doctrine of possession of recently stolen property (see the note under "Misdemeanor Larceny") does not apply to receiving (202 N.C. 9; 227 N.C. 585).

Element (2). The property must have been obtained by "stealing or taking [that] amounts to larceny or a felony" [G.S. 14-71]. Also, a criminal pleading must specifically allege whether the property received was obtained by larceny or taken in violation of another felony statute, such as G.S. 14-74 (larceny by employee) or G.S. 14-90 (embezzlement) (34 N.C. App. 336). The property must be stolen by "another." A person may not be convicted of receiving the property if he or she is the one who stole it (247 N.C. 539); the jury must be instructed on this element (38 N.C. App. 209).

Element (3). This element is satisfied if the person has actual knowledge that the property was stolen, or if the circumstances of receiving it were sufficient to lead him or her to believe that it was stolen (208 N.C. 456), or if the person had "reasonable grounds to believe" that it was stolen (that is, the person should have known it was stolen) (304 N.C. 471; 307 N.C. 1; 316 N.C. 295; 45 N.C. App. 417).

Element (4). See the note for Element (3) under "Misdemeanor Possession of Stolen Goods."

Relationship to larceny and possession of stolen goods. A person may be charged with larceny, receiving, and possession of the same property, but may be convicted of only one of those offenses (302 N.C. 370; 305 N.C. 225; 47 N.C. App. 303). Possession is not a lesser-included offense of receiving (302 N.C. 370).

Attempt. See the discussion under "Attempt" in Chapter 4, "General Crimes." For the offense to constitute an attempt to receive stolen property, the defendant must have committed some overt act with the intent to complete the offense, at the same time knowing or believing that the property was stolen. Attempted receiving is a Class 2 misdemeanor pursuant to G.S. 14-2.5. When the police recovered stolen silver and later a police undercover agent offered to sell the silver to the defendant, telling him that it had been stolen, and the defendant bought it, the receiving was not completed because the silver ceased to be "stolen" once it had been recovered by the police, but the defendant was guilty of attempted receiving (307 N.C. 1).

Receiving stolen lost property. See the note concerning "Larceny of lost property" under "Misdemeanor Larceny."

Limited civil liability for merchant or law enforcement officer. See the note on this topic under "Shoplifting—Concealing Merchandise," below.

Merchant required to make reasonable effort to notify parent of detained minor. See the note on this topic under "Shoplifting—Concealing Merchandise," below.

Related offenses not in this chapter

See the offenses listed under "Misdemeanor Larceny."
"Accessory after the Fact to Felony" (Chapter 4)

Receipt of goods and services fraudulently obtained (G.S. 14-113.15)
Failure to follow pawnbroker requirements (G.S. 91A-11)

Receiving Stolen Goods—Felony

Statute

See G.S. 14-71, reproduced under "Receiving Stolen Goods—Misdemeanor," and G.S. 14-72, reproduced under "Misdemeanor Larceny."

Elements

A person guilty of this offense
- (1) receives or conceals property
- (2) stolen by another
- (3) when that larceny by another was
  - (a) of property worth more than $1,000, *or*
  - (b) from the person, *or*
  - (c) pursuant to burglary, or breaking out of a dwelling, or breaking or entering a building, or burglary by explosives, *or*
  - (d) of an explosive or incendiary device, *or*
  - (e) of a firearm, *or*
  - (f) of a record or paper in the custody of the North Carolina State Archives
- (4) knowing, or with reasonable grounds to believe, that the property was stolen in that manner
- (5) and with a dishonest purpose.

Punishment

Class H felony.

Notes

Felonious possession of stolen goods is a preferable charge. Felonious possession of stolen goods usually will be a preferable charge to felonious receiving stolen goods because "possession" is likely easier to prove than "receiving." Also, for felonious possession of stolen goods, it is not necessary to prove that someone other than the defendant stole the property as long as circumstances would have led a reasonable person to believe it was stolen (305 N.C. 225).

Elements (1) and (2). See the discussion of these same elements under "Receiving Stolen Goods—Misdemeanor."

Element (3) generally. Sub-elements (a) through (f) are identical to sub-elements (a) through (f) of Element (6) of "Felonious Larceny," earlier in this chapter. See the discussion of those elements under that offense for further explanation. Thus the characteristics that distinguish misdemeanor and felonious larceny also distinguish misdemeanor and felonious receipt of stolen goods.

Element (4). See the discussion of Element (3) under "Receiving Stolen Goods—Misdemeanor."

Element (5). See the discussion of Element (4) under "Felonious Possession of Stolen Goods."

Receiving stolen vehicles. Receiving a stolen vehicle, like receiving any other stolen personal property, may be charged as a felony if the vehicle is worth more than $1,000 or is taken from the person or taken pursuant to burglary or breaking and entering; otherwise it is charged as a misdemeanor. Regardless of the vehicle's value, the defendant may also be charged with the felonies of receiving stolen vehicle and possession of stolen vehicle.

Receiving stolen dogs, horses, mules, swine, or cattle. Receiving stolen dogs, horses, mules, swine, or cattle is a felony regardless of their value because the larceny of these animals is a felony regardless of their value. See G.S. 14-81 and 14-71.

Proof of motor vehicle ownership. See the note on "Proof of motor vehicle ownership" under "Misdemeanor Larceny."

Forfeiture of vehicles. See the note on this topic under "Felonious Possession of Stolen Goods."

Attempt. See the note on "Attempt" under "Receiving Stolen Goods—Misdemeanor."

Receiving stolen lost property. See the note concerning "Larceny of lost property" under "Misdemeanor Larceny."

Lesser-included offenses. Receiving stolen goods—misdemeanor is a lesser-included offense of this offense.

Limited civil liability for merchant or law enforcement officer. See the note on this topic under "Shoplifting—Concealing Merchandise," below.

Merchant required to make reasonable effort to notify parent of detained minor. See the note on this topic under "Shoplifting—Concealing Merchandise."

Related offenses not in this chapter

See the offenses listed under "Receiving Stolen Goods—Misdemeanor."
"Accessory after the Fact to Felony" (Chapter 4)

Possession of Stolen Vehicle

Statute

§20-106. Receiving or transferring stolen vehicles.

Any person who, with intent to procure or pass title to a vehicle which he knows or has reason to believe has been stolen or unlawfully taken, receives or transfers possession of the same from or to another, or who has in his possession any vehicle which he knows or has reason to believe has been stolen or unlawfully taken, and who is not an officer of the law engaged at the time in the performance of his duty as such officer shall be punished as a Class H felon.

Elements

A person guilty of this offense
(1) possesses
(2) a vehicle
(3) that he or she knows, or has reason to believe, was stolen or unlawfully taken.

Punishment

Class H felony.

Notes

Element (1). To "have in one's possession" is not the same as to "receive." One who steals a vehicle and keeps it cannot be charged with receiving the stolen vehicle (247 N.C. 539), but the person can be charged with possessing it knowing it to be stolen.

Element (2). G.S. 20-4.01(49) defines "vehicle" to include "every device in, upon, or by which any person or property is or may be transported or drawn upon a highway, excepting devices moved by human power or used exclusively upon fixed rails or tracks; provided, that for the purposes of this Chapter bicycles shall be deemed vehicles. . . ." Thus it would be possible to charge a person who possesses a stolen bicycle received from the thief with the felony of possession of a stolen vehicle, although a more common practice is to charge the misdemeanor of receiving stolen goods if the bicycle is not worth more than $1,000 and was not stolen from the person or pursuant to burglary or breaking or entering (see "Receiving Stolen Goods—Misdemeanor"). The same is true of charging one who possesses a motor vehicle that he received from the thief when the motor vehicle is not worth more than $1,000 and was not stolen from the person or pursuant to burglary or breaking or entering. If a car is stolen and then disassembled, possession of the parts does not constitute possession of a stolen vehicle under this statute; rather, it constitutes possession of stolen goods under G.S. 14-71.1 (70 N.C. App. 555).

Element (3). See the note on Element (3) under "Receiving Stolen Goods—Misdemeanor."

Doctrine of possession of recently stolen property. See the note with this title under "Misdemeanor Larceny." The doctrine of possession of recently stolen property may provide a sufficient basis for concluding that a defendant who possesses a vehicle that has been recently stolen knows that the vehicle was stolen unless, of course, there are circumstances tending to show that the person could have obtained the vehicle innocently (39 N.C. App. 163).

Law enforcement officers exempted. It is not necessary for the state to prove that the defendant was not "an officer of the law engaged at the time in performing his duty," because that provision of the statute is intended as an exemption to protect law enforcement officers and is not an element of the offense (39 N.C. App. 163).

Alternate charge. See the note on "Possessing stolen vehicle" under "Felonious Possession of Stolen Goods."

Proof of motor vehicle ownership. See the note concerning "Proof of motor vehicle ownership" under "Misdemeanor Larceny."

Forfeiture of vehicles. See the note on this topic under "Felonious Possession of Stolen Goods."

Related offenses not in this chapter

None.

Receiving Stolen Vehicle

Statute

See G.S. 20-106, reproduced under "Possession of Stolen Vehicle."

Elements

A person guilty of this offense
(1) receives from another
(2) a vehicle
(3) that he or she knows, or has reason to believe, was stolen or unlawfully taken
(4) with intent to procure or pass title to the vehicle.

Punishment

Class H felony.

Notes

Generally. Possession of stolen vehicle usually will be a preferable charge to this one because "possession" is likely easier to prove than "receiving."

Elements (1) and (3). See the notes on Elements (1) and (3) under "Receiving Stolen Goods—Misdemeanor."

Element (2). See the note on Element (2) under "Possession of Stolen Vehicle."

Element (4). This element makes this offense slightly different from receiving stolen goods; if someone receives stolen goods to help the thief, without intending to procure title (i.e., legal ownership) of them, that person commits the offense of receiving stolen goods. To have committed this offense, the defendant must have received the stolen vehicle intending to procure title or pass title to someone else.

Law enforcement officers exempted. See the note on this topic under "Possession of Stolen Vehicle."

Alternate charge. Receiving stolen goods may also be charged. See the note on "receiving stolen vehicles" under "Receiving Stolen Goods—Felony."

Proof of motor vehicle ownership. See "Proof of motor vehicle ownership" under "Misdemeanor Larceny."

Forfeiture of vehicles. See the note on this topic under "Felonious Possession of Stolen Goods."

Related offenses not in this chapter

None.

Transferring Stolen Vehicle

Statute

See G.S. 20-106, reproduced under "Possession of Stolen Vehicle."

Elements

A person guilty of this offense
 (1) transfers possession
 (2) of a vehicle
 (3) that the person knows, or has reason to believe, was stolen or unlawfully taken
 (4) with intent to procure or pass title to the vehicle.

Punishment

Class H felony.

Notes

Element (1). To commit the offense the defendant must transfer (give or sell) the stolen vehicle to someone else.

Other elements. See the notes under "Receiving Stolen Vehicle."

Law enforcement officers exempted. See the note on this topic under "Possession of Stolen Vehicle."

Proof of motor vehicle ownership. See the note on this topic under "Misdemeanor Larceny."

Forfeiture of vehicles. See the note on this topic under "Felonious Possession of Stolen Goods."

Related offenses not in this chapter

None.

Shoplifting—Concealing Merchandise

Statute

§14-72.1. Concealment of merchandise in mercantile establishments.

(a) Whoever, without authority, willfully conceals the goods or merchandise of any store, not theretofore purchased by such person, while still upon the premises of such store, shall be guilty of a misdemeanor and, upon conviction, shall be punished as provided in subsection (e). Such goods or merchandise found concealed upon or about the person and which have not theretofore been purchased by such person shall be prima facie evidence of a willful concealment.

(b) Repealed by Session Laws 1985 (Regular Session, 1986), c. 841, s. 2.

(c) A merchant, or the merchant's agent or employee, or a peace officer who detains or causes the arrest of any person shall not be held civilly liable for detention, malicious prosecution, false imprisonment, or false arrest of the person detained or arrested, where such detention is upon the premises of the store or in a reasonable proximity thereto, is in a reasonable manner for a reasonable length of time, and, if in detaining or in causing the arrest of such person, the merchant, or the merchant's agent or employee, or the peace officer had at the time of the detention or arrest probable cause to believe that the person committed the offense created by this section. If the person being detained by the merchant, or the merchant's agent or employee, is a minor under the age of 18 years, the merchant or the merchant's agent or employee, shall call or notify, or make a reasonable effort to call or notify the parent or guardian of the minor, during the period of detention. A merchant, or the merchant's agent or employee, who makes a reasonable effort to call or notify the parent or guardian of the minor shall not be held civilly liable for failing to notify the parent or guardian of the minor.

(d) Whoever, without authority, willfully transfers any price tag from goods or merchandise to other goods or merchandise having a higher selling price or marks said goods at a lower price or substitutes or superimposes thereon a false price tag and then presents said goods or merchandise for purchase shall be guilty of a misdemeanor and, upon conviction, shall be punished as provided in subsection (e).

Nothing herein shall be construed to provide that the mere possession of goods or the production by shoppers of improperly priced merchandise for checkout shall constitute prima facie evidence of guilt.

(d1) Notwithstanding subsection (e) of this section, any person who violates subsection (a) of this section by using a lead-lined or aluminum-lined bag, a lead-lined or aluminum-lined article of clothing, or a similar device to prevent the activation of any antishoplifting or inventory control device is guilty of a Class H felony.

(e) Punishment.—For a first conviction under subsection (a) or (d), or for a subsequent conviction for which the punishment is not specified by this subsection, the defendant shall be guilty of a Class 3 misdemeanor. The term of imprisonment may be suspended only on condition that the defendant perform community service for a term of at least 24 hours. For a second offense committed within three years after the date the defendant was convicted of an offense under this section, the defendant shall be guilty of a Class 2 misdemeanor. The term of imprisonment may be suspended only on condition that the defendant be imprisoned for a term of at least 72 hours as a condition of special probation, perform community service for a term of at least 72 hours, or both. For a third or subsequent offense committed within five years after the date the defendant was convicted of two other offenses under this section, the defendant shall be guilty of a Class 1 misdemeanor. The term of imprisonment may be suspended only if a condition of special probation is imposed to require the defendant to serve a term of imprisonment of at least 11 days. However, if the sentencing judge finds that the defendant is unable, by reason of mental or physical infirmity, to perform the service required under this section, and the reasons for such findings are set forth in the judgment, the judge may pronounce such other sentence as the judge finds appropriate.

(f) Community Service Period.—If the judgment requires a defendant sentenced under this section to perform a specified number of hours of community service, the community service must be completed within:

(1) 90 days, if the amount of community service required is 72 hours or more;
(2) 60 days, if the amount of community service required is at least 48 hours but less than 72 hours; and
(3) 30 days, if the amount of community service required is at least 24 hours but less than 48 hours.

The court may extend these time limits upon motion of the defendant if it finds that the defendant has made a good faith effort to comply with the time limits specified in this subsection. Failure to complete the community service requirement within the applicable time limits is a violation of the defendant's probation.

(g) Limitations.—For active terms of imprisonment imposed under this section:

(1) The judge may not give credit to the defendant for the first 24 hours of time spent in incarceration pending trial;
(2) The defendant must serve the mandatory minimum period of imprisonment and good or gain time credit may not be used to reduce that mandatory minimum period; and
(3) The defendant may not be released or paroled unless he is otherwise eligible and has served the mandatory minimum period of imprisonment.

Elements

A person guilty of this offense

(1) willfully conceals goods or merchandise of a store
(2) without authority
(3) without having purchased the goods or merchandise
(4) while still on the premises of the store.

Punishment

The first offense of this statute is a Class 3 misdemeanor. G.S. 14-72.1(e) provides that the term of imprisonment may be suspended only on condition that the defendant perform community service for a term of at least 24 hours. If the judge finds that the defendant is unable to perform community service because of a mental or physical infirmity, the judge may impose such other sentence as he or she finds appropriate, provided the judge sets out reasons for this finding in the judgment. G.S. 14-72.1(g) contains additional limitations on terms of active imprisonment, but it is unclear how those limitations should be applied in light of structured sentencing.

A second offense, within three years of conviction of a first offense, is a Class 2 misdemeanor. G.S. 14-72.1(e) provides that the term of imprisonment may be suspended only on condition that the defendant be imprisoned for at least 72 hours as a condition of special probation, perform community service for at least 72 hours, or both. If the judge finds that the defendant is unable to perform community service because of a mental or physical infirmity, the judge may impose such other sentence as he or she finds appropriate, provided the judge sets out reasons for this finding in the judgment. G.S. 14-72.1(g) contains additional limitations on terms of active imprisonment, but it is unclear how those limitations should be applied in light of structured sentencing.

A third or subsequent offense of this statute within five years of two prior convictions for the same offense is a Class 1 misdemeanor. G.S. 14-72.1(e) provides that the term of imprisonment may be suspended only if one condition of special probation is that the defendant serve a term of imprisonment of at least 11 days. G.S. 14-72.1(g) contains additional limitations on terms of active imprisonment, but it is unclear how those limitations should be applied in light of structured sentencing.

A subsequent offense not falling into either of the above two categories, based on timing of offense, is a Class 3 misdemeanor. The same limits on active imprisonment apply as with a first offense of this statute.

Statutory subsection (d) (see text above) makes a violation of subsection (a) (concealment of goods or merchandise) a Class H felony if a person uses a lead-lined or aluminum-lined bag, a lead-lined or aluminum-lined article of clothing, or a similar device to prevent the activation of an anti-shoplifting or inventory control device.

Notes

Element (1). To convict a person of this offense, it need not be proven that he or she intended to remove the property from the premises (256 N.C. 27). This offense, unlike larceny, does not require proof of the intent to deprive the owner of possession of the property permanently (256 N.C. 27). The concealment is willful when it is done on purpose (256 N.C. 27). This statute applies only when the goods or merchandise are from a store and not when they are from some other kind of premises, such as a residence (18 N.C. App. 652). The statute provides that finding goods concealed on a person is prima facie evidence that the person concealed them willfully [G.S. 14-72.1(a)].

Element (2). If the person has been authorized to conceal the merchandise, the offense has not been committed.

Element (3). Once the person has purchased the goods, he or she may conceal them without committing the offense.

Element (4). If the concealment occurs off the store's premises, this offense has not been committed, even if the goods have not been purchased.

Comparison with "Misdemeanor Larceny" (see the discussion at the beginning of this chapter). Larceny, unlike shoplifting, requires proof that the person intended to permanently deprive the owner (or other lawful possessor) of possession of the property. Shoplifting, unlike larceny, requires proof that the property was willfully concealed on the store's premises. Although it is legally possible to charge a person with larceny who has been stopped in a store's premises with willfully concealed goods, the difficulty of proving the element of intent to permanently deprive under such circumstances makes concealing merchandise the better charge. On the other hand, a person who has willfully concealed goods on a store's premises and then left the store before being stopped is normally charged with larceny because the element of the intent to permanently deprive is readily provable, and larceny is the more serious offense (misdemeanor larceny is a Class 1 misdemeanor, and the first offense of concealing merchandise is a Class 3 misdemeanor). It is unclear whether a person may be convicted and punished for both larceny and concealing merchandise based on the same incident.

Felony if person uses lead-lined or aluminum-lined bag or similar item to commit offense. Statutory subsection (d) (see text above) makes a violation of subsection (a) (concealment of goods or merchandise) a Class H felony if a person uses a lead-lined or aluminum-lined bag, a lead-lined or aluminum-lined article of clothing, or a similar device to prevent the activation of an anti-shoplifting or inventory control device. If evidence of this felony exists, the criminal pleading must allege the appropriate language and the state must offer and prove such evidence as an element of the offense at trial.

Limited civil liability for merchant or law enforcement officer. The statute limits the liability of merchants and law enforcement officers who detain or cause the arrest of a person for this offense. They may not be held civilly liable for detention, malicious prosecution, false imprisonment, or false arrest of the person detained or arrested, when (1) in detaining or in causing the arrest of the person, the merchant, the merchant's agent or employee, or the law enforcement officer had probable cause to believe that the person committed this offense (116 N.C. App. 676); (2) the detention is on store premises or in "a reasonable proximity thereto"; and (3) the detention is determined to have been in a reasonable manner for a reasonable length of time. This provision, by itself, does not give merchants or law enforcement officers authority to conduct "pat down" searches of customers without their consent; thus it does not protect them from civil liability for an alleged assault and battery arising from such a search (115 N.C. App. 680).

Merchant required to make reasonable effort to notify parent of detained minor. According to the statute, if a person detained by a merchant, or the merchant's agent or employee, is a minor under the age of 18 years, the merchant, or the merchant's agent or employee, shall call or notify, or make a reasonable effort to call or notify the parent or guardian of the minor during the period of detention. A merchant, or the merchant's agent or employee, who makes a reasonable effort to call or notify the parent or guardian of the minor shall not be held civilly liable for failing to notify the parent or guardian of the minor.

Related offenses not in this chapter

"Obtaining Property by False Pretenses" (Chapter 14)

Shoplifting—Substitution of Price

Statute

See G.S. 14-72.1, reproduced immediately above.

Elements

A person guilty of this offense
- (1) (a) willfully transfers a price tag from goods or merchandise to other goods or merchandise having a higher selling price, *or*
  - (b) willfully marks goods or merchandise at a lower price, *or*
  - (c) willfully places a false price tag on goods or merchandise
- (2) without authority, *and*
- (3) then presents the goods for purchase.

Punishment

The first offense of this statute is a Class 3 misdemeanor. G.S. 14-72.1(e) provides that the term of imprisonment may be suspended only on condition that the defendant perform community service for a term of at least 24 hours. If the judge finds that the defendant is unable to perform community service because of a mental or physical infirmity, the judge may impose such other sentence as he or she finds appropriate, provided the judge sets out reasons for this finding in the judgment. G.S. 14-72.1(g) contains additional limitations on terms of active imprisonment, but it is unclear how those limitations should be applied in light of structured sentencing.

A second offense within three years of conviction of a first offense is a Class 2 misdemeanor. G.S. 14-72.1(e) provides that the term of imprisonment may be suspended only on condition that the defendant be imprisoned for at least 72 hours as a condition of special probation, perform community service for at least 72 hours, or both. If the judge finds that the defendant is unable to perform community service because of a mental or physical infirmity, the judge may impose such other sentence as he or she finds appropriate, provided the judge sets out reasons for this finding in the judgment. G.S. 14-72.1(g) contains additional limitations on terms of active imprisonment, but it is unclear how those limitations should be applied in light of structured sentencing.

A third or subsequent offense of this statute within five years of two prior convictions for the same offense is a Class 1 misdemeanor. G.S. 14-72.1(e) provides that the term of imprisonment may be suspended only if one condition of special probation is that the defendant serve a term of imprisonment of at least 11 days. G.S. 14-72.1(g) contains additional limitations on terms of active imprisonment, but it is unclear how those limitations should be applied in light of structured sentencing.

A subsequent offense not falling into either of the above two categories, based on timing of offense, is a Class 3 misdemeanor. The same limits on active imprisonment apply as with a first offense of this statute.

Notes

Element (2). If the person has been authorized to alter the price, then no offense has occurred.

Element (3). No offense occurs unless the person, in addition to altering the price, also presents the goods for purchase.

Limited civil liability for merchant or law enforcement officer. See the note on this topic under "Shoplifting—Concealing Merchandise."

Merchant required to make reasonable effort to notify parent of detained minor. See the note on this topic under "Shoplifting—Concealing Merchandise."

Related offenses not in this chapter

"Obtaining Property by False Pretenses" (Chapter 14).

Financial Transaction Card Theft

Statute

§14-113.9. Financial transaction card theft.

(a) A person is guilty of financial transaction card theft when:

(1) He takes, obtains or withholds a financial transaction card from the person, possession, custody or control of another without the cardholder's consent and with the intent to use it; or who, with knowledge that it has been so taken, obtained or withheld, receives the financial transaction card with intent to use it or to sell it, or to transfer it to a person other than the issuer or the cardholder; or

(2) He receives a financial transaction card that he knows to have been lost, mislaid, or delivered under a mistake as to the identity or address of the cardholder, and who retains possession with intent to use it or to sell it or to transfer it to a person other than the issuer or the cardholder; or

(3) He, not being the issuer, sells a financial transaction card or buys a financial transaction card from a person other than the issuer; or

(4) He, not being the issuer, during any 12-month period, receives financial transaction cards issued in the names of two or more persons which he has reason to know were taken or retained under circumstances which constitute a violation of G.S. 14-113.13(a)(3) and subdivision (3) of subsection (a) of this section.

(b) Credit card theft is punishable as provided by G.S. 14-113.17(b).

I. Taking or Withholding Card

Statute

See G.S. 14-113.9(a)(1), reproduced immediately above.

Elements

A person guilty of this offense

(1) takes or obtains or withholds a financial transaction card
(2) from another
(3) without the cardholder's consent, *and*
(4) with the intent to use it.

Punishment

Class I felony.

Notes

Element (1). A "financial transaction card" is a credit card, bank service card, bank card, check guarantee card, debit card, or any other card that allows the cardholder to obtain goods, services, or money on credit; to guarantee a check to the person accepting it; or to deposit, withdraw, or transfer funds from an account. It does not include credit cards for telephone calls [G.S. 14-113.8(4)] (the use of a false or counterfeit telephone credit card and the unauthorized use of a telephone credit card are prohibited by G.S. 14-113.1). Even when the cardholder has consented to the loan of the financial transaction card, this offense can occur if the defendant does not return the card.

Element (3). G.S. 14-113.8(2) defines "cardholder" as "the person or organization named on the face of a financial transaction card to whom or for whose benefit the financial transaction card is issued by an issuer."

Element (4). Notice that conviction for this offense requires proof that the defendant intended to use the financial transaction card. However, it need not be established that he or she actually used the card. A defendant's intent, not always clear, may be shown by conduct, statements, and other circumstances.

Prima facie evidence. G.S. 14-113.10 provides that it is prima facie evidence of this or any other form of financial transaction card theft that "a person has in his possession or under his control financial transaction cards issued in the names of two or more other persons other than members of his immediate family." The jury must be instructed on the prima facie evidence rule if the evidence tends to establish the requirements of G.S. 14-113.10 (283 N.C. 627).

II.
Receiving Wrongfully Obtained Card

Statute

See G.S. 14-113.9(a)(1), reproduced at the beginning of this section.

Elements

A person guilty of this offense
- (1) receives a financial transaction card
- (2) intending to use it, to sell it, or to transfer it to a person other than the issuer or cardholder, *and*
- (3) knowing that it was taken, obtained, or withheld in violation of "I. Taking or Withholding Card," above.

Punishment

Class I felony.

Notes

Element (1). G.S. 14-113.8(8) defines "receives" as "acquiring possession or control or accepting a financial transaction card as security for a loan." For the definition of "financial transaction card," see the note on Element (1) under "I. Taking or Withholding Card," above.

Element (2). G.S. 14-113.8(5) defines "issuer" as "the business organization or financial institution or its duly authorized agent which issues a financial transaction card." For the definition of "cardholder," see the note on Element (3) under "I. Taking or Withholding Card," above.

Element (3). The defendant must know that the financial transaction card was taken, obtained, or withheld from the person, possession, custody, or control of another without the cardholder's consent and with the intent to use it (51 N.C. App. 413).

Prima facie evidence. See the note on this subject under "I. Taking or Withholding Card," above.

III. Wrongful Retention of Misplaced Card

Statute

See G.S. 14-113.9(a)(2), reproduced at the beginning of this section.

Elements

A person guilty of this offense

(1) receives a financial transaction card
(2) that he or she knows to have been lost, mislaid, or delivered under a mistake as to the identity or address of the cardholder, *and*
(3) (a) retains possession intending to use it or sell it, *or*
 (b) retains possession intending to transfer it to a person other than the issuer or the cardholder.

Punishment

Class I felony.

Notes

Element (1). See the note on Element (1) under "I. Taking or Withholding Card," above.

Element (2). This offense applies to situations in which a person finds a lost financial transaction card or one is delivered to a person by mistake.

Element (3). Note that this element is not satisfied if the person merely retains the card; the person must also intend to use it, sell it, or transfer it. For definitions of "issuer" and "cardholder," see the notes on Element (2) under "II. Receiving Wrongfully Obtained Card," above, and on Element (3) under "I. Taking or Withholding Card," above.

Prima facie evidence. See the note on this subject under "I. Taking or Withholding Card," above.

IV. Buying Card

Statute

See G.S. 14-113.9(a)(3), reproduced at the beginning of this section.

Elements

A person guilty of this offense

(1) is not the issuer, *and*
(2) buys a financial transaction card
(3) from a person other than the issuer.

Punishment

Class I felony.

Notes

Elements (1) and (3). For a definition of "issuer," see the note on Element (2) under "II. Receiving Wrongfully Obtained Card," above.

Element (2). "Financial transaction card" is defined in the note on Element (1) under "I. Taking or Withholding Card," above.

Prima facie evidence. See the note on this subject under "I. Taking or Withholding Card," above.

V. Selling Card

Statute

See G.S. 14-113.9(a)(3), reproduced at the beginning of this section.

Elements

A person guilty of this offense
- (1) is not the issuer, *and*
- (2) sells a financial transaction card.

Punishment

Class I felony.

Notes

Element (1). For a definition of "issuer," see the note on Element (2) under "II. Receiving Wrongfully Obtained Card," above.

Element (2). "Financial transaction card" is defined in the note on Element (1) under "I. Taking or Withholding Card," above.

Prima facie evidence. See the note with this title under "I. Taking or Withholding Card," above.

VI. Receiving Two Cards Issued to Different Names

Statute

See G.S. 14-113.9(a)(4), reproduced at the beginning of this section.

Elements

A person guilty of this offense
- (1) is not the issuer, *and*
- (2) receives during a 12-month period
- (3) financial transaction cards issued in the names of two or more persons
- (4) which he or she has reason to know were taken or retained in violation of laws prohibiting buying financial transaction cards or fraudulently taking financial transaction cards as security for debt.

Punishment

Class I felony.

Notes

Element (1). For a definition of "issuer," see the note on Element (2) under "II. Receiving Wrongfully Obtained Card," above.

Element (2). Note that this element is satisfied if the second card is received within 12 months of the first, even if the two are received in different calendar years. Note also that mere possession within the 12 months is insufficient to establish a violation; both cards must be received during that period.

Element (3). One of the financial transaction cards must be issued to a name different from that to which the others were issued.

Element (4). For the law prohibiting buying financial transaction cards, see "IV. Buying Card," above. For the law prohibiting fraudulently taking financial transaction cards as security for a debt, see "V. Obtaining Card as Security for Debt," under "Financial Transaction Card Fraud" (Chapter 14).

Prima facie evidence. See the note with this title under "I. Taking or Withholding Card," above.

Related offenses not in this chapter

"Financial Transaction Card Forgery" (Chapter 14)
"Financial Transaction Card Fraud" (Chapter 14)
Possession of financial transaction card forgery devices (G.S. 14-113.14)
Receipt of goods and services fraudulently obtained (G.S. 14-113.15)

Larceny by Employee

Statute

§14-74. Larceny by servants and other employees.

If any servant or other employee, to whom any money, goods or other chattels, or any of the articles, securities or choses in action mentioned in G.S. 14-75, by his master shall be delivered safely to be kept to the use of his master, shall withdraw himself from his master and go away with such money, goods or other chattels, or any of the articles, securities or choses in action mentioned as aforesaid, or any part thereof, with intent to steal the same and defraud his master thereof, contrary to the trust and confidence in him reposed by his said master; or if any servant, being in the service of his master, without the assent of his master, shall embezzle such money, goods or other chattels, or any of the articles, securities or choses in action mentioned as aforesaid, or any part thereof, or otherwise convert the same to his own use, with like purpose to steal them, or to defraud his master thereof, the servant so offending shall be guilty of a felony: Provided, that nothing contained in this section shall extend to apprentices or servants within the age of 16 years. If the value of the money, goods, or other chattels, or any of the articles, securities, or choses in action mentioned in G.S. 14-75, is one hundred thousand dollars ($100,000) or more, the person is guilty of a Class C felony. If the value of the money, goods, or other chattels, or any of the articles, securities, or choses in action mentioned in G.S. 14-75, is less than one hundred thousand dollars ($100,000), the person is guilty of a Class H felony.

Elements

A person guilty of this offense
- (1) is an employee, *and*
- (2) (a) willfully goes away with a thing of value, *or*
  - (b) willfully embezzles or converts to his or her own use a thing of value
- (3) entrusted with the employee
- (4) with the intent to steal it and defraud the employer.

Punishment

Class H felony. It is a Class C felony if the value of the property taken is $100,000 or more.

Notes

Element (1). This offense may not be charged if the employee is under 16 years old.

Element (2). The statute specifies that the thing taken can be "money, goods . . . chattels, or any of the articles, securities or choses in action mentioned . . . [in G.S. 14-75]." See the note on "Chose in action" under "Larceny of Chose in Action."

Element (3). This offense is not committed when the defendant initially obtains possession of the property without consent or by tricking the employer. Instead, larceny may be the proper charge.

Charging this offense and comparison with common-law larceny. The title of this offense is misleading because it is not an appropriate charge when the facts show that a common-law larceny was committed (34 N.C. App. 336; 34 N.C. App. 589; 101 N.C. 730; 42 N.C. App. 577; 43 N.C. App. 556; 56 N.C. App. 228). Common-law larceny requires a taking from another's lawful possession (42 N.C. App. 577), whereas larceny by employee requires that an employee have lawful possession and then wrongfully take the property. This offense is similar to embezzlement (discussed later in this chapter) because it involves a taking of property in violation of a trust relationship between an employer and employee. Examples include a foreman of a tire store who takes tires from the store (34 N.C. App. 336); a service station attendant who takes money with which he was entrusted (34 N.C. App. 589); a drug store employee who was a section chief and took drugs from the store (257 N.C. 158); a manager of a clothing store who took clothes (36 N.C. App. 332); and a foreman of a farm who took cattle (56 N.C. App. 228). On the other hand, a person hired by a grocery store to bag groceries and sweep up who takes food from the store commits common-law larceny, not embezzlement or larceny by employee, because the person was not entrusted with the food by his employer (42 N.C. App. 577).

Lesser-included offenses. Larceny is not a lesser-included offense of this offense (43 N.C. App. 556; 34 N.C. App. 589).

Charging issues. It is unnecessary to allege that the defendant was at least 16 years old at the time of the offense, because that fact is not an element of the offense (56 N.C. App. 228). Of course, the state may not prosecute this offense if the defendant is less than 16 years old.

Related offenses not in this chapter

"Obtaining Property by False Pretenses" (Chapter 14)

Embezzlement

Statute

§14-90. Embezzlement of property received by virtue of office or employment.

If any person exercising a public trust or holding a public office, or any guardian, administrator, executor, trustee, or any receiver, or any other fiduciary, or any officer or agent of a corporation, or any agent, consignee, clerk, bailee or servant, except persons under the age of 16 years, of any person, shall embezzle or fraudulently or knowingly and willfully misapply or convert to his own use, or shall take, make away with or secrete, with intent to embezzle or fraudulently or knowingly and willfully misapply or convert to his own use any money, goods or other chattels, bank note, check or order for the payment of money issued by or drawn on any bank or other corporation, or any treasury warrant, treasury note, bond or obligation for the payment of money issued by the United States or by any state, or any other valuable security whatsoever belonging to any other person or corporation, unincorporated association or organization which shall have come into his possession or under his care, he shall be guilty of a felony. If the value of the property is one hundred thousand dollars ($100,000) or more, the person is guilty of a Class C felony. If the value of the property is less than one hundred thousand dollars ($100,000), the person is guilty of a Class H felony.

Elements

A person guilty of this offense
- (1) fraudulently or knowingly and willingly
- (2) uses for a purpose other than that for which the defendant received it
- (3) the property of another
- (4) held by the defendant in a fiduciary capacity.

Punishment

Class H felony. It is a Class C felony if the value of the property embezzled is $100,000 or more.

Notes

Defendant must be 16 years old or older. This offense may not be charged if the defendent is under 16 years old.

Element (2). To commit this offense, the person entrusted with the property need not turn it to his or her own use (114 N.C. 842); the offense can occur if the person turns it to someone else's use. It also occurs if a person secretes the property with the intent to misapply it, even though the person never actually uses it (15 N.C. App. 427). Also, it is not a defense to a charge of embezzlement that the defendant intended and was willing to return the property later (294 N.C. 382).

Element (3). The property can include money and paper securities (G.S. 14-90) but does not include services. A business partner cannot be guilty under G.S. 14-90 of embezzlement of partnership funds; instead, the partner may be prosecuted for appropriating partnership funds to personal use, which violates G.S. 14-97 (81 N.C. App. 281).

Element (4). The statute applies only to one who exercises a public trust or holds a public office, a guardian, administrator, executor, trustee, receiver, fiduciary, officer, agent, consignee, clerk, bailee, or servant. For example, an attorney who forged a client's signature on a settlement check from an insurance agent for a car accident, and then cashed the check, was properly charged with embezzlement against his client. The lawyer-defendant lawfully came into possession of the check from the insurer and was entrusted with care of the check by his client (335 N.C. 509). Note: this defendant also may have been guilty of "Obtaining Property by False Pretenses" (Chapter 14) for his actions against the insurance company.

It is not appropriate to use an embezzlement charge against one who does not fall into one of these categories; a debtor, for example, does not embezzle by leaving town without paying a debt. To commit this offense, the defendant must have obtained the property by virtue of his or her position—the defendant must be entrusted with it (239 N.C. 41). An employee who takes property from a part of the store other than the part in which he or she works is guilty of larceny, not embezzlement, since the employee was not entrusted with that property (208 N.C. 661; 42 N.C. App. 577). Also, an employee who merely has access to his or her employer's property, but is not entrusted with it, commits larceny, not embezzlement, if the employee takes the property. Thus defendants who had access to an entire plant as a troubleshooting team (one was an electrician and the other a mechanic), but did not have authority over machinery components, were improperly convicted of embezzlement when they took machinery components—the proper charge was larceny. (64 N.C. App. 529).

Charging one or more embezzlements based on multiple takings. The state has the choice of charging one embezzlement or multiple embezzlements when a person is involved in a continuous course of conduct involving multiple takings of property (129 N.C. App. 506).

Distinction between embezzlement and malfeasance of a corporate agent. Although the offense of embezzlement and that of malfeasance of a corporate agent (G.S. 14-254) may arise from the same conduct, there are significant differences in the definitions of these two similar offenses: (a) to be convicted of embezzlement, a defendant must have received property in the course of employment while acting in a fiduciary capacity, whereas to be convicted of malfeasance (G.S. 14-254), a defendant need only have taken or misapplied any property of the corporation for which he or she is an agent; (b) to be guilty of embezzlement, a defendant must have intended to defraud his or her principal, whereas G.S. 14-254 covers intent to defraud any person; and (c) to be guilty of embezzlement, a defendant need not be an agent or fiduciary of a corporation, whereas G.S. 14-254 applies only to agents or fiduciaries of corporations (313 N.C. 1).

Comparison with larceny offenses (discussed above in this chapter) and "Obtaining Property by False Pretenses" (Chapter 14). As noted in the discussion of Element (4) above, to commit embezzlement a defendant must deprive an owner of property the defendant has been entrusted with. Neither larceny nor obtaining property by false pretenses have such a requirement. See the note on "Relationship to 'Larceny,' and 'Embezzlement'" under "Obtaining Property by False Pretenses" in Chapter 14 for a more detailed discussion of this issue.

Choosing criminal charges and instructing the jury. The state is not required to elect between embezzlement and false pretenses when there is substantial evidence tending to support both charges arising from the same transaction. When both charges are present in a single trial based on a single transaction, the trial court must instruct the jury that it may convict the defendant of only one offense or the other, not of both (326 N.C. 576). A defendant may not be convicted of obtaining property by false pretenses as a lesser-included offense of embezzlement (108 N.C. App. 550). See the note on this topic under "Obtaining Property by False Pretenses" in Chapter 14.

Related offenses not in this chapter

"Obtaining Property by False Pretenses" (Chapter 14)
Embezzlement by treasurer of charitable and religious organizations (G.S. 14-93)
Embezzlement by officers of railroad companies (G.S. 14-94)
Embezzlement by insurance agents and brokers (G.S. 58-2-162)
Appropriation of partnership funds by partner to personal use (G.S. 14-97)
Embezzlement by surviving partner (G.S. 14-98)
Embezzlement of taxes by officers (G.S. 14-99)
Failure to return hired property (G.S. 14-167)
Conversion by bailee (G.S. 14-168.1)
Malfeasance of corporation officers and agents (G.S. 14-254)
Misapplication of bank funds by officer or employee (G.S. 53-129)
Trust funds to be kept separate (G.S. 128-11)

Embezzlement of State Property by Public Officers and Employees

Statute

§14-91. Embezzlement of State property by public officers and employees.

If any officer, agent, or employee of the State, or other person having or holding in trust for the same any bonds issued by the State, or any security, or other property and effects of the same, shall embezzle or knowingly and willfully misapply or convert the same to his own use, or otherwise willfully or corruptly abuse such trust, such offender and all persons knowingly and willfully aiding and abetting or otherwise assisting therein shall be guilty of a felony. If the value of the property is one hundred thousand dollars ($100,000) or more, a violation of this section is a Class C felony. If the value of the property is less than one hundred thousand dollars ($100,000), a violation of this section is a Class F felony.

Elements

A person guilty of this offense
(1) knowingly and willfully
(2) misapplies or converts to his or her own use
(3) property of the state
(4) held in trust by the defendant.

Punishment

Class F felony. It is a Class C felony if the value of the property embezzled is $100,000 or more.

Notes

Element (2). This charge apparently requires no proof that the defendant deprived the owner of the property; it seems sufficient that the defendant either used the property for an improper purpose or converted it to his or her own use.

Element (3). The nature of the property is probably the same as that specified in G.S. 14-90. The property is "of the state" whenever it is in the possession of the state, even if it is not owned by the state.

Element (4). The property has to have come into the defendant's hands by virtue of his or her position. For example, a public employee who took a typewriter from a desk in another person's office at his or her place of work would not be guilty of this offense since the employee was never entrusted with the typewriter as a part of the employee's work.

A defendant's authority to hire school instructors as provided in the school's budget did not entrust him with the funds used to pay the instructors and therefore he did not commit this offense (91 N.C. App. 424). However, because the employee obtained the funds by a deceptive scheme, he probably committed the offense of "Obtaining Property by False Pretenses" (see Chapter 14).

Related offenses not in this chapter

See the related offenses listed under "Embezzlement."
"Welfare Fraud" (Chapter 14)
Private use of publicly owned vehicle (G.S. 14-247)
Obtaining repairs and supplies for private vehicle at state expense (G.S. 14-248)

Embezzlement by Public Officers and Trustees

Statute

§14-92. Embezzlement of funds by public officers and trustees.

If an officer, agent, or employee of an entity listed below, or a person having or holding money or property in trust for one of the listed entities, shall embezzle or otherwise willfully and corruptly use or misapply the same for any purpose other than that for which such moneys or property is held, such person shall be guilty of a felony. If the value of the money or property is one hundred thousand dollars ($100,000) or more, the person is guilty of a Class C felony. If the value of the money or property is less than one hundred thousand dollars ($100,000), the person is guilty of a Class F felony. If any clerk of the superior court or any sheriff, treasurer, register of deeds or other public officer of any county, unit or agency of local government, or local board of education shall embezzle or wrongfully convert to his own use, or corruptly use, or shall misapply for any purpose other than that for which the same are held, or shall fail to pay over and deliver to the proper persons entitled to receive the same when lawfully required so to do, any moneys, funds, securities or other property which such officer shall have received by virtue or color of his office in trust for any person or corporation, such officer shall be guilty of a felony. If the value of the money, funds, securities, or other property is one hundred thousand dollars ($100,000) or more, the person is guilty of a Class C felony. If the value of the money, funds, securities, or other property is less than one hundred thousand dollars ($100,000), the person is guilty of a Class F felony. The provisions of this section shall apply to all persons who shall go out of office and fail or neglect to account to or deliver over to their successors in office or other persons lawfully entitled to receive the same all such moneys, funds and securities or property aforesaid. The following entities are protected by this section: a county, a city or other unit or agency of local government, a local board of education, and a penal, charitable, religious, or educational institution.

Elements

I. Embezzlement by Officials of Local Government, Jail, Charitable, Religious, or Educational Institutions

A person guilty of this offense
(1) (a) embezzles, *or*

(b) (i) willfully and corruptly
(ii) uses or misapplies
(2) money or property
(3) of a county, a city or other unit or agency of local government, a local board of education, or a penal, charitable, religious, or educational institution
(4) held in trust by the defendant.

II. Embezzlement by Clerk of Superior Court, Sheriff, Register of Deeds, and Officials of Boards of Education and Local Government

A person guilty of this offense
(1) is a clerk of superior court, sheriff, treasurer, register of deeds, or other public officer of any county unit or agency of local government, or local board of education, *and*
(2) (a) embezzles, *or*
(b) wrongfully converts to his, *or* her own use, *or*
(c) corruptly uses, *or*
(d) misapplies, *or*
(e) fails to pay over and deliver to the proper person entitled to receive when lawfully required to do so
(3) money, funds, securities, or other property
(4) held in trust by the defendant.

Punishment

Class F felony. It is a Class C felony if the value of the property embezzled is $100,000 or more.

Notes

Generally. These offenses are similar to embezzlement and embezzlement of state property by public officers and employees, but they are specifically aimed at local government officials and officials of quasi-public organizations (churches, charitable organizations, etc.). This statute provides two offenses.

I. Embezzlement by officials of local government, jail, charitable, religious, or educational institutions encompasses embezzlement generally by local government and quasi-public officials. II. Embezzlement by clerk of superior court, sheriff, register of deeds, and officials of boards of education and local government, as the title indicates, forbids certain violations of trust by the named officials. These two offenses overlap to some extent.

Element (1) of "I. Embezzlement by Officials of Local Government, Jail, Charitable, Religious, or Educational Institutions" and Element (2) of "II. Embezzlement by Clerk of Superior Court, Sheriff, Register of Deeds, and Officials of Boards of Education and Local Government." The elements of each offense, despite their slight variation, basically mean to act unlawfully and fraudulently (294 N.C. 382; 33 N.C. App. 496). Generally, the basic criminal act in each of these offenses is the same as that described under "Embezzlement," and "Embezzlement of State Property by Public Officers and Employees," both described above in this chapter. See the notes about Element (2) under each of those offenses. The offense described in II., above, adds some behavior that might not be covered by embezzlement. That is, when one of the named officials fails to pay over and deliver property entrusted to that official to the proper person entitled to receive it when lawfully required to do so, this offense may be committed.

Element (2) of "I. Embezzlement by Officials of Local Government, Jail, Charitable, Religious, or Educational Institutions," and Elements (3) and

(4) under this offense and under II. See the discussion of similar elements under "Embezzlement," and "Embezzlement of State Property by Public Officers and Employees," but remember that these offenses apply to misappropriation of property from local governments and quasi-government organizations. A state official embezzling state property could not be prosecuted under this statute, nor could a fiduciary of a corporation embezzling from the corporation.

Related offenses not in this chapter

See the offenses listed under "Embezzlement" and "Embezzlement of State Property by Public Officers and Employees" in this chapter.

Altering or Removing Serial Number

Statute

§14-160.1. Alteration, destruction or removal of permanent identification marks from personal property.

(a) It shall be unlawful for any person to alter, deface, destroy or remove the permanent serial number, manufacturer's identification plate or other permanent, distinguishing number or identification mark from any item of personal property with the intent thereby to conceal or misrepresent the identity of said item.

(b) It shall be unlawful for any person knowingly to sell, buy or be in possession of any item of personal property, not his own, on which the permanent serial number, manufacturer's identification plate or other permanent, distinguishing number or identification mark has been altered, defaced, destroyed or removed for the purpose of concealing or misrepresenting the identity of said item.

(c) A violation of any of the provisions of this section shall be a Class 1 misdemeanor.

(d) This section shall not in any way affect the provisions of G.S. 20-108, 20-109(a) or 20-109(b).

Elements

A person guilty of this offense

(1) alters or defaces or destroys or removes
(2) the permanent serial number, manufacturer's identification plate, or other permanent distinguishing number or mark
(3) from any item of personal property
(4) with the intent to conceal or misrepresent the identity of that property.

Punishment

Class 1 misdemeanor.

Notes

Element (3). The statute does not specify that the property must belong to someone else in order for this offense to be charged.

Element (4). Although the statute says that the defendant's intent must be to conceal or misrepresent the identity of the property, the statute probably also was intended to cover situations in which the intent is to conceal the true ownership of the property.

Related offenses not in this chapter

"Accessory after the Fact to Felony" (Chapter 4)
See Chapter 13, "Burglary and Breaking or Entering."
"Injury to Personal Property" (Chapter 16)
"Fraudulent Disposal of Security" (Chapter 14)
"Obtaining Property by False Pretenses" (Chapter 14)
Injuring or tampering with vehicle (G.S. 20-107)
Buying, selling, or possessing vehicle without manufacturer's numbers (G.S. 20-108)
Altering or changing engine numbers (G.S. 20-109)

Buying, Selling, or Possessing Property with Altered Serial Number

Statute

See subsection (b) of G.S. 14-160.1, reproduced under "Altering or Removing Serial Number," immediately above.

Elements

A person guilty of this offense

- (1) knowingly
- (2) (a) buys, *or*
  - (b) sells, *or*
  - (c) possesses
- (3) any item of personal property
- (4) that is not his or her own, *and*
- (5) whose permanent serial number, manufacturer's identification plate, or other permanent distinguishing number or mark has been altered, defaced, destroyed, or removed
- (6) when the alteration, defacement, destruction, or removal was for the purpose of concealing or misrepresenting the identity of the property.

Punishment

Class 1 misdemeanor.

Notes

Element (1). It is not clear from the statute what the word "knowingly" refers to—whether the defendant merely needs to know that the serial number has been altered or whether the defendant also needs to know that the alteration was for the purpose of concealing the identity of the property.

Element (2). As with other possession offenses, the property could be constructively possessed—that is, considered in the defendant's possession, even though the defendant had not touched it, if it had been put in some place under the control of the defendant or an agent of the defendant.

Element (4). This offense differs from altering or removing serial numbers in that the violation can occur only if the property involved belongs to someone other than the defendant.

Element (6). See the note under Element (4) of "Altering or Removing Serial Number."

Related offenses not in this chapter

See the offenses listed under "Altering or Removing Serial Number."

12
Robbery, Extortion, and Related Offenses

Chapter Contents

12
Robbery, Extortion, and Related Offenses

Common-Law Robbery

Statute

This is a common-law offense.

Elements

A person guilty of this offense
(1) commits larceny
(2) from the person or from the person's presence
(3) by violence or intimidation.

Punishment

Class G felony (G.S. 14-87.1).

Notes

Element (1). All the elements of larceny from the person must be proven in order to convict someone of robbery (262 N.C. 162). See "Felonious Larceny" (Chapter 11).

Element (2). "From the person" includes taking something from the owner's hand or pocket or taking something that is physically attached to the owner—e.g., pinned or tied to his or her clothes. "From the person's presence" also includes taking something from under the owner's personal protection even though it may not be physically attached to him or her—e.g., taking a bag of groceries that the robber forced the victim to set down on the sidewalk (26 N.C. App. 475) or, after assaulting the victim or rendering the victim helpless in a room, taking personal property that was under his or her control in that room (*Perkins*, p. 346).

A homicide victim can be a person within the meaning of this offense as long as the death and the taking of property are so connected in time and circumstances as to form a continuous chain of events (325 N.C. 607).

Element (3). Violence or intimidation includes injuring or immobilizing the owner so that the owner cannot protect his or her property. It also includes violence or intimidation that occurs after the larceny begins; for example, if a thief snatches a briefcase, the victim resists, and the robber overcomes the resistance by pulling the briefcase away or threatening to hurt the victim, the thief commits robbery (283 N.C. 383; *Perkins*, p. 347). However, robbery is not committed if the only force used is to obtain possession of the property (for example, snatching a purse from a person's shoulder) and there is no violence or threat of violence to induce the victim to part with the property; in such a case, larceny from the person is the appropriate charge (State v. Robertson, 138 N.C. App. ___, June 20, 2000). There need be no actual violence if the victim is put in fear of some immediate injury. The intimidation need not involve a great degree of terror if it makes the victim apprehensive about his or her own physical safety. Such was the case when three sailors in a car were surrounded by five men, without weapons or actual violence, who told them "[t]his is a shakedown" and then took money from their pockets (224 N.C. 61). Intimidation may also occur by asserting authority when the robber does not actually have that authority; for example, pretending to be police officers, the defendants "arrested" the victim, searched him, and took his money (*Perkins*, p. 348).

When a defendant used force against a victim, and the victim eventually died from that force, that force could be the basis of a common-law robbery charge, when the defendant removed items of value from the victim's home near the time of the murder (325 N.C. 607).

Attempt. Attempted common-law robbery is a Class H felony, pursuant to G.S. 14-2.5, which became effective October 1, 1994, as a part of the structured sentencing laws. See Chapter 4, "General Crimes," for further discussion of that statute and penalties for attempts. This rule for attempted common-law robbery replaces a prior court-made rule that attempted common-law robbery was punishable as an "infamous offense" under G.S. 14-3(b) (244 N.C. 737). Under structured sentencing, attempts have specific punishments and are removed from the class of offenses to which G.S. 14-3(b) applies (only offenses with no specific statutory punishment now fall under that statute's "infamous offense" rule). See "Committing an Infamous or Related Misdemeanor" (Chapter 4).

Attempted robbery is committing an overt act with the specific intent to commit robbery; the act must be more than preparation to commit the offense, but it need not be the last act in completing the offense. For example, a defendant entered a store, kept his right hand in his pocket as if he had a gun (although he had none), and threatened to hurt the storekeeper unless she put her money in a bag and gave it to him, but he was apprehended by a customer before he could take the bag and leave; this was sufficient evidence of attempted common-law robbery (4 N.C. App. 407).

Multiple victims. If a robber intimidates two victims and takes personal property from each of them, the robber commits two robberies. If the robber intimidates several people at the same time and takes only their employer's money from their control, only one robbery is committed (280 N.C. 479; 285 N.C. 238). If the robber intimidates only one employee and takes money of the employee and money of the employer, only one robbery is committed (306 N.C. 491).

Lesser-included offenses. Larceny is a lesser-included offense of robbery (322 N.C. 506; 305 N.C. 391).

Related offenses not in this chapter

"Felonious Larceny" (Chapter 11)
Train robbery (G.S. 14-88)

Armed Robbery

Statute

§14-87. Robbery with firearms or other dangerous weapons.

(a) Any person or persons who, having in possession or with the use or threatened use of any firearms or other dangerous weapon, implement or means, whereby the life of a person is endangered or threatened, unlawfully takes or attempts to take personal property from another or from any place of business, residence or banking institution or any other place where there is a person or persons in attendance, at any time, either day or night, or who aids or abets any such person or persons in the commission of such crime, shall be guilty of a Class D felony.

(b) Repealed by Session Laws 1979, c. 760, s. 5.

(c) Repealed by Session Laws 1979, c. 760, s. 5.

(d) Repealed by Session Laws 1993, c. 539, s. 1173.

Elements

A person guilty of this offense
- (1) commits or attempts to commit larceny
- (2) from the person or from the person's presence
- (3) by the possession, use, or threatened use of a firearm or other dangerous weapon
- (4) which endangers or threatens the life of a person.

Punishment

Class D felony.

Notes

Elements (1) and (2). See the notes on Elements (1) and (2) under "Common-Law Robbery."

Element (3). This element distinguishes armed robbery from common-law robbery. A dangerous weapon is the same as a deadly weapon (47 N.C. App. 667; 78 N.C. App. 365; 78 N.C. App. 405); see the discussion of what constitutes a deadly weapon and related issues under "Assault with Deadly Weapon with Intent to Kill," in Chapter 7, "Assaults and Threats." Such a weapon is generally any article, instrument, or substance which is likely to produce death or great bodily harm (304 N.C. 293). Proof of a dangerous weapon may be in many forms, including evidence of an actual weapon; testimony of a victim or witness about seeing or feeling a weapon; evidence of a victim's resulting injuries (313 N.C. 554); and a defendant's statement that he had a firearm (128 N.C. App. 506). Using a firearm as a club to hit the victim on the head and then taking the victim's property satisfies this element (342 N.C. 173). A pellet gun placed against the victim's back, pointed directly at her kidney, and evidence that a projectile from that gun was capable of penetrating a quarter-inch of plywood, satisfies this element (116 N.C. App. 534).

Element (4). Mere possession of a firearm or dangerous weapon does not satisfy the elements of this offense. The defendant must use the weapon in a way that endangers the victim's life (279 N.C. 447; 303 N.C. 484; 85 N.C. App. 319). For example, in one case the defendant confronted the victim with a pocketknife, threatened to cut his head off if the victim did not give the defendant his billfold, and struck at the victim as he tried to escape. In another case the defendant attacked the victim, put him on his back, hit him on the head with a bottle, and later held an opened pocketknife in his hand

and demanded the victim's wallet. In both of these cases, the court found the pocketknife to be a dangerous weapon whereby the life of a person was endangered (264 N.C. 470; 279 N.C. 455). In still another case, a glass vase was held to be a dangerous weapon when the defendant struck the victim's head with it (313 N.C. 554). On the other hand, when a defendant testified that he used the butt of a shotgun to break through a robbery victim's door and then rested the shotgun against a wall during the robbery, the court found insufficient evidence of this element (303 N.C. 484).

It is not necessary to prove that the victim feared for his or her life; nor must the weapon be threatening the victim at the time of the robbery if the defendant had earlier threatened the victim with a weapon and had made it clear that the threat applied to future acts if the victim did not do as the defendant said (295 N.C. 55).

Timing of elements. The elements of this offense may occur in almost any order, as long as: (1) evidence shows that the larceny was *by* use or possession of a dangerous weapon that endangered the victim—that is, that the show of force induced the victim to part with his or her property, or permitted the defendant to take the property (308 N.C. 470; 322 N.C. 559); and (2) the elements take place in a series of events so joined in time and circumstance as to be inseparable—that is, they occur in a single continuous transaction. Evidence is sufficient for armed robbery in each of the following circumstances: (1) where the victim is dead when the property is taken, as long as the robbery and the victim's death occur during a single continuous transaction (315 N.C. 191; 331 N.C. 515); (2) where the defendant's intent to steal is formed after the use or threat of force, as long as the theft and use or threat of force occur during a single continuous transaction (315 N.C. 191; 319 N.C. 577; 321 N.C. 594); (3) where the use or threat of force occurs before or with the theft or during the same time as the theft to constitute a single continuous transaction (317 N.C. 302; 330 N.C. 557; 97 N.C. App. 631; but see 122 N.C. App. 666). For example, there was sufficient evidence of armed robbery when the defendants stole items from a store, ran out of the store to their car, and one of the defendants pointed a handgun at a store employee who was trying to prevent the defendants from leaving (125 N.C. App. 75).

Multiple victims. If the robber threatens the life of two victims by the use of a dangerous weapon and takes each victim's own property, he or she commits two armed robberies (29 N.C. App. 647), but if the robber intimidates several persons at the same time and takes their employer's property from their control, he or she commits only one armed robbery (280 N.C. 479; 285 N.C. 238). If the robber threatens the life of only one employee and takes money of the employee and money of the employer, he or she commits only one armed robbery because there is only a single assault on a single person (306 N.C. 491).

Attempt. The statute makes attempted armed robbery punishable as armed robbery. See "Attempt" in Chapter 4 and the note on "Attempt" under "Common-Law Robbery" for what conduct constitutes an attempt. When a defendant entered a house to rob two men, shot the first and took his wallet, the second man asked the defendant not to shoot him and threw his wallet toward the defendant, and the defendant left without taking the second man's wallet, the defendant committed attempted armed robbery (326 N.C. 31) against the second victim.

Lesser-included offenses. Common-law robbery, assault with a deadly weapon, and larceny are lesser-included offenses of armed robbery (312 N.C. 779; 322 N.C. 506; 335 N.C. 741). A defendant may be charged with and convicted of both armed robbery and felonious assault (done with intent to kill and/or inflicting serious injury) (see Chapter 7) arising out of the same incident, because all of the elements of felonious assault are not elements of armed robbery (279 N.C. 621; 280 N.C. 306).

Separate convictions for armed robbery and larceny. Separate convictions for armed robbery and larceny are permitted if there are separate takings; separate convictions are not permitted if the takings occurred during one continuous transaction (335 N.C. 741). Convictions for both armed robbery and larceny were permitted when the defendant took the murder victim's wallet after shooting the victim and later returned to the murder scene and took the victim's car (342 N.C. 74), and when the defendants killed and robbed the victim, took his car, and later took his firearm from the car's glove compartment (335 N.C. 741). Convictions for both armed robbery and larceny were not permitted when the defendants took the murder victim's personal possessions and loaded them into the victim's two vehicles and drove away; the taking of the personal possessions and the vehicles occurred during one continuous transaction (342 N.C. 249).

"Presumption" of the use of a dangerous weapon and when a judge must instruct the jury on the lesser-included offense of common-law robbery. If the evidence shows that it appeared to the victim that the robber used a firearm or other dangerous weapon, and no evidence to the contrary is presented, then a jury must find that the robber used a firearm or dangerous weapon that threatened or endangered the victim's life [thereby satisfying Elements (3) and (4), above]. In this circumstance the judge is not required to instruct the jury about the charge of common-law robbery (335 N.C. 518).

If there is evidence that it appeared to the victim that the robbery was committed with a dangerous weapon, as well as evidence tending to show that the weapon in question was not dangerous, then the trial court must submit the case to the jury on the lesser-included offense of common-law robbery as well as armed robbery (317 N.C. 119; 109 N.C. App. 518).

If any credible evidence is presented showing that the victim's life was *not* endangered or threatened, the jury may still infer that the use of a firearm or dangerous weapon threatened or endangered the victim's life [thereby satisfying Elements (3) and (4) of armed robbery], but the presumption that the victim's life was endangered disappears (312 N.C. 779; 317 N.C. 119; 335 N.C. 518). For example, if a victim testifies that he or she was robbed with what appeared to be a handgun, the jury may infer that the object used was a handgun. Absent any credible evidence indicating otherwise, the jury must presume that a dangerous weapon threatening or endangering the victim's life was used. However, if the defendant presents evidence showing that the object used was a toy or otherwise not dangerous, the prosecution must prove that the object used was actually a handgun or other dangerous weapon and that the victim's life was endangered (297 N.C. 285; 312 N.C. 779; 111 N.C. App. 775). Even if a dangerous weapon was neither seen at the time of the offense nor found later, the use of a dangerous weapon may be inferred from the victim's testimony about being hit with an object and from the nature of the victim's wound (87 N.C. App. 246) or the defendant's threat to shoot the victim (128 N.C. App. 506).

Related offenses not in this chapter

"Felonious Larceny" (Chapter 11)
See the offenses in Chapter 19, "Weapons Offenses."
Train robbery (G.S. 14-88)

Extortion

Statute

§14-118.4. Extortion.

Any person who threatens or communicates a threat or threats to another with the intention thereby wrongfully to obtain anything of value or any acquittance, advantage, or immunity is guilty of extortion and such person shall be punished as a Class F felon.

Elements

A person guilty of this offense
(1) threatens or communicates a threat to another
(2) with the intent to obtain wrongfully
(3) anything of value, any acquittance, any advantage, or any immunity.

Punishment

Class F felony.

Notes

Element (1). The statute applies both to the person threatening and to any person who transmits the threat (a messenger, for example).

Element (2). It is not necessary that the defendant actually obtain any of the items listed in Element (3); the defendant must only make the threat with the intent to gain something listed (*Perkins*, p. 449). Additionally, it is not necessary that the defendant seek one of the items for himself or herself.

Element (3). The threat or demand need not concern money. The terms "acquittance, advantage, or immunity" can be read to cover almost any action or inaction by the threatened individual that benefits the person who makes or communicates the threat. An offer to refrain from pressing criminal charges in exchange for money constituted threatening a criminal prosecution, satisfying this element (92 N.C. App. 563).

Comparison with blackmail. Most, if not all, fact scenarios fitting the elements of blackmail will also satisfy the elements of this offense. In fact, the North Carolina Court of Appeals has said that the offense of extortion has superseded the offense of blackmail. The court said that by enacting a new law (extortion in 1973) that covered practically the whole subject of a prior law (blackmail, which has been codified since 1854), there was evidence of legislative intent to repeal the prior offense of blackmail (92 N.C. App. 563). Because extortion requires fewer elements of proof, in any case it is likely a preferable charge to blackmail. Also the state may prefer charging extortion over blackmail because extortion is a Class F felony, while blackmail is a Class 1 misdemeanor.

Related offenses not in this chapter

"Communicating Threats" (Chapter 7)
"Harassing Phone Calls" (Chapter 7)
"Computer Fraud: IV. Extortion by Threatening Computer Damage" (Chapter 14)
Simulation of court process to collect claim (G.S. 14-118.1)

Blackmail

Statute

§14-118. Blackmailing.

If any person shall knowingly send or deliver any letter or writing demanding of any other person, with menaces and without any reasonable or probable cause, any chattel, money or valuable security; or if any person shall accuse, or threaten to accuse, or shall knowingly send or deliver any letter or writing accusing or threatening to accuse any other person of any crime punishable by law with death or by imprisonment in the State's prison, with the intent to extort or gain from such person any chattel, money or valuable security, every such offender shall be guilty of a Class 1 misdemeanor.

I. Demanding Valuables without Reasonable Cause

Statute

See the first clause of G.S. 14-118, reproduced above.

Elements

A person guilty of this offense
- (1) knowingly
- (2) sends or delivers any letter or writing
- (3) demanding a chattel, money, or valuable security
- (4) with menaces, *and*
- (5) without reasonable or probable cause.

Punishment

Class 1 misdemeanor.

Notes

Generally. "Extortion" likely is a more appropriate charge for any fact scenario chargeable under this offense. See the note on "Comparison with blackmail," under "Extortion," for further explanation.

Element (1). See the definition of "knowingly" in Chapter 1.

Element (2). To constitute this kind of blackmail, a written demand is necessary. This offense could not be charged if the demand is communicated orally. But it is not necessary that the victim receive or read the message—only that it be sent or delivered.

Element (3). This offense has not been committed if the demand is for something other than one of the items listed. For example, a demand that the victim drop a lawsuit would not satisfy this element.

Element (4). "With menaces" means "with threats." The threat does not have to be a threat to do something illegal; it could be, for example, a threat to reveal that the person had been unfaithful to his or her spouse.

Element (5). If the person has reason to believe that he or she is entitled to the property he or she is demanding, then the offense has not been committed (N.C.P.I.—Crim. 220.60).

Related offenses not in this chapter

See the offenses listed at the end of this section.

II. Accusing of Crime to Extort Valuables

Statute

See the second clause of G.S. 14-118, reproduced above.

Elements

A person guilty of this offense
(1) accuses or threatens to accuse another person of a crime punishable by death or imprisonment in the state prison
(2) with intent to extort or gain from the person a chattel, money, or valuable security.

Punishment

Class 1 misdemeanor.

Notes

Generally. "Extortion" likely is a more appropriate charge for any fact scenario chargeable under this offense. See the note on "Comparison with blackmail," under "Extortion," for further explanation.

Element (1). The threat or accusation need not be made in writing in order for this offense to occur, but the accusation must be of a criminal offense punishable by death or "imprisonment in the State's prison"—which probably means, for historical reasons, that the offense must be a felony (206 N.C. 87).

Element (2). See the note on Element (3) under "I. Demanding Valuables without Reasonable Cause," just above. For the offense to constitute this kind of blackmail, whether the defendant believes he or she is entitled to the property is apparently irrelevant.

Related offenses not in this chapter

"Communicating Threats" (Chapter 7)
"Harassing Phone Calls" (Chapter 7)
Simulation of court process to collect claim (G.S. 14-118.1)

13
Burglary and Breaking or Entering

Chapter Contents

13
Burglary and Breaking or Entering

First-Degree Burglary

Statute

§14-51. First and second degree burglary.

There shall be two degrees in the crime of burglary as defined at the common law. If the crime be committed in a dwelling house, or in a room used as a sleeping apartment in any building, and any person is in the actual occupation of any part of said dwelling house or sleeping apartment at the time of the commission of such crime, it shall be burglary in the first degree. If such crime be committed in a dwelling house or sleeping apartment not actually occupied by anyone at the time of the commission of the crime, or if it be committed in any house within the curtilage of a dwelling house or in any building not a dwelling house, but in which is a room used as a sleeping apartment and not actually occupied as such at the time of the commission of the crime, it shall be burglary in the second degree. For the purposes of defining the crime of burglary, larceny shall be deemed a felony without regard to the value of the property in question.

§14-52. Punishment for burglary.

Burglary in the first degree shall be punishable as a Class D felony, and burglary in the second degree shall be punishable as a Class G felony.

Elements

A person guilty of this offense
(1) breaks, *and*
(2) enters
(3) without consent
(4) the dwelling house or sleeping apartment
(5) of another
(6) while it is actually occupied
(7) at night
(8) with the intent to commit any felony or larceny therein.

Punishment

Class D felony. Pursuant to G.S. 14-2.5, attempted first-degree burglary is punishable as a Class E felony. This statute supersedes prior North Carolina case law, which held that attempted burglary was an infamous misdemeanor punishable under G.S. 14-3(b) as a Class H felony (230 N.C. 272; 307 N.C. 1). G.S. 14-2.5 provides specific punishments for all attempts not given an offense classification by a particular statute.

Notes

Burglary and breaking and entering offenses generally. The law defines grades of burglary and breaking and entering offenses with respect to five factors: (1) the type of building, (2) whether the building is occupied, (3) the manner of entry, (4) the time of day, and (5) the defendant's intent.

Burglary defined by common law. Burglary is defined by common law; the statute breaks the crime into degrees that depend on whether the dwelling is occupied when the breaking and entering occurs (227 N.C. 132; 315 N.C. 191).

Differences between first- and second-degree burglary. The main differences between first- and second-degree burglary are that (1) a charge of first-degree burglary requires that the dwelling actually be occupied when the breaking and entering occurs, whereas a charge of second-degree burglary does not (270 N.C. 588), and (2) second-degree burglary includes the breaking and entering of not only dwellings and sleeping apartments but also "any house within the curtilage of a dwelling" (an outbuilding near the dwelling regularly used by the dweller or members of the household, such as a garage). Except for these differences, the following notes apply to both first- and second-degree burglary.

Element (1). "Breaking" means the making of some kind of opening, however slight, in the building (106 N.C. App. 433). It may be through a usual opening (i.e., door) or an unusual opening (i.e., chimney). Merely going through an open door or window is not "breaking." But opening a door or window, even if unlocked, is "breaking" (35 N.C. 244; 285 N.C. 1; 299 N.C. 335); no destructive force need be used. Opening a partly opened door is a "breaking" (342 N.C. 249). Breaking is sometimes shown by testimony that before the entry, all doors and windows through which the defendant might have entered, or did enter, were closed (291 N.C. 366; 335 N.C. 457; 18 N.C. App. 460; 106 N.C. App. 433). Entering through the chimney is "breaking" even though the chimney is open (52 N.C. 190). The breaking of an inner door of a house or apartment can satisfy this element (313 N.C. 539).

In some instances, there is apparent consent to entry from a victim of a breaking, or the victim actually opens a door and allows the defendant to enter the dwelling. Even though the defendant has not physically done the "breaking" in such cases, courts still find illegal breaking based on fraud, trickery, force, or intimidation directed toward the victim. These are "constructive breaking" cases, and they are discussed more fully under Element (3), below.

Element (2). "Entering" can be accomplished by the offender's putting any part of his or her body into the building, even a finger (*Perkins*, p. 253), such as when the defendant extended his hand and a small pistol through a broken window (297 N.C. 410). Inserting a tool into the building is not "entering" if the insertion is only for the purpose of "breaking" (for example, when a crowbar is shoved an inch or two into the building for the purpose of forcing a window open), but when the tool is inserted for the purpose of committing a felony (for example, when a hook for stealing something or the barrel of a gun for killing an occupant is thrust through a window opening), "entering" occurs (*Perkins*, p. 253).

Element (3). A defendant does not "break" or "enter" if the owner or some other person entitled to possession consents without coercion or trickery to entry (332 N.C. 439; 306 N.C. 683; N.C.P.I.—Crim. 214.10). If a person is given a key and is authorized to enter at any time, for example, the person does not commit "breaking" or "entering," even if he or she uses the key to enter and commit a felony or larceny (*Perkins*, p. 250). However, opening a locked door with a key is "breaking" if the person who uses the key has no permission to enter at the time.

Entry gained by fraud, trick, coercion, threat, or conspiracy constitutes "constructive breaking" (289 N.C. 531; *Perkins*, pp. 248–50). In "constructive breaking" cases, it may appear that consent for entry was obtained or the victim or another occupant may actually open a door for the defendant; however, such consent is not valid and an opening by the victim in such a situation is still attributed to the defendant. Examples of "constructive breaking" include obtaining entry by tricking an occupant into opening the door (344 N.C. 290; 350 N.C. 315; 31 N.C. 463; 68 N.C. 207); by the occupant initially opening the door and then the defendant forcing his or her way inside (297 N.C. 121; 298 N.C. 573; 308 N.C. 357); by having the door opened by an occupant who is an accomplice or co-conspirator in the crime (98 N.C. 629; 311 N.C. 145; *Perkins*, p. 249); or by inducing an occupant to open a door by force or the threat of force (31 N.C. 463; 216 N.C. 572; 289 N.C. 531; *Perkins*, p. 249).

This element may be satisfied by the occupant's testimony that he or she did not consent to the entry or by other circumstantial evidence indicating lack of consent (330 N.C. 579). For example, evidence that the victim told the defendant that she did not want to talk with him, that she did not open a locked door, and that the defendant broke down the locked front door to gain entry was sufficient evidence of the occupant's lack of consent (330 N.C. 579).

Occupants do not always have authority to consent to entry by others. When a defendant and a juvenile resident of a house conspired to commit murder against other residents of the house (the juvenile's parents), and the defendant entered the house at night for that purpose (the juvenile was absent at the time), the juvenile occupant of the house had no authority to give the defendant permission to enter his parent's home in the middle of the night for a criminal purpose—here, to commit murder (332 N.C. 439).

Element (4). A "dwelling" is a structure regularly used by a person or persons for sleeping (129 N.C. 704). "Regularly used" means that use "occurs in ordinary practice or in the ordinary course of events" (112 N.C. App. 262). Homes owned by elderly people were dwellings, even though they lived elsewhere because of health problems, when they intended to return to their homes when they were able to do so and their homes still contained their personal effects (121 N.C. App. 41). A dwelling may be a house; an apartment; a room in a hotel, motel, or rooming house (298 N.C. 573; 3 N.C. App. 571); a condominium (112 N.C. App. 262); a tent; or other habitation with walls and a roof, no matter how crude or squalid (60 N.C. 471; *Perkins*, p. 255). It may also be a house trailer or mobile home (109 N.C. App. 692); it does not matter that the dwelling may be mobile. Courts in other states have ruled that the cabin of a houseboat is a dwelling [264 N.W.2d 406 (Minnesota); 919 P.2d 731 (California)].

A storage room at the back of a house just behind a bedroom that could be entered through either the bedroom window or an outside door is a part of the dwelling (305 N.C. 463). A dwelling also includes: (1) a store or other building if it has been made a "sleeping apartment" by a person's use of it as a regular sleeping place (90 N.C. 724), but not if it is used for sleeping only occasionally; (2) a sleeping apartment in a skating rink (120 N.C. App. 815); and (3) the common areas of a sorority house in which the victim's apartment was located (120 N.C. App. 732). A house used for only part of the year, such as a summer cottage or condominium, is a dwelling if the owner, members of the owner's household, or renters have at some time used it regularly for sleeping and intend to use it again (112 N.C. App. 262). Even a condominium not rented on the night of a break-in qualifies as a dwelling, if "in the ordinary course of events [it is] used as a dwelling by either the owner, the owner's family, or a renter" and it is "regularly available for rent" (112 N.C. App. 265). However, if an owner moves out permanently with no intention of returning, and a new owner or renter has not begun to sleep in the house regularly, the house ceases to be a dwelling (*Perkins*, p. 258).

Element (5). The phrase "of another" means that the property broken into or entered is legally possessed by a person other than the offender, even though that person may not own the property. Even a defendant with an ownership interest in a house can be guilty of burglary if the house is legally and exclusively possessed by another person (312 N.C. 787; 73 N.C. App. 432). A spouse may be convicted of burglary, or breaking or entering, for breaking into the other spouse's dwelling, or of larceny for taking the other spouse's property, if the evidence shows that the other spouse had exclusive possession of the dwelling and the property taken (344 N.C. 95; 73 N.C. App. 432; 81 N.C. App. 490). For example, if a defendant enters a spouse's residence that the defendant has been expressly prohibited from entering by a marital separation agreement, these offenses may be committed. When a building is rented to a tenant who regularly sleeps there, it becomes the tenant's "dwelling," and the landlord who opens the door and enters without the tenant's agreement is breaking and entering the dwelling of another (*Perkins*, p. 261).

Element (6). "Actually occupied" means that some person must be present somewhere inside the dwelling when the breaking and entering occurs. A motel room is not actually occupied when a breaking and entering occurs, for example, if the offense is accomplished by pushing the victim, who is standing outside his or her motel room, into the room while the defendant also is standing outside the door (297 N.C. 121). The element is satisfied regardless of whether the offender *knew* the dwelling was occupied (270 N.C. 588).

Element (7). "At night" is that time after sunset and before sunrise "when it is so dark that a man's face cannot be identified except by an artificial light or moonlight" (284 N.C. 137; 113 N.C. App. 69). Evidence of nighttime may be by judicial notice of sunset and sunrise times for particular dates, as recorded in *U.S. Naval Observatory Nautical Almanac* reports (294 N.C. 270) or the official records of the National Climate Data Center (135 N.C. App. 682).

Element (8). For breaking and entering of a dwelling to be burglary, it is necessary that the intruder, when breaking and entering, intends to commit a felony or larceny. If the intruder does not form the intent to commit the felony or larceny until after he or she breaks and enters, the offense is misdemeanor breaking or entering rather than burglary (313 N.C. 554). The value of property stolen is irrelevant to whether the offense is a felony (216 N.C. 304); any larceny, regardless of property value, is a felony if committed in the course of a breaking or entering a building (G.S. 14-72; see "Felonious Larceny" in Chapter 11). Also, in instructing the jury in such cases, the judge must define larceny (40 N.C. App. 71).

The intention to commit any other felony, such as rape or murder, also makes the breaking and entering constitute burglary. The intruder *need not be successful* in committing the felony in order for the breaking or entering to be burglary; the intruder merely has to *intend* to commit it when he or she breaks and enters (285 N.C. 746; 308 N.C. 181). For example, if a defendant entered a building with intent to commit a felony, but once inside was interrupted or frightened away before committing any felony, this element would still be satisfied (289 N.C. 232). It may be hard to prove exactly what the intruder intended to do when entering; the fact that the intruder actually committed a felony inside would be strong evidence that he or she intended to do it before entering (299 N.C. 377; 330 N.C. 579), as would evidence that he or she attempted or prepared to commit a felony inside (270 N.C. 588). Also, the fact that an intruder broke and entered a dwelling in the nighttime is sufficient, in the absence of contrary evidence, to support a finding that the intruder intended to steal (277 N.C. 65). The fact that an intruder at nighttime broke and entered a dwelling occupied by a woman is *not* sufficient to prove intent to rape (207 N.C. 445; 90 N.C. App. 185). The intruder may offer evidence of his or her innocence by showing entry for some nonfelonious purpose (242 N.C. 700).

Doctrine of possession of recently stolen property. If a defendant possesses property that has recently been stolen following a burglary or a breaking and entering, that possession may be a sufficient basis for concluding that the defendant committed the burglary or breaking and entering if, under the circumstances, it is unlikely that he or she could have acquired the property innocently (282 N.C. 249; 301 N.C. 18). See the more extensive discussion of this topic under "Misdemeanor Larceny" (Chapter 11).

An interval of 30 days between the discovery of theft of someone's property—a television set, towels, linens, and a fan—and the location of the stolen items in the defendant's possession did not support an inference of breaking or entering and larceny, since the items stolen were of a type normally and frequently traded through lawful channels (316 N.C. 41). An interval of 11 to 12 days between the larceny and the defendant's possession of commercial restaurant equipment supported an inference of breaking or entering and larceny, because such equipment is not usually or frequently traded through lawful channels (83 N.C. App. 323). Similarly, an interval of 9 days between the larceny and the defendant's possession of unique tools and metal work supported an inference of breaking or entering and larceny (86 N.C. App. 235).

Lesser-included offenses. Second-degree burglary and felonious and misdemeanor breaking or entering (113 N.C. App. 69) are lesser-included offenses of first-degree burglary.

Charging issues. In a criminal pleading alleging first-degree burglary, it is not necessary to specify the felony that the defendant intended to commit when breaking and entering a dwelling. It need only allege that the defendant intended to commit a felony (336 N.C. 268; 350 N.C. 411).

Related offenses not in this chapter

"First-Degree Trespass" (Chapter 16)
"Second-Degree Trespass" (Chapter 16)
"Forcible Trespass" (Chapter 16)
"Domestic Criminal Trespass" (Chapter 16)
"Felonious Larceny" (Chapter 11)

Second-Degree Burglary

Statute

See G.S. 14-51 and G.S. 14-52, reproduced under "First-Degree Burglary."

Elements

A person guilty of this offense
(1) breaks, *and*
(2) enters
(3) without consent
(4) the dwelling house or sleeping apartment, or any building within the curtilage of the dwelling
(5) of another
(6) at night
(7) with the intent to commit any felony or larceny therein.

Punishment

Class G felony. Attempted second-degree burglary is a Class H felony, pursuant to G.S. 14-2.5. This statute supersedes prior North Carolina case law, which held that attempted burglary was an infamous misdemeanor as defined in G.S. 14-3(b) and punishable as a Class H felony (230 N.C. 272; 307 N.C. 1). G.S. 14-2.5 provides specific punishments for all attempts that are not given an offense classification by a particular statute.

Notes

Compared with first-degree burglary. The elements of second-degree burglary are the same as the elements of first-degree burglary except that (1) the dwelling need not be *occupied* when the breaking and entering occurs and (2) the building broken and entered need not be a dwelling if it is "within the curtilage" of a dwelling. Otherwise, second-degree burglary is the same as first-degree burglary, and the notes under that offense apply here.

Elements (1), (2). "Breaking and entering" a building within the curtilage is defined in the same way as breaking and entering a dwelling. For example, opening a closed garage door and entering is "breaking and entering," but entering through a garage door that is standing open is not.

Element (4). A building "within the curtilage" of a dwelling is a building close to the dwelling and regularly used by the dweller or members of his or her household—for example, a garage, nearby barn, or toolshed (2 N.C. 102). How close the building must be to the dwelling to be "within the curtilage" is not precisely defined, but it should not be across a public road from the dwelling (*Perkins*, p. 259); the area "within the curtilage" is about what we now call the "yard." An unoccupied toolshed located forty-five feet from the dwelling was not within the curtilage, and therefore an entry into the toolshed was not second-degree burglary (315 N.C. 191).

Related offenses not in this chapter

See the offenses listed under "First-Degree Burglary" in this chapter.

Breaking out of a Dwelling

Statute

§14-53. Breaking out of dwelling house burglary.

If any person shall enter the dwelling house of another with intent to commit any felony or larceny therein, or being in such dwelling house, shall commit any felony or larceny therein, and shall, in either case, break out of such dwelling house in the nighttime, such person shall be punished as a Class D felon.

Elements

A person guilty of this offense
- (1) (a) enters
  - (b) without consent
  - (c) the dwelling house
  - (d) of another
  - (e) with the intent to commit any felony or larceny therein, *or*
- (2) (a) commits any felony or larceny
  - (b) in the dwelling house
  - (c) of another, *and*
- (3) then breaks out of the dwelling
- (4) at night.

Punishment

Class D felony.

Notes

Generally. This statute covers a gap in the common-law definition of burglary: it makes the defendant's actions punishable as burglary when the defendant did not have to break to enter (but had to break to escape) or when the entry was made in the daytime but the exit was made at night. Note that there are two possibilities: the offender either may *enter with the intent* to commit a felony or may simply *commit* a felony in the dwelling (even though intent to commit a felony was absent at entry). The notes under "First-Degree Burglary" apply to this offense.

Element (6). "Breaking out" means the same as "breaking" in first-degree burglary, except that it is done for the purpose of leaving the dwelling, not getting inside it. Thus "breaking out" requires that the intruder inside make some sort of opening in the dwelling and then exit through it. This would include, for example, leaving by opening a closed door or window, forcing a locked door open, pushing out a window screen, or knocking a hole in the wall, but not walking out a door that is already standing open.

Related offenses not in this chapter

See the offenses listed under "First-Degree Burglary" in this chapter.

Felonious Breaking or Entering of Building

Statute

§14-54. Breaking or entering buildings generally.

(a) Any person who breaks or enters any building with intent to commit any felony or larceny therein shall be punished as a Class H felon.

(b) Any person who wrongfully breaks or enters any building is guilty of a Class 1 misdemeanor.

(c) As used in this section, "building" shall be construed to include any dwelling, dwelling house, uninhabited house, building under construction, building within the curtilage of a dwelling house, and any other structure designed to house or secure within it any activity or property.

Elements

A person guilty of this offense
(1) breaks or enters
(2) without consent
(3) any building
(4) with the intent to commit any felony or larceny therein.

Punishment

Class H felony.

Notes

Element (1). For felonious breaking or entering to occur, it is not necessary that there be both a "breaking" and an "entering" as in burglary; merely breaking *or* entering the building is enough to constitute the crime if done with intent to commit a felony. For example, it is sufficient simply to walk through an open door into a building with the intent to steal something inside, and it is also sufficient when the intruder opens a closed door, intending to enter and steal, even if he or she is caught or forced to flee without being able to enter (268 N.C. 152; 1 N.C. App. 104). For what constitutes breaking and entering, see the notes for Elements (1) and (2) under "First-Degree Burglary."

Element (2). A defendant does not "break" or "enter" if the owner or some other person entitled to possession consents to entry (N.C.P.I.—Crim. 214.30). For example, a defendant who entered a clothing store during business hours and stole two sweaters did not commit this offense because he entered with the owner's consent (297 N.C. 652); see the notes for Element (3) under "First-Degree Burglary." But another defendant who entered a store during business hours, concealed himself in an area not open to the public, remained there until after the store closed, and then participated in larceny was guilty of felonious entry of the store (44 N.C. App. 59).

Element (3). Unlike burglary, felonious breaking or entering of a building does not require that a *dwelling* be entered; a "building" may be a dwelling, but it may also be a store (266 N.C. 55), boiler room, shop, warehouse, bank, garage, mobile home (51 N.C. App. 594; 54 N.C. App. 85), trailer put up on blocks and used for storage of construction equipment (55 N.C. App. 612), or any other permanent structure with walls and a roof, which need not be occupied or even inhabited.

Element (4). Felonious breaking or entering also requires the intent to commit a felony when the breaking or entry occurs (4 N.C. App. 575); see the notes for Element (8) under "First-Degree Burglary." The value of the property taken is immaterial to whether the theft is a felony (266 N.C. 55); any larceny by breaking or entering of a building is a felony (G.S. 14-72; see "Felonious Larceny" in Chapter 11).

Daytime or nighttime. The breaking or entering need not be done at night. The breaking or entering of a dwelling in the daytime, done with the intent to steal or commit some other felony, is felonious breaking or entering, not burglary.

Lesser-included offense. Misdemeanor breaking or entering of building and first- and second-degree trespass are lesser-included offenses of this offense (264 N.C. 134; G.S. 14-159.14).

Related offenses not in this chapter

See the offenses listed under "First-Degree Burglary."

Misdemeanor Breaking or Entering of Building

Statute

See G.S. 14-54(b) and (c), reproduced under "Felonious Breaking or Entering of Building."

Elements

A person guilty of this offense
(1) breaks or enters
(2) without consent
(3) any building.

Punishment

Class 1 misdemeanor.

Notes

Generally. To constitute misdemeanor breaking or entering, a crime need not involve an intent to commit a felony (272 N.C. 515); all that is required is the breaking *or* entering of any building at any time of day, whether occupied or not. Thus misdemeanor breaking or entering is a lesser-included offense of felonious breaking or entering of building (264 N.C. 134). The "entering" must be *without permission*; it is not a crime to enter with permission to do so.

Element (1). For definitions of "breaking" and "entering," see the notes for Elements (1) and (2) under "First-Degree Burglary."

Element (2). See the notes for Element (3) under "First-Degree Burglary."

Related offenses not in this chapter

See the offenses listed under "First-Degree Burglary."

Possession of Burglar's Tools

Statute

§14-55. Preparation to commit burglary or other housebreakings.

If any person shall be found armed with any dangerous or offensive weapon, with the intent to break or enter a dwelling, or other building whatsoever, and to commit any felony or larceny therein; or shall be found having in his possession, without lawful excuse, any picklock, key, bit, or other implement of housebreaking; or shall be found in any such building, with intent to commit any felony or larceny therein, such person shall be punished as a Class I felon.

Elements

A person guilty of this offense
(1) is found having a picklock, key, bit, or other implement of housebreaking
(2) without lawful excuse.

Punishment

Class I felony.

Notes

Element (1). The statute refers to possession of "any picklock, key, bit, or other implement of housebreaking," but court decisions make it clear that the possession must be for the purpose of breaking in. For example, the fact that the defendants were found with a picklock and homemade telephone box key—as well as hammers, chisels, other tools, and hundreds of coin wrappers—in their car was held to be enough to support a jury finding that they possessed the tools for the purpose of breaking into buildings and stealing from pay telephone boxes (272 N.C. 160). When the defendants were apprehended outside the rear of a drugstore with prescription drugs nearby, the front door having been pried open, a crowbar lying outside the back door, and a tire tool lying inside the building at the rear door, the tools were held to be implements of housebreaking (300 N.C. 736). But in a case in which the defendants had a bolt cutter, a large screwdriver, and brace and bit in their car, plus a pistol and blackjack they admitted carrying for protection while transporting illegal liquor, the court held that they could not be found guilty of violating G.S. 14-55 because there was no evidence that they possessed the tools for the purpose of housebreaking (223 N.C. 79).

Element (2). The state has the burden of proving that the defendant had no lawful excuse for possessing the tools (223 N.C. 79; 272 N.C. 469).

Pleading issue. G.S. 14-55 creates three separate offenses, and the criminal pleading must clearly and individually identify the offense with which a defendant is charged (37 N.C. App. 68).

Related offenses not in this chapter

"Attempt" (Chapter 4)

Being Found in a Building with Intent to Commit Any Felony or Larceny

Statute

See G.S. 14-55, reproduced under "Possession of Burglar's Tools."

Elements

A person guilty of this offense
(1) is found in any building
(2) without consent
(3) with the intent to commit any felony or larceny therein.

Punishment

Class I felony.

Notes

Generally. This offense seems to be rarely charged, probably because it is difficult to establish an intent to commit a felony or larceny merely from a person's unauthorized presence in a building. More proof would be needed, such as evidence that the person committed or attempted to commit a felony or larceny. Moreover, if such evidence is available, a more appropriate charge would be felonious breaking or entering of building.

Related offenses not in this chapter

"Attempt" (Chapter 4)
See the offenses in Chapter 16, "Trespass, Property Damage, and Littering."

Being Found Armed with Intent to Break or Enter

Statute

See G.S. 14-55, reproduced under "Possession of Burglar's Tools."

Elements

A person guilty of this offense
(1) is found armed with any dangerous or offensive weapon
(2) with the intent to break or enter and to commit any felony or larceny
(3) in any building.

Punishment

Class I felony.

Notes

Generally. This offense seems to be rarely charged, probably because it is difficult to prove that a person found armed with a dangerous weapon intends to break or enter a building. If there is evidence that the person actually broke or entered, it would be more appropriate to charge felonious breaking or entering of building.

Related offenses not in this chapter

"Armed Robbery" (Chapter 12)
See the offenses in Chapter 16, "Trespass, Property Damage, and Littering."
See the offenses in Chapter 19, "Weapons Offenses."

Breaking or Entering Vehicle

Statute

§14-56. Breaking or entering into or breaking out of railroad cars, motor vehicles, trailers, aircraft, boats, or other watercraft.

If any person, with intent to commit any felony or larceny therein, breaks or enters any railroad car, motor vehicle, trailer, aircraft, boat, or other watercraft of any kind, containing any goods, wares, freight, or other thing of value, or, after having committed any felony or larceny therein, breaks out of any railroad car, motor vehicle, trailer, aircraft, boat, or other watercraft of any kind containing any goods, wares, freight, or other thing of value, that person is guilty of a Class I felony. It is prima facie evidence that a person entered in violation of this section if he is found unlawfully in such a railroad car, motor vehicle, trailer, aircraft, boat, or other watercraft.

Elements

I. Breaking or Entering Vehicle

A person guilty of this offense
(1) breaks or enters
(2) without consent
(3) any railroad car, motor vehicle, trailer, aircraft, boat, or other watercraft
(4) containing goods, wares, freight, or anything of value
(5) with the intent to commit any felony or larceny therein.

II. Breaking out of Vehicle

A person guilty of this offense
(1) breaks out of
(2) any railroad car, motor vehicle, trailer, aircraft, boat, or other watercraft
(3) containing goods, wares, freight, or anything of value
(4) after having committed any felony or larceny therein.

Punishment

Class I felony.

Notes

Definitions. For the meaning of "breaking," "entering," "without consent," and "intent to commit any felony or larceny," see the notes under "First-Degree Burglary." A defendant was found to have entered a van when he leaned through an open door with the upper part of his body while standing on the street (38 N.C. App. 230), and the defendants who opened and looked under the hood of an automobile were held to have entered the automobile even though a chain lock prevented the hood from being opened more than 18 inches (64 N.C. App. 663). Also, it is a felony to break or enter a vehicle with the intent to commit *any* larceny, whether misdemeanor or felonious larceny (34 N.C. App. 452).

Proof of personal property within vehicle. Element (4) of "Breaking or Entering Vehicle," (I., above), and Element (3) of "Breaking out of Vehicle," (II., above), require proof that a vehicle contained personal property of some value, however trivial (such as a vehicle registration card, hubcap key, papers, cigarettes, or a shoe bag) (321 N.C. 267).

Trailer as dwelling. If the trailer involved is someone's *dwelling* (see "First-Degree Burglary"), the offense is either burglary or felonious breaking or entering, which carry higher penalties than this offense.

Breaking out of vehicle. This statute also applies if the defendant breaks *out* of a vehicle after committing larceny or any other felony in it. See the notes on "Breaking out of a Dwelling."

Prima facie case. The statute provides that being found in a vehicle unlawfully creates a prima facie case that the person entered in violation of this statute.

Larceny pursuant to breaking into a vehicle is not necessarily a felony; value of property taken is relevant. Larceny committed pursuant to burglary, breaking out of a building, breaking or entering a building, or burglary by explosive is a felony regardless of the value of the property taken (G.S. 14-72; see "Felonious Larceny" in Chapter 11). However, larceny is not a felony simply because it was committed pursuant to breaking or entering a vehicle, or breaking out of a vehicle. If a larceny occurs in such a breaking, it would be a felony only if one of the other factors making larceny a felony under G.S. 14-72 is present. For example, if the property taken from the vehicle was valued at more than $1,000 or a firearm was stolen, then it would be felonious larceny.

Relation to other offenses. Tampering with a motor vehicle [G.S. 20-107(a)] is not a lesser-included offense of this offense (96 N.C. App. 230).

Related offenses not in this chapter

See the offenses listed under "First-Degree Burglary."
Injuring or tampering with vehicle [G.S. 20-107(a)]

Breaking into Coin- or Currency-Operated Machine

Statute

§14-56.1. Breaking into or forcibly opening coin- or currency-operated machines.

Any person who forcibly breaks into, or by the unauthorized use of a key or other instrument opens, any coin- or currency-operated machine with intent to steal any property or moneys therein shall be guilty of a Class 1 misdemeanor, but if such person has previously been convicted of violating this section, such person shall be punished as a Class I felon. The term "coin- or currency-operated machine" shall mean any coin- or currency-operated vending machine, pay telephone, telephone coin or currency receptacle, or other coin- or currency-activated machine or device.

There shall be posted on the machines referred to in G.S. 14-56.1 a decal stating that it is a crime to break into vending machines, and that a second offense is a felony. The absence of such a decal is not a defense to a prosecution for the crime described in this section.

Elements

A person guilty of this offense
(1) breaks into
(2) without consent
(3) a coin-operated or currency-operated machine
(4) with the intent to steal property or money therein.

Punishment

The first offense is a Class 1 misdemeanor. A second or subsequent offense is a Class I felony.

Notes

Use of key. The statute provides that this offense is also committed by the unauthorized opening of the machine with a key or other instrument.

Element (2). A defendant does not "break" into a machine if an authorized person consents to his or her opening of the machine (N.C.P.I.—Crim. 214.55).

Element (3). See the last sentence of the statute's first paragraph for the broad definition of "coin- or currency-operated machine."

Notice of penalty. In setting out this crime, the statute says that the coin- or currency-operated machine is to have posted on it a decal stating that breaking into the machine is a crime and that a second offense is a felony. However, it also provides that the absence of the required warning decal is not a defense to a prosecution.

Related offenses not in this chapter

"Injury to Personal Property" (Chapter 16)
"Felonious Larceny" (Chapter 11)
"Misdemeanor Larceny" (Chapter 11)
Breaking into paper currency machines (G.S. 14-56.3)
Obtaining property from vending machine by false token (G.S. 14-108)

Damaging or Destroying Coin- or Currency-Operated Machine

Statute

§14-56.2. Damaging or destroying coin- or currency-operated machines.

Any person who shall willfully and maliciously damage or destroy any coin- or currency-operated machine shall be guilty of a Class 1 misdemeanor. The term "coin- or currency-operated machine" shall be defined as set out in G.S. 14-56.1.

Elements

A person guilty of this offense
(1) willfully, *and*
(2) maliciously

(3) damages or destroys
(4) a coin-operated or currency-operated machine.

Punishment

Class 1 misdemeanor.

Notes

Elements (1) and (2). See the definitions of "willfully" and "maliciously" in Chapter 1, "States of Mind."

Element (4). For the broad definition of "coin- or currency- operated machine," see the last sentence of G.S. 14-56.1's first paragraph, reproduced under "Breaking into Coin- or Currency-Operated Machine."

Related offenses not in this chapter

See the offenses listed under "Breaking into Coin- or Currency-Operated Machine."

Burglary with Explosives

Statute

§14-57. Burglary with explosives.

Any person who, with intent to commit any felony or larceny therein, breaks and enters, either by day or by night, any building, whether inhabited or not, and opens or attempts to open any vault, safe, or other secure place by use of nitroglycerine, dynamite, gunpowder, or any other explosive, or acetylene torch, shall be deemed guilty of burglary with explosives. Any person convicted under this section shall be punished as a Class D felon.

Elements

A person guilty of this offense
(1) breaks, *and*
(2) enters
(3) without consent
(4) any building
(5) with the intent to commit any felony or larceny, *and*
(6) opens or attempts to open any vault, safe, or other secure place
(7) by use of nitroglycerine, dynamite, gunpowder, or any other explosive or acetylene torch.

Punishment

Class D felony.

Notes

Definitions. For the meaning of "breaking," "entering," "without consent," and "intent to commit any felony or larceny," see the notes under "First-Degree Burglary."

Elements (1) and (2). The breaking and entering involved in this offense may occur at any time and in any building, but note that *both* breaking and entering are required to constitute this offense.

Element (5). Almost always, the felony intended will be larceny. Larceny by breaking or entering a building is always a felony, regardless of the value of property involved (G.S. 14-72; see "Felonious Larceny" in Chapter 11).

Element (6). To commit this offense, the intruder must also open, or attempt to open, a vault, safe, or other secure place with explosives or an acetylene torch.

Entry without breaking. Suppose the intruder enters a building through a door standing open, without permission and with the intent to steal, and then forces open a vault or safe inside with dynamite. The intruder has not violated this statute because he or she did not "break" before entering; however, the intruder has violated G.S. 14-54(a) (see "Felonious Breaking or Entering of Building") because he or she entered the building with the intent to commit larceny, and the intruder has also violated G.S. 14-89.1 (see "Safecracking").

Related offenses not in this chapter

See the offenses listed under "First-Degree Burglary" and "Breaking into Coin- or Currency-Operated Machine."

Safecracking

Statute

§14-89.1. Safecracking.

(a) A person is guilty of safecracking if he unlawfully opens, enters, or attempts to open or enter a safe or vault:

(1) By the use of explosives, drills, or tools; or
(2) Through the use of a stolen combination, key, electronic device, or other fraudulently acquired implement or means; or
(3) Through the use of a master key, duplicate key or device made or obtained in an unauthorized manner, stethoscope or other listening device, electronic device used for unauthorized entry in a safe or vault, or other surreptitious means; or
(4) By the use of any other safecracking implement or means.

(b) A person is also guilty of safecracking if he unlawfully removes from its premises a safe or vault for the purpose of stealing, tampering with, or ascertaining its contents.

(c) Safecracking shall be punishable as a Class I felony.

Elements

A person guilty of this offense

(1) unlawfully opens or attempts to open or enters or attempts to enter
(2) a safe or vault
(3) by any of the following means:
    (a) explosives
    (b) drills
    (c) tools
    (d) stolen combination
    (e) stolen key
    (f) stolen electronic device
    (g) other fraudulently acquired implement or means

(h) master key made or obtained in an unauthorized manner
(i) duplicate key made or obtained in an unauthorized manner
(j) other device made or obtained in an unauthorized manner
(k) stethoscope
(l) listening device
(m) electronic device
(n) other surreptitious means, *or*
(o) any other safecracking implement or means.

Punishment

Class I felony.

Notes

Element (2). For the illegal opening of a safe or vault to constitute safecracking, it is not necessary that the safe or vault have a combination type of lock (272 N.C. 312). Under a prior version of the statute, for the crime to be safecracking the safe had to be kept and customarily used for storing money or other valuables when the forcible opening occurred. Thus when a defendant attempted to force open a safe that the owner had just acquired but had not yet begun using to store valuables, the defendant did not commit safecracking (272 N.C. 439). The present statute does not make this a requirement.

Element (3). The courts have considered "tools" to include acetylene torches, blowtorches, chisels, saws, sledgehammers, and the like (280 N.C. 81; 26 N.C. App. 151).

Attempt. Safecracking and attempted safecracking are punishable equally. Thus if an offender attempts to force open a safe, the offender commits safecracking even if he or she fails to open it. Mere preparation (such as obtaining the necessary tools) is not an attempt; for an attempt to be made, some step must be taken toward forcing the safe open, such as cutting off a dial, chiseling out part of the concrete base, or smudging the safe with a blowtorch (280 N.C. 81). See the discussion under "Attempt" in Chapter 4.

Related offenses not in this chapter

See the offenses listed under "First-Degree Burglary" and "Breaking into Coin- or Currency-Operated Machine."

Safecracking by Removing Safe

Statute

See subsection (b) of G.S. 14-89.1, reproduced under "Safecracking."

Elements

A person guilty of this offense
(1) unlawfully removes from its premises
(2) a safe or vault
(3) for the purpose of
  (a) stealing its contents, *or*
  (b) tampering with its contents, *or*
  (c) ascertaining its contents.

Punishment	Class I felony.
Notes	**Element (2).** A prior version of the statute required that the safe or vault be used for storing valuables, but that is no longer necessary for this offense to be charged. See the note on Element (2) under "Safecracking." **Element (3).** It is not necessary that any one of these three purposes actually be accomplished; the defendant need only intend to commit one of these three acts when removing the safe.
Related offenses not in this chapter	See the offenses listed under "First-Degree Burglary" and "Breaking into Coin- or Currency-Operated Machine."

14
Fraud, Forgery, False Pretenses, and Related Offenses

Chapter Contents

14
Fraud, Forgery, False Pretenses, and Related Offenses

Worthless Check—Making or Uttering

Statute

§14-107. Worthless checks.

(a) It is unlawful for any person, firm or corporation, to draw, make, utter or issue and deliver to another, any check or draft on any bank or depository, for the payment of money or its equivalent, knowing at the time of the making, drawing, uttering, issuing and delivering the check or draft, that the maker or drawer of it has not sufficient funds on deposit in or credit with the bank or depository with which to pay the check or draft upon presentation.

(b) It is unlawful for any person, firm or corporation to solicit or to aid and abet any other person, firm or corporation to draw, make, utter or issue and deliver to any person, firm or corporation, any check or draft on any bank or depository for the payment of money or its equivalent, being informed, knowing or having reasonable grounds for believing at the time of the soliciting or the aiding and abetting that the maker or the drawer of the check or draft has not sufficient funds on deposit in, or credit with, the bank or depository with which to pay the check or draft upon presentation.

(c) The word "credit" as used in this section means an arrangement or understanding with the bank or depository for the payment of a check or draft.

(d) A violation of this section is a Class I felony if the amount of the check or draft is more than two thousand dollars ($2,000). If the amount of the check or draft is two thousand dollars ($2,000) or less, a violation of this section is a misdemeanor punishable as follows:

(1) Except as provided in subdivision (3) or (4) of this subsection, the person is guilty of a Class 2 misdemeanor. Provided, however, if the person has been convicted three times of violating this section, the person shall on the fourth and all subsequent convictions (i) be punished as for a Class 1 misdemeanor and (ii) be ordered, as a condition of probation, to refrain from maintaining a checking account or making or uttering a check for three years.

(2) Repealed by Session Laws 1999-408, s. 1, effective December 1, 1999.

(3) If the check or draft is drawn upon a nonexistent account, the person is guilty of a Class 1 misdemeanor.

(4) If the check or draft is drawn upon an account that has been closed by the drawer, or that the drawer knows to have been closed by the bank or depository, prior to time the check is drawn, the person is guilty of a Class 1 misdemeanor.

(e) In deciding to impose any sentence other than an active prison sentence, the sentencing judge shall consider and may require, in accordance with the provisions of

G.S. 15A-1343, restitution to the victim for (i) the amount of the check or draft, (ii) any service charges imposed on the payee by a bank or depository for processing the dishonored check, and (iii) any processing fees imposed by the payee pursuant to G.S. 25-3-506, and each prosecuting witness (whether or not under subpoena) shall be entitled to a witness fee as provided by G.S. 7A-314 which shall be taxed as part of the cost and assessed to the defendant.

Elements

A person guilty of this offense

(1) makes and delivers
(2) a check or draft
(3) without having sufficient funds or credit with the bank for the check or draft to be paid, *and*
(4) knowing that there are insufficient funds or credit available for the payment.

Punishment

Class 2 misdemeanor if the check or draft is for $2,000 or less. For a fourth or subsequent conviction at this misdemeanor level, the offense is a Class 1 misdemeanor. Additionally, the sentencing judge must order, as a part of probation for a repeat offender on his or her fourth offense, that the offender refrain from maintaining a checking account or making or uttering a check for three years. If the check or draft is for more than $2,000, the offense is a Class I felony.

Notes

Element (1). The statute specifically requires that a person "draw, make, utter or issue, *and* [emphasis added] deliver" a worthless check. This phrase's exact meaning is not entirely clear. One interpretation is that evidence of this element shows that a defendant is involved with both creating a worthless check (by writing it, endorsing it, etc.) *and* delivering it to another person. This is probably the best interpretation of the case law as well (see 194 N.C. 498; 220 N.C. 812; 243 N.C. 216; 253 N.C. 459; 81 N.C. App. 499). These courts relied on the General Assembly's words in creating this offense in 1927:

> Whereas, the common practice of giving checks, drafts, and bills of exchange, without first providing funds in or credits with the depository on which the same are drawn to pay and satisfy the same, tends to create the circulation of worthless paper, overdrafts, bad banking, and check kiting, and a mischief to trade and commerce; and it being the purpose of this act to remedy this evil (quoted in 194 N.C. 498).

This legislative language implies that both failing to have adequate funds *and* passing worthless instruments were to be remedied by creation of this criminal statute. Some court decisions emphasize the delivery of bad checks, without mentioning the creation part of the element (see, e.g., 253 N.C. 459). This is probably the exception rather than the norm, however. These courts seem to have simply overlooked the legislative emphasis on the creation part of the element.

The creation or making part of the element may also be described as "writing," "issuing," or "uttering." "Issuing" and "uttering" are confusing as well, because their meaning in this context includes both elements of creation and delivery. For example, issuing means to send forth or produce, and also means delivery (266 N.C. 115) [this meaning of "uttering" differs from that in "Uttering Forged Checks and Securities or Forging Endorsement on Them," discussed below in this chapter, where the term means passing or attempting to pass an item]. Delivering may also be described as "passing" or "giving" (266 N.C. 115).

Element (2). All checks and drafts on a bank or deposit are included, but not IOUs. A *postdated* check does not fall within the purview of this element (198 N.C. 522; 204 N.C. 162).

The North Carolina Supreme Court has issued conflicting rulings concerning whether it is a violation of G.S. 14-107 when there is an agreement between the check writer and the check recipient to hold a check written on an account with insufficient funds for later deposit. One case (220 N.C. 812) ruled it was a violation, and another case (205 N.C. 784) ruled it was not. It would appear that such an agreement is similar to when a person gives a postdated check to another and therefore does not satisfy this element. It also would appear that a delayed deposit check taken by a check-cashing business under G.S. 53-281 does not satisfy this element.

Element (3). For this element to be satisfied, it is necessary only that the funds be insufficient; they need not be totally lacking. "Credit" refers to an arrangement or understanding by which the bank will honor a check even if the actual funds on deposit are insufficient.

Element (4). The defendant must *know* that the funds on deposit are insufficient to cover the check. If the bank declines to honor the check for reasons other than insufficiency (for example, a "stop payment" on the check), this statute is not violated (260 N.C. 542).

While the statute sets out methods by which prima facie evidence of other elements of this offense can be established, there is no such prima facie standard for proving knowledge (106 N.C. App. 334). Return of a check due to insufficient funds or lack of credit does not constitute prima facie evidence that the person issuing the check knew at the time of issuance that there were insufficient funds or lack of credit to pay the check on presentation (106 N.C. App. 334).

Consent not a defense. The fact that anyone, including the payee, consented to the making or uttering of a worthless check does not constitute a defense to the charge (243 N.C. 216).

Soliciting or aiding and abetting. The statute also makes a person who solicits the writing of a bad check or aids and abets it equally guilty with the check writer. See "Aiding and Abetting Felony" in Chapter 3 and "Solicitation of Another to Commit a Felony" in Chapter 4, for descriptions of conduct constituting each of these offenses.

Similar offenses. For this offense to be committed, the defendant need not receive anything of value. If the defendant received anything in return for the check, he or she may also be guilty of "Obtaining Property for Worthless Check," described later in this chapter, which requires proof that the defendant had an intent to cheat and defraud. But uttering a worthless check is not a lesser-included offense of obtaining property by false pretenses (308 N.C. 502); nor is it a lesser-included offense of uttering forged checks (330 N.C. 249).

The North Carolina Supreme Court has ruled that a prosecution for obtaining property by false pretenses is permitted even without an additional representation beyond the presentation of the worthless check (346 N.C. 262, which overruled contrary views in 308 N.C. 502, 79 N.C. App. 177, and 70 N.C. App. 530). Evidence that a defendant paid for a motorcycle and accessories with a check written on an account that the defendant knew was closed was sufficient to convict the defendant of obtaining property by false pretenses (346 N.C. 262; the court did not decide in this case whether a defendant could be convicted of and punished for both obtaining property by false pretenses and making or uttering a worthless check).

Jurisdiction to prosecute if part of offense is committed outside North Carolina. North Carolina has the jurisdiction (jurisdiction means the authority of a government to act) to charge and prosecute this offense as long as one element of the offense occurs in North Carolina (81 N.C. App. 499). Note, however, that G.S. 15A-134 provides that if an offense occurs in part in North Carolina and in part outside North Carolina, a person charged with that offense may be tried in North Carolina only if he or she has not been tried (that is, placed in jeopardy) for the identical offense in another state.

Venue of trial if elements of offense are committed in more than one county in North Carolina. G.S. 15A-132(a) provides that if acts or omissions constituting an offense occurred in more than one county, each county has concurrent venue (venue means the place of a trial). If a defendant writes a worthless check in county A and mails it to county B, then each county has venue to try the offense. G.S. 15A-132(c) provides that when counties have concurrent venue, the first county in which a charge is issued becomes the county with exclusive venue. Thus if county A issues an arrest warrant or criminal summons for this offense, then the offense will be tried in county A. However, if county A dismisses the charge before trial, county B may bring the charge and prosecute in county B (316 N.C. 630).

Use of affidavits at hearing or trial. Subsections (a) through (e) of G.S. 14-107.1 provide that an affidavit (satisfying the statute's detailed requirements) of a person accepting a check is admissible as prima facie evidence in a prosecution of a G.S. 14-107 violation to establish that the defendant was the person who passed the check; the check also may be introduced with its markings (for example, "insufficient funds") as prima facie evidence of the reason why the bank did not accept it. This prima facie evidence rule does not apply unless the affidavit has been filed before issuance of the initial charge.

G.S. 14-107.1(f) provides that an affidavit of a bank employee is admissible at a district court hearing or trial to prove the reason for dishonor of the check, such as whether there were sufficient funds in the account or other related matters. The defendant must be provided with a copy of the affidavit before trial and have the opportunity to subpoena the affiant for trial.

Related offenses not in this chapter

None.

Worthless Check on Nonexistent Account

Statute

See G.S. 14-107, especially subdivision (d)(3), reproduced under "Worthless Check—Making or Uttering."

Elements

A person guilty of this offense

(1) makes and delivers
(2) a check or draft
(3) drawn on a nonexistent account
(4) knowing that the check was drawn on a nonexistent account.

Punishment

Class 1 misdemeanor.

Notes

Elements (1) and (2). See the notes on these same elements under "Worthless Check—Making or Uttering."

Element (3). To prove this offense, it must be shown that the person who made the check did not have a checking account with the institution at the time the check was drawn (N.C.P.I.—Crim. 219.52). This charge probably would not be appropriate if the check was written on an account that simply had been closed, no matter how long it had been closed (see "Worthless Check on Closed Account," immediately following this offense) or if the check was written on someone else's account with the institution. This charge *would* be appropriate if the defendant had written a fictitious account number on a counter check.

Element (4). See the note on Element (4) under "Worthless Check—Making or Uttering."

Similar offenses. See this note under "Worthless Check—Making or Uttering."

Related offenses not in this chapter

None.

Worthless Check on Closed Account

Statute

See G.S. 14-107, especially subdivision (d)(4), reproduced under "Worthless Check—Making or Uttering," above.

Elements

A person guilty of this offense
- (1) makes and delivers
- (2) a check or draft
- (3) drawn on an account that
  - (a) had been closed by the person who wrote the check or draft before the check or draft was written, *or*
  - (b) the person who wrote the check or draft knew to have been closed by the bank or depository before the check or draft was written
- (4) knowing that the check was drawn on such an account.

Punishment

Class 1 misdemeanor.

Notes

Elements (1) and (2). See the notes under "Worthless Check—Making or Uttering."

Element (3). A 1999 legislative amendment added an additional way to prove this element, which is set out in (3)(b). It is no longer required that the person who wrote the check be the one who closed the account. It is sufficient if the person who wrote the check knew the account had been closed by the bank before the check was written.

Element (4). See the note on Element (4) under "Worthless Check—Making or Uttering."

Similar offenses. See this note under "Worthless Check—Making or Uttering."

Related offenses not in this chapter

None.

Obtaining Property for Worthless Check

Statute

§14-106. Obtaining property in return for worthless check, draft or order.

Every person who, with intent to cheat and defraud another, shall obtain money, credit, goods, wares or any other thing of value by means of a check, draft or order of any kind upon any bank, person, firm or corporation, not indebted to the drawer, or where he has not provided for the payment or acceptance of the same, and the same be not paid upon presentation, shall be guilty of a Class 2 misdemeanor. The giving of the aforesaid worthless check, draft, or order shall be prima facie evidence of an intent to cheat and defraud.

Elements

A person guilty of this offense

(1) makes and delivers to another a check, draft, or order of any kind drawn on a bank, person, firm, or corporation in which the person has no money, *and*
(2) the person has made no arrangements for payment or acceptance of the check, *and*
(3) the check is not paid on presentation to the bank, *and*
(4) the person thereby obtains money, credit, goods, wares, or any other thing of value
(5) with the intent to cheat and defraud the other person.

Punishment

Class 2 misdemeanor.

Notes

Element (1). See the note on Element (1) under "Worthless Check—Making or Uttering." Exactly what act the defendant must perform with the worthless check to obtain something of value is not clear from the statute. Examining the legislative intent indicates that the best interpretation might be that a defendant must make and deliver the check. However, there is some authority that simply "giving" the worthless check is sufficient (N.C.P.I.—Crim. 219.40).

Element (2). Even though a person has no money in an account, the person has not committed a crime if he or she has arranged for the bank to cover checks or automatically make a loan to his or her account.

Element (3). The check must have been presented and payment refused before the crime is complete.

Element (4). The statute specifies that this offense includes obtaining money, credit, goods, wares, or any other "thing of value." "Thing of value" could fairly be interpreted to include services. See, for example, G.S. 14-100, which lists "services" as a "thing of value" insofar as obtaining property by false pretenses is concerned.

Element (5). This element is not satisfied unless the defendant intended to defraud the victim. If, for example, the defendant expected to have money in the bank by the time the check was presented, this intent would be absent. However, the statute provides that merely giving a worthless check or draft is prima facie evidence of the intent to defraud.

Similar offenses. Conduct covered by this offense might also be covered by "Worthless Check on Nonexistent Account" or "Worthless Check on Closed Account," described earlier in this chapter. Neither of those offenses requires proof of an intent to cheat and defraud or that the defendant obtained property.

Related offenses not in this chapter

None.

Obtaining Property by False Pretenses

Statute

§14-100. Obtaining property by false pretenses.

(a) If any person shall knowingly and designedly by means of any kind of false pretense whatsoever, whether the false pretense is of a past or subsisting fact or of a future fulfillment or event, obtain or attempt to obtain from any person within this State any money, goods, property, services, chose in action, or other thing of value with intent to cheat or defraud any person of such money, goods, property, services, chose in action or other thing of value, such person shall be guilty of a felony: Provided, that if, on the trial of anyone indicted for such crime, it shall be proved that he obtained the property in such manner as to amount to larceny or embezzlement, the jury shall have submitted to them such other felony proved; and no person tried for such felony shall be liable to be afterwards prosecuted for larceny or embezzlement upon the same facts: Provided, further, that it shall be sufficient in any indictment for obtaining or attempting to obtain any such money, goods, property, services, chose in action, or other thing of value by false pretenses to allege that the party accused did the act with intent to defraud, without alleging an intent to defraud any particular person, and without alleging any ownership of the money, goods, property, services, chose in action or other thing of value; and upon the trial of any such indictment, it shall not be necessary to prove either an intent to defraud any particular person or that the person to whom the false pretense was made was the person defrauded, but it shall be sufficient to allege and prove that the party accused made the false pretense charged with an intent to defraud. If the value of the money, goods, property, services, chose in action, or other thing of value is one hundred thousand dollars ($100,000) or more, a violation of this section is a Class C felony. If the value of the money, goods, property, services, chose in action, or other thing of value is less than one hundred thousand dollars ($100,000), a violation of this section is a Class H felony.

(b) Evidence of nonfulfillment of a contract obligation standing alone shall not establish the essential element of intent to defraud.

(c) For purposes of this section, "person" means person, association, consortium, corporation, body politic, partnership, or other group, entity, or organization.

Elements

A person guilty of this offense
(1) makes a representation of a past or existing fact or a future event
(2) that is false, *and*
(3) is calculated and intended to deceive, *and*
(4) does in fact deceive another person, *and*
(5) the person thereby obtains, or attempts to obtain, money, property, services, or some other thing of value from that other person.

Punishment

Class H felony. It is a Class C felony if the value of the property taken is $100,000 or more.

Notes

Element (1). The representation may be of a past fact, an existing fact, a promise of future performance, or a statement that something will happen in the future. The representation need not be oral or written; it can be communicated by action (4 N.C. App. 484). Examples of false representations include false statements that property pledged as security is free of liens (220 N.C. 113); false statements about the value of security given for a loan (299 N.C. 229); false statements that a person is a broker who will invest money in stocks (111 N.C. App. 569); creation of a false business for the purpose of writing worthless checks (101 N.C. App. 519); false statements as to the defendant's identity (35 N.C. App. 531); use of counterfeit money (35 N.C. App. 95); presentation of a worthless check (346 N.C. 262); and falsified invoices (35 N.C. App. 119). Convictions of this offense were upheld when the defendant created a fictional business for the purpose of inducing merchants to cash worthless checks presented by the defendant's cohorts posing as employees of the business (308 N.C. 502), and when the defendant cashed a worthless check by presenting an identification card representing him to be a present employee of a company when in fact he was an ex-employee and the company was defunct (70 N.C. App. 530).

Element (2). Court decisions in other states suggest that the defendant's honest belief that the representation was true may be a valid defense to a charge of obtaining property by false pretenses (*Perkins*, p. 379).

Element (3). The statute says that "it shall not be necessary to prove . . . an intent to defraud any particular person. . . ." This provision means that this charge may be made even if the defendant did not intend to deceive a specific person (N.C.P.I.—Crim. 219.10; 299 N.C. 229).

Elements (1), (2), and (3). While a false promise to perform an act in the future may satisfy the requirement that a defendant made a false representation with intent to defraud, proof that a defendant failed to fulfill a contractual duty through ineptness or lack of diligence is not sufficient to satisfy these elements (90 N.C. App. 101; 106 N.C. App. 695). The statute itself provides that evidence of nonfulfillment of a contract, standing alone, cannot establish intent to defraud.

Element (4). "Person," either as the defendant or as the victim, is broadly defined in the statute to include corporations, partnerships, associations, organizations, and other groups. The statute provides that the person to whom the false pretense was made need not be the person defrauded. An agent allegedly obtaining anything of value for a corporation by false pretenses may be charged with this offense along with the corporation (36 N.C. App. 271; 106 N.C. App. 695).

Element (5). For this charge to be made, the defendant must gain possession of the property but need not gain title or ownership interest. Thus a defendant who rented a typewriter by falsely representing his identity and saying he would return the machine in one hour, but who did not return it, was properly convicted of this offense (67 N.C. App. 110). Additionally, a defendant who told a car salesman she wanted to test drive a car after falsely representing her identity was properly convicted of this offense after she drove away in the car and did not return it (75 N.C. App. 461).

Whether the defendant intends to pay for the property later is irrelevant for purposes of this element; if he or she intended to defraud the owner of the property to obtain it, the element is satisfied (35 N.C. App. 531). The false representation must be a factor in inducing the victim to part with property, but the false representation need not necessarily be the only inducement to the victim (*Perkins*, p. 383; 220 N.C. 113).

If the defendant makes a false representation for some reason other than to obtain the property, this crime has not occurred. There must be a causal relationship between the false representation and the obtaining of property (299 N.C. 229). For example, when a town official, with the authority to write checks, wrote checks on the town's account to pay for train tickets for unauthorized private travel by herself and others and falsified the check records to conceal the true purpose of the checks (thus making a false representation to the town), there was no causal connection between the false representation (the falsified check records) and the obtaining of the town's money, and the defendant was not guilty of obtaining property by false pretenses (48 N.C. App. 526). If this same defendant had been required to obtain another official's approval of the checks and vouchers before payment, and the defendant submitted a false voucher as described, then prosecution for obtaining property by false pretenses would be proper. In this alternative scenario, the false statement would be causally related to obtaining the town's money. Likewise, if a person required to submit vouchers for reimbursement of work-related expenses makes a false statement on a voucher to receive payment to which the person is not entitled, obtaining property by false pretenses is a proper charge.

Actual loss and absence of compensation not required. This offense can be charged even though the person who gives up the property, services, etc., does not suffer economic loss. If the elements of the offense are established, the fact that this person suffered no loss is not a defense (36 N.C. App. 33). It need not be proved that the defendant obtained the property, services, etc., without paying compensation (299 N.C. 229) in order to convict for this offense.

Attempt. The statute provides that an attempt to commit this offense is treated the same as the completed offense. To convict for this crime, it is not necessary to prove that the intended victim actually was deceived; for example, in one case the defendant attempted to obtain money from a store owner in exchange for below-cost cigarettes (which the evidence showed never existed), gave the store owner a bill of lading, refused to let him see the goods, demanded the money, and was immediately arrested by undercover police who were observing the transaction (57 N.C. App. 40).

Relationship to Larceny (various offenses) and "Embezzlement" (both in Chapter 11). At common law, larceny was committed by a person who, with intent to deprive an owner permanently of property, obtained possession—rather than "title," or actual claim to ownership—of another's property. Larceny remains so defined in North Carolina today. At common law, obtaining property by false pretenses was committed if title to, and not just possession of, property passed as a result of a false representation. For example, if person A asks to borrow a watch from person B, promising to return it in a few hours, but with no intention to do so, and then A does not return it to B, "title" to the watch does not pass (B thinks A has borrowed a watch that B still owns), and A has committed larceny by trick. If, however, person C lies in telling a jeweler he is accepting delivery of a new watch on behalf of another (person D who has paid for the watch) and C takes the watch away, "title" to the watch has passed from the jeweler to C (the jeweler thinks he or she has transferred title, or ownership, to D through C). Person C has obtained property by false pretenses, as defined at common law.

North Carolina's statutory definition of obtaining property by false pretenses, first codified in 1811, has never included the element of passage of title to property. This unique way of defining this offense renders inapplicable—and confusing—comparisons of larceny and obtaining property by false pretenses in general legal treatises. The above examples do not describe legal differences today between larceny and obtaining property by false pretenses in North Carolina. In two cases, the North Carolina Court of Appeals has explicitly said that title to property need not pass for the crime of obtaining property by false pretenses to be committed (67 N.C. App. 110; 75 N.C. App. 461). The court found that because the statute defining this crime does not require passage of title as an element of the statutory offense (67 N.C. App. 110), passage of title need not be shown to convict a person of this offense. The court relied, in part, on the absence of discussion of this element in previous supreme court opinions (67 N.C. App. 110; 299 N.C. 229).

In the absence of the title/possession distinction prevalent in other states, there are only three important differences between larceny and obtaining property by false pretenses in North Carolina: (1) obtaining property by false pretenses requires a false representation, while larceny has no such requirement (of course, a false representation *may* be the basis of larceny by trick; see Larceny (various offenses) in Chapter 11); (2) larceny requires that property be wrongfully taken without the owner's consent, while obtaining property by false pretenses frequently involves the initial consent of the property owner (75 N.C. App. 461); and (3) larceny requires that the defendant intend to permanently deprive the property owner of his or her property, but obtaining false pretenses does not. A defense to larceny might be that the defendant intended to return the property, but such a claim is not a defense to obtaining property by false pretenses (105 N.C. App. 182).

North Carolina's definition of obtaining property by false pretenses leads to at least two problems: (1) North Carolina relies on common law, not statute, to define larceny, and larceny does not encompass criminal activity in which a person obtains title to property (of course, a person who obtained possession and title could be prosecuted for larceny)—consequently, such criminal conduct is not squarely addressed in our law. Additionally, confusion results because the common law suggests that obtaining property by false pretenses should be based on passage of title to property, rather than mere change in possession (see, for example, N.C.P.I.—Crim. 219.10, footnote 2). (2) This definition makes it very difficult to distinguish larceny by trick from obtaining property by false pretenses; it could be used to rationalize elevating an offense which would normally be thought of as misdemeanor larceny by trick (a Class 1 misdemeanor) to the Class H felony of obtaining property by false pretenses.

Embezzlement's most distinguishing feature is that it must be committed by a person who has been entrusted with the care of particular property. See the note on Element (4) under "Embezzlement" in Chapter 11. A person who embezzles does so after legally obtaining the missing property in the course of employment by virtue of a relationship entrusting him or her with the property. However, a person who commits obtaining property by false pretenses wrongfully obtains the property from the start (92 N.C. App. 265). Occasionally, situations arise in which it is not clear whether a person, like a store employee, has been entrusted with property. In these situations, the offense committed may be larceny or obtaining property by false pretenses. On the following facts, obtaining property by false pretenses is the proper charge: a store checkout clerk, who is not normally entrusted with the care of any property in the store, works out an arrangement with a non-employee friend to charge the friend a lesser amount than list price on items at the checkout, and the employee does so without authority. Arguably, the clerk has committed this offense by making a false representation of price for the store's cash register records with the intent to defraud, and thereby obtained the property for a friend. Larceny is probably not the appropriate charge for the employee because the employee does not "carry away" the property, as required by Element (2) of larceny. If there is evidence that a store employee has been entrusted with the property, then embezzlement (62 N.C. App. 12) or larceny by employee could be charged.

Relationship with worthless check offenses. Worthless check—making or uttering, worthless check on a nonexistent account, worthless check on a closed account, and obtaining property for worthless check are not lesser-included offenses of obtaining property by false pretenses (308 N.C. 502). The North Carolina Supreme Court has ruled that a prosecution for obtaining property by false pretenses is permitted even without an additional representation beyond the presentation of the worthless check (346 N.C. 262, which overruled contrary views in 308 N.C. 502, 79 N.C. App. 177, and 70 N.C. App. 530). Evidence that a defendant paid for a motorcycle and accessories with a check written on an account that the defendant knew was closed was sufficient to convict the defendant of obtaining property by false pretenses (346 N.C. 262; the court did not decide in this case whether a defendant could be convicted of and punished for both obtaining property by false pretenses and making or uttering a worthless check). When a defendant wrote checks with insufficient funds in a business checking account the defendant had opened, and there was evidence that the defendant had created the business as a sham for the purpose of writing worthless checks, conviction of obtaining property by false pretenses was appropriate (101 N.C. App. 519).

Choosing criminal charges and instructing the jury. The statute provides ". . . that, if on the trial of anyone indicted for such crime, it shall be proved that he obtained the property in such manner as to amount to larceny or embezzlement, the jury shall have submitted to them such other felony proved; and no person tried for such felony shall be liable to be afterwards prosecuted for larceny or embezzlement upon the same facts. . . ." Nevertheless, it may be possible for the state to charge a defendant with obtaining property by false pretenses after a trial for larceny or embezzlement (75 N.C. App. 461). The state is not required to elect between charges when there is substantial evidence tending to support both embezzlement and false pretenses arising from the same transaction. When both charges are present in a single trial based on a single transaction, the trial court must instruct the jury that it may convict the defendant of only one offense or the other, not of both (326 N.C. 576). A defendant may not be convicted of obtaining property by false pretenses as a lesser-included offense of embezzlement (108 N.C. App. 550).

Related offenses not in this chapter

Larceny (various offenses) (Chapter 11)
"Embezzlement" (Chapter 11)
"Creating Counterfeit Controlled Substance" (Chapter 24)
"Sale or Delivery of Counterfeit Controlled Substance" (Chapter 24)
"Possession of Counterfeit Controlled Substance with Intent to Sell or Deliver" (Chapter 24)
"Obtaining Controlled Substance by Fraud or Forgery" (Chapter 24)
Obtaining signatures by false pretenses (G.S. 14-101)
Obtaining property by false representation of pedigree of animals (G.S. 14-102)
Obtaining advances under promise to work (G.S. 14-104)
Obtaining property from slot machines with false tokens (G.S. 14-108)
Obtaining merchandise on approval (G.S. 14-112)
Obtaining telephone or telegraph service with intent to avoid payment (G.S. 14-113.4)
Obtaining property or services by false or fraudulent use of credit device (G.S. 14-113.1 through -113.7A)
Obtaining money by false representation of physical defect (G.S. 14-113)
Tampering with utility meters (G.S. 14-151.1)
Falsely registering as husband and wife (G.S. 14-186)
Use and production of counterfeit trademark (G.S. 80-11.1)
City ordinance violation: many ordinances prohibit obtaining taxi rides or meals in restaurants without paying

Financial Identity Fraud

Statute

§14-113.20. Financial identity fraud.

(a) A person who knowingly obtains, possesses, or uses personal identifying information of another person without the consent of that other person, with the intent to fraudulently represent that the person is the other person for the purposes of making financial or credit transactions in the other person's name or for the purpose of avoiding legal consequences is guilty of a felony punishable as provided in G.S. 14-113.22(a).

(b) The term "identifying information" as used in this section includes the following:

(1) Social security numbers.
(2) Drivers license numbers.
(3) Checking account numbers.
(4) Savings account numbers.
(5) Credit card numbers.
(6) Debit card numbers.
(7) Personal Identification (PIN) Code as defined in G.S. 14-113.8(6).
(8) Electronic identification numbers.
(9) Digital signatures.
(10) Any other numbers or information that can be used to access a person's financial resources.

(c) It shall not be a violation under this section for a person to do any of the following:

(1) Lawfully obtain credit information in the course of a bona fide consumer or commercial transaction.
(2) Lawfully exercise, in good faith, a security interest or a right of offset by a creditor or financial institution.
(3) Lawfully comply, in good faith, with any warrant, court order, levy, garnishment, attachment, or other judicial or administrative order, decree, or directive, when any party is required to do so.

§14-113.21. Venue of offenses.

In any criminal proceeding brought under G.S. 14-113.20, the crime is considered to be committed in any county in which any part of the financial identity fraud took place, regardless of whether the defendant was ever actually present in that county.

§14-113.22. Punishment and liability.

(a) A violation of G.S. 14-113.20 is punishable as a Class H felony, except if the victim suffers arrest, detention, or conviction as a proximate result of the offense, then the violation is punishable as a Class G felony.

(b) Notwithstanding subsection (a) of this section, any person who knowingly obtains, possesses, or uses personal identifying information of another person without the consent of that other person, with the intent to fraudulently represent that the person is the other person for the purposes of making financial or credit transactions in the other person's name or for the purpose of avoiding legal consequences, shall be liable to the other person for civil damages of up to five thousand dollars ($5,000) for each incident, or three times the amount of actual damages, if any, sustained by the person damaged, whichever amount is greater. A person damaged as set forth in this subsection may also institute a civil action to enjoin and restrain future acts which would constitute a violation of this subsection. The court, in an action brought under this subsection, may award reasonable attorneys' fees to the prevailing party.

(c) In any case in which a person obtains identifying information of another person in violation of G.S. 14-113.20, uses that information to commit a crime in addition to a violation of G.S. 14-113.20, and is convicted of that additional crime, the court records shall reflect that the person whose identity was falsely used to commit the crime did not commit the crime.

Elements

A person guilty of this offense
(1) knowingly obtains, possesses, or uses
(2) personal identifying information of another person
(3) without the consent of that other person
(4) with the intent to fraudulently represent the person is the other person
(5) for the purpose of
  (a) making financial or credit transactions in the other person's name, *or*
  (b) avoiding legal consequences.

Punishment

Class H felony. However, if the victim suffers arrest, detention, or conviction as a proximate result of the offense, then the violation is a Class G felony (note that the state must allege this information in the criminal pleading and prove it at trial).

Notes

Element (2). "Identifying information" is defined in G.S. 14-113.20(b), reproduced above.

Element (5)(b). This offense primarily is aimed at the misuse of another person's identifying information for financial reasons. However, this element (and the other four elements) could be satisfied, for example, by evidence that a person gave a law enforcement officer a driver's license number of another person to avoid the legal consequences of being issued a speeding ticket.

Related offenses not in this chapter

None.

Defrauding Innkeeper or Campground Owner

Statute

§14-110. Defrauding innkeeper or campground owner.

No person shall, with intent to defraud, obtain food, lodging, or other accommodations at a hotel, inn, boardinghouse, eating house, or campground. Whoever violates this section shall be guilty of a Class 2 misdemeanor. Obtaining such lodging, food, or other accommodation by false pretense, or by false or fictitious show of pretense of baggage or other property, or absconding without paying or offering to pay therefor, or surreptitiously removing or attempting to remove such baggage, shall be prima facie evidence of such fraudulent intent, but this section shall not apply where there has been an agreement in writing for delay in such payment.

Elements

A person guilty of this offense
(1) with intent to defraud
(2) obtains food or lodging, or other accommodations
(3) at a hotel, inn, boardinghouse, eating house, or campground
(4) when there is no written agreement to delay payment.

Punishment

Class 2 misdemeanor.

Notes

Element (1). The statute provides that obtaining food or lodging "by false pretense [see "Obtaining Property by False Pretenses"], or by false or fictitious show of pretense of baggage or other property, or absconding without paying or offering to pay therefor, or surreptitiously removing or attempting to remove such baggage, shall be prima facie evidence of such fraudulent intent." Note that this activity is merely evidence of fraudulent intent, not necessarily conclusive proof.

Element (2). The offense includes obtaining food, room, or board, but not other items or services of value.

Element (3). A place is not a hotel, inn, boardinghouse, eating house, or campground unless it is licensed or held out to be such. A place is not necessarily a boardinghouse simply because it received payment for taking someone in (170 N.C. 712).

Element (4). The section does not apply when there is a written agreement to delay payment, even if the person never intended to pay. The statute does not clearly address the effect of payment of the bill by check or credit card, which naturally delays final receipt of cash by the innkeeper. It is also not clear whether the state must prove the absence of an agreement to delay payment unless the defendant claims that there was an agreement.

Related offenses not in this chapter

Obtaining property or services by false or fraudulent use of credit device (G.S. 14-113.1 through -113.7A)
Falsely registering as husband and wife (G.S. 14-186)

Fraudulent Disposal of Security

Statute

§14-114. Fraudulent disposal of personal property on which there is a security interest.

(a) If any person, after executing a security agreement on personal property for a lawful purpose, shall make any disposition of any property embraced in such security agreement, with intent to defeat the rights of the secured party, every person so offending and every person with a knowledge of the security interest buying any property embraced in which security agreement, and every person assisting, aiding or abetting the unlawful disposition of such property, with intent to defeat the rights of any secured party in such security agreement, shall be guilty of a Class 2 misdemeanor.

A person's refusal to turn over secured property to a secured party who is attempting to repossess the property without a judgment or order for possession shall not, by itself, be a violation of this section.

(b) Intent to commit the crime as set forth in subsection (a) may be presumed from proof of possession of the property embraced in such security agreement by the grantor thereof after execution of the security agreement, and while it is in force, the further proof of the fact that the sheriff or other officer charged with the execution of process cannot after due diligence find such property under process directed to him for its seizure, for the satisfaction of such security agreement. However, this presumption may be rebutted by evidence that the property has, through no fault of the defendant, been stolen, lost, damaged beyond repair, or otherwise disposed of by the defendant without intent to defeat the rights of the secured party.

Elements

A person guilty of this offense
(1) executes a security agreement on personal property for a lawful purpose, *and*
(2) while the security agreement is in force, disposes of property "embraced in the security agreement" or assists, aids, or abets the disposition of such property
(3) with the intent to defeat the rights of the secured party.

Punishment

Class 2 misdemeanor.

Notes

Generally. The statute provides that a person's refusal to turn over secured property to a secured party who is attempting to repossess the property without a judgment or order for possession is not, by itself, a violation of the statute.

Element (1). A security agreement is a written agreement that makes specified personal property subject to being claimed by another to whom the owner owes money if the owner should fail to make good on the debt. Any property to which the agreement refers is "embraced" in the agreement.

Element (2). It is not necessary to prove the identity of the person to whom the property was conveyed.

Evidence rule. The statute provides that the intent to commit the offense may be inferred (a) from proof of possession of the property embraced in the security agreement by the grantor after execution of the security agreement, and (b) from the fact that, while the agreement is in force, the sheriff or other officer executing process cannot after due diligence find the property under the process directing the officer to seize it to satisfy the agreement. This inference may be rebutted by evidence that the property has, through no fault of the defendant, been stolen, lost, damaged beyond repair, or otherwise disposed of by the defendant without the intent to defeat the rights of the secured party.

Related offenses not in this chapter

"Altering or Removing Serial Number" (Chapter 11)
Failure to make payment out of designated property (G.S. 14-105)

Fraudulent Purchase of Security

Statute

See G.S. 14-114, reproduced under "Fraudulent Disposal of Security."

Elements

A person guilty of this offense
(1) buys personal property embraced in a security agreement
(2) knowing that the security agreement is in force
(3) with intent to defeat the rights of the secured party.

Punishment

Class 2 misdemeanor.

Notes

Generally. See the notes under "Fraudulent Disposal of Security."

Related offenses not in this chapter

Failure to make payment out of designated property (G.S. 14-105)

Secreting Property to Hinder Enforcement of Security Interest

Statute

§14-115. Secreting property to hinder enforcement of lien or security interest.

Any person who, with intent to prevent or hinder the enforcement of the lien or security interest after a judgment or order has been issued for possession for that personal property subject to said lien or security interest, either refuses to surrender such personal property in his possession to a law enforcement officer, or removes, or exchanges, or secretes such personal property shall be guilty of a Class 2 misdemeanor.

Elements

A person guilty of this offense
- (1) (a) removes, exchanges, or secretes personal property, *or*
  - (b) refuses to surrender to a law enforcement officer personal property in that person's possession
- (2) on which a lien or security interest exists
- (3) after a judgment or order for possession has been issued for possession for that personal property
- (4) with intent to prevent or hinder the enforcement of the lien or security interest.

Punishment

Class 2 misdemeanor.

Notes

Generally. See the notes under "Fraudulent Disposal of Security."

Elements (1) and (2). For this offense to be committed, it is not necessary that the property be sold or disposed of; it need only be hidden or otherwise removed from the one who has a lien on it. Apparently the defendant need not be a party to the security agreement.

Related offenses not in this chapter

Failure to make payment out of designated property (G.S. 14-105)

Common-Law Forgery

Statute

This is a common-law offense.

Elements

A person guilty of this offense
- (1) makes a false writing
- (2) that is apparently capable of effecting a fraud
- (3) with intent to defraud.

Punishment

This is a Class 1 misdemeanor unless the criminal pleading alleges it was done "with deceit and intent to defraud." If deceit and intent to defraud are alleged, it is a Class H felony, pursuant to G.S. 14-3(b) and 317 N.C. 557. See "Committing an Infamous or Related Misdemeanor" (Chapter 4).

Notes

Element (1). This element may be satisfied by the defendant's making a false instrument, such as a railroad pass (94 N.C. 836); by signing a fictitious name to an instrument (256 N.C. 445); by signing a check with a name (fictitious or real) that is not on the signature card for the bank account (47 N.C. App. 623); by altering an instrument so that it is different from what it originally was (253 N.C. 799); by signing one's real name to an instrument intending that it be taken as the signature of someone with the same name (231 N.C. 510); or by signing someone else's name without authority (268 N.C. 522). When a person signs someone else's name, however, the law presumes that he or she has the authority to do so; the state must demonstrate the lack of authority (256 N.C. 445; 37 N.C. App. 40).

Evidence that (a) a defendant uttered a forged instrument and attempted to obtain money from it, or (b) that a defendant possessed a forged instrument, supports an inference that the possessor either forged or consented to forgery of the instrument (266 N.C. 291); that inference does not violate the defendant's rights to due process (42 N.C. App. 156; 51 N.C. App. 221). A jury instruction was unconstitutional, however, when it stated that a person who possesses a forged instrument and endeavors to obtain money with it is *presumed* to have forged or consented to its forgery, when the jury reasonably would have interpreted the presumption to be a conclusive or mandatory presumption; that presumption unconstitutionally shifted the burden of proof to the defendant (708 F. Supp. 730). An instruction on a permissive presumption or inference, permitting the jury to accept or reject an inference of forgery, would be constitutional.

Element (2). For this element to be satisfied, the instrument must be of the kind that either has some legal effect (115 N.C. 76; *Perkins*, p. 415) or can make the person who does the writing subject to legal liability (*Perkins*, p. 416). This means, for example, that a painting, historical document, or letter of introduction could not be the subject of forgery (although a copy of the painting, historical document, or letter of introduction, if used fraudulently to obtain property, can give rise to liability for obtaining property by false pretenses) (*Perkins*, p. 417). For this element to be satisfied, the false writing must appear to be genuine (49 N.C. App. 145; N.C.P.I.—Crim. 221.10). It must be enough like the real thing to mislead a reasonable person (94 N.C. 913), but it need not be a perfect copy; if the name of a person or corporation is misspelled (231 N.C. 510; 80 N.C. 407) or if the writing on the instrument is informal (94 N.C. 913), the false writing is still a forgery.

Element (3). It is not necessary that a person actually be defrauded (291 N.C. 442). The defendant need only *intend* that his or her false writing be used fraudulently. This element is satisfied even if no attempt is ever made to defraud anyone with it (268 N.C. 522).

When forged instrument is check. When the forgery is of a check or security, it is usually better to charge the statutory offense of forgery of notes, checks, and other securities.

Punishment for forgery and uttering. A person can be tried, convicted, and punished for forgery and for uttering the same document; punishment for both offenses does not violate the defendant's double jeopardy rights (42 N.C. App. 156).

Related offenses not in this chapter

"Committing an Infamous or Related Misdemeanor" (Chapter 4)
"Obtaining Controlled Substance by Fraud or Forgery" (Chapter 24)
Counterfeiting (G.S. 14-13 to -16)
Selling certain forged securities (G.S. 14-121)
Forgery of deeds, wills, and certain other instruments (G.S. 14-122)
Forgery of transcripts and diplomas (G.S. 14-122.1)
Forging names to petitions and uttering forged petitions (G.S. 14-123)
Forging certificate of corporate stock and uttering forged certificates (G.S. 14-124)
Forgery of instruments by connecting genuine parts (G.S. 14-125)
Forging vehicle title or registration (G.S. 20-71)
Possession of false vehicle title or registration [G.S. 20-111(2)]
Use and production of counterfeit trademark (G.S. 80-11.1)
Attempting to vote by forging name of registered voter [G.S. 163-237(c)]

Forgery of Notes, Checks, and Other Securities

Statute

§14-119. Forgery of notes, checks, and other securities.

(a) If a person makes, forges, or counterfeits:
(1) Any bill, note, warrant, check, order, or similar instrument in imitation of, or purporting to be, a bill, note, warrant, check, order, or similar instrument of or on any financial institution or governmental unit, or any cashier or officer of such an institution or unit; or
(2) Any security purporting to be issued by, or on behalf of, any corporation, financial institution, or governmental unit, with the intent to injure or defraud any person, corporation, financial institution, or governmental unit, he shall be punished as a Class I felon.

(b) For purposes of this section:
(1) "Financial institution" means any mutual fund, money market fund, credit union, savings and loan association, bank, or similar institution.
(2) "Governmental unit" means the United States, any United States territory, any state of the United States, or any political subdivision of any state.

Elements

A person guilty of this offense
(1) makes, forges, or counterfeits
(2) (a) a bill, note, warrant, check, order, or similar instrument purporting to be a bill, note, warrant, check, order, or similar instrument of or drawn on any financial institution or governmental unit or any officer of such an institution or unit, *or*
(b) a security purporting to be issued by or on behalf of any corporation, financial institution, or governmental unit
(3) with the intent to injure or defraud
(4) any person, corporation, financial institution, or governmental unit.

Punishment

Class I felony.

Notes

Generally. This offense is merely a codified version of common-law forgery (108 N.C. 777), except that it is limited to the specified kinds of written instruments and it is a felony. Forgery of instruments not covered by this statute may be charged under "Common-Law Forgery."

Element (1). See the note on Element (1) under "Common-Law Forgery."

Element (2). The writing that is made, forged, or counterfeited must be *either* a bill, note, warrant, check, etc., purporting to be of or drawn on a financial institution or governmental unit or officer of such an institution or unit *or* a security purporting to be issued by a corporation, financial institution, or governmental unit.

Element (3). See the note on Element (3) under "Common-Law Forgery."

Element (4). "Financial institution" means "any mutual fund, money market fund, credit union, savings and loan association, bank, or similar institution" [G.S. 14-119(b)(1)]. "Governmental unit" means the United States, any state or territory of the United States, or any political subdivision of any state [G.S. 14-119(b)(2)].

Related offenses not in this chapter

See the offenses listed under "Common-Law Forgery."

Common-Law Uttering of Forged Paper

Statute

This is a common-law offense.

Elements

A person guilty of this offense
(1) utters as true
(2) a false writing
(3) that is apparently capable of effecting a fraud
(4) with intent to defraud
(5) knowing that the writing is false.

Punishment

This is a Class 1 misdemeanor unless the criminal pleading alleges it was done "with deceit and intent to defraud." If deceit and intent to defraud are alleged, it is a Class H felony, pursuant to G.S. 14-3(b) and 317 N.C. 557. See "Committing an Infamous or Related Misdemeanor" (Chapter 4).

Notes

Generally. See *Perkins*, pp. 429–31.

Element (1). See the discussion of Element (1) under "Uttering Forged Checks and Securities or Forging Endorsement on Them: I. Uttering."

Elements (2), (3), and (4). See the notes on these topics under "Common-Law Forgery."

Element (5). This element would probably be satisfied if the defendant either knew or should have known that the instrument was forged; this is similar to the knowledge requirement for Receiving Stolen Goods (various offenses) in Chapter 11.

Related offenses not in this chapter

See the offenses listed under "Common-Law Forgery."

Uttering Forged Checks and Securities or Forging Endorsement on Them

Statute

§14-120. Uttering forged paper or instrument containing a forged endorsement.

If any person, directly or indirectly, whether for the sake of gain or with intent to defraud or injure any other person, shall utter or publish any such false, forged or counterfeited instrument as is mentioned in G.S. 14-119, or shall pass or deliver, or attempt to pass or deliver, any of them to another person (knowing the same to be falsely forged or counterfeited) the person so offending shall be punished as a Class I felon. If any person, directly or indirectly, whether for the sake of gain or with intent to defraud or injure any other person, shall falsely make, forge or counterfeit any endorsement on any instrument described in the preceding section, whether such instrument be genuine or false, or shall knowingly utter or publish any such instrument containing a false, forged or counterfeited endorsement or, knowing the same to be falsely endorsed, shall pass or deliver or attempt to pass or deliver any such instrument containing a forged endorsement to another person, the person so offending shall be guilty of a Class I felony.

I. Uttering

Statute

See G.S. 14-120, reproduced above.

Elements

A person guilty of this offense

(1) utters
(2) (a) a bill, note, warrant, check, order, or similar instrument purporting to be a bill, note, warrant, check, order, or similar instrument of or drawn on any financial institution or governmental unit or any officer of such an institution or unit, *or*
    (b) a security purporting to be issued by or on behalf of any corporation, financial institution, or governmental unit that
(3) (a) contains a false endorsement, *or*
    (b) was falsely made
(4) (a) for the sake of gain, *or*
    (b) with intent to defraud or injure another
(5) knowing that it was falsely made.

Punishment

Class I felony.

Notes

Element (1). This element is satisfied when a person passes or attempts to pass a forged instrument (238 N.C. 110; 343 N.C. 285). It can be satisfied by putting the forged instrument in a place where it will be found (101 N.C. 770) or by delivering it to an agent to be passed (27 N.C. 287).

Element (2). This element is satisfied only if the forgery uttered is on one of the instruments specified in G.S. 14-119. See the note on Element (2) under "Forgery of Notes, Checks, and Other Securities." Uttering of other kinds of forged instruments may fit the offense of common-law uttering of forged paper.

Element (3). See the note on Element (1) under "Common-Law Forgery."

Element (4). See the note on Element (3) under "Common-Law Forgery." The defendant need not succeed in defrauding anyone (272 N.C. 651; 90 N.C. App. 368).

Element (5). This element would probably be satisfied if the defendant either knew or should have known that the instrument was forged; this is similar to the knowledge requirement for Receiving Stolen Goods (various offenses) in Chapter 11.

II. Forging Endorsement

Statute

See G.S. 14-120, reproduced above.

Elements

A person guilty of this offense
- (1) falsely makes
- (2) an endorsement
- (3) apparently capable of effecting a fraud
- (4) (a) on a bill, note, warrant, check, order, or similar instrument purporting to be a bill, note, warrant, check, order, or similar instrument of or drawn on any financial institution or governmental unit or any officer of such an institution or unit, *or*
  - (b) on a security purported to be issued by or on behalf of any corporation, financial institution, or governmental unit
- (5) (a) for the sake of gain, *or*
  - (b) with intent to defraud or injure another.

Punishment

Class I felony.

Notes

Element (1). See the note on Element (1) under "Common-Law Forgery."

Element (2). This offense applies to a false endorsement made on an otherwise valid instrument or on a forged instrument. An "endorsement" is the signature by the holder of an instrument that transfers it to another person (*Black's Law Dictionary*).

Element (3). See the note on Element (2) under "Common-Law Forgery."

Element (4). See the note on Element (2) under "Forgery of Notes, Checks, and Other Securities."

Element (5). See the note on Element (3) under "Common-Law Forgery."

Related offenses not in this chapter

See the offenses listed under "Common-Law Forgery."

Financial Transaction Card Forgery

Statute

§14-113.11. Forgery of financial transaction card.

(a) A person is guilty of financial transaction card forgery when:

(1) With intent to defraud a purported issuer, a person or organization providing money, goods, services or anything else of value, or any other person, he falsely makes or falsely embosses a purported financial transaction card or utters such a financial transaction card; or

(2) With intent to defraud a purported issuer, a person or organization providing money, goods, services or anything else of value, or any other person, he falsely encodes, duplicates or alters existing encoded information on a financial transaction card or utters such a financial transaction card; or

(3) He, not being the cardholder or a person authorized by him, with intent to defraud the issuer, or a person or organization providing money, goods, services or anything else of value, or any other person, signs a financial transaction card.

(b) A person falsely makes a financial transaction card when he makes or draws, in whole or in part, a device or instrument which purports to be the financial transaction card of a named issuer but which is not such a financial transaction card because the issuer did not authorize the making or drawing, or alters a financial transaction card which was validly issued.

(c) A person falsely embosses a financial transaction card when, without authorization of the named issuer, he completes a financial transaction card by adding any of the matter, other than the signature of the cardholder, which an issuer requires to appear on the financial transaction card before it can be used by a cardholder.

(d) A person falsely encodes a financial transaction card when, without authorization of the purported issuer, he records magnetically, electronically, electro-magnetically or by any other means whatsoever, information on a financial transaction card which will permit acceptance of that card by any automated banking device. Conviction of financial transaction card forgery shall be punishable as provided in G.S. 14-113.17(b).

I. Forging Card or Uttering Forged Card

Statute

See G.S. 14-113.11(a)(1), reproduced above.

Elements

A person guilty of this offense

(1) (a) falsely makes a purported financial transaction card, *or*
(b) falsely embosses a purported financial transaction card, *or*

(c) utters a falsely made or falsely embossed financial transaction card
(2) with intent to defraud.

Punishment

Class I felony.

Notes

"Financial transaction card." A financial transaction card is a credit card, bank service card, bank card, check guarantee card, debit card, or any other card that allows the cardholder to obtain goods, services, or money on credit; to guarantee a check to the person who accepts it; or to deposit, withdraw, or transfer funds from an account. It does not include credit cards for telephone calls [G.S. 14-113.8(4)].

Element (1). "Falsely makes" is defined in G.S. 14-113.11(b), and "falsely embosses" is defined in G.S. 14-113.11(c), both of which are set out at the beginning of this section.

Element 1(c). For a definition of "uttering" as that term is used with respect to checks, see "Uttering Forged Checks and Securities or Forging Endorsement on Them."

Element (2). Note that the statute specifies various types of persons and organizations that may be the object of the intent to defraud. The list appears to include every possible victim.

Prima facie evidence. G.S. 14-113.12(a) provides that possession of two or more falsely made or falsely embossed financial transaction cards is prima facie evidence that the cards were "obtained" in violation of G.S. 14-113.11(a)(1) or G.S. 14-113.11(a)(2). But because these two subsections do not deal with the illegal obtaining of credit cards, the meaning and effect of this rule on prima facie evidence is unclear.

Related offenses not in this chapter

See the offenses listed at the end of this section.

II. Falsely Encoding Financial Transaction Card

Statute

See G.S. 14-113.11(a)(2), reproduced at the beginning of this section.

Elements

A person guilty of this offense
(1) with intent to defraud
(2) (a) falsely encodes, duplicates, or alters encoded information, *or*
(b) utters a falsely encoded, duplicated, or altered
(3) financial transaction card.

Punishment

Class I felony.

Notes

Element (1). See the note to Element (2) under "I. Forging Card or Uttering Forged Card," above.

Element (2)(a). "Falsely encode" is defined in G.S. 14-113.11(d), reproduced above.

Element (2)(b). For a definition of "uttering" as that term is used with respect to checks, see "Uttering Forged Checks and Securities or Forging Endorsement on Them."

Element (3). See the note on "Financial transaction card" under "I. Forging Card or Uttering Forged Card," above.

Related offenses not in this chapter

See the offenses listed at the end of this section.

III. Signing Card Fraudulently

Statute

See G.S. 14-113.11(a)(3), reproduced at the beginning of this section.

Elements

A person guilty of this offense
(1) not being the cardholder or a person authorized by the cardholder
(2) signs a financial transaction card
(3) with intent to defraud.

Punishment

Class I felony.

Notes

Element (1). G.S. 14-113.8(2) defines "cardholder" as "the person or organization named on the face of a financial transaction card to whom or for whose benefit the financial transaction card is issued by an issuer." It is not clear whether the rule that the signer of someone else's name has the presumed authority to do so [see the note on Element (1) under "Common-Law Forgery"] applies here; the safe course is for the state to demonstrate the lack of authority.

Element (2). See the note on "Financial transaction card" under "I. Forging Card or Uttering Forged Card" (hereafter cited as "I.") above, for a definition of financial transaction card.

Element (3). See the note on Element (2) under "I.," above.

Prima facie evidence. See the discussion on this same topic under "I.," above.

Related offenses not in this chapter

"Financial Transaction Card Theft" (Chapter 11)
Obtaining property or services by false or fraudulent use of credit device (G.S. 14-113.1 through -113.7A)
Possession of financial transaction card forgery devices (G.S. 14-113.14)

Financial Transaction Card Fraud

Statute

§14-113.13. Financial transaction card fraud.

(a) A person is guilty of financial transaction card fraud when, with intent to defraud the issuer, a person or organization providing money, goods, services or anything else of value, or any other person, he

(1) Uses for the purpose of obtaining money, goods, services or anything else of value a financial transaction card obtained or retained, or which was received with knowledge that it was obtained or retained, in violation of G.S. 14-113.9 or 14-113.11 or a financial transaction card which he knows is forged, altered, expired, revoked or was obtained as a result of a fraudulent application in violation of G.S. 14-113.13(c); or

(2) Obtains money, goods, services, or anything else of value by:

a. Representing without the consent of the cardholder that he is the holder of a specified card; or

b. Presenting the financial transaction card without the authorization or permission of the cardholder; or

c. Representing that he is the holder of a card and such card has not in fact been issued; or

d. Using a financial transaction card to knowingly and willfully exceed:

1. The actual balance of a demand deposit account or time deposit account; or

2. An authorized credit line in an amount which exceeds such authorized credit line in the amount of five hundred dollars ($500.00), or fifty percent (50%) of such authorized credit line, whichever is greater; or

(3) Obtains control over a financial transaction card as security for debt; or

(4) Deposits into his account or any account, by means of an automated banking device, a false, fictitious, forged, altered or counterfeit check, draft, money order, or any other such document not his lawful or legal property; or

(5) Receives money, goods, services or anything else of value as a result of a false, fictitious, forged, altered, or counterfeit check, draft, money order or any other such document having been deposited into an account via an automated banking device, knowing at the time of receipt of the money, goods, services, or item of value that the document so deposited was false, fictitious, forged, altered or counterfeit or that the above deposited item was not his lawful or legal property.

(b) A person who is authorized by an issuer to furnish money, goods, services or anything else of value upon presentation of a financial transaction card by the cardholder, or any agent or employee of such person is guilty of a financial transaction card fraud when, with intent to defraud the issuer or the cardholder, he

(1) Furnishes money, goods, services or anything else of value upon presentation of a financial transaction card obtained or retained in violation of G.S. 14-113.9, or a financial transaction card which he knows is forged, expired or revoked; or

(2) Fails to furnish money, goods, services or anything else of value which he represents in writing to the issuer that he has furnished.

Conviction of financial transaction card fraud as provided in subsection (a) or (b) of this section is punishable as provided in G.S. 14-113.17(a) if the value of all money, goods, services and other things of value furnished in violation of this section, or if the difference between the value actually furnished and the value represented to the issuer to have been furnished in violation of this section, does not exceed five hundred dollars ($500.00) in any six-month period. Conviction of financial transaction card fraud as provided in subsection (a) or (b) of this section is punishable as provided in G.S. 14-113.17(b) if such value exceeds five hundred dollars ($500.00) in any six-month period.

(c) A person is guilty of financial transaction card fraud when, upon application for a financial transaction card to an issuer, he knowingly makes or causes to be made a false statement or report relative to his name, occupation, financial condition, assets, or liabilities; or willfully and substantially overvalues any assets, or willfully omits or substantially undervalues any indebtedness for the purpose of influencing the issuer to issue a financial transaction card.

Conviction of financial transaction card fraud as provided in this subsection is punishable as provided in G.S. 14-113.17(a).

(c1) A person authorized by an acquirer to furnish money, goods, services or anything else of value upon presentation of a financial transaction card or a financial transaction card account number by a cardholder, or any agent or employee of such person, who, with intent to defraud the issuer, acquirer, or cardholder, remits to an issuer or acquirer, for payment, a financial transaction card record of a sale, which sale was not made by such person, his agent or employee, is guilty of financial transaction card fraud.

Conviction of financial transaction card fraud as provided in this subsection is punishable as provided in G.S. 14-113.17(a).

(d) A cardholder is guilty of financial transaction card fraud when he willfully, knowingly, and with an intent to defraud the issuer, a person or organization providing money, goods, services, or anything else of value, or any other person, submits, verbally or in writing, to the issuer or any other person, any false notice or report of the theft, loss, disappearance, or nonreceipt of his financial transaction card.

Conviction of financial transaction card fraud as provided in this subsection is punishable as provided in G.S. 14-113.17(a).

(e) In any prosecution for violation of G.S. 14-113.13, the State is not required to establish and it is no defense that some of the acts constituting the crime did not occur in this State or within one city, county, or local jurisdiction.

(f) For purposes of this section, revocation shall be construed to include either notice given in person or notice given in writing to the person to whom the financial transaction card and/or personal identification code was issued. Notice of revocation shall be immediate when notice is given in person. The sending of a notice in writing by registered or certified mail in the United States mail, duly stamped and addressed to such person at his last address known to the issuer, shall be prima facie evidence that such notice was duly received after seven days from the date of the deposit in the mail. If the address is located outside the United States, Puerto Rico, the Virgin Islands, the Canal Zone and Canada, notice shall be presumed to have been received 10 days after mailing by registered or certified mail.

I. Using Illicit Card

Statute

See G.S. 14-113.13(a)(1), reproduced at the beginning of this section.

Elements

A person guilty of this offense

- (1) with intent to defraud
- (2) (a) uses a financial transaction card obtained or retained by financial transaction theft, *or*
  - (b) uses a financial transaction card received with knowledge that it was obtained by credit card fraud, *or*
  - (c) uses a financial transaction card that he or she knows is forged, expired, revoked, or altered, *or*
  - (d) uses a financial transaction card obtained by a fraudulent application

(3) for the purpose of obtaining money, goods, services, or anything else of value.

Punishment

If value of over $500 is obtained in a 6-month period, the offense is a Class I felony. If value of $500 or less is obtained in a 6-month period, the offense is a Class 2 misdemeanor.

Notes

"Financial transaction card." A financial transaction card is a credit card, bank services card, bank card, check guarantee, debit card, or any other card that allows the cardholder to obtain goods, services, or money on credit; to guarantee a check to the person who accepts it; or to deposit, withdraw, or transfer funds from accounts. It does not include telephone credit cards or similar devices covered by Art. 19A of G.S. Ch. 14 [G.S. 14-113.8(4)].

Element (1). Note that the statute specifies various types of persons and organizations that may be the object of the intent to defraud. The list appears to include every possible victim.

Element (2)(a). See "Financial Transaction Card Theft" (Chapter 11) for a description of circumstances when a card is obtained by theft.

Element (2)(c). See "Financial Transaction Card Forgery" for a description of circumstances when a card has been forged. Note that this element also may be satisfied when a person uses a card originally issued to him or her that has expired or been revoked.

Element (2)(d). See G.S. 14-113.13(c) for a description of circumstances when a financial transaction card is obtained by a fraudulent application.

Related offenses not in this chapter

See the offenses listed at the end of this section.

II. False Self-Representation as Cardholder

Statute

See G.S. 14-113.13(a)(2)a. and c., reproduced at the beginning of this section.

Elements

A person guilty of this offense

(1) obtains money, goods, services, or anything else of value
(2) with intent to defraud
(3) by representing that he or she is the holder of a financial transaction card
(4) (a) when he or she does not have the consent of the holder of that card, *or*
    (b) when the card has not in fact been issued.

Punishment

If value of over $500 is obtained in a 6-month period, the offense is a Class I felony. If value of $500 or less is obtained in a 6-month period, the offense is a Class 2 misdemeanor.

Notes

"Financial transaction card." See the note on this topic under "I. Using Illicit Card," above.

Element (2). See the note on Element (1) under "I. Using Illicit Card," above.

Element (3). A person can "represent" himself or herself to be the holder of a financial transaction card merely by presenting it to pay for something; he or she need not claim to be the cardholder.

Related offenses not in this chapter

See the offenses listed at the end of this section.

III. Unauthorized Presentment of Card

Statute

See G.S. 14-113.13(a)(2)b., reproduced at the beginning of this section.

Elements

A person guilty of this offense
 (1) obtains money, goods, services, or anything else of value
 (2) with intent to defraud
 (3) by presenting a financial transaction card without the authorization of the cardholder.

Punishment

If value of over $500 is obtained in a 6-month period, the offense is a Class I felony. If value of $500 or less is obtained in a 6-month period, the offense is a Class 2 misdemeanor.

Notes

"Financial transaction card." See the note on this topic under "I. Using Illicit Card," above.

Element (2). See the note on Element (1) under "I. Using Illicit Card," above.

Element (3). "Present" means to put a card in an automatic banking machine or to display a card with the intent to defraud a person who provides money, goods, or services [G.S. 14-113.8(7)].

Comparison with "II. False Self-Representation as Cardholder." "False Self-Representation as Cardholder," described above, involves representing oneself to be the holder of the financial transaction card. Unauthorized presentment of the card apparently covers not only situations in which the defendant falsely represents that he or she is the cardholder but also situations in which the defendant falsely alleges authorization to make charges on someone else's card or implies such authorization by presenting the other person's card and signing his or her own name.

Related offenses not in this chapter

See the offenses listed at the end of this section.

IV. Using Card to Overdraw Account

Statute

See G.S. 14-113.13(a)(2)d., reproduced at the beginning of this section.

Elements

A person guilty of this offense
- (1) with intent to defraud
- (2) obtains money, services, goods, or anything else of value
- (3) by using a financial transaction card
- (4) to exceed knowingly and willfully
  - (a) the actual balance of a demand or time deposit account, *or*
  - (b) an authorized credit line by 50 percent or $500, whichever is greater.

Punishment

If value of over $500 is obtained in a 6-month period, the offense is a Class I felony. If value of $500 or less is obtained in a 6-month period, the offense is a Class 2 misdemeanor.

Notes

"Financial transaction card." See the note on this topic under "I. Using Illicit Card," above.

Element (1). See the note on Element (1) under "I. Using Illicit Card," above.

Related offenses not in this chapter

See the offenses listed at the end of this section.

V. Obtaining Card as Security for Debt

Statute

See G.S. 14-113.13(a)(3), reproduced at the beginning of this section.

Elements

A person guilty of this offense
- (1) obtains control over a financial transaction card as security for debt
- (2) with intent to defraud.

Punishment

If value of over $500 is obtained in a 6-month period, the offense is a Class I felony. If value of $500 or less is obtained in a 6-month period, the offense is a Class 2 misdemeanor. It is unclear how the value of property or services "furnished in violation of this section" [G.S. 14-113.13(b)] is to be determined, because the offense can be committed even if the only valuable thing obtained is control of the financial transaction card itself. If the latter is the only property "furnished in violation of this section," then the offense probably always will be a Class 2 misdemeanor.

Notes

"Financial transaction card." See the note on this topic under "I. Using Illicit Card," above.

Element (2). See the note to Element (1) under "I. Using Illicit Card," above.

Related offenses not in this chapter

See the offenses listed at the end of this section.

VI. Fraudulent Deposits of Money

Statute

See G.S. 14-113.13(a)(4), reproduced at the beginning of this section.

Elements

A person guilty of this offense
- (1) with intent to defraud
- (2) deposits in an account
- (3) a false, forged, or altered check, draft, money order, or other document
- (4) that is not his or her property
- (5) by using an automated banking machine.

Punishment

If value of over $500 is obtained in a 6-month period, the offense is a Class I felony. If value of $500 or less is obtained in a 6-month period, the offense is a Class 2 misdemeanor.

Notes

Element (1). See the note to Element (1) under "I. Using Illicit Card," above.

Related offenses not in this chapter

See the offenses listed at the end of this section.

VII. Receiving Money Improperly from Bank Machine

Statute

See G.S. 14-113.13(a)(5), reproduced at the beginning of this section.

Elements

A person guilty of this offense
- (1) with intent to defraud
- (2) receives
- (3) money, goods, services, or anything else of value
- (4) as a result of having deposited a false, forged, or altered check, draft, money order, or other document in an account
- (5) by the use of an automated banking machine
- (6) with knowledge
  - (a) that the check, etc., was forged, etc., *or*
  - (b) that the check, etc., was not his or her property.

Punishment

If value of over $500 is obtained in a 6-month period, the offense is a Class I felony. If value of $500 or less is obtained in a 6-month period, the offense is a Class 2 misdemeanor.

Notes

Element (1). See the note to Element (1) under "I. Using Illicit Card," above.

Related offenses not in this chapter

See the offenses listed at the end of this section.

VIII. False Statement to Obtain Card

Statute

See G.S. 14-113.13(c), reproduced at the beginning of this section.

Elements

A person guilty of this offense
- (1) in an application for a financial transaction card to an issuer
- (2) (a) (i) knowingly makes or causes to be made
  - (ii) a false statement or report relative to
  - (iii) the person's name, occupation, financial condition, assets, or liabilities, *or*
  - (b) willfully and substantially overvalues any assets, *or*
  - (c) willfully omits or substantially undervalues any indebtedness
- (3) for the purpose of influencing the issuer to issue a financial transaction card

Punishment

Class 2 misdemeanor.

Notes

"Financial transaction card." See the note on this topic under "I. Using Illicit Card," above.

Related offenses not in this chapter

See the offenses listed at the end of this section.

IX. Submitting False Credit Card Sale

Statute

See G.S. 14-113.13(c1), reproduced at the beginning of this section.

Elements

A person guilty of this offense
- (1) is a merchant, or the merchant's employee or agent authorized by an acquirer to furnish money, goods, services, or anything else of value upon presentation of a financial transaction card or financial transaction card number
- (2) who submits to the acquirer for payment
- (3) with intent to defraud
- (4) any record of a sale based on the use of a financial transaction card or financial transaction card number

(5) that the merchant, merchant's employee, or agent did not transact with the cardholder.

Punishment

Class 2 misdemeanor.

Notes

"Financial transaction card." See the note on this topic under "I. Using Illicit Card," above.

Elements (1) and (2). G.S. 14-113.8 defines "acquirer" as a business or agent of a business that authorizes a merchant to accept payment by financial transaction card for money, goods, services, or anything else of value.

Element (3). See the note on Element (1) under "I. Using Illicit Card," above.

Related offenses not in this chapter

See the offenses listed at the end of this section.

X. Soliciting Submission of False Credit Card Sale (Factoring)

Statute

§14-113.15A. Criminal factoring of financial transaction card records.

Any person who, without the acquirer's express authorization, employs or solicits an authorized merchant, or any agent or employee of such merchant, to remit to an issuer or acquirer, for payment, a financial transaction card record of a sale, which sale was not made by such merchant, his agent or employee, is guilty of a felony punishable as provided in G.S. 14-113.17(b).

Elements

A person guilty of this offense
(1) employs or solicits a merchant
(2) to submit to a bank or credit card issuer
(3) without authorization of the bank or credit card issuer
(4) any record of a credit card sale not made by that merchant, the merchant's agent, or employee.

Punishment

Class I felony.

Notes

"Financial transaction card." See the note on this topic under "I. Using Illicit Card," above.

Element (1). This offense prohibits both solicitation and employment of another to submit a false credit card sale for payment.

Element (2). The statute specifically prohibits submission of false credit card sales to an "acquirer" or "issuer." G.S. 14-113.8 defines "acquirer" as a business or agent of a business that authorizes a merchant to accept payment by financial transaction card for money, goods, services, or anything else of value. It defines "issuer" as the business or its agent that issues a financial transaction card.

Element (4). G.S. 14-113.8(4) provides that a credit card is a kind of financial transaction card.

Related offenses not in this chapter

"Financial Transaction Card Theft" (Chapter 11)
Obtaining property or services by false or fraudulent use of credit device (G.S. 14-113.1 through -113.7A)
Financial transaction card fraud by employee [G.S. 14-113.13(b)]
Filing false report of loss of financial transaction card [G.S. 14-113.13(d)]
Criminal receipt of goods and services obtained by financial transaction card fraud (G.S. 14-113.15)

Medicaid Fraud by Provider

Statute

§108A-63. Medical assistance provider fraud.

(a) It shall be unlawful for any provider of medical assistance under this Part to knowingly and willfully make or cause to be made any false statement or representation of a material fact:

(1) In any application for payment under this Part, or for use in determining entitlement to such payment; or
(2) With respect to the conditions or operation of a provider or facility in order that such provider or facility may qualify or remain qualified to provide assistance under this Part.

(b) It shall be unlawful for any provider of medical assistance to knowingly and willfully conceal or fail to disclose any fact or event affecting:

(1) His initial or continued entitlement to payment under this Part; or
(2) The amount of payment to which such person is or may be entitled.

(c) Any person who violates a provision of this section shall be guilty of a Class I felony.

(d) "Provider" shall include any person who provides goods or services under this Part and any other person acting as an employee, representative or agent of such person.

I. Fraudulent Application by Medicaid Provider

Statute

See G.S. 108A-63(a), reproduced above.

Elements

A person guilty of this offense

(1) is a provider of medical assistance under the state Medical Assistance (Medicaid) Program, *and*
(2) willfully and knowingly
(3) makes or causes to be made
(4) a false statement or a false representation of a material fact
(5) (a) in an application for payment, *or*
    (b) in an application that is used to determine Medicaid eligibility, *or*
    (c) that allows a provider of services to qualify or remain eligible to provide Medicaid services.

Punishment

Class I felony.

Notes

Element (1). A "provider" is any person who provides goods or services in the Medicaid Program and any employee, representative, or agent of such a person [G.S. 108A-63(d)]. It includes a pharmacist who dispenses medicines to Medicaid patients (64 N.C. App. 511).

II.
Concealment of Fact Affecting Medicaid Provider's Eligibility

Statute

See G.S. 108A-63(b), reproduced above.

Elements

A person guilty of this offense
- (1) is a provider of medical assistance under the state Medical Assistance (Medicaid) Program, *and*
- (2) knowingly and willfully
- (3) conceals or fails to disclose a fact or event
- (4) that affects:
  - (a) his or her initial or continued entitlement to Medicaid payment, *or*
  - (b) the amount of Medicaid payment he or she receives.

Punishment

Class I felony.

Notes

Element (1). See the note on Element (1) under "I. Fraudulent Application by Medicaid Provider," above.

Related offenses not in this chapter

Larceny (various offenses) (Chapter 11)
Medicaid conflict of interest (G.S. 108A-65)

Medicaid Fraud by Recipient

Statute

§108A-64. Medical assistance recipient fraud.

(a) It shall be unlawful for any person to knowingly and willfully and with intent to defraud make or cause to be made a false statement or representation of a material fact in an application for assistance under this Part, or intended for use in determining entitlement to such assistance.

(b) It shall be unlawful for any applicant, recipient or person acting on behalf of such applicant or recipient to knowingly and willfully and with intent to defraud, conceal or fail to disclose any condition, fact or event affecting such applicant's or recipient's initial or continued entitlement to receive assistance under this Part.

(b1) It is unlawful for any person knowingly, willingly, and with intent to defraud, to obtain or attempt to obtain, or to assist, aid, or abet another person, either directly or indirectly, to obtain money, services, or any other thing of value to which the person is not entitled as a recipient under this Part, or otherwise to deliberately misuse a Medicaid identification card. This misuse includes the sale, alteration, or lending of the Medicaid identification card to others for services and the use of the card by someone other than the recipient to receive or attempt to receive Medicaid program coverage for services rendered to that individual.

Proof of intent to defraud does not require proof of intent to defraud any particular person.

(c)(1) A person who violates a provision of this section shall be guilty of a Class I felony if the value of the assistance wrongfully obtained is more than four hundred dollars ($400.00).

(2) A person who violates a provision of this section shall be guilty of a Class 1 misdemeanor if the value of the assistance wrongfully obtained is four hundred dollars ($400.00) or less.

(d) For purposes of this section the word "person" includes any natural person, association, consortium, corporation, body politic, partnership, or other group, entity or organization.

I. Fraudulent Application by Medicaid Recipient

Statute

See G.S. 108A-64(a), (c), and (d), reproduced above.

Elements

A person guilty of this offense
(1) knowingly and willfully
(2) with intent to defraud
(3) makes or causes to be made
(4) a false statement or a false representation of a material fact
(5) (a) in an application for Medicaid assistance, *or*
(b) in an application intended for use in determining entitlement for Medicaid assistance.

Punishment

If the value of the assistance wrongfully obtained exceeds $400, this offense is a Class I felony; otherwise it is a Class 1 misdemeanor.

Notes

"Person." For purposes of this offense, a "person" is "any natural person, association, consortium, corporation, body politic, partnership, or other group, entity or organization" [G.S. 108A-64(d)].

II. Concealment of Fact Affecting Medicaid Recipient's Eligibility

Statute

See G.S. 108A-64(b), (c), and (d), reproduced above.

Elements

A person guilty of this offense
(1) (a) is an applicant for, or recipient of, Medicaid assistance, *or*
(b) is a person acting on behalf of such an applicant or recipient, *and*

(2) knowingly and willfully
(3) with intent to defraud
(4) conceals or fails to disclose a condition, fact, or event
(5) that affects his or her initial or continued entitlement to Medicaid assistance.

Punishment

If the value of the assistance wrongfully obtained by the concealment exceeds $400, this offense is a Class I felony; otherwise it is a Class 1 misdemeanor.

Notes

"Person." See the note with this title under "I. Fraudulent Application by Medicaid Recipient," above.

Related offenses not in this chapter

Larceny (various offenses) (Chapter 11)
Medicaid conflict of interest (G.S. 108A-65)

Medicaid Card Fraud

Statute

See subsection (b1) of G.S. 108A-64, reproduced under "Medicaid Fraud by Recipient," above.

Elements

A person guilty of this offense
(1) (a) (i) knowingly, willingly, and with the intent to defraud
(ii) obtains or attempts to obtain or assists, aids, or abets another person to obtain
(iii) money, services, or any other thing of value
(iv) to which the person is not entitled as a Medicaid recipient, *or*
(b) (i) deliberately
(ii) misuses a Medicaid identification card.

Punishment

Class I felony.

Notes

Element (1)(a)(i). The statute specifically states that proof of intent to defraud does not require proof to defraud any particular person.

Element (1)(b)(ii). The statute defines misuse to include the sale, alteration, or lending of a Medicaid identification card to others for services or so that others may attempt to use the card to receive Medicaid coverage for services rendered.

"Person." See the note with this title, under "Medicaid Fraud by Recipient: I. Fraudulent Application by Medicaid Recipient," above.

Related offenses not in this chapter

Larceny (various offenses) (Chapter 11)

Welfare Fraud

Statute

§108A-39. Fraudulent misrepresentation.

(a) Any person whether provider or recipient, or person representing himself as such, who willfully and knowingly and with intent to deceive makes a false statement or representation or who fails to disclose a material fact and as a result of making a false statement or representation or failing to disclose a material fact obtains, for himself or another person, attempts to obtain for himself or another person, or continues to receive or enables another person to continue to receive public assistance in the amount of not more than four hundred dollars ($400.00) is guilty of a Class 1 misdemeanor.

(b) Any person, whether provider or recipient, or person representing himself as such who willfully and knowingly with the intent to deceive makes a false statement or representation or fails to disclose a material fact and as a result of making a false statement or representation or failing to disclose a material fact, obtains for himself or another person, attempts to obtain for himself or another person, or continues to receive or enables another person to continue to receive public assistance in an amount of more than four hundred dollars ($400.00) is guilty of a Class I felony.

(c) As used in this section the word "person" means person, association, consortium, corporation, body politic, partnership, or other group, entity, or organization.

Elements

A person guilty of this offense

(1) is a provider or recipient of public assistance or a person representing himself or herself as such, *and*
(2) willfully and knowingly
(3) with the intent to deceive
(4) (a) makes a false statement or representation, *or*
    (b) fails to disclose a material fact, *and*
(5) as a result he or she
    (a) obtains public assistance for himself or herself, or others, *or*
    (b) attempts to obtain public assistance for himself or herself, or others, *or*
    (c) continues to receive or enables another person to continue to receive public assistance.

Punishment

If the value of the public assistance wrongfully obtained exceeds $400, this offense is a Class I felony; otherwise it is a Class 1 misdemeanor.

Notes

"Person." For purposes of this offense, a "person" is a "person, association, consortium, corporation, body politic, partnership, or other group, entity, or organization" [G.S. 108A-39(c)].

"Public assistance." G.S. 108A-39 does not define "public assistance," but a related statute in the same article (G.S. 108A-25) lists the following programs of public assistance: state-county special assistance for adults, the food stamp program, foster care and adoption assistance, low-income energy assistance, the Work First program, and medical assistance (Medicaid).

Related offenses not in this chapter

Larceny (various offenses) (Chapter 11)

Food Stamp Fraud

Statute

§108A-53. Fraudulent misrepresentation.

(a) Any person, whether provider or recipient or person representing himself as such, who knowingly obtains or attempts to obtain, or aids or abets any person to obtain by means of making a willfully false statement or representation or by impersonation or by failing to disclose material facts or in any manner not authorized by this Part or the regulations issued pursuant thereto, transfers with intent to defraud any food stamps or authorization cards to which that person is not entitled in the amount of four hundred dollars ($400.00) or less shall be guilty of a Class 1 misdemeanor. Whoever knowingly obtains or attempts to obtain, or aids or abets any person to obtain by means of making a willfully false statement or representation or by impersonation or by failing to disclose material facts or in any manner not authorized by this Part or the regulations issued pursuant thereto, transfers with intent to defraud any food stamps or authorization cards to which he is not entitled in an amount more than four hundred dollars ($400.00) shall be guilty of a Class I felony.

(b) Whoever presents, or causes to be presented, food stamps or authorization cards for payment or redemption, knowing the same to have been received, transferred, or used in any manner in violation of the provisions of this Part or the regulations issued pursuant to this Part shall be guilty of a Class 1 misdemeanor.

(c) Whoever receives any food stamps for any consumable item knowing that such food stamps were procured fraudulently under subsections (a) and/or (b) of this section shall be guilty of a Class 1 misdemeanor.

(d) Whoever receives any food stamps for any consumable item whose exchange is prohibited by the United States Department of Agriculture shall be guilty of a Class 1 misdemeanor.

I. Fraudulently Obtaining or Transferring Food Stamps

Statute

See G.S. 108A-53(a), reproduced above.

Elements

A person guilty of this offense
(1) knowingly
(2) (a) (i) obtains or attempts to obtain or aids and abets any person to obtain
(ii) by means of willfully making a false representation or by impersonation or by failing to disclose material facts, *or*

(b) transfers with intent to defraud in any manner not authorized by the food stamp statutes (G.S. Ch. 108A, Art. 2, Part 5) and associated regulations
(3) food stamps or authorization cards
(4) to which the person is not entitled.

Punishment

If the value of the food stamps or authorization cards obtained or transferred exceeds $400, this offense is a Class I felony; otherwise it is a Class 1 misdemeanor.

Notes

Generally. A person need not be a recipient of food stamp assistance to commit this offense.

Element (2). Receiving and transferring stamps are apparently intended to be two separate ways of violating this section; "Presentment of Fraudulently Obtained Food Stamps," below, also treats them separately.

Element (3). "Authorization cards" are cards issued that entitle persons to receive food stamps.

Continuing acts may constitute one offense. When a person made false statements on nine separate occasions over a 4-year period and received food stamps as a result of each misrepresentation, the successive acts of misrepresentation were a continuing act with the same criminal goal. Consequently, the value of the food stamps fraudulently received could be combined to reach the threshold for charging a felony offense under this section (101 N.C. App. 412).

Statutory language. G.S. 108A-53(a) apparently should be read as if there were a comma after the phrase "or by failing to disclose material facts" in both places where it appears.

II. Presentment of Fraudulently Obtained Food Stamps

Statute

See G.S. 108A-53(b), reproduced above.

Elements

A person guilty of this offense
(1) presents for payment or redemption
(2) food stamps or authorization cards
(3) knowing that they have been received, transferred, or used in violation of the food stamp statutes (G.S. Ch. 108A, Art. 2, Part 5) or associated regulations.

Punishment

Class 1 misdemeanor.

III.
Receiving Fraudulently Obtained Food Stamps

Statute

See G.S. 108A-53(c), reproduced above.

Elements

A person guilty of this offense
- (1) receives in exchange for any consumable item
- (2) food stamps
- (3) knowing that they were procured fraudulently in violation of G.S. 108A-53(a) or (b).

Punishment

Class 1 misdemeanor.

IV.
Receiving Food Stamps for Nonexchangeable Item

Statute

See G.S. 108A-53(d), reproduced above.

Elements

A person guilty of this offense
- (1) receives food stamps
- (2) in exchange for any consumable item whose exchange is prohibited by the U.S. Department of Agriculture.

Punishment

Class 1 misdemeanor.

Related offenses not in this chapter

None.

Illegal Possession or Use of Food Stamps

Statute

§108A-53.1. Illegal possession or use of food stamps.

(a) Any person who knowingly buys, sells, distributes, or possesses with the intent to sell, or distribute food stamp coupons, authorization cards, or access devices in any manner contrary to that authorized by this Part or the regulations issued pursuant thereto shall be guilty of a Class H felony.

(b) Any person who knowingly uses, transfers, acquires, alters, or possesses food stamp coupons, authorization cards, or access devices in any manner contrary to that authorized by this Part or the regulations issued pursuant thereto, other than as set forth in subsection (a) of this section, shall be guilty of a Class 1 misdemeanor if the value of such food stamp coupons, authorization cards, or access devices is less than one hundred dollars ($100.00), or a Class A1 misdemeanor if the value of such food stamp coupons, authorization cards, or access devices is equal to at least one hundred dollars ($100.00) but less than five hundred dollars ($500.00), or a Class I felony if the value of such food stamp coupons, authorization cards, or access devices is equal to at least five hundred dollars ($500.00) but less than one thousand dollars ($1,000), or a Class H felony if the value of such food stamp coupons, authorization cards, or access devices equals or exceeds one thousand dollars ($1,000).

I. Illegally Buying, Selling, or Possessing with Intent to Sell Food Stamps

Statute

See G.S. 108A-53.1, reproduced above.

Elements

A person guilty of this offense
- (1) knowingly
- (2) buys, sells, distributes, or possesses with the intent to sell or distribute
- (3) food stamp coupons, authorization cards, or access devices
- (4) in any manner not authorized by the food stamp statutes (G.S. Ch. 108A, Art. 2, Part 5) and associated regulations.

Punishment

Class H felony.

Notes

Element (3). "Authorization cards" are cards issued that entitle people to receive food stamps.

II. Illegally Using or Possessing Food Stamps

Statute

See G.S. 108A-53.1, reproduced above

Elements

A person guilty of this offense
- (1) knowingly
- (2) uses, transfers, acquires, alters, or possesses
- (3) food stamp coupons, authorization cards, or access devices
- (4) in any manner not authorized by the food stamp statutes (G.S. Ch. 108A, Art. 2, Part 5) and associated regulations.

Punishment

This offense is a Class 1 misdemeanor if the value of the illegal food stamp coupons, authorization cards, or access devices is less than $100; a Class A1 misdemeanor if the value is at least $100 but less than $500; a Class I felony if the value is at least $500 but less than $1,000; a Class H felony if the value is at least or exceeds $1,000.

Notes

Element (3). "Authorization cards" are cards issued that entitle people to receive food stamps.

Related offenses not in this chapter

None.

False Statement to Procure Insurance Benefits

Statute

§58-2-161. False statement to procure or deny benefit of insurance policy or certificate.

(a) For the purposes of this section:

(1) "Insurer" has the same meaning as in G.S. 58-1-5(3) and also includes:

a. Any hull insurance and protection and indemnity club operating under Article 20 of this Chapter.
b. Any surplus lines insurer operating under Article 21 of this Chapter.
c. Any risk retention group or purchasing group operating under Article 22 of this Chapter.
d. Any local government risk pool operating under Article 23 of this Chapter.
e. Any risk-sharing plan operating under Article 42 of this Chapter.
f. The North Carolina Insurance Underwriting Association operating under Article 45 of this Chapter.
g. The North Carolina Joint Insurance Underwriting Association operating under Article 46 of this Chapter.
h. The North Carolina Insurance Guaranty Association operating under Article 48 of this Chapter.
i. Any multiple employer welfare arrangement operating under Article 49 of this Chapter.
j. The North Carolina Life and Health Insurance Guaranty Association operating under Article 62 of this Chapter.
k. Any service corporation operating under Article 65 of this Chapter.
l. Any health maintenance organization operating under Article 67 of this Chapter.
m. The Teachers' and State Employees' Comprehensive Major Medical Plan operating under Chapter 135 of the General Statutes.
n. A group of employers self-insuring their workers' compensation liabilities under Article 47 of this Chapter.
o. An employer self-insuring its workers' compensation liabilities under Article 5 of Chapter 97 of the General Statutes.
p. The North Carolina Self-Insurance Guaranty Association under Article 4 of Chapter 97 of the General Statutes.
q. Any reinsurer licensed or accredited under this Chapter.

(2) "Statement" includes any application, notice, statement, proof of loss, bill of lading, receipt for payment, invoice, account, estimate of property damages, bill for services, diagnosis, prescription, hospital or doctor records, X rays, test result, or other evidence of loss, injury, or expense.

(b) Any person who, with the intent to injure, defraud, or deceive an insurer or insurance claimant:

(1) Presents or causes to be presented a written or oral statement, including computer-generated documents as part of, in support of, or in opposition to, a claim for payment or other benefit pursuant to an insurance policy, knowing that the statement contains false or misleading information concerning any fact or matter material to the claim, or

(2) Assists, abets, solicits, or conspires with another person to prepare or make any written or oral statement that is intended to be presented to an insurer or insurance claimant in connection with, in support of, or in opposition to, a claim for payment or other benefit pursuant to an insurance policy, knowing that the statement contains false or misleading information concerning a fact or matter material to the claim

is guilty of a Class H felony. Each claim shall be considered a separate count. Upon conviction, if the court imposes probation, the court may order the defendant to pay restitution as a condition of probation. In determination of the amount of restitution pursuant to G.S. 15A-1343(d), the reasonable costs and attorneys' fees incurred by the victim in the investigation of, and efforts to recover damages arising from, the claim, may be considered part of the damage caused by the defendant arising out of the offense.

In a civil cause of action for recovery based upon a claim for which a defendant has been convicted under this section, the conviction may be entered into evidence against the defendant. The court may award the prevailing party compensatory damages, attorneys' fees, costs, and reasonable investigative costs. If the prevailing party can demonstrate that the defendant has engaged in a pattern of violations of this section, the court may award treble damages.

Elements

A person guilty of this offense

(1) with the intent to injure, defraud, or deceive
(2) an insurer or insurance claimant
(3) presents or causes to be presented a written or oral statement, including computer-generated documents,
(4) as part of, in support of, or in opposition to a claim for payment or other benefit under an insurance policy
(5) knowing that the statement contains
(6) false or misleading information concerning any fact or matter material to the claim.

Punishment

Class H felony.

Notes

Element (1). The term "insurer" is broadly defined in G.S. 58-2-161(a)(1), reproduced above. It includes the specific kinds of insurers set out in a. through q. It also includes insurers defined in G.S. 58-1-5(3): any corporation, association, partnership, society, order, individual or aggregation of individuals engaging or proposing or attempting to engage as principals in any kind of insurance business, including the exchanging of reciprocal or interinsurance contracts between individuals, partnerships and corporations—but not the State of North Carolina or any county, city, or other political subdivision of the State of North Carolina.

Elements (3) and (6). The term "statement" is defined in G.S. 58-2-161(a)(2), reproduced above.

Each fraudulent claim is a separate offense. G.S. 58-2-161(b) provides that each claim is a separate offense.

Conspiracy and solicitation are punished the same as for the completed offense. Under G.S. 58-2-161(b)(2), the punishment for conspiracy and solicitation to commit this offense is the same as for the completed offense. Thus this provision supplants G.S. 14-2.4(a) (conspiracy is punished one class lower) and G.S. 14-2.6 (solicitation is punished two classes lower).

Former statute. The predecessor statute for this offense was G.S. 14-214. It was later recodified and rewritten as the current statute, reproduced above. Examples of cases under G.S. 14-214 include: fraudulently staging a car accident and filing an insurance claim (22 N.C. App. 291); fraudulently reporting in an insurance claim that a boat, motor, and trailer had been stolen (36 N.C. App. 202); fraudulently reporting in an insurance claim more goods than were in fact stolen from a store break-in (101 N.C. App. 691); and insufficient evidence that the defendant "willfully and knowingly" violated G.S. 14-214 (240 N.C. 365; 218 N.C. 258).

Related offenses not in this chapter

Embezzlement by insurance agents (G.S. 58-2-162)
Refusal to exhibit or making false statements about insurance documents (G.S. 58-2-200)
False statements in insurance applications (G.S. 58-33-105)

Computer Fraud

Statute

§14-454. Accessing computers.

(a) It is unlawful to willfully, directly or indirectly, access or cause to be accessed any computer, computer program, computer system, computer network, or any part thereof, for the purpose of:

(1) Devising or executing any scheme or artifice to defraud, unless the object of the scheme or artifice is to obtain educational testing material, a false educational testing score, or a false academic or vocational grade, or

(2) Obtaining property or services other than educational testing material, a false educational testing score, or a false academic or vocational grade for a person, by means of false or fraudulent pretenses, representations or promises.

A violation of this subsection is a Class G felony if the fraudulent scheme or artifice results in damage of more than one thousand dollars ($1,000), or if the property or services obtained are worth more than one thousand dollars ($1,000). Any other violation of this subsection is a Class 1 misdemeanor.

(b) Any person who willfully and without authorization, directly or indirectly, accesses or causes to be accessed any computer, computer program, computer system, or computer network for any purpose other than those set forth in subsection (a) above, is guilty of a Class 1 misdemeanor.

(c) For the purpose of this section, the phrase "access or cause to be accessed" includes introducing, directly or indirectly, a computer program (including a self-replicating or a self-propagating computer program) into a computer, computer program, computer system, or computer network.

I. Accessing Computer to Defraud or Obtain Property

Statute

See G.S. 14-454(a), reproduced immediately above.

Elements

A person guilty of this offense

(1) willfully
(2) accesses or causes to be accessed
(3) a computer, computer program, computer system, computer network, or any part thereof
(4) for the purpose of
    (a) devising or executing a scheme or artifice to defraud, *or*
    (b) obtaining property or services by means of false or fraudulent pretenses, representations, or promises.

Punishment

Class G felony if the fraud results in more than $1,000 in damage or if the property or services obtained are worth more than $1,000. Otherwise, an offense is a Class 1 misdemeanor.

Notes

Element (2). "Access" means to instruct, communicate with, cause input, cause output, cause data processing, or otherwise make use of any resources of a computer, computer system, or computer network [G.S. 14-453(1)]. It also includes the introduction of a computer program, like a "virus," into a computer, computer system, or computer network [G.S. 14-454(c)].

Element (3). A computer is an internally programmed automatic device that performs data processing or telephone switching [G.S. 14-453(2)]. A computer program is an ordered set of data that are coded instructions or statements that when executed by a computer cause the computer to process data [G.S. 14-453(4)]. A computer system is at least one computer together with a set of related, connected, or unconnected peripheral devices [G.S. 14-453(6)]. A computer network is the interconnection of communication systems with a computer through remote terminals, or a complex consisting of two or more connected computers or telephone switching equipment [G.S. 14-453(3)].

Element (4)(b). Property includes financial instruments, information, including electronically processed or produced data, and computer software and computer programs in either machine or human readable form, and any other tangible or intangible item of value [G.S. 14-453(8)]. Services include computer time, data processing, and storage functions [G.S. 14-453(9)].

Exception. G.S. 14-454 expressly provides that this offense does not include (1) accessing a computer to obtain false test scores or course grades or to obtain test questions or (2) accessing a computer to devise a scheme to defraud, the object of which is to obtain a false test score or course grade, or to obtain test questions. Such actions are covered by "Accessing Computer without Authorization," below.

Related offenses not in this chapter

See the offenses listed at the end of this section.

II. Accessing Computer without Authorization

Statute

See G.S. 14-454(b), reproduced under "Computer Fraud."

Elements

A person guilty of this offense
(1) willfully
(2) without authorization
(3) accesses or causes to be accessed
(4) a computer, computer program, computer system, or computer network.

Punishment

Class 1 misdemeanor.

Notes

Generally. This offense differs from accessing computer to defraud or obtain property in the purpose for which the computer is illegally used. It covers unauthorized use for any purpose other than those covered by accessing computer to defraud or obtain property, including the educational fraud purposes specifically exempted from prosecution under that offense.

Element (3). See the note on Element (2) under "Accessing Computer to Defraud or Obtain Property."

Element (4). See the note on Element (3) under "Accessing Computer to Defraud or Obtain Property."

Related offenses not in this chapter

See the offenses listed at the end of this section.

III. Denying Computer to an Authorized User

Statute

§14-456. Denial of computer services to an authorized user.

(a) Any person who willfully and without authorization denies or causes the denial of computer, computer program, computer system, or computer network services to an authorized user of the computer, computer program, computer system, or computer network services is guilty of a Class 1 misdemeanor.

(b) This section also applies to denial of services effectuated by introducing, directly or indirectly, a computer program (including a self-replicating or a self-propagating computer program) into a computer, computer program, computer system, or computer network.

Elements

A person guilty of this offense
(1) willfully
(2) without authorization
(3) denies or causes to be denied
(4) the use of a computer, computer program, computer system, or computer network services

(5) to an authorized user of the computer, computer program, system, or network.

Punishment

Class 1 misdemeanor.

Notes

Element (3). Denial of service includes denial caused by the introduction of a computer "virus" [G.S. 14-456(b)].

Related offenses not in this chapter

See the offenses listed at the end of this section.

IV. Extortion by Threatening Computer Damage

Statute

§14-457. Extortion.

Any person who verbally or by a written or printed communication, maliciously threatens to commit an act described in G.S. 14-455 with the intent to extort money or any pecuniary advantage, or with the intent to compel any person to do or refrain from doing any act against his will, is guilty of a Class H felony.

See G.S. 14-455, reproduced under "Damaging Computer or Related Equipment" in Chapter 16.

Elements

A person guilty of this offense

(1) maliciously
(2) threatens to
(3) alter, damage, or destroy
(4) a computer, computer program, computer system, computer network, or any part thereof
(5) with the intent to
  (a) extort money or any monetary advantage, *or*
  (b) compel another person to do or refrain from doing an act.

Punishment

Class H felony.

Notes

Element (2). The threat can be oral or written. A threat written in a computer communication likely qualifies as well.

Element (3). This offense would include threats to do damage by the introduction of software computer "viruses" [G.S. 14-455(b)].

Element (4). See the note discussing Element (4) under "Damaging Computer or Related Equipment" (Ch. 16).

Related offenses not in this chapter

See the offenses listed at the end of this section.

V.
Computer Trespass

Statute

§14-458. Computer trespass; penalty.

(a) Except as otherwise made unlawful by this Article, it shall be unlawful for any person to use a computer or computer network without authority and with the intent to do any of the following:

(1) Temporarily or permanently remove, halt, or otherwise disable any computer data, computer programs, or computer software from a computer or computer network.
(2) Cause a computer to malfunction, regardless of how long the malfunction persists.
(3) Alter or erase any computer data, computer programs, or computer software.
(4) Cause physical injury to the property of another.
(5) Make or cause to be made an unauthorized copy, in any form, including, but not limited to, any printed or electronic form of computer data, computer programs, or computer software residing in, communicated by, or produced by a computer or computer network.
(6) Falsely identify with the intent to deceive or defraud the recipient or forge commercial electronic mail transmission information or other routing information in any manner in connection with the transmission of unsolicited bulk commercial electronic mail through or into the computer network of an electronic mail service provider or its subscribers.

For purposes of this subsection, a person is "without authority" when (i) the person has no right or permission of the owner to use a computer, or the person uses a computer in a manner exceeding the right or permission, or (ii) the person uses a computer or computer network, or the computer services of an electronic mail service provider to transmit unsolicited bulk commercial electronic mail in contravention of the authority granted by or in violation of the policies set by the electronic mail service provider.

(b) Any person who violates this section shall be guilty of computer trespass, which offense shall be punishable as a Class 3 misdemeanor. If there is damage to the property of another and the damage is valued at less than two thousand five hundred dollars ($2,500) caused by the person's act in violation of this section, the offense shall be punished as a Class 1 misdemeanor. If there is damage to the property of another valued at two thousand five hundred dollars ($2,500) or more caused by the person's act in violation of this section, the offense shall be punished as a Class I felony.

(c) Any person whose property or person is injured by reason of a violation of this section may sue for and recover any damages sustained and the costs of the suit pursuant to G.S. 1-539.2A.

Elements

A person guilty of this offense

(1) uses a computer or computer network
(2) without authority, *and*
(3) with the intent to
  (a) temporarily or permanently remove, halt, or otherwise disable any computer data, computer programs, or computer software from a computer or computer network, *or*
  (b) cause a computer to malfunction, *or*
  (c) alter or erase any computer data, computer programs, or computer software, *or*
  (d) cause physical injury to the property of another, *or*
  (e) make or cause to be made an unauthorized copy, in any form, including, but not limited to, any printed or electronic form of computer data, computer programs, or computer software

residing in, communicated by, or produced by a computer or computer network, *or*

(f) falsely identify with the intent to deceive or defraud the recipient or forge commercial electronic mail transmission information or other routing information in any manner in connection with the transmission of unsolicited bulk commercial electronic mail through or into the computer network of an electronic mail service provider or its subscribers.

Punishment

If there is damage to the property of another of a value of $2,500 or more, this offense is a Class I felony. If there is damage to the property of another of a value of less than $2,500, this offense is a Class 1 misdemeanor. If there is no damage to the property of another, it is a Class 3 misdemeanor.

Notes

Element (2). See the definition of "without authority" in G.S. 14-458(a), reproduced above.

Element (3)(f). "Electronic mail" is defined as the transmission of information or communication by the use of the Internet, a computer, a facsimile machine, a pager, a cellular telephone, a video recorder, or other electronic means sent to a person identified by a unique address or address number and received by that person [G.S. 14-196.3(a)(2); 14-453(6b)].

Related offenses not in this chapter

"Extortion" (Chapter 12)
"Damaging Computer or Related Equipment" (Chapter 16)

Willful Failure to File State Tax Return, Supply State Tax Information, or Pay State Tax

Statute

§105-236. Penalties.

(9) Willful Failure to File Return, Supply Information, or Pay Tax.—Any person required to pay any tax, to make a return, to keep any records, or to supply any information, who willfully fails to pay the tax, make the return, keep the records, or supply the information, at the time or times required by law, or rules issued pursuant thereto, shall, in addition to other penalties provided by law, be guilty of a Class 1 misdemeanor. Notwithstanding any other provision of law, no prosecution for a violation brought under this subdivision shall be barred before the expiration of six years after the date of the violation.

Only one subsection of G.S. 105-236 is reproduced here.

Elements

A person guilty of this offense

(1) is required by G.S. Ch. 105, Subchapter I (Levy of Taxes), to

    (a) pay any tax
    (b) make a return
    (c) keep any records, *or*
    (d) supply any information, *and*
(2) willfully
(3) fails to
    (a) pay such tax
    (b) make such return
    (c) keep such records, *or*
    (d) supply such information.

Punishment

Class 1 misdemeanor.

Notes

Generally. This offense applies to G.S. Ch. 105, Subchapters I, V, and VIII, and to inspection taxes levied under G.S. Ch. 119, Art. 3 [G.S. 105-228.90]. These statutory subchapters encompass many (but not all) of the taxes collected in North Carolina, including corporate and individual income tax, local government sales and use tax, conveyance tax, license tax, gasoline tax, tobacco tax, soft drink tax, alcoholic beverage excise tax, gift tax, and controlled substance tax. It does *not* apply to taxation of real and personal property pursuant to G.S. Ch. 119, Subchapter II.

Element (2). See the definition of "willfully" in Chapter 1, "States of Mind." In addressing this element of this particular offense, the North Carolina Court of Appeals said, a good-faith misunderstanding of the law's requirements may negate willfulness, but a good-faith disagreement with the law does not (96 N.C. App. 545). Thus disagreement with tax laws does not afford tax protesters a defense to this element.

Related offenses not in this chapter

None.

15
Arson and Burning Offenses

Chapter Contents

15 Arson and Burning Offenses

First-Degree Arson

Statute

§14-58. Punishment for arson.

There shall be two degrees of arson as defined at the common law. If the dwelling burned was occupied at the time of the burning, the offense is arson in the first degree and is punishable as a Class D felony. If the dwelling burned was unoccupied at the time of the burning, the offense is arson in the second degree and is punishable as a Class G felony.

Elements

A person guilty of this offense
(1) willfully and maliciously
(2) burns
(3) the dwelling house or other buildings within the curtilage
(4) of another
(5) while someone is present inside the dwelling.

Punishment

Class D felony.

Notes

Common-law offense. Since the elements of the crime of arson are not listed in G.S. 14-58, common law (case law) provides the general definition of arson (306 N.C. 90, 99–100). G.S. 14-58 adds the distinction between first- and Second-Degree arson.

Element (1). To constitute arson, the burning of the dwelling must be done willfully and maliciously (243 N.C. 393). To prove this element, the state must show (1) that the defendant intended to burn the dwelling or that the act committed would probably result in a burning of a dwelling and (2) that the act was done "voluntarily and without excuse or justification and without any bona fide claim or right" (288 N.C. 44). It is not necessary that the person have intended to injure a person; proof of intent to burn a particular house is sufficient (98 N.C. 637).

Element (2). The house need not be destroyed; the requirement is met if any part, however small, is consumed—for example, if the wallpaper is burned (305 N.C. 126; 305 N.C. 327). But there must be actual charring rather than mere discoloration or scorching. Charring occurs when some part of the house—for example, a piece of wood paneling—is reduced to coal and has its identity changed (305 N.C. 126). The words "set fire to" should not be used in charging this offense because they are not the legal equivalent of the word "burn" (93 N.C. 571). See the notes to Element (2) under "Burning Public Building" for a discussion of the phrase "set fire to."

Element (3). The dwelling must be inhabited (243 N.C. 393; 306 N.C. 90). That requirement means only that someone must regularly or frequently use the house as a residence (306 N.C. 90). The value of the dwelling is irrelevant; a shack, as well as a mansion, can be a dwelling. The term "dwelling house," for burglary and probably also for arson, includes all interconnecting portions of any building in which a person habitually sleeps, even if the building's main use is as a store (90 N.C. 724; *Perkins*, p. 280). A person can have more than one dwelling house (90 N.C. 724); burning a summer beach cottage during the winter would be burning a dwelling house. Burning of other buildings within the curtilage is also arson (235 N.C. 173; 97 N.C. 496). Arson has not been committed if only the contents of the dwelling are burned; some part on the structure itself must be burned (25 N.C. 570).

Element (4). The house or dwelling must be possessed by someone other than (or in addition to) the defendant (98 N.C. 637). For example, a defendant who burned his apartment in a building containing other apartments was convicted of arson (rather than of "Burning One's Own Dwelling House") because the entire building was considered the dwelling of the other tenants (296 N.C. 75). A defendant may also be charged with arson for burning a dwelling that the defendant inhabits with another (305 N.C. 327). Possession, not legal ownership, is the important element (187 N.C. 698); thus an owner can be guilty of arson for burning a dwelling rented to and possessed by someone else.

Element (5). For a burning to constitute first-degree arson, someone must physically be present in the dwelling when the burning occurs (333 N.C. 666). Otherwise, the crime is Second-Degree arson.

A case may involve arson and murder, with arson being the underlying felony for a felony murder charge (see "First-Degree Murder" in Chapter 6). If so, and the arson and murder are a part of one continuous transaction, felony murder may be charged even if the victim dies before the arson is committed (332 N.C. 116). A continuous transaction is one so joined in time and circumstances as to be part of a single event. If the dwelling was "occupied" when the continuous transaction involving murder and arson started, and the time between the murder and arson was short, the dwelling is considered occupied for first-degree arson. This continuous transaction doctrine is similar to that applied to murders committed during armed robberies and sex offenses (330 N.C. 557; 329 N.C. 423).

In cases involving murder and arson, when there is evidence that the two offenses are not so joined in time and circumstances as to be a single continuous transaction, it may be necessary to determine whether there was a living occupant in the dwelling at the time of the burning (332 N.C. 116). For example, when one occupant of a dwelling was murdered several days before the burning of a dwelling, the victim's body was removed from the dwelling, and the second, and only other, occupant permanently abandoned the dwelling before the burning, the dwelling was neither inhabited nor occupied. Consequently, the defendant was guilty of burning an uninhabited house rather than of arson (93 N.C. App. 682).

Burning apartment building. A building containing several apartments is a single dwelling. Therefore the charring (burning) of one apartment satisfies

Element (2), and the habitation of another apartment—even though not charred—satisfies Element (3) (48 N.C. App. 709).

Arson not solely a nighttime offense. While burglary can take place only at night, arson can be committed at any time of day.

Confession as evidence. A defendant's confession alone is insufficient to establish the criminal origin of a fire. Corroborating evidence is necessary in addition to a confession (308 N.C. 181; 315 N.C. 222).

Lesser-included offenses. An attempt to commit this offense is a lesser-included offense of First-Degree arson (285 N.C. 751; G.S. 15-170). Burning an uninhabited house (G.S. 14-62) is not a lesser-included offense of arson (132 N.C. App. 173).

Related offenses not in this chapter

"Attempt" (Chapter 4)
See the offenses in Chapter 16, "Trespass, Property Damage, and Littering."
See the offenses in Chapter 7, "Assaults and Threats."
"Malicious Injury by Use of Explosive or Incendiary" (Chapter 7)
"Malicious Damage to Occupied Property by Use of Explosive or Incendiary" (Chapter 16)
"Malicious Damage by Use of Explosive or Incendiary" (Chapter 16)
"Trespass during Emergency" (Chapter 17)
"Looting" (Chapter 17)
Burning ginhouses and tobacco houses (G.S. 14-64)
Injuring houses other than by burning (G.S. 14-144)
Injuring houses (G.S. 14-159)

Second-Degree Arson

Statute

See G.S. 14-58, reproduced under "First-Degree Arson."

Elements

A person guilty of this offense
(1) willfully and maliciously
(2) burns
(3) the dwelling house or other buildings within the curtilage
(4) of another.

Punishment

Class G felony.

Notes

Generally. The elements of arson are defined by common law. G.S. 14-58, however, distinguishes the elements of First-Degree and Second-Degree arson.

Difference from "First-Degree Arson." This offense differs from first-degree arson in that it does not require that someone be present inside the dwelling when the burning occurs.

Elements (1) through (4). See the notes on these elements under "First-Degree Arson." An additional note concerning element (3): a malicious and willful burning of a mobile home used as a dwelling and unoccupied at the time of the burning is second-degree arson (121 N.C. App. 209).

Related offenses not in this chapter

See the offenses listed under "First-Degree Arson."

Arson of Mobile Home

Statute

§14-58.2. Burning of mobile home, manufactured-type house or recreational trailer home.

If any person shall willfully and maliciously burn any mobile home or manufactured-type house or recreational trailer home which is the dwelling house of another and which is occupied at the time of the burning, the same shall constitute the crime of arson in the first degree.

Elements

A person guilty of this offense
(1) willfully and maliciously
(2) burns
(3) a mobile home, manufactured type of home, or recreational trailer home
(4) that is the dwelling house
(5) of another
(6) while someone is present inside the dwelling.

Punishment

Class D felony.

Notes

Generally. The notes for "First-Degree Arson" apply to the corresponding elements of this offense.

Compared with first-degree arson. First-degree arson may be a more appropriate charge than this offense when a mobile home, manufactured-type house, or recreational trailer vehicle used as a dwelling is burned while someone is inside. First-degree arson may be preferable because it requires one less element—Element (3) above is absent under first-degree arson. Neither statutes nor case law clearly state whether one charge is more appropriate than the other. However, the offense of arson of mobile home may have been created because common-law arson covers dwellings that are buildings, and some legislators may have thought that mobile homes, manufactured-type homes, or recreational trailers did not fit the common-law definition of building. Since the enactment of G.S. 14-58.2, the North Carolina Court of Appeals has clearly recognized that mobile homes and manufactured housing are dwellings (121 N.C. App. 211, recognizing burning of unoccupied mobile home as second-degree arson). Thus G.S. 14-58.2 appears unnecessary; that is, the burning of the structures set out in the statute when used as dwellings are included in both first- and Second-Degree arson.

Element (6). "Occupied," as used in the statute, means that the structure has someone physically within when the burning takes place. If no one is present when the burning occurs, the perpetrator is guilty of Second-Degree arson under G.S. 14-58 (121 N.C. App. 209; 93 N.C. App. 682). See the elements of "Second-Degree Arson."

Burning trailer used for purposes other than dwelling. G.S. 14-58.1 provides that for all statutory burning offenses, mobile homes, manufactured types of housing, and recreational trailers are included within the term "building." Thus, for example, a trailer or mobile home used as an annex or temporary office by a local government would be a public building covered by G.S. 14-59, the next offense discussed.

Lesser-included offenses. An attempt to commit this offense is a lesser-included offense of Second-Degree arson (G.S. 15-170). Burning an uninhabited house (G.S. 14-62) is not a lesser-included offense of arson (132 N.C. App. 173).

Related offenses not in this chapter

See the offenses listed under "First-Degree Arson."

Burning Public Building

Statute

§14-59. Burning of certain public buildings.

If any person shall wantonly and willfully set fire to or burn or cause to be burned or aid, counsel or procure the burning of, the State Capitol, the Legislative Building, the Justice Building or any building owned or occupied by the State or any of its agencies, institutions or subdivisions or by any county, incorporated city or town or other governmental or quasi-governmental entity, he shall be punished as a Class F felon.

Elements

A person guilty of this offense
(1) wantonly and willfully
(2) sets fire to, or burns, or causes to be burned, or aids, or counsels, or procures the burning of
(3) the State Capitol, the Legislative Building, the Justice Building, or any other building owned or occupied by any agency of state or local government.

Punishment

Class F felony.

Notes

Element (1). The term "wantonly," as applied to this and other crimes, implies that the act is done "perversely, recklessly without regard to the property or the rights of others, careless of consequence and yet without malice" (98 N.C. 641; 284 N.C. 67). The term "willfully" implies that the act "is done knowingly, and of stubborn purpose, but not of malice" (97 N.C. 465). See also the definitions of "wantonly" and "willfully" in Chapter 1.

Element (2). To aid, counsel, or procure the burning carries the same punishment as the actual burning. For a discussion of aiding and abetting, see "Aiding and Abetting Felony" (Chapter 3). The statute specifies that setting fire to the buildings could constitute a crime. Thus if one "set fire to" one of the buildings mentioned in the statute but the effect of "setting fire to" did not satisfy the traditional test of "burning" (see the notes under "First-Degree Arson"), the crime of burning a public building has still been committed (93 N.C. 571). For example, if the wood on the structure was discolored but was not sufficiently decomposed to be classified as "burned," the defendant has "set fire to" the wood. In charging someone with procuring the burning of a building, the state is alleging actual complicity in the crime. To convict, it must prove that the defendant instructed someone to burn the building and that the building was, in fact, burned (22 N.C. App. 148).

Element (3). The building should be described with enough detail in an indictment to insure that it is included in the class covered by the statute and to insure that the defendant can prepare a defense. Stating that the building was possessed by a named person is sufficient, but not necessary, to identify it (247 N.C. 745).

School buildings. In 17 N.C. App. 550, a defendant was charged and convicted of this offense for burning a former school classroom building that was being used as school board administrative offices. Thus it may be appropriate to charge the burning of a school administration building as "burning public building." Note, however, that the language of "Burning Schoolhouse," discussed below, is sufficiently broad to encompass buildings used by educational institutions for a wide variety of purposes, including education, administration, and recreation.

Burning trailer. G.S. 14-58.1 provides that for all the burning offenses, mobile homes, manufactured types of housing, and recreational trailers are included within the term "building." Thus a trailer or mobile home used as an annex or temporary office by any government agency would be a public building covered by G.S. 14-59.

Relation to other offenses. Burning personal property is not a lesser-included offense of burning public building (208 N.C. 47).

Related offenses not in this chapter

See the offenses listed under "First-Degree Arson."

Burning Schoolhouse

Statute

§14-60. Burning of schoolhouses or buildings of educational institutions.

If any person shall wantonly and willfully set fire to or burn or cause to be burned or aid, counsel or procure the burning of, any schoolhouse or building owned, leased or used by any public or private school, college or educational institution, he shall be punished as a Class F felon.

Elements

A person guilty of this offense
(1) wantonly and willfully
(2) sets fire to, or burns, or causes to be burned, or aids, or counsels, or procures the burning of
(3) any schoolhouse or building used or leased by an educational institution.

Punishment

Class F felony.

Notes

Generally. The notes to "Burning Public Building" apply to the appropriate elements of this offense.

Element (3). The statute covers "any schoolhouse or building owned, leased, or used" by all types of educational institutions, both public and private. This language appears broad enough to cover buildings used for administrative, classroom, or recreational purposes.

Related offenses not in this chapter

See the offenses listed under "First-Degree Arson."

Burning Bridge, Fire Station, Rescue Squad Building, etc.

Statute

§14-61. Burning of certain bridges and buildings.

If any person shall wantonly and willfully set fire to or burn or cause to be burned, or aid, counsel or procure the burning of, any public bridge, or private toll bridge, or the bridge of any incorporated company, or any fire-engine house or rescue-squad building, or any house belonging to an incorporated company or unincorporated association and used in the business of such company or association, he shall be punished as a Class F felon.

Elements

A person guilty of this offense
(1) wantonly and willfully
(2) sets fire to, or burns, or causes to be burned, or aids, or counsels, or procures the burning of a
(3) public bridge, private toll bridge or a corporation bridge, or a fire engine house or rescue squad building, or a house owned and used by a corporation or unincorporated association in its business.

Punishment

Class F felony.

Notes

Generally. The notes to "Burning Public Building" apply to the appropriate elements of this offense.

Private bridges not covered. This statute apparently does not cover private nontoll bridges owned by individuals. The offense of "Burning Building Not Listed in Any Other Statute" would cover such a bridge, however.

Related offenses not in this chapter

See the offenses listed under "First-Degree Arson."
Injuring bridge (G.S. 14-146)

Burning Uninhabited House, Factory, Store, etc.

Statute

§14-62. Burning certain buildings.

If any person shall wantonly and willfully set fire to or burn or cause to be burned, or aid, counsel or procure the burning of, any uninhabited house, or any stable, coach house, outhouse, warehouse, office, shop, mill, barn or granary, or any building, structure or erection used or intended to be used in carrying on any trade or manufacture, or any branch thereof, whether the same or any of them respectively shall then be in the possession of the offender, or in the possession of any other person, he shall be punished as a Class F felon.

Elements

A person guilty of this offense

(1) wantonly and willfully
(2) sets fire to, or burns, or causes to be burned, or aids, or counsels, or procures the burning of
(3) an uninhabited house, outhouse, stable, warehouse, office, shop, mill, barn, or building used or intended to be used in carrying on a trade or manufacture.

Punishment

Class F felony.

Notes

Generally. The notes to "Burning Public Building" apply to the appropriate elements of this offense.

Element (3). "Building" means a structure or other erection built by humans, designed to stand more or less permanently, that can shelter humans or serve some other useful purpose (235 N.C. 173). If a building is still under construction, burning building under construction is the proper charge. To prove this charge when a house is burned, the house must be uninhabited. The defendant has not committed this offense if the house is normally used as a residence even if the tenants are absent at the time of the burning (46 N.C. App. 822); the proper charge in such a case is Second-Degree arson. For this offense, "outhouse" does not mean an outdoor toilet facility (which is more precisely called a privy); instead, it means a building within the curtilage of a dwelling used for storage or other purposes. Thus all privies are outhouses, but all outhouses are not privies (109 N.C. App. 360).

"To be used in carrying on any trade or manufacture" means to be put to its intended purpose for any ordinary occupation or business, whether manual or mercantile, even if the building is used that way only once (235 N.C. 173); the use need not be habitual in order to satisfy Element (3). The statute also covers buildings intended for use in trade or manufacture. It includes any farm buildings not covered by the arson statute, including a tobacco barn (306 N.C. 90).

Burning by possessor. The statute specifies that it covers burnings either by the possessor of the building or by someone else.

Lesser-included offenses. This offense is not a lesser-included offense of arson (132 N.C. App. 173).

Related offenses not in this chapter

See the offenses listed under "First-Degree Arson."

Burning Churches and Certain Other Religious Buildings

Statute

§14-62.2. Burning of churches and certain other religious buildings.

If any person shall wantonly and willfully set fire to or burn or cause to be burned, or aid, counsel or procure the burning of any church, chapel, or meetinghouse, the person shall be punished as a Class E felon.

Elements

A person guilty of this offense
(1) wantonly and willfully
(2) sets fire to, or burns, or causes to be burned, or aids, or counsels, or procures the burning of
(3) a church, chapel, or meetinghouse.

Punishment

Class E felony.

Notes

Elements (1) and (2). See the notes on Elements (1) and (2) under "Burning Public Building."

Related offenses not in this chapter

See the offenses listed under "First-Degree Arson."

Burning Building under Construction

Statute

§14-62.1. Burning of building or structure in process of construction.

If any person shall wantonly and willfully set fire to or burn or cause to be burned, or aid, counsel or procure the burning of, any building or structure in the process of construction for use or intended to be used as a dwelling house or in carrying on any trade or manufacture, or otherwise, whether the same or any of them respectively shall then be in the possession of the offender, or in the possession of any other person, he shall be punished as a Class H felon.

Elements

A person guilty of this offense
(1) wantonly and willfully
(2) sets fire to, or burns, or causes to be burned, or aids, or counsels, or procures the burning of
(3) a building or structure in the process of construction
(4) that is intended for use as a dwelling or in carrying on a trade or business.

Punishment

Class H felony.

Notes

Elements (1) and (2). See the notes for Elements (1) and (2) under "Burning Public Building."

Element (3). This statute includes structures that would become buildings used as dwellings or for business, but which are not yet completed. Note that G.S. 14-58.1 defines mobile homes, manufactured types of housing, and recreational trailers as buildings; burning one of those buildings while it is under construction apparently would violate this statute.

Element (4). See the discussion of dwelling's definition in the note on Element (3) under "First-Degree Arson"; see the discussion of building "used in any trade or manufacture" in the note on Element (3) under "Burning Uninhabited House, Factory, Store, etc."

Burning by possessor. The statute specifies that it covers burnings by either the possessor of the building or someone else.

Related offenses not in this chapter

See the offenses listed under "First-Degree Arson."

Burning Boat, Barge, Ferry, or Float

Statute

§14-63. Burning of boats and barges.

If any person shall wantonly and willfully set fire to or burn or cause to be burned or aid, counsel or procure the burning of, any boat, barge, ferry or float, without the consent of the owner thereof, he shall be punished as a Class H felon. In the event the consent of the owner is given for an unlawful or fraudulent purpose, however, the penalty provisions of this section shall remain in full force and effect.

Elements

A person guilty of this offense
(1) wantonly and willfully
(2) sets fire to, or burns, or causes to be burned, or aids, or counsels, or procures the burning of any
(3) boat, barge, ferry, or float
(4) without the owner's consent, or with owner's consent, if done for a fraudulent purpose.

Punishment

Class H felony.

Notes

Generally. The notes under "Burning Public Building" apply to the appropriate elements of this offense.

Element (4). The fraudulent purpose could, for example, be collection of insurance. See the note for Element (1) under "Burning One's Own Dwelling House."

Burning of houseboats. The willful and malicious burning of a houseboat of another person used as a dwelling probably would constitute arson. To set fire to, cause to be burned, aid, counsel, or procure the burning of such a houseboat would not constitute arson but would violate this statute.

Related offenses not in this chapter

See the offenses listed under "First-Degree Arson."
"Obtaining Property by False Pretenses" (Chapter 14)
False statement to procure insurance benefits (G.S. 58-2-161)

Burning One's Own Dwelling House

Statute

§14-65. Fraudulently setting fire to dwelling houses.

If any person, being the occupant of any building used as a dwelling house, whether such person be the owner thereof or not, or, being the owner of any building designed or intended as a dwelling house, shall wantonly and willfully or for a fraudulent purpose set fire to or burn or cause to be burned, or aid, counsel or procure the burning of such building, he shall be punished as a Class H felon.

Elements

A person guilty of this offense
(1) wantonly and willfully or for a fraudulent purpose
(2) sets fire to, or burns, or causes to be burned, or aids counsels, procures the burning of
(3) a dwelling house occupied by the defendant, whether as owner or not, or a building designed or intended for use as a dwelling and owned by the defendant.

Punishment

Class H felony.

Notes

Element (1). See the note on "wantonly and willfully" under "Burning Public Building." A person who burns his or her own home in circumstances that do not create a danger of injury or loss to others does not act wantonly (306 N.C. 138). "For a fraudulent purpose" describes a mental state of having the desire for illegal monetary gain, usually at the expense of the property's insurer (288 N.C. 44).

Element (2). See the note for Element (2) under "Burning Public Building."

Element (3). See the definition of dwelling house in the note to Element (3) under "First-Degree Arson." Note that G.S. 14-58.1 includes mobile homes, manufactured types of housing, and recreational trailers under the definitions of houses and buildings.

Related offenses not in this chapter

See the offenses listed under "First-Degree Arson."
"Obtaining Property by False Pretenses" (Chapter 14)
False statement to procure insurance benefits (G.S. 58-2-161)

Burning Building Not Listed in Any Other Statute

Statute

§14-67.1. Burning other buildings.

If any person shall wantonly and willfully set fire to or burn or cause to be burned or aid, counsel or procure the burning of any building or other structure of any type not otherwise covered by the provisions of this Article, he shall be punished as a Class H felon.

Elements

A person guilty of this offense
(1) wantonly and willfully
(2) sets fire to, or burns, or causes to be burned, or aids, or counsels, or procures the burning of
(3) any structure of any type not otherwise covered in an offense already listed in this chapter.

Punishment

Class H felony.

Notes

Elements (1) and (2). See the note for Element (1) under "Burning Public Building."

Element (2). See the note for Element (2) under "Burning Public Building."

Element (3). When an offense is charged under this statute, the structure burned must be described. This statute covers any structure not covered in the other burning offenses, such as an uninhabited storage building on a farm (34 N.C. App. 462).

Attempt. In 1993 the General Assembly removed the part of this statute that treated attempts the same as actual burnings under this statute. As a result, an attempt to commit this offense should be treated as attempts are generally treated (see Chapter 4).

Related offenses not in this chapter

See the offenses listed under "First-Degree Arson."

Burning Personal Property

Statute

§14-66. Burning of personal property.

If any person shall wantonly and willfully set fire to or burn, or cause to be burned, or aid, counsel or procure the burning of, any goods, wares, merchandise or other chattels or personal property of any kind, whether or not the same shall at the time be insured by any person or corporation against loss or damage by fire, with intent to injure or prejudice the insurer, the creditor or the person owning the property, or any other person, whether the property is that of such person or another, he shall be punished as a Class H felon.

Elements

A person guilty of this offense
(1) wantonly and willfully
(2) sets fire to, or burns, or causes to be burned, or aids, or counsels, or procures the burning of
(3) any goods, wares, or personal property of any kind
(4) with intent to injure or prejudice the insurer, creditor, person who owns such property, or any other person.

Punishment

Class H felony.

Notes

Generally. The notes under "Burning Public Building" apply to the appropriate elements of this offense.

Element (3). The burned goods need not be insured before this offense can occur, but whether they are insured might be relevant to the defendant's intent under Element (4).

Element (4). This offense can be committed when a person burns his or her own property with the specific intent to injure or prejudice another, such as a creditor or lienholder. This intent may be inferred from such circumstances as the nature of the act and how it was done (59 N.C. App. 527). The injury may be physical or financial.

Relation to other offenses. Burning personal property is not a lesser-included offense of burning public building (208 N.C. 47).

Related offenses not in this chapter

See the offenses listed under "First-Degree Arson."
"Obtaining Property by False Pretenses" (Chapter 14)
Fraudulent disposal of personal property on which there is a security interest (G.S. 14-114)
False statement to procure insurance benefit (G.S. 58-2-161)

Setting Fire to Woods and Fields

Statute

§14-137. Willfully or negligently setting fire to woods and fields.

If any person, firm or corporation shall willfully or negligently set on fire, or cause to be set on fire, any woods, lands or fields, whatsoever, every such offender shall be guilty of a Class 2 misdemeanor. This section shall apply only in those counties under the protection of the Department of Environment and Natural Resources in its work of forest fire control. It shall not apply in the case of a landowner firing, or causing to be fired, his own open, nonwooded lands, or fields in connection with farming or building operations at the time and in the manner now provided by law: Provided, he shall have confined the fire at his own expense to said open lands or fields.

Elements

A person guilty of this offense
(1) willfully or negligently
(2) sets on fire or causes to be set on fire
(3) any woods, land, or fields
(4) in any county that is under the protection of the Department of Environment and Natural Resources in its work of forest fire control.

Punishment

Class 2 misdemeanor.

Notes

Element (1). See the definitions of "willfully" and "negligently" in Chapter 1.

Not applicable to person's own land. This statute does not apply to a landowner who sets on fire his or her own open, nonwooded lands in a farming or building operation, if it is done in compliance with other state laws and if, at his or her own expense, and the landowner has kept the fire confined to his or her land.

Related offenses not in this chapter

See the offenses in Chapter 16, "Trespass, Property Damage, and Littering."
"Malicious Damage by Use of Explosive or Incendiary" (Chapter 16)
Injuring another's timber (G.S. 14-135)
Setting fire to grassland, brushland, or woodland, without extinguishing (G.S. 14-138.1)
Failure to watch fire (G.S. 14-140.1)
Burning or otherwise destroying crops in field (G.S. 14-141)

Setting Fire to Grass, Brushlands, or Woodlands

Statute

§14-136. Setting fire to grass and brushlands and woodlands.

If any person shall intentionally set fire to grassland, brushland or woodland, except it be his own property, or in that case without first giving notice to all persons owning or in charge of lands adjoining the land intended to be fired, and without also taking care to watch such fire while burning and to extinguish it before it shall reach any lands near to or adjoining the lands so fired, he shall for every such offense be guilty of a Class 2 misdemeanor for the first offense, and for a second or any subsequent similar offense shall be guilty of a Class 1 misdemeanor. If intent to damage the property of another shall be shown, said person shall be punished as a Class I felon. This section shall not prevent an action for the damages sustained by the owner of any property from such fires. For the purposes of this section, the term "woodland" is to be taken to include all forest areas, both timber and cutover land, and all second-growth stands on areas that have at one time been cultivated. Any person who shall furnish to the State, evidence sufficient for the conviction of a violation of this section shall receive the sum of five hundred dollars ($500.00) to be paid from the State Fire Suppression Fund.

I. Intentional Burning

Statute

See G.S. 14-136, reproduced immediately above.

Elements

A person is guilty of this offense if he or she
- (1) intentionally
- (2) sets fire to
- (3) any grassland, brushland, or woodland
- (4) (a) of another, *or*
  - (b) owned by the person, unless he or she
    - (1) notifies adjacent property owners, *and*
    - (2) watches the fire and insures that it does not damage the adjoining lands.

Punishment

The first offense is a Class 2 misdemeanor, and a second or subsequent offense is a Class 1 misdemeanor.

Notes

Element (1). If the defendant burns his or her own land out of necessity (i.e., to save a portion of the person's land from an approaching fire), the burning is not voluntary and thus does not constitute this offense (8 N.C. 60).

Element (3). "Woodlands" means all forest areas, both timber and cutover areas, and all second-growth stands on previously cultivated areas.

Element (4)(b). An owner of property may be prosecuted under this statute for burning his or her own property if the owner (1) fails to notify adjoining landowners or those in charge of adjacent land or (2) fails to watch the fire and extinguish it before it reaches the land of another. If the owner does either, he or she has violated this statute (94 N.C. 534).

Civil suits allowed. Besides being tried under this statute, a defendant may be sued by a property owner whose land was damaged by the fire (118 N.C. 991). If a property owner who is burning his or her own property fails to notify adjacent property owners, the owner is liable for damage to the adjacent property, regardless of his or her efforts to stop the fire (94 N.C. 534; 253 N.C. 695).

Reward. The state gives a $500 reward to anyone who provides enough evidence to convict a defendant under this statute.

Related offenses not in this chapter

See the offenses listed under "Setting Fire to Woods and Fields" in this chapter.

II. Burning with Intent to Damage Property

Statute

See G.S. 14-136, reproduced at the beginning of this section.

Elements

A person guilty of this offense
(1) sets fire to
(2) the grassland, brushland, or woodland
(3) of another
(4) with willful or malicious intent
(5) to damage the property.

Punishment

Class I felony.

Notes

Generally. See the notes under "I. Intentional Burning," above.

Related offenses not in this chapter

See the offenses listed under "Setting Fire to Woods and Fields" in this chapter.

16
Trespass, Property Damage, and Littering

Chapter Contents

16
Trespass, Property Damage, and Littering

First-Degree Trespass

Statute

§14-159.12. First degree trespass.

(a) Offense.—A person commits the offense of first degree trespass if, without authorization, he enters or remains:
(1) On premises of another so enclosed or secured as to demonstrate clearly an intent to keep out intruders; or
(2) In a building of another.

(b) Classification.—First degree trespass is a Class 2 misdemeanor.

Elements

A person guilty of this offense
(1) without authorization
(2) (a) enters, *or*
(b) remains
(3) (a) on premises of another so enclosed or secured as to demonstrate an intent to keep out intruders, *or*
(b) in a building of another.

Punishment

Class 2 misdemeanor.

Notes

Generally. The basic distinction between first- and second-degree trespass is the strength of interests in privacy, possession, and control of premises protected by the offenses. The crime of first-degree trespass involves stronger interests and, therefore, more serious violations of privacy, possession, and control of premises. This offense also prohibits many of the same acts (at least those of entering) that are prohibited by "Misdemeanor Breaking or Entering of Building" (Chapter 13).

Element (1). "Without authorization" probably means the same as without consent in breaking or entering offenses—see Element (2) of "Felonious Breaking or Entering of Building" (Chapter 13). The possessor may exclude a person for any reason (247 N.C. 455) except one that rests on a basis (such as race) prohibited by federal civil rights laws.

Element (2). See the note for Element (2) of "First-Degree Burglary" (Chapter 13) for the definition of "entering." "Remains" means stays. It is an affirmative defense to trespass that a defendant entered with reasonable grounds to believe in a legal right to enter, even though the defendant did not have a legal right to enter (231 N.C. 136; 170 N.C. 737).

Element (3)(a). Premises include the entire piece of real estate—not just the building but the land as well. A fenced-in area surrounding all or a part of the premises may satisfy this element.

Element (3)(b). This offense is committed if a person enters a building (home, business, etc.) after previously having been forbidden or remains after having been ordered to leave. For example, if a homeowner tells the defendant—when the defendant is inside his or her house—to leave, and the defendant refuses to do so, or if the homeowner tells the defendant never to come back onto this property again but the defendant comes back and enters the homeowner's house, the defendant has committed first-degree trespass. G.S. 14-159.11 defines "building" as "any structure or part of a structure, other than a conveyance, enclosed so as to permit reasonable entry only through a door and roofed to protect it from the elements."

Spouse forbidding entry to spouse. Applying the law of trespass in domestic disputes has been particularly difficult because of the problem of determining ownership or custody of the property. The offense of "Domestic Criminal Trespass" usually will be the more appropriate charge to consider.

Invitation by tenant after landlord forbids entry. Unless the tenant's lease denies the tenant the authority to invite, a guest who enters premises at the invitation of the tenant is not guilty of this offense even if the landlord has told the guest not to enter (101 N.C. 717).

Asserting rights of free speech on shopping mall property. A defendant was properly convicted of trespass when he refused to leave the parking lot of a shopping mall after he was asked to stop soliciting signatures against the draft. The mall parking lot was private property, and it had not been dedicated to public use in a way that would guarantee rights to free speech under federal or state constitutions (302 N.C. 173).

Lesser-included offenses. G.S. 14-159.14 provides that first- and second-degree trespass are lesser-included offenses of breaking or entering in G.S. 14-54 (felonious and misdemeanor breaking or entering building, discussed in Chapter 13) and G.S. 14-56 (breaking or entering motor vehicle, railroad car, etc., also discussed in Chapter 13), even though there appears to be no difference in the elements of misdemeanor breaking or entering under G.S. 14-54(b) and first-degree trespass with respect to unauthorized entry of a building.

Offenses involving health care facilities. If facts involve a hospital, clinic, or other facility licensed to administer medical treatment, and it is unclear that a trespass offense has been committed, consider the applicability of G.S. 14-277.4 (Obstruction of health care facilities). This statute specifically addresses a situation in which one person blocks another's access or egress from a health care facility or adjoining property in a manner that deprives or delays the latter person from obtaining or providing health care services in the facility. The statute specifies that it is does not prohibit a person from engaging in lawful speech or picketing which does not impede the access or egress of others to the facility or interfere with the delivery of health care at the facility. The statute permits injunctive relief to prevent violation of this statute. Violation of this statute is a Class 2 misdemeanor. A second conviction within 3 years of the first is a Class 1 misdemeanor. A third, or subsequent, conviction, within 3 years of the last is a Class I felony. This statute is not unconstitutionally overbroad or vague (126 F.3d 575; see also 530 U.S. 703).

Offenses involving animal research facilities. If the alleged trespass offense involves such a facility, consider the applicability of G.S. 14-159.2 (Interference with animal research). This statute specifically addresses a situation in which a person trespasses at a research facility where animals are used for medical, veterinary, dental, or biological research. This offense would apply if the defendant (1) had the intent to (a) disrupt the facility's operation, (b) damage the facility or any personal property inside, (c) release any research animal from an enclosure within the facility, or (d) interfere with the care of animals within, and (2) the defendant actually carried out at least one of the listed intended acts. Violation of this statute is a Class 1 misdemeanor. If an animal having an infectious disease is released during commission of this offense, the act is a Class I felony.

Offenses involving entering or remaining on another's land to engage in recreational activities. In a handful of counties, the offense of third-degree trespass applies. A person commits this offense if, without authorization, the person enters or remains on the premises of another for the purpose of hunting, fishing, trapping, loitering, or operating an all-terrain vehicle. This offense is a Class 3 misdemeanor. The offense permits a prosecution for trespass where the elements of first- and second-degree trespass warning trespassors to stay away are not present. Land need not be posted or securely enclosed for this offense to apply, nor does a person need to be warned to stay off the property. This law is stated in Chapter 862 of the 1991 Session Laws of North Carolina. As of 2000, this law applied only in Iredell, Rowan, Wilkes, and Yadkin Counties (see Chapters 593 and 659 of the 1993 Session Laws of North Carolina).

Trespassing to remove pine needles or pine straw. It is a Class 1 misdemeanor under G.S. 14-159.6(b) if a person (1) willfully goes on land upon which signs prohibiting the raking or removal of pine needles or pine straw have been posted in accordance with G.S. 14-159.7, (2) for the purpose of raking or removing pine needles or pine straw, and (3) without the written consent of the owner or owner's agent.

Trespassing with motorized all-terrain vehicle. It is a Class 2 misdemeanor under G.S. 14-159.3 if a person (1) operates a motorized all-terrain vehicle (as defined in the statute); (2) on private property not owned by the operator of the vehicle or within the banks of any stream or waterway (other than a sound or the Atlantic Ocean), the adjacent lands of which are not owned by the operator; and (3) without the owner's consent or outside the restrictions imposed by the owner.

Related offenses not in this chapter

"Stalking" (Chapter 7)
"Misdemeanor Breaking or Entering of Building" (Chapter 13)
"Being Found in a Building with Intent to Commit Any Felony or Larceny" (Chapter 13)
"Trespass during Emergency" (Chapter 17)
"Picketing Courthouse" (Chapter 18)
Taking wild plants (G.S. 14-129)
Trespass on public lands (G.S. 14-130)
Trespass on land under option by the federal government (G.S. 14-131)

Operating motor vehicle on utility easements after being forbidden (G.S. 14-134.2)
Unlawful posting of advertisements (G.S. 14-145)
Taking unlawful possession of a house (G.S. 14-159)
Interference with animal research (G.S. 14-159.2)
Trespassing for purpose of hunting (G.S. 14-159.6)
Trespass on railroad right-of-way (G.S. 14-280.1)
Airport obstruction (G.S. 63-37.1)

Second-Degree Trespass

Statute

§14-159.13. Second degree trespass.

(a) Offense.—A person commits the offense of second degree trespass if, without authorization, he enters or remains on premises of another:

(1) After he has been notified not to enter or remain there by the owner, by a person in charge of the premises, by a lawful occupant, or by another authorized person; or

(2) That are posted, in a manner reasonably likely to come to the attention of intruders, with notice not to enter the premises.

(b) Classification.—Second degree trespass is a Class 3 misdemeanor.

Elements

A person guilty of this offense

(1) without authorization

(2) (a) enters, *or*

(b) remains

(3) on premises of another

(4) (a) after having been notified not to enter or remain there by the owner, a person in charge of premises, a lawful occupant, or another authorized person, *or*

(b) when the premises are posted, in a manner reasonably likely to come to the attention of intruders, with notice not to enter the premises.

Punishment

Class 3 misdemeanor.

Notes

Elements (1) and (2). See the notes for Elements (1) and (2) under "First-Degree Trespass."

Element (3). Premises include the entire piece of real estate—not just the building, but the land as well.

Element (4)(a). This element would be satisfied if a homeowner tells a defendant to leave the homeowner's front yard and the defendant refuses, or if a homeowner tells a defendant never to come back onto the homeowner's property again, but the defendant re-enters the property. However, if the unauthorized entering or remaining occurs in a building, first-degree trespass should be charged. "Another authorized person" could include an agent of the owner or occupant of the premises.

Element (4)(b). This element may be satisfied by posting "No trespassing" or similar signs in a manner reasonably likely to come to an intruder's attention. Proof that the intruder actually saw the signs is not required.

Lesser-included offenses. G.S. 14-159.14 provides that first- and second-degree trespass are lesser-included offenses of breaking or entering in G.S. 14-54 (felonious and misdemeanor breaking or entering building, discussed in Chapter 13) and G.S. 14-56 (breaking or entering motor vehicle, railroad car, etc., also discussed in Chapter 13).

Offenses involving health care facilities. See this note under "First-Degree Trespass."

Offenses involving animal research facilities. See this note under "First-Degree Trespass."

Offenses involving entering or remaining on another's land to engage in recreational activities. See this note under "First-Degree Trespass."

Trespassing to remove pine needles or pine straw. See this note under "First-Degree Trespass."

Trespassing with motorized all-terrain vehicle. See this note under "First-Degree Trespass."

Related offenses not in this chapter

See the related offenses under "First-Degree Trespass" in this chapter.

Domestic Criminal Trespass

Statute

§14-134.3. Domestic criminal trespass.

(a) Any person who enters after being forbidden to do so or remains after being ordered to leave by the lawful occupant, upon the premises occupied by a present or former spouse or by a person with whom the person charged has lived as if married, shall be guilty of a misdemeanor if the complainant and the person charged are living apart; provided, however, that no person shall be guilty if said person enters upon the premises pursuant to a judicial order or written separation agreement which gives the person the right to enter upon said premises for the purpose of visiting with minor children. Evidence that the parties are living apart shall include but is not necessarily limited to:

(1) A judicial order of separation;
(2) A court order directing the person charged to stay away from the premises occupied by the complainant;
(3) An agreement, whether verbal or written, between the complainant and the person charged that they shall live separate and apart, and such parties are in fact living separate and apart; or
(4) Separate places of residence for the complainant and the person charged.

Except as provided in subsection (b) of this section, upon conviction, said person is guilty of a Class 1 misdemeanor.

(b) A person convicted of a violation of this section is guilty of a Class G felony if the person is trespassing upon property operated as a safe house or haven for victims of domestic violence and the person is armed with a deadly weapon at the time of the offense.

Elements

A person guilty of this offense

(1) (a) after having been forbidden to enter, *or*
(b) after having been ordered to leave
(2) by the lawful occupant
(3) (a) enters, *or*
(b) refuses to leave
(4) the premises occupied by
(a) the charged person's present or former spouse, *or*
(b) another person with whom the charged person has lived as if married
(5) at a time when the charged person and the present or former spouse (or person with whom the charged person has lived as if married) are living apart.

Punishment

Class 1 misdemeanor. However, it is a Class G felony if the person trespassed upon property operated as a safe house or haven for victims of domestic violence and the person was armed with a deadly weapon at the time of the offense (note that the state must allege this information in the criminal pleading and prove it at trial).

Notes

Element (2). The lawful occupant apparently may be someone other than the present or former spouse or person with whom the defendant has lived as if married; for example, the lawful occupant could be the new spouse or partner of the former spouse.

Element (3). The statute provides that a person who enters the premises pursuant to a court order that allows the person entry to visit his or her children may not be convicted of this offense for that entry. Presumably if the person entered at a time not authorized by the court order, he or she could commit this offense if all other elements are satisfied.

Element (4). The statute requires that the former or present spouse or person with whom the defendant has lived as if married have occupied the premises at the time of the offense. It is not clear whether "occupied" requires that the complainant actually be present at the premises when the defendant entered or refused to leave.

Element (5). The statute specifies that the following evidence may be used to prove the fact that the parties are living apart: (1) a judicial order of separation; (2) a court order directing the defendant to stay away from the complainant's premises; (3) an agreement (written or oral) between the parties that they will live apart; and (4) the fact that the parties have separate residences.

Relationship with first- and second-degree trespass. In situations involving spouses, former spouses, and parties who have been living together as if married, it may be difficult to establish the accused trespasser's lack of legal authority to be present on the property—a necessary element of both first- and second-degree trespass. Consequently, this may be a more appropriate charge in such situations.

Related offenses not in this chapter

"Simple Assault" (Chapter 7)
"Communicating Threats" (Chapter 7)
"Stalking" (Chapter 7)
Illegal purchase of firearm by person subject to domestic violence order (G.S. 14-269.8)
"Violation of Domestic Violence Protective Order" (Chapter 7)

Forcible Trespass

Statute

This is a common-law offense.

Elements

A person guilty of this offense

(1) (a) makes an unpermitted and unlawful entry on premises, *or*
    (b) willfully refuses to leave the premises after being ordered to do so
(2) (a) using force against the occupant, *or*
    (b) threatening to use force, *or*
    (c) appearing so as to inspire fear
(3) when the occupant is present on the premises
(4) and is in peaceful possession of the premises.

Punishment

Class 1 misdemeanor.

Notes

Element (1)(b). Even if the defendant originally gains entry peaceably, he or she can commit this offense by later refusing to leave (61 N.C. 558; 39 N.C. L. Rev. 121, 149).

Element (2). Mere entry unaccompanied by a show of force normally does not satisfy this element (136 N.C. 578). Thus the entry must be one that could or does cause a breach of the peace (36 N.C. App. 207). Appearing with weapons or a multitude of people may be sufficient to satisfy Element 2 (b) or (c) (70 N.C. 71). The peaceful entry into property and staging of a sit-in by a multitude of people is sufficient to constitute the required force when the lawful occupant must yield possession in order to avoid a breach of the peace (48 N.C. App. 575).

Element (3). If the premises are unoccupied when the trespass takes place, this element is not satisfied (87 N.C. 535) unless the occupant appears while the trespasser is still present (119 N.C. 836).

Element (4). "Peaceful possession" means that the person present had occupied the premises for some time without the use of force, but it does not mean that the person must have title or a lease to the premises (125 N.C. 649).

Offenses involving health care facilities. See this note under "First-Degree Trespass."

Offenses involving entering or remaining on another's land to engage in recreational activities. See this note under "First-Degree Trespass."

Trespassing to remove pine needles or pine straw. See this note under "First-Degree Trespass."

Trespassing with motorized all-terrain vehicle. See this note under "First-Degree Trespass."

Related offenses not in this chapter

See the related offenses under "First-Degree Trespass."
"Simple Assault" (Chapter 7)
"Misdemeanor Breaking or Entering of Building" (Chapter 13)
"Being Found in a Building with Intent to Commit Any Felony or Larceny" (Chapter 13)
"Trespass during Emergency" (Chapter 17)
"Demonstration in Public Building" (Chapter 17)
"Picketing Courthouse" (Chapter 18)
Taking wild plants (G.S. 14-129)
Trespass on public lands (G.S. 14-130)
Trespass on land under option by the federal government (G.S. 14-131)
Trespassing on school bus (G.S. 14-132.2)
Operating motor vehicle on utility easements after being forbidden (G.S. 14-134.2)
Unlawful posting of advertisements (G.S. 14-145)
Taking unlawful possession of a house (G.S. 14-159)
Trespassing for purpose of hunting (G.S. 14-159.6)

Injury to Real Property

Statute

§14-127. Willful and wanton injury to real property.

If any person shall willfully and wantonly damage, injure or destroy any real property whatsoever, either of a public or private nature, he shall be guilty of a Class 1 misdemeanor.

Elements

A person guilty of this offense
(1) willfully and wantonly
(2) damages, injures, or destroys
(3) the real property of another.

Punishment

Class 1 misdemeanor.

Notes

Element (1). "Willfully and wantonly" means "intentionally and without justification or excuse and without regard for the consequences or rights of others" (N.C.P.I.—Crim. 222.15). See the definitions of "willfully" and "wantonly" in Chapter 1.

Element (3). For purposes of this statute, real property may be regarded as land and anything fixed to it or a part of it, such as buildings, fences, water, growing things, and minerals in the ground. The real property may be publicly or privately owned.

Offenses involving health care facilities. See this note under "First-Degree Trespass."

Offenses involving animal research facilities. If the alleged property damage involves such a facility, consider the applicability of G.S. 14-159.2 (Interference with animal research). This statute specifically addresses a situation in which a person trespasses at a research facility where animals are used for medical, veterinary, dental, or biological research. This offense would apply if the defendant (1) had the intent to: (a) disrupt the facility's operation, (b) damage the facility or any personal property inside, (c) release any research animal from an enclosure within the facility, or (d) interfere with the care of animals within, and (2) the defendant actually carried out at least one of the listed intended acts. Violation of this statute is a Class 1 misdemeanor. If an animal having an infectious disease is released during commission of this offense, the act is a Class I felony.

Offenses involving entering or remaining on another's land to engage in recreational activities. See this note under "First-Degree Trespass."

Trespassing to remove pine needles or pine straw. See this note under "First-Degree Trespass."

Trespassing with motorized all-terrain vehicle. See this note under "First-Degree Trespass."

Related offenses not in this chapter

See the offenses listed in Chapter 15, "Arson and Burning Offenses."
"Throwing Objects at Sporting Events" (Chapter 7)
"Damaging or Destroying Coin- or Currency-Operated Machine" (Chapter 13)
"Safecracking" (Chapter 13)
"Looting" (Chapter 17)
"Picketing Courthouse" (Chapter 18)
Injuring dams and channels (G.S. 14-142)
Injuring buildings (G.S. 14-144)
Injuring bridges (G.S. 14-146)
Removing or defacing landmarks (G.S. 14-147)
Defacing or desecrating grave sites (G.S. 14-148)
Desecrating graves (G.S. 14-149)
Interference with electric, gas, or water meters (G.S. 14-151.1)
Injuring property of gas companies (G.S. 14-152)
Injuring fixtures of utility companies (G.S. 14-154, -156, -158)
Injuring buildings or fences (G.S. 14-159)
Contaminating a public water system (G.S. 14-159.1)
Interference with animal research (G.S. 14-159.2)
Poisoning livestock (G.S. 14-163)
Injury to hired personal property (G.S. 14-165)
Willful injury to property of railroads (G.S. 14-278)
Unlawful injury to property of railroads (G.S. 14-279)
Injuring hatcheries and other aquaculture operations (G.S. 113-269)

Defacing Public Building

Statute

§14-132. Disorderly conduct in and injuries to public buildings and facilities.

(a) It is a misdemeanor if any person shall:

(1) Make any rude or riotous noise, or be guilty of any disorderly conduct, in or near any public building or facility; or

(2) Unlawfully write or scribble on, mark, deface, besmear, or injure the walls of any public building or facility, or any statue or monument situated in any public place; or

(3) Commit any nuisance in or near any public building or facility.

(b) Any person in charge of any public building or facility owned or controlled by the State, any subdivision of the State, or any other public agency shall have authority to arrest summarily and without warrant for a violation of this section.

(c) The term "public building or facility" as used in this section includes any building or facility which is:

(1) One to which the public or a portion of the public has access and is owned or controlled by the State, any subdivision of the State, any other public agency, or any private institution or agency of a charitable, educational, or eleemosynary nature; or

(2) Dedicated to the use of the general public for a purpose which is primarily concerned with public recreation, cultural activities, and other events of a public nature or character.

(3) Designated by the Attorney General in accordance with G.S. 114-20.1.

The term "building or facility" as used in this section also includes the surrounding grounds and premises of any building or facility used in connection with the operation or functioning of such building or facility.

(d) Any person who violates any provision of this section is guilty of a Class 2 misdemeanor.

Elements

A person guilty of this offense

(1) writes on, marks, defaces, or injures

(2) the walls of any public building or facility or statue or monument in a public place.

Punishment

Class 2 misdemeanor.

Notes

Element (2). For the broad meaning the statute gives to the term "public building or facility," see the notes under "Disorderly Conduct in Public Building," in Chapter 17.

Related offenses not in this chapter

"Throwing Objects at Sporting Events" (Chapter 7)
"Disorderly Conduct in Public Building" (Chapter 17)
"Trespass during Emergency" (Chapter 17)
"Picketing Courthouse" (Chapter 18)

Malicious Damage to Occupied Property by Use of Explosive or Incendiary

Statute

§14-49.1. Malicious damage of occupied property by use of explosive or incendiary; punishment.

Any person who willfully and maliciously damages any real or personal property of any kind or nature, being at the time occupied by another, by the use of any explosive or incendiary device or material is guilty of a felony punishable as a Class D felony.

Elements

A person guilty of this offense
(1) willfully and maliciously
(2) damages
(3) real or personal property occupied at the time by another
(4) by use of an explosive or incendiary device or material.

Punishment

Class D felony.

Notes

Elements generally. See the notes on these elements under "Malicious Injury by Use of Explosive or Incendiary," in Chapter 7.

Element (2). The state must prove "measurable damage" to satisfy this element; the defendant's burning of his blue jeans that only left a slightly visible mark on a jail's floor after it was stripped and waxed was insufficient evidence of measurable damage (132 N.C. App. 187).

Element (3). This element is satisfied only if someone is actually present in the premises or property when the damage occurs (see 270 N.C. 588, a burglary case). Also see the notes on this element under "First-Degree Burglary," in Chapter 13.

Related offenses not in this chapter

"Malicious Injury by Use of Explosive or Incendiary" (Chapter 7)
"Discharging Barreled Weapon or Firearm into Occupied Property" (Chapter 7)
"Burglary with Explosives" (Chapter 13)
"Transporting, Possessing Weapon during Emergency" (Chapter 17)
"Manufacture, Possession, etc., of Machine Gun, Sawed-Off Shotgun, or Weapon of Mass Destruction" (Chapter 19)
Shooting or throwing at trains (G.S. 14-280)
Exploding dynamite cartridges or bombs (G.S. 14-283)
Sale, use of pyrotechnics (G.S. 14-410)

Malicious Damage by Use of Explosive or Incendiary

Statute

§14-49. Malicious use of explosive or incendiary; punishment.

(a) Any person who willfully and maliciously injures another by the use of any explosive or incendiary device or material is guilty of a Class D felony.

(b) Any person who willfully and maliciously damages any real or personal property of any kind or nature belonging to another by the use of any explosive or incendiary device or material is guilty of a Class G felony.

(b1) Any person who willfully and maliciously damages, aids, counsels, or procures the damaging of any church, chapel, synagogue, mosque, masjid, or other building of worship by the use of any explosive or incendiary device or material is guilty of a Class E felony.

(c) Repealed by Session Laws 1993, c. 539, s. 1149, effective January 1, 1995.

Elements

A person guilty of this offense
- (1) willfully and maliciously
- (2) damages
- (3) real or personal property belonging to another
- (4) by use of an explosive or incendiary device or material.

Punishment

Class G felony. However, this offense is a Class E felony if the property damaged is a building of worship described in G.S. 14-49(b1) (note that the state must allege this information in the criminal pleading and prove it at trial).

Notes

Element (3). If a single explosion damages two or more pieces of property, even if one piece is real property and one personal, only one offense has occurred (275 N.C. 342).

Other elements. See the notes on the elements under "Malicious Injury by Use of Explosive or Incendiary," in Chapter 7.

Related offenses not in this chapter

See the related offenses under "Malicious Damage to Occupied Property by Use of Explosive or Incendiary."

Making False Bomb Report

Statute

§14-69.1. Making a false report concerning destructive device.

(a) Except as provided in subsection (c) of this section, any person who, by any means of communication to any person or group of persons, makes a report, knowing or having reason to know the report is false, that there is located in any building, house or other structure whatsoever or any vehicle, aircraft, vessel or boat any device designed to destroy or damage the building, house or structure or vehicle, aircraft, vessel or boat by explosion, blasting or burning, is guilty of a Class H felony.

(b) Repealed by S.L. 1997-443, s. 19.25(cc).

(c) Any person who, by any means of communication to any person or groups of persons, makes a report, knowing or having reason to know the report is false, that there is located in any public building any device designed to destroy or damage the public building by explosion, blasting, or burning, is guilty of a Class H felony. Any person who receives a second conviction for a violation of this subsection within five years of the first conviction for violation of this subsection is guilty of a Class G felony. For purposes of this subsection, "public building" means educational property as defined in G.S. 14-269.2(a)(1), a hospital as defined in G.S. 131E-76(3), a building housing only State, federal, or local government offices, or the offices of State, federal, or local government located in a building that is not exclusively occupied by the State, federal, or local government.

(d) The court may order a person convicted under this section to pay restitution, including costs and consequential damages resulting from the disruption of the normal activity that would have otherwise occurred on the premises but for the false report, pursuant to Article 81C of Chapter 15A of the General Statutes.

(e) For purposes of this section, the term "report" shall include making accessible to another person by computer.

Elements

A person guilty of this offense
- (1) makes a report
- (2) knowing or having reason to know
- (3) that the report is false
- (4) that there is located
  - (a) in any building or house or other structure or vehicle or aircraft or vessel or boat [G.S. 14-69.1(a)], *or*
  - (b) in any public building [G.S. 14-69.1(c)]
- (5) any device designed to destroy or damage [a building or other object set out in (4)(a) or (4)(b)]
- (6) by explosion or blasting or burning.

Punishment

Class H felony. A person who is convicted of G.S. 14-69.1(c) (making false report in public building) within 5 years of the first conviction of G.S. 14-69.1(c) is guilty of a Class G felony (note that the prior conviction must be alleged and proved under G.S. 15A-928).

Notes

Elements (4)(a) and (4)(b). If a public building is involved, a person should be charged with a violation of G.S. 14-69.1(c). See that subsection for a definition of public building. Otherwise, a person should be charged with a violation of G.S. 14-69.1(a).

Related offenses not in this chapter

Perpetrating hoax by use of false bomb or other device (G.S. 14-69.2)

Injury to Trees, Crops, or Lands of Another

Statute

§14-128. Injury to trees, crops, lands, etc., of another.

Any person, not being on his own lands, who shall without the consent of the owner thereof, willfully commit any damage, injury, or spoliation to or upon any tree, wood, underwood, timber, garden, crops, vegetables, plants, lands, springs, or any other matter or thing growing or being thereon, or who cuts, breaks, injures, or removes any tree, plant, or flower, shall be guilty of a Class 1 misdemeanor: Provided, however, that this section shall not apply to the officers, agents, and employees of the Department of Transportation while in the discharge of their duties within the right-of-way or easement of the Department of Transportation.

Elements

A person guilty of this offense
- (1) willfully
- (2) (a) damages any land or growing thing, *or*
  - (b) cuts, breaks, injures, or removes from the land a tree, plant, or flower
- (3) without the consent of the owner.

Punishment

Class 1 misdemeanor.

Notes

Element (1). See the definition of "willfully" in Chapter 1.

Element (2). The statute speaks of committing any "damage, injury, or spoliation to or upon any tree, wood, underwood, timber, garden, crops, vegetables, plants, lands, springs, or any other matter or thing growing or being thereon."

Element (3). Although no cases on this point appear, it seems that the consent could be implied as well as express.

Offenses involving entering or remaining on another's land to engage in recreational activities. See this note under "First-Degree Trespass."

Related offenses not in this chapter

"Setting Fire to Woods and Fields" (Chapter 15)
"Setting Fire to Grass, Brushlands, or Woodlands" (Chapter 15)
Larceny of ungathered crops (G.S. 14-78)
Larceny of ginseng (G.S. 14-79)
Larceny of wood (G.S. 14-80)
Taking certain wild plants (G.S. 14-129)
Cutting, injuring, or removing another's timber (G.S. 14-135)
Setting fire to grassland, brushland, or woodland, without extinguishing (G.S. 14-138.1)
Failure to watch fire (G.S. 14-140.1)
Burning or otherwise destroying crops in field (G.S. 14-141)
Injuring hatcheries and other aquaculture operations (G.S. 113-269)

Injury to Personal Property

Statute

§14-160. Willful and wanton injury to personal property; punishments.

(a) If any person shall wantonly and willfully injure the personal property of another he shall be guilty of a Class 2 misdemeanor.

(b) Notwithstanding the provisions of subsection (a), if any person shall wantonly and willfully injure the personal property of another, causing damage in an amount in excess of two hundred dollars ($200.00), he shall be guilty of a Class 1 misdemeanor.

(c) This section applies to injuries to personal property without regard to whether the property is destroyed or not.

Elements

A person guilty of this offense
(1) willfully and wantonly
(2) injures
(3) the personal property of another.

Punishment

If the damage is over $200, the offense is a Class 1 misdemeanor. If the damage is not more than $200, the offense is a Class 2 misdemeanor.

Notes

Element (1). "Willfully and wantonly" means "intentionally and without justification or excuse and without regard for the consequences or rights of others" (N.C.P.I.—Crim. 222.15). See the definitions of "willfully" and "wantonly" in Chapter 1. It need not be proved that the defendant acted with malice (60 N.C. App. 414).

Element (2). The statute specifies that property need not be destroyed in order for a violation to occur.

Element (3). Personal property is property other than real property. See the note on Element (3) under "Injury to Real Property."

Amount of damage. The extent of the damages is determined by the differential in market value just before and just after the injury (220 N.C. 721). In the absence of an established market value, the measure is the cost of repair (261 N.C. 710).

Offenses involving animal research facilities. If the alleged property damage offense involves such a facility, consider the applicability of G.S. 14-159.2 (Interference with animal research). This statute specifically addresses a situation in which a person trespasses at a research facility where animals are used for medical, veterinary, dental, or biological research. This offense would apply if the defendant (1) had the intent to: (a) disrupt the facility's operation, (b) damage the facility or any personal property inside, (c) release any research animal from an enclosure within the facility, or (d) interfere with the care of animals within, and (2) the defendant actually carried out at least one of the listed intended acts. Violation of this statute is a Class 1 misdemeanor. If an animal having an infectious disease is released during commission of this offense, the act is a Class I felony.

Offenses involving entering or remaining on another's land to engage in recreational activities. See this note under "First-Degree Trespass."

Related offenses not in this chapter

See the related offenses under "Injury to Real Property."
"Altering or Removing Serial Number" (Chapter 11)

Littering

Statute

§14-399. Littering.

(a) No person, including but not limited to, any firm, organization, private corporation, or governing body, agents or employees of any municipal corporation shall intentionally or recklessly throw, scatter, spill or place or intentionally or recklessly cause to be blown, scattered, spilled, thrown or placed or otherwise dispose of any litter upon any public property or private property not owned by him within this State or in the waters of this State including, but not limited to, any public highway, public park, lake, river, ocean, beach, campground, forest land, recreational area, trailer park, highway, road, street or alley except:

(1) When such property is designated by the State or political subdivision thereof for the disposal of garbage and refuse, and such person is authorized to use such property for such purpose; or

(2) Into a litter receptacle in such a manner that the litter will be prevented from being carried away or deposited by the elements upon any part of such private or public property or waters.

(b) When litter is blown, scattered, spilled, thrown or placed from a vehicle or watercraft, the operator thereof shall be presumed to have committed such offense. This presumption, however, does not apply to a vehicle transporting agricultural products or supplies when the litter from that vehicle is a nontoxic, biodegradable agricultural product or supply.

(c) Any person who violates this section in an amount not exceeding 15 pounds and not for commercial purposes is guilty of a Class 3 misdemeanor punishable by a fine of not less than two hundred fifty dollars ($250.00) nor more than one thousand dollars ($1,000) for the first offense. In addition, the court may require the violator to perform community service of not less than eight hours nor more than 24 hours. The community service required shall be to pick up litter if feasible, and if not feasible, to perform other labor commensurate with the offense committed. Any second or subsequent offense within three years after the date of a prior offense is punishable by a fine of not less than five hundred dollars ($500.00) nor more than two thousand dollars ($2,000). In addition, the court may require the violator to perform community service of not less than 16 hours nor more than 50 hours. The community service required shall be to pick up litter if feasible, and if not feasible, to perform other labor commensurate with the offense committed.

(d) Any person who violates this section in an amount exceeding 15 pounds but not exceeding 500 pounds and not for commercial purposes is guilty of a Class 3 misdemeanor punishable by a fine of not less than five hundred dollars ($500.00) nor more than two thousand dollars ($2,000). In addition, the court shall require the violator to perform community service of not less than 24 hours nor more than 100 hours. The community service required shall be to pick up litter if feasible, and if not feasible, to perform other community service commensurate with the offense committed.

(e) Any person who violates this section in an amount exceeding 500 pounds or in any quantity for commercial purposes, or who discards litter that is a hazardous waste as defined in G.S. 130A-290 is guilty of a Class I felony. In addition, the court shall order the violator to:

(1) Remove, or render harmless, the litter that he discarded in violation of this section;
(2) Repair or restore property damaged by, or pay damages for any damage arising out of, his discarding litter in violation of this section; or
(3) Perform community public service relating to the removal of litter discarded in violation of this section or to the restoration of an area polluted by litter discarded in violation of this section.

(f) A court may enjoin a violation of this section.

(f1) If a violation of this section involves the operation of a motor vehicle, upon a finding of guilt, the court shall forward a record of the finding to the Department of Transportation, Division of Motor Vehicles, which shall record a penalty of one point on the violator's drivers license pursuant to the point system established by G.S. 20-16. There shall be no insurance premium surcharge or assessment of points under the classification plan adopted under G.S. 58-36-65 for a finding of guilt under this section.

(g) A motor vehicle, vessel, aircraft, container, crane, winch, or machine involved in the disposal of more than 500 pounds of litter in violation of this section is declared contraband and is subject to seizure and summary forfeiture to the State.

(h) If a person sustains damages arising out of a violation of this section that is punishable as a felony, a court, in a civil action for such damages, shall order the person to pay the injured party threefold the actual damages or two hundred dollars ($200.00), whichever amount is greater. In addition, the court shall order the person to pay the injured party's court costs and attorney's fees.

(i) For the purpose of the section, unless the context requires otherwise:
(1) "Aircraft" means a motor vehicle or other vehicle that is used or designed to fly, but does not include a parachute or any other device used primarily as safety equipment.
(2) Repealed by Session Laws 1999-454, s. 1, effective December 1, 1999.
(2a) "Commercial purposes" means litter discarded by a business, corporation, association, partnership, sole proprietorship, or any other entity conducting business for economic gain, or by an employee or agent of such entity.
(3) "Law enforcement officer" means any officer of the North Carolina Highway Patrol, the State Bureau of Investigation, the Division of Motor Vehicles of the Department of Transportation, a county sheriff's department, a municipal law enforcement department, a law enforcement department of any other political subdivision, the Department, or the North Carolina Wildlife Resources Commission. In addition, and solely for the purposes of this section, "law enforcement officer" means any employee of a county or municipality designated by the county or municipality as a litter enforcement officer; or wildlife protectors as defined in G.S. 113-128(9);
(4) "Litter" means any garbage, rubbish, trash, refuse, can, bottle, box, container, wrapper, paper, paper product, tire, appliance, mechanical equipment or part, building or construction material, tool, machinery, wood, motor vehicle or motor vehicle part, vessel, aircraft, farm machinery or equipment, sludge from a waste treatment facility, water supply treatment plant, or air pollution control facility, dead animal, or discarded material in any form resulting from domestic, industrial, commercial, mining, agricultural, or governmental operations. "Litter" does not include political pamphlets, handbills, religious tracts, newspapers, and other such printed materials the unsolicited distribution of which is protected by the Constitution of the United States or the Constitution of North Carolina.
(5) "Vehicle" has the same meaning as in G.S. 20-4.01(49); and
(6) "Watercraft" means any boat or vessel used for transportation across the water.

(j) It shall be the duty of all law enforcement officers to enforce the provisions of this section.

(k) This section does not limit the authority of any State or local agency to enforce other laws, rules or ordinances relating to litter or solid waste management.

Elements

A person guilty of this offense
- (1) intentionally or recklessly
- (2) (a) throws, scatters, spills, places, or disposes of, *or*
  - (b) causes to be blown, scattered, spilled, thrown, placed, or disposed of
- (3) litter
- (4) on public property or private property not owned by the person, *and*
- (5) (a) the amount of litter does not exceed 15 pounds and the littering is not for a commercial purpose, *or*
  - (b) the amount of litter exceeds 15 pounds but does not exceed 500 pounds and the littering is not for a commercial purpose, *or*
  - (c) (i) the amount of litter exceeds 500 pounds, *or*
    - (ii) the littering is for a commercial purpose, *or*
    - (iii) the litter is hazardous waste as defined in G.S. 130A-290.

Punishment

For (5)(a), it is a Class 3 misdemeanor punishable by a fine of not less than $250 nor more than $1,000. For a second or subsequent offense within 3 years after the date of a prior offense, it is a Class 3 misdemeanor punishable by a fine of not less than $500 nor more than $2,000 (note that a prior conviction must be alleged in the criminal pleading and proved at trial under G.S. 15A-928). For (5)(b), it is a Class 3 misdemeanor punishable by a fine of not less than $500 nor more than $2,000. For (5)(c), it is a Class I felony. See G.S. 14-399(c), (d), and (e), reproduced above, for additional obligations that may or must be imposed on a person convicted of littering.

Notes

Element (1). "Intentionally" is defined in Chapter 1. Although not defined in the statute or by case law concerning this offense, "recklessly" probably means being careless and indifferent to consequences.

Element (3). "Litter" is defined in G.S. 14-399(i)(4), reproduced above.

Element (4). This offense does not apply when a person disposes of litter on property owned by him or her. This offense applies to the waters of North Carolina, and the statute explicitly includes the ocean—so it would include that part of the ocean over which the state exercises territorial jurisdiction.

Element (5)(c)(ii). "Commercial purpose" is defined in G.S. 14-399(i)(2a) as "litter discarded by a business, corporation, association, partnership, sole proprietorship, or any other entity conducting business for economic gain, or by an employee or agent of such entity."

Exceptions. G.S. 14-399(a)(1) and (2) explicitly permit the disposal of litter (1) on property designated by the state or a political subdivision for the disposal of garbage and refuse, when the person is authorized to use such property for that purpose, and (2) in a litter receptacle in such a manner that the litter will be prevented from being carried away or deposited by the elements on any part of private or public property or waters.

Presumption relating to operator of vehicle or watercraft. G.S. 14-399(b) provides that when "litter is blown, scattered, spilled, thrown or placed from a vehicle or watercraft, the operator thereof shall be presumed to have committed such offense. This presumption, however, does not apply to a vehicle transporting agricultural products or supplies when the litter from that vehicle is a nontoxic, biodegradable agricultural product or supply." Because of constitutional problems with a mandatory presumption in criminal cases (for example, if it is irrebuttable or shifts the burden of proof), it is likely that this provision will be treated as a permissive presumption or inference (a discussion of this issue is beyond the scope of this book; for appellate cases on this issue, see 300 N.C. 494; 442 U.S. 140).

Forfeiture of vehicle for disposing of more than 500 pounds of litter. G.S. 14-399(g) provides that a motor vehicle, vessel, aircraft, and other specified objects that are involved in the unlawful disposal of more than 500 pounds of litter may be seized and forfeited to the state.

Related offenses not in this chapter

Certain plastic yoke and ring type holding devices prohibited (G.S. 14-399.2)
Various offenses in Art. 9 (solid waste management) of G.S. Ch. 130A; Art. 21 (water and air resources), Art. 21A (oil pollution and hazardous substances control), and Art. 21B (air pollution control) of G.S. Ch. 143.

Damaging Computer or Related Equipment

Statute

§14-455. Damaging computers, computer programs, computer systems, computer networks, and resources.

(a) It is unlawful to willfully and without authorization alter, damage, or destroy a computer, computer program, computer system, computer network, or any part thereof. A violation of this subsection is a Class G felony if the damage caused by the alteration, damage, or destruction is more than one thousand dollars ($1,000). Any other violation of this subsection is a Class 1 misdemeanor.

(b) This section applies to alteration, damage, or destruction effectuated by introducing, directly or indirectly, a computer program (including a self-replicating or self-propagating computer program) into a computer, computer program, computer system or computer network.

Elements

A person guilty of this offense
(1) willfully
(2) without authorization
(3) alters, damages, or destroys
(4) a computer, computer program, computer system, computer network, or any part thereof.

Punishment

Class G felony if the damage caused by the alteration, damage, or destruction is greater than $1,000. Otherwise, an offense is a Class 1 misdemeanor.

Notes

Element (3). This offense includes damage caused by the introduction of software computer "viruses" [G.S. 14-455(b)].

Element (4). A computer is an internally programmed automatic device that performs data processing or telephone switching [G.S. 14-453(2)]. A computer program is an ordered set of data that are coded instructions or statements that when executed by a computer cause the computer to process data [G.S. 14-453(4)]. A computer system is at least one computer together with a set of related, connected, or unconnected peripheral devices [G.S. 14-453(6)]. A computer network is the interconnection of communication systems with a computer through remote terminals, or a complex consisting of two or more connected computers or telephone switching equipment [G.S. 14-453(3)]. "Any part thereof" likely includes stored data. Data is broadly defined to include all information, facts, knowledge, concepts or instructions intended for use on computers, computer systems, and computer networks; it may be embodied in printouts, magnetic storage media, internal hardware storage, punch cards, or any other form [G.S. 14-453(6a)].

Related offenses not in this chapter

"Computer Fraud" (Chapter 14)

17
Disorderly Conduct and Riot

Chapter Contents

17 Disorderly Conduct and Riot

Drunk and Disruptive

Statute

§14-444. Intoxicated and disruptive in public.

(a) It shall be unlawful for any person in a public place to be intoxicated and disruptive in any of the following ways:

(1) Blocking or otherwise interfering with traffic on a highway or public vehicular area, or
(2) Blocking or lying across or otherwise preventing or interfering with access to or passage across a sidewalk or entrance to a building, or
(3) Grabbing, shoving, pushing or fighting others or challenging others to fight, or
(4) Cursing or shouting at or otherwise rudely insulting others, or
(5) Begging for money or other property.

(b) Any person who violates this section shall be guilty of a Class 3 misdemeanor. Notwithstanding the provisions of G.S. 7A-273(1), a magistrate is not empowered to accept a guilty plea and enter judgment for this offense.

Elements

A person guilty of this offense

(1) is drunk
(2) in a public place
(3) and is disruptive by
  (a) blocking or otherwise interfering with traffic on a highway or public vehicular area, *or*
  (b) interfering with passage across a sidewalk, *or*
  (c) interfering with entrance to any building, *or*
  (d) grabbing, shoving, or pushing others, *or*
  (e) fighting or challenging others to fight, *or*
  (f) cursing, shouting at, or rudely insulting others, *or*
  (g) begging.

Punishment

Class 3 misdemeanor.

Notes

Element (1). The statute uses the word "intoxicated" instead of "drunk" and defines the term to mean "the condition of a person whose mental or physical functioning is presently substantially impaired as a result of the use of alcohol" (G.S. 14-443). This is largely the same as the case-law definition of "drunk" under the old public drunkenness statute. That definition considered "drunk" to be a state of intoxication greater than being under the influence (261 N.C. 332). The intoxication must be from alcohol; being high on drugs does not constitute this offense.

Element (2). "Public place" is defined as "a place which is open to the public, whether it is publicly or privately owned" (G.S. 14-443)—a definition substantially similar to the case-law definition under the old public drunkenness statute; a business establishment can be a public place (263 N.C. 694).

Element (3)(a). Public vehicular area is defined in the motor vehicle statutes to include driveways, parking lots, and similar places—whether publicly or privately owned—open to customers or other members of the public [G.S. 20-4.01(32)].

Guilty pleas. Magistrates may not accept guilty pleas to a charge of this offense; the defendant must appear in district court [G.S. 14-444(b)].

Alcoholism defense. A complete defense to this charge is that the defendant is an alcoholic (G.S. 14-445). Alcoholism is defined as "the state of a person who habitually lacks self-control as to the use of alcoholic beverages, or uses alcoholic beverages to the extent that his health is substantially impaired or endangered or his social or economic function is substantially disrupted" (G.S. 14-443). This defense may be considered by the judge even if not raised by the defendant (G.S. 14-445). A defendant found not guilty by reason of alcoholism is subject to possible civil commitment for that alcoholism (G.S. 14-446).

Simple drunkenness. For this offense to be committed, the defendant must be both drunk *and* disruptive. Prosecutions for simple public drunkenness are prohibited (G.S. 14-447); thus a local ordinance making that a crime would be invalid.

Assistance without arrest. A separate statute authorizes officers to assist the nondisruptive public drunk without arresting him or her; depending on the person's condition, the assistance may be to take the person home, to a detoxification center, or to a hospital or other medical facility (G.S. 122C-301). If no other place is readily available and the intoxicated person does not need medical attention, he or she may be taken to the jail and released as soon as sober but not more than 24 hours later; the person may be released from the jail at any time to a relative or other individual willing to be responsible for his or her care (G.S. 122C-303).

Related offenses not in this chapter

See the offenses in Chapter 7, "Assaults and Threats."
"First-Degree Trespass" (Chapter 16)
"Second-Degree Trespass" (Chapter 16)
"Resisting, Delaying, or Obstructing an Officer" (Chapter 18)
"Indecent Exposure" (Chapter 9)
Using profane language on highway (G.S. 14-197)
Disorderly conduct at bus station, airport (G.S. 14-275.1)

Disorderly Conduct

Statute

§14-288.4. Disorderly conduct.

(a) Disorderly conduct is a public disturbance intentionally caused by any person who:

(1) Engages in fighting or other violent conduct or in conduct creating the threat of imminent fighting or other violence; or

(2) Makes or uses any utterance, gesture, display or abusive language which is intended and plainly likely to provoke violent retaliation and thereby cause a breach of the peace; or

(3) Takes possession of, exercises control over, or seizes any building or facility of any public or private educational institution without the specific authority of the chief administrative officer of the institution, or his authorized representative; or

(4) Refuses to vacate any building or facility of any public or private educational institution in obedience to:

a. An order of the chief administrative officer of the institution, or his representative, who shall include for colleges and universities the vice chancellor for student affairs or his equivalent for the institution, the dean of students or his equivalent for the institution, the director of the law enforcement or security department for the institution, and the chief of the law enforcement or security department for the institution; or

b. An order given by any fireman or public health officer acting within the scope of his authority; or

c. If a state of emergency is occurring or is imminent within the institution, an order given by any law-enforcement officer acting within the scope of his authority; or

(5) Shall, after being forbidden to do so by the chief administrative officer, or his authorized representative, of any public or private educational institution:

a. Engage in any sitting, kneeling, lying down, or inclining so as to obstruct the ingress or egress of any person entitled to the use of any building or facility of the institution in its normal and intended use; or

b. Congregate, assemble, form groups or formations (whether organized or not), block, or in any manner otherwise interfere with the operation or functioning of any building or facility of the institution so as to interfere with the customary or normal use of the building or facility; or

(6) Disrupts, disturbs or interferes with the teaching of students at any public or private educational institution or engages in conduct which disturbs the peace, order or discipline at any public or private educational institution or on the grounds adjacent thereto.

(7) Disrupts, disturbs or interferes with a religious service or assembly or engages in conduct which disturbs the peace or order at any religious service or assembly.

As used in this section the term "building or facility" includes the surrounding grounds and premises of any building or facility used in connection with the operation or functioning of such building or facility.

(b) Any person who willfully engages in disorderly conduct is guilty of a Class 2 misdemeanor.

I.
Disorderly Conduct by Fighting

Statute

See subsection (a)(1) of G.S. 14-288.4, reproduced at the beginning of this section.

Elements

A person guilty of this offense
(1) intentionally causes a public disturbance
(2) by fighting or other violent conduct or conduct creating an imminent threat of fighting or other violence.

Punishment

Class 2 misdemeanor.

Notes

Generally. Although this offense is included in the Riot and Civil Disorder Act, it applies even when no riot or state of emergency exists.

Element (1). G.S. 14-288.1(8) defines a "public disturbance" as "any annoying, disturbing, or alarming act . . . exceeding the bounds of social toleration normal for the time and place in question. . . ." The disturbance must take place in a public place, a phrase that includes but is not limited to "highways, transport facilities, schools, prisons, apartment houses, places of business or amusement, or any neighborhood."

Related offenses not in this chapter

See the offenses listed at the end of this section.

II.
Disorderly Conduct by Abusive Language Provoking Retaliation

Statute

See subdivision (a)(2) of G.S. 14-288.4, reprodued at the beginning of this section.

Elements

A person guilty of this offense
(1) intentionally causes a public disturbance
(2) by making or using any utterance, gesture, display, or abusive language
(3) that is intended to and is plainly likely to provoke violent retaliation and thereby cause a breach of the peace.

Punishment

Class 2 misdemeanor.

Notes

Generally. Although this offense is included in the Riot and Civil Disorder Act, it may be applied even in circumstances when no riot or state of emergency exists.

Element (1). See the note on Element (1) of "Disorderly Conduct by Fighting," immediately above.

Element (2). To establish the provocative nature of the language used, a criminal pleading for this offense should set out the exact words spoken.

Element (3). When the defendant, who was being given a traffic ticket, told the officer to "get his goddam ass out of the way" or the defendant "would run over him," his language was sufficient for conviction under this statute. Those were plainly fighting words even though the officer was not likely to retaliate (34 N.C. App. 72).

Constitutionality. Constitutional First Amendment protection of free speech does not bar punishment for use of insulting or fighting words that are likely to cause an immediate breach of the peace (282 N.C. 157, overruled on other grounds, 324 N.C. 539).

Related offenses not in this chapter

See the offenses listed at the end of this section.

III. Disorderly Conduct by Seizing or Blocking a School Building

Statute

See subdivisions (a)(3) through (a)(5) of G.S. 14-288.4, reproduced at the beginning of this section.

Elements

A person guilty of this offense

(1) intentionally causes a public disturbance

(2) by engaging in the following conduct in a building or on the grounds of a public or private educational institution:

(3) (a) seizing or otherwise taking control of the building without specific authorization, *or*

(b) refusing to vacate the building after being ordered to do so by (i) the chief administrative officer of the institution or the officer's representative, (ii) a firefighter or public health officer, or (iii) a law enforcement officer acting within the officer's scope of authority when a state of emergency is occurring or imminent, *or*

(c) obstructing entrance and exit from the building by sitting, lying down, etc., or interfering with normal use by blocking, etc., *after* being forbidden to do so by the chief administrative officer of the institution or the officer's representative.

Punishment

Class 2 misdemeanor.

Notes

Generally. Although this offense is included in the Riot and Civil Disorder Act, it may be applied even in circumstances when no riot or state of emergency exists.

Element (1). See the note on Element (1) of "Disorderly Conduct by Fighting," above.

Element (2). The statute does not require that the building be one used for classroom purposes.

Element (3). The statute specifically describes who may be the representative of a college or university's chief administrative officer. That representative may be the vice chancellor for student affairs or an equivalent officer, the dean of students or an equivalent officer, or the director or chief of the campus law enforcement or security department.

Related offenses not in this chapter

See the offenses listed at the end of this section.

IV. Disorderly Conduct by Disrupting Students

Statute

See subdivision (a)(6) of G.S. 14-288.4, reproduced at the beginning of this section.

Elements

A person guilty of this offense

(1) intentionally causes a public disturbance
(2) by disrupting, disturbing, interfering with the teaching of students, or otherwise disrupting or disturbing the peace
(3) at any public or private educational institution or on the grounds of such an institution.

Punishment

Class 2 misdemeanor.

Notes

Generally. Although this offense is included in the Riot and Civil Disorder Act, it may be applied even in circumstances when no riot or state of emergency exists.

Element (1). See the note on Element (1) of "Disorderly Conduct by Fighting," above.

Element (2). Evidence was insufficient to support a juvenile adjudication of delinquency of this offense when a high school student during class talked to another student in a loud and disruptive voice, she continued to talk after her teacher reprimanded her, other students were distracted by the episode and started looking up from their work, the teacher asked her a second time to stop talking, and the student looked at her, made a face, and shrugged her shoulders; the court ruled that this conduct did not substantially interfere with the operation of the school (103 N.C. App. 452). Evidence was insufficient to support a juvenile adjudication of delinquency of this offense. When a student made a move toward another student, who was separated by an aisle, causing the other student to dodge the student's move, the teacher approached the student and asked her to show her what was in her hand, she willingly gave her a carpenter's nail; the court ruled that this conduct did not substantially interfere with the operation of the school (331 N.C. 714). Evidence was insufficient to support two juveniles' adjudications of delinquency of this offense when two high school students each struck a radiator at least once during class instruction, and each time contact was made, a rattling, metallic noise was produced that caused the other students to look toward where the sound was coming from and caused the teacher to interrupt her teaching for fifteen to twenty seconds, and each time the noise was made she stared at the students and then continued her lecture; the court ruled that this conduct did not substantially interfere with the operation of the school (331 N.C. 714).

Related offenses not in this chapter

See the offenses listed at the end of this section.

V. Disorderly Conduct by Disrupting Religious Service or Assembly

Statute

See subdivision (a)(7) of G.S. 14-288.4, reproduced at thebeginning of this section.

Elements

A person guilty of this offense
(1) intentionally causes a public disturbance
(2) by disrupting, disturbing, or interfering with a religious service or assembly or otherwise disturbing the peace at any religious service or assembly.

Punishment

Class 2 misdemeanor.

Notes

Generally. Although this offense is included in the Riot and Civil Disorder Act, it may be applied even in circumstances when no riot or state of emergency exists.

Related offenses not in this chapter

See the offenses in Chapter 7, "Assaults and Threats."
"Misdemeanor Breaking or Entering of Building" (Chapter 13)
"First-Degree Trespass" (Chapter 16)
"Second-Degree Trespass" (Chapter 16)
"Injury to Real Property" (Chapter 16)
"Injury to Personal Property" (Chapter 16)
"Defacing Public Building" (Chapter 16)
"Resisting, Delaying, or Obstructing an Officer" (Chapter 18)
"Picketing Courthouse" (Chapter 18)
"Carrying Concealed Weapon" (Chapter 19)
"Possession of Weapon on School Grounds" (Chapter 19)
Using profane language on highway (G.S. 14-197)
Disorderly conduct at bus station, airport (G.S. 14-275.1)
Standing, sitting, or lying upon highway (G.S. 20-174.1)

Disorderly Conduct in Public Building

Statute

§14-132. Disorderly conduct in and injuries to public buildings and facilities.

(a) It is a misdemeanor if any person shall:

(1) Make any rude or riotous noise, or be guilty of any disorderly conduct, in or near any public building or facility; or

(2) Unlawfully write or scribble on, mark, deface, besmear, or injure the walls of any public building or facility, or any statue or monument situated in any public place; or

(3) Commit any nuisance in or near any public building or facility.

(b) Any person in charge of any public building or facility owned or controlled by the State, any subdivision of the State, or any other public agency shall have authority to arrest summarily and without warrant for a violation of this section.

(c) The term "public building or facility" as used in this section includes any building or facility which is:

(1) One to which the public or a portion of the public has access and is owned or controlled by the State, any subdivision of the State, any other public agency, or any private institution or agency of a charitable, educational, or eleemosynary nature; or

(2) Dedicated to the use of the general public for a purpose which is primarily concerned with public recreation, cultural activities, and other events of a public nature or character.

(3) Designated by the Attorney General in accordance with G.S. 114-20.1.

The term "building or facility" as used in this section also includes the surrounding grounds and premises of any building or facility used in connection with the operation or functioning of such building or facility.

(d) Any person who violates any provision of this section is guilty of a Class 2 misdemeanor.

Elements

A person guilty of this offense

(1) makes any rude or riotous noise or engages in disorderly conduct or commits a nuisance

(2) in or near any public building or facility.

Punishment

Class 2 misdemeanor.

Notes

Generally. Because the conduct prohibited by this statute is also prohibited by a more specific statute, "Disorderly Conduct" (G.S. 14-288.4), it would be advisable for law enforcement officers and prosecutors to proceed under G.S. 14-288.4 rather than under this statute.

Element (2). "Public building or facility" is broadly defined by the statute to include all facilities owned or controlled by a public agency or by a private charitable or educational agency. The definition also includes privately owned facilities used for recreational or cultural purposes or for other public events. The statute also specifies that it covers the grounds surrounding such buildings.

Related offenses not in this chapter

See the offenses listed under "Disorderly Conduct."

Simple Affray

Statute

§14-33. Misdemeanor assaults, batteries, and affrays, simple and aggravated; punishments.

(a) Any person who commits a simple assault or a simple assault and battery or participates in a simple affray is guilty of a Class 2 misdemeanor.

(b) Unless his conduct is covered under some other provision of law providing greater punishment, any person who commits any assault, assault and battery, or affray is guilty of a Class 1 misdemeanor if, in the course of the assault, assault and battery, or affray, he:

(1) through (3) Repealed by Session Laws 1995, c. 507, s. 19.5(b);
(4) through (7) Repealed by Session Laws 1991, c. 525, s. 1;
(8) Repealed by Session Laws 1995, c. 507, s. 19.5(b);
(9) Commits an assault and battery against a sports official when the sports official is discharging or attempting to discharge official duties at a sports event, or immediately after the sports event at which the sports official discharged official duties. A "sports official" is a person at a sports event who enforces the rules of the event, such as an umpire or referee, or a person who supervises the participants, such as a coach. A "sports event" includes any interscholastic or intramural athletic activity in a primary, middle, junior high, or high school, college, or university, any organized athletic activity sponsored by a community, business, or nonprofit organization, any athletic activity that is a professional or semiprofessional event, and any other organized athletic activity in the State.

(c) Unless the conduct is covered under some other provision of law providing greater punishment, any person who commits any assault, assault and battery, or affray is guilty of a Class A1 misdemeanor if, in the course of the assault, assault and battery, or affray, he or she:

(1) Inflicts serious injury upon another person or uses a deadly weapon;
(2) Assaults a female, he being a male person at least 18 years of age;
(3) Assaults a child under the age of 12 years;
(4) Assaults an officer or employee of the State or any political subdivision of the State, when the officer or employee is discharging or attempting to discharge his official duties;
(5) Repealed by Session Laws 1999-105, s. 1, effective December 1, 1999; or
(6) Assaults a school employee or school volunteer when the employee or volunteer is discharging or attempting to discharge his or her duties as an employee or volunteer, or assaults a school employee or school volunteer as a result of the discharge or attempt to discharge that individual's duties as a school employee or school volunteer. For purposes of this subdivision, the following definitions shall apply:
   a. "Duties" means:
      1. All activities on school property;
      2. All activities, wherever occurring, during a school authorized event or the accompanying of students to or from that event; and
      3. All activities relating to the operation of school transportation.
   b. "Employee" or "volunteer" means:
      1. An employee of a local board of education; or a charter school authorized under G.S. 115C-238.29D, or a nonpublic school which has filed intent to operate under Part 1 or Part 2 of Article 39 of Chapter 115C of the General Statutes;
      2. An independent contractor or an employee of an independent contractor of a local board of education, charter school authorized under G.S. 115C-238.29D, or a nonpublic school which has filed intent to operate under Part 1 or Part 2 of Article 39 of Chapter 115C

of the General Statutes, if the independent contractor carries out duties customarily performed by employees of the school; and

3. An adult who volunteers his or her services or presence at any school activity and is under the supervision of an individual listed in sub-sub-subdivision 1. or 2. of this sub-subdivision.

Elements

A person guilty of this offense
 (1) engages in fighting
 (2) in a public place
 (3) to the terror of the citizens.

Punishment

Class 2 misdemeanor.

Notes

Element (1). A mere scuffle (friendly play, rather than being "mad and fighting") does not satisfy this element (127 N.C. 544). A person who has agreed to fight but never lands a blow can be guilty of affray (73 N.C. 150). The person must have engaged in the fighting willingly and without a lawful excuse (107 N.C. 944). The person who deliberately brings on a fight by words or action may be guilty of affray even though he or she never gets in a blow (94 N.C. 940). To have a fight requires more than one person, so normally when one person is charged with affray, at least one other person also would be charged.

Element (2). Although this element is not clear, it probably is to be interpreted to mean a place that is readily visible from a location generally open to the public, even if the site of the fight is not itself open to the public (*Perkins*, p. 480).

Element (3). Although North Carolina has not specifically resolved this point, another jurisdiction [35 Ala. 392 (Alabama)] has established that the terror of the citizens is presumed from the fact that a fight is occurring in a public place; no proof is necessary that citizens were actually put in terror by the fight.

Relationship to assault. In most affrays, parties to the fight could be charged with assault. However, a person who provoked a fight but never got in a blow could properly be charged with affray, though not with assault.

Related offenses not in this chapter

See the offenses in Chapter 7, "Assaults and Threats."
"Resisting, Delaying, or Obstructing an Officer" (Chapter 18)
Using profane language on highway (G.S. 14-197)

Aggravated Misdemeanor Affray

Statute

See G.S. 14-33, reproduced under "Simple Affray."

Elements

A person guilty of this offense
 (1) engages in fighting

(2) in a public place
(3) to the terror of the citizens, *and*
(4) (a) inflicts serious injury *or*
(b) uses a deadly weapon, *or*
(c) being a male at least 18 years old, assaults a female, *or*
(d) assaults a child under the age of 12 years, *or*
(e) assaults an officer or employee of the state or any political subdivision of the state who is discharging or attempting to discharge official duties, *or*
(f) assaults a school employee or school volunteer who is discharging or attempting to discharge duties or as a result of the employee's or volunteer's discharge or attempt to discharge duties, *or*
(g) commits an assault and battery against a sports official when the sports official is discharging or attempting to discharge official duties at a sports event, or immediately after the sports event at which the sports official discharged official duties.

Punishment

An aggravated affray involving sub-elements (a), (b), (c), (d), (e), or (f) is a Class A1 misdemeanor. An aggravated affray involving sub-element (g) is a Class 1 misdemeanor.

Notes

Elements (1) through (3). See the notes on Elements (1) through (3) under "Simple Affray."

Element (4) generally. See the notes on these elements under "Simple Assault," "Assault Inflicting Serious Injury," "Assault with a Deadly Weapon," "Assault on a Female," "Assault on a Child under 12," and "Assault on a Governmental Officer or Employee" (all in Chapter 7).

Aggravated misdemeanor and felony affray involving firefighters and medical personnel. For a discussion of aggravated misdemeanor and felony affray involving firefighters and medical personnel under G.S. 14-34.6, see "Simple Assault and Aggravated Assaults on Firefighters or Specified Medical Personnel" in Chapter 7.

Related offenses not in this chapter

See the offenses listed under "Simple Affray."

Unlawful Assembly

Statute

This is a common-law offense.

Elements

A person guilty of this offense
(1) assembles with two or more other persons
(2) with the common intent to commit disorderly acts that will interfere with the rights of others, *or*

(3) for the purpose of committing acts in such a manner as would cause a firm person to apprehend a breach of peace.

Punishment

Class 1 misdemeanor.

Notes

Generally. This offense has been recognized as a component of the crime of riot, both under the common law (249 N.C. 733) and under the 1969 Riot and Civil Disorder Act (G.S. 14-288.3; 287 N.C. 392). G.S. 14-288.3 specifies that passage of the riot act was not intended to abolish this offense. Some of the notes under "Misdemeanor Riot," below, apply to this offense as well. The prohibited assembly must have been for an unlawful purpose—that is, it was for the purpose of either doing an unlawful act or doing a lawful act in an unlawful manner; the purpose may be formed before or during the assembly; the unlawful assembly may be created deliberately or by chance (249 N.C. 733). In some other states it has been held that there must be some act in furtherance of the unlawful purpose before this offense has been committed.

Constitutionality. Because of potential interference with First Amendment rights of free speech, officers should avoid using this charge and instead should charge such other offenses as disorderly conduct, conspiracy, and riot, as the facts dictate.

Related offenses not in this chapter

See the offenses listed under "Disorderly Conduct."

Misdemeanor Riot

Statute

§14-288.2. Riot; inciting to riot; punishment.

(a) A riot is a public disturbance involving an assemblage of three or more persons which by disorderly and violent conduct, or imminent threat of disorderly and violent conduct, results in injury or damage to persons or property or creates a clear and present danger of injury or damage to persons or property.

(b) Any person who willfully engages in a riot is guilty of a Class 1 misdemeanor.

(c) Any person who willfully engages in a riot is guilty of a Class H felony, if:
(1) In the course and as a result of the riot there is property damage in excess of fifteen hundred dollars ($1,500) or serious bodily injury; *or*
(2) Such participant in the riot has in his possession any dangerous weapon or substance.

(d) Any person who willfully incites or urges another to engage in a riot, so that as a result of such inciting or urging a riot occurs or a clear and present danger of a riot is created, is guilty of a Class 1 misdemeanor.

(e) Any person who willfully incites or urges another to engage in a riot, and such inciting or urging is a contributing cause of a riot in which there is property damage in excess of fifteen hundred dollars ($1,500) or serious bodily injury, shall be punished as a Class F felon.

Elements

A person guilty of this offense
(1) assembles
(2) with two or more other persons, *and*
(3) engages in a public disturbance
(4) that by disorderly and violent conduct or by the imminent threat of disorderly and violent conduct
(5) (a) causes injury or damage to persons or property, *or*
(b) creates a clear and present danger of injury or damage to persons or property.

Punishment

Class 1 misdemeanor.

Notes

Element (1). For this element to be satisfied, participants must have assembled for an unlawful purpose; the unlawful purpose can be formed either before or during the assembly (249 N.C. 733; 264 N.C. 51). A meeting of the Ku Klux Klan for purposes of intimidating and coercing other citizens is an unlawful assembly (249 N.C. 733).

Element (2). A defendant can be convicted even if other participants are not named, if the evidence establishes and the jury finds that there were two or more other participants. Defendants need not have acted in concert so long as they all participated in the riot (264 N.C. 51).

Element (3). To "engage in" means to actively participate in the riotous activity (110 N.C. App. 250). Mere presence at the scene of a riot does not establish a defendant's participation in the riot (45 N.C. App. 34). G.S. 14-288.1(8) defines a "public disturbance" as "any annoying, disturbing, or alarming act . . . exceeding the bounds of social toleration normal for the time and place." The disturbance must take place in or affect persons in a public place, which the same section defines as including but not limited to "highways, transport facilities, schools, prisons, apartment houses, places of business or amusement, or any neighborhood."

Element (4). G.S. 14-288.4 provides that a person engages in "disorderly conduct" by engaging in "fighting or other violent conduct or in conduct creating the threat of imminent fighting or other violence" or by making or using "any utterance, gesture, display or abusive language which is intended and plainly likely to provoke violent retaliation and thereby cause a breach of the peace." Note, though, that this statute specifies that there must be both disorderly *and* violent conduct.

Element (5). The defendant need not have personally caused the injury or damage; the person can be convicted of riot as long as the injury or damage occurred or was threatened as part of the public disturbance in which he or she participated.

Not unconstitutionally vague. This statute is not unconstitutionally vague; it simplifies and sets out in concrete form the elements of the common-law crime of riot (287 N.C. 392).

Related offenses not in this chapter

See the offenses listed under "Disorderly Conduct."

Felony Riot

Statute

See G.S. 14-288.2, reproduced under "Misdemeanor Riot."

Elements

A person guilty of this offense
- (1) assembles
- (2) with two or more other persons, *and*
- (3) engages in a public disturbance
- (4) that by disorderly and violent conduct
- (5) (a) results in property damage in excess of $1,500, *or*
  - (b) results in serious bodily injury, *or*
  - (c) (i) results in damage or injury or creates a clear and present danger of damage or injury, *and*
    - (ii) the defendant possesses a dangerous weapon or substance.

Punishment

Class H felony.

Notes

Elements (1) through (4). See the notes on these elements under "Misdemeanor Riot."

Element (5)(a). Presumably the same rule applies as in larceny cases, so that if there is a question of how much damage was done in the riot, the jury decides the issue.

Element (5)(b). For the offense of assault inflicting serious injury, "serious injury" includes physical injury causing great pain and suffering as well as serious mental injury (326 N.C. 777). However, this statute specifies that "bodily" injury must be caused. Consequently, it is unlikely that mental injury would satisfy this element.

Element (5)(c). The defendant need not have personally caused the property damage or physical injury in Element (5)(a) or (b), but he or she must have had personal possession of the dangerous weapon or substance to be convicted of felony riot for that reason. G.S. 14-288.1(2) defines "dangerous weapon or substance" to include "any deadly weapon, ammunition, explosive, incendiary device, radioactive material or device . . . or any instrument or substance designed for a use that carries a threat of serious bodily injury or destruction of property . . . or any part or ingredient in any [such] instrument or substance . . . when the circumstances indicate a probability that such part or ingredient will be so used."

Related offenses not in this chapter

"Assault Inflicting Serious Injury" (Chapter 7)
See the offenses listed under "Disorderly Conduct."

Misdemeanor Inciting to Riot

Statute

See G.S. 14-288.2, reproduced under "Misdemeanor Riot."

Elements

A person guilty of this offense
(1) incites or urges another
(2) to engage in a riot, *and*
(3) a riot consequently occurs or a clear and present danger of a riot is created.

Punishment

Class 1 misdemeanor.

Notes

Definition of riot. See the notes under "Misdemeanor Riot" for the elements of a riot.

Element (1). "Incite" has its plain and accepted meaning—to arouse, stir up, urge, provoke, encourage, spur on, goad. To incite means to use words, signs, or any other means that would naturally lead others to engage in conduct that would constitute a riot (249 N.C. 733; 24 N.C. App. 338). The defendant need not have participated in the riot itself to be guilty of this offense.

Element (2). A Ku Klux Klan rally, even if organized for a lawful purpose, became an unlawful assembly when used to preach racial dissension and to intimidate and coerce other citizens (249 N.C. 733).

Element (3). Under the common-law crime of inciting to riot, it was necessary to prove that a riot actually had occurred (249 N.C. 733), but the present statute also allows a conviction for inciting even if the inciting merely creates a clear and present danger of a riot.

Constitutionality. The statutory offense of inciting to riot does not infringe the federal constitutional right of free speech (287 N.C. 392).

Related offenses not in this chapter

See the offenses listed under "Disorderly Conduct."

Felony Inciting to Riot

Statute

See G.S. 14-288.2, reproduced under "Misdemeanor Riot."

Elements

A person guilty of this offense
(1) incites or urges another
(2) to engage in a riot, *and*
(3) a riot consequently occurs that

(4) (a) results in property damage of $1,500 or more, *or*
(b) results in serious bodily injury to someone.

Punishment

Class F felony.

Notes

Elements (1), (2), and (3). See the notes on these elements under "Misdemeanor Inciting to Riot."

Element (4). See the notes on Elements (5)(a) and (5)(b) under "Felony Riot."

Related offenses not in this chapter

See the offenses listed under "Disorderly Conduct."

Failure to Disperse on Command

Statute

§14-288.5. Failure to disperse when commanded a misdemeanor; prima facie evidence.

(a) Any law-enforcement officer or public official responsible for keeping the peace may issue a command to disperse in accordance with this section if he reasonably believes that a riot, or disorderly conduct by an assemblage of three or more persons, is occurring. The command to disperse shall be given in a manner reasonably calculated to be communicated to the assemblage.

(b) Any person who fails to comply with a lawful command to disperse is guilty of a Class 2 misdemeanor.

(c) If any person remains at the scene of any riot, or disorderly conduct by an assemblage of three or more persons, following a command to disperse and after a reasonable time for dispersal has elapsed, it is prima facie evidence that the person so remaining is willfully engaging in the riot or disorderly conduct, as the case may be.

Elements

A person guilty of this offense
(1) fails to comply with a command to disperse
(2) given in a manner reasonably calculated to be heard by those assembled
(3) by a law enforcement officer or public official responsible for keeping the peace
(4) when that officer reasonably believes that a riot or disorderly conduct by three or more persons is occurring.

Punishment

Class 2 misdemeanor.

Notes

Element (3). G.S. 14-288.1(5) defines "law enforcement officer" to include any officer with the power of arrest and any member of the armed forces or state militia called to duty in a state of emergency to preserve the peace.

Element (4). See the notes under "Misdemeanor Riot" and "Disorderly Conduct" for definitions of riot and disorderly conduct. The statute does not require that a person participate in the riot or disorderly conduct to be charged with this offense.

Presumption of participation in riot. Subsection (c) of G.S. 14-288.5 provides that failure by anyone to disperse after a reasonable time is prima facie evidence that the person is willfully participating in the riot or disorderly conduct.

Constitutionality. This statute is constitutional (24 N.C. App. 338).

Related offenses not in this chapter

"Resisting, Delaying, or Obstructing an Officer" (Chapter 18)

Trespass during Emergency

Statute

§14-288.6. Looting; trespass during emergency.

(a) Any person who enters upon the premises of another without legal justification when the usual security of property is not effective due to the occurrence or aftermath of riot, insurrection, invasion, storm, fire, explosion, flood, collapse, or other disaster or calamity is guilty of a Class 1 misdemeanor of trespass during an emergency.

(b) Any person who commits the crime of trespass during emergency and, without legal justification, obtains or exerts control over, damages, ransacks, or destroys the property of another is guilty of the felony of looting and shall be punished as a Class H felon.

Elements

A person guilty of this offense

(1) enters upon the premises of another
(2) without legal justification
(3) when the usual security of the property is not effective because of riot, insurrection, storm, fire, explosion, flood, or other disaster or calamity.

Punishment

Class 1 misdemeanor.

Notes

Element (2). Firefighters, law enforcement officers, and similar public officers would have legal justification for entering.

Element (3). See the notes under "Misdemeanor Riot" for a definition of riot. Note that this statute does not cover all premises within an area where a state of emergency has been declared, only those where security has become ineffective.

Related offenses not in this chapter

"Misdemeanor Breaking or Entering of Building" (Chapter 13)
"First-Degree and Second-Degree Trespass" (Chapter 16)
"Injury to Real Property" (Chapter 16)
"Injury to Personal Property" (Chapter 16)

Looting

Statute

See section (b) of G.S. 14-288.6, reproduced under "Trespass during Emergency."

Elements

A person guilty of this offense
- (1) enters upon the premises of another
- (2) without legal justification
- (3) when the usual security of the property is not effective because of riot, insurrection, storm, fire, explosion, flood, or other disaster or calamity, *and*
- (4) without legal justification
  - (a) obtains or exerts control over the property of another, *or*
  - (b) damages or ransacks the property of another, *or*
  - (c) destroys the property of another.

Punishment

Class H felony.

Notes

Generally. Elements (1) through (3) constitute the lesser-included offense of "Trespass during Emergency," discussed above.

Element (4). This crime differs from larceny (various offenses; Chapter 11) in that a conviction is possible without showing a carrying away of the property or an intent to deprive the owner of the use of his or her property permanently. This statute covers damage, etc., to both real and personal property.

Related offenses not in this chapter

"Felonious Breaking or Entering of Building" (Chapter 13)
"Injury to Real Property" (Chapter 16)
"Injury to Personal Property" (Chapter 16)
"Felonious Larceny" (Chapter 11)

Transporting, Possessing Weapon during Emergency

Statute

§14-288.7. Transporting dangerous weapon or substance during emergency; possessing off premises; exceptions.

(a) Except as otherwise provided in this section, it is unlawful for any person to transport or possess off his own premises any dangerous weapon or substance in any area:
(1) In which a declared state of emergency exists; or
(2) Within the immediate vicinity of which a riot is occurring.

(b) This section does not apply to persons exempted from the provisions of G.S. 14-269 with respect to any activities lawfully engaged in while carrying out their duties.

(c) Any person who violates any provision of this section is guilty of a Class 1 misdemeanor.

Elements

A person guilty of this offense

(1) transports or possesses off the person's own premises
(2) a dangerous weapon or substance
(3) in an area in which a state of emergency has been declared or within the immediate vicinity of a riot.

Punishment

Class 1 misdemeanor.

Notes

Element (1). It is not necessary that the weapon be concealed in order to make this charge.

Element (2). G.S. 14-288.1(2) defines "dangerous weapon or substance" to include "any deadly weapon, ammunition, explosive, incendiary device, radioactive material . . . or any instrument or substance designed for . . . a threat of serious bodily injury or destruction of property . . . or any part or ingredient in any instrument or substance . . . when the circumstances indicate a probability that such part or ingredient will be so used."

Element (3). A state of emergency may be declared by certain municipal and county officials and by the Governor under the authority of the Riots and Civil Disorders Act (G.S. Ch. 14, Art. 36A) when an emergency exists because of civil disorder or a natural disaster. See the notes under "Misdemeanor Riot" for the elements of riot.

Law enforcement officers exempted. Subsection (b) of the statute exempts the same persons who are exempted from the prohibition of G.S. 14-269 on carrying concealed weapons. Primarily, this means law enforcement and military officers who are discharging their official duties.

Related offenses not in this chapter

"Carrying Concealed Weapon" (Chapter 19)
"Possession of Weapon on School Grounds" (Chapter 19)
"Possession of Firearm by Felon" (Chapter 19)
"Manufacture, Possession, etc., of Machine Gun, Sawed-Off Shotgun, or Weapon of Mass Destruction" (Chapter 19)
"Carrying Gun into Assembly or Establishment Where Alcoholic Beverages Are Sold and Consumed" (Chapter 19)
Possession of machine guns (G.S. 14-409 and -409.9)

Failure to Evacuate Building on Governor's Order

Statute

§14-288.19. Governor's power to order evacuation of public building.

(a) When it is determined by the Governor that a great public crisis, disaster, riot, catastrophe, or any other similar public emergency exists, or the occurrence of any such condition is imminent, and, in the Governor's opinion it is necessary to evacuate any building owned or controlled by any department, agency, institution, school, college, board, division, commission or subdivision of the State in order to maintain public order and safety or to afford adequate protection for lives or property, the Governor is hereby authorized to issue an order of evacuation directing all persons within the building to leave the building and its premises forthwith. The order shall be delivered to any law-enforcement officer or officer of the national guard, and such officer shall, by a suitable public address system, read the order to the occupants of the building and demand that the occupants forthwith evacuate said building within the time specified in the Governor's order.

(b) Any person who willfully refuses to leave the building as directed in the Governor's order shall be guilty of a Class 2 misdemeanor.

Elements

A person guilty of this offense
(1) willfully refuses to leave within the time set in the order
(2) a public building
(3) upon having an order to do so read over a public address system by a law enforcement or national guard officer,
(4) the order having been issued by the Governor
(5) upon a determination that a great public crisis, disaster, riot, catastrophe, or similar public emergency requires evacuation of the building in order to protect lives or property.

Punishment

Class 2 misdemeanor.

Notes

Element (2). The statute is worded broadly to be applicable to any building owned or controlled by a public agency.

Element (5). See the notes under "Misdemeanor Riot" for the elements of riot. The statute specifies that the order may also be issued when a public emergency is imminent.

Related offenses not in this chapter

"Resisting, Delaying, or Obstructing an Officer" (Chapter 18)

Violation of State-of-Emergency Ordinance

G.S. 14-288.12 (municipalities) and G.S. 14-288.13 (counties) give local governments authority to enact ordinances to become effective when a state of civil emergency is declared by the appropriate local official. Ideally, these ordinances will have been passed well before the emergency, but they may be promulgated and made effective immediately (G.S. 14-288.17). The ordinance can restrict use of public places, operation of businesses, possession of liquor, possession of weapons and gasoline, and similar activities. The most common example of such an emergency ordinance is the setting of a general curfew for all persons. The ordinance may delegate authority to the mayor or the chair of the county commissioners to issue a proclamation declaring the state of emergency and imposing the restrictions. If an ordinance has been enacted and a state of emergency proclaimed, violation of the ordinance is a Class 3 misdemeanor. Greater punishment—a Class 2 misdemeanor—may be imposed for violating a restriction imposed by proclamation of the Governor in those emergencies in which the Governor intervenes because the local governments cannot handle the situation (G.S. 14-288.15).

18
Perjury, Bribery, and Other Crimes against the Administration of Justice

Chapter Contents

18 Perjury, Bribery, and Other Crimes against the Administration of Justice

Common-Law Obstruction of Justice

Statute

This is a common-law offense.

Elements

A person guilty of this offense
(1) unlawfully and willfully
(2) obstructs justice.

Punishment

This is a Class 1 misdemeanor unless the criminal pleading alleges it was done "with deceit and intent to defraud." If deceit and intent to defraud are alleged and proved, it is a Class H felony, pursuant to G.S. 14-3(b) and 317 N.C. 557. See "Committing an Infamous or Related Misdemeanor" (Chapter 4).

Before the structured sentencing laws became effective, there was contradictory case law about whether common-law obstruction of justice was a misdemeanor offense punishable under G.S. 14-3(b) as a Class H felony because it is done with "deceit and intent to defraud." In 73 N.C. App. 174, the court ruled that evidence of "deceit and intent to defraud" was not present in a charge of common-law obstruction of justice, so the charge could not be elevated from a misdemeanor to a felony. In 100 N.C. App. 286, the court ruled that evidence of "deceit and intent to defraud" was sufficient to raise the offense to a felony.

Notes

Element (1). See the definition of "willfully" in Chapter 1, "States of Mind," and in 113 N.C. App. 347.

Element (2). Obstructing justice consists of any act that prevents, obstructs, impedes, or hinders public or legal justice, and it may take many forms. It may consist of conduct covered by a statute [for example, offenses in G.S. Ch. 14, Art. 30, like G.S. 14-221.2 (Altering court documents or entering unauthorized judgments) and G.S. 14-226.1 (Violating court orders)]. Or, conduct not covered by an existing statute may constitute this offense. For example, cases addressing the following situations implicitly or explicitly recognized this offense: when a defendant attempted to prevent the convening of a grand jury (309 N.C. 635); when a defendant attempted to intimidate a prospective witness for a trial de novo in superior court (4 N.C. App. 475); when a defendant supplied money to pay a fine and costs to another person who pled guilty in court to a criminal offense, and the defendant knew that the person pleading guilty was not the person actually charged with the offense (73 N.C. App. 174); and when a defendant offered to pay money to a prosecuting witness in exchange for the witness requesting dismissal of a criminal charge (100 N.C. App. 286).

Comparison with statutory offense concerning witness intimidation. G.S. 14-226, discussed below under "Intimidating Witnesses," is limited to intimidating a person who is summoned or acting as a witness. The common-law offense of obstruction of justice covers all forms of witness intimidation, including intimidation of prospective witnesses not "summoned" or "acting" as witnesses (4 N.C. App. 475). If the specific offenses described in G.S. 14-226 were allegedly committed, they may be charged under that statute. However, other types of witness intimidation (as well as offenses that fit within G.S. 14-226) may be charged as common-law obstruction of justice.

Related offenses not in this chapter

"Extortion" (Chapter 12)
"Committing an Infamous or Related Misdemeanor" (Chapter 4)
"Communicating Threats" (Chapter 7)
"Harassing Phone Calls" (Chapter 7)
Bribery of jurors (G.S. 14-220)
Altering, destroying, or stealing evidence of criminal conduct (G.S. 14-221.1)
Altering court documents or entering unauthorized judgments (G.S. 14-221.2)
Harassment of and communication with jurors (G.S. 14-225.2)
Violating orders of court (G.S. 14-226.1)

Intimidating Witnesses

Statute

§14-226. Intimidating or interfering with witnesses.

If any person shall by threats, menaces or in any other manner intimidate or attempt to intimidate any person who is summoned or acting as a witness in any of the courts of this State, or prevent or deter, or attempt to prevent or deter any person summoned or acting as such witness from attendance upon such court, he shall be guilty of a Class H felony.

Elements

A person guilty of this offense
(1) threatens, menaces, or in any other manner
(2) (a) (i) intimidates or attempts to intimidate
(ii) a person who is summoned or acting as a witness
(iii) in any North Carolina state court, *or*
(b) (i) prevents or deters, or attempts to prevent or deter
(ii) a person who is summoned or acting as a witness
(iii) from attendance in any North Carolina state court.

Punishment

Class H felony.

Notes

Element (1). A defendant's threat to kill a witness's daughter if the witness did not "drop the charges" after the defendant's conviction in district court and appeal for trial de novo in superior court was sufficient evidence for conviction (52 N.C. App. 331).

Elements (2)(a)(ii) and (3)(b)(ii). A defendant was properly convicted of this offense when he threatened a witness after the witness had testified in district court and the defendant had appealed for trial de novo in superior court; the witness—although not under subpoena—was a prospective witness when the threats were made as a result of the defendant's appeal for trial de novo (4 N.C. App. 475). A defendant-lawyer's inducement of a state's witness to leave the courthouse so the defendant-lawyer could attempt to obtain a dismissal of the charges against his client was sufficient evidence to support a conviction of an attempt to commit this offense (68 N.C. App. 358). The term "acting as a witness" does not appear to require that the witness have been actually subpoenaed to testify. See the facts in 68 N.C. App. 358. See also 347 N.C. 143, 182–83, in which the court, in interpreting a capital sentencing aggravating circumstance, ruled that a murder victim who was the complainant in arrest warrants issued against the defendant was a "witness" under G.S. 15A-2000(e)(8) because she would be testifying against him. That ruling may be applied by analogy in interpreting "acting as a witness" in G.S. 14-226.

Related offenses not in this chapter

See the related offenses listed under "Common-Law Obstruction of Justice" in this chapter.

Perjury

Statute

§14-209. Punishment for perjury.

If any person shall willfully and corruptly commit perjury, on his oath or affirmation, in any suit, controversy, matter or cause, depending in any of the courts of the State, or in any deposition or affidavit taken pursuant to law, or in any oath or affirmation duly administered of or concerning any matter or thing whereof such person is lawfully required to be sworn or affirmed, every person so offending shall be punished as a Class F felon.

Elements

A person guilty of this offense

(1) willfully and corruptly
(2) while under oath or affirmation in proceedings requiring the oath or affirmation
(3) gives testimony or makes a statement
(4) that is false
(5) and material.

Punishment

Class F felony.

Notes

Element (1). To commit this offense, the defendant must know that the statement is false and must make the statement intentionally (201 N.C. 714; 230 N.C. 198; 110 N.C. App. 449; N.C.P.I.—Crim. 228.1).

Element (2). The statute specifies that the statement be made "in any suit, controversy, matter, or cause, depending in any of the courts of the State, or in any deposition or affidavit taken pursuant to law, or in an oath or affirmation duly administered of or concerning any matter or thing whereof such person is lawfully required to be sworn or affirmed." In short, a statement can be perjury only if made under oath in circumstances in which it is legally required to be under oath.

Element (3). Perjury can apply to both oral and written statements. Statements of qualification like "I don't think so," or "I don't recall saying that," do not prevent testimony from being considered perjury (110 N.C. App. 449).

Element (4). To establish perjury, the falsity of the statement must be proved by the testimony of two witnesses or by one witness and other corroborating testimony (260 N.C. 220; 110 N.C. App. 149). For example, a doctor's opinion that a wound was inflicted by a sharp-edged instrument corroborated a witness's testimony that the defendant had lied when he said he had not used an ax in a fight (115 N.C. 712).

Element (5). To constitute perjury, the false statement must bear directly on a matter at issue in the proceedings; a false statement about something else is not perjury (230 N.C. 198; 247 N.C. 208). The federal constitution requires that the state prove the element of materiality to a jury beyond a reasonable doubt (515 U.S. 506; 138 N.C. App. 169).

Related offenses not in this chapter

False swearing to question of indigency (G.S. 7A-456)
Perjury before legislative committees (G.S. 14-211)
False statement to Commissioner of Insurance (G.S. 58-2-180)
False statement to procure benefit of insurance policy (G.S. 58-2-161)
False oath to statement required of fraternal benefit societies (G.S. 58-24-180)
False oath to certificate of mutual insurance company (G.S. 58-8-1)
Altering court documents or entering unauthorized judgments (G.S. 14-221.2)
Swearing falsely to official reports (G.S. 14-232)
Making false oath on matters required by Driver's License Act (G.S. 20-31)
Making false oath on matters required by Motor Vehicle Act of 1937 (G.S. 20-112)
False swearing to creditor's oath (G.S. 23-9)
False taking of debtor's oath (G.S. 23-43)
False swearing in fire investigation by Attorney General (G.S. 58-79-10)
False swearing by person responding to investigation of trusts and monopolies (G.S. 75-12)
Swearing to false statement in hunting license application (G.S. 113-275)
False certification that bids submitted without collusion (G.S. 143-54)
False swearing before city council investigation (G.S. 160A-80)
False statement under oath to matter required for absentee ballot (G.S. 163-237)

Subornation of Perjury

Statute

§14-210. Subornation of perjury.

If any person shall, by any means, procure another person to commit such willful and corrupt perjury as is mentioned in G.S. 14-209, the person so offending shall be punished as a Class I felon.

Elements

A person guilty of this offense
(1) willfully procures or induces another to commit perjury, *and*
(2) that other person commits perjury.

Punishment

Class I felony.

Notes

Element (1). To commit this offense, the defendant must believe (a) that the testimony or statement he or she procures is false (240 N.C. 113) and (b) that the person testifying believes it to be false (*Perkins*, p. 524).

Element (2). To establish this offense, it must be proved that the person who testified actually committed perjury, satisfying each of the elements of the separate offense of perjury (267 N.C. 631; 56 N.C. App. 721). If the person who testified did not commit perjury, the defendant can be charged with solicitation to commit perjury (56 N.C. App. 721). Solicitation to commit perjury is a Class 2 misdemeanor under G.S. 14-2.6. See "Solicitation of Another to Commit a Felony" (Chapter 4) for a discussion of what conduct constitutes solicitation.

Related offenses not in this chapter

"Solicitation of Another to Commit a Felony" (Chapter 4)
See the related offenses listed under "Perjury" in this chapter.

Bribery of Official

Statute

§14-217. Bribery of officials.

(a) If any person holding office under the laws of this State who, except in payment of his legal salary, fees or perquisites, shall receive, or consent to receive, directly or indirectly, anything of value or personal advantage, or the promise thereof, for performing or omitting to perform any official act, which lay within the scope of his official authority and was connected with the discharge of his official and legal duties, or with the express or implied understanding that his official action, or omission to act, is to be in any degree influenced thereby, he shall be punished as a Class F felon.

(b) Indictments issued under these provisions shall specify:
(1) The thing of value or personal advantage sought to be obtained; and
(2) The specific act or omission sought to be obtained; and
(3) That the act or omission sought to be obtained lay within the scope of the defendant's official authority and was connected with the discharge of his official and legal duties.

(c) Repealed by Session Laws 1993, c. 539, s. 1207.

Elements

A person guilty of this offense
(1) while holding a public office
(2) receives or agrees to receive
(3) something of value or personal advantage
(4) for performing an official act or omitting to perform an official act in the scope of his or her official duties and authority
(5) with the express or implied understanding
(6) that the defendant's official action or inaction was to be influenced by the thing of value or personal advantage.

Punishment

Class F felony.

Notes

Element (1). No cases explain what constitutes "public office" in this statute; but for purposes of other statutes (prohibiting dual officeholding), public officers are persons who hold "public positions to which a portion of the sovereignty of the country, either legislative, executive, or judicial, attaches for the time being, and which is exercised for the benefit of the public. . . . The most important characteristic which distinguishes an office from an agency is that the conferring of the office carries with it a delegation to the individual of some of the sovereign functions of the government" (145 N.C. 476).

The key, then, is that the officer must exercise some portion of the sovereign power of the state. Any person elected to a government post is a public officer, and some persons who are not in top-level elected positions are also public officers. Examples of some persons held to be public officers include law enforcement officers (127 N.C. 518; 264 N.C. 149); judicial officials (186 N.C. 127); members of county boards and commissions (182 N.C. 865); county commissioners (201 N.C. 661); city council members (207 N.C. 293); and county alcohol beverage control (ABC) officers (114 N.C. App. 464).

Element (2). An agreement to receive something of value or a personal advantage may be either expressed or implied (*Perkins*, p. 534).

Element (3). The thing received by the public officer need not be of monetary value if it is valuable to the person being bribed. If the subject of the bribe is a promise, the promise need not be legally enforceable. The thing of value can take the form of a regular transaction; for example, a piece of land can be sold to a public official at substantially below the market price, and the difference between the market price and the sale price can be the thing of value that is the subject of the bribe (*Perkins*, p. 533).

Element (4). It is not a defense to this charge that the public official would have taken the same action even if he or she had not accepted the bribe; "an officer who has determined upon a certain course of public action might change his mind if free from corrupting influences" (*Perkins*, p. 537). For this crime to be committed, the act to be influenced must be within the scope of the officer's official authority, and it must be a legal duty and not just a moral one (238 N.C. 325). An example of an act within an officer's duties and authority is an arrest by a law enforcement officer (60 N.C. App. 568).

Element (5). It is no defense that the public official's action was not, in fact, influenced by the bribe. The offense is completed when the official receives or agrees to receive the thing of value, intending to modify his or her behavior because of it (*Perkins*, p. 537).

Conspiracy to bribe. Conspiracy to bribe is established by the general North Carolina rule on conspiracy. See the discussion of "Conspiracy" in Chapter 4. For acts completed only before October 1, 1994, a special rule applies, requiring an overt act for an offense to constitute conspiracy to bribe [see repealed subsection (c) of G.S. 14-217 for the requirements].

Related offenses not in this chapter

"Extortion" (Chapter 12)
Bribery of jurors (G.S. 14-220)
Buying and selling offices (G.S. 14-228)
Willfully failing to discharge duties (G.S. 14-230)
Bribery of players, managers, coaches, referees, umpires, and officials (G.S. 14-373)
Acceptance of bribes by players, managers, coaches, referees, umpires, and officials (G.S. 14-374)
Bribery of horse show judges or officials (G.S. 14-380.1)
Bribery of legislators (G.S. 120-86)
Bargains for office void (G.S. 128-3)
Receiving compensation of subordinates for appointment or retention (G.S. 128-4)
Failure of building inspector to perform duties (G.S. 153A-356)

Offering Bribe to Official

Statute

§14-218. Offering bribes.

If any person shall offer a bribe, whether it be accepted or not, he shall be punished as a Class F felon.

Elements

A person guilty of this offense
(1) with a corrupt intent
(2) offers something of value
(3) to a public official
(4) knowing that person to be a public official
(5) for the purpose of influencing the official in performing an official act.

Punishment

Class F felony.

Notes

Element (1). "Corrupt intent" means a wrongful design to acquire some pecuniary profit or other advantage (114 N.C. App. 464). It does not necessarily mean requesting that an officer perform a duty in an illegal manner; this offense can be committed by offering a bribe to an officer to do something within the officer's legal authority. This element can be satisfied even if the person who offers the bribe does not benefit from the official action he or she is trying to influence and even if the public is not actually harmed; it is enough if the person offering the bribe intends to achieve either of these objectives (*Perkins*, p. 537).

Element (2). See the note on Element (3) of "Bribery of Official." The statute defining this offense specifies that whether the public official accepts the offer is immaterial in establishing a violation.

Element (3). See the note on Element (1) of "Bribery of Official." The statute does not specify that this offense applies only to bribes offered to public officials, but cases interpreting the statute suggest that result (238 N.C. 325). Note, however, this statute has been applied to offering bribes to jurors (204 N.C. 329).

Element (4). Case law (238 N.C. 325) requires that this element be satisfied, but an indictment is sufficient if requisite knowledge can merely be reasonably inferred from the other allegations in the indictment.

Element (5). The act to be influenced must be within the scope of the officer's official authority, and it must be a legal duty, not just a moral one (238 N.C. 325). "Duty" does not mean that an officer is *required* to perform that act; it means that the act is within the officer's authority (114 N.C. App. 464).

Related offenses not in this chapter

See the offenses listed under "Bribery of Official."

Resisting, Delaying, or Obstructing an Officer

Statute

§14-223. Resisting officers.

If any person shall willfully and unlawfully resist, delay or obstruct a public officer in discharging or attempting to discharge a duty of his office, he shall be guilty of a Class 2 misdemeanor.

Elements

A person guilty of this offense

(1) willfully
(2) resists or delays or obstructs
(3) a person the defendant knows to be a public officer
(4) while that officer is discharging or attempting to discharge a duty of his or her office.

Punishment

Class 2 misdemeanor.

Notes

Element (1). See the definition of "willfully" in Chapter 1, "States of Mind."

Element (2). For this offense to be committed, the defendant's conduct must keep the officer from performing an official duty. This offense can occur even if there is no assault or other physical interference, but something more than merely questioning or criticizing an officer (278 N.C. 243; 14 N.C. App. 485) or failing to give one's Social Security number after arrest (126 N.C. App 712) is necessary to constitute a violation. For example, a defendant violated this statute when he cursed and threatened an officer after receiving a parking ticket *and* had to be forcibly removed from his truck with Mace and a black-jack so that he could be arrested for disorderly conduct (34 N.C. App. 72). This statute prohibits communications intended to hinder or prevent an officer from carrying out an official duty, though not communication intended to express disagreement or criticism, to clarify a misunderstanding, or to obtain information. A conviction was proper in a case in which two defendants, despite being ordered to halt, approached within 6 feet of officers who were trying to arrest a man on a narcotics charge and began to shout; one defendant raised his fists into the air and shouted, "No, no, no, he ain't going nowhere," and the other yelled, "Stop it, he ain't going." The court concluded that the defendants' conduct showed their determination to prevent the officers from arresting the man and that their acts caused the officers temporarily to lose control of that man. A citizen has a right to resist unlawful conduct by an officer (65 N.C. 327; 1 N.C. App. 479), but if the officer is acting lawfully, as in making a lawful arrest, the person is required to submit peacefully (13 N.C. App. 1). A person does not have a right to resist an arrest by an officer who, without illegal entry or use of excessive force, attempts to make an arrest pursuant to an arrest warrant that appears regular on its face but fails properly to state a crime (44 N.C. App. 53).

Element (3). A person may resist if the person does not know of the officer's authority to undertake the act in question (76 N.C. 10). In a case involving an assault on a law enforcement officer that also would likely apply to this offense, the North Carolina Supreme Court ruled that the state must prove that the defendant knew that the person he or she was assaulting was a law enforcement officer (315 N.C. 1). By its terms the statute is not limited to law enforcement officers but applies to all public officers. Few cases have considered the question of who is a public officer, but see the discussion of the meaning of "public office" under Element (1) of "Bribery of Official." This statute's broad language apparently prohibits resistance to any public employee who is required to regulate the conduct of others, such as a firefighter or a building inspector.

Element (4). Rather than generally allege that the officer was performing some duty of his or her office (37 N.C. App. 133), a criminal pleading must specifically allege what particular duty the officer was performing (256 N.C. 203; 263 N.C. 694). The duty being discharged can be one other than arrest, such as making a search, questioning a suspect (278 N.C. 243), or fighting a fire.

Charging both resisting arrest and assault on a governmental officer or employee. This offense is not a lesser-included offense of "Assault on Governmental Officer or Employee" (Chapter 7) when the governmental employee involved is a law enforcement officer. The general rule is that a person may not be convicted of both this offense and assault on a governmental officer or employee if the same assaultive conduct is the basis of both offenses (282 N.C. 157; 298 N.C. 191; 33 N.C. App. 698; 33 N.C. App. 722), because double jeopardy prohibits a person from being punished twice for the same criminal conduct, absent a contrary legislative intent (see the discussion of double jeopardy as a bar to prosecution in Chapter 2, "Bars and Defenses"). The best practice may be to charge both offenses based on the same conduct and permit the prosecutor to: (a) choose the best offense for prosecution, (b) determine whether, given the facts, separate charges based on different conduct are possible, or (c) attempt to prosecute for both offenses based on the following argument. It may be argued that the legislature has clearly expressed "its intent to prescribe and punish exactly the same conduct under two separate statutes," so the general rule should no longer stand (315 N.C. 444, 450–63). Consequently, a trial court in a single trial may impose punishment for conviction of each statute separately even though the same conduct is the basis for each charge (315 N.C. 444, 450–63; 322 N.C. 666, 678). It is clear that a defendant may be convicted of resisting, delaying, or obstructing a public officer and assault on a governmental officer on the basis of *different* conduct arising out of the same incident (298 N.C. 191). For example, the defendant's hitting an officer and later resisting that officer's attempt to handcuff the defendant may be two episodes of conduct arising out of the same incident that led to two separate convictions.

Constitutionality. This statute is not unconstitutionally vague (73 N.C. App. 612).

Related offenses not in this chapter

"Assault on Governmental Officer or Employee" (Chapter 7)
"Assault with Firearm or Other Deadly Weapon on Governmental Officers or Employees" (Chapter 7)
"Assault on Emergency Personnel" (Chapter 7)
"Failure to Yield for Emergency Vehicle" (Chapter 25)
"Failure to Stop for Emergency Vehicle" (Chapter 25)
"Speeding to Elude Arrest" (Chapter 25)
Surrender of driver's license (G.S. 20-29)
Willful failure to obey traffic officer (G.S. 20-114.1)
Interference with firefighter (G.S. 58-82-1)

False Report to Law Enforcement Agencies or Officers

Statute

§14-225. False reports to law enforcement agencies or officers.

Any person who shall willfully make or cause to be made to a law enforcement agency or officer any false, misleading or unfounded report, for the purpose of interfering with the operation of a law enforcement agency, or to hinder or obstruct any law enforcement officer in the performance of his duty, shall be guilty of a Class 2 misdemeanor.

Elements

A person guilty of this offense
- (1) willfully
- (2) makes or causes to be made
- (3) to a law enforcement agency or officer
- (4) a false or misleading or unfounded report
- (5) for the purpose of
  - (a) interfering with the operation of a law enforcement agency, *or*
  - (b) hindering or obstructing any law enforcement officer in performing official duties.

Punishment

Class 2 misdemeanor.

Notes

Generally. The General Assembly enlarged this offense in 1994 from a statute prohibiting much narrower conduct (false reports to police radio stations). This offense prohibits provision of false, misleading, or unfounded information to law enforcement officials. It includes a situation in which a person lies to or misleads a law enforcement officer, as well as false reports by phone or radio to law enforcement officials.

Element (4). This statute prohibits "false," "misleading," or "unfounded" statements. A dictionary definition of "unfounded" is "without basis in fact."

Element (5). This offense is committed only if the defendant acts with one of the required purposes.

Related offenses not in this chapter

None.

Picketing Courthouse

Statute

§14-225.1. Picketing or parading.

Any person who, with intent to interfere with, obstruct, or impede the administration of justice, or with intent to influence any justice or judge of the General Court of Justice, juror, witness, district attorney, assistant district attorney, or court officer, in the discharge of his duty, pickets, parades, or uses any sound truck or similar device within 300 feet of an exit from any building housing any court of the General Court of Justice, or within 300 feet of any building or residence occupied or used by such justice, judge, juror, witness, district attorney, assistant district attorney, or court officer, shall upon plea or conviction be guilty of a Class 1 misdemeanor.

Elements

A person guilty of this offense
- (1) pickets or parades or uses a sound truck or similar device
- (2) within 300 feet of
- (3) (a) the exit of any building that houses a North Carolina court, *or*
  - (b) any building occupied or used by a North Carolina judge or justice, juror, witness, district attorney, assistant district attorney, or other court officer
- (4) with the intent to
  - (a) interfere with the administration of justice, *or*
  - (b) obstruct the administration of justice, *or*
  - (c) impede the administration of justice, *or*
  - (d) influence a North Carolina judge or justice, juror, witness, district attorney, assistant district attorney, or other court officer in discharging his or her duty.

Punishment

Class 1 misdemeanor.

Notes

Element (2). Apparently the offense is not committed if the picketing, parading, or use of sound truck is located more than 300 feet from the courthouse even though the demonstration might be heard from the courthouse.

Element (3)(a). A building satisfying this element need not be a courthouse so long as court is held there.

Element (3)(b). The offense would be committed if the picketing, parading, or use of a sound truck took place within 300 feet or a motel where a judge, jurors, witnesses, or other specified officials were housed.

Element (4). The offense is committed only if the defendant acts with the required specific intent.

Related offenses not in this chapter

"Communicating Threats" (Chapter 7)
"Harassing Phone Calls" (Chapter 7)
First-Degree and Second-Degree Trespass (Chapter 16)
"Injury to Real Property" (Chapter 16)
"Defacing Public Building" (Chapter 16)
"Injury to Personal Property" (Chapter 16)
"Disorderly Conduct" (Chapter 17)
"Disorderly Conduct in Public Building" (Chapter 17)
Trespass on public lands (G.S. 14-130)

Prison Breach and Escape from County or Municipal Confinement Facilities or Officers

Statute

§14-256. Prison breach and escape from county or municipal confinement facilities or officers.

If any person shall break any prison, jail or lockup maintained by any county or municipality in North Carolina, being lawfully confined therein, or shall escape from the lawful custody of any superintendent, guard or officer of such prison, jail or lockup, he shall be guilty of a Class 1 misdemeanor, except that the person is guilty of a Class H felony if:

(1) He has been convicted of a felony and has been committed to the facility pending transfer to the State prison system; or
(2) He is serving a sentence imposed upon conviction of a felony.

Elements

A person guilty of this offense

(1) escapes from
(2) (a) lawful confinement in a prison, jail, or lockup maintained by a county or municipality, *or*
    (b) lawful custody of any superintendent, guard, or officer of a prison, jail, or lockup maintained by a county or municipality.

Punishment

Class 1 misdemeanor. Class H felony if the defendant (1) has been convicted of a felony and has been committed to the facility pending transfer to the state prison system or (2) is serving a sentence imposed on conviction of a felony.

Notes

Generally. This statute does not apply if a person escapes from an officer before being confined to jail (82 N.C. 585).

Duress as a defense. See the note on duress as a defense under "Escape from State Prison System."

Escape while on local work release. A related statute, G.S. 14-255, provides that a prisoner who escapes from the custody of his or her work supervisor while on limited release from a local confinement facility or a county's satellite jail/work release unit, pursuant to authorized release for work under G.S. 162-58, commits a Class 1 misdemeanor.

Related offenses not in this chapter

Allowing prisoners to escape (G.S. 14-239)
Escape of working prisoners from custody (G.S. 14-255)
Escape from private correctional facility (G.S. 14-256.1)
Conveying messages and weapons to or trading with convicts and other prisoners (G.S. 14-258)
Furnishing poison, controlled substances, deadly weapons, cartridges, ammunition, or alcoholic beverages to inmates of charitable, mental, or penal institutions or local confinement facilities (G.S. 14-258.1)
Taking of hostage by prisoner (G.S. 14-258.3)
Harboring or aiding certain persons (G.S. 14-259)

Escape from State Prison System

Statute

§148-45. Escaping or attempting escape from State prison system; failure of conditionally and temporarily released prisoners and certain youthful offenders to return to custody of Department of Correction.

(a) Any person in the custody of the Department of Correction in any of the classifications hereinafter set forth who shall escape from the State prison system, shall for the first such offense, except as provided in subsection (g) of this section, be guilty of a Class 1 misdemeanor:

(1) A prisoner serving a sentence imposed upon conviction of a misdemeanor;
(2) A person who has been charged with a misdemeanor and who has been committed to the custody of the Department of Correction under the provisions of G.S. 162-39;
(3) Repealed by Session Laws 1985, c. 226, s. 4.
(4) A person who shall have been convicted of a misdemeanor and who shall have been committed to the Department of Correction for presentence diagnostic study under the provisions of G.S. 15A-1332(c).

(b) Any person in the custody of the Department of Correction, in any of the classifications hereinafter set forth, who shall escape from the State prison system, shall, except as provided in subsection (g) of this section, be punished as a Class H felon.

(1) A prisoner serving a sentence imposed upon conviction of a felony;
(2) A person who has been charged with a felony and who has been committed to the custody of the Department of Correction under the provisions of G.S. 162-39;
(3) Repealed by Session Laws 1985, c. 226, s. 5.
(4) A person who shall have been convicted of a felony and who shall have been committed to the Department of Correction for presentence diagnostic study under the provisions of G.S. 15A-1332(c); or
(5) Any person previously convicted of escaping or attempting to escape from the State prison system.

(c) Repealed by Session Laws 1979, c. 760, s. 5.

(d) Any person who aids or assists other persons to escape or attempt to escape from the State prison system shall be guilty of a Class 1 misdemeanor.

(e) Repealed by Session Laws 1983, c. 465, s. 5.

(f) Any person convicted of an escape or attempt to escape classified as a felony by this section shall be immediately classified and treated as a convicted felon even if such person has time remaining to be served in the State prison system on a sentence or sentences imposed upon conviction of a misdemeanor or misdemeanors.

(g)(1) Any person convicted and in the custody of the North Carolina Department of Correction and ordered or otherwise assigned to work under the work-release program, G.S. 148-33.1, or any convicted person in the custody of the North Carolina Department of Correction and temporarily allowed to leave a place of confinement by the Secretary of Correction or his designee or other authority of law, who shall fail to return to custody of the North Carolina Department of Correction, shall be guilty of the crime of escape and subject to the applicable provisions of this section and shall be deemed an escapee. For the purpose of this subsection, escape is defined to include, but is not restricted to, willful failure to return to an appointed place and at an appointed time as ordered.

(2) If a person, who would otherwise be guilty of a first violation of G.S. 148-45(g)(1), voluntarily returns to his place of confinement within 24 hours of the time at which he was ordered to return, such person shall not be charged with an escape as provided in this section but shall be subject to such administrative action as may be deemed appropriate for an escapee by the Department of Correction; said escapee shall not be allowed to be placed on work release for a four-month period or for the balance of his term if less than four months; provided, however, that if such person commits a subsequent violation of this section then such person shall be charged with that offense and, if convicted, punished under the provisions of this section.

Elements

A person guilty of this offense
(1) escapes
(2) from the custody of the Department of Correction.

Punishment

For an escapee who was in the Department of Correction's custody because of a misdemeanor conviction, or while charged with a misdemeanor, this offense is a Class 1 misdemeanor. For a person in custody because of a felony conviction, in custody while charged with a felony, or previously convicted of this offense, the offense is a Class H felony.

Notes

Element (1). "Escape" is not limited to breaking free of confinement from a state prison facility. It includes failure to return to the Department of Correction's custody at the appropriate time by persons on work release or temporary parole. It also includes failure to return to custody after having been temporarily released by the Secretary of Correction under G.S. 148-4. For example, a prisoner's failure to return after having been instructed to clean a chapel located just beyond the prison fence was an offense under this statute (30 N.C. App. 217). A person "on escape" from work release, early parole, or temporary release may avoid being charged with escape by returning to confinement within 24 hours of the time he or she was ordered to report. While returning within 24 hours will not be treated as an escape for purposes of this offense, the person may be subject to administrative action by the department. If a person fails to return more than once, a subsequent nonreturn is an escape even if the person eventually returns within 24 hours [G.S. 148-45(g)(2)].

Element (2). The statute applies to all prisoners in the department's custody. For example, (1) if they are serving a sentence for a conviction; (2) if they are being held by the department for a local confinement facility because of overcrowding or for safekeeping (G.S. 162-39); (3) if they are being held by the department pending appeal [G.S. 15A-1353(a)]; and (4) if they are being held by the department for presentence diagnostic study (G.S. 148-49.13).

Aiders and assisters guilty of misdemeanor. People who aid and assist inmates to escape are guilty of a Class 1 misdemeanor [G.S. 148-45(d)]. This offense would apply to both other inmates and people outside the prison system who help the inmate escape. If the assistance is furnishing deadly weapons, cartridges, or ammunition to prisoners, the aider might also violate G.S. 14-258.1 (furnishing poison, controlled substances, deadly weapons, cartridges, ammunition, or alcoholic beverages to inmates of charitable, mental, or penal institutions or local confinement facilities) and G.S. 14-258 (conveying messages and weapons to or trading with convicts and other prisoners).

Duress as a defense. "Duress or Necessity" (Chapter 2) is available as a defense to escape if five criteria are satisfied: (1) the prisoner has been threatened with death, forcible sexual attack, or substantial bodily injury in the immediate future; (2) the prisoner had no time to complain to prison officials or a history of futile complaints exists; (3) the prisoner had no time to resort to the courts; (4) the prisoner did not use force or violence against prison personnel or other innocent people in the escape; and (5) the prisoner immediately reported to proper authorities when he or she was safe from the immediate threat of the criteria set out in (1) (60 N.C. App. 191; 67 N.C. App. 128).

Attempt to escape. An attempt to escape would be treated under the general rule concerning "Attempt" (see Chapter 4).

Related offenses not in this chapter

See the offenses listed under "Prison Breach and Escape from County or Municipal Confinement Facilities or Officers" in this chapter.

19
Weapons Offenses

Chapter Contents

19
Weapons Offenses

Possession of Firearm by Felon

Statute

§14-415.1. Possession of firearms, etc., by felon prohibited.

(a) It shall be unlawful for any person who has been convicted of a felony to purchase, own, possess, or have in his custody, care, or control any handgun or other firearm with a barrel length of less than 18 inches or an overall length of less than 26 inches, or any weapon of mass death and destruction as defined in G.S. 14-288.8(c).

Every person violating the provisions of this section shall be punished as a Class G felon.

Nothing in this subsection would prohibit the right of any person to have possession of a firearm within his own home or on his lawful place of business.

(b) Prior convictions which cause disentitlement under this section shall only include:

(1) Felony convictions in North Carolina that occur before, on, or after December 1, 1995; and

(2) Repealed by Session Laws 1995, c. 487, s. 3.

(3) Violations of criminal laws of other states or of the United States that occur before, on, or after December 1, 1995, and that are substantially similar to the crimes covered in subdivision (1) which are punishable where committed by imprisonment for a term exceeding one year.

When a person is charged under this section, records of prior convictions of any offense, whether in the courts of this State, or in the courts of any other state or of the United States, shall be admissible in evidence for the purpose of proving a violation of this section. The term "conviction" is defined as a final judgment in any case in which felony punishment, or imprisonment for a term exceeding one year, as the case may be, is permissible, without regard to the plea entered or to the sentence imposed. A judgment of a conviction of the defendant or a plea of guilty by the defendant to such an offense certified to a superior court of this State from the custodian of records of any state or federal court shall be prima facie evidence of the facts so certified.

(c) The indictment charging the defendant under the terms of this section shall be separate from any indictment charging him with other offenses related to or giving rise to a charge under this section. An indictment which charges the person with violation of this section must set forth the date that the prior offense was committed, the type of offense and the penalty therefor, and the date that the defendant was convicted or plead guilty to such offense, the identity of the court in which the conviction or plea of guilty took place and the verdict and judgment rendered therein.

Elements

A person guilty of this offense

(1) has previously been convicted of:
   (a) a felony in North Carolina, *or*
   (b) a violation of the criminal law of another state or the United States for an offense substantially similar to one in subdivision (a) and carrying a maximum punishment of more than one year imprisonment, *and*

(2) purchases, owns, possesses, or has in his or her custody, care, or control outside his or her own home or place of business

(3) any handgun, any weapon of mass death and destruction, or any other firearm with a barrel length of less than 18 inches or an overall length of less than 26 inches.

Punishment

Class G felony.

Notes

Generally. In 1995 the General Assembly amended this offense, effective for offenses committed on or after December 1, 1995. Felony status invoking the offense was expanded to apply to previous conviction of *any* felony in North Carolina, or a similar offense in another state or under the federal law (there had been some limits on what felony convictions were covered). More significantly, the legislature repealed the portion of the statute that made this offense only applicable within five years of the date of a covered felony conviction. Effectively, the legislature extended this offense to cover a person convicted of a felony in North Carolina at any point in his or her lifetime. How long ago the felony conviction occurred is no longer relevant.

Element (2). The exception from criminal liability for possession of a firearm in one's own home does not apply to possession of a firearm in the common areas of a motel (83 N.C. App. 529) or an apartment house—such as stairways, halls, and parks (78 N.C. App. 514)—or the yard of a trailer that a person owns but does not live in (121 N.C. App. 355). The state does not have to prove that a defendant was *not* in his or her home or business; the defendant has the burden of showing that this exception applies (119 N.C. App. 695; 78 N.C. App. 514). There was insufficient evidence to prove that the defendant possessed a firearm located on the console between the driver's and front passenger's seats of a car where the defendant was sitting in the front passenger seat, his wife was driving the car that was registered to the defendant's brother, and the firearm was purchased by and registered to his wife (131 N.C. App. 514).

Element (3). A firearm is a weapon that propels shot, shell, or bullets by the action of an explosion within it (*Black's Law Dictionary*, p. 648). However, for firearms other than handguns or weapons of mass destruction, the statute applies only to those with a barrel length of less than 18 inches or an overall length of less than 26 inches. Therefore it does not apply to long rifles or long shotguns. Apparently the definition also does not include air rifles or pistols or blank cartridge pistols. The prosecution need not prove the barrel length or overall length of a handgun; these measurement requirements are only elements for possession of other kinds of firearms (83 N.C. App. 529). The firearm must be operable, but if the defendant presents no evidence that it is inoperable, the jury can find that it is operable and convict the defendant (34 N.C. App. 307).

For a definition of a weapon of mass death and destruction, see the statute reproduced under "Manufacture, Possession, etc., of Machine Gun, Sawed-Off Shotgun, or Weapon of Mass Destruction."

Repeal of offense's application for five years after conviction. Historically, this statute had applied to any felon who had not yet had his or her citizenship restored. When the restoration-of-citizenship statutes were changed to make restoration automatic on final discharge from custody, this statute was rewritten to apply for five years after the completion of punishment. Under that version of the law, possession of a firearm after the five-year post-release period had expired was not a crime (935 F.2d 28). Effective for offenses committed on or after December 1, 1995, the date of the pertinent felony conviction is irrelevant. If a person has ever been convicted of a felony under Element (1), this offense bars purchase, ownership, possession, etc. (outside the person's home or business) of any weapon listed in Element (3).

Constitutionality. G.S. 14-415.1, as previously codified, was not unconstitutionally vague, nor did it deny equal protection of the laws (39 N.C. App. 668).

Disposition of seized weapons. G.S. 14-269.1 and G.S. 15-11.1 govern disposition of seized weapons. G.S. 14-269.1 applies to disposition of deadly weapons after a defendant's conviction. G.S. 15-11.1 applies to disposition of other kinds of seized property, which may include non-deadly weapons. However, G.S. 15-11.1(b1) also provides a disposition procedure for firearms. These statutes overlap in applying to firearms that may be deadly weapons within the meaning of G.S. 14-269.1. How they should be applied together is not completely clear.

Similar ban on possession of weapons by insanity acquittees and persons determined to lack capacity to stand trial. G.S. 14-415.3 makes it a Class H felony for a particular class of people to purchase, own, possess, or have in the person's custody, care, or control, any firearm or any weapon of mass death and destruction as defined by G.S. 14-288.8(c). This prohibition applies to (1) a person who has been acquitted by reason of insanity of any offense listed in G.S. 14-415.1(b) [listed under Element (1), above] or any violation of G.S. 14-33(b)(1) (misdemeanor assault with a deadly weapon and assault inflicting serious injury), G.S. 14-33(b)(8) (misdemeanor assault on governmental officer or employee, or company or campus police officer), or G.S. 14-34 (misdemeanor assault by pointing gun); and (2) any person who has been determined to lack capacity to proceed as a criminal defendant in a criminal prosecution by the procedure provided in G.S. 15A-1002 for any of the offenses listed under Element (1). Note that this prohibition applies to a broader set of criminal offenses than "Possession of firearm by felon," including some misdemeanors. G.S. 14-415.3 specifies that weapons confiscated in relation to a violation of this prohibition must be disposed of in accordance with G.S. 15-11.1.

Broader federal firearms statute. A federal statute, 18 U.S.C. § 922(g), prohibits the possession, receipt, or transportation in interstate or foreign commerce of any firearm by a person who has been convicted in any state or federal court of a crime punishable by more than one year's imprisonment. However, 18 U.S.C. § 921(a)(20) excludes from 18 U.S.C. § 922(g)'s coverage conviction of a state offense classified by that state as a misdemeanor and punishable by a maximum of 2 years imprisonment or less; a conviction for certain offenses relating to the regulation of business practices; and a conviction which has been expunged, set aside, or for which the person has been pardoned or has had civil rights restored (see G.S. 13-1), unless the pardon, expungement, or civil rights restoration expressly provides that the person may not ship, transport, possess, or receive firearms.

This federal statute also prohibits the possession, receipt, or transportation in interstate or foreign commerce of any firearm by a person who (1) is subject to a court order such as a civil domestic violence protective order issued under G.S. 50B-3 or (2) has been convicted of a "misdemeanor crime of domestic violence." The term "misdemeanor crime of domestic violence" means a misdemeanor under federal or state law that has, as an element, the use or attempted use of physical force, or the threatened use of a deadly weapon, committed by (a) a current or former spouse, parent, or guardian of the victim; (b) a person with whom the victim shares a child in common; or (c) a person who is cohabiting with or has cohabited with the victim as a spouse, parent, or guardian, or a person similarly situated to a spouse, parent, or guardian of the victim. However, it is not considered a conviction unless the person was represented by counsel in the case or knowingly and intelligently waived the right to counsel. It also is not a conviction if the conviction has been expunged or the person has received a pardon. See 18 U.S.C. § 921(a)(33) for the complete definition of "misdemeanor crime of domestic violence." The statutory firearm prohibition discussed in this paragraph has been found to be constitutional (168 F.3d 718; 209 F.3d 319).

Federal cases have ruled that certificates of civil rights restoration must be interpreted in light of applicable state criminal law prohibitions. So, for example, under the pre–December 1, 1995, version of this offense, it was a violation of federal firearms law for a person to possess a firearm within the five-year period under G.S. 14-415.1, even though his or her civil rights had been restored for a particular felony conviction (904 F.2d 216). Also, a federal court ruled that a defendant properly may be convicted under the federal statute for possessing a firearm in his or her home, although possessing a firearm in one's home is permitted by G.S. 14-415.1, when the defendant's civil rights had not yet been restored under North Carolina state law (119 F.3d 290). Conversely, a certificate restoring civil rights could not deny a person rights he or she had pursuant to state law. Thus, for example, a federal court ruled that a defendant's federal conviction for possession of firearms in his home in violation of 18 U.S.C. § 922(g)(1) was not valid, even though his North Carolina restoration certificate stated he was not entitled to "own, possess, receive, buy, or otherwise acquire firearms of any description," because G.S. 14-415.1 does not prohibit a defendant's possession of a firearm in the defendant's home or place of business (2 F.3d 53). For offenses committed on or after December 1, 1995, the federal firearms law would likely apply no matter when a person's felony conviction occurred.

This federal statute also prohibits the possession, receipt, or transportation in interstate or foreign commerce of any firearm by a person who is a fugitive from justice, is a narcotics user or addict, has been adjudged mentally defective or has been committed to a mental institution, is an illegal alien, has been dishonorably discharged from the armed forces, or has renounced United States citizenship.

"Firearm" in 18 U.S.C. § 921(a)(3) is defined to include "any weapon (including a starter gun) which will or is designed to or may readily be converted to expel a projectile by the action of an explosive; the frame or receiver of any such weapon; any firearm muffler or silencer; or any destructive device," with the exception of antique firearms. Note that this federal law is broader than G.S. 14-415.1; it includes all firearms (handguns, rifles, shotguns, etc.) with no restrictions as to barrel length, and there is no time limit on its prohibition of firearm possession by convicted felons. However, a convicted felon can obtain relief from the federal prohibitions by applying under 18 U.S.C. § 925(c) to the Secretary of the Treasury for permission to possess firearms; this is done by applying to the Alcohol, Tobacco, and Firearms Bureau (ATF) of the U.S. Treasury Department. Note that no such relief is possible with the prohibition imposed by G.S. 14-415.1.

Related offenses not in this chapter

"Transporting, Possessing Weapon during Emergency" (Chapter 17)
Conveying weapon to convict (G.S. 14-258)
Furnishing weapon to inmate (G.S. 14-258.1)
Possession of dangerous weapon by prisoner (G.S. 14-258.2)
Weapons on state property and in courthouses (G.S. 14-269.4)
Purchase of firearm by person subject to domestic violence order prohibited (G.S. 14-269.8)
Selling or giving weapons to minors (G.S. 14-315)
Permitting child to use firearm (G.S. 14-316)
Purchasing weapon without permit (G.S. 14-402)
Possession of machine gun (G.S. 14-409)
Purchase of rifles and shotguns out of state (G.S. 14-409.10)

Carrying Concealed Weapon

Statute

§14-269. Carrying concealed weapons.

(a) It shall be unlawful for any person willfully and intentionally to carry concealed about his person any bowie knife, dirk, dagger, slung shot, loaded cane, metallic knuckles, razor, shurikin, stun gun, or other deadly weapon of like kind, except when the person is on the person's own premises.

(a1) It shall be unlawful for any person willfully and intentionally to carry concealed about his person any pistol or gun except in the following circumstances:

(1) The person is on the person's own premises.
(2) The deadly weapon is a handgun, and the person has a concealed handgun permit issued in accordance with Article 54B of this Chapter.

(b) This prohibition shall not apply to the following persons:

(1) Officers and enlisted personnel of the armed forces of the United States when in discharge of their official duties as such and acting under orders requiring them to carry arms and weapons;
(2) Civil officers of the United States while in the discharge of their official duties;
(3) Officers and soldiers of the militia and the national guard when called into actual service;
(4) Officers of the State, or of any county, city, or town, charged with the execution of the laws of the State, when acting in the discharge of their official duties;
(5) Sworn law-enforcement officers, when off-duty if:
   a. Written regulations authorizing the carrying of concealed weapons have been filed with the clerk of superior court in the county where the law-enforcement unit is located by the sheriff or chief of police or other superior officer in charge; and
   b. Such regulations specifically prohibit the carrying of concealed weapons while the officer is consuming or under the influence of alcoholic beverages.

(b1) It is a defense to a prosecution under this section that:

(1) The weapon was not a firearm;
(2) The defendant was engaged in, or on the way to or from, an activity in which he legitimately used the weapon;
(3) The defendant possessed the weapon for that legitimate use; and

(4) The defendant did not use or attempt to use the weapon for an illegal purpose.

The burden of proving this defense is on the defendant.

(c) Any person violating the provisions of subsection (a) of this section shall be guilty of a Class 2 misdemeanor. Any person violating the provisions of subsection (a1) of this section shall be guilty of a Class 2 misdemeanor for the first offense. A second or subsequent offense is punishable as a Class I felony.

(d) This section does not apply to an ordinary pocket knife carried in a closed position. As used in this section, 'ordinary pocket knife' means a small knife, designed for carrying in a pocket or purse, that has its cutting edge and point entirely enclosed by its handle, and that may not be opened by a throwing, explosive, or spring action.

Elements

A person guilty of this offense

(1) willfully and intentionally
(2) carries
(3) concealed about his or her person
(4) a bowie knife, dirk, dagger, slung shot, loaded cane, metallic knuckles, razor, shurikin, stun gun, pistol, gun, or other deadly weapon of like kind
(5) (a) while off his or her own premises, *or*
    (b) if the deadly weapon is a handgun, the person does not have a concealed handgun permit issued in accordance with G.S. Ch. 14, Art. 54B.

Punishment

Class 2 misdemeanor if the weapon is a deadly weapon other than a pistol or gun. If the improperly possessed weapon is a pistol or gun, a first offense is also a Class 2 misdemeanor; however, a second or subsequent offense is a Class I felony (the prior conviction must be alleged and proved under G.S. 15A-928).

Notes

Element (1). To constitute a violation of this statute the concealment must be willful and intentional. To convict, it is not necessary to show any intent to use the weapon (121 N.C. 556).

Element (3). The weapon must be concealed (116 N.C. 1049); if it is carried openly, the statute is not violated (125 N.C. 704). A weapon probably is not concealed if it is partly exposed to view (121 N.C. 556; but see 187 N.C. 477). Whether the weapon was concealed is a factual question for the jury (121 N.C. 556). The purpose of the statute is to reduce the likelihood that a concealed weapon will be used in a fit of anger (273 N.C. 620).

The concealment need not be *on* the person but may be "about" the person, in a position providing ready access (273 N.C. 620). Consider the following cases to define "about" the person. In one case, a defendant was properly convicted of this offense when a police officer found a gun under the driver's seat of a car driven by the defendant, after the defendant was seen to reach under the seat as though placing something there after an accident (75 N.C. App. 637). In comparison, evidence was found insufficient to support a conviction on this charge when a defendant was in the driver's seat of a car and a gun was found under the car's back seat (273 N.C. 620).

Element (4). Cases on "Assault with a Deadly Weapon" (Chapter 7) indicate that a weapon may be deadly either because of its character (e.g., a large knife) or because of the way it is used (e.g., a stick used by powerful man against a frail old woman). A butcher knife has been held to be a deadly weapon of the same kind as those specified in the statute (91 N.C. 545).

A "slung shot" is a flexible weapon loaded at one end, to be swung at another, such as a sock with a heavy paperweight in one end. A "shurikin" is a star-shaped martial arts throwing weapon. A "dirk" is a short, straight dagger.

This offense does not apply to an ordinary pocket knife carried in a closed position. An "ordinary pocket knife" is defined as a small knife, designed for carrying in a pocket or purse, which has its cutting edge and point entirely enclosed by its handle and which may not be opened by throwing, explosive, or spring action. "Small" has not been precisely defined by our appellate courts or legislature, but a pocket knife that was 4 1/2 inches in overall length was an "ordinary pocket knife" as defined by this statute (96 N.C. App. 375).

Element (5)(a). A private security guard is on his or her own premises and exempt from the statute when on premises he or she has been employed to watch (129 N.C. 521). A person is not on his or her own premises while in his or her car on a public highway (273 N.C. 620).

Element (5)(b). In its 1995 session the General Assembly passed laws permitting citizens to carry concealed handguns off their premises in some circumstances. The concealed handgun permit laws are described in G.S. Ch. 14, Art. 54B. A person carrying a concealed handgun by a lawful permit would not commit this offense.

If a person *has been issued a permit* for carrying a concealed handgun but carries the concealed handgun without possessing the permit, he or she is guilty of an infraction under G.S. 14-415.21. A second offense is a Class 2 misdemeanor.

Restrictions apply to a person carrying a concealed handgun with a permit [see G.S. 14-415.11(c)]. For example, "Possession of Weapons on School Grounds," "Carrying Gun into Assembly or Establishment Where Alcoholic Beverages Are Sold and Consumed," and "Weapons at Parades, etc. Prohibited," all discussed later in this chapter, prohibit a person with a handgun permit from carrying that weapon in certain places. Additionally, G.S. 14-269.4, which prohibits possession of deadly weapons on some state property and in courthouses, applies to such a person. Other federal and state laws may also restrict the rights of a person carrying a concealed weapon with a proper permit.

Exemptions from prohibition. Law enforcement and military personnel are exempt from the statute when performing their official duties (G.S. 14-269). "Law enforcement officers" includes those with the power of arrest. Private investigators are not exempt from the statute even if they have been sworn as deputies, unless they are discharging the official law enforcement duties of the sheriff.

The statute allows a law enforcement officer to carry a concealed weapon while off duty if the officer's department has a written regulation allowing officers to carry weapons off duty, the regulation has been filed with the clerk of superior court, and the officer is not drinking or under the influence of any alcoholic beverage. Effective December 1, 1995, the General Assembly repealed requirements that an officer be a full-time officer and be within his or her territorial jurisdiction while carrying a concealed weapon.

Disposition of weapons. Upon conviction of a person for this offense, any deadly weapon providing the basis of that conviction should be disposed of in accordance with G.S. 14-269.1.

Affirmative defense. Subsection (b1) of the statute provides that a defense to a prosecution for this offense is to show evidence that the weapon was not a firearm, that the defendant was engaged in or on the way to or from an activity involving a legitimate use of the weapon, that the defendant possessed the weapon for that legitimate use, and that the defendant did not use or attempt to use the weapon for an illegal purpose.

Related offenses not in this chapter

See the offenses listed under "Possession of Firearm by Felon."
Possession and sale of spring-loaded projectile knifes (G.S. 14-269.6)
Concealed handgun permit (G.S. Ch. 14, Art. 54B)

Possession of Handgun by Minor

Statute

§14-269.7. Prohibition on handguns for minors.

(a) Any minor who possesses or carries a handgun is guilty of a Class 2 misdemeanor.

(b) This section does not apply:

(1) To officers and enlisted personnel of the armed forces of the United States when in discharge of their official duties or acting under orders requiring them to carry handguns.

(2) To a minor who possesses a handgun for educational or recreational purposes while the minor is supervised by an adult who is present.

(3) To an emancipated minor who possesses such handgun inside his or her residence.

(4) To a minor who possesses a handgun while hunting or trapping outside the limits of an incorporated municipality if he has on his person written permission from a parent, guardian, or other person standing in loco parentis.

(c) The following definitions apply in this section:

(1) Handgun.—A firearm that has a short stock and is designed to be fired by the use of a single hand, or any combination of parts from which such a firearm can be assembled.

(2) Minor.—Any person under the age of 18 years of age.

Elements

A person guilty of this offense

(1) is a minor, *and*
(2) possesses or carries
(3) a handgun.

Punishment

Class 2 misdemeanor.

Notes

Element (1). The statute defines a minor as a person under the age of 18.

Element (3). The statute defines a handgun as a firearm with a short stock designed to be fired by the use of a single hand, or any combination of parts from which such a firearm can be assembled. Pistols and revolvers fit this definition, but it may also include weapons modified to be fired with a single hand. See Element (3) under "Possession of Firearm by Felon" for a definition of "firearm."

Exceptions. Subsection (b) of the statute provides a number of exceptions to this prohibition: a minor in the United States armed forces carrying out official duties; a minor possessing such a weapon for educational or recreation purposes while supervised by an adult; an emancipated minor possessing such a weapon inside his or her residence; and a minor hunting or trapping outside the limits of an incorporated municipality while in possession of written permission from a parent or guardian authorizing possession of the weapon.

Disposition of seized weapons. See the note on this topic under "Possession of Firearm by Felon."

Related offenses not in this chapter

See the offenses listed under "Possession of Firearm by Felon."
Selling or giving weapons to minors (G.S. 14-315)
Permitting child to use firearm (G.S. 14-316)

Possession of Weapons on School Grounds

Statute

§14-269.2 Weapons on campus or other educational property.

(a) The following definitions apply to this section:

(1) Educational property.—Any school building or bus, school campus, grounds, recreational area, athletic field, or other property owned, used, or operated by any board of education or school board of trustees, or directors for the administration of any school.

(1a) Employee.—A person employed by a local board of education or school whether the person is an adult or a minor.

(1b) School.—A public or private school, community college, college, or university.

(2) Student.—A person enrolled in a school or a person who has been suspended or expelled within the last five years from a school, whether the person is an adult or a minor.

(3) Switchblade knife.—A knife containing a blade that opens automatically by the release of a spring or a similar contrivance.

(4) Weapon.—Any device enumerated in subsection (b), (b1), or (d) of this section.

(b) It shall be a Class I felony for any person to possess or carry, whether openly or concealed, any gun, rifle, pistol, or other firearm of any kind on educational property or to a curricular or extracurricular activity sponsored by a school. However, this subsection does not apply to a BB gun, stun gun, air rifle, or air pistol.

(b1) It shall be a Class G felony for any person to possess or carry, whether openly or concealed, any dynamite cartridge, bomb, grenade, mine, or powerful explosive as defined in G.S. 14-284.1, on educational property or to a curricular or extracurricular activity sponsored by a school. This subsection shall not apply to fireworks.

(c) It shall be a Class I felony for any person to cause, encourage, or aid a minor who is less than 18 years old to possess or carry, whether openly or concealed, any gun, rifle, pistol, or other firearm of any kind on educational property. However, this subsection does not apply to a BB gun, stun gun, air rifle, or air pistol.

(c1) It shall be a Class G felony for any person to cause, encourage, or aid a minor who is less than 18 years old to possess or carry, whether openly or concealed, any dynamite cartridge, bomb, grenade, mine, or powerful explosive as defined in G.S. 14-284.1 on educational property. This subsection shall not apply to fireworks.

(d) It shall be a Class 1 misdemeanor for any person to possess or carry, whether openly or concealed, any BB gun, stun gun, air rifle, air pistol, bowie knife, dirk, dagger, slungshot, leaded cane, switchblade knife, blackjack, metallic knuckles, razors and razor blades (except solely for personal shaving), firework, or any sharp-pointed or edged instrument except instructional supplies, unaltered nail files and clips and tools used solely for preparation of food, instruction, and maintenance, on educational property.

(e) It shall be a Class 1 misdemeanor for any person to cause, encourage, or aid a minor who is less than 18 years old to possess or carry, whether openly or concealed, any BB gun, stun gun, air rifle, air pistol, bowie knife, dirk, dagger, slung shot, leaded cane, switchblade knife, blackjack, metallic knuckles, razors and razor blades (except solely for personal shaving), firework, or any sharp-pointed or edged instrument except instructional supplies, unaltered nail files and clips and tools used solely for preparation of food, instruction, and maintenance, on educational property.

(f) Notwithstanding subsection (b) of this section it shall be a Class 1 misdemeanor rather than a Class I felony for any person to possess or carry, whether openly or concealed, any gun, rifle, pistol, or other firearm of any kind, on educational property or to a curricular or extracurricular activity sponsored by a school if:

(1) The person is not a student attending school on the educational property or an employee employed by the school working on the educational property; and

(1a) The person is not a student attending a curricular or extracurricular activity sponsored by the school at which the student is enrolled or an employee attending a curricular or extracurricular activity sponsored by the school at which the employee is employed; and

(2) Repealed by Session Laws 1999-211, s. 1, effective December 1, 1999, and applicable to offenses committed on or after that date.

(3) The firearm is not loaded, is in a motor vehicle, and is in a locked container or a locked firearm rack.

(4) Repealed by Session Laws 1999-211, s. 1, effective December 1, 1999, and applicable to offenses committed on or after that date.

(g) This section shall not apply to:

(1) A weapon used solely for educational or school-sanctioned ceremonial purposes, or used in a school-approved program conducted under the supervision of an adult whose supervision has been approved by the school authority;

(1a) A person exempted by the provisions of G.S. 14-269(b);

(2) Firefighters, emergency service personnel, North Carolina Forest Service personnel, and any private police employed by an educational institution, when acting in the discharge of their official duties; or

(3) Home schools as defined in G.S. 115C-563(a).

(h) No person shall be guilty of a criminal violation of this section so long as both of the following apply:

(1) The person comes into possession of a weapon by taking or receiving the weapon from another person or by finding the weapon.

(2) The person delivers the weapon, directly or indirectly, as soon as practical to law enforcement authorities.

I.
Possession of Firearms

Statute

See G.S. 14-269.2(b), reproduced above.

Elements

A person guilty of this offense

(1) possesses or carries

(2) a gun, rifle, pistol, or other firearm of any kind

(3) (a) on educational property, *or*

(b) to a curricular or extracurricular activity sponsored by a school.

Punishment

Class I felony. However, it is a Class 1 misdemeanor under certain conditions (see the note below).

Notes

Element (1). This offense is committed whether or not the weapon was concealed.

Element (2). A gun need not be operable to satisfy this element (120 N.C. App. 274). The statute specifically provides that this offense does not include a BB gun, stun gun, air rifle, or air pistol. These weapons are included in "II. Possession of Weapons Other than Firearms and Explosives," discussed below.

Element (3)(a). Educational property is defined in G.S. 14-269.2(a)(1) to include a school building or bus, school campus, grounds, recreational area, athletic field, or other property owned, used, or operated by any board of education or school board of trustees, or directors for the administration of any school. A school is defined in G.S. 14-269.2(a)(1b) as a public or private school, community college, college, or university.

Element (3)(b). This element could be satisfied by evidence, for example, that a person took a gun to a school-sponsored prom that was held at a hotel.

Aiding minor to commit offense. Subsection (c) of this statute makes it a Class I felony for a person to cause, encourage, or aid a minor less than 18 years old to commit this offense on educational property.

Offense is Class 1 misdemeanor under certain conditions. Subsection (f) of this statute makes it a Class 1 misdemeanor instead of a Class I felony if (1) the person is not a student attending school on the educational property or an employee employed by the school working on the educational property; (2) the person is not a student attending a curricular or extracurricular activity sponsored by the school at which the student is enrolled or an employee attending a curricular or extracurricular activity sponsored by the school at which the employee is employed; and (3) the firearm is not loaded, is in a motor vehicle, and is in a locked container or a locked firearm rack. A student is defined in G.S. 14-269.2(a)(2), reproduced above.

Exemptions. Subsection (g) of this statute provides that this offense does not apply to (1) a weapon used solely for educational or school-sanctioned ceremonial purposes, or used in a school-approved program conducted under the supervision of an adult whose supervision has been approved by the school authority; (2) a person exempted by the provisions of G.S. 14-269(b) (see "Carrying Concealed Weapon," earlier in this chapter); (3) firefighters, emergency service personnel, North Carolina Forest Service personnel, and any private police employed by an educational institution, when acting in the discharge of their official duties; and (4) home schools as defined in G.S. 115C-563(a). Subsection (h) of this statute provides that this offense is not committed if the person comes into possession of a weapon by taking or receiving the weapon from another person or by finding the weapon and the person delivers the weapon, directly or indirectly, as soon as practical to law enforcement authorities.

Disposition of seized weapons. See the note on this topic under "Possession of Firearm by Felon."

Related offenses not in this chapter

See the offenses listed under "Possession of Firearm by Felon" and "Possession of Handgun by Minor."

II.
Possession of Weapons Other than Firearms and Explosives

Statute

See G.S. 14-269.2(d), reproduced above.

Elements

A person guilty of this offense
(1) possesses or carries
(2) a BB gun, stun gun, air rifle, air pistol, bowie knife, dirk, dagger, slung shot, leaded cane, switchblade knife, blackjack, metallic knuckles, razors and razor blades (except solely for personal shaving), firework, or any sharp-pointed or edged instrument except instructional supplies, unaltered nail files and clips and tools used solely for preparation of food, instruction, and maintenance,
(3) on educational property.

Punishment

Class 1 misdemeanor.

Notes

Element (1). See the note on Element (1) in I., above.

Element (2). There was sufficient evidence to prove a student's constructive possession of a pellet gun when it was found in his book bag (136 N.C. App. 648). A switchblade knife is defined in G.S. 14-269.2(a)(3) as a knife containing a blade that opens automatically by the release of a spring or a similar contrivance.

There are several aspects of the weapons prohibited in this statutory subsection that suggest that the legislature did not intend pocket knives to be included. The statute describes several specific knives—bowie knife, dirk, dagger, switchblade knife—but does not include pocket knives. Although the catchall phrase "any sharp-pointed or edged instrument" may include other types of knives that are not specifically named, it would not arguably include an ordinary pocket knife whose cutting edge (or edges) is fully enclosed in its handle, because such a pocket knife, in its enclosed position, is not a "sharp-pointed or edged instrument." When considering the wording of this statute and the common knowledge of legislators that pocket knives are possessed by many school employees, parents, and others who are on educational property daily, the most reasonable interpretation is that this offense does not apply to a pocket knife in its closed position. (Although 32 N.C. App. 492 involved a pocket knife at a school, the issue of whether it constituted an offense was not decided in the case.)

The fact that the legislature in 1985 (Ch. 432 of the Session Laws of 1985) enacted a specific exemption for pocket knives in the concealed weapon statute (G.S. 14-269) and did not also amend the weapon-on-educational-property statute does not necessarily support an argument that pocket knives are prohibited by the latter statute. The legislature may have responded to what it considered improper interpretations of the law (that is, people were wrongly being charged with carrying a concealed weapon when possessing pocket knives) and wanted to make clear that pocket knives were not included within the statute. In fact, the title of the 1985 law was "AN ACT TO *CLARIFY* THE LAW AGAINST CARRYING CONCEALED WEAPONS" (*emphasis added*). Reasons for a legislative amendment to one statute, absent legislative history or other concrete information, are too varied to place much weight when interpreting other statutes.

Element (3). See the note on Element (3)(a) in I., above.

Aiding minor to commit offense. Subsection (e) of this statute makes it a Class 1 misdemeanor for a person to cause, encourage, or aid a minor less than 18 years old to commit this offense on educational property.

Exemptions. See the note in I., above.

Disposition of seized weapons. See the note in I., above.

Related offenses not in this chapter

None.

III. Possession of Explosives

Statute

See G.S. 14-269.2(b1), reproduced above.

Elements

A person guilty of this offense
- (1) possesses or carries
- (2) a dynamite cartridge, bomb, grenade, mine, or powerful explosive as defined in G.S. 14-284.1
- (3) (a) on educational property, *or*
  - (b) to a curricular or extracurricular activity sponsored by a school.

Punishment

Class G felony.

Notes

Element (1). See the note on Element (1) in I., above.

Elements (3)(a) and (3)(b). See the notes on Elements (3a) and (3)(b) in I., above.

Aiding minor to commit offense. Subsection (c1) of this statute makes it a Class G felony for a person to cause, encourage, or aid a minor less than 18 years old to commit this offense on educational property.

Exemptions. See the note in I., above.

Disposition of seized weapons. See the note in I., above.

Fireworks inapplicable to this offense. G.S. 14-269.2(b1) specifically excludes fireworks from its coverage. Possessing or carrying fireworks is, however, a Class 1 misdemeanor under G.S. 14-269.2(d)—see II., above.

Related offenses not in this chapter

None.

Storing Firearm in a Manner Accessible to a Minor

Statute

§14-315.1 Storage of firearms to protect minors.

(a) Any person who resides in the same premises as a minor, owns or possesses a firearm, and stores or leaves the firearm (i) in a condition that the firearm can be discharged and (ii) in a manner that the person knew or should have known that an unsupervised minor would be able to gain access to the firearm, is guilty of a Class 1 misdemeanor if a minor gains access to the firearm without the lawful permission of the minor's parents or a person having charge of the minor and the minor:

(1) Possesses it in violation of G.S. 14-269.2(b);
(2) Exhibits it in a public place in a careless, angry, or threatening manner;
(3) Causes personal injury or death with it not in self defense; or
(4) Uses it in the commission of a crime.

(b) Nothing in this section shall prohibit a person from carrying a firearm on his or her body, or placed in such close proximity that it can be used as easily and quickly as if carried on the body.

(c) This section shall not apply if the minor obtained the firearm as a result of an unlawful entry by any person.

(d) "Minor" as used in this section means a person under 18 years of age who is not emancipated.

Elements

A person guilty of this offense

(1) (a) resides in the same premises as a minor
(b) owns or possesses a firearm, *and*
(c) stores or leaves the firearm
(i) in a condition that the firearm can be discharged, *and*
(ii) in a manner that the person knew or should have known that an unsupervised minor would be able to gain access to the firearm, *and*

(2) a minor gains access to the firearm without lawful permission of the minor's parents or person having charge of the minor, *and*

(3) the minor
(a) illegally possesses the firearm on school grounds in violation of G.S. 14-269.2(b), *or*
(b) exhibits the firearm in a public place in a careless, angry, or threatening manner, *or*
(c) causes personal injury or death with the firearm not in self-defense, *or*
(d) uses it in the commission of a crime.

Punishment

Class 1 misdemeanor.

Notes

Generally. A minor is defined by the statute as a person under 18 years of age who has not been emancipated.

Element (3). A number of activities by the minor can satisfy this element, including commission of the offense "Possession of Weapon on School Grounds." It is not necessary that the minor commit another criminal offense in order to satisfy this element. For example, carelessly exhibiting a weapon in public can satisfy this element, even if such activity does not result in a criminal charge against the minor.

Exception. This statute does not apply if a minor obtains a firearm as a result of an unlawful entry by any person. So, for example, if an adult has improperly stored a firearm and a minor obtains the firearm by breaking into the adult's home and then commits one of the acts listed in Element (3), the adult may not be charged with this offense. Also, if that minor obtains the firearm from another person who broke in and stole the weapon, the adult could not be charged with this offense.

Firearm storage notification mandated. G.S. 14-315.2 requires retailers and transferors of firearms to deliver a written copy of G.S. 14-315.1 to any purchaser or recipient of a firearm. Also, it requires that retail or wholesale merchants selling firearms must post the following warning sign: "It Is Unlawful to Store or Leave a Firearm That Can Be Discharged in a Manner That a Reasonable Person Should Know Is Accessible to a Minor." Failure to follow either of these warning requirements is a Class 1 misdemeanor.

Disposition of seized weapons. See the note on this topic under "Possession of Firearm by Felon."

Related offenses not in this chapter

See the offenses listed under "Possession of Firearm by Felon" and "Possession of Handgun by Minor."

Carrying Gun into Assembly or Establishment Where Alcoholic Beverages Are Sold and Consumed

Statute

§14-269.3. Carrying weapons into assemblies and establishments where alcoholic beverages are sold and consumed.

(a) It shall be unlawful for any person to carry any gun, rifle, or pistol into any assembly where a fee has been charged for admission thereto, or into any establishment in which alcoholic beverages are sold and consumed. Any person violating the provisions of this section shall be guilty of a Class 1 misdemeanor.

(b) This section shall not apply to the following:

(1) A person exempted from the provisions of G.S. 14-269;
(2) The owner or lessee of the premises or business establishment;
(3) A person participating in the event, if he is carrying a gun, rifle, or pistol with the permission of the owner, lessee, or person or organization sponsoring the event; and
(4) A person registered or hired as a security guard by the owner, lessee, or person or organization sponsoring the event.

Elements

A person guilty of this offense

(1) carries into
(2) (a) any assembly where an admission fee has been charged, *or*

(b) any establishment in which alcoholic beverages are sold and consumed

(3) a gun, rifle, or pistol.

Punishment

Class 1 misdemeanor.

Notes

Element (1). The statute apparently does not cover the person who simply has possession of a gun, rifle, or pistol in one of the named establishments; there must be proof by direct or circumstantial evidence that the person *carried* the weapon into the place.

Element (2)(a). Examples of such assemblies are athletic events with admission fees, stock car races, concerts, movie theaters, dances, and fairs.

Element (2)(b). "Alcoholic beverage" includes any beverage with at least 1/2 of 1 percent alcohol [G.S. 18B-101(4)]. Thus beer and wine are covered. Note that the establishment must be licensed for both the sale *and* consumption of alcoholic beverages. Therefore neither a store with only an off-premises beer permit nor an ABC store would be covered by the statute. A restaurant with a brown-bagging permit (which authorizes only consumption, not sale) would be covered only if it also had a permit allowing the sale of some kind of alcoholic beverage, such as beer or wine. It is not clear whether the statute is limited to establishments that are *legally* permitted to sell alcoholic beverages for consumption on their premises.

Persons exempted. Exempted from the statute are law enforcement officers, the lawful possessor of the premises, participants in some event for which the gun will be used, and security guards.

Relationship to other offenses. Although this statute concerns only guns, rifles, and pistols, in some situations the same conduct that gives rise to this charge would justify a charge of "Carrying Concealed Weapon" or "Possession of Weapon on School Grounds," both covered earlier in this chapter.

Related offenses not in this chapter

See the offenses listed under "Possession of Firearm by Felon," covered earlier in this chapter.

Weapons at Parades, etc., Prohibited

Statute

§14-277.2. Weapons at parades, etc., prohibited.

(a) It shall be unlawful for any person participating in, affiliated with, or present as a spectator at any parade, funeral procession, picket line, or demonstration upon any private health care facility or upon any public place owned or under the control of the State or any of its political subdivisions to willfully or intentionally possess or have immediate access to any dangerous weapon. Violation of this subsection shall be a Class 1 misdemeanor. It shall be presumed that any rifle or gun carried on a rack in a pickup truck at a holiday parade or in a funeral procession does not violate the terms of this act.

(b) For the purposes of this section the term "dangerous weapon" shall include those weapons specified by G.S. 14-269, 14-269.2, 14-284.1, or 14-288.8 or any other object capable of inflicting serious bodily injury or death when used as a weapon.

(c) The provisions of this section shall not apply to a person exempted by the provisions of G.S. 14-269(b) or to persons authorized by State or federal law to carry dangerous weapons in the performance of their duties or to any person who obtains a permit to carry a dangerous weapon at a parade, funeral procession, picket line, or demonstration from the sheriff or police chief, whichever is appropriate, of the locality where such parade, funeral procession, picket line, or demonstration is to take place.

Elements

A person guilty of this offense
- (1) willfully or intentionally
- (2) possesses or has immediate access to
- (3) any dangerous weapon
- (4) while participating in, affiliated with, or present as a spectator at any
  - (a) parade, *or*
  - (b) funeral procession, *or*
  - (c) picket line, *or*
  - (d) demonstration at any private health care facility, *or*
  - (e) demonstration in a public place owned or controlled by the state or a local government.

Punishment

Class 1 misdemeanor.

Notes

Element (3). The statute defines "dangerous weapon" to include weapons specified by G.S. 14-269, -269.2, -284.1, and -288.8 and any other object capable of causing serious bodily injury or death when used as a weapon. A "dangerous weapon" is the same as a "deadly weapon" (78 N.C. App. 405). For a more complete discussion of what constitutes a deadly weapon see the note on Element (2) under "Assault with a Deadly Weapon" in Chapter 7.

Element (4)(d). A "health care facility" is any hospital, clinic, or other facility licensed to administer medical treatment, or the primary function of which is to provide medical treatment in this state [G.S. 14-277.4(f)].

Exceptions. The statute does not apply to a person (1) exempted under G.S. 14-269(b) (see "Carrying Concealed Weapon," covered earlier in this chapter), (2) authorized by state or federal law to carry a dangerous weapon in performing his or her duties, or (3) who obtains a permit to carry a dangerous weapon during the event from the sheriff or police chief of the jurisdiction in which the event will occur. The statute also does not apply to a rifle or gun carried in a gun rack in a pickup truck at a holiday parade or in a funeral procession; the language "shall be presumed" in G.S. 14-277.2(b) appears to be a mandatory presumption that may not be rebutted.

Disposition of seized weapons. See the note on this topic under "Possession of Firearm by Felon."

Related offenses not in this chapter

See the offenses listed under "Possession of Firearm by Felon."

Manufacture, Possession, etc., of Machine Gun, Sawed-Off Shotgun, or Weapon of Mass Destruction

Statute

§14-288.8. Manufacture, assembly, possession, storage, transportation, sale, purchase, delivery, or acquisition of weapon of mass death and destruction; exceptions.

(a) Except as otherwise provided in this section, it is unlawful for any person to manufacture, assemble, possess, store, transport, sell, offer to sell, purchase, offer to purchase, deliver or give to another, or acquire any weapon of mass death and destruction.

(b) This section does not apply to:

(1) Persons exempted from the provisions of G.S. 14-269 with respect to any activities lawfully engaged in while carrying out their duties.

(2) Importers, manufacturers, dealers, and collectors of firearms, ammunition, or destructive devices validly licensed under the laws of the United States or the State of North Carolina, while lawfully engaged in activities authorized under their licenses.

(3) Persons under contract with the United States, the State of North Carolina, or any agency of either government, with respect to any activities lawfully engaged in under their contracts.

(4) Inventors, designers, ordnance consultants and researchers, chemists, physicists, and other persons lawfully engaged in pursuits designed to enlarge knowledge or to facilitate the creation, development, or manufacture of weapons of mass death and destruction intended for use in a manner consistent with the laws of the United States and the State of North Carolina.

(c) The term "weapon of mass death and destruction" includes:

(1) Any explosive, incendiary, poison gas or radioactive material:

a. Bomb; or

b. Grenade; or

c. Rocket having a propellant charge of more than four ounces; or

d. Missile having an explosive or incendiary charge of more than one-quarter ounce; or

e. Mine; or

f. Device similar to any of the devices described above; or

(2) Any type of weapon (other than a shotgun or a shotgun shell of a type particularly suitable for sporting purposes) which will, or which may be readily converted to, expel a projectile by the action of an explosive or other propellant, and which has any barrel with a bore of more than one-half inch in diameter; or

(3) Any firearm capable of fully automatic fire, any shotgun with a barrel or barrels of less than 18 inches in length or an overall length of less than 26 inches, any rifle with a barrel or barrels of less than 16 inches in length or an overall length of less than 26 inches, any muffler or silencer for any firearm, whether or not such firearm is included within this definition. For the purposes of this section, rifle is defined as a weapon designed or redesigned, made or remade, and intended to be fired from the shoulder.

(4) Any combination of parts either designed or intended for use in converting any device into any weapon described above and from which a weapon of mass death and destruction may readily be assembled;

(5) Radioactive material, which means any solid, liquid or gas which emits or may emit ionizing radiation spontaneously or which becomes capable of producing radiation or nuclear particles when controls or triggering mechanisms of any associated device are operable.

The term "weapon of mass death and destruction" does not include any device which is neither designed nor redesigned for use as a weapon; any device, although originally designed for use as a weapon, which is redesigned for use as a signaling, pyrotechnic, line-throwing, safety, or similar device; surplus ordnance sold, loaned, or given by the Secretary of the Army pursuant to the provisions of section 4684(2), 4685, or 4686 of Title 10 of the United States Code; or any other device which the Secretary of the Treasury finds is not likely to be used as a weapon, is an antique, or is a rifle which the owner intends to use solely for sporting purposes, in accordance with Chapter 44 of Title 18 of the United States Code.

(d) Any person who violates any provision of this section is guilty of a Class F felony.

Elements

A person guilty of this offense

(1) manufactures or assembles or possesses or stores or transports or sells or offers to sell or purchases or offers to purchase or delivers or gives to another or acquires

(2) (a) any explosive, incendiary, poison gas, or radioactive material: bomb, grenade, rocket with propellant of more than 4 ounces, missile with a charge of more than 1/4 ounce, mine, or similar device, *or*

(b) a weapon that expels a projectile by action of an explosive and has a barrel with a bore of more than 1/2 inch in diameter, *or*

(c) any firearm capable of fully automatic fire, *or*

(d) any shotgun with a barrel length of less than 18 inches or an overall length of less than 26 inches, *or*

(e) any rifle with a barrel length of less than 16 inches or an overall length of less than 26 inches, *or*

(f) any muffler or silencer for any firearm, whether or not such firearm is a weapon of mass death and destruction, *or*

(g) parts from which one of these weapons could be assembled, *or*

(h) radioactive material.

Punishment

Class F felony.

Notes

Generally. Although this offense is included in the Riot and Civil Disorder Act, it also applies when no riot or state of emergency exists.

Element (1). For this offense, it is not necessary that the weapon be concealed or that the defendant be off his or her own premises in possession of the weapon.

Element (2). The state is not required to prove that the weapon is operable or may readily be made operable. However, a defendant may, as an affirmative defense, assert that a weapon is inoperable. Such evidence may disprove that a particular weapon is a weapon of mass destruction (95 N.C. App. 140). Also, the last part of subsection (c) of the statute exempts specific weapons from this statute's coverage.

Persons exempted. Subsection (b) of the statute specifically exempts from its coverage law enforcement and military officers performing their official duties, licensed dealers and collectors, government contractors, and inventors, designers, and researchers.

Disposition of seized weapons. See the note on this topic under "Possession of Firearm by Felon."

Federal assault weapons ban. The Public Safety and Recreational Firearms Use Protection Act [Pub. L. 103-322, §§ 110101–110106 (1994)], passed by the United States Congress in 1994, modifies 18 U.S.C. §§ 921 and 922 to prohibit the manufacture, transfer, or possession of semiautomatic assault weapons not lawfully possessed under federal law on September 13, 1994 (when the law was enacted). The ban covers nineteen military-style assault weapons, assault weapons with specific combat features, and "copy-cat" models. The act specifically exempts over 600 firearm models used for hunting and sporting purposes. The act also prohibits the transfer or possession of large capacity ammunition feeding devices not lawfully possessed on the date of its enactment. Such devices are defined to include a magazine, feed strip, or similar device that can accept more than 10 rounds of ammunition or be readily restored or converted to accept more than 10 rounds. This ban on both semiautomatic assault weapons and large capacity ammunition feeding devices is subject to a sunset provision that will cause its repeal in 10 years. In addition, semiautomatic assault weapons and large capacity ammunition feeding devices lawfully possessed on the date of the Act's enactment may be lawfully transferred to another person.

Related offenses not in this chapter

See the offenses listed under "Possession of Firearm by Felon" in this chapter.

20
Prostitution and Loitering for Prostitution

Chapter Contents

20 Prostitution and Loitering for Prostitution

Prostitution and Assignation

Statute

§14-203. Definition of terms.

The term "prostitution" shall be construed to include the offering or receiving of the body for sexual intercourse for hire, and shall also be construed to include the offering or receiving of the body for indiscriminate sexual intercourse without hire. The term "assignation" shall be construed to include the making of any appointment or engagement for prostitution or any act in furtherance of such appointment or engagement.

§14-204. Prostitution and various acts abetting prostitution unlawful.

It shall be unlawful:

(1) To keep, set up, maintain, or operate any place, structure, building or conveyance for the purpose of prostitution or assignation.

(2) To occupy any place, structure, building, or conveyance for the purpose of prostitution or assignation; or for any person to permit any place, structure, building or conveyance owned by him or under his control to be used for the purpose of prostitution or assignation, with knowledge or reasonable cause to know that the same is, or is to be, used for such purpose.

(3) To receive, or to offer or agree to receive any person into any place, structure, building, or conveyance for the purpose of prostitution or assignation, or to permit any person to remain there for such purpose.

(4) To direct, take, or transport, or to offer or agree to take or transport, any person to any place, structure, or building or to any other person, with knowledge or reasonable cause to know that the purpose of such directing, taking, or transporting is prostitution or assignation.

(5) To procure, or to solicit, or to offer to procure or solicit for the purpose of prostitution or assignation.

(6) To reside in, enter, or remain in any place, structure, or building, or to enter or remain in any conveyance, for the purpose of prostitution or assignation.

(7) To engage in prostitution or assignation, or to aid or abet prostitution or assignation by any means whatsoever.

Elements

A person guilty of this offense
(1) (a) engages in prostitution, *or*
(b) engages in assignation.

Punishment

Class 1 misdemeanor.

Notes

Generally. Under the definitions of "prostitution" and "assignation" in G.S. 14-203 a person of either sex and either the "seller" or the "buyer" can be guilty of engaging in prostitution or assignation.

Element (1). G.S. 14-203 defines "prostitution" as "the offering or receiving of the body for sexual intercourse for hire . . . or for indiscriminate sexual intercourse without hire." Prostitution does not include masturbation, sodomy, fellatio, or cunnilingus for hire (307 N.C. 692), although those acts could be charged as "Crime against Nature" (Chapter 9). G.S. 14-203 defines "assignation" to include "the making of an appointment or engagement for prostitution or any act in furtherance of such appointment or engagement."

Evidence of purpose. For an example of circumstantial evidence establishing the purpose of prostitution, see 220 N.C. 712.

"Pyramiding" punishment invalid. Where a person is convicted of several violations of G.S. 14-204 that arise out of the same transaction (for example, occupying a place for prostitution, agreeing to receive a person in a place for prostitution, and entering a place for prostitution), consecutive sentences may not be imposed; although the multiple convictions do not amount to unconstitutional double jeopardy, consecutive sentences are contrary to legislative intent (26 N.C. App. 14).

Related offenses not in this chapter

"Crime against Nature" (Chapter 9)
"Fornication and Adultery" (Chapter 9)
Occupying room for immoral purposes (G.S. 14-186)
Keeping bawdy house (G.S. 14-188)
Occupying a place for prostitution [G.S. 14-204(2)]
Receiving person on premises for prostitution [G.S. 14-204(3)]
Arranging transportation for prostitution [G.S. 14-204(4)]
Entering place for prostitution [G.S. 14-204(6)]
Aiding or abetting prostitution [G.S. 14-204(7)]

Procuring for Prostitution

Statute

See subsection (5) of G.S. 14-204, reproduced under "Prostitution and Assignation."

Elements

A person guilty of this offense
(1) procures or solicits or offers to procure or solicit
(2) for the purpose of prostitution or assignation.

Punishment

Class 1 misdemeanor.

Notes

Generally. See the notes under "Prostitution and Assignation."

Element (1). It is not necessary that particular words be spoken for solicitation to take place. The fact of solicitation is proved by the circumstances, giving everyday meanings to the words used by the parties (59 N.C. App. 727).

Related offenses not in this chapter

See the offenses listed under "Prostitution and Assignation" in this chapter.

Maintaining a Place of Prostitution

Statute

See subsection (1) of G.S. 14-204, reproduced under "Prostitution and Assignation."

Elements

A person guilty of this offense
(1) keeps, sets up, maintains, or operates
(2) any place, structure, building, or conveyance
(3) for the purpose of prostitution or assignation.

Punishment

Class 1 misdemeanor.

Notes

Generally. See the notes under "Prostitution and Assignation."

Related offenses not in this chapter

See the offenses listed under "Prostitution and Assignation" in this chapter.

Permitting Use of Place for Prostitution

Statute

See subsection (2) of G.S. 14-204, reproduced under "Prostitution and Assignation."

Elements

A person guilty of this offense
(1) permits use of a place under his or her control
(2) for the purpose of prostitution or assignation
(3) with knowledge, or reasonable cause to know, of that use.

Punishment

Class 1 misdemeanor.

Notes

Generally. See the notes under "Prostitution and Assignation."

Element (1). This element is satisfied if the defendant merely allows the use of a place when the defendant could have disallowed it, even if he or she makes no money from the operation or does not otherwise participate (223 N.C. 208).

Element (3). This offense has occurred only if the defendant knew of the use or if circumstances were such that the defendant should have known of it. This element may be proved by showing facts about the use without showing the defendant's actual knowledge (175 N.C. 791; 223 N.C. 208).

Related offenses not in this chapter

See the related offenses listed under "Prostitution and Assignation."

Loitering for Prostitution

Statute

§14-204.1. Loitering for the purpose of engaging in prostitution offense.

(a) For the purposes of this section, "public place" means any street, sidewalk, bridge, alley or alleyway, plaza, park, driveway, parking lot or transportation facility, or the doorways and entrance ways to any building which fronts on any of those places, or a motor vehicle in or on any of those places.

(b) If a person remains or wanders about in a public place and
- (1) Repeatedly beckons to, stops, or attempts to stop passers-by, or repeatedly attempts to engage passers-by in conversation; or
- (2) Repeatedly stops or attempts to stop motor vehicles; or
- (3) Repeatedly interferes with the free passage of other persons for the purpose of violating any subdivision of G.S. 14-204 or 14-177, that person is guilty of a Class 1 misdemeanor.

Elements

A person guilty of this offense
- (1) (a) repeatedly beckons to, stops, or attempts to stop passers-by or engage them in conversation, *or*
  - (b) repeatedly stops or attempts to stop motor vehicles, *or*
  - (c) repeatedly interferes with the free passage of other persons
- (2) in a public place
- (3) for the purpose of prostitution, assignation, or crime against nature.

Punishment

Class 1 misdemeanor.

Notes

Element (2). "Public place" is defined in subsection (a) of the statute.

Constitutionality. This statute is not unconstitutionally vague (73 N.C. App. 214).

Related offenses not in this chapter

See the offenses listed under "Prostitution and Assignation."

Promoting Prostitution of a Minor

Statute

§14-190.13. Definitions for certain offenses concerning minors.

The following definitions apply to G.S. 14-190.14, displaying material harmful to minors; G.S. 14-190.15, disseminating or exhibiting to minors harmful material or performances; G.S. 14-190.16, first degree sexual exploitation of a minor; G.S. 14-190.17, second degree sexual exploitation of a minor; G.S. 14-190.17A, third degree sexual exploitation of a minor; G.S. 14-190.18, promoting prostitution of a minor; and G.S. 14-190.19, participating in prostitution of a minor.

(1) Harmful to Minors.—That quality of any material or performance that depicts sexually explicit nudity or sexual activity and that, taken as a whole, has the following characteristics:
  a. The average adult person applying contemporary community standards would find that the material or performance has a predominant tendency to appeal to a prurient interest of minors in sex; and
  b. The average adult person applying contemporary community standards would find that the depiction of sexually explicit nudity or sexual activity in the material or performance is patently offensive to prevailing standards in the adult community concerning what is suitable for minors; and
  c. The material or performance lacks serious literary, artistic, political, or scientific value for minors.

(2) Material.—Pictures, drawings, video recordings, films or other visual depictions or representations but not material consisting entirely of written words.

(3) Minor.—An individual who is less than 18 years old and is not married or judicially emancipated.

(4) Prostitution.—Engaging or offering to engage in sexual activity with or for another in exchange for anything of value.

(5) Sexual Activity.—Any of the following acts:
  a. Masturbation, whether done alone or with another human or an animal.
  b. Vaginal, anal, or oral intercourse, whether done with another human or with an animal.
  c. Touching, in an act of apparent sexual stimulation or sexual abuse, of the clothed or unclothed genitals, pubic area, or buttocks of another person or the clothed or unclothed breasts of a human female.
  d. An act or condition that depicts torture, physical restraint by being fettered or bound, or flagellation of or by a person clad in undergarments or in revealing or bizarre costume.
  e. Excretory functions; provided, however, that this sub-division shall not apply to G.S. 14-190.17A.
  f. The insertion of any part of a person's body, other than the male sexual organ, or of any object into another person's anus or vagina, except when done as part of a recognized medical procedure.

(6) Sexually Explicit Nudity.—The showing of:
  a. Uncovered, or less than opaquely covered, human genitals, pubic area, or buttocks, or the nipple or any portion of the areola of the human female breast, except as provided in G.S. 14-190.9(b); or
  b. Covered human male genitals in a discernibly turgid state.

§14-190.18. Promoting prostitution of a minor.

(a) Offense.—A person commits the offense of promoting prostitution of a minor if he knowingly:

(1) Entices, forces, encourages, or otherwise facilitates a minor to participate in prostitution; or

(2) Supervises, supports, advises, or protects the prostitution of or by a minor.

(b) Mistake of Age.—Mistake of age is not a defense to a prosecution under this section.

(c) Punishment and Sentencing.—Violation of this section is a Class D felony.

Elements

I. Facilitating Minor's Prostitution—G.S. 14-190.18(a)(1)

A person guilty of this offense

(1) knowingly
(2) entices or forces or encourages or otherwise facilitates
(3) a minor
(4) to participate in prostitution.

II. Protecting Minor's Prostitution—G.S. 14-190.18(a)(2)

A person guilty of this offense

(1) knowingly
(2) supervises or supports or advises or protects
(3) the prostitution
(4) of a minor or by a minor.

Punishment

Class D felony.

Notes

Elements I.(1) and II.(1). "Knowingly" applies to knowledge of the prostitution activity that the defendant's action is promoting. As will be seen below, the state need not prove that the defendant knew of the prostitute's age.

Subdivisions overlap. The differences between the offenses in the two subdivisions of this statute are not self-evident. Subdivision (1) (set out in I. above) may be aimed more at the pimp or other person who directly deals with the prostitute; and subdivision (2) (set out in II. above) may be aimed more at the organizer of the prostitution business who mainly deals indirectly with the prostitute and whose activities of support and protection are given to persons in the network rather than to the prostitute personally. This may also explain the choice of prepositions in Element (4) of the protection offense. The prostitution "of" a minor could refer to the minor's status as a prostitute rather than to specific acts of prostitution; the phrase "prostitution by a minor" would cover the latter situation. The distinctions are not clear-cut and the subdivisions do overlap. Most conceivable offenses of promoting prostitution of a minor could be charged under either subdivision. A person may be guilty of this offense even if the minor does not actually commit an act of prostitution; the mere attempt to corrupt a minor by knowingly promoting such prostitution satisfies the elements of the offense (87 N.C. App. 499).

Broad definition of "prostitution." Perhaps the most important thing about this section is the extremely broad definition of "prostitution" set out in G.S. 14-190.13(4) to mean "engaging or offering to engage in sexual activity with or for another in exchange for anything of value." Several points should be made:

(1) The broad definition of "sexual activity" in G.S. 14-190.13(5) means that prostitution of a minor will cover many more acts than the sexual intercourse that is the basis for "Prostitution and Assignation."

(2) Sexual activity for another is also included in this definition. Thus a voyeur who pays a minor to masturbate or commit some other act under the broad definition of "sexual activity" would be participating in prostitution. Anyone who facilitates this arrangement could be prosecuted under this section.

(3) Sexual activity performed—or an agreement to perform it—in exchange for anything of value constitutes prostitution under this definition. A person who agrees to give a minor a marijuana cigarette in exchange for sexual favors short of intercourse is undoubtedly covered as participating in prostitution, and anyone who facilitates this arrangement can be prosecuted under this section.

Elements I.(3) and II.(4). Under G.S. 14-190.13, a minor is a person less than 18 years old who is not married or judicially emancipated.

Element I.(4). In interpreting this element, use the dictionary definition of "participate." G.S. 14-190.19 (reproduced below) includes this word in its caption, "Participating in prostitution of a minor," but there the word is not used in defining the elements of the offense. Moreover, that offense is aimed exclusively at customers of the minor prostitute, whereas the word in this subdivision appears to refer to the minor's participation in prostitution.

Mistake of age no defense. Subsection (b) provides that mistake as to the age of an involved minor is not a defense to a prosecution under this section.

Comparison with other prostitution offenses. Note that while other offenses in this chapter are punishable as misdemeanors, "Promoting Prostitution of a Minor" and "Participating in Prostitution of a Minor" are punished as felonies.

Related offenses not in this chapter

See the offenses listed under "Prostitution and Assignation."
"Indecent Liberties with a Child" (Chapter 8)
"Failure to Register as Sex Offender" (Chapter 8)

Participating in Prostitution of a Minor

Statute

See G.S. 14-190.13, reproduced under "Promoting Prostitution of a Minor."

§14-190.19. Participating in prostitution of a minor.

(a) Offense.—A person commits the offense of participating in the prostitution of a minor if he is not a minor and he patronizes a minor prostitute. As used in this section, "patronizing a minor prostitute" means:

(1) Soliciting or requesting a minor to participate in prostitution;
(2) Paying or agreeing to pay a minor, either directly or through the minor's agent, to participate in prostitution; or

(3) Paying a minor, or the minor's agent, for having participated in prostitution, pursuant to a prior agreement.

(b) Mistake of Age.—Mistake of age is not a defense to a prosecution under this section.

(c) Punishment and Sentencing.—Violation of this section is a Class F felony.

Elements

I. Soliciting—G.S. 14-190.19(a)(1)

A person guilty of this offense

(1) solicits or requests
(2) a minor
(3) to participate in prostitution
(4) when the person soliciting or requesting is not a minor.

II. Paying/Agreeing to Pay—G.S. 14-190.19(a)(2)

A person guilty of this offense

(1) pays or agrees to pay
(2) a minor
(3) to participate in prostitution
(4) when the person who pays or agrees to pay is not a minor.

III. Paying Afterward under Prior Agreement—G.S. 14-190.19(a)(3)

A person guilty of this offense

(1) pays
(2) a minor
(3) for having participated in prostitution
(4) pursuant to a prior agreement
(5) when the person who pays is not a minor.

Punishment

Class F felony.

Notes

Minor not punishable under this section. This section is aimed at adults who patronize minor prostitutes. The minor is not subject to prosecution under this section, even though, for example, a 17-year-old prostitute may look mature and may have initiated the sexual encounter.

Statutory subdivision overlap. The statutory subdivisions of this offense overlap. It is not clear that the offense set out in subdivision (a)(3) of the statute (described in III., above, as "Paying Afterward under Prior Agreement") covers anything not also covered by the offense set out in subdivision (a)(2) (described in II., above, as "Paying/Agreeing to Pay").

Dealing through agent specified in statute. Subdivisions (a)(2) and (a)(3) of the statute specify that paying through the minor's agent or making the agreement to pay with the minor's agent is covered. This is probably unnecessary because general legal principles would cover these indirect dealings. The wording of these subdivisions raises the issue of whether soliciting a minor prostitute through the minor's agent would be covered by subdivision (a)(1) of the statute (set out in I., above, as "Soliciting"). The answer is almost certainly yes.

Definition of "minor." For the offenses described in I., II., and III., above, G.S. 14-190.13(3) defines a minor as a person less than 18 years old who is not married or judicially emancipated.

Broad definition of "prostitution." Refer to the discussion under this heading in "Promoting Prostitution of a Minor," just above.

Mistake of age no defense. In common with several other child-protection offenses (see Chapter 21, "Obscenity and Related Offenses"), subsection (b) specifies that mistake as to the age of an involved minor is not a defense to prosecution under this section.

Comparison with "Prostitution and Assignation." While this offense does not punish activity by a participating minor, prostitution and assignation applies to sexual intercourse for hire on the part of both the supplier of the service and the recipient.

Comparison with other prostitution offenses. Note that while other offenses in this chapter are punishable as misdemeanors, promoting prostitution of a minor and participating in prostitution of a minor are felonies.

Related offenses not in this chapter

See the offenses listed under "Promoting Prostitution of a Minor" in this chapter.

21
Obscenity and Related Offenses

Chapter Contents

21 Obscenity and Related Offenses

Disseminating Obscenity

Statute

§14-190.1. Obscene literature and exhibitions.

(a) It shall be unlawful for any person, firm or corporation to intentionally disseminate obscenity. A person, firm or corporation disseminates obscenity within the meaning of this Article if he or it:

(1) Sells, delivers or provides or offers or agrees to sell, deliver or provide any obscene writing, picture, record or other representation or embodiment of the obscene; or

(2) Presents or directs an obscene play, dance or other performance or participates directly in that portion thereof which makes it obscene; or

(3) Publishes, exhibits or otherwise makes available anything obscene; or

(4) Exhibits, presents, rents, sells, delivers or provides; or offers or agrees to exhibit, present, rent or to provide: any obscene still or motion picture, film, filmstrip, or projection slide, or sound recording, sound tape, or sound track, or any matter or material of whatever form which is a representation, embodiment, performance, or publication of the obscene.

(b) For purposes of this Article any material is obscene if:

(1) The material depicts or describes in a patently offensive way sexual conduct specifically defined by subsection (c) of this section; and

(2) The average person applying contemporary community standards relating to the depiction or description of sexual matters would find that the material taken as a whole appeals to the prurient interest in sex; and

(3) The material lacks serious literary, artistic, political, or scientific value; and

(4) The material as used is not protected or privileged under the Constitution of the United States or the Constitution of North Carolina.

(c) As used in this Article, "sexual conduct" means:

(1) Vaginal, anal, or oral intercourse, whether actual or simulated, normal or perverted; or

(2) Masturbation, excretory functions, or lewd exhibition of uncovered genitals; or

(3) An act or condition that depicts torture, physical restraint by being fettered or bound, or flagellation of or by a nude person or a person clad in undergarments or in revealing or bizarre costume.

(d) Obscenity shall be judged with reference to ordinary adults except that it shall be judged with reference to children or other especially susceptible audiences if it appears from the character of the material or the circumstances of its dissemination to be especially designed for or directed to such children or audiences.

(e) It shall be unlawful for any person, firm or corporation to knowingly and intentionally create, buy, procure or possess obscene material with the purpose and intent of disseminating it unlawfully.

(f) It shall be unlawful for a person, firm or corporation to advertise or otherwise promote the sale of material represented or held out by said person, firm or corporation as obscene.

(g) Violation of this section is a Class I felony.

(h) Obscene material disseminated, procured, or promoted in violation of this section is contraband.

(i) Nothing in this section shall be deemed to preempt local government regulation of the location or operation of sexually oriented businesses to the extent consistent with the constitutional protection afforded free speech.

Elements

A person guilty of this offense
(1) intentionally
(2) disseminates obscenity.

Punishment

Class I felony.

Notes

Element (1). The defendant must intend to disseminate the material, rather than intend that the material or performance be obscene. Whether material is intended to be obscene is a mixed matter of fact and law. It is no defense that a defendant mistakenly thought the material was not legally obscene. The cases do require, however, that the defendant know the character or content of the material or performance disseminated (361 U.S. 147; 322 N.C. 22; 88 N.C. App. 624; 88 N.C. App. 69; 87 N.C. App. 217; 83 N.C. App. 544, affirmed, 320 N.C. 485). The term "intentionally" requires that the person who disseminates do so purposefully—that is, with a more specific intent than "knowingly" or "wantonly" or "recklessly" (see the discussion of states of mind in Chapter 1). The acts covered by the term "disseminating obscenity" will vary substantially so that the element of intention will require different forms of proof in different types of cases, but in each instance it will take proof of intent that the obscenity be communicated in some fashion to someone or to a generalized audience.

Element (2). The product of dissemination can be either material or a performance. G.S. 14-190.1(a) sets out four broad and overlapping categories that delineate differing ways of disseminating obscene material and performances. Category (1) is aimed at physical transfers of obscene material. Category (2) refers to live performances. Category (3) is aimed at distributions of material in which there is no clear-cut transfer to a specific person; the term "publishes" probably will be interpreted to refer to publication in the legal sense—that is, *making public* rather than just printing material. Category (4) is aimed at the transmission of obscenity via electronic media. It would cover videotapes, laser discs, television and radio broadcasts, and cable transmissions, as well as motion pictures, still photographs, and audio or audio-visual recordings distributed via radio, TV, telephonic devices, or computer.

Under general principles of law, those who aid and abet the dissemination may be prosecuted for the offense of disseminating obscenity. However, the willing recipient or buyer is not an aider and abettor; according to a rule of statutory interpretation, when a statute makes only one party in a two-party transaction criminally liable, the other party may not be prosecuted as an aider and abettor.

"Obscene" defined. The statute sets out in subsection (b) a definition of "obscene" material that essentially tracks the case-law definitions. Because of its case-law derivation, this definition would also apply to obscene performances; the word "performance" is then interchangeable with "material." For simplicity, the word "material" will be used in most of this discussion, but most points will apply to performances also.

A number of commentators take the position that the definition of obscenity covers only hard-core pornography—that is, something that goes so far beyond what the community will tolerate that it may be banned totally. Under the statute, material is obscene if all four of the following criteria apply:

(1) *"The material depicts or describes in a patently offensive way sexual conduct specifically defined. . . ."* "Sexual conduct" must be specifically defined by statute or case law. Subsection (c) of this statute contains a definition of sexual conduct, which will be separately analyzed below. No matter how offensive the material may be, unless it involves sexual conduct, it is not obscene. Whether the material is patently offensive is a jury question and is to be judged by contemporary community standards (322 N.C. 22; 88 N.C. App. 624). The statute does not specify the geographical limits of the relevant community and a trial judge may permit jurors to apply the standards of their local communities (323 N.C. 159; 322 N.C. 22).

(2) *"The average person applying contemporary community standards relating to the depiction or description of sexual matters would find that the material taken as a whole appeals to the prurient interest in sex."* The jury decides what the contemporary community standards are. As stated above, a trial judge may permit jurors to apply the standards of their local communities (323 N.C. 159; 322 N.C. 22), and the state is not required to present evidence of what constitutes contemporary community standards (123 N.C. App. 292). Jurors will be asked to apply not *their* standards but the standards of the average person in the community as to sexual matters. The material must be taken as a whole. Many works of art or literature have some pornographic content, but before material may be declared obscene, it is essential that jurors find that as a whole it appeals to the prurient interest in sex. "Prurient" means a morbid or unhealthy interest; cases indicate that some sexually explicit material may only appeal to a healthy curiosity about sex. The statute also specifies "the" prurient interest in sex. This means that a jury could find that the material appeals to the prurient interest in sex of the special audience to which the material is directed, even though it has no such appeal to any juror, as for example the case of material intended specifically for sadomasochists, deviants, or children. Subsection (d) makes this principle explicit.

(3) *"The material lacks serious literary, artistic, political, or scientific value."* The value of material must be decided with reference to the work as a whole (413 U.S. 15; 89 N.C. App. 19; 88 N.C. App. 624). Also, in contrast to the criteria of patent offensiveness and appeal to the prurient interest in sex, the criterion of value must be assessed by reference to the standards of a "reasonable person," not by reference to community standards (481 U.S. 497; 322 N.C. 22; 89 N.C. App. 19, rev'd on other grounds, 323 N.C. 439; 88 N.C. App. 624; 88 N.C. App. 19; 87 N.C. App. 217). The word "or" means that if the material has serious value of the sort defined by any of the four adjectives, it is not obscene. Some material does deal heavily with prurient themes but nevertheless has serious value. Many commentators, for example, believe that most issues of *Playboy* contain enough items of serious literary and artistic interest to forestall a claim that the magazine lacks "serious literary" or

"artistic" value—even though a local jury may find that the magazine taken as a whole appeals to the prurient interest in sex. In this case, *Playboy* could not be banned, because subdivision (3) does not apply.

(4) *"The material as used is not protected or privileged under the Constitution of the United States or the Constitution of North Carolina."* This provision is apparently added as a precaution. The other three subdivisions of the statute spell out the currently applicable constitutional standards of obscenity. The phrase "as used" might protect serious researchers who are collecting pornographic material that has no inherent serious value. This is a special case, however, and generally subdivision (4) need not concern judges when they charge juries. Note that such protection has been held to include possession of obscene material in one's own home, although the statute does not expressly address the issue (83 N.C. App. 544, aff'd, 320 N.C. 485; 89 N.C. App. 19).

"Sexual conduct" defined. Subsection (c) sets out the definition of sexual conduct that the material or performance must depict or describe or embody. It lists a variety of acts under three subdivisions. Any act included as an alternative in a subdivision will satisfy the requirement of specificity in the definition of "obscene." This is in contrast to the definition of "obscene" itself, which requires that all four elements of the definition be present. The statute covers:

(1) *"Vaginal, anal, or oral intercourse, whether actual or simulated, normal or perverted."* This means that the material or performance may only simulate intercourse and still meet the definition of sexual conduct.

(2) *"Masturbation, excretory functions, or lewd exhibition of uncovered genitals."* Although "simulated" is not repeated here, the basic statutory definition of obscene material covers material that "depicts or describes" sexual conduct. So if the material depicts masturbation, the fact that the actor or model portrayed was only simulating masturbation would be no defense. As to excretory functions, the depiction or description should be in a sexual context—even though the statute does not so specify. In observing this precaution, keep in mind that the sexual context may be deviant or sadomasochistic.

(3) *"An act or condition that depicts torture, physical restraint by being fettered or bound, or flagellation of or by a nude person or a person clad in undergarments or in revealing or bizarre costume."* This subdivision covers sadomasochism that depicts or describes torture, bondage, or flagellation in which either the abuser or the victim is nude, clad in undergarments, or clad in a revealing or bizarre costume. The statute does not specify that the subdivision must be limited to sadomasochism, but this would be wise, for the subdivision is part of a definition of sexual conduct. Sadomasochistic torture, bondage, or flagellation in which the parties are fully and normally clothed is not covered by this subdivision. Normally, though, such material will include sexual activity specified in subdivision (1) or (2) as part of the activity and thus will fit into the definition of obscenity.

Approval of search warrant and criminal process application. The offense of disseminating obscenity is subject to G.S. 14-190.20, which requires that a prosecutor (either a district attorney or an assistant district attorney) make the request that a search warrant or criminal process be issued. Criminal process includes the citation, criminal summons, arrest warrant, and order for arrest. The major purpose of this provision is to allow a prosecutor to screen the evidence before criminal process is applied for. The statute does not cover arrests without criminal process, and the law is not clear whether such arrests in obscenity cases are valid. No such arrests should be made except in true emergencies.

Note that in 1985 the General Assembly repealed the statutory requirement that material be declared obscene in a civil adversary hearing before a person may be prosecuted for disseminating it. The repeal of that requirement has been upheld as constitutional (83 N.C. App. 544, aff'd, 320 N.C. 485; 87 N.C. App. 217), though a defendant has a constitutional nonstatutory right under the First and Fourteenth Amendments to a prompt, post-seizure adversary hearing on the obscenity of seized material pending trial. The burden is on the person seeking return of the material to request a hearing (83 N.C. App. 544, aff'd, 320 N.C. 485). Now the only statutory precondition for prosecution is a prosecutor's request for issuance of a search warrant or criminal process.

Material contraband. Subsection (h) provides that obscene material disseminated in violation of G.S. 14-190.1 is contraband. An exception to this statute by case law concerns the possession of obscene material in the *home* for personal use; such material may not be seized. The statute sets out no disposition procedure for contraband obscene material, and therefore a court order should be obtained to dispose of it.

Only one offense committed during single transaction. When a person disseminates several obscene items during a single transaction, only one offense is committed (323 N.C. 439).

Constitutionality. This section has been upheld as not facially overbroad or vague (83 N.C. App. 544, aff'd, 320 N.C. 485; 98 N.C. App. 628).

Related offenses not in this chapter

Depending on the facts of the situation, consider offenses in Chapter 8 ("Sexual Assaults"), Chapter 9 ("Crime against Nature," "Incest, Indecent Exposure," and related offenses), and Chapter 20 ("Prostitution and Loitering for Prostitution").

Creating, Buying, Procuring, or Possessing Obscenity with Intent to Distribute

Statute

See G.S. 14-190.1(e), reproduced under "Disseminating Obscenity."

Elements

A person guilty of this offense

(1) creates or buys or procures or possesses

(2) obscene material

(3) with the purpose and intent of disseminating it unlawfully.

Punishment

Class I felony.

Notes

Element (1). The alternative activities in Element (1) obviously overlap. Buying and procuring would overlap with one another. Possession would overlap with the other three.

Element (2). See the discussion under Element (2) of "Disseminating Obscenity" for a definition of "obscene" material.

Element (3). Before October 1, 1985, only disseminations that occurred in a public place were unlawful. Since that date, any dissemination is unlawful. This distinction should be kept in mind in proving the intent to disseminate unlawfully. See the discussion under Element (2) of "Disseminating Obscenity" of the broad meaning of "disseminate" with respect to obscene material. There is no crime in simple possession of obscenity, and proof of the intent and purpose required by this element is essential for conviction.

Approval of search warrant and criminal process application. G.S. 14-190.20 applies to all offenses in G.S. 14-190.1. Refer to the discussion in the parallel section under "Disseminating Obscenity."

Procured material contraband. Statutory subsection (h) makes obscene material that is "procured" in violation of G.S. 14-190.1 contraband. This would logically cover obscene material that was unlawfully bought as well as material otherwise procured, but it would be safer to have the pleading allege "procure" and to have the jury specify in its verdict the counts on which it is finding a defendant guilty. Such specification will prevent arguments over whether the material is subject to destruction after a conviction. The statute does not state that the obscene material is contraband when the conviction is for possession for the purpose of unlawful dissemination. But it may be possible in a hearing to establish that the obscene material had been unlawfully disseminated, procured, or promoted in North Carolina. If so, the judge should be entitled to find the material contraband following a conviction for the possession offense.

Related offenses not in this chapter

See this same heading under "Disseminating Obscenity" in this chapter.

Advertising or Promoting Sale of Material as Obscene

Statute

See G.S. 14-190.1(f), reproduced under "Disseminating Obscenity."

Elements

A person guilty of this offense
- (1) advertises or otherwise promotes the sale of
- (2) material
- (3) that the person represents or holds out
- (4) as obscene.

Punishment

Class I felony.

Notes

Generally. This statutory subsection does not require proof that the material advertised or promoted was in fact obscene; it is sufficient if the advertising or promotion represents or holds it out to be obscene. The purpose of this method of drafting is to allow prosecution of promoters even if the obscene material is not found. As a practical matter, though, it may be difficult to secure a conviction under this subsection without introducing the material into evidence. The definition of obscenity requires that the material be judged as a whole and that it lack substantial redeeming value. Most advertisements or promotions will stress the sexual explicitness of the material but may not be detailed enough about the overall character of the material to constitute proof beyond a reasonable doubt that the material is being held out as obscene. The promises of an advertisement or promotion taken in conjunction with the material being hawked put matters into context and help prove the case. If the promotion promises that the material is even more explicit than some other hard-core obscenity, conviction may be possible through introducing into evidence the referred-to material. Even if the material advertised is located and introduced into evidence and is unquestionably obscene, the case is not thereby won. A simple advertisement for obscene material that does not imply that the material is obscene fails to fit the elements of this offense. The clear innuendo of the promotion must be that the material is obscene. The advertisement or promotion will rarely explicitly say that the material is "obscene" or that hard-core pornography is the exclusive subject, so proof by innuendo will be the norm in cases under the statute.

Approval of search warrant and criminal process application. As noted in the discussion of the previous offense, G.S. 14-190.20 applies to all offenses in G.S. 14-190.1.

Promoted material contraband. Subsection (h) states that obscene material that is "promoted" in violation of G.S. 14-190.1 is contraband. Because a conviction for this offense may be had without proving that the advertised or promoted material was obscene in fact, it will be necessary to establish as a matter of record that the material is obscene before the court may order its destruction.

Related offenses not in this chapter

See this same heading under "Disseminating Obscenity" in this chapter.

Preparing Obscene Photographs, Slides, and Motion Pictures

Statute

§14-190.5. Preparation of obscene photographs, slides and motion pictures.

Every person who knowingly:

(1) Photographs himself or any other person, for purposes of preparing an obscene film, photograph, negative, slide or motion picture for the purpose of dissemination; or

(2) Models, poses, acts, or otherwise assists in the preparation of any obscene film, photograph, negative, slide or motion picture for the purpose of dissemination,

shall be guilty of a Class 1 misdemeanor.

Elements

I. Photographing—G.S. 14-190.5(1)

A person guilty of this offense
(1) knowingly
(2) photographs
(3) himself, herself, or another person
(4) for purposes of preparing an obscene film or photograph or negative or slide or motion picture
(5) for the purpose of dissemination.

II. Assisting the Photographer—G.S. 14-190.5(2)

A person guilty of this offense
(1) knowingly
(2) models or poses or acts or otherwise assists in the preparation of
(3) an obscene film or photograph or negative or slide or motion picture
(4) for the purpose of dissemination.

Punishment

Class 1 misdemeanor.

Notes

Elements I.(1) and II.(1). For each offense the structure of the statute puts the word "knowingly" first, and the word arguably modifies all of the succeeding elements. Proof that an act is done "knowingly" beyond reasonable doubt is often difficult, but the statutory wording probably creates no special problems. The cases establish that knowledge of the obscene nature of material may be proved by proof of knowledge of the material's character or content (361 U.S. 147; 322 N.C. 22; 88 N.C. App. 624; 88 N.C. App. 69; 87 N.C. App. 217; 83 N.C. App. 544, aff'd, 320 N.C. 485). Nevertheless, whether material is obscene is a mixed issue of fact and law, and the defendant's belief with respect to the material's obscenity is irrelevant. Probably the crucial bit of knowledge to prove in these offenses is knowledge that the material is being made for the purpose of dissemination.

Elements I.(2, 4) and II.(3). This section was drafted before the widespread use of videotape, laser discs, cable television, etc. This raises an issue of the meaning of the verb "photograph" and the term "motion picture." The obvious legislative intent was to cover all forms of material that capture reproductions of still and moving images, and a court would be justified in interpreting this section to effectuate that intent.

Approval of search warrant and criminal process application. This section is covered by G.S. 14-190.20, which requires that a prosecutor request the issuance of any search warrant or criminal process. Refer to the discussion in the parallel section under "Disseminating Obscenity."

No contraband statute applies. The only criminal statute governing the contraband status of obscenity is G.S. 14-190.1(h), and it applies to obscene material "disseminated, procured, or promoted in violation of this section." Thus there is no statute directly applying to this offense that would authorize destruction of the obscene material prepared in violation of this section. After conviction, a judge may have inherent power under the common law to order destruction of the obscene material, but there is no clear North Carolina law on this point. Given the uncertainties, a prosecutor may consider bringing a concurrent civil nuisance proceeding in factually appropriate cases under G.S. Ch. 19, in addition to the criminal charge under this section.

Comparison with "Creating, Buying, Procuring, or Possessing Obscenity with Intent to Distribute" above. The offense of creation appears to provide for a much broader, completely overlapping offense. Everyone covered by the offense of "Preparing obscene photographs, slides, and motion pictures" is in some way creating or assisting in the creation of obscene material. Under general principles of law, a prosecutor may choose either the felony or the misdemeanor charge, or both.

Related offenses not in this chapter

See the offenses listed under "Disseminating Obscenity" in this chapter.

Using Minor to Assist in Obscenity Offense

Statute

§14-190.6. Employing or permitting minor to assist in offense under Article.

Every person 18 years of age or older who intentionally, in any manner, hires, employs, uses or permits any minor under the age of 16 years to do or assist in doing any act or thing constituting an offense under this Article and involving any material, act or thing he knows or reasonably should know to be obscene within the meaning of G.S. 14-190.1, shall be guilty of a Class I felony.

Elements

A person guilty of this offense
(1) is 18 years of age or older, *and*
(2) intentionally
(3) hires or employs or uses or permits
(4) a minor under the age of 16
(5) to do or assist in doing
(6) any act or thing
(7) constituting an offense under Article 26 of G.S. Chapter 14
(8) involving any obscene material, or act, or thing
(9) that the person knows or reasonably should know
(10) is obscene within the meaning of G.S. 14-190.1.

Punishment

Class I felony.

Notes

Element (2). The intentional state of mind clearly applies to the act of hiring, employing, using, or permitting. See the discussion of "intention" in Element (1) under "Disseminating Obscenity." An important question is whether this element of intent also applies to the defendant's state of mind about the minor's age. See the discussion concerning mistake of age in Element (4), below.

Element (4). As noted above, the statute can be interpreted to require that the element "intentionally" apply to the age of the minor involved. If it is so interpreted, no issue of a *defense* based on mistake of age will arise, for the State would have to prove that the defendant both knew and intended to hire, etc., the minor under age 16. The more usual interpretation of the statute would restrict the element of intent to the act done rather than to a surrounding circumstance, such as the minor's age. If the courts adopt this approach, the law on mistake of age is germane. This section has never contained a provision relating to mistake of age, and it was not changed in this respect by the 1985 revisions of the obscenity laws. The question of whether a mistake of age would be a defense therefore remains unsettled. The General Assembly in 1985 specified in some of the child-protection sections that mistake of age is no defense, but it is not clear that the legislators focused on the mistake issue in 1985 when it amended this section. If mistake of age is a defense, the defendant will have to demonstrate a reasonable and mistaken belief that the minor was not under age 16. Indifference to, or disregard of, the minor's age would be no basis for a defense. In most cases this discussion may be academic, because overlapping offenses that disallow the defense of mistake of age will often be available. See the discussion below on comparison with "First-Degree Sexual Exploitation of a Minor."

Elements (8), (9), and (10). The statute does not specify that the material, act, or thing must in fact be obscene; it says only that the defendant must have the required knowledge of its obscene character. But the implication is that the material, act, or thing must be obscene and that the state must prove it. In this connection, see the note on "'Obscene' defined" under the offense of "Disseminating Obscenity."

Comparison with "First-Degree Sexual Exploitation of a Minor" (G.S. 14-190.16). First-degree sexual exploitation may be charged in almost every instance in which a charge could be brought under this section. That offense is punished more heavily and provides that mistake of age is no defense.

Related offenses not in this chapter

See the offenses listed under "Disseminating Obscenity" in this chapter.
"Failure to Register as Sex Offender" (Chapter 8)

Disseminating Obscene Material to Minor under 16

Statute

§14-190.7. Dissemination to minors under the age of 16 years.

Every person 18 years of age or older who knowingly disseminates to any minor under the age of 16 years any material which he knows or reasonably should know to be obscene within the meaning of G.S. 14-190.1 shall be guilty of a Class I felony.

Elements

A person guilty of this offense
(1) is 18 years of age or older, *and*
(2) knowingly
(3) disseminates

(4) to a minor under the age of 16 years
(5) obscene material
(6) that the person knows or reasonably should know
(7) is obscene within the meaning of G.S. 14-190.1.

Punishment

Class I felony.

Notes

Elements (2) and (3). The word "knowingly" clearly applies to the dissemination. See the note on Element (2) under "Disseminating Obscenity" for a parallel discussion, keeping in mind that the standard "knowingly" is a lesser one than "intentionally" (also refer to Chapter 1, "States of Mind"). As in the previous offense, "Using Minor to Assist in Obscenity Offense," the important issue is whether the element "knowingly" also applies to the defendant's state of mind with respect to the minor's age. See the discussion below on mistake of age.

Element (4). Most of the discussion on mistake of age set out for the previous offense, "Using Minor to Assist in Obscenity Offense," applies here. This section was amended in 1985, and it may be important to note that the amendments deleted a defense for counseling professionals. This deletion could be interpreted as evidence of the General Assembly's intent not to allow defenses to this section, although a defendant could assert that mistake of age is a special application of the common-law defense of reasonable mistake of fact—and therefore one that applies unless withheld by the General Assembly.

Element (5). The statute literally says "material . . . he [the defendant] knows or reasonably should know to be obscene. . . ." The fair implication of these words, however, is that the material must be obscene material in fact, and this interpretation is reflected in the listing of elements above. Refer to the discussion under "Disseminating Obscenity," above, for the definition of "obscene" material. It should be noted that this section is limited to the dissemination of "obscene" material. The dissemination of an obscene performance to a minor would be charged under "Disseminating Obscenity" (G.S. 14-190.1).

Related offenses not in this chapter

See the offenses listed under "Disseminating Obscenity" in this chapter.

Disseminating Obscene Material to Minor under 13

Statute

§14-190.8. Dissemination to minors under the age of 13 years.

Every person 18 years of age or older who knowingly disseminates to any minor under the age of 13 years any material which he knows or reasonably should know to be obscene within the meaning of G.S. 14-190.1 shall be punished as a Class I felon.

Elements

A person guilty of this offense
(1) is 18 years of age or older, *and*
(2) knowingly
(3) disseminates
(4) to a minor under the age of 13 years
(5) obscene material
(6) that the person knows or reasonably should know
(7) is obscene within the meaning of G.S. 14-190.1.

Punishment

Class I felony.

Notes

Parallel to "Disseminating Obscene Material to Minor under 16." This offense is identical to the one above except that it covers a younger victim.

Related offenses not in this chapter

See the offenses listed under "Disseminating Obscenity" in this chapter.

Displaying Material Harmful to Minors

Statute

§14-190.13. Definitions for certain offenses concerning minors.

The following definitions apply to G.S. 14-190.14, displaying material harmful to minors; G.S. 14-190.15, disseminating or exhibiting to minors harmful material or performances; G.S. 14-190.16, first degree sexual exploitation of a minor; G.S. 14-190.17, second degree sexual exploitation of a minor; G.S. 14-190.17A, third degree sexual exploitation of a minor; G.S. 14-190.18, promoting prostitution of a minor; and G.S. 14-190.19, participating in prostitution of a minor.

(1) Harmful to Minors.—That quality of any material or performance that depicts sexually explicit nudity or sexual activity and that, taken as a whole, has the following characteristics:
  a. The average adult person applying contemporary community standards would find that the material or performance has a predominant tendency to appeal to a prurient interest of minors in sex; and
  b. The average adult person applying contemporary community standards would find that the depiction of sexually explicit nudity or sexual activity in the material or performance is patently offensive to prevailing standards in the adult community concerning what is suitable for minors; and
  c. The material or performance lacks serious literary, artistic, political, or scientific value for minors.

(2) Material.—Pictures, drawings, video recordings, films or other visual depictions or representations but not material consisting entirely of written words.

(3) Minor.—An individual who is less than 18 years old and is not married or judicially emancipated.

(4) Prostitution.—Engaging or offering to engage in sexual activity with or for another in exchange for anything of value.

(5) Sexual Activity.—Any of the following acts:
  a. Masturbation, whether done alone or with another human or an animal.

b. Vaginal, anal, or oral intercourse, whether done with another human or with an animal.
c. Touching, in an act of apparent sexual stimulation or sexual abuse, of the clothed or unclothed genitals, pubic area, or buttocks of another person or the clothed or unclothed breasts of a human female.
d. An act or condition that depicts torture, physical restraint by being fettered or bound, or flagellation of or by a person clad in undergarments or in revealing or bizarre costume.
e. Excretory functions; provided, however, that this sub-division shall not apply to G.S. 14-190.17A.
f. The insertion of any part of a person's body, other than the male sexual organ, or of any object into another person's anus or vagina, except when done as part of a recognized medical procedure.

(6) Sexually Explicit Nudity.—The showing of:
a. Uncovered, or less than opaquely covered, human genitals, pubic area, or buttocks, or the nipple or any portion of the areola of the human female breast, except as provided in G.S. 14-190.9(b); or
b. Covered human male genitals in a discernibly turgid state.

§14-190.14. Displaying material harmful to minors.

(a) Offense.—A person commits the offense of displaying material that is harmful to minors if, having custody, control, or supervision of a commercial establishment and knowing the character or content of the material, he displays material that is harmful to minors at that establishment so that it is open to view by minors as part of the invited general public. Material is not considered displayed under this section if the material is placed behind "blinder racks" that cover the lower two thirds of the material, is wrapped, is placed behind the counter, or is otherwise covered or located so that the portion that is harmful to minors is not open to the view of minors.

(b) Punishment.—Violation of this section is a Class 2 misdemeanor. Each day's violation of this section is a separate offense.

Elements

A person guilty of this offense
(1) displays
(2) material
(3) that is harmful to minors
(4) at a commercial establishment
(5) so that it is open to view by minors as part of the invited general public, *and*
(6) has custody, control, or supervision
(7) of the commercial establishment, *and*
(8) knows the material's character or content.

Punishment

Class 2 misdemeanor. Each day's violation is a separate offense.

Notes

Element (1). This section does not give any definitional examples of the word "displays." It does provide certain exceptions to display, but for the most part one must turn to the dictionary or to case law defining the word in other statutes. No mental element such as "intentionally" or "knowingly" is set out in this statute, but the inherent meaning of display is inconsistent with any accidental showing or disclosure of the material.

The statute does not address one issue that may frequently arise. Assume that the contents of an adult magazine are unquestionably "harmful to minors," but the fully displayed cover picture—though provocative—does not show either "sexually explicit nudity" or "sexual activity." Does display of the cover constitute an offense? This issue is treated below under the exceptions to the display offense.

Element (2). "Material" is defined in G.S. 14-190.13(2) to mean "pictures, drawings, video recordings, films or other visual depictions or representations but not material consisting entirely of written words."

Element (3). The term *harmful to minors* is defined in G.S. 14-190.13(1) to mean "[t]hat quality of any material or performance that depicts sexually explicit nudity or sexual activity and that, taken as a whole, has the following characteristics: . . . ." The statute then sets out a three-pronged test, (1)a., (1)b., and (1)c., similar to the test established by the United States Supreme Court (413 U.S. 15), except that it is tied to the community standards applicable to minors. Each word in this three-pronged test is important, and the statute must be studied. All three prongs must be satisfied before any material (or performance) can be regulated. The term only applies to "sexually explicit nudity" or "sexual activity." It is essential to understand the special definitions for these phrases.

Definition of "sexually explicit nudity." This phrase is defined in G.S. 14-190.13(6)a. and (6)b. Subparagraph a., which designates portions of the body revealed, actually covers mere nudity rather than sexually explicit nudity, but this potential overbreadth is immaterial because demonstrating any nudity in a material or a performance would be only the first step in determining whether it is "harmful to minors." The material or performance would still have to meet the three-pronged test mentioned above.

Definition of "sexual activity." This phrase, defined in G.S. 14-190.13(5), is a crucial one used in several sections in the child-protection provisions of the 1985 amendments governing obscenity and related offenses. As before, satisfying this definition is only the first step in determining whether any material or performance is "harmful to minors"; application of the three-pronged test probably will enable the statute to survive any constitutional challenges on grounds of overbreadth. The prohibition against depictions of persons portrayed as minors in romantic encounters involving apparent sexual touching has been upheld constitutionally as not facially overbroad (83 N.C. App. 544, aff'd, 320 N.C. 485).

Definition of "minor." G.S. 14-190.13(3) defines a minor as "[a]n individual who is less than 18 years old and is not married or judicially emancipated."

Element (5)—minors as part of the invited general public. The wording of this element would require proof that the commercial establishment welcomed the general public and made no attempt to exclude minors from the area of the establishment in which material harmful to minors was open to view. Mere evidence that a minor viewed the material would be insufficient. The precautions an establishment may have to take may depend on the public that it normally welcomes. A for-profit art gallery that almost never has any minor patrons may need to take few precautions. Commercial establishments that can expect minors as patrons, or accompanying adult patrons, would need to be far more careful. Note that under this section it is no defense that a minor's parent or guardian may have consented or encouraged the display of the material. In fact, that parent or guardian would probably be guilty as an aider and abettor of the offense set out here.

Exceptions to "display." To qualify as an exception to the statute, material must be "placed behind 'blinder racks' that cover the lower two-thirds of the material, . . . wrapped, . . . placed behind the counter, or . . . otherwise covered or located so that the portion that is harmful to minors is not open to the view of minors." Given the context of these exceptions, the word "wrapped" should be interpreted to mean covered with an opaque wrapper that hides the portion of the material harmful to minors. These exceptions, with the catch-all authorizing just a covering of the portion of material harmful to minors, probably answer the question asked above under Element (1) concerning the basic meaning of "display." There is probably no display in the first place if the cover of a book or magazine contains no material harmful to minors—so long as the contents that fall within the definition are not revealed. The statute merely states that material is "not considered" to be displayed if the provisions of the exception sentence quoted above are met. The statute does not say so explicitly, but avoidance of display probably is an affirmative defense to be raised and proved by the defendant (see the note on "Affirmative defenses" under the next offense, "Disseminating Harmful Material to Minors").

Aiders and abettors; use of related offense. Any person who is free to act independently and who aids and abets the manager or owner or other person in supervision or control may be charged with this offense under general principles of law (see Chapter 3, "Participants in Crimes"). There might be more difficulty, though, in prosecuting any employee who is in the establishment at the same time as the supervisor. If the supervisor leaves and the employee then has custody of the establishment, the employee may be prosecuted. An employee who notices a minor browsing through adult material and fails to stop the perusal may be subject to prosecution under G.S. 14-190.15(a), which is discussed in the offense below.

Related offenses not in this chapter

See the offenses listed under "Disseminating Obscenity" in this chapter.

Disseminating Harmful Material to Minors

Statute

§14-190.15. Disseminating harmful material to minors; exhibiting harmful performances to minors.

(a) Disseminating Harmful Material.—A person commits the offense of disseminating harmful material to minors if, with or without consideration and knowing the character or content of the material, he:

(1) Sells, furnishes, presents, or distributes to a minor material that is harmful to minors; or
(2) Allows a minor to review or peruse material that is harmful to minors.

(b) Exhibiting Harmful Performance.—A person commits the offense of exhibiting a harmful performance to a minor if, with or without consideration and knowing the character or content of the performance, he allows a minor to view a live performance that is harmful to minors.

(c) Defenses.—Except as provided in subdivision (3), a mistake of age is not a defense to a prosecution under this section. It is an affirmative defense to a prosecution under this section that:

(1) The defendant was a parent or legal guardian of the minor.
(2) The defendant was a school, church, museum, public library, governmental agency, medical clinic, or hospital carrying out its legitimate function; or an

employee or agent of such an organization acting in that capacity and carrying out a legitimate duty of his employment.

(3) Before disseminating or exhibiting the harmful material or performance, the defendant requested and received a driver's license, student identification card, or other official governmental or educational identification card or paper indicating that the minor to whom the material or performance was disseminated or exhibited was at least 18 years old, and the defendant reasonably believed the minor was at least 18 years old.

(4) The dissemination was made with the prior consent of a parent or guardian of the recipient.

(d) Punishment.—Violation of this section is a Class 1 misdemeanor.

Elements

I. Furnishing the Material—G.S. 14-190.15(a)(1)

A person guilty of this offense

(1) sells or furnishes or presents or distributes
(2) material
(3) that is harmful to minors
(4) to a minor
(5) with knowledge of the material's character or content.

II. Permitting Browsing—G.S. 14-190.15(a)(2)

A person guilty of this offense

(1) allows
(2) a minor
(3) to review or peruse
(4) material
(5) that is harmful to minors
(6) with knowledge of the material's character or content.

Punishment

Class 1 misdemeanor.

Notes

Element II.(1). Although there is no mental element of "knowledge" specified in the browsing offense, the word "allows" that is used in the statute implies knowledge and control over the situation and a conscious decision to allow the act in question to occur.

Elements I.(2, 3, and 4), and II.(2, 4, and 5). The important definitions of "material," "harmful to minors," and "minor" are covered in the notes for Elements (2) and (3) of the offense, "Displaying Material Harmful to Minors," just above.

Offense applies everywhere. Whereas displaying material harmful to minors is limited to commercial establishments, this offense applies everywhere, and the statute specifically notes that the dissemination is an offense whether done for compensation or not. Thus a person who shows a neighbor's 17-year-old the latest issue of *Playboy* commits an offense under this section.

Mistake of age no defense except in one instance. Subsection (c) provides that mistake of age is not a defense to a prosecution except in one situation covered by the affirmative defenses treated below.

Affirmative defenses. Statutory subsection (c) sets out four affirmative defenses. The defendant must raise the affirmative defense, and then must prove it to the satisfaction of the finder of the fact. Subdivision (3) regarding request of identification papers represents the only defense of mistake of age allowed. Subdivision (4) requires the prior consent of the parent or guardian.

Related offenses not in this chapter

See the offenses listed under "Disseminating Obscenity" in this chapter.

Exhibiting Harmful Performances to Minors

Statute

See G.S. 14-190.15(b), reproduced under "Disseminating Harmful Material to Minors."

Elements

A person guilty of this offense
(1) allows
(2) a minor
(3) to view
(4) a live performance
(5) that is harmful to minors
(6) with knowledge of the performance's character or content.

Punishment

Class 1 misdemeanor.

Notes

Element (1). See the note on Element II.(1) under "Disseminating Harmful Material to Minors," just above.

Elements (2) and (5). The important definitions of "material," "harmful to minors," and "minor" are covered in the notes for Elements (2) and (3) of the offense "Displaying Material Harmful to Minors."

Private noncommercial performances prohibited. Like the offense of disseminating harmful material to minors, this offense applies everywhere—to both public and private performances and without regard to whether any admission is charged for entry.

Mistake of age no defense except in one instance. See the discussion of this note heading under "Disseminating Harmful Material to Minors," just above. The same rule applies.

Affirmative defenses. See the discussion of this note heading under "Disseminating Harmful Material to Minors," just above. The same affirmative defenses are available here.

Related offenses not in this chapter

See the offenses listed under "Disseminating Obscenity" in this chapter.

First-Degree Sexual Exploitation of a Minor

Statute

§14-190.16. First degree sexual exploitation of a minor.

(a) Offense.—A person commits the offense of first degree sexual exploitation of a minor if, knowing the character or content of the material or performance, he:

(1) Uses, employs, induces, coerces, encourages, or facilitates a minor to engage in or assist others to engage in sexual activity for a live performance or for the purpose of producing material that contains a visual representation depicting this activity; or

(2) Permits a minor under his custody or control to engage in sexual activity for a live performance or for the purpose of producing material that contains a visual representation depicting this activity; or

(3) Transports or finances the transportation of a minor through or across this State with the intent that the minor engage in sexual activity for a live performance or for the purpose of producing material that contains a visual representation depicting this activity; or

(4) Records, photographs, films, develops, or duplicates for sale or pecuniary gain material that contains a visual representation depicting a minor engaged in sexual activity.

(b) Inference.—In a prosecution under this section, the trier of fact may infer that a participant in sexual activity whom material through its title, text, visual representations, or otherwise represents or depicts as a minor is a minor.

(c) Mistake of Age.—Mistake of age is not a defense to a prosecution under this section.

(d) Punishment and Sentencing.—Violation of this section is a Class D felony.

Elements

I. Facilitating Production—G.S. 14-190.16(a)(1)

A person guilty of this offense

(1) uses or employs or induces or coerces or encourages or facilitates
(2) a minor
(3) to engage in or to assist others to engage in
(4) sexual activity
(5) for a live performance or for the purpose of producing material that contains a visual representation depicting sexual activity
(6) with knowledge of the character or content
(7) of the performance or material.

II. Permitting Sexual Activity for Production—G.S. 14-190.16(a)(2)

A person guilty of this offense

(1) permits
(2) a minor
(3) under the person's custody or control
(4) to engage in sexual activity
(5) for a live performance or for the purpose of producing material that contains a visual representation depicting sexual activity
(6) with knowledge of the character or content
(7) of the performance or material.

III. Transporting Minor for Production—G.S. 14-190.16(a)(3)

A person guilty of this offense
(1) transports or finances the transportation of
(2) a minor
(3) through North Carolina or across North Carolina
(4) with the intent that the minor engage in sexual activity
(5) for a live performance or for the purpose of producing material that contains a visual representation depicting sexual activity
(6) with knowledge of the character or content
(7) of the performance or material.

IV. Producing Material Commercially—G.S. 14-190.16(a)(4)

A person guilty of this offense
(1) records or photographs or films or develops or duplicates
(2) for sale or pecuniary gain
(3) material that contains a visual representation depicting a minor engaged in sexual activity
(4) with knowledge of the material's character or content.

Punishment

Class D felony.

Notes

Purpose of section. The purpose of this section is to punish severely persons who engage in the production of pornography in which minors are used as actors or models. In every instance under this section the "visual representation" must be tied to the actual exposure of a minor to sexual activity (83 N.C. App. 544, aff'd, 320 N.C. 485). The word "material" is defined in G.S. 14-190.13(2) [see the statute under "Displaying Material Harmful to Minors"] to include drawings and other pictures, but this aspect of the definition must be disregarded unless there is clear proof that a minor's participation in sexual activity was necessary to the creation of the drawing or picture.

Territorial jurisdiction. For North Carolina's courts to have jurisdiction, at least one of the elements of the offense must occur within North Carolina. The encouraging, facilitating, permitting, transporting, or financing may well take place here for the purpose of sexual activity by the minor outside the state; the North Carolina courts will have jurisdiction over the offense even though the sexual activity takes place in another jurisdiction that does not punish the particular sexual activity involved. (Indeed, under the first three subdivisions, if the purpose is proved, the offense is committed even when the minor never does in fact engage in the sexual activity anywhere.) Of special importance is the offense under subdivision (4), producing material commercially. If material is duplicated in North Carolina, it is apparently immaterial that the minor's sexual activity may have occurred long ago and even in a foreign country. The United States Supreme Court has ruled that a state's interest in stopping the sexual exploitation of its children is so strong that it may act to punish the production and distribution of pornography that was produced with the use of children without having to be concerned about proving time of occurrence or place of origin (458 U.S. 747). There may not be a violation if the material was produced without any sexual exploitation of the minor, such as pictures of children engaged in rites widely approved by their cultures, such as those pictures that might appear in *National Geographic* (see concurring opinion in 458 U.S. 747).

Sexual activity. The definition of "sexual activity" is provided in G.S. 14-190.13(5); see "Displaying Material Harmful to Minors." The broad definition may cause constitutional problems, and courts may give certain of its phrases a narrow interpretation. The parts of the definition that cause particular concern are:

Certain touchings under subparagraph (5)c. The subparagraph covers touchings, in an act of apparent sexual stimulation, of the clothed buttocks of another person or the clothed breasts of a human female. It has been upheld constitutionally as not being facially overbroad (83 N.C. App. 544, aff'd, 320 N.C. 485). One can imagine a serious, nonobscene drama on sexual abuse of children that might portray such a touching of a child actor. Courts may rule that if the production of serious, nonobscene material or performances nevertheless causes the sexual exploitation of a child actor or model, the state may ban the activity. But to ban relatively harmless touchings of the clothed buttocks or breasts of a professional child actor in the course of a drama, when the sexual stimulation depicted is only simulated, may raise serious constitutional problems.

Certain depictions of torture or physical restraint under subparagraph (5)d. Subparagraph d. is aimed at sadomasochistic torture, bondage, or flagellation in which either the abuser or the victim is "clad in undergarments or in revealing or bizarre costume." The statute, however, does not restrict the subparagraph only to sadomasochism. As a matter of caution, anyone attempting a prosecution under this section should consider using this part of the definition of "sexual activity" only for material and performances in which the sexual or sadomasochistic context is clear.

Excretory functions under subparagraph (5)e. Literally, a photograph of a small boy urinating against a playground fence would be sexual activity by a minor, and anyone who dealt commercially with a photograph of the boy would be subject to prosecution under this section. However, this part of the definition of sexual activity should probably be restricted to excretory functions shown in a sexual context or in a setting in which the depiction is clearly intended to stimulate the viewer sexually. Note that if material is designed for the sexual stimulation of a deviant audience, it may come under the definition of "sexual activity" even though it would not stimulate a normal person sexually.

Application of section to material and performances involving "minors." This section applies to material and performances involving all minors as defined in G.S. 14-190.13(3)(see the statute under "Displaying Material Harmful to Minors")—anyone under age 18 who is not married or judicially emancipated.

Inference that model or actor was a minor. Subsection (b) of G.S. 14-190.16 states that "the trier of fact may infer that a participant in sexual activity whom material through its title, text, visual representations, or otherwise represents or depicts as a minor is a minor." The constitutionality of this inference has been upheld (83 N.C. App. 544, aff'd, 320 N.C. 485).

Mistake of age no defense. Subsection (c) of the statute states that mistake of age is not a defense to a prosecution under this section.

Related offenses. Compare with creating, buying, procuring, or possessing obscenity with intent to distribute, G.S. 14-190.1(e), which makes it a Class I felony to create obscene material with the purpose and intent of disseminating it unlawfully; preparing obscene photographs, slides, and motion pictures, G.S. 14-190.5(1) and (2), which makes it a Class 1 misdemeanor (a) to photograph oneself or another for the purpose of preparing obscene material intended for dissemination or (b) to model, pose, act, or otherwise assist in the preparation of photographic obscene material for the purpose of dissemination; and using minor to assist in obscenity offense, G.S. 14-190.6, which makes it a Class I felony to hire, employ, use, or permit a minor under age 16 to do anything in violation of Article 26 involving any obscene material, act, or thing. It should be noted that this section on first-degree sexual exploitation of a minor does not, in specific terms, cover the person who photographs the minor engaged in sexual activity; but it is difficult to conceive of a situation in which the photographer of child pornography would not be guilty under subdivision (1) of using, employing, inducing, etc., the minor to engage in sexual activity for the purpose of producing the material. In this connection, note that the offense under subdivision (4) is that of photographing the material for sale or pecuniary gain. Compare subdivision (4) with photographing under "Second-Degree Sexual exploitation of a Minor," G.S. 14-190.17(a)(1), below, which is substantially identical except for omission of the element "for sale or pecuniary gain." Also compare with "Third-Degree Sexual Exploitation of a Minor," below. The latter offense is aimed primarily at possession of exploitative material, and it is broad enough to cover the activities listed in this, the offense of first-degree sexual exploitation of a minor.

Related offenses not in this chapter

See the offenses listed under "Disseminating Obscenity" in this chapter.
"Failure to Register as Sex Offender" (Chapter 8)

Second-Degree Sexual Exploitation of a Minor

Statute

§14-190.17. Second degree sexual exploitation of a minor.

(a) Offense.—A person commits the offense of second degree sexual exploitation of a minor if, knowing the character or content of the material, he:

(1) Records, photographs, films, develops, or duplicates material that contains a visual representation of a minor engaged in sexual activity; or
(2) Distributes, transports, exhibits, receives, sells, purchases, exchanges, or solicits material that contains a visual representation of a minor engaged in sexual activity.

(b) Inference.—In a prosecution under this section, the trier of fact may infer that a participant in sexual activity whom material through its title, text, visual representations or otherwise represents or depicts as a minor is a minor.

(c) Mistake of Age.—Mistake of age is not a defense to a prosecution under this section.

(d) Punishment and Sentencing.—Violation of this section is a Class F felony.

Elements

I. Producing Material Noncommercially—G.S. 14-190.17(a)(1)

A person guilty of this offense

(1) records or photographs or films or develops or duplicates
(2) material that contains a visual representation of a minor engaged in sexual activity

(3) with knowledge of the material's character or content.

II. Circulating Material—G.S. 14-190.17(a)(2)

A person guilty of this offense
- (1) distributes or transports or exhibits or receives or sells or purchases or exchanges or solicits
- (2) material that contains a visual representation of a minor engaged in sexual activity
- (3) with knowledge of the material's character or content.

Punishment

Class F felony.

Notes

Purpose of section. Subdivision (1) is aimed at noncommercial production of child pornography; it is identical to "IV. Producing Material Commercially G.S. 14-190. 16(a)(4)," under "First-Degree Sexual Exploitation of a Minor," except that the first-degree offense adds the element "for sale or pecuniary gain." Hearings before legislative committees have discussed the cottage industry in which children are sexually exploited by deviants who then swap the material they produce with other deviants. Subdivision (2) is aimed at circulation of the child pornography—whether done commercially or noncommercially.

Application of section to material produced elsewhere. See the note about territorial jurisdiction under "First-Degree Sexual Exploitation of a Minor." The points made there pertain to this offense, and this section is intended to apply to child pornography without regard to when and where it was produced.

Sexual activity. See the note of this same heading under "First-Degree Sexual Exploitation of a Minor." The cautions stated there apply to this offense with even greater force, because this offense covers noncommercial transactions by persons far removed from any personal involvement in sexual exploitation of a minor.

Inference that model or actor was a minor. See the note of this same heading under "First-Degree Sexual Exploitation of a Minor." Subsection (b) of this statutory section is a provision on inference as to the age of the apparent minor who participated in sexual activity identical to the one set out in the first-degree offense. The constitutionality of this inference has been upheld (83 N.C. App. 544, aff'd, 320 N.C. 485).

Mistake of age no defense. Subsection (c) of this section provides that mistake of age is not a defense. This rule may apply more harshly here than in the first-degree offense, because the noncommercial producers and circulators of child pornography will typically have had no dealings with the child involved and may have no basis for knowing the age of the participant in the sexual activity. Whereas commercial dealers and direct participants logically should take the risk of mistake of age, the logic is less strong here.

Related offenses. See the note of this heading under "First-Degree Sexual Exploitation of a Minor" for a pertinent discussion of this issue.

Related offenses not in this chapter

See this same heading under "First-Degree Sexual Exploitation of a Minor" in this chapter.

Third-Degree Sexual Exploitation of a Minor

Statute

§14-190.17A. Third degree sexual exploitation of a minor.

(a) Offense.— A person commits the offense of third degree sexual exploitation of a minor if, knowing the character or content of the material, he possesses material that contains a visual representation of a minor engaging in sexual activity.

(b) Inference.— In a prosecution under this section, the trier of fact may infer that a participant in sexual activity whom material through its title, text, visual representations or otherwise represents or depicts as a minor a minor.

(c) Mistake of Age.— Mistake of age is not defense to a prosecution under this section.

(d) Punishment and Sentencing.— Violation of this section is a Class I felony.

Elements

A person guilty of this offense
- (1) possesses
- (2) material that contains a visual representation of a minor engaged in sexual activity
- (3) with knowledge of the material's character or content.

Punishment

Class I felony.

Notes

Generally. This section would apply to anyone who knowingly possesses child pornography. The concept of "possession" would also encompass the activities prohibited by first- and second-degree sexual exploitation of a minor. This offense may be an alternative charge to those more serious offenses, based on the facts of an individual case and the adequacy of evidence to prove the greater offenses.

Sexual activity. See the notes of this same heading under "First-Degree Sexual Exploitation of a Minor" and "Second-Degree Sexual Exploitation of a Minor." The cautions stated there apply to this offense, possibly with even greater force, given that possession may be far removed from any personal involvement in sexual exploitation of a minor. Sexual activity for purposes of this offense is distinguishable from first-degree and second-degree sexual exploitation of a minor in that G.S. 14-190.13(5)e. explicitly states that "excretory functions" is not a sexual activity reachable by this offense. That means, for example, that possession of a photograph of a small boy urinating against a playground fence would not violate this statute, while commercially dealing, producing, or circulating such a photo could violate the first- or second-degree exploitation offenses.

Inference that model or actor was a minor. See the notes of this same heading under "First-Degree Sexual Exploitation of a Minor" and "Second-Degree Sexual Exploitation of a Minor." Subsection (b) of this statutory section is an inference provision identical to that contained in those offenses.

Mistake of age no defense. Subsection (c) of this section provides that mistake of age is not a defense. See the note of this same heading under "Second-Degree Sexual Exploitation of a Minor." Just as with that offense, the no-defense rule may have harsh application to offenders under this statute.

Related offenses. See the note of this same heading under "First-Degree Sexual Exploitation of a Minor."

Related offenses not in this chapter

See this same heading under "First-Degree Sexual Exploitation of a Minor" in this chapter.

Permitting Facility to Contain Multiple Adult Establishments

Statute

§14-202.10. Definitions.

As used in this Article:

(1) "Adult bookstore" means a bookstore:

a. Which receives a majority of its gross income during any calendar month from the sale or rental of publications (including books, magazines, other periodicals, videotapes, compact discs, other photographic, electronic, magnetic, digital, or other imaging medium) which are distinguished or characterized by their emphasis on matter depicting, describing, or relating to specified sexual activities or specified anatomical areas, as defined in this section; or

b. Having as a preponderance (either in terms of the weight and importance of the material or in terms of greater volume of materials) of its publications (including books, magazines, other periodicals, videotapes, compact discs, other photographic, electronic, magnetic, digital, or other imaging medium) which are distinguished or characterized by their emphasis on matter depicting, describing, or relating to specified sexual activities or specified anatomical areas, as defined in this section.

(2) "Adult establishment" means an adult bookstore, adult motion picture theatre, adult mini motion picture theatre, adult live entertainment business, or massage business as defined in this section.

(3) "Adult live entertainment" means any performance of or involving the actual presence of real people which exhibits specified sexual activities or specified anatomical areas, as defined in this section.

(4) "Adult live entertainment business" means any establishment or business wherein adult live entertainment is shown for observation by patrons.

(5) "Adult motion picture theatre" means an enclosed building or premises used for presenting motion pictures, a preponderance of which are distinguished or characterized by an emphasis on matter depicting, describing, or relating to specified sexual activities or specified anatomical areas, as defined in this section, for observation by patrons therein. "Adult motion picture theatre" does not include any adult mini motion picture theatre as defined in this section.

(6) "Adult mini motion picture theatre" means an enclosed building with viewing booths designed to hold patrons which is used for presenting motion pictures, a preponderance of which are distinguished or characterized by an emphasis on matter depicting, describing or relating to specified sexual activities or specified anatomical areas as defined in this section, for observation by patrons therein.

(7) "Massage" means the manipulation of body muscle or tissue by rubbing, stroking, kneading, or tapping, by hand or mechanical device.

(8) "Massage business" means any establishment or business wherein massage is practiced, including establishments commonly known as health clubs, physical culture studios, massage studios, or massage parlors.

(9) "Sexually oriented devices" means without limitation any artificial or simu-

lated specified anatomical area or other device or paraphernalia that is designed principally for specified sexual activities but shall not mean any contraceptive device.

(10) "Specified anatomical areas" means:
   a. Less than completely and opaquely covered: (i) human genitals, pubic region, (ii) buttock, or (iii) female breast below a point immediately above the top of the areola; or
   b. Human male genitals in a discernibly turgid state, even if completely and opaquely covered.

(11) "Specified sexual activities" means:
   a. Human genitals in a state of sexual stimulation or arousal;
   b. Acts of human masturbation, sexual intercourse or sodomy; or
   c. Fondling or other erotic touchings of human genitals, pubic regions, buttocks or female breasts.

§14-202.11. Restrictions as to adult establishments.

(a) No person shall permit any building, premises, structure, or other facility that contains any adult establishment to contain any other kind of adult establishment. No person shall permit any building, premises, structure, or other facility in which sexually oriented devices are sold, distributed, exhibited, or contained to contain any adult establishment.

(b) No person shall permit any viewing booth in an adult mini motion picture theatre to be occupied by more than one person at any time.

(c) Nothing in this section shall be deemed to preempt local government regulation of the location or operation of adult establishments or other sexually oriented businesses to the extent consistent with the constitutional protection afforded free speech.

§14-202.12. Violations; penalties.

Any person who violates G.S. 14-202.11 shall be guilty of a Class 3 misdemeanor. Any person who has been previously convicted of a violation of G.S. 14-202.11, upon conviction for a second or subsequent violation of G.S. 14-202.11, shall be guilty of a Class 2 misdemeanor.

As used herein, "person" shall include:

(1) The agent in charge of the building, premises, structure or facility; or
(2) The owner of the building, premises, structure or facility when such owner knew or reasonably should have known the nature of the business located therein, and such owner refused to cooperate with the public officials in reasonable measures designed to terminate the proscribed use; provided, however, that if there is an agent in charge, and if the owner did not have actual knowledge, the owner shall not be prosecuted; or
(3) The owner of the business; or
(4) The manager of the business.

Elements

A person guilty of this offense

(1) (a) is the agent in charge of any building, premises, structure, or facility, *or*
   (b) is the owner of any building, premises, structure, or facility when:
      (i) the owner knew or reasonably shown have known
      (ii) the nature of the business located therein, *and*
      (iii) refused to cooperate with public officials in reasonable measures designed to terminate the proscribed use, *or*
   (c) is the owner of the business [operating an offending adult establishment], *or*

(d) is the manager of the business [operating an offending adult establishment], *and*
(2) permits
(3) the building, premises, structure, or other facility
(4) that contains any adult establishment
(5) to contain any other kind of adult establishment.

Punishment

Class 3 misdemeanor. A person who previously has been convicted of any offense within G.S. 14-202.11 is guilty of a Class 2 misdemeanor.

Notes

Element (1). The penalty provision applicable to this section is G.S. 14-202.12, which states that any "person" who violates G.S. 14-202.11 is criminally punishable as indicated. The second paragraph of G.S. 14-202.12 states, "As used herein, 'person' shall include"—and then sets out four classes: (1) agents in charge of facilities, (2) owners of facilities, (3) owners of businesses, and (4) managers of businesses. The word "herein" strictly means only G.S. 14-202.12; but the word "person" is also used in connection with each offense in G.S. 14-202.11, and the penalty provision is interconnected with that section. The statute is unclear whether the word "includes" signifies merely an illustrative list or sets out a closed list of "persons" who can be responsible for violations. The listing of elements above follows a conservative interpretation by setting out the material characterizing the "person" responsible in Element (1). It may be that the list is only illustrative and that the state need not allege or prove any of the matter in Element (1). (If this is true, the restrictions on when a facility owner may be a "person" should be treated as defenses to be asserted by owners of facilities. Refer to the treatment below of a proviso concerning the facility owner, "Defense for owner of facility.")

Element (2). The word "permit" implies that the person who permits the activity has a basic awareness of the facts involved, has some power of control, and makes a conscious determination to permit it. Given this, it is not important that, in regard to owners of facilities, the statute sets out detailed provisions about that owner's knowledge and says nothing about the state of knowledge of the other people specified.

Element (3). For convenience, in the following discussion the term "facility" will be used instead of the phrase "building, premises, structure, or other facility."

Element (4). G.S. 14-202.10(2) lists five kinds of adult establishments:
(1) "Adult bookstore"
(2) "Adult motion picture theatre"
(3) "Adult mini-motion picture theatre"
(4) "Adult live entertainment business"
(5) "Massage business"

G.S. 14-202.10 sets out detailed definitions for each of these kinds of adult establishments. These definitions must be studied in detail in the process of investigating and proving a case, but they will not be repeated here.

The term "preponderance" used in the definition of "adult mini-motion picture theatre" in G.S. 14-202.10(6) is not unconstitutionally vague (612 F.2d 821; 128 N.C. App. 703; 129 N.C. App. 282).

Element (5). The wording of the statute indicates that a facility that *contains* an adult establishment is not permitted to contain any other kind of adult establishment. This apparently means that the first adult establishment has priority over other kinds that may be located in the facility later. It does not limit the number of adult establishments of the *same* kind in any facility, however.

The idea of priority is reflected in the wording of Element (1), in which bracketed matter is added to define the owners and managers of businesses who can be prosecuted as responsible parties. The safest interpretation is to prosecute owners and managers of adult establishments if they locate in the same facility *after* another kind of adult establishment is already contained there. Often, of course, a business will run two different kinds of adult establishments as part of the same operation. There is nothing unlawful about this so long as the different kinds of establishments are in different facilities. But when, as is often the case, they are in the same facility, the owner and the manager of the business may be prosecuted for violating this offense.

Defense for owner of facility. A proviso to subdivision (2) of the second paragraph of G.S. 14-202.12 states that the owner of the facility may not be prosecuted unless the owner has *actual* knowledge of the violation if there is an agent in charge of the facility. This is in contrast with the knew-or-reasonably-should-have-known standard otherwise applicable to that owner under the wording set out above in Element (1). Note, however, that Element (1) also requires that the facility owner has refused to cooperate with the authorities before the owner can be prosecuted. This would seem to make the proviso redundant in most cases; in the course of refusing to cooperate, the owner would surely have gained the requisite actual knowledge.

Aiding and abetting. Any person with independence of action who aids and abets one of the parties named in Element (1) to commit the offense may be prosecuted as an aider and abettor under general principles of law (see Chapter 3, "Participants in Crimes"). The naming of these four categories of "persons," however, does raise a question about the liability of employees of a facility or of a business operating an adult establishment that is violating the law. If, as noted above, the listing of persons set out in Element (1) is merely illustrative—so that it is not in fact an element of the crime—a knowing and complicit employee may well be subject to prosecution as an aider and abettor. But if the list is interpreted as a closed list, employees who do not fall within the four categories will probably not be subject to prosecution.

Related offenses not in this chapter

See the offenses listed under "Disseminating Obscenity" in this chapter.

Permitting Adult Establishment in Facility Where Sexually Oriented Devices Are Contained

Statute

See G.S. 14-202.11, reproduced under "Permitting Facility to Contain Multiple Adult Establishments," above.

Elements

A person guilty of this offense

(1) (a) is the agent in charge of any building, premises, structure, or facility, *or*

   - (b) is the owner of any building, premises, structure, or facility when:
     - (i) the owner knew or reasonably should have known
     - (ii) the nature of the business located therein, *and*
     - (iii) the owner refused to cooperate with public officials in reasonable measures designed to terminate the proscribed use, *or*
   - (c) is the owner of the business [operating an offending adult establishment], *or*
   - (d) is the manager of the business [operating an offending adult establishment], *and*
- (2) permits
- (3) any building, premises, structure, or other facility
- (4) in which sexually oriented devices are sold or distributed or exhibited or contained
- (5) to contain any adult establishment.

Punishment

Class 3 misdemeanor. A person who previously has been convicted of any offense within G.S. 14-202.11 is guilty of a Class 2 misdemeanor.

Notes

Element (1). Note the discussion of the concept of priority in "Permitting Facility to Contain Multiple Adult Establishments." In the vast majority of cases it will be an ongoing adult establishment that would wish to maximize its profits by installing a line of sexually oriented devices, which the statute clearly forbids. The person responsible for operating the adult establishment will have to choose between carrying sexually oriented devices and operating the adult establishment.

Element (2). Refer to the discussion of "permit" under this heading in "Permitting Facility to Contain Multiple Adult Establishments."

Elements (3), (4). See G.S. 14-202.10, reproduced under "Permitting Facility to Contain Multiple Adult Establishments" for definitions of the various kinds of adult establishments and of "sexually oriented devices." Note that the definition of "sexually oriented devices" excludes contraceptive devices. For convenience, in the following discussion the term "facility" will be used instead of the phrase "building, premises, structure, or other facility."

Defense for owner of facility. See the note with this same heading under "Permitting Facility to Contain Multiple Adult Establishments."

Aiding and abetting. See the note with this same heading under "Permitting Facility to Contain Multiple Adult Establishments."

Related offenses not in this chapter

See this same heading under "Disseminating Obscenity" in this chapter.

Permitting Multiple Occupancy in Viewing Booth

Statute

See G.S. 14-202.11, reproduced under "Permitting Facility to Contain Multiple Adult Establishments."

Elements

A person guilty of this offense
- (1) (a) is the agent in charge of any building, premises, structure, or facility, *or*
  - (b) is the owner of the building, premises, structure, or facility when:
    - (i) the owner knew or reasonably should have known
    - (ii) the nature of the business located therein, *and*
    - (iii) the owner refused to cooperate with public officials in reasonable measures designed to terminate the proscribed use, *or*
  - (c) is the owner of the business [controlling the viewing booth], *or*
  - (d) is the manager of the business [controlling the viewing booth], *and*
- (2) permits
- (3) any viewing booth
- (4) in an adult mini–motion picture theater
- (5) to be occupied by more than one person.

Punishment

Class 3 misdemeanor. A person who previously has been convicted of any offense within G.S. 14-202.11 is guilty of a Class 2 misdemeanor.

Notes

Element (1). For convenience, in the following discussion the term "facility" will be used instead of the phrase "building, premises, structure, or other facility."

Element (2). Refer to the discussion of the level of awareness and control implied by the word "permit" under Element (2) in "Permitting Facility to Contain Multiple Adult Establishments." The owner or the agent in charge of a facility with multiple stores in it would seldom have the requisite knowledge and power of control over the viewing booths to bring them within the meaning of "permit." Examples could be posed of a continual practice that comes to the attention of the facility owner or manager, but proof of this knowledge rarely would be available. Of course, the "facility" may be a building owned by a participant in the business of operating a single adult mini–motion picture theater in it; in this instance it may be more feasible to charge the owner, though the wording of the statute as to owners set forth in Element (1) does not fit well.

Discussions in the two previous offenses generally applicable here. Because this offense is in the same section as the two previous offenses, is subject to the same definitions, and carries the same penalty, most of the previous points are applicable to this offense also and will not be repeated.

Particular problem as to employees. Refer to the discussions of the definition of "person" under Element (1) and the issue of aiding and abetting in

"Permitting Facility to Contain Multiple Adult Establishments." The ambiguities cited there cause particular problems with this offense. Suppose that while the manager of an adult mini-motion picture theater is in an office on the premises, an employee sees more than two persons occupying a viewing booth, does nothing about it, and says nothing to the manager. If the listing of persons is a closed list, only the manager may be directly charged. But in this instance the manager does not have the knowledge to do the requisite "permitting"; only the employee has that knowledge. With the other two offenses discussed above, a strong argument can be made for not holding mere employees liable if they have no control over the business operations. To establish that principle, however, may seriously hinder enforcement of this viewing-booth provision.

Related offenses not in this chapter

See the offenses listed under "Disseminating Obscenity" in this chapter.

22

Gambling, Bingo, and Raffles

Chapter Contents

22
Gambling, Bingo, and Raffles

Advertising Lotteries

Statute

§14-289. Advertising lotteries.

Except in connection with a lawful raffle as provided in Part 2 of this Article, if anyone by writing or printing or by circular or letter or in any other way, advertise or publish an account of a lottery, whether within or without this State, stating how, when or where the same is to be or has been drawn, or what are the prizes therein or any of them, or the price of a ticket or any share or interest therein, or where or how it may be obtained, he shall be guilty of a Class 2 misdemeanor.

Elements

A person guilty of this offense
- (1) advertises or publishes an account
- (2) of a lottery
- (3) (a) stating how, when, or where the lottery is drawn, *or*
  - (b) stating the prizes in the lottery, *or*
  - (c) stating the price of a lottery ticket, *or*
  - (d) stating where or how to obtain entry in the lottery.

Punishment

Class 2 misdemeanor.

Notes

Element (1). The statute provides that the element is satisfied if the advertising or publishing is done "by writing or printing or by circular or letter or in any other way."

Element (2). A lottery is any scheme by which a person gives some benefit in order to be considered for winning a prize and the selection of the prize winner is predominantly by chance (169 N.C. 265; 59 N.C. App. 287).

Element (3). The advertised price of a ticket may be of "a ticket or any share or interest therein."

Legal raffles. See "Legal Bingo and Raffles."

Related offenses not in this chapter

Participation in pyramid and chain schemes (G.S. 14-291.2)
Allowing gambling in houses of public entertainment (G.S. 14-293)

Gambling with faro banks and tables (G.S. 14-294)
Keeping or gambling at gaming tables, punchboards, or slot machines on premises (G.S. 14-295)
Allowing gaming tables, punchboards, or slot machines on premises (G.S. 14-297)
Opposing destruction or seizure of gambling material (G.S. 14-300)
Possession of slot machine for operation (G.S. 14-301)
Possession of punchboards or gambling machine for operation (G.S. 14-302)
Agreeing to provide slot machine users a reward (G.S. 14-305)
Limitations on video gaming machines (G.S. 14-306.1)
Participating in illegal futures contract (G.S. 16-4)
Opening office for sale of futures (G.S. 16-5)

Dealing in Lotteries

Statute

§14-290. Dealing in lotteries.

Except in connection with a lawful raffle as provided in Part 2 of this Article, if any person shall open, set on foot, carry on, promote, make or draw, publicly or privately, a lottery, by whatever name, style or title the same may be denominated or known; or if any person shall, by such way and means, expose or set to sale any house, real estate, goods, chattels, cash, written evidence of debt, certificates of claims or any other thing of value whatsoever, every person so offending shall be guilty of a Class 2 misdemeanor which may include a fine not to exceed two thousand dollars ($2,000). Any person who engages in disposing of any species of property whatsoever, including money and evidences of debt, or in any manner distributes gifts or prizes upon tickets, bottle crowns, bottle caps, seals on containers, other devices or certificates sold for that purpose, shall be held liable to prosecution under this section. Any person who shall have in his possession any tickets, certificates or orders used in the operation of any lottery shall be held liable under this section, and the mere possession of such tickets shall be prima facie evidence of the violation of this section.

Elements

A person guilty of this offense
(1) operates
(2) a lottery.

Punishment

Class 2 misdemeanor, which may include a fine not to exceed $2,000.

Notes

Element (2). See the note on Element (2) under "Advertising Lotteries."

Legal raffles. See "Legal Bingo and Raffles."

Related offenses not in this chapter

See the offenses listed under "Advertising Lotteries."

Possession of Lottery Tickets

Statute

See G.S. 14-290, reproduced under "Dealing in Lotteries."

Elements

A person guilty of this offense
(1) knowingly possesses lottery tickets
(2) used in operating any lottery.

Punishment

Class 2 misdemeanor, which may include a fine not to exceed $2,000.

Notes

Element (1). To satisfy this element, the possession need not be immediate personal possession; it is sufficient if tickets are in the defendant's place of business under his or her control (213 N.C. 640). The statute provides that a person commits this offense by possessing tickets, certificates, or orders used in a lottery. It is unclear whether possession in North Carolina of an otherwise legal lottery ticket purchased in another state is a violation of this statute (but see the discussion of G.S. 14-290 and other criminal statutes in 114 N.C. App. 424).

Element (2). The statute has been interpreted to provide that mere possession of the ticket provides an inference that it was used in operating the lottery (N.C.P.I.—Crim. 237.20).

Legal raffles. See "Legal Bingo and Raffles."

Related offenses not in this chapter

See the offenses listed under "Advertising Lotteries."

Selling Lottery Tickets

Statute

§14-291. Selling lottery tickets and acting as agent for lotteries.

Except in connection with a lawful raffle as provided in Part 2 of this Article, if any person shall sell, barter or otherwise dispose of any lottery ticket or order for any number of shares in any lottery, or shall in anywise be concerned in such lottery, by acting as agent in the State for or on behalf of any such lottery, to be drawn or paid either out of or within the State, such person shall be guilty of a Class 2 misdemeanor.

Elements

A person guilty of this offense
(1) sells or disposes of
(2) tickets
(3) for a lottery.

Punishment

Class 2 misdemeanor.

Notes

Elements (1) and (2). The statute provides that the act is to "sell, barter, or otherwise dispose of" any lottery ticket or any order for share(s) in a lottery.

Element (3). See the note on Element (2) under "Advertising Lotteries."

Legal raffles. See "Legal Bingo and Raffles."

Related offenses not in this chapter

See the offenses listed under "Advertising Lotteries."

Acting as Agent for Lottery

Statute

See G.S. 14-291, reproduced under "Selling Lottery Tickets."

Elements

A person guilty of this offense
(1) acts as agent in this state
(2) for a lottery.

Punishment

Class 2 misdemeanor.

Notes

Element (1). In a civil case that likely would apply to this offense, an agent has been said not to be "a subordinate employee without discretion, but must be one having some charge or measure of control over the business entrusted to him, or of some feature of it." (153 N.C. 76).

Element (2). See the note on Element (2) under "Advertising Lotteries." The statute covers lotteries drawn or paid either within or outside the state.

Legal raffles. See "Legal Bingo and Raffles."

Related offenses not in this chapter

See the offenses listed under "Advertising Lotteries."

Selling Numbers Tickets

Statute

§14-291.1. Selling "numbers" tickets; possession prima facie evidence of violation.

Except in connection with a lawful raffle as provided in Part 2 of this Article, if any person shall sell, barter or cause to be sold or bartered, any ticket, token, certificate or order for any number or shares in any lottery, commonly known as the numbers or butter and egg lottery, or lotteries of similar character, to be drawn or paid within or without the State, such person shall be guilty of Class 2 misdemeanor. Any person who shall have in his possession any tickets, tokens, certificates or orders used in the operation of any such lottery shall be guilty under this section, and the possession of such tickets shall be prima facie evidence of the violation of this section.

Elements

A person guilty of this offense
- (1) sells or barters a ticket, token, certificate, or order
- (2) used in a "numbers" or "butter and egg" lottery, or a lottery of similar character.

Punishment

Class 2 misdemeanor.

Notes

Element (1). The offense may be committed by obtaining either money (sale) or goods (barter) for the tickets (238 N.C. 130).

Element (2). The statute apparently does not apply to all lotteries; it applies only to "numbers" or "butter and egg" lotteries. A "butter and egg" lottery is one in which the winning numbers are determined by closing prices in the commodities markets. A "numbers" lottery is similar; the winning numbers may be determined from a variety of sources, such as the number of shares traded on the New York Stock Exchange. The statute specifies that it applies whether the lottery is drawn or paid within or outside the state.

Legal raffles. See "Legal Bingo and Raffles."

Related offenses not in this chapter

See the offenses listed under "Advertising Lotteries."

Possession of Numbers Tickets

Statute

See G.S. 14-291.1, reproduced under "Selling Numbers Tickets."

Elements

A person guilty of this offense
- (1) knowingly possesses tickets, certificates, or orders
- (2) used in the operation of a "numbers" or "butter and egg" lottery, or a lottery of a similar character.

Punishment

Class 2 misdemeanor.

Notes

Element (1). For this offense to occur, the defendant must know that the items he or she possesses are numbers tickets, certificates, or orders used in a lottery (27 N.C. App. 336). See the note on Element (2) under "Advertising Lotteries" for a definition of lottery.

Element (2). G.S. 14-291.1 does not seem to apply to all lotteries, but only to "numbers" or "butter and egg" lotteries.

Legal raffles. See "Legal Bingo and Raffles."

Related offenses not in this chapter

See the offenses listed under "Advertising Lotteries."

Gambling

Statute

§14-292. Gambling.

Except as provided in Part 2 of this Article, any person or organization that operates any game of chance or any person who plays at or bets on any game of chance at which any money, property or other thing of value is bet, whether the same be in stake or not, shall be guilty of a Class 2 misdemeanor.

Elements

A person guilty of this offense
(1) operates, plays, or bets
(2) at a game of chance
(3) at which any money, property, or other thing of value is bet.

Punishment

Class 2 misdemeanor.

Notes

Element (1). A defendant may be guilty as one who operates, plays, or bets on a game of chance. On the meaning of "bet," Justice R. Hunt Parker remarked in State v. Stroupe, 238 N.C. 34, 41 (1953):

> We might say in passing that the word "bet" is so universally understood and used that for a court to attempt to define it would be
>
> To gild refined gold, to paint the lily
> To throw a perfume on the violet.
>
> Shakespeare, *King John*, IV, II, 11–12

Element (2). In a game of chance it is the element of chance that determines the outcome of the game, dominating the element of skill (238 N.C. 34). It has been suggested that all card games are games of chance (111 N.C. 680). Blackjack is considered a game of chance (16 N.C. App. 532). The fact that the money of the defendant and other bettors was converted into a prize for the winner does not change the character of the game (117 N.C. 702). Even if the game is one of skill to the participants in it, it is a game of chance for others; thus betting on a horse race, which is a game, violates the statute (221 N.C. 301). In a discussion of what is a game of chance, dice and card games are stated to be games of chance, but shuffleboard and tenpins are not (238 N.C. 34). Video poker is a game of chance; the elements of chance dominate any element of skill that may be used to play the game (117 N.C. App. 405), but statutes amended (G.S. 14-306) and enacted (G.S. 14-306.1) since that appellate case permit the use of video gaming machines, including video poker, under certain circumstances.

Element (3). To satisfy this element, the defendant need not personally place a bet; if he or she operates or plays a game of chance on which someone else bets, this element is satisfied.

Legal bingo and raffles. See "Legal Bingo and Raffles."

Related offenses not in this chapter

"Encouraging or Betting on Prearranged Race" (Chapter 25)
See the offenses listed under "Advertising Lotteries."

Possession of Slot Machine

Statute

§14-304. Manufacture, sale, etc., of slot machines and devices.

It shall be unlawful to manufacture, own, store, keep, possess, sell, rent, lease, let on shares, lend or give away, transport, or expose for sale or lease, or to offer to sell, rent, lease, let on shares, lend or give away, or to permit the operation of, or for any person to permit to be placed, maintained, used or kept in any room, space or building owned, leased or occupied by him or under his management or control, any slot machine or device where the user may become entitled to receive any money, credit, allowance, or any thing of value, as defined in G.S. 14-306.

§14-306. Slot machine or device defined.

(a) Any machine, apparatus or device is a slot machine or device within the provisions of G.S. 14-296 through 14-309, if it is one that is adapted, or may be readily converted into one that is adapted, for use in such a way that, as a result of the insertion of any piece of money or coin or other object, such machine or device is caused to operate or may be operated in such manner that the user may receive or become entitled to receive any piece of money, credit, allowance or thing of value, or any check, slug, token or memorandum, whether of value or otherwise, or which may be exchanged for any money, credit, allowance or any thing of value, or which may be given in trade, or the user may secure additional chances or rights to use such machine, apparatus or device; or any other machine or device designed and manufactured primarily for use in connection with gambling and which machine or device is classified by the United States as requiring a federal gaming device tax stamp under applicable provisions of the Internal Revenue Code. This definition is intended to embrace all slot machines and similar devices except slot machines in which is kept any article to be purchased by depositing any coin or thing of value, and for which may be had any article of merchandise which makes the same return or returns of equal value each and every time it is operated, or any machine wherein may be seen any pictures or heard any music by depositing therein any coin or thing of value, or any slot weighing machine or any machine for making stencils by the use of contrivances operated by depositing in the machine any coin or thing of value, or any lock operated by slot wherein money or thing of value is to be deposited, where such slot machines make the same return or returns of equal value each and every time the same is operated and does not at any time it is operated offer the user or operator any additional money, credit, allowance, or thing of value, or check, slug, token or memorandum, whether of value or otherwise, which may be exchanged for money, credit, allowance or thing of value or which may be given in trade or by which the user may secure additional chances or rights to use such machine, apparatus, or device, or in the playing of which the operator does not have a chance to make varying scores or tallies.

(b) The definition contained in subsection (a) of this section and G.S. 14-296, 14-301, 14-302, and 14-305 does not include coin-operated machines, video games, pinball machines, and other computer, electronic or mechanical devices that are operated and played for amusement, that involve the use of skill or dexterity to solve problems or tasks or to make varying scores or tallies and that:

(1) Do not emit, issue, display, print out, or otherwise record any receipt, paper, coupon, token, or other form of record which is capable of being redeemed, exchanged, or repurchased for cash, cash equivalent, or prizes, or award free replays; or

(2) In actual operation, limit to eight the number of accumulated credits or replays that may be played at one time and which may award free replays or paper coupons that may be exchanged for prizes or merchandise with a value not exceeding ten dollars ($10.00), but may not be exchanged or converted to money.

(c) Any video machine, the operation of which is made lawful by subsection (b)(2) of this section, shall have affixed to it in view of the player a sticker informing that person that it is a criminal offense with the potential of imprisonment to pay more than that which is allowed by law. In addition, if the machine has an attract chip which allows programming, the static display shall contain the same message.

(d) The exception in subsection (b)(2) of this section does not apply to any machine that pays off in cash. The exemption in subsection (b)(2) of this section does not apply where the prizes, merchandise, credits, or replays are (i) repurchased for cash or rewarded by cash, (ii) exchanged for merchandise of a value of more than ten dollars ($10.00), or (iii) where there is a cash payout of any kind, by the person operating or managing the machine or the premises, or any agent or employee of that person. It is also a criminal offense, punishable under G.S. 14-309, for the person making the unlawful payout to the player of the machine to violate this section, in addition to any other person whose conduct may be unlawful.

Elements

A person guilty of this offense

(1) possesses

(2) a slot machine.

Punishment

Class 1 misdemeanor. Class I felony for second conviction, and Class H felony for third or subsequent convictions (G.S. 14-309).

Notes

Element (1). There are no reported appellate cases defining what constitutes possession of a slot machine; presumably the possession may be either actual or constructive (e.g., when the machine is found in a store owned by the defendant but the defendant is not present). For cases on what constitutes possession of an item generally, see the notes under "Possession of Controlled Substance" (Chapter 24).

Element (2). G.S. 14-306(a) provides a thorough definition of a slot machine. In general the statute defines slot machines as devices that allow a user, by inserting money or tokens, to receive something of value in return, including chances to continue playing (see also 218 N.C. 470). The statute specifically exempts from the definition of slot machine vending machines in which the same amounts of goods are sold to all purchasers. The definition of a slot machine is not unconstitutionally vague (126 N.C. App. 729).

G.S. 14-306(b) provides that the following are not illegal slot machines: coin-operated machines, video games, pinball machines, and other computer, electronic, or mechanical devices that are operated and played for amusement, that involve the use of skill or dexterity to solve problems or tasks or to make varying scores or tallies and (1) do not issue or otherwise record any receipt or other form of record that is capable of being redeemed for cash, cash equivalent, or prizes, or award free replays, or (2) in actual operation, limit to eight the number of accumulated credits or replays that may be played at one time and which may award free replays or paper coupons that may be exchanged for prizes or merchandise with a value not exceeding ten dollars ($10.00), but may not be exchanged or converted to money. However, the exemption from an illegal slot machine in (2), above, does not apply to any machine that pays off in cash or when the prizes, merchandise, credits, or replays are (i) repurchased for cash or rewarded by cash, (ii) exchanged for merchandise of a value of more than ten dollars ($10.00), or (iii) when there is a cash payout of any kind by the person operating or managing the machine or the premises, or any agent or employee of that person.

Limitations on the use of video gaming machines, including video poker, are contained in G.S. 14-306.1, which was enacted in the 2000 legislative session.

Constitutionality. The constitutionality of G.S. 14-304 has been upheld in a case that also includes a history of North Carolina gambling laws (213 N.C. 1).

Other activities prohibited. G.S. 14-304 also prohibits almost any other kind of activity that uses a slot machine, including manufacture, sale, leasing, and allowing operation.

Relationship to other slot machine statutes. Simple possession is sufficient for conviction under this statute. For a conviction under G.S. 14-301, it is necessary to show that the defendant possessed the slot machine for purposes of operation. The punishment for the two offenses is the same, but charges made under G.S. 14-304 would be easier to prove. Because the elements are different, a defendant may be tried and convicted under both statutes for the same act (219 N.C. 545).

Possession of revenue license. The statutes requiring revenue licenses for slot machines do not make possession lawful (188 N.C. 470; 218 N.C. 470).

Related offenses not in this chapter

See the offenses listed under "Advertising Lotteries" in this chapter.

Legal Bingo and Raffles

Statute

§14-309.5. Bingo.

(a) The purpose of the conduct of bingo is to insure a maximum availability of the net proceeds exclusively for application to the charitable, nonprofit causes and undertakings specified herein; that the only justification for this Part is to support such charitable, nonprofit causes; and such purpose should be carried out to prevent the operation of bingo by professionals for profit, prevent commercialized gambling, prevent the disguise of bingo and other game forms or promotional schemes, prevent participation by criminal and other undesirable elements, and prevent the diversion of funds for the purpose herein authorized.

(b) It is lawful for an exempt organization to conduct bingo games in accordance with the provisions of this Part. Any licensed exempt organization who conducts a bingo game in violation of any provision of this Part shall be guilty of a Class 2 misdemeanor. Upon conviction such person shall not conduct a bingo game for a period of one year. It is lawful to participate in a bingo game conducted pursuant to this Part. It shall be a Class I felony for any person: (i) to operate a bingo game without a license; (ii) to operate a bingo game while license is revoked or suspended; (iii) to willfully misuse or misapply any moneys received in connection with any bingo game; or (iv) to contract with or provide consulting services to any licensee. It shall not constitute a violation of any State law to advertise a bingo game conducted in accordance with this Part.

§14-309.6. Definitions.

For purposes of this Part, the term:

(1) "Exempt organization" means an organization that has been in continuous existence in the county of operation of the bingo game for at least one year and that is exempt from taxation under section 501(c)(3), 501(c)(4), 501(c)(8), 501(c)(10), 501(c)(19), or 501(d) of the Internal Revenue Code and is exempt under similar provisions of the General Statutes as a bona fide nonprofit charitable, civic, religious, fraternal, patriotic or veterans' organization or as a nonprofit volunteer fire department, or as a nonprofit volunteer rescue squad or a bona fide homeowners' or property owners' association. (If the organization has local branches or chapters, the term "exempt organization" means the local branch or chapter operating the bingo game);

(2) "Bingo game" means a specific game of chance played with individual cards having numbered squares ranging from one to 75, in which prizes are awarded on the basis of designated numbers on such cards conforming to a predetermined pattern of numbers (but shall not include "instant bingo" which is a game of chance played by the selection of one or more prepackaged cards, with winners determined by the appearance of a preselected designation on the card);

(3) Repealed by Session Laws 1983 (Regular Session 1984), c. 1107, s. 5.

(4) "Local law-enforcement agency" means for any bingo game conducted outside the corporate limits of a municipality or inside the corporate limits of a municipality having no municipal police force:

a. The county police force; or

b. The county sheriff's office in a county with no county police force;

(5) "Local law-enforcement agency" means the municipal police for any bingo game conducted within the corporate limits of a municipality having a police force;

(6) "Beach bingo games" means bingo games which have prizes of ten dollars ($10.00) or less or merchandise that is not redeemable for cash and that has a value of ten dollars ($10.00) or less; and

(7) "Licensed exempt organization" means an exempt organization which possesses a currently valid license.

§14-309.7. Licensing procedure.

(a) An exempt organization may not operate a bingo game at a location without a license. Application for a bingo license shall be made to the Department of Health and Human Services on a form prescribed by the Department. The Department shall charge an annual application fee of one hundred dollars ($100.00) to defray the cost of issuing bingo licenses and handling bingo audit reports. The fees collected shall be deposited in the General Fund of the State. This license shall expire one year after the granting of the license. This license may be renewed yearly, if the applicant pays the application fee and files an audit with the Department pursuant to G.S. 14-309.11. A copy of the application and license shall be furnished to the local law-enforcement agency in the county or municipality in which the licensee intends to operate before bingo is conducted by the licensee.

(b) Each application and renewal application shall contain the following information:

(1) The name and address of the applicant and if the applicant is a corporation, association or other similar legal entity, the name and home address of each of the officers of the organization as well as the name and address of the directors, or other persons similarly situated, of the organization.

(2) The name and home address of each of the members of the special committee.

(3) A copy of the application for recognition of exemptions and a determination letter from the Internal Revenue Service and the Department of Revenue that indicates that the organization is an exempt organization and stating the section under which that exemption is granted; except that if the organization is a State or local branch, lodge, post, or chapter of a national organization, a copy of the determination letter of the national organization satisfies this requirement.

(4) The location at which the applicant will conduct the bingo games. If the premises are leased, a copy of the lease or rental agreement.

(c) In order for an exempt organization to have a member familiar with the operation of bingo present on the premises at all times when bingo is being played and for this member to be responsible for the receiving, reporting and depositing of all revenues received, the exempt organization may pay one member for conducting a bingo game. Such pay shall be on an hourly basis only for the time bingo is actually being played and shall not exceed one and one-half times the existing minimum wage in North Carolina. The member paid under this provision shall be a member in good standing of the exempt organization for at least one year and shall not be the lessor or an employee or agent of the lessor. No other person may be compensated for conducting a bingo game from funds derived from any activities occurring in, or simultaneously with, the playing of bingo, including funds derived from concessions. An exempt organization shall not contract with any person for the purpose of conducting a bingo game. Except as provided in subsection (e) of this section, an exempt organization may hold a bingo game only in or on property owned (either legally or equitably and the buildings must be of a permanent nature with approved plumbing for bathrooms and not movable or of a temporary nature such as a tent or lean-to) or leased by the organization from the owner or bona fide property management agent (no subleasing is permitted) at a total monthly rental in an amount not to exceed one and one-quarter percent (1 1/4%) of the total assessed ad valorem tax value of the portion of the building actually used for the bingo games and the land value on which the building is located (not to exceed two acres) for all activities conducted therein including the playing of bingo for a period of not less than one year and actually occupied and used by that organization on a regular basis for purposes other than bingo for at least six months before the game; and all equipment used by the exempt organization in conducting the bingo game must be owned by the organization. Unless the exempt organization leases the property in accordance with this subsection, an exempt organization may conduct a bingo game only in or on property that is exempt from property taxes levied under Subchapter II of Chapter 105 of the General Statutes, or that is classified and not subject to any property taxes levied under Subchapter II of Chapter 105 of the General Statutes. It shall be unlawful for any person to operate beach bingo games at a location which is being used by any licensed exempt organization for the purpose of conducting bingo games.

(d) Conduct of a bingo game or raffle under this Part on such property shall not operate to defeat an exemption or classification under Subchapter II of Chapter 105 of the General Statutes.

(e) An exempt organization that wants to conduct only an annual or semiannual bingo game may apply to the Department of Health and Human Services for a limited occasion permit. The Department of Health and Human Services may require such information as is reasonable and necessary to determine that the bingo game is conducted in accordance with the provisions of this Part but may not require more information than previously specified in this section for application of a regular license. The application shall be made to the Department on prescribed forms at least 30 days prior to the scheduled date of the bingo game. In lieu of the reporting requirements of G.S. 14-309.11(b) the exempt organization shall file with the licensing agency and local law-enforcement a report on prescribed forms no later than 30 days following the conduct of the bingo game for which the permit was obtained. Such report may require such information as is reasonable and necessary to determine that the bingo game was conducted in accordance with the provisions of this Part but may not require more information than specified in G.S. 14-309.11(b). Any licensed exempt organization may donate or loan its equipment or use of its premises to an exempt organization which has secured a limited occasion permit provided such arrangement is disclosed in the limited occasion permit application and is approved by the Department of Health and Human Services. Except as stated above, all provisions of this Part shall apply to any exempt organization operating a bingo game under this provision.

§14-309.8. Limit on sessions.

The number of sessions of bingo conducted or sponsored by an exempt organization shall be limited to two sessions per week and such sessions must not exceed a period of five hours each per session. No two sessions of bingo shall be held within a 48-hour period of time. No more than two sessions of bingo shall be operated or conducted in any one building, hall or structure during any one calendar week and if two sessions are held, they must be held by the same exempt organization. This section shall not apply to bingo games conducted at a fair or other exhibition conducted pursuant to Article 45 of Chapter 106 of the General Statutes.

§14-309.9. Bingo prizes.

(a) The maximum prize in cash or merchandise that may be offered or paid for any one game of bingo is five hundred dollars ($500.00). The maximum aggregate amount of prizes, in cash and/or merchandise, that may be offered or paid at any one session of bingo is one thousand five hundred dollars ($1,500). Provided, however, that if an exempt organization holds only one session of bingo during a calendar week, the maximum aggregate amount of prizes, in cash and/or merchandise, that may be offered or paid at any one session is two thousand five hundred dollars ($2,500).

(b) Repealed by Session Laws 1983 (Regular Session 1984), c. 1107, s. 8.

(c) This section shall not apply to bingo games conducted at a fair or other exhibition conducted pursuant to Article 45 of Chapter 106 of the General Statutes.

§14-309.10. Operation of bingo.

The operation of bingo games shall be the direct responsibility of, and controlled by, a special committee selected by the governing body of the exempt organization in the manner provided by the rules of the exempt organization.

§14-309.11. Accounting and use of proceeds.

(a) All funds received in connection with a bingo game shall be placed in a separate bank account. No funds may be disbursed from this account except the exempt organization may expend proceeds for prizes, advertising, utilities, and the purchase of supplies and equipment used [in conducting the raffle and] in playing bingo, taxes and license fees related to bingo and the payment of compensation as authorized by G.S. 14-309.7(c) and for the purposes set forth below for the remaining proceeds. Such payments shall be made by consecutively numbered checks. Any proceeds available in the account after payment of the above expenses shall inure to the exempt organization to be used for religious, charitable, civic, scientific, testing, public safety, literary, or educational purposes or for purchasing, constructing, maintaining, operating or using equipment or land or a building or improvements thereto owned by and for the exempt organization and used for civic purposes or made available by the exempt organization for use by the general public from time to time, or to foster amateur sports competition, or for the prevention of cruelty to children or animals, provided that no proceeds shall be used or expended for social functions for the members of the exempt organization.

(b) An audit of the account required by subsection (a) of this section shall be prepared annually for the period of January 1 through December 31 or otherwise as directed by the Department of Health and Human Services and shall be filed with the Department of Health and Human Services and the local law-enforcement agency at a time directed by the Department of Health and Human Services. The audit shall be prepared on a form approved by the Department of Health and Human Services and shall include the following information:

(1) The number of bingo games conducted or sponsored by the exempt organization;
(2) The location and date at which each bingo game was conducted and the prize awarded;
(3) The gross receipts of each bingo game;
(4) The cost or amount of any prize given at each bingo game;
(5) The amount paid in prizes at each session;
(6) The net return to the exempt organization; and
(7) The disbursements from the separate account and the purpose of those disbursements, including the date of each transaction and the name and address of each payee.

(c) Any person who shall willfully furnish, supply, or otherwise give false information in any audit or statement filed pursuant to this section shall be guilty of a Class 2 misdemeanor.

(d) All books, papers, records and documents relevant to determining whether an organization has acted or is acting in compliance with this section shall be open to inspection by the law-enforcement agency or its designee, or the district attorney or his designee, or the Department of Health and Human Services at reasonable times and during reasonable hours.

§14-309.12. Violation is gambling.

A bingo game conducted otherwise than in accordance with the provisions of this Part is "gambling" within the meaning of G.S. 19-1 et seq., and proceedings against such bingo game may be instituted as provided for in Chapter 19 of the General Statutes.

§14-309.13. Public sessions.

Any exempt organization operating a bingo game which is open to persons other than members of the exempt organization, their spouses, and their children shall make such bingo game open to the general public.

§14-309.14. Beach bingo.

Nothing in this Article shall apply to "beach bingo" games except for the following subsections:

(1) No beach bingo game may offer a prize having a value greater than ten dollars ($10.00). Any person offering a greater than ten-dollar ($10.00) but less than fifty-dollar ($50.00) prize is guilty of a Class 2 misdemeanor. Any person offering a prize of fifty dollars ($50.00) or greater is guilty of a Class I felony.
(2) No beach bingo game may be held in conjunction with any other lawful bingo game, with any "promotional bingo game", or with any offering of an opportunity to obtain anything of value, whether for valuable consideration or not. No beach bingo game may offer free bingo games as a promotion, for prizes or otherwise. Any person who violates this subsection is guilty of a Class I felony.
(3) G.S. 18B-308 shall apply to beach bingo games.
(4) Upon conviction under any provision of this section, such person shall not conduct a bingo game for a period of at least one year.

§14-309.15. Raffles.

(a) It is lawful for any nonprofit organization or association, recognized by the Department of Revenue as tax-exempt pursuant to G.S. 105-130.11(a), to conduct raffles in accordance with this section. Any person who conducts a raffle in violation of any provision of this section shall be guilty of a Class 2 misdemeanor. Upon conviction that person shall not conduct a raffle for a period of one year. It is lawful to participate in a raffle conducted pursuant to this section. It shall not constitute a violation of State law to advertise a raffle conducted in accordance with this section. A raffle conducted pursuant to this section is not "gambling".

(b) For purposes of this section "raffle" means a game in which the prize is won by random drawing of the name or number of one or more persons purchasing chances.

(c) Raffles shall be limited to two per nonprofit organization per year.

(d) The maximum cash prize that may be offered or paid for any one raffle is ten thousand dollars ($10,000) and if merchandise is used as a prize, and it is not redeemable for cash, the maximum fair market value of that prize may be fifty thousand dollars ($50,000). No real property may be offered as a prize in a raffle. The total cash prizes offered or paid by any nonprofit organization or association may not exceed ten thousand dollars ($10,000) in any calendar year. The total fair market value of all prizes offered by any nonprofit organization or association, either in cash or in merchandise that is not redeemable for cash, may not exceed fifty thousand dollars ($50,000) in any calendar year.

(e) Raffles shall not be conducted in conjunction with bingo.

(f) As used in this subsection, "net proceeds of a raffle" means the receipts less the cost of prizes awarded. No less than ninety percent (90%) of the net proceeds of a raffle shall be used by the nonprofit organization or association for charitable, religious, educational, civic, or other nonprofit purposes. None of the net proceeds of the raffle may be used to pay any person to conduct the raffle, or to rent a building where the tickets are received or sold or the drawing is conducted.

Notes

Generally. The relevant statutes, printed above, apply to bingo and raffles statewide. No local exceptions are now in force. Any bingo game or raffle not conducted in accordance with these statutes constitutes a violation of the state's gambling laws.

Bingo. Bingo games are legal if conducted pursuant to Part 2 of Article 37, G.S. Chapter 14 (G.S. 14-309.5 through 14-309.15). "Beach bingo" games are exempt from all statutes in Article 37 other than G.S. 14-309.14. "Beach bingo" is a bingo game offering maximum prizes of $10.00 or merchandise with a maximum value of $10.00 that is not redeemable for cash [G.S. 14-309.6(6)]. If a person operating a beach bingo game offers a prize greater than $10.00 but less than $50.00, he or she is guilty of a Class 2 misdemeanor. If such a person offers a prize of $50.00 or more (126 N.C. App. 729), he or she is guilty of a Class I felony. G.S. 14-309.14(2) prohibits holding a beach bingo game in conjunction with any other lawful bingo game, with any promotional bingo game, or with any offering of an opportunity to obtain anything of value, whether or not the players pay anything for the opportunity. It also prohibits a beach bingo game operator from offering free games as a promotion. Violation of G.S. 14-309.14(2)'s prohibitions is a Class I felony. If a person is convicted of violating any part of G.S. 14-309.14, he or she cannot conduct a bingo game for at least one year after conviction.

For games in which prizes larger than $10.00 are awarded (up to $500 per game, with a cumulative limit per session of $1,500 if two sessions per week are held or $2,500 if a single weekly session is held), the law imposes numerous restrictions. First, the game must be conducted by an organization exempt from taxes by the federal Internal Revenue Service and the state Department of Revenue. Eligible organizations include charitable, civic, religious, fraternal, and veterans' groups, as well as volunteer fire departments, and volunteer rescue squads. Second, the organization must obtain a license from the Department of Health and Human Services before it conducts a game. Third, the organization must use bona fide members of its organization to conduct the game, and no more than one of its members may be paid for his or her work during the game. The rate of pay for that person is limited to 1.5 times the prevailing minimum wage. A special committee must be appointed to supervise the game's operation. Fourth, the organization must use its own equipment and facilities to conduct the game, and any building used must be a permanent structure. If the building is leased, the lease must be at no more than fair market value, and the building must be used for purposes other than bingo. Fifth, the organization may not conduct more than two sessions (each with a 5-hour maximum) per week, and no session may be held within 48 hours of another. Finally, the net proceeds of the bingo games must be used for specified nonprofit purposes, and the manner in which the money is spent is strictly regulated and required to be audited annually.

A scheme in which a person purchases a comb for $5.00 (when its retail value is 19 cents) or candy for $1.00 (when its retail value is one cent) and then is given "free" bingo game cards with substantial prizes for winners constitutes bingo (95 N.C. App. 258).

Raffles. G.S. 14-309.15 legalizes raffles under certain conditions. The raffle must be conducted by a tax-exempt organization. The prize offered in any one raffle may not exceed $10,000 in cash or if merchandise is offered as a prize, its fair market value may not exceed $50,000. The total cash prizes an organization may offer in any calendar year may not exceed $10,000, and the total fair market value of any merchandise awarded in any calendar year may not exceed $50,000. Real property may not be offered as a prize. The organization may not conduct more than two raffles per year. Ninety percent of the raffle's net proceeds must be used to further the charitable or other nonprofit purpose of the organization. Finally, no one may be paid for services rendered in conducting the raffle, and none of the net proceeds may be used to rent a building where raffle tickets are sold or received or the drawing is held.

It should also be noted that Chapter 219 of the 1993 Session Laws provides that for the purposes of that act (which set the maximum cash prize for any one raffle at $5,000 and the maximum fair market value of merchandise that may be offered as a prize at $25,000), government entities in North Carolina shall be considered nonprofit as defined in G.S. 105-130.11(a). Thus government entities may run raffles under the terms of that act.

A raffle's randomness, as required by G.S. 14-309.15(b), was destroyed when cards for all ticket holders were placed on a wall; as tickets were removed from a cage purportedly holding all tickets, names were removed from the wall; upon discovering that the number of names on the wall did not match the number of tickets left in the cage (only three tickets were in the cage, while four names remained on the wall), one more ticket containing the missing name was added to the cage (109 N.C. App. 384). Consequently, the event properly was declared void as a raffle pursuant to G.S. 14-292.

G.S. 14-309.6, which expressly designates homeowners' and property owners' associations as organizations eligible to conduct bingo games or raffles, has been declared unconstitutional (65 N.C. App., aff'd, 311 N.C. 397).

The licensing criteria under G.S. 14-309.7(c) for bingo games that limit rent, prohibit subleasing, and prohibit contracting with bingo operators are constitutional, since they are rationally related to the legitimate goal of ensuring that the money earned by an exempt organization is used for a charitable purpose

(79 N.C. App. 156). Under G.S. 14-309.7(c) the requirements about the minimum term of a lease and other uses of a building used for bingo are constitutional, in that they are rationally related to the legitimate goal of ensuring that an exempt organization has community roots (79 N.C. App. 156). The rules under G.S. 14-309.8 prohibiting more than two games a week in a building and requiring the same organization to conduct the games are rationally related to the legitimate goal of ensuring that bingo games are not operated by full-time professionals for a profit (79 N.C. App. 156). The provision of G.S. 14-309.8 prohibiting an exempt organization from conducting two bingo sessions within a 48-hour period is not unconstitutionally vague. Also, it does not violate equal protection rights, since it is rationally related to the legitimate interest of limiting bingo to a brief, occasional chance for harmless recreation (82 N.C. App. 583).

Related offenses not in this chapter

None.

23
Abandonment and Nonsupport

Chapter Contents

23
Abandonment and Nonsupport

Abandonment and Failure to Support Spouse

Statute

§14-322. Abandonment and failure to support spouse and children.

(a) For purposes of this Article:
- (1) "Supporting spouse" means a spouse, whether husband or wife, upon whom the other spouse is actually substantially dependent or from whom such other spouse is substantially in need of maintenance and support.
- (2) "Dependent spouse" means a spouse, whether husband or wife, who is actually substantially dependent upon the other spouse for his or her maintenance and support or is substantially in need of maintenance and support from the other spouse.

(b) Any supporting spouse who shall willfully abandon a dependent spouse without providing that spouse with adequate support shall be guilty of a Class 1 or 2 misdemeanor and upon conviction shall be punished according to subsection (f).

(c) Any supporting spouse who, while living with a dependent spouse, shall willfully neglect to provide adequate support for that dependent spouse shall be guilty of a misdemeanor and upon conviction shall be punished according to subsection (f).

(d) Any parent who shall willfully neglect or refuse to provide adequate support for that parent's child, whether natural or adopted, and whether or not the parent abandons the child, shall be guilty of a misdemeanor and upon conviction shall be punished according to subsection (f). Willful neglect or refusal to provide adequate support of a child shall constitute a continuing offense and shall not be barred by any statute of limitations until the youngest living child of the parent shall reach the age of 18 years.

(e) Upon conviction for an offense under this section, the court may make such order as will best provide for the support, as far as may be necessary, of the abandoned spouse or child, or both, from the property or labor of the defendant. If the court requires the payment of child support, the amount of the payments shall be determined as provided in G.S. 50-13.4(c). For child support orders initially entered on or after January 1, 1994, the immediate income withholding provisions of G.S. 110-136.5(c1) shall apply.

(f) A first offense under this section is a Class 2 misdemeanor. A second or subsequent offense is a Class 1 misdemeanor.

Elements

A person guilty of this offense
- (1) is a supporting spouse, *and*

(2) willfully
(3) abandons his or her dependent spouse
(4) without providing that spouse with adequate support.

Punishment

The first offense is a Class 2 misdemeanor. A second or subsequent offense is a Class 1 misdemeanor.

Notes

Man or woman may commit offense. A husband or a wife may commit this offense.

Element (1). A supporting spouse is a spouse from whom a dependent spouse, as a matter of fact, substantially needs support.

Element (2). "Willful," in this offense, means that both the abandonment and the nonsupport of the dependent spouse are intentional and without excuse or mitigation (164 N.C. 475; 242 N.C. 84). A defendant's inability to provide support is a defense, though the defendant may not be excused if he or she is able to work and simply refuses to do so (55 N.C. App. 255; *Perkins*, p. 673).

Element (3). If a husband and wife consent to separate, neither may be charged with abandoning the other under this statute (164 N.C. 475). The duty to support also ends with divorce. Adultery by the dependent spouse is a defense to a charge of abandonment (194 N.C. 378). If the defendant cohabits with the dependent spouse after having been convicted of this offense, the defendant may be charged again under this offense if he or she again willfully abandons and fails to support the dependent spouse (79 N.C. 603; 181 N.C. 597). Evidence was sufficient to prove that the defendant abandoned his wife when he left the marital residence and returned the next day to gather his remaining things. In addition, the defendant's acts of cruelty toward her constituted constructive abandonment (123 N.C. App. 698).

Element (4). A supporting spouse has not committed this offense if he or she abandons his or her spouse but continues to provide support (228 N.C. 151; 242 N.C. 84). The support required is clothing, food, lodging, medical attention, and other necessities for a person of the dependent spouse's social position and circumstances and commensurate with the supporting spouse's ability to provide (234 N.C. 192).

Where crime occurs. This offense has been committed only if the abandonment occurred in North Carolina.

Order for support. On conviction, the defendant may be ordered to pay a regular amount into court for support of his or her dependent spouse [G.S. 14-322(e); 196 N.C. 239]. If a court orders child support, the amount of payments must be determined according to G.S. 50-13.4(c). For orders initially entered on or after January 1, 1994, a person obligated to pay child support may also be immediately subject to income withholding under G.S. 110-136.5(c1).

Related offenses not in this chapter

None.

Failure to Support Dependent Spouse While Living Together

Statute

See subsection (c) of G.S. 14-322, reproduced under "Abandonment and Failure to Support Spouse."

Elements

A person guilty of this offense
(1) is a supporting spouse, *and*
(2) while living with a dependent spouse
(3) willfully neglects to provide adequate support for that spouse.

Punishment

The first offense is a Class 2 misdemeanor. A second or subsequent offense is a Class 1 misdemeanor.

Notes

Man or woman may commit offense. See this same note under "Abandonment and Failure to Support Spouse."

Element (1). See the note on Element (1) under "Abandonment and Failure to Support Spouse."

Element (2). This crime covers nonsupport when the defendant continues to live with his or her spouse; if the defendant abandons his or her spouse, the crime is abandonment and failure to support spouse.

Element (3). See the notes on Elements (2) and (4) under "Abandonment and Failure to Support Spouse."

Continuing offense. This is a continuing offense, and the offending spouse may be prosecuted for subsequent failure to support after a first conviction, as in nonsupport of an illegitimate child (212 N.C. 566).

Related offenses not in this chapter

None.

Nonsupport of Child

Statute

See subsection (d) of G.S. 14-322, reproduced under "Abandonment and Failure to Support Spouse."

Elements

A parent guilty of this offense
(1) willfully
(2) (a) neglects, *or*
    (b) refuses
(3) to support adequately
(4) his or her child.

Punishment

The first offense is a Class 2 misdemeanor. A second or subsequent offense is a Class 1 misdemeanor.

Notes

Father or mother may commit offense. A father or mother may commit this offense.

Elements (1) and (2). See the note on Element (2) under "Abandonment and Failure to Support Spouse," above, and the notes on Elements (2) and (3) under "Nonsupport of Illegitimate Child (Bastardy)," below.

Element (3). The duty to support continues even though others, such as grandparents, might be providing for the child (*Perkins*, p. 675). Abandonment is *not* an element of this offense. The parent may not relieve himself or herself of the obligation to support by contract (257 N.C. 374). For a definition of support, see the note to Element (4) under "Nonsupport of Illegitimate Child (Bastardy)."

Element (4). The statute applies to both natural and adopted children; it does not apply to illegitimate children (219 N.C. 331); nonsupport of an illegitimate child is punished as a separate offense (this offense is covered immediately below). A putative father may defend a nonsupport charge on grounds that the child is not his (300 N.C. 494); if the husband has access to the wife during the time when the child could have been conceived, there is a strong presumption that he is the child's father (300 N.C. 494). The husband may rebut this presumption by presenting evidence that raises a factual issue as to the paternity of the child (300 N.C. 494). Blood tests to prove or disprove parentage, including the statistical likelihood of the alleged parent's parentage, are admissible in a criminal action (G.S. 8-50.1). See the discussion of blood tests in the note on Element (1) under "Nonsupport of Illegitimate Child."

Continuing offense. This is a continuing offense. As with nonsupport of an illegitimate child (212 N.C. 566), the parent may be prosecuted for subsequent failure to support after a first conviction, or even after a prior acquittal (51 N.C. App. 553). Generally a parent's duty to support his or her child ceases when that child reaches the age of 18 or is emancipated (20 N.C. App. 550). However, if the child is still in primary or secondary school when he or she reaches age 18, payments shall continue until the child graduates, ceases to attend school on a regular basis, fails to make satisfactory progress toward graduation, or reaches age 20, unless the court, in its discretion orders that payments cease [G.S. 50-13.4(c)]. Upon the child's graduation or attainment of age 20, payments terminate without court order, but the child has the right to show that he or she has neither reached age 20 nor graduated. A parent's duty to support a child who is physically or mentally incapable of self-support also ends when that child reaches age 18 (G.S. 50-13.8). No statute of limitations is a bar until the youngest child who might be supported reaches age 18.

Effect of divorce. The duty to support a child continues even after a divorce of the parents (184 N.C. 701) and even if the other parent has custody (*Perkins*, p. 676).

Order for support. Upon conviction, the defendant may be ordered to pay child support [G.S. 14-322(e)]; the court may order that payments be made to the clerk of court (G.S. 15A-1344.1). If the defendant fails to comply with the order, it may be enforced through income withholding (G.S. 110-136.3).

Where offense committed. G.S. 14-325.1 provides that a parent commits this offense if the child resides in North Carolina, regardless of where the parent resides.

Related offenses not in this chapter

"Contributing to a Juvenile's Being Delinquent, Undisciplined, Abused, or Neglected" (Chapter. 7)
Illegally receiving or giving compensation for placing child for adoption (G.S. 48-10-102)

Nonsupport of Illegitimate Child (Bastardy)

Statute

§49-2. Nonsupport of illegitimate child by parents made misdemeanor.

Any parent who willfully neglects or who refuses to provide adequate support and maintain his or her illegitimate child shall be guilty of a Class 2 misdemeanor. A child within the meaning of this Article shall be any person less than 18 years of age and any person whom either parent might be required under the laws of North Carolina to support and maintain if such child were the legitimate child of such parent.

Elements

A person guilty of this offense
- (1) is a parent, *and*
- (2) willfully
- (3) (a) neglects, *or*
  (b) refuses
- (4) to support adequately
- (5) his or her illegitimate child.

Punishment

Class 2 misdemeanor. In addition, a person convicted of this offense must make support payments for the child's benefit in a sum determined by the court (G.S. 49-8).

Notes

Generally. It is not a crime to father or give birth to an illegitimate child, but failure to support the child is a crime (208 N.C. 231; 262 N.C. 446).

Statute is gender-neutral. Mothers as well as fathers may be prosecuted for this offense (G.S. 49-4).

Element (1). Proof that the defendant is the parent is essential to a conviction for this offense (210 N.C. 271; 311 N.C. 727). The results of a blood test are admissible in evidence in cases in which paternity is disputed; a test that excludes the defendant as a father is conclusive evidence if the jury believes that it was administered properly; if the test result does not exclude the defendant, the statistical probability that the defendant could have been the parent is admissible (G.S. 8-50.1; G.S. 49-7).

Elements (2) and (3). "Willful" as used in this offense refers to the "intentional neglect or refusal to support the illegitimate child" (232 N.C. 388), "without any lawful justification or excuse" (228 N.C. 137). See the note on Element (2) under "Abandonment and Failure to Support Spouse." A refusal to support an illegitimate child is not willful unless the parent has first refused a demand for support of the child (241 N.C. 119; 262 N.C. 446).

Element (4). To support means to provide food, clothing, and other necessities, including medical care (238 N.C. 283). This offense does not cover the failure to provide either medical care for the mother during pregnancy or the expenses of birth, but a judge may require the defendant to pay those expenses as a part of a judgment (228 N.C. 137).

Element (5). A child is "any person less than eighteen years of age and any person whom either parent might be required under the law of North Carolina to support and maintain as if the child were the legitimate child of such parent" (G.S. 49-2). Where the child was born is irrelevant; the only requirement is that the child now reside in North Carolina (G.S. 49-3; 238 N.C. 206). Failure to support a legitimate child is punishable under nonsupport of child.

Statute of Limitations. A reputed father may be prosecuted for this offense at any time within the first 3 years after the child is born or any time before the child is 18 if the child was declared to be his child within 3 years after the child's birth (68 N.C. App. 268). If a finding of paternity has not been made, the prosecution may commence at any time before the child reaches 18 if the father has made a support payment for the child's support within 3 years of the child's birth and if the criminal pleading charging the offense was issued within 3 years from the date of the last payment (269 N.C. 280). A mother may be prosecuted at any time before the child reaches 18 (G.S. 49-4).

Who may bring charges. Prosecutions for this offense may be initiated by the supporting parent, or by that parent's personal representative if he or she is dead or incompetent, or by the county director of social services if the child is likely to "become a public charge" (G.S. 49-5).

Continuing offense. If a person again does not support his or her illegitimate child after being released from prison or probation for a previous conviction of this offense, the person may be prosecuted again for the same offense (212 N.C. 566).

Order for support. Upon finding that the defendant is a parent of the child for whom the proceeding has been initiated and that the defendant has neglected or refused to provide adequate support for that child, the court is required to order future support (G.S. 49-7; 41 N.C. App. 281). Such an order is subject to modification and increase, and the amount of child support must be determined according to guidelines established pursuant to G.S. 50-13.4(c) (G.S. 49-7). If the defendant does not comply with the court order for support, the order may be enforced through income withholding (G.S. 110-136.3).

Where offense committed. G.S. 49-3 provides that a parent commits this offense if the child resides in North Carolina, regardless of where the parent resides or if the child was born outside of the state.

Related offenses not in this chapter

Illegally receiving or giving compensation for placing child for adoption (G.S. 48-10-102)

Abandonment of Child for Six Months

Statute

§14-322.1. Abandonment of child or children for six months.

Any man or woman who, without just cause or provocation, willfully abandons his or her child or children for six months and who willfully fails or refuses to provide adequate means of support for his or her child or children during the six months' period, and who attempts to conceal his or her whereabouts from his or her child or children with the intent of escaping his lawful obligation for the support of said child or children, shall be punished as a Class I felon.

Elements

A person guilty of this offense
- (1) willfully
- (2) abandons
- (3) his or her child, *and*
- (4) willfully fails or refuses to provide adequate support for that child
- (5) for six months, *and*
- (6) the person attempts to conceal his or her whereabouts from the child
- (7) with the intent to escape the obligation to support.

Punishment

Class I felony.

Notes

Father or mother may commit offense. A father or mother may commit this offense.

Element (1). See the note on Element (2) under "Abandonment and Failure to Support Spouse."

Element (4). See the note on Element (4) under "Abandonment and Failure to Support Spouse" and the note on Element (3) under "Nonsupport of Child."

Element (3). It is not clear whether this offense applies to nonsupport of illegitimate children.

Order for support. While child-support orders and income withholding are authorized upon conviction of nonsupport of child as well as conviction of abandonment and failure to support spouse, there is no clear statutory authority for such remedies upon conviction of this offense.

Related offenses not in this chapter

"Contributing to a Juvenile's Being Delinquent, Undisciplined, Abused, or Neglected" (Chapter 7)

Illegally receiving or giving compensation for placing child for adoption (G.S. 48-10-102)

Failure to Support Parent

Statute

§14-326.1. Parents; failure to support.

If any person being of full age, and having sufficient income after reasonably providing for his or her immediate family shall, without reasonable cause, neglect to maintain and support his or her parent or parents, if such parent or parents be sick or not able to work and have not sufficient means or ability to maintain or support themselves, such person shall be deemed guilty of a Class 2 misdemeanor; upon conviction of a second or subsequent offense such person shall be guilty of a Class 1 misdemeanor.

If there be more than one person bound under the provisions of the next preceding paragraph to support the same parent or parents, they shall share equitably in the discharge of such duty.

Elements

A person guilty of this offense

(1) is 18 years of age or more, *and*
(2) has sufficient income after providing for his or her immediate family, *and*
(3) without reasonable cause
(4) neglects to support his or her parent
(5) when the parent is sick or unable to work and support himself or herself.

Punishment

The first offense is a Class 2 misdemeanor. The second or subsequent offense is a Class 1 misdemeanor.

Notes

Son or daughter may commit offense. A son or daughter may commit this offense.

Element (4). The definition of support is probably similar to that set out under "Nonsupport of Child" and "Abandonment and Failure to Support Spouse."

Children share costs equally. If more than one child is at fault, they must share the financial cost of parental support equally.

Jurisdiction. Both statutory and case law expressly provide that the defendant's state of residence is irrelevant to the commission of the offense of nonsupport of child; for this offense, there is no such provision. However, G.S. 15A-134, which permits prosecution of a person for an offense that occurs only partly in North Carolina, should permit prosecution of a nonresident for failure to support a parent who resides in North Carolina.

Related offenses not in this chapter

"Domestic Abuse, Neglect, or Exploitation of Disabled or Elder Adults" (Chapter 7)

24
Drug Offenses

Chapter Contents

24
Drug Offenses

Part I. Controlled Substances

Scheduling of Controlled Substances

Some examples of the drugs listed under the different schedules of the Controlled Substances Act (G.S. Ch. 90, Art. 5):

Schedule I (G.S. 90-89):

Heroin (and other specified opium derivatives)
Lysergic acid diethylamide (LSD)
Mescaline
Methaqualone
3, 4-methylenedioxyamphetamine (MDA)
3, 4-methylenedioxymethamphetamine (MDMA)
Peyote

Schedule II (G.S. 90-90):

Amphetamine (Dexedrine)
Cocaine
Coca leaves
Codeine
Methadone (Dolophine)
Methamphetamine (Desoxyn)
Methylphenidate (Ritalin)
Morphine
Opium
Pentobarbital (Nembutal) (see also Schedule III, below)
Phencyclidine (PCP)
Phenmetrazine (Preludin)
Secobarbital (Seconal) (see also Schedule III, below)

Schedule III (G.S. 90-91):

Anabolic steroids
Methyprylon (Noludar)
Nalorphine
Pentobarbital in suppository dosage form

Secobarbital in suppository dosage form

Schedule IV (G.S. 90-92):
Barbital
Chloral hydrate (Noctec)
Chlordiazepoxide (Librium)
Diazepam (Valium)
Ethclorvynol (Placidyl)
Meprobamate (Miltown, Equanil)
Methohexital (Brevital)
Phenobarbital

Schedule V (G.S. 90-93):
Includes compounds containing mixtures of certain narcotic drugs with other, nonnarcotic, medicinal ingredients to give the compound valuable medicinal qualities. For example, it includes a compound with not more than 200 milligrams of codeine per 100 milliliters or per 100 grams, or a compound with not more than 100 milligrams of opium per 100 milliliters or per 100 grams.

Schedule VI (G.S. 90-94):
Marijuana
Tetrahydrocannabinols

Manufacture of Controlled Substance

Statute

§90-95. Violations; penalties.

(a) Except as authorized by this Article, it is unlawful for any person:

(1) To manufacture, sell or deliver, or possess with intent to manufacture, sell or deliver, a controlled substance;

(2) To create, sell or deliver, or possess with intent to sell or deliver, a counterfeit controlled substance;

(3) To possess a controlled substance.

(b) Except as provided in subsections (h) and (i) of this section, any person who violates G.S. 90-95(a)(1) with respect to:

(1) A controlled substance classified in Schedule I or II shall be punished as a Class H felon, except that the sale of a controlled substance classified in Schedule I or II shall be punished as a Class G felon;

(2) A controlled substance classified in Schedule III, IV, V, or VI shall be punished as a Class I felon, except that the sale of a controlled substance classified in Schedule III, IV, V, or VI shall be punished as a Class H felon. The transfer of less than 5 grams of marijuana for no remuneration shall not constitute a delivery in violation of G.S. 90-95(a)(1).

(c) Any person who violates G.S. 90-95(a)(2) shall be punished as a Class I felon.

(d) Except as provided in subsections (h) and (i) of this section, any person who violates G.S. 90-95(a)(3) with respect to:

(1) A controlled substance classified in Schedule I shall be punished as a Class I felon;

(2) A controlled substance classified in Schedule II, III, or IV shall be guilty of a Class 1 misdemeanor. If the controlled substance exceeds four tablets, capsules, or other dosage units or equivalent quantity of hydromorphone or if the quantity of the controlled substance, or combination of the controlled substances, exceeds one hundred tablets, capsules or other dosage units, or

equivalent quantity, the violation shall be punishable as a Class I felony. If the controlled substance is methamphetamine, amphetamine, phencyclidine, or cocaine and any salt, isomer, salts of isomers, compound, derivative, or preparation thereof, or coca leaves and any salt, isomer, salts of isomers, compound, derivative, or preparation of coca leaves, or any salt, isomer, salts of isomers, compound, derivative or preparation thereof which is chemically equivalent or identical with any of these substances (except decocanized coca leaves or any extraction of coca leaves which does not contain cocaine or ecgonine), the violation shall be punishable as a Class I felony.

(3) A controlled substance classified in Schedule V shall be guilty of a Class 2 misdemeanor;

(4) A controlled substance classified in Schedule VI shall be guilty of a Class 3 misdemeanor, but any sentence of imprisonment imposed must be suspended and the judge may not require at the time of sentencing that the defendant serve a period of imprisonment as a special condition of probation. If the quantity of the controlled substance exceeds one-half of an ounce (avoirdupois) of marijuana or one-twentieth of an ounce (avoirdupois) of the extracted resin of marijuana, commonly known as hashish, the violation shall be punishable as a Class 1 misdemeanor. If the quantity of the controlled substance exceeds one and one-half ounces (avoirdupois) of marijuana or three-twentieths of an ounce (avoirdupois) of the extracted resin of marijuana, commonly known as hashish, or if the controlled substance consists of any quantity of synthetic tetrahydrocannabinols or tetrahydrocannabinols isolated from the resin of marijuana, the violation shall be punishable as a Class I felony.

(d1) Except as authorized by this Article, it is unlawful for any person to:

(1) Possess an immediate precursor chemical with intent to manufacture a controlled substance; or

(2) Possess or distribute an immediate precursor chemical knowing, or having reasonable cause to believe, that the immediate precursor chemical will be used to manufacture a controlled substance.

Any person who violates this subsection shall be punished as a Class H felon.

(d2) The immediate precursor chemicals to which subsection (d1) of this section applies are those immediate precursor chemicals designated by the Commission pursuant to its authority under G.S. 90-88, and the following (until otherwise specified by the Commission):

(1) Anhydrous ammonia.
(1a) Anthranilic acid.
(2) Benzyl cyanide.
(3) Chloroephedrine.
(4) Chloropseudoephedrine.
(5) D-lysergic acid.
(6) Ephedrine.
(7) Ergonovine maleate.
(8) Ergotamine tartrate.
(9) Ethyl Malonate.
(10) Ethylamine.
(10a) Iodine.
(11) Isosafrole.
(11a) Lithium.
(12) Malonic acid.
(13) Methylamine.
(14) N-acetylanthranilic acid.
(15) N-ethylephedrine.
(16) N-ethylepseudoephedrine.
(17) N-methylephedrine.
(18) N-methylpseudoephedrine.
(19) Norpseudoephedrine.
(20) Phenyl-2-propane.
(21) Phenylacetic acid.

(22) Phenylpropanolamine.
(23) Piperidine.
(24) Piperonal.
(25) Propionic anhydride.
(26) Pseudoephedrine.
(27) Pyrrolidine.
(27a) Red phosphorous.
(28) Safrole.
(28a) Sodium.
(29) Thionylchloride.
(30) Gamma-butyrolactone.

(e) The prescribed punishment and degree of any offense under this Article shall be subject to the following conditions, but the punishment for an offense may be increased only by the maximum authorized under any one of the applicable conditions:

(1), (2) Repealed by Session Laws 1979, c. 760, s. 5.

(3) If any person commits a Class 1 misdemeanor under this Article and if he has previously been convicted for one or more offenses under any law of North Carolina or any law of the United States or any other state, which offenses are punishable under any provision of this Article, he shall be punished as a Class I felon. The prior conviction used to raise the current offense to a Class I felony shall not be used to calculate the prior record level;

(4) If any person commits a Class 2 misdemeanor, and if he has previously been convicted for one or more offenses under any law of North Carolina or any law of the United States or any other state, which offenses are punishable under any provision of this Article, he shall be guilty of a Class 1 misdemeanor. The prior conviction used to raise the current offense to a Class 1 misdemeanor shall not be used to calculate the prior conviction level;

(5) Any person 18 years of age or over who violates G.S. 90-95(a)(1) by selling or delivering a controlled substance to a person under 16 years of age but more than 13 years of age or a pregnant female shall be punished as a Class D felon. Any person 18 years of age or over who violates G.S. 90-95(a)(1) by selling or delivering a controlled substance to a person who is 13 years of age or younger shall be punished as a Class C felon. Mistake of age is not a defense to a prosecution under this section. It shall not be a defense that the defendant did not know that the recipient was pregnant.

(6) For the purpose of increasing punishment under G.S. 90-95(e)(3) and (e)(4), previous convictions for offenses shall be counted by the number of separate trials at which final convictions were obtained and not by the number of charges at a single trial;

(7) If any person commits an offense under this Article for which the prescribed punishment requires that any sentence of imprisonment be suspended, and if he has previously been convicted for one or more offenses under any law of North Carolina or any law of the United States or any other state, which offenses are punishable under any provision of this Article, he shall be guilty of a Class 2 misdemeanor;

(8) Any person 21 years of age or older who commits an offense under G.S. 90-95(a)(1) on property used for an elementary or secondary school or within 300 feet of the boundary of real property used for an elementary or secondary school shall be punished as a Class E felon. For purposes of this subdivision, the transfer of less than five grams of marijuana for no remuneration shall not constitute a delivery in violation of G.S. 90-95(a)(1).

(9) Any person who violates G.S. 90-95(a)(3) on the premises of a penal institution or local confinement facility shall be guilty of a Class H felony.

(f) Any person convicted of an offense or offenses under this Article who is sentenced to an active term of imprisonment that is less than the maximum active term that could have been imposed may, in addition, be sentenced to a term of special probation. Except as indicated in this subsection, the administration of special probation shall be the same as probation. The conditions of special probation shall be fixed in the same manner as probation, and the conditions may include requirements for rehabilitation treatment. Special probation shall follow the active sentence. No term of special probation shall exceed five years. Special probation may be revoked in the same manner as probation; upon revocation, the original term of imprisonment may be increased by no more than the difference between the active term of imprisonment actually served and the maximum active term that could have been imposed at trial for the offense or offenses for which the person was convicted, and the resulting term of imprisonment need not be diminished by the time spent on special probation.

(g) Whenever matter is submitted to the North Carolina State Bureau of Investigation Laboratory, the Charlotte, North Carolina, Police Department Laboratory or to the Toxicology Laboratory, Reynolds Health Center, Winston-Salem for chemical analysis to determine if the matter is or contains a controlled substance, the report of that analysis certified to upon a form approved by the Attorney General by the person performing the analysis shall be admissible without further authentication in all proceedings in the district court and superior court divisions of the General Court of Justice as evidence of the identity, nature, and quantity of the matter analyzed. Provided, however, that a report is admissible in a criminal proceeding in the superior court division or in an adjudicatory hearing in juvenile court in the district court division only if:

(1) The State notifies the defendant at least 15 days before trial of its intention to introduce the report into evidence under this subsection and provides a copy of the report to the defendant, and
(2) The defendant fails to notify the State at least five days before trial that the defendant objects to the introduction of the report into evidence.

Nothing in this subsection precludes the right of any party to call any witness or to introduce any evidence supporting or contradicting the evidence contained in the report.

(g1) Procedure for establishing chain of custody without calling unnecessary witnesses.—

(1) For the purpose of establishing the chain of physical custody or control of evidence consisting of or containing a substance tested or analyzed to determine whether it is a controlled substance, a statement signed by each successive person in the chain of custody that the person delivered it to the other person indicated on or about the date stated is prima facie evidence that the person had custody and made the delivery as stated, without the necessity of a personal appearance in court by the person signing the statement.
(2) The statement shall contain a sufficient description of the material or its container so as to distinguish it as the particular item in question and shall state that the material was delivered in essentially the same condition as received. The statement may be placed on the same document as the report provided for in subsection (g) of this section.
(3) The provisions of this subsection may be utilized by the State only if:
    a. The State notifies the defendant at least 15 days before trial of its intention to introduce the statement into evidence under this subsection and provides the defendant with a copy of the statement, and
    b. The defendant fails to notify the State at least five days before trial that the defendant objects to the introduction of the statement into evidence.
(4) Nothing in this subsection precludes the right of any party to call any witness or to introduce any evidence supporting or contradicting the evidence contained in the statement.

(h) Notwithstanding any other provision of law, the following provisions apply except as otherwise provided in this Article.

(1) Any person who sells, manufactures, delivers, transports, or possesses in excess of 10 pounds (avoirdupois) of marijuana shall be guilty of a felony which felony shall be known as "trafficking in marijuana" and if the quantity of such substance involved:
    a. Is in excess of 10 pounds, but less than 50 pounds, such person shall be punished as a Class H felon and shall be sentenced to a minimum term of 25 months and a maximum term of 30 months in the State's prison and shall be fined not less than five thousand dollars ($5,000);

b. Is 50 pounds or more, but less than 2,000 pounds, such person shall be punished as a Class G felon and shall be sentenced to a minimum term of 35 months and a maximum term of 42 months in the State's prison and shall be fined not less than twenty-five thousand dollars ($25,000);
c. Is 2,000 pounds or more, but less than 10,000 pounds, such person shall be punished as a Class F felon and shall be sentenced to a minimum term of 70 months and a maximum term of 84 months in the State's prison and shall be fined not less than fifty thousand dollars ($50,000);
d. Is 10,000 pounds or more, such person shall be punished as a Class D felon and shall be sentenced to a minimum term of 175 months and a maximum term of 219 months in the State's prison and shall be fined not less than two hundred thousand dollars ($200,000).

(2) Any person who sells, manufactures, delivers, transports, or possesses 1,000 tablets, capsules or other dosage units, or the equivalent quantity, or more of methaqualone, or any mixture containing such substance, shall be guilty of a felony which felony shall be known as "trafficking in methaqualone" and if the quantity of such substance or mixture involved:
a. Is 1,000 or more dosage units, or equivalent quantity, but less than 5,000 dosage units, or equivalent quantity, such person shall be punished as a Class G felon and shall be sentenced to a minimum term of 35 months and a maximum term of 42 months in the State's prison and shall be fined not less than twenty-five thousand dollars ($25,000);
b. Is 5,000 or more dosage units, or equivalent quantity, but less than 10,000 dosage units, or equivalent quantity, such person shall be punished as a Class F felon and shall be sentenced to a minimum term of 70 months and a maximum term of 84 months in the State's prison and shall be fined not less than fifty thousand dollars ($50,000);
c. Is 10,000 or more dosage units, or equivalent quantity, such person shall be punished as a Class D felon and shall be sentenced to a minimum term of 175 months and a maximum term of 219 months in the State's prison and shall be fined not less than two hundred thousand dollars ($200,000).

(3) Any person who sells, manufactures, delivers, transports, or possesses 28 grams or more of cocaine and any salt, isomer, salts of isomers, compound, derivative, or preparation thereof, or any coca leaves and any salt, isomer, salts of isomers, compound, derivative, or preparation of coca leaves, and any salt, isomer, salts of isomers, compound, derivative or preparation thereof which is chemically equivalent or identical with any of these substances (except decocainized coca leaves or any extraction of coca leaves which does not contain cocaine) or any mixture containing such substances, shall be guilty of a felony, which felony shall be known as "trafficking in cocaine" and if the quantity of such substance or mixture involved:
a. Is 28 grams or more, but less than 200 grams, such person shall be punished as a Class G felon and shall be sentenced to a minimum term of 35 months and a maximum term of 42 months in the State's prison and shall be fined not less than fifty thousand dollars ($50,000);
b. Is 200 grams or more, but less than 400 grams, such person shall be punished as a Class F felon and shall be sentenced to a minimum term of 70 months and a maximum term of 84 months in the State's prison and shall be fined not less than one hundred thousand dollars ($100,000);
c. Is 400 grams or more, such person shall be punished as a Class D felon and shall be sentenced to a minimum term of 175 months and a maximum term of 219 months in the State's prison and shall be fined at least two hundred fifty thousand dollars ($250,000).

(3a) Repealed by Session Laws 1999-370, s. 1, effective December 1, 1999.

(3b) Any person who sells, manufactures, delivers, transports, or possesses 28 grams or more of methamphetamine or amphetamine shall be guilty of a felony which felony shall be known as "trafficking in methamphetamine or amphetamine" and if the quantity of such substance or mixture involved:

a. Is 28 grams or more, but less than 200 grams, such person shall be punished as a Class F felon and shall be sentenced to a minimum term of 70 months and a maximum term of 84 months in the State's prison and shall be fined not less than fifty thousand dollars ($50,000);
b. Is 200 grams or more, but less than 400 grams, such person shall be punished as a Class E felon and shall be sentenced to a minimum term of 90 months and a maximum term of 117 months in the State's prison and shall be fined not less than one hundred thousand dollars ($100,000);
c. Is 400 grams or more, such person shall be punished as a Class C felon and shall be sentenced to a minimum term of 225 months and a maximum term of 279 months in the State's prison and shall be fined at least two hundred fifty thousand dollars ($250,000).

(4) Any person who sells, manufactures, delivers, transports, or possesses four grams or more of opium or opiate, or any salt, compound, derivative, or preparation of opium or opiate (except apomorphine, nalbuphine, analoxone and naltrexone and their respective salts), including heroin, or any mixture containing such substance, shall be guilty of a felony which felony shall be known as "trafficking in opium or heroin" and if the quantity of such controlled substance or mixture involved:
a. Is four grams or more, but less than 14 grams, such person shall be punished as a Class F felon and shall be sentenced to a minimum term of 70 months and a maximum term of 84 months in the State's prison and shall be fined not less than fifty thousand dollars ($50,000);
b. Is 14 grams or more, but less than 28 grams, such person shall be punished as a Class E felon and shall be sentenced to a minimum term of 90 months and a maximum term of 117 months in the State's prison and shall be fined not less than one hundred thousand dollars ($100,000);
c. Is 28 grams or more, such person shall be punished as a Class C felon and shall be sentenced to a minimum term of 225 months and a maximum term of 279 months in the State's prison and shall be fined not less than five hundred thousand dollars ($500,000).

(4a) Any person who sells, manufactures, delivers, transports, or possesses 100 tablets, capsules, or other dosage units, or the equivalent quantity, or more, of Lysergic Acid Diethylamide, or any mixture containing such substance, shall be guilty of a felony, which felony shall be known as "trafficking in Lysergic Acid Diethylamide". If the quantity of such substance or mixture involved:
a. Is 100 or more dosage units, or equivalent quantity, but less than 500 dosage units, or equivalent quantity, such person shall be punished as a Class G felon and shall be sentenced to a minimum term of 35 months and a maximum term of 42 months in the State's prison and shall be fined not less than twenty-five thousand dollars ($25,000);
b. Is 500 or more dosage units, or equivalent quantity, but less than 1,000 dosage units, or equivalent quantity, such person shall be punished as a Class F felon and shall be sentenced to a minimum term of 70 months and a maximum term of 84 months in the State's prison and shall be fined not less than fifty thousand dollars ($50,000);
c. Is 1,000 or more dosage units, or equivalent quantity, such person shall be punished as a Class D felon and shall be sentenced to a minimum term of 175 months and a maximum term of 219 months in the State's prison and shall be fined not less than two hundred thousand dollars ($200,000).

(4b) Any person who sells, manufactures, delivers, transports, or possesses 100 or more tablets, capsules, or other dosage units, or 28 grams or more of 3,4-methylenedioxyamphetamine (MDA), including its salts, isomers, and salts of isomers, or 3,4-methylenedioxymethamphetamine (MDMA), including its salts, isomers, and salts of isomers, or any mixture containing such substances, shall be guilty of a felony, which felony shall be known as "trafficking in MDA/MDMA." If the quantity of the substance or mixture involved:
a. Is 100 or more tablets, capsules, or other dosage units, but less than

500 tablets, capsules, or other dosage units, or 28 grams or more, but less than 200 grams, the person shall be punished as a Class G felon and shall be sentenced to a minimum term of 35 months and a maximum term of 42 months in the State's prison and shall be fined not less than twenty-five thousand dollars ($25,000);

b. Is 500 or more tablets, capsules, or other dosage units, but less than 1,000 tablets, capsules, or other dosage units, or 200 grams or more, but less than 400 grams, the person shall be punished as a Class F felon and shall be sentenced to a minimum term of 70 months and a maximum term of 84 months in the State's prison and shall be fined not less than fifty thousand dollars ($50,000);

c. Is 1,000 or more tablets, capsules, or other dosage units, or 400 grams or more, the person shall be punished as a Class D felon and shall be sentenced to a minimum term of 175 months and a maximum term of 219 months in the State's prison and shall be fined not less than two hundred fifty thousand dollars ($250,000).

(5) Except as provided in this subdivision, a person being sentenced under this subsection may not receive a suspended sentence or be placed on probation. The sentencing judge may reduce the fine, or impose a prison term less than the applicable minimum prison term provided by this subsection, or suspend the prison term imposed and place a person on probation when such person has, to the best of his knowledge, provided substantial assistance in the identification, arrest, or conviction of any accomplices, accessories, co-conspirators, or principals if the sentencing judge enters in the record a finding that the person to be sentenced has rendered such substantial assistance.

(6) Sentences imposed pursuant to this subsection shall run consecutively with and shall commence at the expiration of any sentence being served by the person sentenced hereunder.

(i) The penalties provided in subsection (h) of this section shall also apply to any person who is convicted of conspiracy to commit any of the offenses described in subsection (h) of this section.

Elements

A person guilty of this offense
(1) knowingly
(2) manufactures
(3) a controlled substance.

Punishment

For a Schedule I or II substance, the crime is a Class H felony. For a Schedule III, IV, V, or VI substance, the crime is a Class I felony.

Notes

Element (1). The knowledge required for the various drug crimes is that the defendant knew in fact (a) what the defendant was doing was *manufacturing, possessing, selling, etc.*, a controlled substance, and (b) what the defendant was manufacturing, possessing, selling, etc., was a *controlled substance*. However, the state must prove knowledge of (a) and/or (b) at trial only if evidence of lack of knowledge is produced at trial (310 N.C. 284; 55 N.C. App. 92; 24 N.C. App. 732).

North Carolina does not recognize the doctrine, recognized in some jurisdictions, that knowledge includes willful blindness of a highly probable fact (that is, deliberate avoidance of knowledge) (324 N.C. 190).

Element (2). Manufacturing is broadly defined by G.S. 90-87(15) to include any method, direct or indirect, of producing, propagating, preparing, compounding, converting, or processing and also to include packaging or repackaging the substance and labeling or relabeling its container. But manufacturing does not include preparation or compounding for one's own use. However, if the act that constitutes manufacturing is *not* preparing or compounding, it is manufacturing even if the defendant intended to keep the controlled substance for his or her own use (310 N.C. 563; 41 N.C. App. 729).

A defendant's close proximity to the place where a substance is being manufactured (by growing, labeling, relabeling, packaging, or repackaging) will establish sufficient evidence of manufacturing (310 N.C. 563; 54 N.C. App. 660; 34 N.C. App. 115). Evidence was sufficient to show that the defendant constructively possessed marijuana and was guilty of manufacturing (by growing) marijuana when he lived in a trailer that was near a path leading to a marijuana patch, that the person who lived in an adjacent trailer knew nothing about the marijuana, and there were no residences within a half-mile of the patch (51 N.C. App. 429; see also 316 N.C. 87; 105 N.C. App. 175). Evidence of two sets of scales and Ziploc bags found with marijuana was sufficient to prove manufacturing (55 N.C. App. 205; see also 97 N.C. App. 189).

Element (3). Trial testimony must establish the actual chemical name of the controlled substance if an abbreviation generally is used, such as "MDA" for "3, 4-methylenedioxyamphetamine" (296 N.C. 652).

Lesser-included offenses. Possession of a controlled substance is not a lesser-included offense of manufacture. A defendant may be convicted and punished for both offenses (74 N.C. App. 295).

Restitution for cleanup of drug manufacturing laboratory. G.S. 90-95.3(c) provides that when a defendant is convicted of an offense involving the manufacturing of controlled substances, the court must order the defendant to make restitution for the actual cost of cleanup to the law enforcement agency that cleaned up any clandestine laboratory used to manufacture the controlled substances, including personnel overtime, equipment, and supplies.

Defense of authorized use. A defendant has the burden of proving that he or she was authorized by the Controlled Substances Act to possess, deliver, manufacture, etc., a controlled substance (G.S. 90-113.1; 47 N.C. App. 30). See G.S. 90-101 for descriptions of authorized persons. See also "Proof of Exemption from Controlled Substances Act."

Related offenses not in this chapter

Contaminating food or drink with controlled substance to render one mentally incapacitated or physically helpless (G.S. 14-401.16)

Sale or Delivery of Controlled Substance

Statute

See subsections (a)(1) and (b) of G.S. 90-95, reproduced under "Manufacture of Controlled Substance."

Elements

A person guilty of this offense
- (1) knowingly
- (2) (a) sells, *or*
  - (b) delivers
- (3) a controlled substance
- (4) to another person.

Punishment

For the sale of a Schedule I or II substance, the crime is a Class G felony. For the delivery of a Schedule I or II substance, the crime is a Class H felony. For the sale of a Schedule III, IV, V, or VI substance, the crime is a Class H felony. For the delivery of a Schedule III, IV, V, or VI substance, the crime is a Class I felony. For all substances, there are offenses with increased punishments if the defendant is 18 years old or older and sells or delivers a controlled substance to a person under 16 or a pregnant female—see the discussions later in this chapter of "Sale or Delivery of Controlled Substance to Person Under 16 by Person 18 or Older," "Sale or Delivery of Controlled Substance to Person Under 13 by Person 18 or Older," and "Sale or Delivery of Controlled Substance to Pregnant Female by Person 18 or Older."

Notes

Element (1). See the note on Element (1) under "Manufacture of Controlled Substance."

Element (2). "Sell" means to transfer for remuneration (i.e., compensation) (327 N.C. 378). "Deliver" means actual or constructive transfer to another person and includes attempts to transfer [G.S. 90-87(7)]. Each sale is also a delivery. The statute provides that it is not a delivery to transfer less than 5 grams of marijuana for no remuneration [G.S. 90-95(b)(2)]; such activity could be punished only as possession. The sale and delivery of the same controlled substance under G.S. 90-95(a)(1) may be punished as only one offense (327 N.C. 378); to impose the more severe punishment for the act of sale, jury instructions must distinguish between sale and delivery to ensure that the jury in fact reached a unanimous verdict on the act of sale. Note, however, that trafficking by sale and trafficking by delivery of the same controlled substance are separate punishable offenses (330 N.C. 298; 317 N.C. 545; 316 N.C. 87).

Element (4). An indictment charging the sale of a controlled substance must allege the name of the purchaser or that the purchaser's name is unknown (280 N.C. 167). If the defendant sells the drug to Jones who was acting as an intermediary for Smith, the ultimate purchaser, the indictment must allege the purchaser as Jones if the defendant did not know that he or she was selling to Smith (102 N.C. App. 434; 96 N.C. App. 45).

Evidence of prior purchase. Evidence of drug transactions by the defendant before the drug offense with which he or she is charged is admissible for the limited purposes of showing the defendant's intent in possessing the drugs and that the defendant knew the character of the substance (309 N.C. 451).

Restitution for drug purchases and for expenses to analyze controlled substance. G.S. 90-95.3(a) allows a court to order a convicted defendant to make restitution to a law enforcement agency for reasonable expenditures made in purchasing controlled substances from the defendant or his or her agent as part of an investigation leading to the defendant's conviction (316 N.C. 535). G.S. 90-95.3(b) allows a court to order a convicted defendant to make restitution in the amount of $100.00 to the state of North Carolina for the expense of analyzing any controlled substance possessed by the defendant or his or her agent as part of an investigation leading to the defendant's conviction (124 N.C. App. 462).

Identification of substance. See the note on "Identification of marijuana by officer" under "Possession of Controlled Substance."

Defense of authorized use. See the note on this subject under "Manufacture of Controlled Substance."

Prosecution of physician. A physician who writes a prescription for a controlled substance outside the normal course of professional practice does not violate this statute but may be charged under G.S. 90-108(a)(2) (unlawful distribution of controlled substance by registrant or practitioner) (292 N.C. 294).

Possession not lesser-included offense. Possession of a substance (or possession with intent to sell or deliver) is not a lesser-included offense of sale of the substance, since possession is not necessary to a sale; a defendant may be convicted and punished for both (283 N.C. 191; 59 N.C. App. 656). Although the North Carolina Court of Appeals has ruled that possession of a substance is a lesser-included offense of delivery of the substance (71 N.C. App. 55), there is some doubt whether the North Carolina Supreme Court would agree with that ruling (see 327 N.C. 378).

A defendant may be convicted and punished for (1) possession with intent to sell, deliver, and manufacture and (2) sale and delivery (59 N.C. App. 656), but not for possession of the same controlled substance.

Related offenses not in this chapter

None.

Sale or Delivery of Controlled Substance to Person under 16 by Person 18 or Older

Statute

See subdivision (e)(5) of G.S. 90-95, reproduced under "Manufacture of Controlled Substance."

Elements

A person guilty of this offense
- (1) is 18 years old or older, *and*
- (2) knowingly
- (3) (a) sells, *or*
  - (b) delivers
- (4) a controlled substance to
- (5) a person under 16 but more than 13.

Punishment

Class D felony.

Notes

Element (2). See the note on Element (1) under "Manufacture of Controlled Substance."

Element (3). See the note on Element (2) under "Sale or Delivery of Controlled Substance." See also the note on Element (5), below.

Element (5). The statute provides that it is no defense that the person who sold or delivered a controlled substance did not know that the recipient was under 16.

Criminal pleading. A criminal pleading charging this offense must allege the defendant was 18 years old or older and that the recipient was under 16 but more than 13.

Related offenses not in this chapter

None.

Sale or Delivery of Controlled Substance to Person Under 13 by Person 18 or Older

Statute

See subdivision (e)(5) of G.S. 90-95, reproduced under "Manufacture of Controlled Substance"

Elements

A person guilty of this offense
- (1) is 18 years old or older, *and*
- (2) knowingly
- (3) (a) sells, *or*
  - (b) delivers
- (4) a controlled substance to
- (5) a person under 13.

Punishment

Class C felony.

Notes

Element (2). See the note on Element (1) under "Manufacture of Controlled Substance."

Element (3). See the note on Element (2) under "Sale or Delivery of Controlled Substance." See also the note on Element (5), below.

Element (5). The statute provides that it is no defense that the person who sold or delivered a controlled substance did not know that the recipient was under 13.

Criminal pleading. A criminal pleading charging this offense must allege the defendant was 18 years old or older and that the recipient was under 13.

Related offenses not in this chapter

None.

Sale or Delivery of Controlled Substance to Pregnant Female by Person 18 or Older

Statute

See subdivision (e)(5) of G.S. 90-95, reproduced under "Manufacture of Controlled Substance."

Elements

A person guilty of this offense
- (1) is 18 years old or older, *and*
- (2) knowingly
- (3) (a) sells, *or*
  - (b) delivers
- (4) a controlled substance to
- (5) a pregnant female.

Punishment

Class D felony.

Notes

Element (2). See the note on Element (1) under "Manufacture of Controlled Substance."

Element (3). See the note on Element (2) under "Sale or Delivery of Controlled Substance." See also the note on Element (5), below.

Element (5). The statute provides that it is no defense that the person who sold or delivered a controlled substance did not know that the recipient was pregnant.

Criminal pleading. A criminal pleading charging this offense must allege the defendant was 18 years old or older and that the recipient was a pregnant female.

Related offenses not in this chapter

None.

Manufacture, Sale, Delivery, or Possession of Controlled Substance with Intent to Manufacture, Sell, or Deliver at or Near School by Person 21 or Older

Statute

See subdivision (e)(8) of G.S. 90-95, reproduced under "Manufacture of Controlled Substance."

Elements

A person guilty of this offense
- (1) is 21 years old or older, *and*
- (2) knowingly
- (3) (a) manufactures, *or*
  - (b) sells, *or*
  - (c) delivers, *or*
  - (d) possesses with intent to sell or deliver or manufacture
- (4) a controlled substance
- (5) on property
  - (a) used for an elementary or secondary school, *or*
  - (b) within 300 feet of the boundary of real property used for an elementary or secondary school.

Punishment

Class E felony.

Notes

Element (2). See the note on Element (1) under "Manufacture of Controlled Substance."

Element (3)(a). See the note on Element (2) under "Manufacture of Controlled Substance."

Elements (3)(b) and (c). See the note on Element (2) under "Sale or Delivery of Controlled Substance," above. The statute specifically provides that the transfer of less than 5 grams of marijuana for no remuneration does not constitute a delivery.

Element (3)(d). See the note on Element (2) under "Possession of Controlled Substance" and Element (4) under "Possession of Controlled Substance with Intent to Manufacture, Sell, or Deliver," below.

Element (5). This statute includes both private and public elementary and secondary schools, kindergarten through twelfth grade. The drug transaction does not have to involve school students or personnel (911 F.2d 50, interpreting similar federal law). The state does not have to prove that the defendant intended to sell or deliver drugs at or near the school (948 F.2d 1422, interpreting similar federal law). The measurement of the distance to the school is by a straight line from the school's boundary line to the place of the drug transaction, not by the pedestrian route of travel (887 F.2d 980, interpreting similar federal law). Evidence was sufficient to prove the distance was within 300 feet, based on the testimony of school employees (111 N.C. App. 416; 106 N.C. App. 371). The property need not be located on the school campus to be included within this offense; for example, it would include a high school football field located at a different place than the high school, since the property is used for a secondary school.

Criminal pleading. A criminal pleading charging this offense must allege the defendant was 21 years old or older and that the offense occurred on property used for, or within 300 feet of the boundary of real property used for, an elementary or secondary school.

Related offenses not in this chapter

None.

Possession of Controlled Substance with Intent to Manufacture, Sell, or Deliver

Statute

See subdivision (a)(1) and subsection (b) of G.S. 90-95, reproduced under "Manufacture of Controlled Substance."

Elements

A person guilty of this offense

(1) knowingly
(2) possesses
(3) a controlled substance
(4) with the intent to manufacture or sell or deliver it.

Punishment

For a Schedule I or II substance, the crime is a Class H felony. For a Schedule III, IV, V, or VI substance, the crime is a Class I felony.

Notes

Element (1). See the note on Element (1) under "Manufacture of Controlled Substance."

Element (2). See the discussion of this element under "Possession of Controlled Substance."

Element (4). See the discussion of Element (2) under "Manufacture of Controlled Substance" for a broad definition of manufacture. See the discussion of Element (2) under "Sale or Delivery of Controlled Substance" for definitions of sale and delivery. There is no specific amount that automatically proves that a person possesses a controlled substance with the intent to sell, deliver, or manufacture, although quantity alone may sometimes be sufficient (329 N.C. 654). Possession of certain kinds and amounts of drugs along with drug paraphernalia may be sufficient evidence to prove an intent to sell, deliver, or manufacture. For example, an intent to "distribute" (the term under present law is "deliver") a substance was inferred from the amount found (219 grams of marijuana), the manner in which it was packaged (in sixteen separate envelopes), and the presence of other packaging materials (another twenty-eight empty envelopes, tape, cigarette papers) (285 N.C. 735). A total of 2.7 grams of heroin was a substantial amount—more than an individual would possess for personal consumption—when drug paraphernalia and ten to fifteen tinfoil squares were found in addition to the heroin; the evidence was sufficient to show possession with intent to sell or deliver (307 N.C. 452). Three-quarters of an ounce of cocaine, along with evidence of prior purchases, was sufficient (329 N.C. 654). When a defendant possessed 4.27 grams of cocaine packaged in twenty separate envelopes and also possessed a large amount of cash, there was sufficient evidence of intent to sell the cocaine (91 N.C. App. 707). In contrast, possession of 215.5 grams of marijuana was not by itself sufficient evidence to raise an inference that it was possessed with intent to distribute (33 N.C. App. 291), nor was the possession of seventy phenobarbital tablets when there was no other evidence of an intent to distribute (42 N.C. App. 210).

A verdict finding a defendant guilty of possession of a controlled substance with intent to "sell or deliver" was not fatally ambiguous, since possession with intent to sell or deliver is only one offense (313 N.C. 572; 313 N.C. 122).

Lesser-included offenses. Possession of a controlled substance is a lesser-included offense of possession with intent to manufacture, sell, or deliver the same substance, except as discussed below; a defendant may be sentenced for one or the other, but not both (286 N.C. 202). Possession of more than one-half ounce of marijuana (Class 1 misdemeanor) or one and one-half ounces of marijuana (Class I felony) are not lesser-included offenses of possession with intent to sell or deliver, since these possession offenses (unlike simple misdemeanor possession, a Class 3 misdemeanor) require additional proof that the amount possessed was more than one-half ounce or one and one-half ounces, as the case may be. (This same principle applies to other controlled substances in Schedules II through V when the felony possession offense depends on the amount of the substance possessed.) However, if the state in a criminal pleading charging possession with intent to sell and deliver alleges the amount possessed, the jury may be instructed on the offenses of felony and misdemeanor possession even though these offenses may not be lesser-included offenses (84 N.C. App. 309).

If the controlled substance in question is the same, the defendant may be sentenced for only possession with intent to sell, deliver, and manufacture *or* possession, but not both. The state need not elect which charge to proceed on; instead the jury can be given alternative verdicts to choose from (296 N.C. 564; 84 N.C. App. 309).

Defense of authorized use. See the note on this subject under "Manufacture of Controlled Substance."

Related offenses not in this chapter

None.

Creating Counterfeit Controlled Substance

Statute

See subdivision (a)(2) and subsection (c) of G.S. 90-95, reproduced under "Manufacture of Controlled Substance."

Elements

A person guilty of this offense
(1) knowingly
(2) creates
(3) a counterfeit controlled substance.

Punishment

Class I felony.

Notes

Element (1). See the note on Element (1) under "Manufacture of Controlled Substance."

Element (2). "Create" is not defined by statute; according to *Webster's Third New International Dictionary*, the term means "to bring into existence."

Element (3). A "counterfeit controlled substance" is defined in G.S. 90-87(6). The term includes two quite different kinds of substances. One is a controlled substance labeled or otherwise marked to indicate that it is manufactured, distributed, or dispensed by someone (usually a company) other than the actual manufacturer, distributor, or dispenser. The other is a substance intentionally represented as a controlled substance even though it is not. Thus a counterfeit controlled substance exists, for example, when a person puts oregano into a plastic bag and asserts that it is marijuana or puts flour in tin foil and asserts that it is heroin.

Defense of authorized use. See the note on this subject under "Manufacture of Controlled Substance."

Related offenses not in this chapter

"Obtaining Property by False Pretenses" (Chapter 14)

Sale or Delivery of Counterfeit Controlled Substance

Statute

See subdivision (a)(2) and subsection (c) of G.S. 90-95, reproduced under "Manufacture of Controlled Substance."

Elements

A person guilty of this offense
(1) knowingly
(2) sells or delivers
(3) a counterfeit controlled substance
(4) to another person.

Punishment

Class I felony.

Notes

Element (1). See the note on Element (1) under "Manufacture of Controlled Substance."

Element (2). See the note on Element (2) under "Sale or Delivery of Controlled Substance" for definitions of sale and delivery.

Element (3). See the note on Element (3) under "Creating Counterfeit Controlled Substance" for a definition of counterfeit substance.

Element (4). A criminal pleading charging sale of a controlled substance (and, presumably, sale of counterfeit substance) must allege the name of the purchaser or, if not known, that the purchaser's name is unknown (280 N.C. 167).

Defense of authorized use. See the note on this subject under "Manufacture of Controlled Substance."

Related offenses not in this chapter

"Obtaining Property by False Pretenses" (Chapter 14)

Possession of Counterfeit Controlled Substance with Intent to Sell or Deliver

Statute

See subsections (a)(2) and (c) of G.S. 90-95, reproduced under "Manufacture of Controlled Substance."

Elements

A person guilty of this offense
(1) knowingly
(2) possesses
(3) a counterfeit controlled substance
(4) with the intent to sell or deliver it.

Punishment

Class I felony.

Notes

Element (1). See the note on Element (1) under "Manufacture of Controlled Substance."

Element (2). See the discussion of this element under "Possession of Controlled Substance."

Element (3). See the note on Element (3) of "Creating Counterfeit Controlled Substance" for a definition of counterfeit substance.

Element (4). For a discussion of this element, see the notes on Element (4) under "Possession of Controlled Substance with Intent to Manufacture, Sell, or Deliver."

Defense of authorized use. See the note on this subject under "Manufacture of Controlled Substance."

Related offenses not in this chapter

"Obtaining Property by False Pretenses" (Chapter 14)

Possession of Controlled Substance

Statute

See subsections (a)(3) and (d) of G.S. 90-95, rerproduced under "Manufacture of Controlled Substance."

Elements

A person guilty of this offense
(1) knowingly
(2) possesses
(3) a controlled substance.

Punishment

For a Schedule I substance, the crime is a Class I felony. *For a Schedule II, III, or IV substance*, if the amount possessed is (a) more than 100 tablets, capsules, or dosage units, (b) more than four tablets, capsules, dosage units of dilaudid (chemically known as "hydromorphone"), or (c) any amount of cocaine or phencyclidine, the crime is a Class I felony. For possession of a lesser amount of a Schedule II, III, or IV substance, the crime is a Class 1 misdemeanor. *For a Schedule V substance*, the crime is a Class 2 misdemeanor. *For a Schedule VI substance*, (a) a defendant's first conviction for possession of up to a half-ounce of marijuana or up to one-twentieth of an ounce of hashish is punishable as a Class 3 misdemeanor and any sentence of imprisonment must be suspended and the defendant may not be required to serve active time as a special condition of probation; (b) possession of more than a half-ounce of marijuana and up to one and a half ounces of marijuana or more than one-twentieth of an ounce and up to three-twentieths of an ounce of hashish is a Class 1 misdemeanor; (c) possession of more than one and a half ounces of marijuana, more than three-twentieths of an ounce of hashish, or any amount of synthetic tetrahydrocannabinols or tetrahydrocannabinols isolated from marijuana resin is a Class I felony.

Notes

Element (1). See the note on Element (1) under "Manufacture of Controlled Substance."

Element (2). Possession of a substance may be either actual or constructive; constructive possession is established by showing the defendant's power and intent to control disposition of the substance (279 N.C. 406). The fact that a controlled substance is found on premises controlled by the defendant permits an inference that the defendant knowingly possessed the substance (281 N.C. 1). Whether the evidence is sufficient to create an inference of constructive possession depends on the totality of circumstances in each case (81 N.C. App. 91). Although it is not necessary to show that a defendant exclusively possesses the premises where the controlled substance was found, when the possession of the premises is nonexclusive, constructive possession of the substance may not be inferred without other incriminating circumstances (310 N.C. 563).

Cases in which there was sufficient evidence of constructive possession.

North Carolina Supreme Court cases:

- Even though the defendant was not at the house when the heroin was found, the evidence was sufficient that he possessed heroin when utilities for the house were listed in his name, his ID card and personal papers were found in the bedroom where the heroin was found, and there was testimony that he directed others to sell the heroin (279 N.C. 406).
- An inference existed that the defendant possessed marijuana when he was in control of the house and he was found within 3 to 4 feet of the marijuana and no one else was present (281 N.C. 1).
- Evidence supported a conviction of possession of marijuana when the marijuana was found in a shed 20 yards directly behind the defendant's residence, he had been seen near the shed often, and marijuana seeds were found in his bedroom (281 N.C. 121).
- A male defendant constructively possessed marijuana found in his apartment even though he was not present at the time it was found, when marijuana was found in a dresser drawer under men's clothing and in a man's coat in the closet and no one other than the defendant and his wife lived in the apartment (285 N.C. 735).
- Evidence was sufficient to prove a defendant's constructive possession of a marijuana field 300 yards behind his house, because the defendant admitted knowing marijuana was growing there, he was coming from the field when officers first saw him, and he was wearing work clothes and sweating heavily (317 N.C. 643).
- Evidence was sufficient to prove a defendant's constructive possession of drugs in a mobile home although he did not have exclusive possession of the mobile home and others were present with the defendant when officers found the drugs, because the defendant's name was on a bill of sale for a mobile home that matched this particular home's description and a bottle of prescription drugs with the defendant's name was found on a coffee table beside the chair in which he was sitting when the officers arrived (325 N.C. 693).
- Evidence was sufficient to prove a defendant's constructive possession of drugs when the defendant owned and controlled a game room where the drugs were found and sold and the defendant directed the undercover agent (who had asked to buy drugs) to another person inside the game room who actually sold the drugs to the agent (326 N.C. 451).

North Carolina Court of Appeals cases:

- Evidence was sufficient to prove constructive possession of cocaine found in an apartment bathroom when officers saw two males in the bathroom as they approached the apartment, one male ran from the bathroom as officers entered the apartment, and the other male was in the bathroom where the cocaine was found on the top of the toilet (109 N.C. App. 684).
- Evidence was sufficient to prove constructive possession of cocaine when the defendant was standing with two other people in a kitchen that measured 6 by 8 feet and on the kitchen table were four packages of cocaine, $47 in cash, a semi-automatic pistol, and a leather jacket nearby, and the defendant claimed the jacket and cash (101 N.C. App. 245).
- Evidence was sufficient to prove constructive possession of marijuana when undercover officers set up a drug deal in which the defendant was to place marijuana in a ditch beside a road and when the officers went there, the defendant gestured the officers toward the ditch and the officers found marijuana there (102 N.C. App. 541).
- Evidence was sufficient to prove constructive possession of cocaine found in a building (where the defendant and three others were present) when the defendant exercised some control of the premises by answering the door and telling someone that the business was closed and they were not selling beer, the defendant was in the same room where officers found cocaine in plain view, and the defendant had previously used cocaine in the building (95 N.C. App. 72).
- Evidence was sufficient to prove a defendant's constructive possession of cocaine when an officer heard glass breaking on the other side of a closed door and opened the door to find the defendant and another person in the room; the defendant was standing near a broken window and 3 feet from a table which had cocaine and drug paraphernalia on it. A jury could infer that the defendant was either attempting to escape from the house or was preparing to dispose of the cocaine through the broken window (93 N.C. App. 496).
- Evidence was sufficient to prove a defendant's constructive possession of cocaine found in a room where the defendant and others were present when the defendant's key fit a padlock on the building's front door and a rent receipt for the premises along with $10,638 were found in his pocket (91 N.C. App. 707).
- Evidence was sufficient to prove a female defendant's constructive possession when cocaine was found in the bedroom of a house while the defendant was in the kitchen during the search, evidence showed that she lived there, women's clothes were in the bedroom and in the dresser where the cocaine was found, and letters with the defendant's name on them were also in the bedroom (87 N.C. App. 380).
- Evidence was sufficient to prove a defendant's constructive possession of marijuana and cocaine found in four different rooms in a house, some of it hidden and some in plain view, even though she was not present when the drugs were found, because a telephone bill and other mail addressed to the defendant at the house address were found in the bedroom, the defendant's minor son (who did not live there) appeared at the house during the course of the officers' search, and an acquaintance of the defendant (who did not live there) was in the living room when officers arrived; this defendant was arrested in the house 10 days after the search (89 N.C. App. 123).
- Evidence was sufficient to show constructive possession when the defendant knew that a substantial quantity of marijuana was growing on the land he cultivated and frequented (60 N.C. App. 604).
- Evidence was sufficient to show constructive possession when the defen-

dant was found pinned in a wrecked stolen car and drug capsules were found in a bag under the hood (34 N.C. App. 131).

- Evidence was sufficient to prove the defendant's possession of marijuana when he drove a borrowed car with a bag of marijuana just inside the door on the driver's side in a place where a person entering the car could see it (24 N.C. App. 54).
- Evidence was sufficient to prove a defendant's construction possession of cocaine and drug paraphernalia when the defendant was the driver and owner of the car (which also contained a front seat female passenger), the cocaine was found in a tissue box on the passenger side, which was surrounded by other items belonging to the defendant (his wallet and sales and insurance documents in his name), a black travel bag containing drug paraphernalia was located in the back of the car, and the bag also contained a number of personal items, including men's underwear and shaving items (134 N.C. App. 546).
- Evidence was sufficient to support the defendant's constructive possession of cocaine found in two adjoining motel rooms when he was sole occupant, he rented both rooms and retained the keys to them, and all of the personal belongings seized from the rooms—his birth certificate, two diplomas, and a traffic citation—were his (136 N.C. App. 218).

Cases in which there was insufficient evidence of constructive possession:

- Evidence was insufficient to prove a female defendant's constructive possession of drug paraphernalia found in her house, because officers had seen two adult males enter and leave the house the day it was searched and adult male clothes were found in the closets and, therefore, the defendant's control over the premises was not exclusive; there was no incriminating evidence linking her to the paraphernalia (320 N.C. 143).
- The fact that the defendant was leasing an apartment was not sufficient to establish his constructive possession of marijuana found in the apartment when he had not been present in the apartment for 44 days before the officers found the marijuana; there was evidence that he had sublet the apartment and another person was living there (290 N.C. 755).
- Evidence was insufficient to establish constructive possession where it showed only that the defendant was a friend and visitor of a co-defendant who was leasing land on which marijuana was found growing and he was a passenger in the co-defendant's car when marijuana was found in it (290 N.C. 68).
- Evidence was insufficient to prove a defendant's constructive possession of cocaine when the defendant did not have either exclusive or nonexclusive control of the premises, the defendant was found upstairs in a small hallway, and opening into the hallway was a bedroom where two other people were found with the cocaine (101 N.C. App. 245).
- Evidence was insufficient to prove a defendant's constructive possession of cocaine found in a building (where he and three others were present) when evidence did not show that he exercised ownership or possession of the building; even though there was evidence that he knew cocaine was there, there was insufficient evidence that he had the capability to exercise control and dominion over it (95 N.C. App. 72).
- When the defendants had no control over the premises, the evidence was insufficient to convict them; they were transients who merely slept at the premises (17 N.C. App. 655).
- Evidence was insufficient to show the defendant's possession of a package of cocaine when an undercover officer handed the defendant a package of cocaine during a drug deal in a car; the defendant then gave the package to an accomplice sitting in the front seat; and after the accomplice tested the cocaine, he handed the package back to the undercover officer and told him

that they did not want to purchase the cocaine because of its poor quality (138 N.C. App. 163).

- Evidence was insufficient to prove the defendant possessed a trafficking amount of marijuana when an officer intercepted a package containing a trafficking amount of marijuana, removed most of the marijuana so there was no longer a trafficking amount, and then delivered the package of marijuana to the defendant; instead, the defendant was guilty of attempted trafficking by possession (137 N.C. App. 90).

Proof of possession of prescription controlled substance was insufficient. Officers found a white plastic bottle containing 78 five-milligram tablets of diazepam (Valium) in the pocket of a coat in a bedroom. This evidence was insufficient, since the state failed to show that the tablets were not issued pursuant to a valid prescription (the bottle was not submitted as an exhibit on appeal) or that the quantity of diazepam possessed was larger than amounts normally prescribed (109 N.C. App. 235).

Testimony concerning identity of drugs. An SBI chemist was permitted to testify that all 400 tablets found in the defendant's trailer were phencyclidine, although he had tested a random sample of only five tablets, when he also testified that all the tablets appeared the same to him; the same rule was followed on testimony concerning eight bags of vegetable matter identified as marijuana from a sample of only one bag (34 N.C. App. 197). Similar cases have involved the testing of pills (276 N.C. 361; 59 N.C. App. 298).

Identification of marijuana by officer. An officer who had been trained to recognize marijuana and had investigated 60 to 70 cases involving marijuana was qualified as an expert witness to identify a substance as marijuana (30 N.C. App. 253). An officer's testimony that the substance was marijuana was sufficient to uphold a conviction (92 N.C. App. 50).

Track marks evidence admissible. Track marks on the defendant's arm were admissible evidence to show that he knowingly possessed a small amount of heroin; the possession statute covers possession of even a mere trace of heroin (20 N.C. App. 255).

Lesser-included offenses. Possession of a controlled substance is not a lesser-included offense of sale of that substance, since possession is not necessary for a sale to be made; a defendant may be tried and sentenced for both (283 N.C. 191). Possession of a controlled substance is a lesser-included offense of possession with intent to manufacture, sell, or deliver, except as discussed below; a defendant may be sentenced for one or the other, but not both (286 N.C. 202). Possession of more than one-half ounce of marijuana (Class 1 misdemeanor) or one and one-half ounces of marijuana (Class I felony) are not lesser-included offenses of possession with intent to sell or deliver, since these possession offenses (unlike simple misdemeanor possession, a Class 3 misdemeanor) require additional proof that the amount possessed was more than one-half ounce or one and one-half ounces, as the case may be. (This same principle applies to other controlled substances in Schedules II through IV when the felony possession offense depends on the amount of the substance possessed.) However, if the state in a criminal pleading charging possession with intent to sell and deliver alleges the amount possessed, the jury may be instructed on the offenses of felony and misdemeanor possession even though these offenses may not be lesser-included offenses (84 N.C. App. 309).

Although the North Carolina Court of Appeals has ruled that possession of a controlled substance is a lesser-included offense of delivery of the substance, there is some doubt whether the North Carolina Supreme Court would agree with that ruling (see 327 N.C. 378).

A defendant may be convicted and punished for (1) possession with intent to sell, deliver, and manufacture and (2) sale and delivery (59 N.C. App. 656), but not also for possession of the same controlled substance.

Multiple punishment. A person may be convicted and punished for both possession of a controlled substance under G.S. 90-95(a)(3) and trafficking by possessing a controlled substance, even though the offenses are based on the same controlled substance (337 N.C. 431).

No double jeopardy bar to prosecuting drug offense after imposition of drug tax. There is no double jeopardy bar to prosecuting a drug offense after a defendant has been assessed and paid a drug tax under Ch. 105 of the General Statutes (132 N.C. App. 819).

Related offenses not in this chapter

None.

Possession of Controlled Substance on Premises of Prison or Local Confinement Facility

Statute

See subdivision (e)(9) of G.S. 90-95, reproduced under "Manufacture of Controlled Substance."

Elements

A person guilty of this offense
(1) knowingly
(2) possesses
(3) a controlled substance
(4) on the premises of a penal institution or local confinement facility.

Punishment

Class H felony.

Notes

Element (1). See the note on Element (1) under "Manufacture of Controlled Substance."

Element (2). See the note on Element (2) under "Possession of Controlled Substance."

Element (4). This offense may occur anywhere on the property, not just the confinement areas, of a prison, jail, or other kind of confinement facility. It also applies to any person, not just an inmate. This offense most likely would be charged when the possession offense would otherwise be a misdemeanor.

Criminal pleading. A criminal pleading charging this offense must allege that the possession of the controlled substance occurred on the premises of a penal institution or local confinement facility.

Related offenses not in this chapter

None.

Possession of Immediate Precursor Chemical with Intent to Manufacture, Sell, or Deliver Controlled Substance

Statute

See subsection (d1) of G.S. 90-95, reproduced under "Manufacture of Controlled Substance."

Elements

A person guilty of this offense
(1) knowingly
(2) possesses
(3) an immediate precursor chemical
(4) with intent to manufacture
(5) a controlled substance.

Punishment

Class H felony.

Notes

Element (1). See the note on Element (1) under "Manufacture of Controlled Substance."

Element (2). See the note on Element (2) under "Possession of Controlled Substance."

Element (3). Immediate precursor is defined in G.S. 90-87(14). It is a substance that is the principal compound commonly used or produced primarily for use (and which is an immediate chemical intermediary used or likely to be used) in manufacturing a controlled substance. The Commission for Mental Health, Developmental Disabilities, and Substance Abuse Services has the authority to designate chemicals as immediate precursor chemicals. In addition, G.S. 90-95(d2) lists specific chemicals as immediate precursor chemicals.

Element (4). See the note on Element (2) under "Manufacture of Controlled Substance" for the definition of manufacturing.

Related offense. A related offense in G.S. 90-95(d1) is possessing or distributing an immediate precursor chemical knowing, or having reasonable cause to believe, that the immediate precursor chemical will be used to manufacture a controlled substance.

Related offenses not in this chapter

None.

Employing or Intentionally Using Minor to Commit Controlled Substance Offense

Statute

§90-95.4. Employing or intentionally using minor to commit a drug law violation.

(a) A person who is at least 18 years old but less than 21 years old who hires or intentionally uses a minor to violate G.S. 90-95(a)(1) shall be guilty of a felony. An offense under this subsection shall be punishable as follows:

(1) If the minor was more than 13 years of age, then as a felony that is one class more severe than the violation of G.S. 90-95(a)(1) for which the minor was hired or intentionally used.

(2) If the minor was 13 years of age or younger, then as a felony that is two classes more severe than the violation of G.S. 90-95(a)(1) for which the minor was hired or intentionally used.

(b) A person 21 years of age or older who hires or intentionally uses a minor to violate G.S. 90-95(a)(1) shall be guilty of a felony. An offense under this subsection shall be punishable as follows:

(1) If the minor was more than 13 years of age, then as a felony that is three classes more severe than the violation of G.S. 90-95(a)(1) for which the minor was hired or intentionally used.

(2) If the minor was 13 years of age or younger, then as a felony that is four classes more severe than the violation of G.S. 90-95(a)(1) for which the minor was hired or intentionally used.

(c) Mistake of Age.—Mistake of age is not a defense to a prosecution under this section.

(d) The term "minor" as used in this section is defined as an individual who is less than 18 years of age.

I. Employing or Intentionally Using Minor to Commit Controlled Substance Offense by Defendant Who Is 21 Years Old or Older

Statute

See G.S. 90-95.4(b), reproduced above.

Elements

A person guilty of this offense

(1) is 21 years old or older, *and*
(2) hires or intentionally uses
(3) (a) a minor who is more than 13 years old, *or*
    (b) a minor who is 13 years old or younger
(4) to violate G.S. 90-95(a)(1) by
    (a) selling or delivering or manufacturing a controlled substance, *or*
    (b) possessing a controlled substance with the intent to sell or deliver or manufacture.

Punishment

For an offense including Element (3)(a) (a minor who is more than 13 years old), the punishment is three classes more severe than the violation of G.S. 90-95(a)(1) for which the minor was hired or intentionally used. For example, a Class H felony becomes a Class E felony. For an offense including Element

(3)(b) (a minor who is 13 years old or younger), the punishment is four classes more severe than the violation of G.S. 90-95(a)(1) for which the minor was hired or intentionally used. For example, a Class H felony becomes a Class D felony.

Notes

Element (2). "Hires" means to pay someone to do something; payment would include money and other things of value. The term "intentionally uses" would not require payment.

Element (3). The statute defines minor as a person under 18 years old and provides that it is no defense that the defendant did not know the person hired or intentionally used was under 18.

Element (4). See "Sale or Delivery of Controlled Substance" and "Possession of Controlled Substance with Intent to Manufacture, Sell, or Deliver."

Criminal pleading. A criminal pleading must allege all the elements listed above for the increased punishments to apply.

II. Employing or Intentionally Using Minor to Commit Controlled Substance Offense by Defendant Who Is At Least 18 Years Old but Less Than 21 Years Old

Statute

See G.S. 90-95.4(a), reproduced above.

Elements

A person guilty of this offense

(1) is at least 18 years old but less than 21 years old, *and*
(2) hires or intentionally uses
(3) (a) a minor who is more than 13 years old, *or*
    (b) a minor who is 13 years old or younger
(4) to violate G.S. 90-95(a)(1) by
    (a) selling or delivering or manufacturing a controlled substance, *or*
    (b) possessing a controlled substance with the intent to sell or deliver or manufacture.

Punishment

For an offense including Element (3)(a) (a minor who is more than 13 years old), the punishment is one class more severe than the violation of G.S. 90-95(a)(1) for which the minor was hired or intentionally used. For example, a Class H felony becomes a Class G felony. For an offense including Element (3)(b) (a minor who is 13 years old or younger), the punishment is two classes more severe than the violation of G.S. 90-95(a)(1) for which the minor was hired or intentionally used. For example, a Class H felony becomes a Class F felony.

Notes

See the notes under "I. Employing or Intentionally Using Minor to Commit Drug Law Violation by Defendant Who Is 21 Years Old or Older," above.

Related offenses not in this chapter

None.

Promoting Drug Sales by Minor

Statute

§90-95.6. Promoting drug sales by a minor.

(a) A person who is 21 years of age or older is guilty of promoting drug sales by a minor if the person knowingly:

(1) Entices, forces, encourages, or otherwise facilitates a minor in violating G.S. 90-95(a)(1).

(2) Supervises, supports, advises, or protects the minor in violating G.S. 90-95(a)(1).

(b) Mistake of age is not a defense to a prosecution under this section.

(c) A violation of this section is a Class D felony.

Elements

A person guilty of this offense

(1) is 21 years old or older, *and*
(2) knowingly
(3) entices, forces, encourages, or otherwise facilitates
(4) a minor
(5) to violate G.S. 90-95(a)(1) by
 (a) selling or delivering or manufacturing a controlled substance *or*
 (b) possessing a controlled substance with the intent to sell or deliver or manufacture, *and*
(6) supervises, supports, advises, or protects
(7) the minor
(8) to violate G.S. 90-95(a)(1) by
 (a) selling or delivering or manufacturing a controlled substance, *or*
 (b) possessing a controlled substance with the intent to sell or deliver or manufacture.

Punishment

Class D felony.

Notes

Elements (3) and (6). Although this statute contains no conjunction between subdivisions (a)(1) and (a)(2)—that is, no "and" or "or"—it appears to require proof of both subdivisions for a conviction. If proof of only one subdivision was required, the listed acts (enticing, supervising, and so on) could have been set out in a single clause. Further, subdivision (a)(1) refers to "a" minor, and subdivision (a)(2) refers to "the" minor, suggesting that a defendant must enlist a minor's assistance and then oversee that minor's activities. Finally, the punishment for this offense is potentially greater than the punishment for "Employing or Intentionally Using Minor to Commit Controlled Substance Offense" under G.S. 90-95.4, discussed earlier in this chapter, suggesting that more is required for conviction than the acts listed in subdivision (a)(1) alone.

Element (4). Because the statute does not specify the minor's age, the general definition of "minor" in G.S. 48A-2 (a person under 18 years of age) probably applies to this offense. The statute provides that mistake of age is not a defense.

Elements (5) and (8). See "Sale or Delivery of Controlled Substance" and "Possession of Controlled Substance with Intent to Manufacture, Sell, or Deliver."

Related offenses not in this chapter

None.

Participating in Drug Violation by Minor

Statute

§90-95.7. Participating in a drug violation by a minor.

(a) A person 21 years of age or older who purchases or receives a controlled substance from a minor 13 years of age or younger who possesses, sells, or delivers the controlled substance in violation of G.S. 90-95(a)(1) is guilty of participating in a drug violation of a minor.

(b) Mistake of age is not a defense to a prosecution under this section.

(c) A violation of this section is a Class G felony.

Elements

A person guilty of this offense

(1) is 21 years old or older, *and*
(2) purchases or receives
(3) a controlled substance
(4) from a minor 13 years old or younger
(5) who sells or delivers or possesses with intent to sell, deliver or manufacture the controlled substance in violation of G.S. 90-95(a)(1).

Punishment

Class G felony.

Notes

Element (3). The statute provides that mistake of age is not a defense.

Element (5). Although the statute uses the word "possesses," its linkage to a violation of G.S. 90-95(a)(1) requires that the defendant possess the controlled substance with the intent to sell, deliver, or manufacture. Of course, if the person who is 21 years old or older purchases or receives the controlled substance from the minor, the minor always will have possessed the controlled substance with the intent to sell or deliver.

Related offenses not in this chapter

None.

Trafficking in Marijuana

Statute

See subdivision (h)(1) and subsection (i) of G.S. 90-95, reproduced under "Manufacture of Controlled Substance."

Elements

A person guilty of this offense
- (1) knowingly
- (2) (a) sells or manufactures or delivers or transports or possesses, *or*
  - (b) conspires to sell or manufacture or deliver or transport or possess
- (3) marijuana
- (4) to another person (if the person sells or delivers), *and*
- (5) the quantity of marijuana is
  - (a) in excess of 10 pounds but less than 50 pounds, *or*
  - (b) 50 pounds or more but less than 2,000 pounds, *or*
  - (c) 2,000 pounds or more but less than 10,000 pounds, *or*
  - (d) 10,000 pounds or more.

Punishment

For the amount in (5)(a), the crime is a Class H felony punishable by a mandatory minimum imprisonment of 25 months and a mandatory maximum imprisonment of 30 months and a mandatory minimum fine of $5,000. *For the amount in (5)(b)*, the crime is a Class G felony punishable by mandatory minimum imprisonment of 35 months and a mandatory maximum imprisonment of 42 months and a mandatory minimum fine of $25,000. *For the amount in (5)(c)*, the crime is a Class F felony punishable by a mandatory minimum imprisonment of 70 months and a mandatory maximum imprisonment of 84 months and a mandatory minimum fine of $50,000. *For the amount in (5)(d)*, the crime is a Class D felony punishable by a mandatory minimum imprisonment of 175 months and a mandatory maximum imprisonment of 219 months and a mandatory minimum fine of $200,000. Sentences must run consecutively to any sentence being served at the time of sentencing [G.S. 90-95(h)(6)].

The punishment for this offense under structured sentencing is exactly as set out above and is not affected by a defendant's prior record level or aggravating and mitigating factors. However, a sentencing judge under G.S. 90-95(h)(5) may impose a lesser sentence if the defendant has provided substantial assistance in the identification, arrest, or conviction of any accomplices, accessories, co-conspirators, or principals involved in controlled substances offenses (see generally 104 N.C. App. 274).

Notes

Element (1). See the note on Element (1) under "Manufacture of Controlled Substance."

Element (2). See the discussion of manufacture, sell, deliver, and possess in the notes under "Manufacture of Controlled Substance," "Sale or Delivery of Controlled Substance," and "Possession of Controlled Substance." See the discussion of conspiracy under "Conspiracy" (Chapter 4). Transport means "any real carrying about or movement from one place to another." The following was sufficient evidence of transportation: the defendant removed drugs from a dwelling and brought them to an undercover agent in a car (110 N.C. App. 643); when officers surrounded a house, the defendant zipped up the bag containing cocaine and tossed it in the yard next door (102 N.C. App. 447); the defendant carried cocaine from his house to his truck in the driveway and began to back out of the driveway (96 N.C. App. 192); the defendant threw a package of cocaine from a car into some bushes to avoid being caught by law enforcement officers and so he could retrieve the cocaine later (124 N.C. App. 136).

Element (3). "Marijuana" is defined in G.S. 90-87(16) to mean "all parts of the plant of the genus *Cannabis*, whether growing or not; the seeds thereof; the resin extracted from any part of such plant; and every compound, manufacture, salt, derivative, mixture, or preparation of such plant, its seeds or resin, but shall not include the mature stalks of such plant, fiber produced from such stalks, oil, or cake made from the seeds of such plant, any other compound, manufacture, salt, derivative, mixture, or preparation of such mature stalks (except the resin extracted therefrom), fiber, oil, or cake, or the sterilized seed of such plant which is incapable of germination."

Element (4). See the note on Element (4) under "Sale or Delivery of Controlled Substance."

Element (5). In a case in which the weight of marijuana, seized from a field that was wet and included dirt and mature stalks [excludable under G.S. 90-87(16)], was 16,620 pounds and another pickup truckload had not been weighed because it had been plowed under, the evidence was sufficient to prove that the amount of marijuana was over 10,000 pounds (66 N.C. App. 402).

A drug trafficking conspiracy includes the cumulative amount of controlled substances sold during the course of an open-ended conspiracy, even though the conspirators' agreement was silent about the exact quantity (110 N.C. App. 626). Evidence was insufficient to prove the defendant possessed a trafficking amount of marijuana when an officer intercepted a package containing a trafficking amount of marijuana, removed most of the marijuana so there was no longer a trafficking amount, and then delivered the package of marijuana to the defendant; instead, the defendant was guilty of attempted trafficking by possession (137 N.C. App. 90).

Multiple convictions and punishments. Trafficking by sale, manufacture, delivery, transportation, and possession are separate offenses for which a defendant may be separately convicted and punished (330 N.C. 298; 317 N.C. 545; 316 N.C. 87). A person may be convicted and punished for both possession of a controlled substance under G.S. 90-95(a)(3) and trafficking by possessing a controlled substance, even though the offenses are based on the same controlled substance (337 N.C. 431); this principle would also apply to convictions for sale, delivery, and manufacture under G.S. 90-95(a)(1) and the corresponding trafficking offenses of sale, delivery, and manufacture.

When only one agreement encompasses a conspiracy to sell, deliver, manufacture, transport, and possess, only one trafficking conspiracy may be charged and punished (84 N.C. App. 150).

Related offenses not in this chapter

None.

Trafficking in Methaqualone

Statute

See subdivision (h)(2) and subsection (i) of G.S. 90-95, reproduced under "Manufacture of Controlled Substance."

Elements

A person guilty of this offense
- (1) knowingly
- (2) (a) sells or manufactures or delivers or transports or possesses, *or*
  - (b) conspires to sell or manufacture or deliver or transport or possess
- (3) tablets, capsules, or other dosage units, or the equivalent quantity, or methaqualone, or any mixture containing methaqualone
- (4) to another person (if the person sells or delivers), *and*
- (5) the quantity of methaqualone or mixture containing methaqualone is
  - (a) 1,000 or more dosage units or equivalent quantity, but less than 5,000, *or*
  - (b) 5,000 or more dosage units or equivalent quantity, but less than 10,000, *or*
  - (c) 10,000 or more dosage units or equivalent quantity.

Punishment

For the amount in (5)(a), the crime is a Class G felony punishable by a mandatory minimum imprisonment of 35 months and a mandatory maximum imprisonment of 42 months and a mandatory minimum fine of $25,000. *For the amount in (5)(b)*, the crime is a Class F felony punishable by a mandatory minimum imprisonment of 70 months and a mandatory maximum imprisonment of 84 months and a mandatory minimum fine of $50,000. *For the amount in (5)(c)*, the crime is a Class D felony punishable by a mandatory minimum imprisonment of 175 months and a mandatory maximum imprisonment of 219 months and a mandatory minimum fine of $200,000. Sentences must run consecutively to any sentence being served at the time of sentencing [G.S. 90-95(h)(6)].

The punishment for this offense under structured sentencing is exactly as set out above and is not affected by a defendant's prior record level or aggravating and mitigating factors. However, a sentencing judge under G.S. 90-95(h)(5) may impose a lesser sentence if the defendant has provided substantial assistance in the identification, arrest, or conviction of any accomplices, accessories, co-conspirators, or principals involved in controlled substances offenses (see generally 104 N.C. App. 274).

Notes

Element (1). See the note on Element (1) under "Manufacture of Controlled Substance."

Element (2). See the discussion of manufacture, sell, deliver, and possess in the notes under "Manufacture of Controlled Substance," "Sale or Delivery of Controlled Substance," and "Possession of Controlled Substance." See the discussion of conspiracy in "Conspiracy" (Chapter 4). For a discussion of transport, see the note on Element (2) under "Trafficking in Marijuana."

Element (3). This element is satisfied if the tablet, capsule, other dosage unit, or equivalent quantity has any mixture containing methaqualone. The dosage unit need not contain pure methaqualone (for similar rulings involving heroin, see 92 N.C. App. 651; 75 N.C. App. 632). Random sampling and testing of tablets is sufficient to establish that all similar-appearing tablets contain methaqualone (61 N.C. App. 554).

Element (4). See the note on Element (4) under "Sale or Delivery of Controlled Substance."

Element (5). A drug trafficking conspiracy includes the cumulative amount of controlled substances sold during the course of an open-ended conspiracy, even though the conspirators' agreement was silent about the exact quantity (110 N.C. App. 626).

Multiple convictions and punishments. See the note on this subject under "Trafficking in Marijuana."

Related offenses not in this chapter

None.

Trafficking in Cocaine

Statute

See subdivision (h)(3) and subsection (i) of G.S. 90-95, reproduced under "Manufacture of Controlled Substance."

Elements

A person guilty of this offense
- (1) knowingly
- (2) (a) sells or manufactures or delivers or transports or possesses, *or*
  - (b) conspires to sell or manufacture or deliver or transport or possess
- (3) cocaine or any mixture containing cocaine
- (4) to another person (if the person sells or delivers), *and*
- (5) the quantity of cocaine or mixture containing cocaine is
  - (a) 28 grams or more, but less than 200 grams, *or*
  - (b) 200 grams or more, but less than 400 grams, *or*
  - (c) 400 grams or more.

Punishment

For the amount in (5)(a), the crime is a Class G felony punishable by a mandatory minimum imprisonment of 35 months and a mandatory maximum imprisonment of 42 months and a mandatory minimum fine of $50,000. *For the amount in (5)(b)*, the crime is a Class F felony punishable by a mandatory minimum imprisonment of 70 months and a mandatory maximum imprisonment of 84 months and a mandatory minimum fine of $100,000. *For the amount in (5)(c)*, the crime is a Class D felony punishable by a mandatory minimum imprisonment of 175 months and a mandatory maximum imprisonment of 219 months and a mandatory minimum fine of $250,000. Sentences must run consecutively to any sentence being served at the time of sentencing [G.S. 90-95(h)(6)].

The punishment for this offense under structured sentencing is exactly as set out above and is not affected by a defendant's prior record level or aggravating and mitigating factors. However, a sentencing judge under G.S. 90-

95(h)(5) may impose a lesser sentence if the defendant has provided substantial assistance in the identification, arrest, or conviction of any accomplices, accessories, co-conspirators, or principals involved in controlled substances offenses (see generally 104 N.C. App. 274).

Notes

Element (1). See the note on Element (1) under "Manufacture of Controlled Substance."

Element (2). See the discussion of manufacture, sell, deliver, and possess in the notes under "Manufacture of Controlled Substance," "Sale or Delivery of Controlled Substance," and "Possession of Controlled Substance." See the discussion of conspiracy under "Conspiracy" (Chapter 4). For a discussion of transport, see the note on Element (2) under "Trafficking in Marijuana."

Element (3). The statute prohibits trafficking in the following substances: "cocaine and any salt, isomer, salts of isomers, compound, derivative, or preparation thereof, or any coca leaves and any salt, isomer, salts of isomers, compound, derivative, or preparation of coca leaves, and any salt, isomer, salts of isomers, compound, derivative or preparation thereof which is chemically equivalent or identical with any of these substances (except decocainized coca leaves or any extraction of coca leaves which does not contain cocaine) or any mixture containing such substances. . . ."

This element is satisfied if any mixture contains a prohibited substance. Thus a defendant who sold an undercover agent a powdery mixture weighing 37.1 grams, of which only 5.565 grams were cocaine, was properly convicted of trafficking in cocaine by delivering over 28 grams of cocaine (55 N.C. App. 57).

Element (4). See the note on Element (4) under "Sale or Delivery of Controlled Substance."

Element (5). A drug trafficking conspiracy includes the cumulative amount of controlled substances sold during the course of an open-ended conspiracy, even though the conspirators' agreement was silent about the exact quantity (110 N.C. App. 626).

Multiple convictions and punishments. See the note on this subject under "Trafficking in Marijuana."

Related offenses not in this chapter

None.

Trafficking in Opium or Heroin

Statute

See subdivision (h)(4) and subsection (i) of G.S. 90-95, reproduced under "Manufacture of Controlled Substance."

Elements

A person guilty of this offense
(1) knowingly
(2) (a) sells or manufactures or delivers or transports or possesses, *or*
(b) conspires to sell or manufacture or deliver or transport or possess

(3) opium, including heroin, or any mixture containing opium or heroin
(4) to another person (if the person sells or delivers), *and*
(5) the quantity of opium, including heroin, or any mixture containing opium or heroin is
  (a) 4 grams or more, but less than 14 grams, *or*
  (b) 14 grams or more, but less than 28 grams, *or*
  (c) 28 grams or more.

Punishment

For the amount in (5)(a), the crime is a Class F felony punishable by a mandatory minimum imprisonment of 70 months and a mandatory maximum imprisonment of 84 months and a mandatory minimum fine of $50,000. *For the amount in (5)(b)*, the crime is a Class E felony punishable by a mandatory minimum imprisonment of 90 months and a mandatory maximum imprisonment of 117 months and a mandatory minimum fine of $100,000. *For the amount in (5)(c)*, the crime is a Class C felony punishable by a mandatory minimum imprisonment of 225 months and a mandatory maximum imprisonment of 279 months and a mandatory minimum fine of $500,000. Sentences must run consecutively to any sentence being served at the time of sentencing [G.S. 90-95(h)(6)].

The punishment for this offense under structured sentencing is exactly as set out above and is not affected by a defendant's prior record level or aggravating and mitigating factors. However, a sentencing judge under G.S. 90-95(h)(5) may impose a lesser sentence if the defendant has provided substantial assistance in the identification, arrest, or conviction of any accomplices, accessories, co-conspirators, or principals involved in controlled substances offenses (see generally 104 N.C. App. 274).

Notes

Element (1). See the note on Element (1) under "Manufacture of Controlled Substance."

Element (2). See the discussion of manufacture, sell, deliver, and possess in the notes under "Manufacture of Controlled Substance," "Sale or Delivery of Controlled Substance," and "Possession of Controlled Substance." See the discussion of conspiracy under "Conspiracy" (Chapter 4). For a discussion of transport, see the note on Element (2) under "Trafficking in Marijuana."

Element (3). The statute prohibits trafficking in the following substances: "opium or opiate, or any salt, compound, derivative, or preparation of opium or opiate (except apomorphine, nalbuphine, analoxone and naltrexone and their respective salts), including heroin, or any mixture containing such substance. . . ."

This element is satisfied if the mixture contains any amount of a prohibited substance. It is the weight of the entire mixture, not the weight of the controlled substance in the mixture, that determines liability and punishment under this statute. Thus white powder that weighed 13.2 grams but contained only 30 percent pure heroin was sufficient to prove trafficking by possessing at least 4 grams, since the weight of the entire mixture was at least 4 grams (61 N.C. App. 23). A heroin mixture that weighed 22 grams was sufficient for a trafficking conviction even though the amount of pure heroin in the mixture was less than 4 grams (94 N.C. App. 710; for similar rulings, see 92 N.C. App. 651; 75 N.C. App. 632).

Element (4). See the note on Element (4) under "Sale or Delivery of Controlled Substance."

Element (5). A drug trafficking conspiracy includes the cumulative amount of controlled substances sold during the course of an open-ended conspiracy, even though the conspirators' agreement was silent about the exact quantity (110 N.C. App. 626).

Multiple convictions and punishments. See the note on this subject under "Trafficking in Marijuana."

Related offenses not in this chapter

None.

Trafficking in Amphetamine

Statute

See subdivision (h)(3b) and subsection (i) of G.S. 90-95, reproduced under "Manufacture of Controlled Substance."

Elements

A person guilty of this offense
- (1) knowingly
- (2) (a) sells or manufactures or delivers or transports or possesses, *or*
  - (b) conspires to sell or manufacture or deliver or transport or possess
- (3) amphetamine or any mixture containing such substance
- (4) to another person (if the person sells or delivers), *and*
- (5) the quantity of amphetamine or mixture containing such substance is
  - (a) 28 grams or more, but less than 200 grams, *or*
  - (b) 200 grams or more, but less than 400 grams, *or*
  - (c) 400 grams or more.

Punishment

For the amount in (5)(a), the crime is a Class F felony punishable by a mandatory minimum imprisonment of 70 months and a maximum term of 84 months and a mandatory minimum fine of $50,000. *For the amount in (5)(b),* the crime is a Class E felony punishable by a mandatory minimum imprisonment of 90 months and a maximum term of 117 months and a mandatory minimum fine of $100,000. *For the amount in (5)(c),* the crime is a Class C felony punishable by a mandatory minimum imprisonment of 225 months and a maximum term of 279 months and a mandatory minimum fine of $250,000. Sentences must run consecutively to any sentence being served at the time of sentencing [G.S. 90-95(h)(6)].

The punishment for this offense under structured sentencing is exactly as set out above and is not affected by a defendant's prior record level or aggravating and mitigating factors. However, a sentencing judge under G.S. 90-95(h)(5) may impose a lesser sentence if the defendant has provided substantial assistance in the identification, arrest, or conviction of any accomplices, accessories, co-conspirators, or principals involved in controlled substances offenses (see generally 104 N.C. App. 274).

Notes

Element (1). See the note on Element (1) under "Manufacture of Controlled Substance."

Element (2). See the discussion of manufacture, sell, deliver, and possess in the notes under "Manufacture of Controlled Substance," "Sale or Delivery of Controlled Substance," and "Possession of Controlled Substance." See the discussion of conspiracy under "Conspiracy" (Chapter 4). For a discussion of transport, see the note on Element (2) under "Trafficking in Marijuana."

Element (3). The statute prohibits trafficking in amphetamine or any mixture containing amphetamine. When a mixture containing amphetamine is involved, it is the weight of the mixture, not the amphetamine alone, that determines whether this element is satisfied (for similar rulings involving heroin, see 92 N.C. App. 651; 75 N.C. App. 632).

Element (4). See the note on Element (4) under "Sale or Delivery of Controlled Substance."

Element (5). A drug trafficking conspiracy includes the cumulative amount of controlled substances sold during the course of an open-ended conspiracy, even though the conspirators' agreement was silent about the exact quantity (110 N.C. App. 626).

Multiple convictions and punishments. See the note on this subject under "Trafficking in Marijuana."

Related offenses not in this chapter

None.

Trafficking in Methamphetamine

Statute

See subdivision (h)(3b) and subsection (i) of G.S. 90-95, reproduced under "Manufacture of Controlled Substance."

Elements

A person guilty of this offense

(1) knowingly
(2) (a) sells or manufactures or delivers or transports or possesses, *or*
    (b) conspires to sell or manufacture or deliver or transport or possess
(3) methamphetamine or any mixture containing such substance
(4) to another person (if the person sells or delivers), *and*
(5) the quantity of methamphetamine or mixture containing such substance is
    (a) 28 grams or more, but less than 200 grams, *or*
    (b) 200 grams or more, but less than 400 grams, *or*
    (c) 400 grams or more.

Punishment

For the amount in (5)(a), the crime is a Class F felony punishable by a mandatory minimum imprisonment of 70 months and a maximum term of 84 months and a mandatory minimum fine of $50,000. *For the amount in (5)(b),* the crime is a Class E felony punishable by a mandatory minimum imprisonment of 90 months and a maximum term of 117 months and a mandatory minimum fine of $100,000. *For the amount in (5)(c),* the crime is a Class C felony punishable by a mandatory minimum imprisonment of 225 months and a maximum term of 279 months and a mandatory minimum fine of $250,000. Sentences must run consecutively to any sentence being served at the time of sentencing [G.S. 90-95(h)(6)].

The punishment for this offense under structured sentencing is exactly as set out above and is not affected by a defendant's prior record level or aggravating and mitigating factors. However, a sentencing judge under G.S. 90-95(h)(5) may impose a lesser sentence if the defendant has provided substantial assistance in the identification, arrest, or conviction of any accomplices, accessories, co-conspirators, or principals involved in controlled substances offenses (see generally 104 N.C. App. 274).

Notes

Element (1). See the note on Element (1) under "Manufacture of Controlled Substance."

Element (2). See the discussion of manufacture, sell, deliver, and possess in the note on Element (1) under "Manufacture of Controlled Substance," "Sale or Delivery of Controlled Substance," and "Possession of Controlled Substance." See the discussion of conspiracy under "Conspiracy" (Chapter 4). For a discussion of transport, see the note on Element (2) under "Trafficking in Marijuana."

Element (3). The statute prohibits trafficking in methamphetamine or any mixture containing methamphetamine. When a mixture containing methamphetamine is involved, it is the weight of the mixture, not the methamphetamine alone, that determines whether this element is satisfied (for similar rulings involving heroin, see 92 N.C. App. 651; 75 N.C. App. 632).

Element (4). See the note on Element (4) under "Sale or Delivery of Controlled Substance."

Element (5). A drug trafficking conspiracy includes the cumulative amount of controlled substances sold during the course of an open-ended conspiracy, even though the conspirators' agreement was silent about the exact quantity (110 N.C. App. 626).

Multiple convictions and punishments. See the note on this subject under "Trafficking in Marijuana."

Related offenses not in this chapter

None.

Trafficking in LSD

Statute

See subdivision (h)(4a) and subsection (i) of G.S. 90-95, reproduced under "Manufacture of Controlled Substance."

Elements

A person guilty of this offense

(1) knowingly

(2) (a) sells or manufactures or delivers or transports or possesses, *or*

(b) conspires to sell or manufacture or deliver or transport or possess

(3) tablets, capsules, or other dosage units, or the equivalent quantity, of lysergic acid diethylamide, or any mixture containing such substance
(4) to another person (if the person sells or delivers), *and*
(5) the quantity of lysergic acid diethylamide, or any mixture containing such substance is
   (a) 100 or more dosage units or equivalent quantity, but less than 500 dosage units or equivalent quantity, *or*
   (b) 500 or more dosage units or equivalent quantity, but less than 1,000 dosage units or equivalent quantity, *or*
   (c) 1,000 or more dosage units or equivalent quantity.

Punishment

For the amount in (5)(a), the crime is a Class G felony punishable by a mandatory minimum imprisonment of 35 months and a mandatory maximum imprisonment of 42 months and a mandatory minimum fine of $25,000. *For the amount in (5)(b)*, the crime is a Class F felony with a mandatory minimum imprisonment of 70 months and a mandatory maximum imprisonment of 84 months and a mandatory minimum fine of $50,000. *For the amount in (5)(c)*, the crime is a Class D felony with a mandatory minimum imprisonment of 175 months and a mandatory maximum imprisonment of 219 months and a mandatory minimum fine of $200,000. Sentences must run consecutively to any sentence being served at the time of sentencing [G.S. 90-95(h)(6)].

The punishment for this offense under structured sentencing is exactly as set out above and is not affected by a defendant's prior record level or aggravating and mitigating factors. However, a sentencing judge under G.S. 90-95(h)(5) may impose a lesser sentence if the defendant has provided substantial assistance in the identification, arrest, or conviction of any accomplices, accessories, co-conspirators, or principals involved in controlled substances offenses (see generally 104 N.C. App. 274).

Notes

Element (1). See the note on Element (1) under "Manufacture of Controlled Substance."

Element (2). See the discussion of manufacture, sell, deliver, and possess under "Manufacture of Controlled Substance," "Sale or Delivery of Controlled Substance," and "Possession of Controlled Substance." See the discussion of conspiracy under "Conspiracy" (Chapter 4). For a discussion of transport, see the note on Element (2) under "Trafficking in Marijuana."

Element (3). This element is satisfied if the tablet, capsule, other dosage unit, or equivalent quantity has any mixture containing LSD. The dosage unit need not contain pure LSD (for similar rulings involving heroin, see 92 N.C. App. 651; 75 N.C. App. 632). Random sampling and testing of tablets is sufficient to establish that all similar-appearing tablets contain LSD (see 61 N.C. App. 554, a case involving methaqualone but equally applicable to LSD).

Element (4). See the note on Element (4) under "Sale or Delivery of Controlled Substance."

Element (5). A drug trafficking conspiracy includes the cumulative amount of controlled substances sold during the course of an open-ended conspiracy, even though the conspirators' agreement was silent about the exact quantity (110 N.C. App. 626).

Multiple convictions and punishments. See the note on this subject under "Trafficking in Marijuana."

Related offenses not in this chapter

None.

Trafficking in MDA and MDMA

Statute

See subdivision (h)(4b) and subsection (i) of G.S. 90-95, reproduced under "Manufacture of Controlled Substance."

Elements

A person guilty of this offense

(1) knowingly

(2) (a) sells or manufactures or delivers or transports or possesses, *or*

(b) conspires to sell or manufacture or deliver or transport or possess

(3) grams, tablets, capsules, or other dosage units, or the equivalent quantity, of 3,4-methylenedioxyamphetamine (MDA) or 3,4-methylenedioxymethamphetamine (MDMA), including its salts, isomers, and salts of isomers, or any mixture containing such substances

(4) to another person (if the person sells or delivers), *and*

(5) the weight or quantity of 3,4-methylenedioxyamphetamine (MDA) *or* 3,4-methylenedioxymethamphetamine (MDMA), including its salts, isomers, and salts of isomers, or any mixture containing such substances is

(a) 100 or more tablets, capsules, or other dosage units, but less than 500 tablets, capsules, or other dosage units, or 28 grams or more, but less than 200 grams, *or*

(b) 500 or more tablets, capsules, or other dosage units, but less than 1,000 tablets, capsules, or other dosage units, or 200 grams or more, but less than 400 grams, *or*

(c) 1,000 or more tablets, capsules, or other dosage units, or 400 grams or more.

Punishment

For the amount in (5)(a), the crime is a Class G felony punishable by a mandatory minimum imprisonment of 35 months and a maximum term of 42 months and a mandatory minimum fine of $25,000. *For the amount in (5)(b)*, the crime is a Class F felony punishable by a mandatory minimum imprisonment of 70 months and a maximum term of 84 months and a mandatory minimum fine of $50,000. *For the amount in (5)(c)*, the crime is a Class D felony punishable by a mandatory minimum imprisonment of 175 months and a maximum term of 219 months and a mandatory minimum fine of $250,000. Sentences must run consecutively to any sentence being served at the time of sentencing [G.S. 90-95(h)(6)].

Notes

Element (1). See the note on Element (1) under "Manufacture of Controlled Substance."

Element (2). See the discussion of manufacture, sell, deliver, and possess in the notes under "Manufacture of Controlled Substance," "Sale or Delivery of Controlled Substance," and "Possession of Controlled Substance." See the discussion of conspiracy under "Conspiracy" (Chapter 4). For a discussion of transport, see the note on Element (2) under "Trafficking in Marijuana."

Element (3). This element is satisfied if the grams, tablet, capsule, other dosage unit, or equivalent quantity has any mixture containing MDA or MDMA. The dosage unit need not contain pure MDA or MDMA (for similar rulings involving heroin, see 92 N.C. App. 651; 75 N.C. App. 632). Random sampling and testing of tablets is sufficient to establish that all similar-appearing tablets contain MDA or MDMA (see 61 N.C. App. 554, a case involving methaqualone but equally applicable to MDA or MDMA). Also, it is the weight of the mixture in grams, not the MDA or MDMA alone, that determines whether this element is satisfied (for similar rulings involving heroin, see 92 N.C. App. 651; 75 N.C. App. 632).

Element (4). See the note on Element (4) under "Sale or Delivery of Controlled Substance."

Element (5). A drug trafficking conspiracy includes the cumulative amount of controlled substances sold during the course of an open-ended conspiracy, even though the conspirators' agreement was silent about the exact quantity (110 N.C. App. 626).

Multiple convictions and punishments. See the note on this subject under "Trafficking in Marijuana."

Related offenses not in this chapter

None.

Continuing Criminal Enterprise—Drug Offenses

Statute

§90-95.1. Continuing criminal enterprise.

(a) Any person who engages in a continuing criminal enterprise shall be punished as a Class C felon and in addition shall be subject to the forfeiture prescribed in subsection (b) of this section.

(b) Any person who is convicted under subsection (a) of engaging in a continuing criminal enterprise shall forfeit to the State of North Carolina:

(1) The profits obtained by him in such enterprise, and

(2) Any of his interest in, claim against, or property or contractual rights of any kind affording a source of influence over, such enterprise.

(c) For purposes of this section, a person is engaged in a continuing criminal enterprise if:

(1) He violates any provision of this Article, the punishment of which is a felony; and

(2) Such violation is a part of a continuing series of violations of this Article;

a. Which are undertaken by such person in concert with five or more other persons with respect to whom such person occupies a position of organizer, a supervisory position, or any other position of management; and

b. From which such person obtains substantial income or resources.

(d) Repealed by Session Laws 1979, c. 760, s. 5.

Elements

A person guilty of this offense
(1) commits any felony under Article 5 of G.S. Ch. 90 (Controlled Substances Act)
(2) that is part of a continuing series of violations of Art. 5
(3) that are undertaken in concert with five or more other persons
(4) over whom the person occupies a position of organizer, supervisor, or other position of management, *and*
(5) the person obtains substantial income or other resources from the continuing violations.

Punishment

Class C felony. In addition, property set out in G.S. 90-95.1(b) must be forfeited.

Notes

Generally. No state appellate cases have interpreted this statute. For federal appellate cases interpreting a similar federal statute, see 526 U.S. 813; 517 U.S. 292; 135 F.3d 291; 471 U.S. 773; 885 F.2d 195; 791 F.2d 1120; 751 F.2d 250; 506 F.2d 1323; and 621 F. Supp. 383.

Related offenses not in this chapter

None.

Obtaining Controlled Substance by Misrepresenting Oneself as Licensed Practitioner

Statute

§90-108. Prohibited acts; penalties.

(a) It shall be unlawful for any person:
(1) Other than practitioners licensed under Articles 1, 2, 4, 6, 11, 12A of this Chapter to represent to any registrant or practitioner who manufactures, distributes, or dispenses a controlled substance under the provision of this Article that he is a licensed practitioner in order to secure or attempt to secure any controlled substance as defined in this Article or to in any way impersonate a practitioner for the purpose of securing or attempting to secure any drug requiring a prescription from a practitioner as listed above and who is licensed by this State;
(2) Who is subject to the requirements of G.S. 90-101 or a practitioner to distribute or dispense a controlled substance in violation of G.S. 90-105 or 90-106;
(3) Who is a registrant to manufacture, distribute, or dispense a controlled substance not authorized by his registration to another registrant or other authorized person;
(4) To omit, remove, alter, or obliterate a symbol required by the Federal Controlled Substances Act or its successor;

(5) To refuse or fail to make, keep, or furnish any record, notification, order form, statement, invoice or information required under this Article;
(6) To refuse any entry into any premises or inspection authorized by this Article;
(7) To knowingly keep or maintain any store, shop, warehouse, dwelling house, building, vehicle, boat, aircraft, or any place whatever, which is resorted to by persons using controlled substances in violation of this Article for the purpose of using such substances, or which is used for the keeping or selling of the same in violation of this Article;
(8) Who is a registrant or a practitioner to distribute a controlled substance included in Schedule I or II of this Article in the course of his legitimate business, except pursuant to an order form as required by G.S. 90-105;
(9) To use in the course of the manufacture or distribution of a controlled substance a registration number which is fictitious, revoked, suspended, or issued to another person;
(10) To acquire or obtain possession of a controlled substance by misrepresentation, fraud, forgery, deception, or subterfuge;
(11) To furnish false or fraudulent material information in, or omit any material information from, any application, report, or other document required to be kept or filed under this Article, or any record required to be kept by this Article;
(12) To make, distribute, or possess any punch, die, plate, stone, or other thing designed to print, imprint, or reproduce the trademark, trade name, or other identifying mark, imprint, or device of another or any likeness of any of the foregoing upon any drug or container or labeling thereof so as to render such drug a counterfeit controlled substance;
(13) To obtain controlled substances through the use of legal prescriptions which have been obtained by the knowing and willful misrepresentation to or by the intentional withholding of information from one or more practitioners;
(14) Who is an employee of a registrant or practitioner and who is authorized to possess controlled substances or has access to controlled substances by virtue of his employment, to embezzle or fraudulently or knowingly and willfully misapply or divert to his own use or other unauthorized or illegal use or to take, make away with or secrete, with intent to embezzle or fraudulently or knowingly and willfully misapply or divert to his own use or other unauthorized or illegal use any controlled substance which shall have come into his possession or under his care.

(b) Any person who violates this section shall be guilty of a Class 1 misdemeanor. Provided, that if the criminal pleading alleges that the violation was committed intentionally, and upon trial it is specifically found that the violation was committed intentionally, such violations shall be a Class I felony. A person who violates subdivision (7) of subsection (a) of this section and also fortifies the structure, with the intent to impede law enforcement entry, (by barricading windows and doors) shall be punished as a Class I felon.

Elements

A person guilty of this offense
(1) is not licensed as a physician, dentist, pharmacist, optometrist, veterinarian, or podiatrist, *but*
(2) (a) represents to a manufacturer, distributor, or dispenser of controlled substances, *or*
(b) in any other way impersonates
(3) that he or she is such a licensed practitioner
(4) in order to secure any controlled substance.

Punishment

Class 1 misdemeanor. If it is alleged and proved that the act was committed intentionally, the offense is a Class I felony [G.S. 90-108(b)].

Related offenses not in this chapter

"Obtaining Property by False Pretenses" (Chapter 14)

Unlawful Distribution of Controlled Substance by Registrant or Practitioner

Statute

See subdivision (a)(2) of G.S. 90-108, reproduced under "Obtaining Controlled Substance by Misrepresenting Oneself as Licensed Practitioner."

Elements

A person guilty of this offense

(1) (a) is licensed under G.S. 90-101 to manufacture, distribute, dispense, or conduct research with a controlled substance, *or*
    (b) is a licensed practitioner (physician, dentist, pharmacist, veterinarian, etc.), *and*
(2) distributes or dispenses a controlled substance
(3) (a) other than pursuant to an order form as required by G.S. 90-105, *or*
    (b) as a practitioner he or she dispenses a Schedule II substance other than by written prescription [as required by G.S. 90-106(a)], unless an emergency oral prescription is allowed under G.S. 90-106(b), *or*
    (c) refills a prescription for a Schedule II substance contrary to G.S. 90-106(b), *or*
    (d) as a pharmacist he or she dispenses a Schedule III or IV substance directly to an ultimate user without a prescription, contrary to G.S. 90-106(c) (unless the substance is paregoric, U.S.P.), *or*
    (e) refills a prescription for a Schedule III or IV substance more than five times or more than 6 months after the date of the prescription, contrary to G.S. 90-106(c), *or*
    (f) distributes or dispenses a Schedule V substance or paregoric, U.S.P., other than for a medical purpose, contrary to G.S. 90-106(d), *or*
    (g) as a licensee for a scientific or research project with a Schedule VI substance, he or she distributes or dispenses such a substance for other than a scientific or research purpose, contrary to G.S. 90-106 (e), *or*
    (h) places such a substance in a container other than one clearly labeled as required by the federal government or the Commission for Mental Health, Developmental Disabilities, and Substance Abuse Services under G.S. 90-106(f), *or*
    (i) fills or refills a copy of a prescription contrary to G.S. 90-106(g), *or*
    (j) as a pharmacist, he or she fails to enter the date of dispensing or fails to sign on the face of a prescription for a controlled substance contrary to G.S. 90-106(h), *or*

(k) as a manufacturer's sales representative, he or she distributes a controlled substance as a complimentary sample to a practitioner without the written request required by G.S. 90-106(i).

Punishment

Class 1 misdemeanor. If it is alleged and proved that the act was committed intentionally, the offense is a Class I felony [G.S. 90-108(b)].

Notes

Prosecution of physician. A physician who writes a prescription for a controlled substance outside the normal professional practice and not for a legitimate medical purpose must be charged under this section rather than charged with unlawful sale or delivery under G.S. 90-95(a)(1) (292 N.C. 294).

Related offenses not in this chapter

None.

Maintaining Store, Dwelling, Vehicle, Boat, or Other Place for Use, Storage, or Sale of Controlled Substances

Statute

See subdivision (a)(7) of G.S. 90-108, reproduced under "Obtaining Controlled Substance by Misrepresenting Oneself as Licensed Practitioner."

Elements

A person guilty of this offense

(1) knowingly keeps or maintains

(2) a store, shop, warehouse, dwelling house, building, vehicle, boat, aircraft, or other place

(3) (a) being resorted to by persons unlawfully using controlled substances, *or*

(b) being used for unlawfully keeping or selling controlled substances.

Punishment

Class 1 misdemeanor. If it is alleged and proved that the act was committed intentionally, the offense is a Class I felony [G.S. 90-108(b)]. Unlike "Obtaining Controlled Substance by Fraud or Forgery," discussed below, this offense may be either a felony (when committed "intentionally") or a misdemeanor (78 N.C. App. 239).

Notes

Element (1). A defendant had sufficient control over a building to be convicted of keeping and maintaining it for the purpose of selling controlled substances when he financed the store there; considered himself married to the woman who controlled the lease, utilities, and liquor license; gave directions to people who were in the store; and was present each time undercover law enforcement officers visited the store (94 N.C. App. 270).

Element (3). This element focuses on the use, not the contents, of the vehicle or other place. Although the contents are clearly relevant in determining its use, its contents are not dispositive in proving this element. When the state's evidence only showed that the defendant had two bags of marijuana while in his car, that his car contained a marijuana cigarette the following day, and that his home contained marijuana and drug paraphernalia, the evidence was insufficient to show that the vehicle was used for selling or keeping a controlled substance (336 N.C. 22; but court approvingly notes cases in which evidence was sufficient: 102 N.C. App. 598; 94 N.C. App. 270; 87 N.C. App. 380; 78 N.C. App. 239). Evidence was sufficient to support a conviction when a package of cocaine was delivered to a house and there were implements of drug paraphernalia inside the house that are used to cut and package cocaine (120 N.C. App. 821).

Multiple convictions. Multiple convictions of this offense were not permitted when the evidence showed that the defendant continuously maintained the dwelling for using a controlled substance; that is, there was no evidence indicating a termination and later resumption of drug trafficking at the dwelling that might otherwise permit multiple convictions (136 N.C. App. 394).

Related offenses not in this chapter

None.

Using False Registration Number in Manufacture or Distribution of Controlled Substance

Statute

See subdivision (a)(9) of G.S. 90-108, reproduced under "Obtaining Controlled Substance by Misrepresenting Oneself as Practitioner."

Elements

A person guilty of this offense
(1) uses a registration number that is fictitious, revoked, suspended, or issued to another person
(2) in the course of manufacturing or distributing a controlled substance.

Punishment

Class 1 misdemeanor. If it is alleged and proved that the act was committed intentionally, the offense is a Class I felony [G.S. 90-108(b)].

Related offenses not in this chapter

None.

Obtaining Controlled Substance by Fraud or Forgery

Statute

See subdivision (a)(10) of G.S. 90-108, reproduced under "Obtaining Controlled Subtance by Misrepresenting Oneself as Licensed Practitioner."

Elements

A person guilty of this offense
(1) obtains possession
(2) of a controlled substance
(3) by misrepresentation or fraud or forgery or deception or subterfuge.

Punishment

Class I felony. By definition, the conduct prohibited by this subdivision—a specific intention to deceive—can only be done intentionally; therefore a violation of this provision can only be a felony [78 N.C. App. 239; 73 N.C. App. 645; G.S. 90-108(b)].

Notes

Element (1). See the discussion of possession under "Possession of Controlled Substance."

Element (3). This statute is most often violated by the use of a forged prescription. A defendant who forges a prescription would be guilty of this offense by forgery; someone who copies a legitimate prescription or uses one forged by someone else would be guilty by misrepresentation, fraud, deception, or subterfuge. When the defendant possesses a forged prescription, a jury may infer that the defendant either forged it or knew that it was forged (52 N.C. App. 563).

Obtaining other drugs. If fraud or forgery is used to obtain a prescription drug that is *not* a controlled substance, the proper charge is under G.S. 106-122(19) (obtaining or attempting to obtain prescription drug by fraud, forgery, misrepresentation, etc.).

Related offenses not in this chapter

"Obtaining Property by False Pretenses" (Chapter 14)
"Common-Law Forgery" (Chapter 14)

Attempt and Conspiracy to Violate Controlled Substances Act

Statute

§90-98. Attempt and conspiracy; penalties.

Except as otherwise provided in this Article, any person who attempts or conspires to commit any offense defined in this Article is guilty of an offense that is the same class as the offense which was the object of the attempt or conspiracy and is punishable as specified for that class of offense and prior record or conviction level in Article 81B of Chapter 15A of the General Statutes.

Punishment

Except as otherwise provided in another statute (for example, conspiracy to commit drug trafficking, discussed in the paragraph below), a person who attempts or conspires to commit any of the offenses in Article 5 of G.S. Chapter 90, the Controlled Substances Act, is guilty of an offense that is the same class that was the object of the attempt or conspiracy and is punished accordingly. This statute overrides the provisions in G.S. 14-2.4 and 14-2.5 that set lower classifications for attempts and conspiracies than the completed offenses themselves.

A drug trafficking conspiracy is the same class of offense *and* is punished the same as a completed trafficking offense with its mandatory minimum provisions (which override the Structured Sentencing Act) because mandatory minimum punishment is specifically required by G.S. 90-95(i). However, an attempt to commit a drug trafficking offense, although the same class of offense as a completed trafficking offense, is not punished with mandatory minimum provisions because there is no statutory provision to require that result. Instead, the punishment is determined under the provisions of the Structured Sentencing Act (137 N.C. App. 90).

Notes

Generally. For additional notes on "Attempt" and "Conspiracy," see Chapter 4. Note that the definition of "deliver" and "delivery" in G.S. 90-87(7) includes an attempt to transfer a substance. Thus a drug offense that charges "deliver" or "delivery" would also include an attempt to deliver.

Attempt to possess controlled substance based on sale of fake controlled substance. A defendant may be convicted of attempting to possess cocaine when (1) the defendant intends to possess cocaine; (2) the defendant acts in a manner to accomplish that intent by driving to an area known for drug sales, approaching people the defendant believed were cocaine dealers, and exchanging money for what the defendant thought was cocaine (but was in fact pieces of Brazil nut represented by undercover officers to be rock cocaine); and (3) the defendant's efforts fall short of completing the offense of possession of cocaine (122 N.C. App. 294).

Related offenses not in this chapter

None.

Proof of Exemption from Controlled Substances Act

Statute

§90-113.1. Burden of proof; liabilities.

(a) It shall not be necessary for the State to negate any exemption or exception set forth in this Article in any complaint, information, indictment, or other pleading or in any trial, hearing, or other proceeding under this Article, and the burden of proof of any such exemption or exception shall be upon the person claiming its benefit.

(b) In the absence of proof that a person is the duly authorized holder of an appropriate registration or order form issued under this Article, he shall be presumed not to be the holder of such registration or form, and the burden of proof shall be upon him to rebut such presumption.

(c) No liability shall be imposed by virtue of this Article upon any duly authorized officer, engaged in the lawful enforcement of this Article.

Notes

Explanation. In criminal pleadings for the offenses in Art. 5 of G.S. Ch. 90, the Controlled Substances Act, it is not necessary to allege that the defendant is *not* a practitioner, licensed registrant, or other person who is entitled to possess, manufacture, sell, etc., controlled substances. At trial, the burden of proof of such an exemption rests with the person who claims the exemption (47 N.C. App. 30).

Related offenses not in this chapter

None.

Possession of Drug Paraphernalia

Statute

§90-113.21. General provisions.

(a) As used in this Article, "drug paraphernalia" means all equipment, products and materials of any kind that are used to facilitate, or intended or designed to facilitate, violations of the Controlled Substances Act, including planting, propagating, cultivating, growing, harvesting, manufacturing, compounding, converting, producing, processing, preparing, testing, analyzing, packaging, repackaging, storing, containing, and concealing controlled substances and injecting, ingesting, inhaling, or otherwise introducing controlled substances into the human body. "Drug paraphernalia" includes, but is not limited to, the following:

(1) Kits for planting, propagating, cultivating, growing, or harvesting any species of plant which is a controlled substance or from which a controlled substance can be derived;
(2) Kits for manufacturing, compounding, converting, producing, processing, or preparing controlled substances;
(3) Isomerization devices for increasing the potency of any species of plant which is a controlled substance;
(4) Testing equipment for identifying, or analyzing the strength, effectiveness, or purity of controlled substances;
(5) Scales and balances for weighing or measuring controlled substances;
(6) Diluents and adulterants, such as quinine, hydrochloride, mannitol, mannite, dextrose, and lactose for mixing with controlled substances;
(7) Separation gins and sifters for removing twigs and seeds from, or otherwise cleaning or refining, marijuana;
(8) Blenders, bowls, containers, spoons, and mixing devices for compounding controlled substances;
(9) Capsules, balloons, envelopes and other containers for packaging small quantities of controlled substances;
(10) Containers and other objects for storing or concealing controlled substances;

(11) Hypodermic syringes, needles, and other objects for parenterally injecting controlled substances into the body;
(12) Objects for ingesting, inhaling, or otherwise introducing marijuana, cocaine, hashish, or hashish oil into the body, such as:
  a. Metal, wooden, acrylic, glass, stone, plastic, or ceramic pipes with or without screens, permanent screens, hashish heads, or punctured metal bowls;
  b. Water pipes;
  c. Carburetion tubes and devices;
  d. Smoking and carburetion masks;
  e. Objects, commonly called roach clips, for holding burning material, such as a marijuana cigarette, that has become too small or too short to be held in the hand;
  f. Miniature cocaine spoons and cocaine vials;
  g. Chamber pipes;
  h. Carburetor pipes;
  i. Electric pipes;
  j. Air-driven pipes;
  k. Chillums;
  l. Bongs;
  m. Ice pipes or chillers.

(b) The following, along with all other relevant evidence, may be considered in determining whether an object is drug paraphernalia:
(1) Statements by the owner or anyone in control of the object concerning its use;
(2) Prior convictions of the owner or other person in control of the object for violations of controlled substances law;
(3) The proximity of the object to a violation of the Controlled Substances Act;
(4) The proximity of the object to a controlled substance;
(5) The existence of any residue of a controlled substance on the object;
(6) The proximity of the object to other drug paraphernalia;
(7) Instructions provided with the object concerning its use;
(8) Descriptive materials accompanying the object explaining or depicting its use;
(9) Advertising concerning its use;
(10) The manner in which the object is displayed for sale;
(11) Whether the owner, or anyone in control of the object, is a legitimate supplier of like or related items to the community, such as a seller of tobacco products or agricultural supplies;
(12) Possible legitimate uses of the object in the community;
(13) Expert testimony concerning its use;
(14) The intent of the owner or other person in control of the object to deliver it to persons whom he knows or reasonably should know intend to use the object to facilitate violations of the Controlled Substances Act.

§90-113.22. Possession of drug paraphernalia.

(a) It is unlawful for any person to knowingly use, or to possess with intent to use, drug paraphernalia to plant, propagate, cultivate, grow, harvest, manufacture, compound, convert, produce, process, prepare, test, analyze, package, repackage, store, contain, or conceal a controlled substance which it would be unlawful to possess, or to inject, ingest, inhale, or otherwise introduce into the body a controlled substance which it would be unlawful to possess.

(b) Violation of this section is a Class 1 misdemeanor.

Elements

A person guilty of this offense
(1) knowingly
(2) uses or possesses with intent to use

(3) drug paraphernalia
(4) for any of the following purposes:
  (a) to plant or propagate or cultivate or grow or harvest *or*
  (b) to manufacture or compound or convert or produce or process or prepare, *or*
  (c) to test or analyze, *or*
  (d) to package or repackage or store or contain or conceal, *or*
  (e) to inject or ingest or inhale or otherwise introduce into the body
(5) a controlled substance that is unlawful to possess.

Punishment

Class 1 misdemeanor.

Notes

Element (3). "Drug paraphernalia" is defined in G.S. 90-113.21(a), reproduced above. It includes a hypodermic needle and syringe, which previously was exempted from the definition by a specific statute (G.S. 90-113.4), now repealed. Triple-beam weighing scales found in a car's trunk in a box next to a suitcase containing cocaine constituted sufficient evidence of drug paraphernalia (96 N.C. App. 389).

Related offenses not in this chapter

Advertisement of drug paraphernalia (G.S. 90-113.24)

Manufacture or Delivery of Drug Paraphernalia

Statute

§90-113.23. Manufacture or delivery of drug paraphernalia.

(a) It is unlawful for any person to deliver, possess with intent to deliver, or manufacture with intent to deliver, drug paraphernalia knowing that it will be used to plant, propagate, cultivate, grow, harvest, manufacture, compound, convert, produce, process, prepare, test, analyze, package, repackage, store, contain, or conceal a controlled substance which it would be unlawful to possess, or that it will be used to inject, ingest, inhale, or otherwise introduce into the body a controlled substance which it would be unlawful to possess.

(b) Delivery, possession with intent to deliver, or manufacture with intent to deliver, of each separate and distinct item of drug paraphernalia is a separate offense.

(c) Violation of this section is a Class 1 misdemeanor. However, delivery of drug paraphernalia by a person over 18 years of age to someone under 18 years of age who is at least three years younger than the defendant shall be punishable as a Class I felony.

Elements

A person guilty of this offense
(1) delivers or possesses with intent to deliver or manufactures with intent to deliver
(2) drug paraphernalia
(3) knowing it will be used

(4) for any of the following purposes:
  (a) to plant or propagate or cultivate or grow or harvest, *or*
  (b) to manufacture or compound or convert or produce or process or prepare, *or*
  (c) to test *or* analyze, *or*
  (d) to package or repackage or store or contain or conceal, *or*
  (e) to inject or ingest or inhale or otherwise introduce into the body
(5) a controlled substance that is unlawful to possess.

Punishment

Class 1 misdemeanor. However, delivery of drug paraphernalia by a person over 18 to a person under 18 who is at least three years younger than the defendant is a Class I felony.

Notes

Element (2). "Drug paraphernalia" is defined in G.S. 90-113.21(a), which is reproduced under "Possession of Drug Paraphernalia."

Separate offenses. G.S. 113-23(b) provides that when items of drug paraphernalia are delivered, possessed with intent to deliver, or manufactured with intent to deliver, the delivery, possession, or manufacture of each separate and distinct item is a separate offense.

Related offenses not in this chapter

Advertisement of drug paraphernalia (G.S. 90-113.24)

Punishment for Second and Subsequent Offenses

Statute

See subdivisions (e)(3), (e)(4), and (e)(7) of G.S. 90-95 reproduced under "Manufacture of Controlled Substance."

Notes

Explanation. An offense punishable as a Class 1 misdemeanor is punished as a Class I felony if the defendant has any prior convictions, felony or misdemeanor, under the Controlled Substances Act or a similar law of another state or the United States [G.S. 90-95(e)(3)]. An offense punishable as a Class 2 misdemeanor is punished as a Class 1 misdemeanor if the defendant has any prior convictions, felony or misdemeanor, under the Controlled Substances Act or a similar law of another state or the United States [G.S. 90-95(e)(4)]. An offense punishable by a mandatory suspended sentence (the only such offense is Class 3 misdemeanor possession of marijuana or hashish) is punished as a Class 2 misdemeanor if the defendant has any prior convictions, felony or misdemeanor, under the Controlled Substances Act or a similar law of another state or the United States [G.S. 90-95(e)(7)].

Prior convictions must be alleged in the criminal pleading to authorize the greater punishment set out in this statute. Even if a defendant is charged with a felony, the state may want to allege a prior conviction in the criminal pleading because the defendant may be convicted of a lesser-included misdemeanor, and the prior conviction would raise the punishment for that misdemeanor.

Related offenses not in this chapter

None.

Other Controlled Substance Offenses

Statute

See G.S. 90-108, reproduced under "Obtaining Controlled Substance by Misrepresenting Oneself as Licensed Practitioner."

Other offenses under G.S. Ch. 90, Art. 5

Registrant who manufactures, distributes or dispenses to another registrant or authorized person a controlled substance not authorized by one's registration [G.S. 90-108(a)(3)].
Omitting, removing, altering, or obliterating symbol required by Federal Controlled Substances Act [G.S. 90-108(a)(4)].
Refusing or failing to make or keep record, order form, etc., required by Controlled Substances Act [G.S. 90-108(a)(5)].
Refusing entry or inspection authorized by Controlled Substances Act [G.S. 90-108(a)(6)].
Registrant or practitioner who fails to distribute a Schedule I or II controlled substance pursuant to an order form required by G.S. 90-105 [G.S. 90-108(a)(8)].
Furnishing false information or omitting material information in application or records required by Controlled Substances Act [G.S. 90-108(a)(11)].
Making, distributing, or possessing punch, die, plate, etc. for printing trademark or other mark on drug or container so as to make it a counterfeit controlled substance [G.S. 90-108(a)(12)].
Obtaining controlled substances by using legal prescriptions that have been obtained by the knowing and willful misrepresentation to, or by the intentional withholding of, information from a practitioner [G.S. 90-108(a)(13)].
Employee of registrant or practitioner who embezzles a controlled substance that has come into one's possession or under one's care [G.S. 90-108(a)(14)].

Punishment

Class 1 misdemeanor. If it is alleged and proved that the act was committed intentionally, the offense is a Class I felony.

Related offenses not in this chapter

None.

Furnishing Controlled Substance to Inmate

Statute

§14-258.1. Furnishing poison, controlled substances, deadly weapons, cartridges, ammunition or alcoholic beverages to inmates of charitable, mental or penal institutions or local confinement facilities.

(a) If any person shall give or sell to any inmate of any charitable, mental or penal institution, or local confinement facility, or if any person shall combine, confederate, conspire, aid, abet, solicit, urge, investigate, counsel, advise, encourage, attempt to procure, or procure another or others to give or sell to any inmate of any charitable, mental or penal institution, or local confinement facility, any deadly weapon, or any cartridge or ammunition for firearms of any kind, or any controlled substances included in Schedules I through VI contained in Article 5 of Chapter 90 of the General Statutes except under the general supervision of a practitioner, poison or poisonous substance, except upon the prescription of a physician, he shall be punished as a Class H felon; and if he be an officer or employee of any institution of the State, or of any local confinement facility, he shall be dismissed from his position or office.

(b) Any person who shall knowingly give or sell any alcoholic beverages to any inmate of any State mental or penal institution, or to any inmate of any local confinement facility, except for medical purposes as prescribed by a duly licensed physician and except for an ordained minister or rabbi who gives sacramental wine to an inmate as part of a religious service; or any person who shall combine, confederate, conspire, procure, or procure another or others to give or sell any alcoholic beverages to any inmate of any such State institution or local confinement facility, except for medical purposes as prescribed by a duly licensed physician and except for an ordained minister or rabbi who gives sacramental wine to an inmate as part of a religious service; or any person who shall bring into the buildings, grounds or other facilities of such institution any alcoholic beverages, except for medical purposes as prescribed by a duly licensed physician or sacramental wine brought by an ordained minister or rabbi for use as part of a religious service, shall be guilty of a Class 1 misdemeanor. If such person is an officer or employee of any institution of the State, such person shall be dismissed from office.

Elements

A person guilty of this offense
(1) gives or sells
(2) any controlled substance
(3) to an inmate of any charitable, mental, or penal institution, including a local confinement facility.

Punishment

Class H felony. If the defendant is employed by any state institution or a local confinement facility, he or she also is to be dismissed from employment.

Notes

Element (1). Since giving is easier to prove than selling, a defendant normally would be charged with giving a substance to an inmate.

Element (2). The statute specifically covers any substance in Schedules I through VI. The amount given or sold is irrelevant.

Element (3). "Penal institution" would include any unit of the state prison system. "Local confinement facility" would include any jail or other confinement facility.

Conspiring, aiding and abetting, etc. The statute specifies that the same punishment applies to the person who conspires, aids and abets, solicits, urges, or otherwise is involved with providing the substance.

Exception. The statute specifies that the offense is not committed when the substance is given under the supervision of a physician.

Related offenses not in this chapter

Providing alcoholic beverage to inmate (G.S. 14-258.1, same statute as above).

Part II. Toxic Vapors Act

Inhaling Toxic Fumes

Statute

§90-113.10. Inhaling fumes for purpose of causing intoxication.

It is unlawful for any person to knowingly breathe or inhale any compound, liquid, or chemical containing toluol, hexane, trichloroethane, isopropanol, methyl isobutyl ketone, methyl cellosolve acetate, cyclohexanone, or any other substance for the purpose of inducing a condition of intoxication. This section does not apply to any person using as an inhalant any chemical substance pursuant to the direction of a physician or dentist.

Elements

A person guilty of this offense
(1) knowingly
(2) breathes or inhales
(3) any compound, liquid, or chemical containing toluol, hexane, trichloroethane, isopropanol, methyl isobutyl ketone, methyl cellosolve acetate, cyclohexanone or a similar substance
(4) to induce intoxication.

Punishment

Class 1 misdemeanor (G.S. 90-113.13).

Notes

Element (3). Although the statute refers to "any other substance," the rule of statutory construction is that the other substance should be of the same general character as the ones listed. The kinds of products likely to contain these substances include fast-drying glues and cements; many paints; lacquers and varnishes; thinners and removers; gasoline; kerosene; lighter and dry-cleaning fluid; fingernail polish remover; and various aerosol products.

Element (4). A separate statute defines "intoxication" as "drunkenness, stupefaction, depression, giddiness, paralysis, irrational behavior, or other change, distortion, or disturbance of the auditory, visual or mental processes" (G.S. 90-113.9).

Exception for medical use. The statute specifically exempts the inhaling of such chemicals when directed by a physician or dentist. For example, these substances might be used as anesthetics.

Related offenses not in this chapter

None.

Possession of Toxic Substance

Statute

§90-113.11. Possession of substances.

It is unlawful for any person to possess any compound, liquid, or chemical containing toluol, hexane, trichloroethane, isopropanol, methyl isobutyl ketone, methyl cellosolve acetate, cyclohexanone, or any other substance which will induce a condition of intoxication through inhalation for the purpose of violating G.S. 90-113.10.

Elements

A person guilty of this offense
(1) possesses
(2) any compound, liquid, or chemical containing toluol, hexane, trichloroethane, isopropanol, methyl isobutyl ketone, methyl cellosolve acetate, cyclohexanone, or a similar substance
(3) for the purpose of violating G.S. 90-113.10.

Punishment

Class 1 misdemeanor (G.S. 90-113.13).

Notes

Element (1). Presumably possession for this statute would be the same as possession for the Controlled Substances Act, which means that the possession may be either actual or constructive. See the notes under "Possession of Controlled Substance" for an extensive discussion of this element.

Element (2). See the note under Element (3) of "Inhaling Toxic Fumes."

Element (3). The reference to G.S. 90-113.10 means that the possession must be for purposes of illegally breathing or inhaling the substance in order to become intoxicated.

Related offenses not in this chapter

None.

Sale of Toxic Substance

Statute

§90-113.12. Sale of substance.

It is unlawful for any person to sell, offer to sell, deliver, give, or possess with the intent to sell, deliver, or give any other person any compound, liquid, or chemical containing toluol, hexane, trichloroethane, isopropanol, methyl isobutyl ketone, methyl cellosolve acetate, cyclohexanone, or any other substance which will induce a condition of intoxication through inhalation if he has reasonable cause to suspect that the product sold, offered for sale, given, delivered, or possessed with the intent to sell, give, or deliver, will be used for the purpose of violating G.S. 90-113.10.

Elements

A person guilty of this offense
(1) sells or gives
(2) a compound, liquid, or chemical containing tuluol, hexane, trichloroethane, isopropanol, methyl isobutyl ketone, methyl cellosolve acetate, cyclohexanone, or a similar substance
(3) to another person
(4) having reasonable grounds to believe that it will be used in violation of G.S. 90-113.10.

Punishment

Class 1 misdemeanor (G.S. 90-113.13).

Notes

Element (1). "Sell" means to transfer for remuneration (i.e., compensation) (327 N.C. 378). "Give" does not necessarily involve any remuneration, nor does "delivery," another term used in the statute. The sale, giving, or delivery might involve constructive rather than actual transfer. The statute also prohibits offers to sell.

Element (2). See the note on Element (3) under "Inhaling Toxic Fumes."

Element (4). The reference to G.S. 90-113.10 means that the defendant must have reason to believe that the person to whom he or she sells or gives the toxic substance will breathe or inhale it illegally in order to become intoxicated.

Related offenses not in this chapter

None.

Possession of Toxic Substance with Intent to Sell

Statute

See G.S. 90-113.12, reproduced under "Sale of Toxic Substance," immediately above.

Elements

A person guilty of this offense

(1) possesses
(2) a compound, liquid, or chemical containing tuluol, hexane, trichloroethane, isopropanol, methyl isobutyl ketone, methyl cellosolve acetate, cyclohexanone, or a similar substance
(3) with the intent to sell or give that substance
(4) to another person
(5) having reasonable grounds to believe that the other person will use it in violation of G.S. 90-113.10.

Punishment

Class 1 misdemeanor (G.S. 90-113.13).

Notes

Element (1). Presumably possession under this statute would be the same as possession under the Controlled Substances Act, which means that the possession may be either actual or constructive. See the notes under "Possession of Controlled Substance" for an extensive discussion of this element.

Element (2). See the note on Element (3) under "Inhaling Toxic Fumes."

Element (3). The intent might be shown by the amount of the toxic substance possessed or the circumstances under which it is possessed, such as being hidden or being near paraphernalia that might indicate illegal use. On this subject, see the notes on Element (4) under "Possession of Controlled Substance with Intent to Manufacture, Sell, or Deliver."

Element (5). The reference to G.S. 90-113.10 means that the defendant who possesses the toxic substance must have some reason to believe that the person to whom the defendant intends to give or sell the substance will breathe or inhale it illegally in order to become intoxicated.

Related offenses not in this chapter

None.

25
Motor Vehicle Offenses

Chapter Contents

25 Motor Vehicle Offenses

Driving While License Revoked

Statute

§20-28. Unlawful to drive while license revoked or while disqualified.

(a) Driving While License Revoked.—Except as provided in subsection (a1) of this section, any person whose drivers license has been revoked who drives any motor vehicle upon the highways of the State while the license is revoked is guilty of a Class 1 misdemeanor. Upon conviction, the person's license shall be revoked for an additional period of one year for the first offense, two years for the second offense, and permanently for a third or subsequent offense.

The restoree of a revoked drivers license who operates a motor vehicle upon the highways of the State without maintaining financial responsibility as provided by law shall be punished as for driving without a license.

(a1) Driving Without Reclaiming License.—A person convicted under subsection (a) shall be punished as if the person had been convicted of driving without a license under G.S. 20-35 if the person demonstrates to the court that either subdivisions (1) and (2), or subdivision (3) of this subsection is true:

(1) At the time of the offense, his license was revoked solely under G.S. 20-16.5; and

(2) a. The offense occurred more than 30 days after the effective date of a revocation order issued under G.S. 20-16.5(f) and the period of revocation was 30 days as provided under subdivision (3) of that subsection; or

b. The offense occurred more than 10 days after the effective date of the revocation order issued under any other provision of G.S. 20-16.5; or

(3) At the time of the offense the person had met the requirements of G.S. 50-13.12, or G.S. 110-142.2 and was eligible for reinstatement of the person's drivers license privilege as provided therein.

In addition, a person punished under this subsection shall be treated for drivers license and insurance rating purposes as if the person had been convicted of driving without a license under G.S. 20-35, and the conviction report sent to the Division must indicate that the person is to be so treated.

(b) Repealed by Session Laws 1993 (Reg. Sess. 1994), c. 761, s. 3.

(c) When Person May Apply for License.—A person whose license has been revoked under this section for one year may apply for a license after 90 days. A person whose license has been revoked under this section for two years may apply for a license after 12 months. A person whose license has been revoked under this section permanently may apply for a license after three years. Upon the filing of an application the Division may, with or without a hearing, issue a new license upon satisfactory proof that the former licensee has not been convicted of a moving violation under this Chapter or the laws of another state, a violation of any provision of the alcoholic beverage laws of this State or another state, or a violation of any provisions of the drug laws of this State or another state when any of these violations occurred during the revocation period. The Division may impose any restrictions or conditions on the new license that the Division considers appropriate for the balance of the revocation period. When the revocation period is permanent, the restrictions and conditions imposed by the Division may not exceed three years.

(d) Driving While Disqualified.—A person who was convicted of a violation that disqualified the person and required the person's drivers license to be revoked who drives a motor vehicle during the revocation period is punishable as provided in the other subsections of this section. A person who has been disqualified who drives a commercial motor vehicle during the disqualification period is guilty of a Class 1 misdemeanor and is disqualified for an additional period as follows:

(1) For a first offense of driving while disqualified, a person is disqualified for a period equal to the period for which the person was disqualified when the offense occurred.
(2) For a second offense of driving while disqualified, a person is disqualified for a period equal to two times the period for which the person was disqualified when the offense occurred.
(3) For a third offense of driving while disqualified, a person is disqualified for life.

The Division may reduce a disqualification for life under this subsection to 10 years in accordance with the guidelines adopted under G.S. 20-17.4(b). A person who drives a commercial motor vehicle while the person is disqualified and the person's drivers license is revoked is punishable for both driving while the person's license was revoked and driving while disqualified.

Elements

A person guilty of this offense
(1) drives
(2) a motor vehicle
(3) on a highway
(4) while the person's driver's license is revoked.

Punishment

Class 1 misdemeanor. (See the note on "Special punishment," below.)

Notes

Special punishment. In two instances, the punishment described above is not applicable. First, when a person drives while the person's license is revoked solely under G.S. 20-16.5 (the immediate, pretrial revocation for persons charged with impaired driving or related offenses) and the license has been revoked for more than 10 days, the punishment is reduced to that applicable to driving without a license (Class 2 misdemeanor). Second, when a person's license was revoked for failure to meet child support obligations under G.S. 50-13.12 and G.S. 110-142.2, and the person was eligible for reinstatement of his or her driver's license when charged with this offense, the punishment is reduced in the same manner. In addition to the reduced punishment, in both situations driver's license and insurance classification points are assessed as if the driver had been convicted of driving without a license (G.S. 20-7) under G.S. 20-35 [G.S. 20-28(a1)] and the conviction is not treated as a moving violation for purposes of G.S. 20-28.1.

Element (1). A person drives, according to G.S. 20-4.01(7) and (25), when he or she is "in actual physical control of a vehicle which is in motion or which has the engine running." A person may be convicted of this and other offenses requiring operation of a vehicle even when the only evidence of this element is circumstantial (15 N.C. App. 391). Driving and operating are synonymous terms (312 N.C. 432).

Element (2). G.S. 20-4.01(23) defines "motor vehicle": "Every vehicle which is self-propelled and every vehicle designed to run upon the highways which is pulled by a self-propelled vehicle. This shall not include mopeds as defined in G.S. 20-4.01(27)d1." G.S. 20-4.01(27)d1 refers to the definition of moped in G.S. 105-164.3: a vehicle that has two or three wheels, no external shifting device, and a motor that does not exceed 50 cubic centimeters piston displacement and cannot propel the vehicle at a speed greater than 20 miles per hour on a level surface.

Element (3). G.S. 20-4.01(13) defines "highway": "The entire width between property or right-of-way lines of every way or place of whatever nature, when any part thereof is open to the use of the public as a matter of right for the purposes of vehicular traffic." The definitions of "street" and "highway" are identical. G.S. 20-4.01(46). This offense may occur only on a highway and not on another type of public vehicular area. G.S. 20-4.01(32) defines public vehicular area. See the note on Element (3) under "Impaired Driving" for a discussion of public vehicular area.

Element (4). G.S. 20-4.01(36) defines revocation: "Termination of a licensee's or permittee's privilege to drive or termination of the registration of a vehicle for a period of time stated in an order of revocation or suspension. The terms 'revocation' or 'suspension' or a combination of both terms shall be used synonymously." G.S. 20-4.01(17) defines license: "Any driver's license or any other license or permit to operate a motor vehicle issued under or granted by the laws of this State including:

a. Any temporary license or learner's permit;
b. The privilege of any person to drive a motor vehicle whether or not such person holds a valid license; and
c. Any nonresident's operating privilege."

Thus a nonresident or unlicensed resident who is convicted of a motor vehicle offense and has his or her driving privilege revoked in this state as a result of the conviction may be charged under this offense, even though he or she has never been issued a North Carolina driver's license.

Additional license revocations. If a person is convicted of this offense, G.S. 20-28(a) requires that the person's driver's license be revoked for an additional period of time, unless the revocation is subject to the special punishment provisions of G.S. 20-28(a1).

Repeal of driving while license permanently revoked. The General Assembly in 1994 repealed the offense of driving while license permanently revoked. Thus when a person's license has been permanently revoked, the appropriate charge is driving while license revoked under G.S. 20-28(a).

Related offenses not in this chapter

None.

Driving While Commercial Driver's License Disqualified

Statute

See subsection (d) of G.S. 20-28, reproduced under "Driving While License Revoked."

Elements

A person guilty of this offense
(1) drives
(2) a commercial motor vehicle
(3) on a highway
(4) while the person's commercial driver's license is disqualified.

Punishment

Class 1 misdemeanor.

Notes

Element (1). See the discussion of Element (1) under "Driving While License Revoked."

Element (2). G.S. 20-4.01(3d) defines "commercial motor vehicle":

> Any of the following motor vehicles that are designed or used to transport passengers or property:
> a. A Class A motor vehicle that has a combined GVWR of at least 26,001 pounds and includes as a part of the combination a towed unit that has a GVWR of at least 10,001 pounds.
> b. A Class B motor vehicle.
> c. A Class C motor vehicle that meets either of the following descriptions:
> 1. Is designed to transport 16 or more passengers, including the driver.
> 2. Is transporting hazardous materials and is required to be placarded in accordance with 49 C.F.R. Part 172, Subpart F.
>
> d. Repealed by Session Laws 1999, c. 330, effective December 1, 1999.

G.S. 20-4.01(2b) defines a Class B Motor Vehicle as any of the following:

> a. A single motor vehicle that has a GVWR of at least 26,001 pounds.
> b. A combination of motor vehicles that includes as part of the combination a towing unit that has a GVWR of at least 26,001 pounds and a towed unit that has a GVWR of less than 10,001 pounds.

G.S. 20-4.01(2a) and (2c) define Class A and Class C Motor Vehicles, respectively. G.S. 20-4.01(12a) defines Gross Vehicle Weight Rating (GVWR).

Element (3). G.S. 20-28(d) does not explicitly require that this offense occur on a highway. However, a person is not required to have a commercial driver's license to operate a commercial vehicle in areas that are not included in the definition of highway (G.S. 20-37.12). Therefore, that this offense must occur on a highway seems implicit. See the discussion of Element (3) under "Driving While License Revoked."

Element (4). A commercial driver's license authorizes an individual to drive a particular class of commercial motor vehicle [G.S. 20-4.01(3c)]. Disqualification means that a person may not legally drive a commercial vehicle. However, the person may drive a noncommercial vehicle if the person's license to drive the noncommercial vehicle is not otherwise revoked [see G.S. 20-4.01(5a) and 20-17.5].

Additional license disqualification. If a person is convicted of this offense, G.S. 20-28(d) requires that the person's commercial driver's license be disqualified for an additional period of time. The additional period depends on whether the person has committed a first, second, or third offense.

Effect if offense occurs while noncommercial driver's license is revoked. A person who drives a commercial motor vehicle while the person is disqualified and the person's driver's license is revoked may be punished for both driving while the person's license was revoked and driving while disqualified [G.S. 20-28(d)].

Related offenses not in this chapter

Possession of driver's license in addition to commercial driver's license [G.S. 20-30(8)]

Impaired Driving

Statute

§20-138.1. Impaired driving.

(a) Offense.—A person commits the offense of impaired driving if he drives any vehicle upon any highway, any street, or any public vehicular area within this State:

(1) While under the influence of an impairing substance; or
(2) After having consumed sufficient alcohol that he has, at any relevant time after the driving, an alcohol concentration of 0.08 or more.

(b) Defense Precluded.—The fact that a person charged with violating this section is or has been legally entitled to use alcohol or a drug is not a defense to a charge under this section.

(c) Pleading.—In any prosecution for impaired driving, the pleading is sufficient if it states the time and place of the alleged offense in the usual form and charges that the defendant drove a vehicle on a highway or public vehicular area while subject to an impairing substance.

(d) Sentencing Hearing and Punishment.—Impaired driving as defined in this section is a misdemeanor. Upon conviction of a defendant of impaired driving, the presiding judge must hold a sentencing hearing and impose punishment in accordance with G.S. 20-179.

(e) Exception.—Notwithstanding the definition of "vehicle" pursuant to G.S. 20-4.01(49), for purposes of this section the word "vehicle" does not include a horse, bicycle, or lawnmower.

Elements

A person guilty of this offense

(1) drives
(2) a vehicle
(3) on a highway or public vehicular area
(4) (a) while under the influence of an impairing substance, *or*

(b) after consuming a sufficient quantity of alcohol that the person has an alcohol concentration of 0.08 or more at any relevant time after the driving.

Punishment

This offense is a misdemeanor to which the structured sentencing laws do not apply. It has five different levels of punishment; the level depends on the presence of and weight assigned to certain specified aggravating and mitigating factors found by the court. Punishment for each level, set forth in G.S. 20-179, is as follows:

Level One: Minimum imprisonment of 30 days, maximum imprisonment of 2 years, and a maximum fine of $4,000.

Level Two: Minimum imprisonment of 7 days, maximum imprisonment of 1 year, and a maximum fine of $2,000.

Level Three: Minimum imprisonment of 72 hours, maximum imprisonment of 6 months, and a maximum fine of $1,000. The original sentence may be suspended on the condition that the defendant meet at least one of these conditions: at least 72 hours of community service, imprisonment for at least 72 hours, or nonoperation of a motor vehicle for at least 90 days.

Level Four: Minimum imprisonment of 48 hours, maximum imprisonment of 120 days, and a maximum fine of $500. The original sentence may be suspended on the condition that the defendant meet at least one of these conditions: at least 48 hours of community service, imprisonment for 48 hours, or nonoperation of a motor vehicle for 60 days.

Level Five: Minimum imprisonment of 24 hours, maximum imprisonment of 60 days, and a maximum fine of $200. The original sentence may be suspended on the condition that the defendant meet at least one of these conditions: at least 24 hours of community service, imprisonment for 24 hours, or nonoperation of a motor vehicle for 30 days.

For each of the above levels of punishment, special probation may be imposed in which a person serves a term of imprisonment equal to that level's minimum imprisonment period. Also, under G.S. 20-179(k1), inpatient treatment may substitute for jail time if the treatment occurred after the commission of the offense for which the defendant is being sentenced. If a defendant is placed on probation in any of the levels, the sentencing judge must impose a requirement that the defendant obtain a substance abuse assessment and education or treatment required by G.S. 20-17.6 for license restoration.

Notes

Institute of Government publication on impaired driving. For an extensive discussion of this offense and other impaired driving offenses, see pages 77–152 of the Institute of Government publication: Ben F. Loeb, Jr., and James C. Drennan, *Motor Vehicle Law and the Law of Impaired Driving in North Carolina* (Chapel Hill: The University of North Carolina at Chapel Hill, 2000 edition).

Element (1). See the note on Element (1) under "Driving While License Revoked."

Element (2). G.S. 20-4.01(49) defines vehicle: "Every device in, upon, or by which any person or property is or may be transported or drawn upon a highway, excepting devices moved by human power or used exclusively upon fixed rails or tracks." Mopeds are also vehicles but not motor vehicles. See G.S. 20-4.01(21a), (23), (27d1). G.S. 20-138.1(e) provides that bicycles, horses, and lawnmowers are not vehicles for purposes of the impaired driving offense only.

Element (3). See the note on Element (3) under "Driving While License Revoked." G.S. 20-4.01(32) defines public vehicular area:

> Any area within the State of North Carolina that is generally open to and used by the public for vehicular traffic, including by way of illustration and not limitation any drive, driveway, road, roadway, street, alley, or parking lot upon the grounds and premises of:
>
> a. Any public or private hospital, college, university, school, orphanage, church, or any of the institutions, parks or other facilities maintained and supported by the State of North Carolina or any of its subdivisions; or
>
> b. Any service station, drive-in theater, supermarket, store, restaurant, or office building, or any other business, residential, or municipal establishment providing parking space for customers, patrons, or the public; or
>
> c. Any property owned by the United States and subject to the jurisdiction of the State of North Carolina. (The inclusion of property owned by the United States in this definition shall not limit assimilation of North Carolina law when applicable under the provisions of Title 18, United States Code, section 13.)
>
> The term "public vehicular area" shall also include any beach area used by the public for vehicular traffic as well as any road opened to vehicular traffic within or leading to a subdivision for use by subdivision residents, their guests, and members of the public, whether or not the subdivision roads have been offered for dedication to the public. The term "public vehicular area" shall not be construed to mean any private property not generally open to and used by the public.

A privately owned mobile home park in which the streets are marked and open for the use of residents and visitors is a public vehicular area (117 N.C. App. 457). A private nightclub's parking lot was a public vehicular area because the lot could generally be used as a thoroughfare by the general public to access the club or an adjacent motel (343 N.C. 61).

Element (4)(a). G.S. 20-4.01(14a) defines "impairing substance": "Alcohol, controlled substance under Chapter 90 of the General Statutes, any other drug or psychoactive substance capable of impairing a person's physical or mental faculties, or any combination of these substances." G.S. 20-4.01(48b) defines "under the influence": "The state of a person having his physical or mental faculties, or both, appreciably impaired by an impairing substance." Note that this is an alternative to (4)(b) as a way of establishing impairment.

Element (4)(b). G.S. 20-4.01(1a) defines "alcohol" as "any substance containing any form of alcohol, including ethanol, methanol, propanol, and isopropanol." G.S. 20-4.01(1b) defines "alcohol concentration": "The concentration of alcohol in a person, expressed either as: Grams of alcohol per 100 milliliters of blood; or grams of alcohol per 210 liters of breath." G.S. 20-4.01(33a) defines "relevant time after the driving": "Any time after the driving in which the driver still has in his body alcohol consumed before or during the driving."

The practical effect of these definitions is that the state proves this element if it shows that the defendant had an alcohol concentration of 0.08 or more when the chemical analysis was made as long as the alcohol was in the defendant's body when the driving stopped. The alcohol concentration at the time of the driving is not relevant for this element.

Even if a defendant's blood alcohol concentration at a relevant time after driving is less than 0.08, the defendant may still be convicted of impaired driving under Element (4)(a), an alternative way to establish impairment. For example, when a law enforcement officer's testimony includes observations supporting a finding of impairment, such as the quality of the defendant's driving, the odor of alcohol about the defendant's person, and the defendant's poor performance on sobriety tests, a defendant may still be convicted of this offense (74 N.C. App. 479; 104 N.C. App. 529).

License revocations. A person convicted of this offense will have his or her license revoked for at least one year [G.S. 20-17(2); G.S. 20-19]. For most first offenders who submit to a substance abuse assessment, a judge may issue a limited driving privilege (G.S. 20-179.3). However, a limited driving privilege may not authorize a person to drive a commercial vehicle.

Forfeiture of motor vehicle. A motor vehicle is subject to forfeiture if it is driven by a person who is committing the offense of impaired driving or habitual impaired driving and the person's license was revoked as a result of a prior impaired driver's license revocation. See G.S. 20-28.2 through -28.9 and the discussion on pages 137–49 of the Institute of Government publication cited at the beginning of these notes.

Prayer for judgment continued is not authorized sentence. A judge is not authorized to enter a prayer for judgment continued (PJC) for the offense of impaired driving; the judge must enter a sentence pursuant to G.S. 20-179 (348 N.C. 677).

Reckless driving is not a lesser-included offense. Reckless driving is not a lesser-included offense of impaired driving (351 N.C. 601).

Multiple punishments. A defendant may be convicted and punished for both impaired driving and second-degree murder based on a vehicular homicide committed while driving while impaired (138 N.C. App. 252).

Constitutionality. This statute is not unconstitutionally vague (312 N.C. 441).

Related offenses not in this chapter

Murder (various offenses) (Chapter 6)
Manslaughter (various offenses) (Chapter 6)
Death by vehicle (various offenses) (Chapter 6)
Impaired instruction (G.S. 20-12.1)
Transporting open container of alcoholic beverage (G.S. 20-138.7)
Possessing alcoholic beverage while operating commercial motor vehicle (G.S. 20-138.2C)
Transporting open container of fortified wine or spirituous liquor (G.S. 18B-401)
Driving motor vehicle while consuming malt beverage or unfortified wine (G.S. 18B-401)

Impaired Driving in Commercial Vehicle

Statute

§20-138.2. Impaired driving in commercial vehicle.

(a) Offense.—A person commits the offense of impaired driving in a commercial vehicle if he drives a commercial motor vehicle upon any highway, any street, or any public vehicular area within the State:

(1) While under the influence of an impairing substance; or

(2) After having consumed sufficient alcohol that he has, at any relevant time after the driving, an alcohol concentration of 0.04 or more.

(b) Defense Precluded.—The fact that a person charged with violating this section is or has been legally entitled to use alcohol or a drug is not a defense to a charge under this section.

(c) Pleading.—To charge a violation of this section, the pleading is sufficient if it states the time and place of the alleged offense in the usual form and charges the defendant drove a commercial motor vehicle on a highway, street, or public vehicular area while subject to an impairing substance.

(d) Implied Consent Defense.—An offense under this section is an implied consent offense subject to the provisions of G.S. 20-16.2

(e) Punishment.—The offense in this section is a misdemeanor and any defendant convicted under this section shall be sentenced under G.S. 20-179. This offense is not a lesser included offense of impaired driving under G.S. 20-138.1, and if a person is convicted under this section and of an offense involving impaired driving under G.S. 20-138.1 arising out of the same transaction, the aggregate punishment imposed by the Court may not exceed the maximum punishment applicable to the offense involving impaired driving under G.S. 20-138.1.

(f) Repealed by Sessions Laws 1991, c. 726, s. 19.

(g) Chemical Analysis Provisions.—The provisions of G.S. 20-139.1 shall apply to the offense of impaired driving in a commercial vehicle.

Elements

A person guilty of this offense
(1) drives
(2) a commercial vehicle
(3) on a highway or public vehicular area
(4) (a) while under the influence of an impairing substance, *or*
(b) after consuming a sufficient quantity of alcohol that the person has an alcohol concentration of 0.04 or more at any relevant time after the driving.

Punishment

This offense is punished the same as impaired driving under G.S. 20-138.1; see the discussion under the heading "Punishment," under "Impaired Driving."

Notes

Element (1). See the discussion of Element (1) under "Driving While License Revoked."

Element (2). See the discussion of Element (2) under "Driving While Commercial Driver's License Disqualified."

Element (3). See the discussion of Element (3) under "Impaired Driving."

Elements (4)(a) and (b). The alcohol concentration triggering an impaired driving in commercial vehicle offense under the Element 4(b) prong is lower than the alcohol concentration triggering an impaired driving offense—it is 0.04 rather than 0.08. See the discussion of Elements (4)(a) and (b) under "Impaired Driving" (substituting 0.04 for references to 0.08).

Effect when impaired driving is also charged. Impaired driving in commercial vehicle is not a lesser-included offense of impaired driving. However, if a person is convicted of impaired driving in commercial vehicle and an impaired driving offense arising out of the same incident, a court may not impose an aggregate punishment greater than the maximum punishment applicable to the impaired driving offense [see subsection (e) of the statute, above].

Disqualification. A person is disqualified from driving a commercial vehicle if convicted of this offense. The person's license will be revoked as well [G.S. 20-17(2)b.]. In some instances in which a license is revoked, a person may be given a limited driving privilege to drive a noncommercial vehicle. A person who has an alcohol concentration of 0.04 or more at any relevant time after the driving of a commercial vehicle is subject to immediate pretrial civil revocation of his or her driver's license [G.S. 20-16.5(b)(4)c.].

Lesser-included offense. The offense of operating commercial vehicle after consuming alcohol (G.S. 20-138.2A) is a lesser-included offense of impaired driving in commercial vehicle.

Related offenses not in this chapter

See the offenses listed under "Impaired Driving."

Operating Commercial Vehicle After Consuming Alcohol

Statute

§20-138.2A. Operating a commercial vehicle after consuming alcohol.

(a) Offense.—A person commits the offense of operating a commercial motor vehicle after consuming alcohol if the person drives a commercial motor vehicle, as defined in G.S. 20-4.01(3d)a. and b., upon any highway, any street, or any public vehicular area within the State while consuming alcohol or while alcohol remains in the person's body.

(b) Implied-Consent Offense.—An offense under this section is an implied-consent offense subject to the provisions of G.S. 20-16.2. The provisions of G.S. 20-139.1 shall apply to an offense committed under this section.

(b1) Odor Insufficient.—The odor of an alcoholic beverage on the breath of the driver is insufficient evidence by itself to prove beyond a reasonable doubt that alcohol was remaining in the driver's body in violation of this section unless the driver was offered an alcohol screening test or chemical analysis and refused to provide all required samples of breath or blood for analysis.

(b2) Alcohol Screening Test.—Notwithstanding any other provision of law, an alcohol screening test may be administered to a driver suspected of violation of subsection (a) of this section, and the results of an alcohol screening test or the driver's refusal to submit may be used by a law enforcement officer, a court, or an administrative agency in determining if alcohol was present in the driver's body. No alcohol screening tests are valid under this section unless the device used is one approved by the Commission for Health Services, and the screening test is conducted in accordance with the applicable regulations of the Commission as to its manner and use.

(c) Punishment.—Except as otherwise provided in this subsection, a violation of the offense described in subsection (a) of this section is a Class 3 misdemeanor and, notwithstanding G.S. 15A-1340.23, is punishable by a penalty of one hundred dollars ($100.00). A second or subsequent violation of this section is a misdemeanor punishable under G.S. 20-179. This offense is a lesser included offense of impaired driving of a commercial vehicle under G.S. 20-138.2.

(d) Second or Subsequent Conviction Defined.—A conviction for violating this offense is a second or subsequent conviction if at the time of the current offense the person has a previous conviction under this section, and the previous conviction occurred in the seven years immediately preceding the date of the current offense. This definition of second or subsequent conviction also applies to G.S. 20-17(a)(13) and G.S. 20-17.4(a)(6).

Elements

A person guilty of this offense
(1) drives
(2) a commercial motor vehicle, but excluding a commercial motor vehicle defined in G.S. 20-4.01(3d)(c) (see note below)
(3) on a highway or public vehicular area
(4) while consuming alcohol or while alcohol remains in his or her body.

Punishment

Class 3 misdemeanor, but apparently the only authorized punishment is a $100 fine [see G.S. 20-138.2A(c)]. Second and subsequent convictions are punishable under G.S. 20-179 in the same manner as impaired driving convictions; see "Impaired Driving." A conviction is a second or subsequent conviction if it occurs within the seven years preceding the date of the current offense.

Notes

Element (1). See the discussion of Element (1) under "Driving While License Revoked."

Element (2). See the discussion of Element (2) under "Driving While Commercial Driver's License Disqualified." However, this offense excludes a commercial motor vehicle defined in G.S. 20-4.01(3d)(c), which is a Class C motor vehicle that (a) is designed to transport 16 or more passengers, including the driver, or (b) is transporting hazardous materials and is required to be placarded in accordance with 49 C.F.R. Part 172, Subpart F.

Element (3). See the discussion of Element (3) under "Impaired Driving."

Element (4). The result of an alcohol screening test (or the driver's refusal to submit to the test) may be used to prove this element if the test is conducted under the requirements set out in G.S. 20-138.2A(b2). The odor of an alcoholic beverage on the driver's breath is insufficient by itself to prove beyond a reasonable doubt that alcohol was remaining in the driver's body unless the driver was offered an alcohol screening test or chemical analysis and refused to provide the appropriate samples [G.S. 20-138.2A(b1)].

Lesser-included offense. This offense is a lesser-included offense of impaired driving in commercial vehicle, G.S. 20-138.2.

Disqualification. For a first conviction, the defendant is disqualified from driving a commercial motor vehicle for 10 days. For a second or subsequent conviction occurring within seven years of the date of the current offense, the disqualification is for 1 year and, in addition, the defendant's driver's license is revoked for 1 year.

Related offenses not in this chapter

See the offenses listed under "Impaired Driving."

Operating School Bus or Child Care Vehicle after Consuming Alcohol

Statute

§20-138.2B. Operating a school bus, school activity bus, or child care vehicle after consuming alcohol.

(a) Offense.—A person commits the offense of operating a school bus, school activity bus, or child care vehicle after consuming alcohol if the person drives a school bus, school activity bus, or child care vehicle upon any highway, any street, or any public vehicular area within the State while consuming alcohol or while alcohol remains in the person's body.

(b) Implied-Consent Offense.—An offense under this section is an implied-consent offense subject to the provisions of G.S. 20-16.2. The provisions of G.S. 20-139.1 shall apply to an offense committed under this section.

(b1) Odor Insufficient.—The odor of an alcoholic beverage on the breath of the driver is insufficient evidence by itself to prove beyond a reasonable doubt that alcohol was remaining in the driver's body in violation of this section unless the driver was offered an alcohol screening test or chemical analysis and refused to provide all required samples of breath or blood for analysis.

(b2) Alcohol Screening Test.—Notwithstanding any other provision of law, an alcohol screening test may be administered to a driver suspected of violation of subsection (a) of this section, and the results of an alcohol screening test or the driver's refusal to submit may be used by a law enforcement officer, a court, or an administrative agency in determining if alcohol was present in the driver's body. No alcohol screening tests are valid under this section unless the device used is one approved by the Commission for Health Services, and the screening test is conducted in accordance with the applicable regulations of the Commission as to its manner and use.

(c) Punishment.—Except as otherwise provided in this subsection, a violation of the offense described in subsection (a) of this section is a Class 3 misdemeanor and, notwithstanding G.S. 15A-1340.23, is punishable by a penalty of one hundred dollars ($100.00). A second or subsequent violation of this section is a misdemeanor punishable under G.S. 20-179. This offense is a lesser included offense of impaired driving of a commercial vehicle under G.S. 20-138.1.

(d) Second or Subsequent Conviction Defined.—A conviction for violating this offense is a second or subsequent conviction if at the time of the current offense the person has a previous conviction under this section, and the previous conviction occurred in the seven years immediately preceding the date of the current offense. This definition of second or subsequent conviction also applies to G.S. 20-19(c2).

Elements

A person guilty of this offense
(1) drives
(2) a school bus or school activity bus or child care vehicle
(3) on a highway or public vehicular area
(4) while consuming alcohol or while alcohol remains in his or her body.

Punishment

Class 3 misdemeanor, but apparently the only authorized punishment is a $100 fine [see G.S. 20-138.2B(c)]. Second and subsequent convictions are punishable under G.S. 20-179 in the same manner as impaired driving convictions; see "Impaired Driving." A conviction is a second or subsequent conviction if it occurs within the seven years preceding the date of the current offense.

Notes

Element (1). See the discussion of Element (1) under "Driving While License Revoked."

Element (2). A "school bus" is defined in G.S. 20-4.01(27)(d4) as a vehicle whose primary purpose is to transport students over an established route to and from a public, private, or parochial school for the regularly scheduled school day. A "school activity bus" in defined in G.S. 20-4.01(27)(d3) as a vehicle whose primary purpose is to transport public, private, or parochial students and others to or from a place for participation in an event other than regular classroom work. A "child care vehicle" is defined in G.S. 20-4.01(27)(c1) as a vehicle under the direction and control of a child care facility, as defined in G.S. 110-86(3), and driven by an owner, employee, or agent of the facility for the primary purpose of transporting children to or from the facility, or to and from an event or activity in connection with the facility.

Element (3). See the discussion of Element (3) under "Impaired Driving."

Element (4). The result of an alcohol screening test (or the driver's refusal to submit to the test) may be used to prove this element if the test is conducted under the requirements set out in G.S. 20-138.2B(b2). The odor of an alcoholic beverage on the driver's breath is insufficient by itself to prove beyond a reasonable doubt that alcohol was remaining in the driver's body unless the driver was offered an alcohol screening test or chemical analysis and refused to provide the appropriate samples [G.S. 20-138.2B(b1)].

Lesser-included offense. This offense is a lesser-included offense of impaired driving in commercial vehicle, G.S. 20-138.2.

License revocation. For a first conviction, the person's driver's license is revoked for 10 days. For a second or subsequent conviction occurring within seven years of the date of the current offense, the revocation is for 1 year.

Related offenses not in this chapter

See the offenses listed under "Impaired Driving."

Habitual Impaired Driving

Statute

§20-138.5. Habitual impaired driving.

(a) A person commits the offense of habitual impaired driving if he drives while impaired as defined in G.S. 20-138.1 and has been convicted of three or more offenses involving impaired driving as defined in G.S. 20-4.01(24a) within seven years of the date of this offense.

(b) A person convicted of violating this section shall be punished as a Class F felon and shall be sentenced to a minimum active term of not less than 12 months of imprisonment, which shall not be suspended. Sentences imposed under this subsection shall run consecutively with and shall commence at the expiration of any sentence being served.

(c) An offense under this section is an implied consent offense subject to the provisions of G.S. 20-16.2.

(d) A person convicted under this section shall have his license permanently revoked.

(e) If a person is convicted under this section, the motor vehicle that was driven by the defendant at the time the defendant committed the offense of impaired driving becomes property subject to forfeiture in accordance with the procedure set out in G.S. 20-28.2. In applying the procedure set out in that statute, an owner or a holder of a security interest is considered an innocent party with respect to a motor vehicle subject to forfeiture under this subsection if any of the following applies:

(1) The owner or holder of the security interest did not know and had no reason to know that the defendant had been convicted within the previous seven years of three or more offenses involving impaired driving.
(2) The defendant drove the motor vehicle without the consent of the owner or the holder of the security interest.

Elements

A person guilty of this offense

(1) drives
(2) a vehicle
(3) on a highway or public vehicular area
(4) (a) while under the influence of an impairing substance, *or*
    (b) after consuming a sufficient quantity of alcohol so that the person has an alcohol concentration of 0.08 or more at any relevant time after the driving, *and*
(5) within seven years of the date of this offense, the person has had convictions of three or more offenses involving impaired driving.

Punishment

Class F felony, and a minimum sentence of 12 months' imprisonment must be imposed, which may not be suspended (this provision overrides the Structured Sentencing Act, which sometimes allows a suspended sentence for a Class F felony). The sentence must commence at the expiration of any sentence being served.

Notes

Elements (1) through (4). See the notes to Elements (1) through (4) under "Impaired Driving."

Element (5). G.S. 20-4.01(24a) defines offenses involving impaired driving. They include impaired driving; habitual imparied driving; impaired driving in commercial vehicle; death by vehicle under G.S. 20-141.4 based on impaired driving; first-degree or second-degree murder under G.S. 14-17 based on impaired driving; involuntary manslaughter under G.S. 14-18 based on impaired driving; and substantially similar offenses committed in another state or jurisdiction.

References in a criminal pleading to prior convictions should include the date and court of conviction. For example, the portion of a charge covering Element (5) might be: "Within seven years of the date of this offense, the defendant has been convicted of three or more offenses involving impaired driving. The defendant has been previously convicted on (1) March 12, 2000, of impaired driving in Durham County District Court; (2) April 6, 1999, of felony death by vehicle in Guilford County Superior Court; and (3) January 10, 1998, of impaired driving in Cumberland County District Court." The impaired driving convictions within seven years do not need to occur consecutive to each other as under the habitual felon statute (G.S. 14-7.1); for example, they could have occurred on the same date (117 N.C. App. 713).

In alleging and proving prior convictions in superior court, a prosecutor must comply with G.S. 15A-928. G.S. 15A-928(b) requires that an indictment or information for this kind of offense allege prior convictions in either

(1) a separate count of the indictment or information charging the substantive offense or (2) in a separate indictment or information.

Under G.S. 15A-928(c), a defendant on trial for this offense in superior court must be arraigned during the trial before the close of the state's case and in the absence of the jury. If the defendant admits the prior convictions, Element (5) is established, and proof of the convictions and jury instructions about this element are not permitted. If the defendant denies the prior convictions or a particular conviction, then the state has the burden of proving the conviction(s) before the jury.

Comparison with habitual felon statute. The offense of habitual impaired driving constitutes a separate substantive felony offense, unlike the habitual felon statute (G.S. 14-7.1), which is a punishment enhancement statute (115 N.C. App. 547). A habitual impaired driving conviction may be used as a felony conviction to establish habitual felon status (117 N.C. App. 713).

License revocation. A person convicted of this offense will have his or her license permanently revoked. No statutory provision authorizes reinstatement of a license so revoked (137 N.C. App. 755).

Motor vehicle forfeiture. If a person is convicted of this offense, the motor vehicle driven by the defendant at the time of the offense is property subject to forfeiture according to the procedure set out in G.S. 20-28.2 (forfeiture of motor vehicle for impaired driving after impaired driving license revocation). For a discussion of forfeiture issues, see page 105 and pages 137–49 of the Institute of Government publication: Ben F. Loeb, Jr., and James C. Drennan, *Motor Vehicle Law and the Law of Impaired Driving in North Carolina* (Chapel Hill: The University of North Carolina at Chapel Hill, 2000 edition).

Related offenses not in this chapter

See the offenses listed under "Impaired Driving."

Driving by Person under 21 Years of Age after Consuming Alcohol or Drugs

Statute

§20-138.3. Driving by person less than 21 years old after consuming alcohol or drugs.

(a) Offense.—It is unlawful for a person less than 21 years old to drive a motor vehicle on a highway or public vehicular area while consuming alcohol or at any time while he has remaining in his body any alcohol or controlled substance previously consumed, but a person less than 21 years old does not violate this section if he drives with a controlled substance in his body which was lawfully obtained and taken in therapeutically appropriate amounts.

(b) Subject to Implied-Consent Law.—An offense under this section is an alcohol-related offense subject to the implied-consent provisions of G.S. 20-16.2.

(b1) Odor Insufficient.—The odor of an alcoholic beverage on the breath of the driver is insufficient evidence by itself to prove beyond a reasonable doubt that alcohol was remaining in the driver's body in violation of this section unless the driver was offered an alcohol screening test or chemical analysis and refused to provide all required samples of breath or blood for analysis.

(b2) Alcohol Screening Test.—Notwithstanding any other provision of law, an alcohol screening test may be administered to a driver suspected of violation of subsection (a) of this section, and the results of an alcohol screening test or the driver's refusal to submit may be used by a law enforcement officer, a court, or an administrative agency in determining if alcohol was present in the driver's body. No alcohol screening tests are valid under this section unless the device used is one approved by the Commission on Health Services, and the screening test is conducted in accordance with the applicable regulations of the Commission as to its manner and use.

(c) Punishment; Effect When Impaired Driving Offense Also Charged.—The offense in this section is a Class 2 misdemeanor. It is not, in any circumstances, a lesser included offense of impaired driving under G.S. 20-138.1, but if a person is convicted under this section and of an offense involving impaired driving arising out of the same transaction, the aggregate punishment imposed by the court may not exceed the maximum applicable to the offense involving impaired driving, and any minimum punishment applicable shall be imposed.

(d) Limited Driving Privilege.—A person who is convicted of violating subsection (a) of this section and whose drivers license is revoked solely based on that conviction may apply for a limited driving privilege as provided in G.S. 20-179.3. This subsection shall apply only if the person meets both of the following requirements:

(1) Is 18, 19, or 20 years old on the date of the offense.
(2) Has not previously been convicted of a violation of this section.

The judge may issue the limited driving privilege only if the person meets the eligibility requirements of G.S. 20-179.3, other than the requirement in G.S. 20-179.3(b)(1)c. G.S. 20-179.3(e) shall not apply. All other terms, conditions, and restrictions provided for in G.S. 20-179.3 shall apply. G.S. 20-179.3, rather than this subsection, governs the issuance of a limited driving privilege to a person who is convicted of violating subsection (a) of this section and of driving while impaired as a result of the same transaction.

Elements

A person guilty of this offense

(1) is less than 21 years old, *and*
(2) drives
(3) a motor vehicle
(4) on a highway or public vehicular area
(5) (a) while the person is consuming alcohol, *or*
    (b) while the person has remaining in his or her body any alcohol, *or*
    (c) while the person has remaining in his or her blood any controlled substance.

Punishment

Class 2 misdemeanor.

Notes

Element (1). This element requires proof of the defendant's age at the time of the offense; his or her age when the trial takes place is irrelevant.

Element (2). See the note to Element (1) under "Driving While License Revoked."

Element (3). See the note to Element (2) under "Driving While License Revoked."

Element (4). See the note to Element (3) under "Impaired Driving."

Element (5). Any amount of alcohol satisfies this element. The result of an alcohol screening test (or the driver's refusal to submit to the test) may be used to prove whether alcohol was present in the driver's body if the test is conducted under the requirements set out in G.S. 20-138.3(b2). The odor of an alcoholic beverage on the driver's breath is insufficient by itself to prove beyond a reasonable doubt that alcohol was remaining in the driver's body unless the driver was offered an alcohol screening test or chemical analysis and refused to provide the appropriate samples [G.S. 20-138.3(b1)]. Element 5(c) does not apply to a defendant who lawfully obtains the controlled substance and takes it in therapeutically appropriate amounts.

Not lesser-included of impaired driving. G.S. 20-138.3(c) proves that this offense is not a lesser-included offense of impaired driving under G.S. 20-138.1.

License revocation. A person convicted of this offense will have his or her license revoked for one year (G.S. 20-13.2). Subsection (d) of G.S. 20-138.3, above, authorizes a limited driving privilege under certain circumstances.

Related offenses not in this chapter

Purchase of alcohol by underage person (G.S. 18B-302)
Impaired instruction (G.S. 20-12.1)
Transporting open alcohol container of alcoholic beverage (G.S. 20-138.7)

Reckless Driving

Statute

§20-140. Reckless driving.

(a) Any person who drives any vehicle upon a highway or any public vehicular area carelessly or heedlessly in willful or wanton disregard of the rights or safety of others shall be guilty of reckless driving.

(b) Any person who drives any vehicle upon a highway or any public vehicular area without due caution and circumspection and at a speed or in a manner so as to endanger or be likely to endanger any person or property shall be guilty of reckless driving.

(c) Repealed by Session Laws 1983, c. 435, s. 23.

(d) Reckless driving as defined in subsections (a) and (b) is a Class 2 misdemeanor.

(e) Repealed by Session Laws 1983, c. 435, s. 23.

I. Carelessly and Heedlessly

Statute

See subsection (a) of G.S. 20-140, reproduced at the beginning of this section.

Elements

A person guilty of this offense
(1) drives
(2) a vehicle
(3) on a highway or public vehicular area
(4) carelessly and heedlessly
(5) in willful or wanton disregard
(6) of the rights and safety of others.

Punishment

Class 2 misdemeanor.

Notes

Element (1). See the note on Element (1) under "Driving While License Revoked."

Element (2). Any vehicle satisfies this element. G.S. 20-4.01(49) defines "vehicle": "Every device in, upon, or by which any person or property is or may be transported or drawn upon a highway, excepting devices moved by human power or used exclusively upon fixed rails or tracks; provided, that . . . bicycles shall be deemed vehicles. . . ." Mopeds are also vehicles, but they are not motor vehicles. See G.S. 20-4.01(21a), (23), (27)(d1). Bicycles, lawnmowers, and horses are considered vehicles for all motor vehicles offenses *except* impaired driving [G.S. 20-138.1(e)]. Notwithstanding this specific exception concerning impaired driving, generally a person riding or driving any animal will be treated as a driver of a vehicle (G.S. 20-171). See the note on Element (2) under "Impaired Driving."

Element (3). See the note on Element (3) under "Impaired Driving."

Generally. The courts, in discussing the elements of reckless driving, rarely discuss them individually. Instead, the issue is usually whether the defendant committed an act of culpable (or criminal) negligence. The elements of the reckless driving statutes in effect amount to culpable negligence. The concept is used in motor vehicle manslaughter, reckless driving, and assault cases, and the courts frequently cite cases dealing with one kind of offense in cases dealing with these other kinds of offenses. One formulation of culpable negligence is that it is the intentional or willful violation of a statute regulating traffic (204 N.C. 28); or it can be the unintentional violation of a statute regulating traffic, "accompanied by such recklessness or carelessness of probable consequences of a dangerous nature, when tested by the rule of reasonable prevision, amounting to a thoughtless disregard of consequences or a heedless indifference to the safety of others" (264 N.C. 463).

Evidence was sufficient to prove reckless driving when (1) a defendant drove at night on a highway at 70 m.p.h. in a 60 m.p.h. zone and in attempting to elude a law enforcement officer, traveled down a dirt road at 45 m.p.h. with the vehicle lights cut off, and then skidded to a stop (256 N.C. 430); (2) a defendant drove 70 m.p.h. in a 45 m.p.h. zone in a residential area, suddenly applied brakes, came down the road sideways with the car's back end coming across the road, slowed down to 5 m.p.h., and then accelerated and swerved left and right three times (15 N.C. App. 438); (3) a defendant in a 25 m.p.h. zone drove his vehicle into the rear of a truck, which was propelled by the collision for 125 feet, and there was a tire mark made by one of the defendant's rear wheels extending back 20 feet from the point of impact, indicating that the vehicle had slid on one wheel for that distance (228 N.C. 634; see also 218 N.C. 769 for a similar case). Evidence was insufficient to prove reckless driving when the defendant's vehicle was on the left of the center line in the direction in which it was traveling when it collided with another vehicle but there was no evidence that the defendant's vehicle was being operated at a dangerous speed or in a perilous manner (264 N.C. 463).

Alternative kinds of reckless driving. Although there are two kinds of reckless driving, a person may be convicted of only one for each occasion in which the person drives recklessly, even if his or her behavior meets both descriptions of reckless driving (256 N.C. 430).

II.
Endangering Persons or Property

Statute

See subsection (b) of G.S. 20-140, reproduced at the beginning of this section.

Elements

A person guilty of this offense
(1) drives
(2) a vehicle
(3) on a highway or public vehicular area
(4) without due caution and circumspection
(5) at a speed or in a manner
(6) that could or does endanger other persons or property.

Punishment

Class 2 misdemeanor.

Notes

Element (1). See the note on Element (1) under "Driving While License Revoked."

Element (2). Any vehicle satisfies this element. See the note on Element (2) under "I. Carelessly and Heedlessly," just above.

Element (3). See the note on Element 3 under "Impaired Driving."

Element (4). "Without due caution" means without due prudence in regard to danger, and "without circumspection" means without looking around. Although the language is different from the language in Element (4) under "Carelessly and Heedlessly," just above, the meaning is the same.

Element (5). A person can commit this offense even while not exceeding the speed limit if the person drives his or her vehicle in a manner that will endanger others (181 N.C. 530; 249 N.C. 228). Also, a person can violate the speeding statute (G.S. 20-141) and not be guilty of reckless driving (273 N.C. 275).

Element (6). This element, unlike Element (5) under "Carelessly and Heedlessly," does not depend on the driver's intent. Instead, if the driver actually endangers others or drives at a speed or in a manner that a reasonable person would say could endanger others, the driver can be guilty of this offense even with innocent intentions.

Related offenses not in this chapter

None.

Willful Racing

Statute

§20-141.3. Unlawful racing on streets and highways.

(a) It shall be unlawful for any person to operate a motor vehicle on a street or highway willfully in prearranged speed competition with another motor vehicle. Any person violating the provisions of this subsection shall be guilty of a Class 1 misdemeanor.

(b) It shall be unlawful for any person to operate a motor vehicle on a street or highway willfully in speed competition with another motor vehicle. Any person willfully violating the provisions of this subsection shall be guilty of a Class 2 misdemeanor.

(c) It shall be unlawful for any person to authorize or knowingly permit a motor vehicle owned by him or under his control to be operated on a public street, highway, or thoroughfare in prearranged speed competition with another motor vehicle, or to place or receive any bet, wager, or other thing of value from the outcome of any prearranged speed competition on any public street, highway, or thoroughfare. Any person violating the provisions of this subsection shall be guilty of a Class 1 misdemeanor.

(d) The Commissioner of Motor Vehicles shall revoke the drivers license or privilege to drive of every person convicted of violating the provisions of subsection (a) or subsection (c) of this section, said revocation to be for three years; provided any person whose license has been revoked under this section may apply for a new license after 18 months from revocation. Upon filing of such application the Division may issue a new license upon satisfactory proof that the former licensee has been of good behavior for the past 18 months and that his conduct and attitude are such as to entitle him to favorable consideration and upon such terms and conditions which the Division may see fit to impose for the balance of the three-year revocation period, which period shall be computed from the date of the original revocation.

(e) The Commissioner may suspend the drivers license or privilege to drive of every person convicted of violating the provisions of subsection (b) of this section. Such suspension shall be for a period of time within the discretion of the Commissioner, but not to exceed one year.

(f) All suspensions and revocations made pursuant to the provisions of this section shall be in the same form and manner and shall be subject to all procedures as now provided for suspensions and revocations made under the provisions of Article 2 of Chapter 20 of the General Statutes.

(g) When any officer of the law discovers that any person has operated or is operating a motor vehicle willfully in prearranged speed competition with another motor vehicle on a street or highway, he shall seize the motor vehicle and deliver the same to the sheriff of the county in which such offense is committed, or the same shall be placed under said sheriff's constructive possession if delivery of actual possession is impractical, and the vehicle shall be held by the sheriff pending the trial of the person or persons arrested for operating such motor vehicle in violation of subsection (a) of this section. The sheriff shall restore the seized motor vehicle to the owner upon execution by the owner of a good and valid bond, with sufficient sureties, in an amount double the value of the property, which bond shall be approved by said sheriff and shall be conditioned on the return of the motor vehicle to the custody of the sheriff on the day of trial of the person or persons accused. Upon the acquittal of the person charged with operating said motor vehicle willfully in prearranged speed competition with another motor vehicle, the sheriff shall return the motor vehicle to the owner thereof.

Notwithstanding the provisions for sale set out above, on petition by a lienholder, the court, in its discretion and upon such terms and conditions as it may prescribe, may allow reclamation of the vehicle by the lienholder. The lienholder shall file with the court an accounting of the proceeds of any subsequent sale of the vehicle and pay into the court any proceeds received in excess of the amount of the lien.

Upon conviction of the operator of said motor vehicle of a violation of subsection (a) of this section, the court shall order a sale at public auction of said motor vehicle and the officer making the sale, after deducting the expenses of keeping the motor vehicle, the fee for the seizure, and the costs of the sale, shall pay all liens, according to their priorities, which are established, by intervention or otherwise, at said hearing or in other proceeding brought for said purpose, as being bona fide, and shall pay the balance of the proceeds to the proper officer of the county who receives fines and forfeitures to be used for the school fund of the county. All liens against a motor vehicle sold under the provisions of this section shall be transferred from the motor vehicle to the proceeds of its sale. If, at the time of hearing, or other proceeding in which the matter is considered, the owner of the vehicle can establish to the satisfaction of the court that said motor vehicle was used in prearranged speed competition with another motor vehicle on a street or highway without the knowledge or consent of the owner, and that the owner had no reasonable grounds to believe that the motor vehicle would be used for such purpose, the court shall not order a sale of the vehicle but shall restore it to the owner, and the said owner shall, at his request, be entitled to a trial by jury upon such issues.

If the owner of said motor vehicle cannot be found, the taking of the same, with a description thereof, shall be advertised in some newspaper published in the city or county where taken, or, if there be no newspaper published in such city or county, in a newspaper having circulation in the county, once a week for two weeks and by handbills posted in three public places near the place of seizure, and if said owner shall not appear within 10 days after the last publication of the advertisement, the property shall be sold, or otherwise disposed of in the manner set forth in this section.

When any vehicle confiscated under the provisions of this section is found to be specially equipped or modified from its original manufactured condition so as to increase its speed, the court shall, prior to sale, order that the special equipment or modification be removed and destroyed and the vehicle restored to its original manufactured condition. However, if the court should find that such equipment and modifications are so extensive that it would be impractical to restore said vehicle to its original manufactured condition, then the court may order that the vehicle be turned over to such governmental agency or public official within the territorial jurisdiction of the court as the court shall see fit, to be used in the performance of official duties only, and not for resale, transfer, or disposition other than as junk: Provided, that nothing herein contained shall affect the rights of lienholders and other claimants to said vehicles as set out in this section.

Elements

A person guilty of this offense
(1) drives
(2) a motor vehicle
(3) on a highway
(4) willfully
(5) in speed competition with another motor vehicle.

Punishment

Class 2 misdemeanor.

Notes

Element (1). "Operate" and "drive" mean the same thing (312 N.C. 432). See the note on Element (1) under "Driving While License Revoked."

Element (2). This offense applies only to *motor* vehicles. See the note on Element (2) under "Driving While License Revoked."

Element (3). See the note on Element (3) under "Driving While License Revoked."

Element (4). See the definition of "willfully" in Chapter 1.

License revocation for conviction. A person convicted of this charge may have his or her driver's license suspended for up to one year [G.S. 20-141.3(e)].

Lesser-included offense. This offense is a lesser-included offense of prearranged racing.

Related offenses not in this chapter

None

Prearranged Racing

Statute

See subsection (a) of G.S. 20-141.3, reproduced under "Willful Racing."

Elements

A person guilty of this offense
(1) operates
(2) a motor vehicle
(3) on a highway
(4) willfully
(5) in prearranged speed competition with another.

Punishment

Class 1 misdemeanor.

Notes

Elements (1) through (4). See the notes to Elements (1) through (4) under "Willful Racing."

Element (5). This offense is different from willful racing only in its requirement that the race be "prearranged."

Vehicle to be seized. Motor vehicles used in prearranged racing in violation of this statute should be seized by the law enforcement officer who makes the arrest, and the vehicles should be delivered to the local sheriff for sale. Vehicles can be returned if a bond is posted, if the defendant is acquitted, or if the owner can prove that he or she did not know his or her vehicle was being used illegally [G.S. 20-141.3(g)].

License revocation for conviction. A person convicted of this offense will have his or her driver's license revoked for three years [G.S. 20-141.3(d)].

Related offenses not in this chapter

None.

Encouraging or Betting on Prearranged Race

I.
Permitting Use of Vehicle for Prearranged Racing

Statute

See subsection (c) of G.S. 20-141.3, reproduced under "Willful Racing."

Elements

A person guilty of this offense
(1) owns a motor vehicle or has one under his or her control, *and*

(2) authorizes or knowingly permits
(3) it to be used in prearranged racing
(4) on a highway.

Punishment

Class 1 misdemeanor.

Notes

Element (2). A person would not be guilty if the person's motor vehicle was used for racing without his or her knowledge.

Element (3). The racing must be prearranged.

Element (4). See the note on Element (3) under "Driving While License Revoked."

License revocation for conviction. A person convicted of this offense will have his or her driver's license revoked for three years [G.S. 20-141.3(d)].

II. Betting on Prearranged Race

Statute

See subsection (c) of G.S. 20-141.3, reproduced under "Willful Racing."

Elements

A person guilty of this offense
(1) places or receives
(2) a bet
(3) on the outcome of a prearranged race
(4) conducted on a highway.

Punishment

Class 1 misdemeanor.

Notes

Element (1). Note that this offense applies to both a bettor and a stakeholder.

Element (2). This includes bets or wagers of anything of value.

Element (3). Note that the offense occurs only if the race being bet on is *prearranged*. If it is not prearranged, a charge of "Gambling" (Chapter 22) might be used. Although the statute does not state that the race must be between motor vehicles, it probably would be so interpreted.

Element (4). See the note on Element (3) under "Driving While License Revoked."

License revocation for conviction. A person convicted of this offense will have his or her driver's license revoked for three years [G.S. 20-141.3(d)].

Related offenses not in this chapter

"Gambling" (Chapter 22)

Hit and Run: Failure to Stop or Remain at Scene When Personal Injury or Death Occurs

Statute

§20-166. Duty to stop in event of accident or collision; furnishing information or assistance to injured person, etc.; persons assisting exempt from civil liability.

(a) The driver of any vehicle who knows or reasonably should know:

(1) That the vehicle which he is operating is involved in an accident or collision; and

(2) That the accident or collision has resulted in injury or death to any person; shall immediately stop his vehicle at the scene of the accident or collision. He shall remain at the scene of the accident until a law-enforcement officer completes his investigation of the accident or collision or authorizes him to leave; Provided, however, that he may leave to call for a law-enforcement officer or for medical assistance or medical treatment as set forth in (b), but must return to the accident scene within a reasonable period of time. A willful violation of this subsection shall be punished as a Class H felony.

(b) In addition to complying with the requirement of (a), the driver as set forth in (a) shall give his name, address, drivers license number and the license plate number of his vehicle to the person struck or the driver or occupants of any vehicle collided with, provided that such person or persons are physically and mentally capable of receiving such information, and shall render to any person injured in such accident or collision reasonable assistance, including the calling for medical assistance if it is apparent that such assistance is necessary or is requested by the injured person. A violation of this subsection is a Class 1 misdemeanor.

(c) The driver of any vehicle, when he knows or reasonably should know that the vehicle which he is operating is involved in an accident or collision, which accident or collision, results:

(1) Only in damage to property; or

(2) In injury or death to any person, but only if the operator of the vehicle did not know and did not have reason to know of the death or injury; shall immediately stop his vehicle at the scene of the accident or collision. A violation of this subsection is a Class 1 misdemeanor.

(c1) In addition to complying with the requirement of (c), the driver as set forth in (c) shall give his name, address, drivers license number and the license plate number of his vehicle to the driver or occupants of any other vehicle involved in the accident or collision or to any person whose property is damaged in the accident or collision. If the damaged property is a parked and unattended vehicle and the name and location of the owner is not known to or readily ascertainable by the driver of the responsible vehicle, the said driver shall furnish the information required by this subsection to the nearest available peace officer, or, in the alternative, and provided he thereafter within 48 hours fully complies with G.S. 20-166.1(c), shall immediately place a paper-writing containing said information in a conspicuous place upon or in the damaged vehicle. If the damaged property is a guardrail, utility pole, or other fixed object owned by the Department of Transportation, a public utility, or other public service corporation to which report cannot readily be made at the scene, it shall be sufficient if the responsible driver shall furnish the information required to the nearest peace officer or make written report thereof containing said information by U.S. certified mail, return receipt requested, to the North Carolina Division of Motor Vehicles within five days following said collision. A violation of this subsection is a Class 1 misdemeanor.

(d) Any person who renders first aid or emergency assistance at the scene of a motor vehicle accident on any street or highway to any person injured as a result of such accident, shall not be liable in civil damages for any acts or omissions relating to such services rendered, unless such acts or omissions amount to wanton conduct or intentional wrongdoing.

Elements

A person guilty of this offense
- (1) drives
- (2) a vehicle
- (3) involved in an accident or collision
- (4) causing personal injury or death, *and*
- (5) the person knows or reasonably should have known that the vehicle is involved in the accident or collision, *and*
- (6) (a) the person willfully fails to stop at the scene of the accident or collision, *or*
  - (b) willfully fails to remain at the scene until authorized to leave by a law enforcement officer, *or*
  - (c) willfully fails to return to the scene after temporarily leaving to call for an officer or for medical assistance.

Punishment

Class H felony.

Notes

Element (1). See the note on Element (1) under "Driving While License Revoked."

Element (2). See the note on Element (2) under "Impaired Driving."

Element (3). The meaning of the word "involved" as it is used in this statute is not clear. It may include situations in which the driver's vehicle does not actually collide with another vehicle, such as when (1) a passenger is injured in a one-car accident or (2) improper passing causes an oncoming vehicle to leave the highway and crash into a tree. The definition of "crash" in G.S. 20-4.01(4b) includes the terms "accident" and "collision" and their cognates (words related in origin), and a crash is defined as "[a]ny event that results in injury or property damage attributable directly to the motion of a motor vehicle or its load."

Element (6)(c). The statute authorizes a driver to leave the scene temporarily to call a law enforcement officer or to seek medical assistance, but the driver must return within a "reasonable period of time." G.S. 20-166(b) requires that a driver seek medical assistance if it appears such assistance is necessary or such assistance is requested by an injured person.

Alternative kinds of hit and run. Failure to do any of the three actions listed under Element (6) satisfies that element, but if a person fails to do all three in the same accident, he or she still may be convicted of only one offense (58 N.C. App. 141).

Application to accidents off public highways. This statute is not restricted to public highways. Thus it covers accidents that occur, for example, on public vehicular areas and private roads (264 N.C. 575). See the note on Element (3) under "Impaired Driving" for the definition of public vehicular area.

Fault not relevant. The driver's duties under this statute exist whether or not he or she is at fault (264 N.C. 575).

Related offenses not in this chapter

Death by Vehicle (various offenses) (Chapter 6)
"Assault with a Deadly Weapon" (Chapter 7)

Hit and Run: Failure to Give Information or Assistance When Injury or Death Occurs

Statute

See subsection (b) of G.S. 20-166, reproduced under "Hit and Run: Failure to Stop or Remain at Scene When Personal Injury or Death Occurs."

Elements

A person guilty of this offense
- (1) drives
- (2) a vehicle
- (3) involved in an accident or collision
- (4) causing personal injury or death, *and*
- (5) the person knows or reasonably should have known that the vehicle is involved in the accident or collision, *and*
- (6) (a) the person fails to give his or her name, address, and driver's license and registration numbers to any person struck and to the driver or occupants of any vehicle collided with, *or*
  - (b) the person fails to render reasonable assistance to any person injured in the accident or collision.

Punishment

Class 1 misdemeanor.

Notes

Element (1). See the note on Element (1) under "Driving While License Revoked."

Element (2). See the note on Element (2) under "Impaired Driving."

Element (3). See the note on Element (3) under "Hit and Run: Failure to Stop or Remain at Scene When Personal Injury or Death Occurs."

Element (6)(a). The duty to give information applies only if the person to receive the information is mentally and physically able to receive it.

Element (6)(b). The driver must render medical assistance as well as any other type of reasonable assistance. That duty includes calling for professional medical assistance if it is apparent that such aid is necessary or if the injured party requests it. G.S. 20-166(d) provides for immunity for negligent assistance rendered in motor vehicle accidents on highways.

Application to accidents off public highways. This statute is not restricted to public highways. Thus it covers accidents that occur, for example, on public vehicular areas and private roads (264 N.C. 575). See the note on this topic under the previous offense.

Fault not relevant. A driver involved in an accident covered by this statute must comply with this statute, even if he or she is not at fault in the accident (264 N.C. 575).

Related offenses not in this chapter

"Injury to Personal Property" (Chapter 16)

Hit and Run: Failure to Stop or Give Information When Injury or Death Not Apparent or Only Property Damage Occurs

Statute

See G.S. 20-166(c) and (c1) reproduced under "Hit and Run: Failure to Stop or Remain at Scene When Personal Injury or Death Occurs."

Elements

A person guilty of this offense
- (1) drives
- (2) a vehicle
- (3) involved in an accident or collision causing
- (4) (a) only property damage, *or*
  - (b) personal injury or death that is not apparent, *and*
- (5) the person knows or reasonably should have known that the vehicle was involved in the accident or collision, *and*
- (6) (a) the person fails to stop at the scene of the accident, *or*
  - (b) fails to give his or her name, address, and driver's license and registration numbers to any person in any other vehicle involved in the accident and to any person whose property is damaged in the accident or collision.

Punishment

Class 1 misdemeanor.

Notes

Element (1). See the note on Element 1 under "Driving While License Revoked."

Element (2). See the note on Element 2 under "Impaired Driving."

Element (3). See the note on Element (3) under "Hit and Run: Failure to Stop or Remain at Scene When Personal Injury or Death Occurs."

Element (6)(b). G.S. 20-166(c1) provides detailed requirements that must be complied with when the collision involved parked vehicles or fixed objects like guardrails and utility poles. If a parked vehicle is struck, the driver has two alternatives: (1) The driver may give the required information to the nearest law enforcement officer or (2) the driver may place the required written information on the struck vehicle; the driver must also notify the vehicle's owner within 48 hours. If a utility pole or highway sign or other fixed object is struck, the driver must immediately notify a law enforcement officer or notify the Division of Motor Vehicles within five days of the accident. Failure to comply with the proper procedure is the same as not providing the information in an accident in which the other parties are present.

Related offenses not in this chapter

"Injury to Personal Property" (Chapter 16)

Hit and Run: Failure to Notify Authorities

Statute

§20-4.01. Definitions.

Only two subsections are reproduced here.

(4b) Crash.—Any event that results in injury or property damage attributable directly to the motion of a motor vehicle or its load. The terms collision, accident, and crash and their cognates are synonymous.

(33b) Reportable Crash. — A crash involving a motor vehicle that results in one or more of the following:
a. Death or injury of a human being.
b. Total property damage of one thousand dollars ($1,000) or more.

§20-166.1. Reports and investigations required in event of accident.

(a) Notice of Accident. — The driver of a vehicle involved in a reportable accident must immediately, by the quickest means of communication, notify the appropriate law enforcement agency of the accident. If the accident occurred in a city or town, the appropriate agency is the police department of the city or town. If the accident occurred outside a city or town, the appropriate agency is the State Highway Patrol or the sheriff's office or other qualified rural police of the county where the accident occurred.

(b) Insurance Verification. — When requested to do so by the Division, the driver of a vehicle involved in a reportable accident must furnish proof of financial responsibility.

(c) Parked Vehicle. — The driver of a motor vehicle that collides with another motor vehicle left parked or unattended on a highway of this State must report the collision to the owner of the parked or unattended motor vehicle. This requirement applies to an accident that is not a reportable accident as well as to one that is a reportable accident. The report may be made orally or in writing, must be made within 48 hours of the accident, and must include the following:
(1) The time, date, and place of the accident.
(2) The driver's name, address, and drivers license number.
(3) The registration plate number of the vehicle being operated by the driver at the time of the accident.

If the driver makes a written report to the owner of the parked or unattended vehicle and the report is not given to the owner at the scene of the accident, the report must be sent to the owner by certified mail, return receipt requested, and a copy of the report must be sent to the Division.

(d) Repealed by Session Laws 1995, c. 191, s. 2.

(e) Investigation by Officer. — The appropriate law enforcement agency must investigate a reportable accident. A law-enforcement officer who investigates a reportable accident, whether at the scene of the accident or by subsequent investigations and interviews, must make a written report of the accident within 24 hours of the accident and must forward it as required by this subsection. The report must contain information on financial responsibility for the vehicle driven by the person whom the officer identified as at fault for the accident.

If the officer writing the report is a member of the State Highway Patrol, the officer must forward the report to the Division. If the officer is not a member of the State Highway Patrol, the officer must forward the report to the local law enforcement agency for the area where the accident occurred. A local law enforcement agency that receives an accident report must forward it to the Division within 10 days after receiving the report.

When a person injured in a reportable accident dies as a result of the accident within 12 months after the accident and the death was not reported in the original report, the law enforcement officer investigating the accident must file a supplemental report that includes the death.

(f) Medical Personnel. — A county medical examiner must report to the Division the death of any person in a reportable accident and the circumstances of the accident. The medical examiner must file the report within five days after the death. A hospital must notify the medical examiner of the county in which the accident occurred of the death within the hospital of any person who dies as a result of injuries apparently sustained in a reportable accident.

(g) Repealed by Session Laws 1987, c. 49.

(h) Forms.—The Division shall provide forms or procedures for submitting crash data to persons required to make reports under this section and the reports shall be made in a format approved by the Commissioner. The following information shall be included about a reportable crash:

(1) The cause of the crash.
(2) The conditions existing at the time of the crash.
(3) The persons and vehicles involved.
(4) Whether the vehicle has been seized and is subject to forfeiture under G.S. 20-28.2.

(i) Effect of Report. — A report of an accident made under this section by a person who is not a law enforcement officer is without prejudice, is for the use of the Division, and shall not be used in any manner as evidence, or for any other purpose in any trial, civil or criminal, arising out of the accident. Any other report of an accident made under this section may be used in any manner as evidence, or for any other purpose, in any trial, civil or criminal, as permitted under the rules of evidence. At the demand of a court, the Division must give the court a properly executed certificate stating that a particular accident report has or has not been filed with the Division solely to prove a compliance with this section.

The reports made by persons who are not law enforcement officers or medical examiners are not public records. The reports made by law enforcement officers and medical examiners are public records and are open to inspection by the general public at all reasonable times. The Division must give a certified copy of one of these reports to a member of the general public who requests a copy and pays the fee set in G.S. 20-42.

(j) Statistics. — The Division may periodically publish statistical information on motor vehicle accidents based on information in accident reports. The Division may conduct detailed research to determine more fully the cause and control of accidents and may conduct experimental field tests within areas of the State from time to time to prove the practicability of various ideas advanced in traffic control and accident prevention.

(k) Punishment. — A violation of any provision of this section is a misdemeanor of the Class set in G.S. 20-176.

Elements

A person guilty of this offense
(1) drives
(2) a vehicle
(3) involved in an accident or collision resulting in personal injury or death, or property damage of $1,000 or more, *and*
(4) fails to immediately notify a law enforcement officer
(5) by the quickest means of communication.

Punishment

Class 2 misdemeanor.

Notes

Element (1). See the note on Element (1) under "Driving While License Revoked."

Element (2). See the note on Element (2) under "Impaired Driving."

Element (3). Although there are no cases construing this element, it is likely that not knowing that an accident or collision occurred is a defense (see 229

N.C. 40). The definition of a crash in G.S. 20-4.01(4b), reproduced above, applies to the terms collision and accident. That definition includes any event resulting "in injury or property damage attributable directly to the motion of a motor vehicle or its load." Thus a reportable crash includes an event when the driver's motor vehicle did not collide with another vehicle or person.

Element (4). If the accident or collision occurred within a municipality, the driver must notify the police department. If it occurred outside a municipality, the State Highway Patrol, the local sheriff, or county police must be notified.

Element (5). The "quickest means of communication" in a particular case depends on the circumstances. If a person made a good-faith effort to notify the authorities promptly, it is unlikely that the person would be convicted just because there was a quicker way to notify them.

Duty if parked car is involved. If the accident or collision involves a parked car, the driver must notify the owner of that car in addition to the notice to law enforcement agencies required by this statute. See "Hit and Run: Failure to Stop or Give Information When Injury or Death Not Apparent or Only Property Damage Occurs."

Related offenses not in this chapter

"Injury to Personal Property" (Chapter 16)
Providing false information in accident report [G.S. 20-279.31(b)]

Passing a Stopped School Bus

Statute

§20-217. Motor vehicles to stop for properly marked and designated school buses in certain instances; evidence of identity of driver.

(a) The driver of a vehicle upon approaching from any direction on the same street, highway, or public vehicular area any school bus (including privately owned buses transporting children and school buses transporting senior citizens under G.S. 115C-243), while the bus is displaying its mechanical stop signal or flashing red stoplights, and is stopped for the purpose of receiving or discharging passengers, shall bring the vehicle to a full stop before passing or attempting to pass the bus, and shall remain stopped until the mechanical stop signal has been withdrawn, the flashing red stoplights have been turned off, and the bus has moved on.

(b) The provisions of this section are applicable only in the event the school bus bears upon the front and rear a plainly visible sign containing the words "school bus" in letters not less than eight inches in height.

(c) Notwithstanding the provisions of subsection (a) of this section, the driver of a vehicle traveling in the opposite direction from the school bus, upon any road, highway or city street which has been divided into two roadways, so constructed as to separate vehicular traffic between the two roadways by an intervening space (including a center lane for left turns if the roadway consists of at least four more lanes) or by a physical barrier, need not stop upon meeting and passing any school bus which has stopped in the roadway across such dividing space or physical barrier.

(d) It shall be unlawful for any school bus driver to stop and receive or discharge passengers or for any principal or superintendent of any school, routing a school bus, to authorize the driver of any school bus to stop and receive or discharge passengers upon any roadway described by subsection (c) of this section where passengers would be required to cross the roadway to reach their destination or to board the bus; provided, that passengers may be discharged or received at points where pedestrians and vehicular traffic are controlled by adequate stop-and-go traffic signals.

(e) Any person violating the provisions of this section shall be guilty of a Class 2 misdemeanor.

Elements

A person guilty of this offense

(1) while driving a vehicle
(2) on a highway or public vehicular area
(3) passes or attempts to pass from any direction on the same highway
(4) a school bus
(5) that is
  (a) displaying its mechanical stop signal or flashing red stoplights, *and*
  (b) is stopped for the purpose of receiving or discharging passengers.

Punishment

Class 2 misdemeanor.

Notes

Element (1). Note that the statute applies to *any* vehicle, not just a motor vehicle. See the notes on Elements (1) and (2) under "Driving While License Revoked." See the note on Element (2) under "Impaired Driving."

Element (2). See the note on Element (3) under "Impaired Driving."

Element (3). This statute does not apply if the vehicle is on the opposite side of a divided highway. A highway is divided if it has separate roadways for both directions of travel, if it has four lanes plus a center left-turn lane, or if it has a physical barrier between the lanes in each direction.

Element (4). Unless the bus is plainly marked a "school bus" in letters at least eight inches high on both the front and rear, this statute does not apply. The signs can be temporary. The bus also must have a mechanical stop signal and/or flashing red stoplights. This statute applies to both public school buses and private school buses that transport children, but not to Sunday School buses (G.S. 20-218.1). It also includes school buses that transport senior citizens.

Related offenses not in this chapter

None.

Failure to Remain Stopped for School Bus

Statute

See G.S. 20-217, reproduced under "Passing a Stopped School Bus."

Elements

A person guilty of this offense

(1) while driving a vehicle
(2) on a highway or public vehicular area
(3) fails to remain stopped until
(4) a school bus
(5) that has
    (a) displayed its mechanical stop signal or its flashing red stoplights, *and*
    (b) stopped for the purpose of receiving or discharging passengers
(6) has
    (a) withdrawn its stop signal,
    (b) turned off its flashing red stoplights, *and*
    (c) moved on.

Punishment

Class 2 misdemeanor.

Notes

Generally. The notes to "Passing a Stopped School Bus" also apply to this offense.

Element (6). A 1991 amendment to this statute requires that a driver remain stopped until a school bus turns off all its stop signals *and* the bus moves on. Under previous law, when a school bus either withdrew its stop signal *or* began to move, a stopped driver could move on. Possibly, the amendment was meant to prevent stopped drivers from passing school buses after they had turned off their stop signal but had not yet started to move. This statute does not expressly address the situation in which a school bus has a stop signal but not flashing red stoplights, or vice versa. However, if a school bus does not have a stop signal, Element (6)(a) would be inapplicable. If a school bus does not have flashing red stoplights, Element (6)(b) would be inapplicable. The statute is ambiguous as to whether a driver commits this offense by failing to remain stopped when a school bus moves on without withdrawing its stop sign or turning off its flashing red stoplights.

Related offenses not in this chapter

None.

Failure to Yield for Emergency Vehicle

Statute

§20-156. Exceptions to the right-of-way rule.

(a) The driver of a vehicle about to enter or cross a highway from an alley, building entrance, private road, or driveway shall yield the right-of-way to all vehicles approaching on the highway to be entered.

(b) The driver of a vehicle upon the highway shall yield the right-of-way to police and fire department vehicles and public and private ambulances, vehicles used by an organ procurement organization or agency for the recovery or transportation of human tissues and organs for transplantation or a vehicle operated by a transplant coordinator who is an employee of an organ procurement organization or agency when the transplant coordinator is responding to a call to recover or transport human tissues or organs for transplantation, and to rescue squad emergency service vehicles and vehicles operated by county fire marshals and civil preparedness coordinators when the operators of said vehicles are giving a warning signal by appropriate light and by bell, siren or exhaust whistle audible under normal conditions from a distance not less than 1,000 feet. When appropriate warning signals are being given, as provided in this subsection, an emergency vehicle may proceed through an intersection or other place when the emergency vehicle is facing a stop sign, a yield sign, or a traffic light which is emitting a flashing strobe signal or a beam of steady or flashing red light. This provision shall not operate to relieve the driver of a police or fire department vehicle or public or private ambulance or vehicles used by an organ procurement organization or agency for the recovery or transportation of human tissues and organs for transplantation or a vehicle operated by a transplant coordinator who is an employee of an organ procurement organization or agency when the transplant coordinator is responding to a call to recover or transport human tissues or organs for transplantation, or rescue squad emergency service vehicle or county fire marshals or civil preparedness coordinators from the duty to drive with due regard for the safety of all persons using the highway, nor shall it protect the driver of any such vehicle or county fire marshal or civil preparedness coordinator from the consequence of any arbitrary exercise of such right-of-way.

Elements

A person guilty of this offense
(1) while driving
(2) a vehicle
(3) on a highway
(4) fails to yield the right of way
(5) to a police vehicle, fire department vehicle, rescue squad vehicle, ambulance, vehicle used for the recovery or transportation of human tissues or organs, vehicle responding to a call to recover or transport human tissues or organs for transplantation, vehicle operated by county fire marshals, or vehicle operated by county civil preparedness coordinators
(6) that is giving a warning signal by appropriate lights and horns or sirens.

Punishment

Class 2 misdemeanor (G.S. 20-176).

Notes

Generally. A driver must yield to emergency vehicles even if a traffic signal gives the driver the right of way. An emergency vehicle, while giving appropriate warning signals, may proceed through stop signs, yield signs, and red lights.

Element (1). See the note on Element (1) under "Driving While License Revoked."

Element (2). See the note on Element (2) under "Impaired Driving."

Element (3). See the note on Element (3) under "Driving While License Revoked."

Element (4). This statute covers only the situation in which the driver fails to yield the right of way—for example, when a driver does not allow an emergency vehicle to pass or otherwise impedes its progress. For the offense of failure to stop, see "Failure to Stop for Emergency Vehicle," below.

Element (6). The audible signal being given by the emergency vehicle must be audible for at least 1,000 feet; note also that both the warning light *and* the audible signal (bell, horn, siren, or whistle) must be used before a driver is required to yield.

Related offenses not in this chapter

"Resisting, Delaying, or Obstructing an Officer" (Chapter 18)

Failure to Stop for Emergency Vehicle

Statute

§20-157. Approach of police, fire department or rescue squad vehicles or ambulances; driving over fire hose or blocking fire-fighting equipment; parking, etc., near police, fire department, or rescue squad vehicle or ambulance.

(a) Upon the approach of any police or fire department vehicle or public or private ambulance or rescue squad emergency service vehicle giving warning signal by appropriate light and by audible bell, siren or exhaust whistle, audible under normal conditions from a distance not less than 1,000 feet, the driver of every other vehicle shall immediately drive the same to a position as near as possible and parallel to the right-hand edge or curb, clear of any intersection of streets or highways, and shall stop and remain in such position unless otherwise directed by a police or traffic officer until police or fire department vehicle or public or private ambulance or rescue squad emergency service vehicle shall have passed. Provided, however, this subsection shall not apply to vehicles traveling in the opposite direction of the vehicles herein enumerated when traveling on a four-lane limited access highway with a median divider dividing the highway for vehicles traveling in opposite directions, and provided further that the violation of this subsection shall not be negligence per se. Violation of this subsection is a Class 2 misdemeanor.

(b) It shall be unlawful for the driver of any vehicle other than one on official business to follow any fire apparatus traveling in response to a fire alarm closer than one block or to drive into or park such vehicle within one block where fire apparatus has stopped in answer to a fire alarm.

(c) Outside of the corporate limits of any city or town it shall be unlawful for the driver of any vehicle other than one on official business to follow any fire apparatus traveling in response to a fire alarm closer than 400 feet or to drive into or park such vehicle within a space of 400 feet from where fire apparatus has stopped in answer to a fire alarm.

(d) It shall be unlawful to drive a motor vehicle over a fire hose or any other equipment that is being used at a fire at any time, or to block a fire-fighting apparatus or any other equipment from its source of supply regardless of its distance from the fire.

(e) It shall be unlawful for the driver of a vehicle, other than one on official business, to park and leave standing such vehicle within 100 feet of police or fire department vehicles, public or private ambulances, or rescue squad emergency service vehicles which are engaged in the investigation of an accident or engaged in rendering assistance to victims of such accident.

Elements

A person guilty of this offense
(1) while driving
(2) a vehicle
(3) on a highway

(4) upon the approach of a police vehicle or fire department vehicle or ambulance or rescue squad vehicle
(5) that is giving a warning signal by appropriate light *and* bell or siren
(6) either
  (a) fails to drive his or her vehicle to the right-hand curb or shoulder and stop, *or*
  (b) fails to remain stopped until the emergency vehicle has passed.

Punishment

Class 2 misdemeanor.

Notes

Generally. The notes to "Failure to Yield for Emergency Vehicle" apply to the appropriate elements of this offense. This offense is commonly called failure to stop for a blue light. This statute requires that a driver pull to the right-hand curb or shoulder and stop *if possible*. If such a maneuver is not possible (e.g., on a two-lane road without a shoulder), then G.S. 20-156 appears to require that the driver at least yield the right of way to the emergency vehicle (see "Failure to Yield for Emergency Vehicle").

Element (6). The statute specifies that a driver must not stop his or her vehicle in a place that blocks an intersection.

Vehicle in opposite direction not required to stop. If the emergency vehicle is traveling on a four-lane limited-access highway with a median dividing the highway, drivers traveling in the opposite direction need not stop.

Related offenses not in this chapter

"Resisting, Delaying, or Obstructing an Officer" (Chapter 18)

Speeding to Elude Arrest

Statute

§20-141.5. Speeding to elude arrest.

(a) It shall be unlawful for any person to operate a motor vehicle on a street, highway, or public vehicular area while fleeing or attempting to elude a law enforcement officer who is in the lawful performance of his duties. Except as provided in subsection (b) of this section, violation of this section shall be a Class 1 misdemeanor.

(b) If two or more of the following aggravating factors are present at the time the violation occurs, violation of this section shall be a Class H felony.
(1) Speeding in excess of 15 miles per hour over the legal speed limit.
(2) Gross impairment of the person's faculties while driving due to:
  a. Consumption of an impairing substance; or
  b. A blood alcohol concentration of 0.14 or more within a relevant time after the driving.
(3) Reckless driving as proscribed by G.S. 20-140.
(4) Negligent driving leading to an accident causing:
  a. Property damage in excess of one thousand dollars ($1,000); or
  b. Personal injury.
(5) Driving when the person's drivers license is revoked.

(6) Driving in excess of the posted speed limit, during the days and hours when the posted limit is in effect, on school property or in an area designated as a school zone pursuant to G.S. 20-141.1, or in a highway work zone as defined in G.S. 20-141(j2).
(7) Passing a stopped school bus as proscribed by G.S. 20-217.
(8) Driving with a child under 12 years of age in the vehicle.

(c) Whenever evidence is presented in any court or administrative hearing of the fact that a vehicle was operated in violation of this section, it shall be prima facie evidence that the vehicle was operated by the person in whose name the vehicle was registered at the time of the violation, according to the Division's records. If the vehicle is rented, then proof of that rental shall be prima facie evidence that the vehicle was operated by the renter of the vehicle at the time of the violation.

(d) The Division shall suspend, for up to one year, the driver's license of any person convicted of a misdemeanor under this section. The Division shall revoke, for two years, the driver's license of any person convicted of a felony under this section if the person was convicted on the basis of the presence of two of the aggravating factors listed in subsection (b) of this section. The Division shall revoke, for three years, the drivers license of any person convicted of a felony under this section if the person was convicted on the basis of the presence of three or more aggravating factors listed in subsection (b) of this section. In the case of a first felony conviction under this section where only two aggravating factors were present, the licensee may apply to the sentencing court for a limited driving privilege after a period of 12 months of revocation, provided the operator's license has not also been revoked or suspended under any other provision of law. A limited driving privilege issued under this subsection shall be valid for the period of revocation remaining in the same manner and under the terms and conditions prescribed in G.S. 20-16.1(b). If the person's license is revoked under any other statute, the limited driving privilege issued pursuant to this subsection is invalid.

(e) When the probable cause of the law enforcement officer is based on the prima facie evidence rule set forth in subsection (c) above, the officer shall make a reasonable effort to contact the registered owner of the vehicle prior to initiating criminal process.

(f) Each law enforcement agency shall adopt a policy applicable to the pursuit of fleeing or eluding motorists. Each policy adopted pursuant to this subsection shall specifically include factors to be considered by an officer in determining when it is advisable to break off a chase to stop and apprehend a suspect. The Attorney General shall develop a model policy or policies to be considered for use by law enforcement agencies.

I. Felony Speeding to Elude Arrest

Statute

See G.S. 20-141.5(d), reproduced above.

Elements

A person guilty of this offense
(1) operates
(2) a motor vehicle
(3) on a highway or public vehicular area
(4) while fleeing or attempting to elude
(5) a law enforcement officer
(6) who is lawfully performing his or her duties, *and*
(7) two more of the following aggravating factors are present when the violation occurs
  (a) speeding in excess of 15 miles per hour over the legal speed limit;
  (b) gross impairment of the person's faculties while driving due to

1. consumption of an impairing substance, *or*
2. a blood alcohol concentration of 0.14 or more within a relevant time after the driving;

(c) reckless driving as proscribed by G.S. 20-140;
(d) negligent driving leading to an accident causing
1. property damage in excess of one thousand dollars ($1,000), *or*
2. personal injury;

(e) driving when the person's driver's license is revoked;
(f) driving in excess of the posted speed limit, during the days and hours when the posted limit is in effect, on school property or in an area designated as a school zone pursuant to G.S. 20-141.1, or in a highway work zone as defined in G.S. 20-141(j2);
(g) passing a stopped school bus as proscribed by G.S. 20-217;
(h) driving with a child under 12 years of age in the vehicle.

Punishment

Class H felony.

Notes

Element (1). See the note on "drives," which is the same as "operates," in Element (1) under "Driving While License Revoked."

Element (2). See the note on "motor vehicle" in Element (2) under "Driving While License Revoked."

Element (3). See the note on "highway" in Element (3) under "Driving While License Revoked" and the note on "public vehicular area" in Element (3) under "Impaired Driving."

Element (4). Although the statutory title of this offense includes the word "speeding," proof of speeding in not necessary to satisfy this element, although in most cases the proof of this element may include evidence of speeding. A defense to this charge is that a defendant did not know that he or she was being chased by a law enforcement officer and was afraid to stop the vehicle because the defendant did not know who was in pursuit (21 N.C. App. 559). For this reason, an officer should consider using both warning lights *and* siren when engaging in a high-speed chase.

Element (5). See the note on Element (3) of "Assault with Firearm on Law Enforcement Officer, Probation or Parole Officer, or Detention Facility Employee" in Chapter 7.

Element (6). See the note on Element (4) under "Assault with Firearm or Other Deadly Weapon on Governmental Officers or Employees, or Company or Campus Police Officers" in Chapter 7.

License revocation for conviction. The Division of Motor Vehicles must revoke the driver's license of a defendant who is convicted of this offense. The length of a driver's license revocation depends on whether the conviction was based on the finding of two aggravating factors (2 years' revocation) or three or more aggravating factors (3 years' revocation). It would be impossible to know if a jury found three or more aggravating factors unless it made a specific finding in its verdict. Under certain circumstances, a defendant may obtain a limited driving privilege after the first year of a 2-year revocation; see G.S. 20-141.5(d), above.

Prima facie evidence about driver of vehicle. G.S. 20-141.5(c) provides that it is prima facie evidence that the vehicle was operated by the person in whose name the vehicle was registered with Division of Motor Vehicles at the time of the violation. If the vehicle was rented, then proof of that rental is prima facie evidence that the vehicle was operated by the renter of the vehicle at the time of the violation. G.S. 20-141.5(e) provides that when a law enforcement officer's probable cause to charge is based on this prima facie evidence provision, the officer must make a reasonable effort to contact the registered owner before initiating criminal process. There is no such requirement that an officer contact a vehicle's renter of record.

II. Misdemeanor Speeding to Elude Arrest

Statute

See G.S. 20-141.5(d), reproduced above.

Elements

A person guilty of this offense
(1) operates
(2) a motor vehicle
(3) on a highway or public vehicular area
(4) while fleeing or attempting to elude
(5) a law enforcement officer
(6) who is lawfully performing his or her duties.

Punishment

Class 1 misdemeanor.

Notes

Elements (1) through (6). See the notes on the felony offense, immediately above.

License revocation for conviction. The Division of Motor Vehicles must revoke, for up to one year, the driver's license of a defendant who is convicted of this offense.

Prima facie evidence about driver of vehicle. See the note on prima facie evidence in the felony offense discussed above.

Related offenses not in this chapter

None.

Directory of Statutes

Directory of Statutes

Statute	Topic / Page
14-32.3	Domestic abuse, neglect, or exploitation of disabled or elder adults / 118
14-32.4	Assault inflicting serious bodily injury / 101
14-33(a)	Simple affray / 367
	Simple assault / 79
14-33(b)	Aggravated misdemeanor affray / 368
14-33(b)(9)	Assault against sports official / 81
14-33(c)(1)	Assault inflicting serious injury / 82
	Assault with deadly weapon / 83
14-33(c)(2)	Assault on a female / 84
14-33(c)(3)	Assault on child under 12 / 85
14-33(c)(4)	Assault on governmental officer or employee / 85
14-33(c)(6)	Assault on school personnel / 87
14-33.2	Habitual misdemeanor assault / 97
14-34	Assault by pointing gun / 96
14-34.1	Discharging barreled weapon or firearm into occupied property / 106
14-34.2	Assault with firearm or other deadly weapon on governmental officers or employees, or company or campus police officers / 88
14-34.5	Assault with firearm on law enforcement officer, probation or parole officer, or detention facility employee / 90
14-34.6	Simple assault and aggravated assault on firefighters or specified medical personnel / 91
14-34.7	Assault inflicting serious bodily injury on law enforcement officer, probation or parole officer, or detention facility employee / 102
14-39	First-degree kidnapping / 185
	Second-degree kidnapping / 189
14-41	Abduction of children / 192
14-43.3	Felonious restraint / 190
14-44	Abortion / 66
14-49(a)	Malicious injury by use of explosive or incendiary / 123
14-49(b)	Malicious damage by use of explosive or incendiary / 348
14-49.1	Malicious damage to occupied property by use of explosive or incendiary / 347
14-51	First-degree burglary / 245
	Second-degree burglary / 250
14-51.1	Use of deadly physical force against intruder / 13
14-52	First-degree burglary / 245
	Second-degree burglary / 250
14-53	Breaking out of a dwelling / 251
14-54(a),(c)	Felonious breaking or entering of building / 252
14-54(b),(c)	Misdemeanor breaking or entering of building / 253
14-55	Possession of burglar's tools / 254
	Being found in a building with intent to commit any felony or larceny / 255
	Being found armed with intent to break or enter / 255
14-56	Breaking or entering vehicle / 256
14-56.1	Breaking into coin- or currency-operated machine / 257
14-56.2	Damaging or destroying coin- or currency-operated machine / 258
14-57	Burglary with explosives / 259
14-58	First-degree arson / 319
	Second-degree arson / 321
14-58.2	Arson of mobile home / 322
14-59	Burning public building / 323
14-60	Burning schoolhouse / 324
14-61	Burning bridge, fire station, rescue squad building, etc. / 325
14-62	Burning uninhabited house, store, etc. / 326
14-62.1	Burning building under construction / 328
14-62.2	Burning churches and certain other religious buildings / 327

Statute	Topic / Page
14-63	Burning boat, barge, ferry, or float / 328
14-65	Burning one's own dwelling house / 329
14-66	Burning personal property / 331
14-67.1	Burning building not listed in any other statute / 330
14-69.1	Making false bomb report / 348
14-71	Receiving stolen goods—misdemeanor / 207
	Receiving stolen goods—felony / 209
14-71.1	Misdemeanor possession of stolen goods / 204
	Felonious possession of stolen goods / 205
14-72	Misdemeanor larceny / 195
	Felonious larceny / 200
14-72(a)	Misdemeanor possession of stolen goods / 204
14-72(a)	Felonious possession of stolen goods / 205
	Receiving stolen goods—misdemeanor / 207
	Receiving stolen goods—felony / 209
14-72.1	Shoplifting—concealing merchandise / 213
	Shoplifting—substitution of price / 217
14-72.2	Unauthorized use of motor-propelled conveyance / 203
14-74	Larceny by employee / 222
14-75	Larceny of chose in action / 202
14-81(a)	Larceny of horses, mules, swine, or cattle / 198
14-81(a1)	Larceny of dog / 198
14-84	Larceny of animals / 196
14-87	Armed robbery / 237
14-89.1	Safecracking / 260
14-89.1(b)	Safecracking by removing safe / 261
14-90	Embezzlement / 224
14-91	Embezzlement of state property by public officers and employees / 226
14-92	Embezzlement by public officers and trustees / 227
14-100	Obtaining property by false pretenses / 271
14-106	Obtaining property for worthless check / 270
14-107	Worthless check—making or uttering / 265
14-107(3)	Worthless check on nonexistent account / 268
14-107(4)	Worthless check on closed account / 269
14-110	Defrauding innkeeper or campground owner / 278
14-113.9	Financial transaction card theft / 218
14-113.11	Financial transaction card forgery / 287
14-113.13	Financial transaction card fraud / 290
14-113.15A	Financial transaction card fraud; soliciting submission of false credit card sale / 297
14-113.20	Financial identity fraud / 276
14-114	Fraudulent disposal of security / 279
	Fraudulent purchase of security / 280
14-115	Secreting property to hinder enforcement of security interest / 281
14-118	Blackmail / 241
14-118.4	Extortion / 240
14-119	Forgery of notes, checks, and other securities / 283
14-120	Uttering forged checks and securities or forging endorsement on them / 285
14-127	Injury to real property / 344
14-128	Injury to trees, crops, or lands of another / 350
14-132	Defacing public building / 346
	Disorderly conduct in public building / 366
14-134.3	Domestic criminal trespass / 341
14-136	Setting fire to grass, brushlands, and woodlands / 333
14-137	Setting fire to woods and fields / 332
14-159.2	Interference with animal research / 339

Statute	Topic / Page
14-225	False report to law enforcement agency or officer / 392
14-225.1	Picketing courthouse / 393
14-226	Witness intimidation / 384
14-255	Inmate escape from work release / 395
14-256	Prison breach and escape from county or municipal confinement facilities or officers / 394
14-258	Conveying messages or weapons to, or trading with, inmates / 397
14-258.1	Furnishing controlled substance to inmate / 547
14-269	Carrying concealed weapon / 405
14-269.1	Disposition of seized weapons / 407
14-269.2	Possession of weapon on school grounds / 409
14-269.3	Carrying gun into assembly or establishment where alcoholic beverages are sold and consumed / 415
14-269.4	Weapons on state property, in courthouses / 407
14-269.7	Possession of handgun by minor / 408
14-277.1	Communicating threats / 127
14-277.2	Weapons at parades, etc., prohibited / 416
14-277.3	Stalking / 134
14-277.4	Obstruction of health care facilities / 338
14-281.1	Throwing objects at sporting events / 136
14-288.1(2)	Dangerous weapon or substance, definition / 108
14-288.2	Misdemeanor riot / 370
	Felony riot / 372
	Misdemeanor inciting to riot / 373
	Felony inciting to riot / 373
14-288.4	Disorderly conduct / 361
14-288.5	Failure to disperse on command / 374
14-288.6(a)	Trespass during emergency / 375
14-288.6(b)	Looting / 376
14-288.7	Transporting, possessing weapon during emergency / 376
14-288.8	Manufacture, possession, etc., of machine gun, sawed-off shotgun, or weapon of mass destruction / 418
14-288.9	Assault on emergency personnel / 107
	Assault on emergency personnel with dangerous weapon / 108
14-288.12	Municipal authority to create state-of-emergency laws / 378
14-288.13	County authority to create state-of-emergency laws / 378
14-288.19	Failure to evacuate building on governor's order / 377
14-289	Advertising lotteries / 467
14-290	Dealing in lotteries / 468
	Possession of lottery tickets / 469
14-291	Selling lottery tickets / 469
	Acting as agent for lottery / 470
14-291.1	Selling numbers tickets / 471
	Possession of numbers tickets / 471
14-292	Gambling / 472
14-304	Possession of slot machine / 473
14-306	Possession of slot machine, definition / 473
14-309.5–15	Legal bingo and raffles / 475
14-315.1	Storing firearm in manner accessible to minor / 414
14-315.2	Firearm storage notification requirement / 415
14-316.1	Contributing to a juvenile's being delinquent, undisciplined, abused, or neglected / 114
14-318.2	Child abuse (misdemeanor) / 109
14-318.4(a)	Child abuse inflicting serious injury (felony) / 110
14-318.4(a1)	Child abuse—prostitution (felony) / 112
14-318.4(a2)	Child abuse—sexual act (felony) / 113

Descriptive-Word Index

Descriptive-Word Index

Descriptive-Word Index